The Descendants of

Philip Pendleton

A Virginia Colonist

David Ellis Pendleton

HERITAGE BOOKS
2019

HERITAGE BOOKS

AN IMPRINT OF HERITAGE BOOKS, INC.

Books, CDs, and more—Worldwide

For our listing of thousands of titles see our website
at
www.HeritageBooks.com

Published 2019 by
HERITAGE BOOKS, INC.
Publishing Division
5810 Ruatan Street
Berwyn Heights, Md. 20740

International Standard Book Number
Paperbound: 978-0-7884-4457-9

Acknowledgements

This book is a completely revised and expanded version of the original May 2001 edition entitled "Descendants of Philip Pendleton." The genealogy of this Pendleton family in America has been the subject of many past studies (Refs. 1 to 5). Those efforts have provided a solid foundation for the current work. However, it is the magic of this technology age that has really made this work possible. This includes on-line database searches provided freely by many organizations as well as commercial sources. And the maps showing the locations of Pendleton households were produced by Tony Moya using digital technology. Finally, much of the information herein, especially more recent family histories, comes from correspondence with cousins near and far mostly be email. Like the first version, this book is dedicated to these members of our Pendleton family.

As is the case for most family trees, the descendancy information presented herein is not without controversy. For recent family information, my approach has been to lean toward the inclusion of information provided by cousins about their own Pendleton branch. Much information would be lost if only those data that can be vigorously "proved" were to be included. By the same token, the original genealogical studies of the Pendleton family are not without error. It is my belief that any difference that can be found between those original studies and this work represents a correction.

David Ellis Pendleton

Table of Contents

Introduction

Philip Pendleton immigrated to the Virginia colony from Norwich, England in 1674. The descendants of Philip and his wife Isabella Hurt now number in the tens of thousands and are scattered throughout the United States. This is a description of their family line.

This Pendleton line can be traced back to 1500 in Manchester, England. The second through fourth generations spent their lives in Norwich, England. It is the fifth generation that included the Virginia immigrants Philip and his older brother Nathaniel. Since Nathaniel died without issue it is Philip and Isabella who are the progenitors of the prestigious Pendleton family of Colonial Virginia.

The earliest studies (Refs. 1 to 3) of the Pendleton family of Virginia focused on the descendants of Henry Pendleton, the eldest son of Philip. Henry's children and grandchildren were certainly central figures in Colonial Virginia society and were important leaders in the developing country throughout the eighteenth century. More recently, the descendants of Philip Jr., the youngest son of Philip (Ref. 4), and John, the middle son (Ref. 5), have been considered in some detail. This work gives equal attention to the descendants of all three sons of Philip in America up to about 1920.

John and Philip Jr., following traditional rules of inheritance, apparently did not have the advantage of the eldest son Henry whose sons had such remarkable success and who remained in relative comfort and prestige within the Old Dominion. The descendants of John and Philip, in contrast, were the ones who first ventured west beyond the Blue Ridge Mountains in search of new lands and new opportunities. They were the pioneers and adventurers who risked all in the continued search for their own promised land.

The descendancy format used throughout this book, including the numbering system for heads of families, is taken from Family Tree Maker ®. Heads of families are listed twice; once as children and again as heads of families. For example, the immigrant Philip Pendleton (fifth generation) is listed as a child of Henry Pendleton, Jr. (fourth generation). The number 7 next to Philip, as a child of Henry, indicates he is included again as the head of household number 7 in the next generation. Those persons without offspring, such as Nathaniel Pendleton, Philip's brother, are listed only once. In Nathaniel's case as a child of Henry Pendleton, Jr. (fourth generation).

Pendleton Origins

The English surname Pendleton is derived from the place where a man once lived or where he once held land. The place name and surname Pendleton is a combination of Old English words "pendle" and "ton." Pendle itself is a combination of the Celtic term "penn" (hill or head) and the Old English word "leah" (wood or clearing). The Old English word "ton," means "farm" or "place." The form of the word pendle is similar to other words of middle or early English origins such as bundle, handle, spindle, etc. Considering that Pendle is located in ancient northern Saxony there is little doubt of its Old English origins.

Today, the place name Pendleton is applied to a small hamlet within the Pendle area in the county of Lancashire between the towns of Nelson, Clitheroe and Accrington about 25 north of Manchester (Fig. 1). Dominant features in maps of the area surrounding the ancient hamlet of Pendleton are the Forest of Pendle and Pendle Hill (Fig. 2). The name Pendleton is also applied to an ancient district of Salford about 2 miles from downtown Manchester. George Pendleton, Esquire, of Manchester, the earliest known ancestor of Philip Pendleton, was perhaps associated in some way with this Pendleton township near Manchester.

Figure 1. The Pendle area northwest of Manchester and Norwich, the birthplace of Philip Pendleton, are indicated.

Figure 2. Pendle Hill in Lancashire, England (Photo by N. Dewar). The hill has captivated the imaginations of many. The Pendle Witches are connected with many villages in Pendle and the hill itself. On the other side of the religious spectrum, Pendle Hill is famous for it's links to the Quakers. George Fox founded the Quaker movement after climbing Pendle Hill in 1652 (Ref. 9).

The following Pendleton references are taken from the Lancashire, England records office (Ref. 6) and from Gottschalk and Nicklin (Ref. 3) who apparently derived much of their information from an earlier Pendleton researcher, Everett Pendleton (Ref. 7) who, in turn, cited ancient Lancashire court records (Ref. 8).

- An early 13-century charter records that Sabastus-de-Pendleton granted land to Thomas son of Ellis-de-Pendleton at a rent of 1d (less than 1 cent today).

- Agnes-de-Pendleton, the daughter of Thomas-de-Pendleton, in her widowhood gave her daughter Aviel and to the heirs of Siward-de-Pendleton 1d to be paid on each St. Oswalds day.

- The Clitheroe family had acquired land in Pendleton as Reginald-de-Pendleton gave an oxgang[1] of land in the village of little Pendleton to Ralph the son of Karnwarth in marriage with his sister Quenild although a rent of 18s was to be paid and Robert, the son of Reginald-de-Pendleton gave 4 oxgangs of land in the same place to Hugh son of Ralph.

- In 1241£3.7s.10d (about $7 today) was rendered to a john-de-lacy from the farm of Penilton. The spelling was Penelton in 1246.

---

[1] An oxgang was probably one eighth to one tenth the size of a plowland which was roughly the amount of land a farmer with a team of eight oxen could plough in one year.

- In 1246 on the death of Siward-de-Pendleton the moiety of 2 oxgangs of land in Pendleton was given to Querderay and Isold Pendleton his daughter.

- Also in the year 1246 in the Assize rolls of Lancashire, mention was made of Thomas de Parva Pendleton who was surety for Adam, Richard and Roger de Penelton, sons of Matilda de Penelton, who was probably the widow of Siward de Penelton.

- In 1295 the annual return for the farm of Pendleton was £6.4s.2d. (about $12 today).

- In the inquest of 1311 there were 16 oxgangs of land held in bondage for the farm of Pennulton.

- In 1324 the Pendleton farm had increased to £6.10s.4d, Baron Henry-de-Blackburn levied 1d additional rent towards the war with Scotland.

- In 1332 Adam de Penholton paid taxes in Salford and Robert and Thomas de Penholton of Penholton paid taxes there.

- In 1469 Thomas Pendleton was living in Lancashire, near Manchester, England.

The First Four Generations – Manchester to Norwich

Although the name Pendleton is derived from the Pendle area north of Manchester, it is Manchester itself that can be traced directly as the "ancestral home" of both Philip Pendleton and Brian Pendleton. These two early Pendleton immigrants to the new world are the ancestors of many if not most of the Pendletons in America today. Major Brian Pendleton first settled in Watertown, Massachusetts and was made a freeman there in 1634. The descendancy of Brian Pendleton is provided in considerable detail by Everett Pendleton in his classic work (Ref. 7). The subject of this history, Philip Pendleton, Sr., immigrated from Norwich to Virginia in 1674 with his brother Nathaniel.

George Pendleton, Esq., Sr. of Manchester, England in 1500 was Philip's great great grandfather. The fact that the township of Pendleton is near Manchester makes the claim that George Pendleton was from Pendleton township especially compelling. David J. Mays previously came to this conclusion and stated it more poetically, although perhaps not as accurately, in his biography of Edmund Pendleton, a grandson of Philip Pendleton (Ref. 10).

Had he [Edmund Pendleton] searched the Heralds Office [in England] he would have found, duly registered, the family coat of arms, bearing the escallop shells won by two ancestors in the Crusades, for the family was an ancient one and well established in the hills of Lancashire in remote times. Moreover, if he had returned to the seat of his ancestors, he would have found the family coat of arms still doing service over an inn, and, a little distance off, the old manor-house which some of the Pendletons still occupied, and the old churchyard with the tombs of Pendletons who, centuries before, had walked the earth as members of the gentry of England. This churchyard was a spot where many of the denizens of the place would not have lingered in olden days because of the ghosts and witches that abounded in that region, for Pendleton township stretched along and across Pendle-hill and dark Pendle forest. [Mays is apparently referring to the small hamlet of Pendleton 25 miles north of Manchester].

Possibly it was the bleak character of this land that induced one of the Pendletons to move from the western to the easternmost part of England – to the County of Norfolk which bulges into the North Sea. At any rate, we find George Pendleton in the records of Lancashire, while George, Jr. (1542-1603), a scrivener, was admitted in 1578 [during the reign of Queen Elizabeth I] to the freedom of the town of Norwich, and lived on in the town until they laid him in St Stephen's churchyard. His son Henry (1575-1635) married Susan Camden, granddaughter of Sir Thomas Pettus, who had served as mayor. This Henry Pendleton was a man of consequence in the community. He is described as "Henry Pendleton of Norwich, gentleman." He and his son Henry (1614 – 1682) were apparently Loyalists, i.e., they supported the Crown during the long struggle between Parliament and King. Henry, Jr. subscribed to a loan to his King when nearly three hundred of his fellow-townsmen refused.

There is little doubt that at that time the family was substantial, for among the records of Norfolk are scattered references to the Pendletons – their conveyances, bequests, charities and pedigrees – and it is probable that their fortunes began to decline with the coming of the Commonwealth, although it was not until after the Restoration that Henry Jr.'s sons, Nathaniel and Philip, turned their eyes to America. Nathaniel, the older of the two, graduated from Corpus Christi College, Cambridge, in 1672. Having been educated in the ministry, he was ordained Deacon by the Bishop of Norwich the following year. But since many of the churches in Norfolk County could not supply a living for their pastors it is probable that that circumstance induced him to migrate to Virginia, where he hardly had time to preach his first sermon in South Farnham Parish before he sickened and died. It was the younger brother Philip, who had been educated to be a schoolmaster, who subsequently founded the Pendleton family in Virginia.

Generation No. 1

1. GEORGE^1 PENDLETON, ESQ., SR. was born about 1500, of Manchester, England. His wife is unknown.

Little is known of George Pendleton of Manchester although the title "Esquire" suggests a man of wealth and prestige.

Child of GEORGE PENDLETON, ESQ., SR. is:
2.	i.	GEORGE^2 PENDLETON JR., b. 1553, Manchester, England; d. Oct 27, 1603, Norwich, England.

Generation No. 2

2. GEORGE^2 PENDLETON JR. *(GEORGE^1)* was born 1553 Manchester, England, and died Oct 27, 1603 in Norwich, England. He married ELIZABETH PETTINGALE Jul 29, 1579 in St. Peter's Mancroft, Norwich, England, daughter of JOHN PETTINGALE, GENT. She was born 1550 in Swardeston, Norfolk, England, and died Jan 1624/25 in Norwich, England.

George Pendleton Jr. was admitted to the Freedom of Norwich as a Scrivener's apprentice on September 21, 1578.

Children of GEORGE PENDLETON and ELIZABETH PETTINGALE are:
	i.	GEORGE^3 PENDLETON, b. Norwich, England.
3.	ii.	HENRY PENDLETON, b. Aug 12, 1580, Norwich, England; d. Jul 1635, Norwich, England.
4.	iii.	FRANCIS PENDLETON, b. Oct 06, 1581, Norwich, England.
	iv.	AGNES PENDLETON, b. Aug 28, 1583, Norwich, England.
5.	v.	GEORGE PENDLETON, d. Jun 01, 1621.

Generation No. 3

3. HENRY[3] PENDLETON *(GEORGE[2], GEORGE[1])* was born Aug 12, 1580 in Norwich, England, and died Jul 1635 in Norwich, England. He married SUSAN CAMDEN Sep 30, 1605 in St. Simon & St. Judes-Norwich, daughter of HUMPHREY CAMDEN and CECILY PETTUS and granddaughter of THOMAS PETTUS, Mayor of Norwich (1591), member of an opulent family. She was born Abt. 1584 in Norwich, England.

Henry Pendleton had the Freedom of Norwich as a Scriptor on September 6, 1605.

Children of HENRY PENDLETON and SUSAN CAMDEN are:
- i. GEORGE[4] PENDLETON, b. Mar 1606/07.
- ii. CECILY PENDLETON, b. Jul 1608.
- iii. JOHN PENDLETON, b. Jul 1609.
- iv. SUSAN PENDLETON, b. Jul 1609.
- v. HENRY PENDLETON, b. Sep 1613.
- 6. vi. JR. HENRY PENDLETON, b. Dec 1614, Norwich, England; d. 1682, Norwich, England.
- vii. ANNE PENDLETON, b. Jun 1615.
- viii. ABIGAIL PENDLETON, b. Oct 1617.
- ix. THOMAS PENDLETON, b. Feb 1618/19.
- x. MATILDA PENDLETON, b. Aug 04, 1620.
- xi. MARY PENDLETON, b. Jul 1623.
- xii. MATTHEW PENDLETON, b. Nov 1624.
- xiii. GEORGE PENDLETON, b. Dec 1626.

4. FRANCIS[3] PENDLETON *(GEORGE[2], GEORGE[1])* was born Oct 06, 1581 in Norwich, England. He married ANNE 1610 in St. Stephen's.

Children of FRANCIS PENDLETON and ANNE are:
- i. ELIZABETH[4] PENDLETON, b. 1611.
- ii. ANNE PENDLETON, b. 1612.
- iii. SUSAN PENDLETON, b. 1613.
- iv. MARY PENDLETON, b. 1615.
- v. ELIZABETH PENDLETON.
- vi. ENOCH PENDLETON, b. 1618; d. 1651.

5. GEORGE[3] PENDLETON *(GEORGE[2], GEORGE[1])* died Jun 01, 1621. He married ELIZABETH OSBORNE Feb 13, 1613/14.

Children of GEORGE PENDLETON and ELIZABETH OSBORNE are:
- i. RICHARD[4] PENDLETON, b. 1618.
- ii. MARY PENDLETON, b. 1621.

Generation No. 4

6. JR. HENRY[4] PENDLETON *(HENRY[3], GEORGE[2], GEORGE[1])* was born Dec 1614 in Norwich, England, and died 1682 in Norwich, England. He married (1) HANNA. She died in Norwich, England. He married (2) ELIZABETH DOUGLASS 1649 in Norwich, England. She died Aft. 1682 in Norwich, England?

Henry Pendleton Jr. had the Freedom of Norwich as a grocer on September 8, 1637.

Children of HENRY PENDLETON and HANNA are:
    i. HENRY[5] PENDLETON, b. Mar 1636/37.
    ii. JOHN PENDLETON, b. Dec 1640.
    iii. MATTHEW PENDLETON, b. Dec 1642.
    iv. SAMUEL PENDLETON, b. Sep 06, 1647, Norwich, England.

Children of HENRY PENDLETON and ELIZABETH DOUGLASS are:
    v. NATHANIEL[5] PENDLETON, b. Mar 31, 1650, Norwich, England; d. Abt. 1674, VA.

    Nathaniel Pendleton was baptized at St. Peter's Mancroft, Norwich, England, April 7, 1650. He was admitted to the Merchant Taylor's School, London, in 1661; In 1669 he was admitted sizar Corpus Christi College, Cambridge as a son of "Henry Pendleton, Merchant, of Norwich." He was an A. B. of Corpus Christi in 1672; on September 20, 1673 he was ordained Deacon by the Bishop of Norwich; he became Curate of Badwell Ash in Suffolk and in 1674 came to Virginia with his younger brother Philip. He died not long after.

7.   vi. PHILIP PENDLETON, b. Mar 26, 1654, Norwich, England; d. Nov 09, 1721, King & Queen Co., VA.

Generation No. 5 – Norwich to Virginia

The fifth generation of Pendletons, the first in the New World, consists of Philip Pendleton and his wife Isabella Hurt as well as Philip's brother Nathaniel who left no offspring. Refer to Generation 4 on Page 8 for a brief summary of Nathaniel's life. The fate of the Pendletons who remained in Norwich, England is not considered in this study. The following commentary on Philip and his descendants is from the William and Mary College Quarterly Historical Magazine (Ref. 11).

Whatever may have been the status in England of the branch of the Pendleton family to which the emigrants Nathaniel and Philip Pendleton belonged, or whatever may have been the reasons for their seeking a home in the new world, the social and economic status of the first two generations of the family is known quite definitely to have been that of the 'planter class' (technically speaking) as distinguished from the 'gentry.' They were people of moderate means, living quiet lives, members of the Established Church, probably above the average in point of education, doubtless taking part in the more strictly local affairs and on the whole most desirable citizens: dignified, industrious, clean. If there is anything in the theory of heredity the Pendleton family is a very good example thereof. In the third and fourth generations great ability was exhibited in one instance at least (Judge Edmund Pendleton) and marked ability in several instances. This 'ability' made itself known at a time when there was real opportunity for the reward of 'merit,' and at a time when it was known that the Pendletons were people of certainly not more than comfortable circumstances. Their offices were not 'purchased' and they were not allied by marriage, or otherwise to the really powerful families of the last days of the colony or of the early days of the state. Space forbids our going into details here (though they have been fully worked out) and a brief summary must suffice.

In the third generation we have Edmund Pendleton, jurist and statesman, and Henry and John Pendleton and in the fourth and fifth generations Nathaniel Pendleton of New York, a lawyer of note, Henry, of South Carolina, jurist, another Edmund, jurist and member of Congress, Nathaniel Greene Pendleton, a member of Congress, Philip Clayton Pendleton, a United States District Judge. Through Pendleton women such names may be added to this list as those of James and Philip Pendleton Barbour, John Esten Cooke, Edmund Pendleton Gaines, David Hunter Strother, John Pendleton Kennedy, Anthony Kennedy, Philip Clayton, and his sons George Rootes Clayton, and Augustin Smith Clayton.

Later generations of the family have also added their full quota to the record of 'ability:' men prominent in the affairs of state, members of the bench and bar, physicians of both soul and body, teachers and soldiers. Of the women of the race, let us note in passing, that only political disability has perhaps prevented them from obtaining the distinctions which have fallen to the men of the family. The women have, however, been truly distinguished: qualities of mind, in many instances far above the ordinary and in some instances amounting to genius, certainly 'ability,' and qualities of heart which in the real work of Life are so very necessary.

It is but fair to state also that the Pendleton family numbers among its members just as many mediocre people as one generally discovers in the histories of large houses. This is but the natural course of human families and really serves but to intensify the interest of the student of heredity and environment in the history of this family as a whole and particularly when due consideration is given to the really more than expected 'ability' which it has produced.

Since the Church of England was the official state church - in colonial Virginia as in the mother country - there was much interlocking of the political and ecclesiastical structures. The leading families dominated in both areas and there was frequent overlapping. Approximately one hundred families, whose members frequently intermarried over the years, dominated the public life of colonial and revolutionary Virginia for some two centuries (Ref. 12). The Pendleton family was not part of this "gentry." Later the famous jurist Edmund Pendleton, however, owed much of his success to his association with Benjamin Robinson, a wealthy Virginia planter. Many of Edmund's brothers and cousins also held positions of trust and authority granted by the gentry.

The economic situation in Virginia in the middle 1670s was ominous. The disastrous effect of England's Navigation Acts (that required that all Virginia and Maryland tobacco be shipped to England, rather than the continent, and stipulated a special duty to the king) on the tobacco growers, plus the havoc wrought by storms and floods and the seizures of tobacco ships by the Dutch, had combined to create widespread suffering and discontent. On top of all else, war with the Indians broke out. Between January and May 1676, more than 500 white settlers were killed. The Indian war led directly to Bacon's rebellion against Governor Berkeley and a temporary end to the governor's autocracy. The overwhelming mass of the people, together with some of the principal planters, supported Nathaniel Bacon but the rebellion died with his death in October 1676 due to illness (Ref. 12).

Both Nathaniel Bacon and Philip Pendleton, Sr. arrived in Virginia in 1674. Nathaniel Bacon led a popular rebellion and died within two years. Philip led an apparently quiet existence and was the founder of a very long and successful line of Pendletons in the New World.

Finally, in 1682, the long depression in the tobacco market came to an end. It had lasted for a quarter of a century. The upturn in the fortunes of the planters would continue for about two decades, and during that time the colonists were to move farther and farther away from the rebellion and its divisive aftereffects (Ref. 12). It was about this time that Philip Pendleton returned from England after having completed his five years as an indentured servant and ready to "make his fortune."

The passage over from England to the colonies during those early days was no doubt a difficult journey. The ships were small (see Fig. 3) and the voyage took months. Brian Pendleton of Massachusetts and Philip and Nathaniel of Virginia were not the only Pendleton immigrants to the New World in the 17th century. Notable examples are the early Pendletons of North Carolina. A Henry Pendleton and a Thomas Pendleton appear in a list of "Some Early Residents in Pasquotank, NC (New Begun Crk.)," approximately 1697 (Ref. 13). And a number of Pendletons subsequently appear in the records of Pasquotank County, North Carolina in the 1700s and 1800s. Although a family connection with the Virginia Pendletons has been presumed, there is apparently no documented evidence of such a link.

Figure 3 (Photo by Paul S. Marley). The Elizabeth II is a replicate of the ships that brought the first Englishmen to the New World. It is a wooden 70' bark (English sailing ship). The beam width is 16 ½ feet!

There are other enigmatic references of Pendletons who show up in records of the New World that reflect the fact that the name was not uncommon in England. The earliest may be a Francis Pendleton who is listed in an index of early census, tax records, rent rolls, etc. for Virginia as "Pendleton, Francis, Virginia Colony, Va. 1607." That is the year Jamestown was founded! Fifteen years later in Jamestown, a John Pindleton (sic) is included (Ref. 14) in a 1622 list of "A Declaration of How the Monies were Disposed…(towards the building of a free schoole in Virginia)." In 1658, a Thomas Brewer was granted 350 acres in Virginia and the "transport of 7 persons, Thomas Pindleton, George Pindleton, William Harbutt, Elizabeth Reinalls, and 3 Negroes." [Again, note the spelling].

On June 1635, persons to be transported [from London] to Bermuda [a stopover to the New World] by the "True Love" of London, Mr. Robert Dennis included William Pendleton 27, Richard Hurt 17, and James Taylor 28, (Ref. 15). Almost fifty years later, in about 1682, the emigrant Philip Pendleton married Isabella Hurt. And this James Taylor could very well be the ancestor of Mary Taylor who in 1701 married Henry Pendleton, eldest son of Philip Pendleton.

Ellen Pendleton, lawbreaker, is included in the Signet Office Docquet Book (1639), Virginia Colonial Records. The docquet book appears to be a passenger list. At least two other English women bearing the Pendleton name were among those who braved that long ocean voyage (Ref. 15):

- 1686. 23 Sep - 6 Oct. The following apprenticed in Liverpool to Edmund Croston of Liverpool, Mariner, to serve 4 years in Virginia or Maryland: Amy Pendleton of Manchester, spinster aged 26.

- 1679. 1-8 Sept. By the Trent [a sailing ship]: Mary Pendleton with Joseph Pollard and Mr. George Munjoy from Barbados to Boston.

The name Pollard is closely associated with the Pendletons of Virginia by the early 1700s. The Trent passage suggests the Pollards and Pendletons were associated even at this early date. And could this trip be in any way associated with Philip Pendleton's reputed trip to England and his return to Virginia in 1680? Philip apparently had 3 aunts named Mary Pendleton.

Generation No. 5

7. PHILIP[5] PENDLETON *(HENRY[4], HENRY[3], GEORGE[2], GEORGE[1])* was born Mar 26, 1654 in Norwich, England, and died Nov 09, 1721 in King & Queen Co., VA. He married ISABELLA HURT 1682 in VA, daughter of WILLIAM HURT and MARGARET.

Records show Philip Pendleton's baptism in St. Peter's, Mancroft, Norwich, England, as of April 2, 1654. When he came to Virginia under a 5-year contract he lived in Old Rappahannock County (Fig. 4). Philip worked out his contract, returned to England, where it is said by some authorities that he married but within a year lost his wife, and after the death of his father (Henry Pendleton Jr.) in 1682 he returned to Virginia where he married Isabella Hurt and had seven children. Philip owned property in Essex Co. and King and Queen Co. where he died in 1721. All seven children married and had families of their own.

The first extant record of Philip Pendleton in the new world is in a Deed of Record for Thomas Newman conveying one-half of his real and personal property to his son, as attested by Philip Pendleton, Tappahanock, VA, 1677 (Ref. 16). Twenty-three years later "To establish the facts in the case, depositions were taken before Henry Tandy, Phil. Pendleton, and Richard Gregory at the Court House of King and Queen Co., Virginia on 6 May 1700" from William Leigh, Mr. John Walker, James Edwards, and Mr. William Seamore – Taken from court records in a case involving Thomas Starke and William Bates (Ref. 17). Not long after, Philip Pendleton was a witness in Court records of King William Co. on Jun 20, 1702 (Ref. 18): "John Hill Junr and Jane his wife of St. Stephens Parish in King and Queen County, sell to John Walker of the same parish and county, Gent." Other witnesses were Rob't Robinson and Sam'l Clayton. In 1704 Philip and his son Henry are included in the Rent Rolls of King and Queen Co.

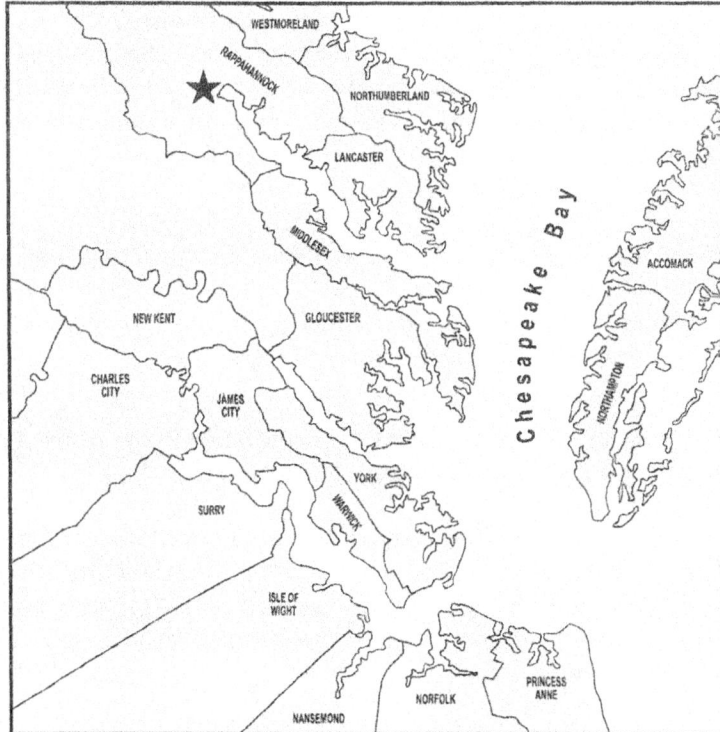

Figure 4. Virginia Counties in 1676. Old Rappahannock County, the site of Philip Pendleton's indentured status from 1674 to 1679, was located along both sides of the Rappahannock River above Lancaster and Middlesex Counties. In 1692, Old Rappahannock was split into Richmond County northeast of the river and Essex County southwest of the river. Philip lived in South Farnham Parish which was included in that portion that became Essex Co.

The following deposition given in 1708 was discovered (along with another similar deposition) in an unindexed volume of records in Essex County, Virginia by a descendant of the Pendleton Family and was published in the William and Mary College Quarterly Historical Magazine (Ref. 11). It establishes among other important facts that Philip and Nathaniel Pendleton immigrated to Virginia in 1674.

Essex County Court, Deeds, &c. No. 13, pages 118-119 and Order Book 1708-1714, page 46: VIRGINIA Sct. George Ward aged fifty Seven yeares or there abouts of South Farnham Parish in the county of Essex in Virginia Planter being examined & Sworn at ye request of Phillip Pendleton deposeth and Saith:

That on or about ye year of our Lord One Thousand Six hundred Seventy & foure their came Consigned to Capt Edmund Crask then liveing in the Said Parish Two reputed Brothers called & known by the name of Nathaniell Pendleton & Phillip Pendleton sent as this Depont heard by their Mother in the Ship whereof was Master Capt John Plover and this Depont Saith that she said Nathaniell was Reputed as a Minister and preached a Sermon in the above said parish Church Soon after his arrival and Imediately thereupon Sickened & dyed And this Depont further Saith that he was a Servant in the House where the said Nathaniell Pendleton dyed and did see the said Nathaniell interred in the

13

Earth, and never heard that the said Nathaniell Pendleton had either wife or child, and this Depont further Saith that the said Phillip Pendleton went for England at the end of five years servitude, and came to Virginia again the Same year and Since marryed & had severall children all now resident in King & Queen County in Virginia, aforesd, And further this Depont Saith not.

George Ward

I Richard Buckner Clerk of Essex County Court do hereby Certifie that George Ward made oath to the above Deposition in Essex County Court the 10th day of August 1708 and on Motion of Phillip Pendleton was ordered to be recorded, and is recorded.

Test Richard Buckner C. Cur.

The following comments were provided as an adjunct to the deposition in the William and Mary College Quarterly Historical Magazine (Ref. 11):

The facts given in the depositions quoted above are, with a few exceptions, given in Doctor Slaughter's history, and by Bishop Meade in his 'Old Churches, Ministers and Families of Virginia' (1861), the latter stating that he derived his information from 'a brief autobiography of Judge [Edmund] Pendleton...and from a genealogy by the same, both executed not long before his death.'

Doctor Slaughter says that Nathaniel and Philip Pendleton were sons of Henry Pendleton of Norwich, England, but gives no authority for his statement. Mrs. Mary Dunnica Micou in her revised edition of Doctor Slaughter's account says that 'Philip Pendleton was son of Henry Pendleton, 3rd son of Henry Pendleton, son and heir of George Pendleton, Gentleman, who married Elizabeth Pettingall, daughter of John Pettingall, Gentleman, of Norwich, England.'

The following is taken from Walter Rye's, *Norfolk Families,* Part IV, Norwich, 1913, p. 661. 'Pendleton: A Visitation Family which bore [arms] gu. an escutcheon arg. between four escallops in saltire, or. George Pendleton, of a Manchester family, was father of George Pendleton, of Norwich, who married Elizabeth Pettingall, of Swardeston, father of (i.a.) Henry Pendleton, of Norwich, who married Susan Camden, of London, father of [1] George (s.p.), [2] John, and [3] Henry. I do not find any of them mentioned in the index to Blomefield nor in the Norwich Freeman Rolls.'

The compiler of these notes has had no way of either verifying the statements relating to the English pedigree of the Pendleton family nor of conducting a research into the records in Norwich. The statements are doubtless substantially correct but more detail would be interesting.

That Nathaniel Pendleton was in 'orders' is certainly evidence that he was a man of education. Bishop Meade makes the statement that Philip Pendleton was 'a teacher.' The Bishop doubtless drew this piece of information from the autobiography of Judge Edmund Pendleton; so here we have evidence that Philip, the progenitor of the Virginia Pendletons was also an educated man. Judge Pendleton was a grandson of the first Philip and certainly had every opportunity of knowing about his forbears and occupations.

The depositions of the Waggoners and of George Ward, given above, reveal the fact that Philip Pendleton was an indentured servant to Edmund Crask of Essex County but the nature of his servitude is not stated and it is a much too risky business to venture a statement in regard to the employments of any man at the time that Philip Pendleton lived, particularly when he was under 'indentures.' The statement made by George Ward that he understood that the Pendletons were sent to the colony by their mother, is very interesting and one cannot but speculate as to the reasons for their being sent. Philip Pendleton evidently did not break off relations with his family in England for 'at the end of five years servitude' he returned to the mother country. After a brief sojourn there he came again to Virginia.

Why the depositions of Ward and the Waggoners were made and recorded at the request of Philip Pendleton is another matter of interest, but, as yet, no record has been discovered which tells why this was done. One cannot help but wonder, however, if it was necessary for Philip Pendleton to prove the points therein on account of family matters in England. Philip Pendleton evidently spent much of his remaining days in King & Queen County, the total destruction of whose records has limited our knowledge of him.

The ancestry of Isabella Hurt has not been well established but the following provides a clue (Ref. 19): "600 acres was patented to John Maddison on the Mattaponi River on 4 Jan. 1653/54. It further shows that John Maddison and Mary, his wife, assigned the land to Thomas Jones in 1659. Thomas Jones assigned the land to William Hurt on 10 May 1660 and William Hurt and his wife, Margaret, assigned the land to William Nichalls (sic) on 3 Feb. 1682/83. New Kent Co. was divided in 1691 to form King and Queen Co. and again in 1702 to form King William Co. Each time the Hurt property was in the newly formed county. This places William and Margaret Hurt at a location and time consistent with the claim that they are the parents of Isabella Hurt."

Children of PHILIP PENDLETON and ISABELLA HURT are:
8.   i.   HENRY[6] PENDLETON, b. 1683, Old Rappahannock Co., VA; d. May 1721, King & Queen Co., VA.
9.   ii. ELIZABETH PENDLETON, b. 1685, Old Rappahannock Co., Virginia; d. 1761, Essex Co., Virginia.
10.   iii. ISABELLA PENDLETON, b. Abt. 1688, Old Rappahannock Co., VA; d. Aft. 1748, VA.
11.   iv. JOHN PENDLETON, b. 1691, Old Rappahannock Co., VA; d. 1776, VA.
12.   v.   RACHEL PENDLETON, b. Abt. 1693, Essex Co., VA.
13.   vi. PHILIP PENDLETON, JR., b. 1695, Essex Co., VA; d. 1753, VA.
14.   vii. CATHERINE PENDLETON, b. 1699, Essex Co., VA; d. 1774, VA.

Generation No. 6 – Early Colonial Virginia

The sixth generation consists of the 7 children of the immigrant, Philip Pendleton and Isabella Hurt each of whom established families of their own in VA (Fig. 5). Henry resided in King & Queen Co., Elizabeth and Rachel apparently in Essex Co., and Isabella apparently in Caroline Co. John and probably Philip Jr. spent at least their early days in Essex Co. The time period is from about 1704, when Henry, Philip's eldest son became 21, up to 1776 when John, his middle son died, the year of the Declaration of Independence from England.

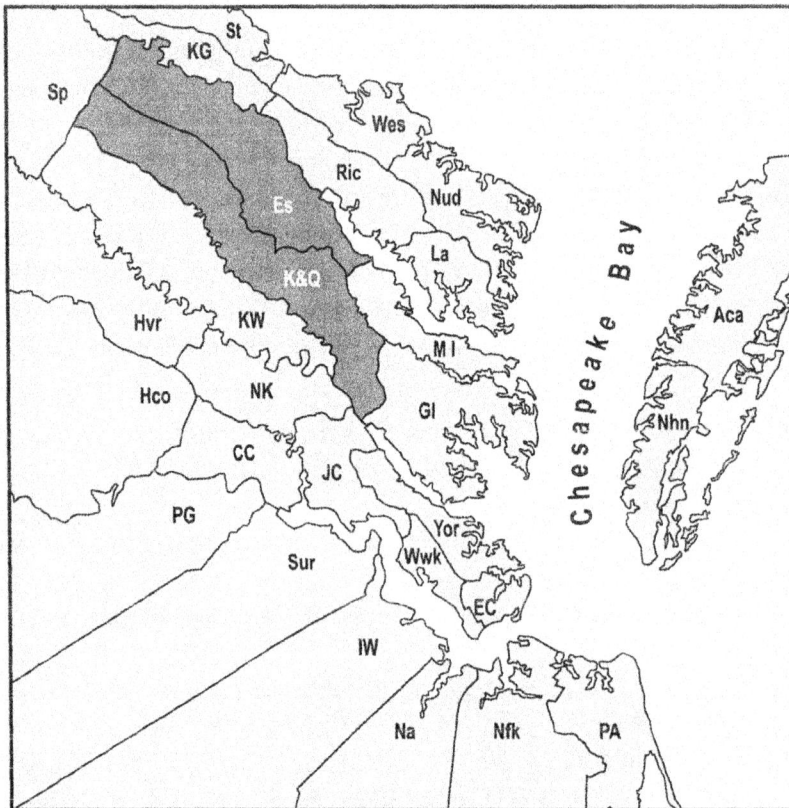

Figure 5. Virginia Counties in 1721. The first generation born in Virginia held property in King & Queen (KQ) and Essex (Es) Cos. which were formed in 1691 and 1692, respectively. Caroline Co., where Isabella Pendleton Thomas resided, was formed from northwestern portions of King & Queen, Essex, and King William Cos. (KW) in 1728. South Farnham Parish is located in the lower (southeastern) portion of Essex Co.

Much has been written about Virginia's large landed proprietors, luxuriating on their baronial estates in the seventeenth and eighteenth centuries. While they constituted the ruling group in the colony, too little has been said of the vastly more numerous group who held a few hundred acres each. There were thousands of them and they were in many ways the backbone of the colony. These owners of medium-sized farms, who often lived in modest clapboard houses with dormer windows, were especially strong and prosperous in the latter years of the seventeenth and the early years of the eighteenth century (Ref. 20). The Virginia rent roll for 1704, which included everything except the Northern Neck, showed that their holdings averaged roughly from three hundred to five hundred acres. Philip Pendleton and his eldest son, Henry, are included in the 1704 Virginia rent rolls for King and Queen County, holding 300 and 700 acres, respectively.

There were few, if any, slaves on these plantations in those years and few indentured servants. This group of sturdy tobacco growers had to depend mainly on themselves and their families for the long, arduous and involved process of raising and curing the leaf. Many tobacco fields adjoined swamps and bogs, and the death rate of tobacco farmers was dismayingly high. But so long as these farmers were able to operate on this self-reliant basis - rigorous though it was - they could maintain a decent standard of living.

Yet the condition was a temporary one. The competing slave economy of the large planters was still in its infancy, since only about six thousand slaves had been brought into the colony by 1700. However, the flow of Africans became a torrent in the succeeding decades, and the great plantation owners were able to grow and market tobacco much more cheaply. In addition, they increased their landholdings to the maximum degree possible, and instituted a system of mass production. This put more and more pressure on the small growers who found such competition increasingly severe. By the middle of the eighteenth century, the result was greatly reduced incomes for these agriculturists. Many were impoverished, and a class of "poor whites," living in squalor, sprang up (Ref. 20).

Wertenbaker (Ref. 21) rightly terms the "undermining of the yeoman class by the importation of slaves one of the great crimes of history." And he adds: "The wrong done the Negro himself has been universally condemned; the wrong done the white man has attracted less attention. It effectively deprived him of his American birthright - the high return for his labor. It transformed Virginia and the South from a land of hard-working, self-respecting yeomen to a land of slaves and slaveholders." It is not likely that all of Philip Pendleton descendants escaped the grave difficulties brought about by the steep decline of tobacco farm income. And in fact, it likely contributed to the great expansion westward shared by the general population and members of the Pendleton clan, where land could still be obtained.

Generation No. 6

8. HENRY[6] PENDLETON *(PHILIP[5], HENRY[4], HENRY[3], GEORGE[2], GEORGE[1])* was born 1683 in Old Rappahannock Co., VA, and died May 1721 in King & Queen Co., VA. He married MARY TAYLOR 1701, daughter of JAMES TAYLOR and MARY GREGORY. She was born Jun 02, 1688 in VA, and died Jun 10, 1770 in King and Queen Co., VA.

Henry was born in Old Rappahannock Co. and by 1704 was taxed as owner of 300 acres in King and Queen County at the age of 21. Henry's marriage with Mary Taylor probably occurred in St. Stephens Parish, King and Queen Co. He died in 1721 the same year his father died and the same year his famous son, the jurist Edmund Pendleton, was born.

Henry Pendleton owned land in South Farnham Parish, Essex Co. in 1707. South Farnham Parish, once a part of Old Rappahanock Co. was included in the new Essex Co. established in 1692. A 1707 Essex Co. deed (Ref. 22) describes a parcel of land, being sold by Edward and Anne Eastham of St. Stephens Parish, King and Queen Co. to William Croudus and Robert Moody, as "225 acres woodland ground, South Farnham Parish, in Essex Co." The parcel was further described as being part of 740 acres of land left to Anne Taylor by her deceased father James Taylor, and the current wife of Edward Eastham. The parcel bordered on the property of John Waggener, Henry Pendleton and John Burnett. It was apparently this property described in a 1742/43 Essex Co. deed (Ref. 23): "Francis Taylor of Drysdale parish, King and Queen Co. sells Robt Spilsbe Coleman of So. Farnham parish, 112 acres in So Farnham parish. Adjoins William Bradburns plantation, Jno Waggenors land, Henry Pendleton's land."

As the eldest son, Henry Pendleton's heirs apparently had the advantage of his father's estate although Henry died 6 months before his father. Henry's sons James, Nathaniel, John and the famous Judge Edmund Pendleton all rose to great prominence in Virginia. The descendants of Henry continued to hold high office and positions of prestige throughout the 18th and 19th centuries.

The exact wealth of Henry and his brothers, John and Philip Jr. is not known with certainty but the fact that Philip Sr., their father, and Henry, the eldest brother, as well as John had land and taxable property typical of the "planter class" indicates that all the early Virginia Pendletons maintained at least a moderate standard of living for the times. The fact that Judge Edmund was apprenticed at a young age indicates that the family was not wealthy. In the mid 1700s yeoman farm families still comprised the great majority of Virginia's population. They owned farms small enough to be worked by the family alone, perhaps with the help of an indentured white servant or one or two slaves. The husband and his children and perhaps his wife worked in the fields. Although they grew some tobacco for cash, their principal crops were corn, wheat, and vegetables for their own use. A few hogs, cattle, and poultry provided meat. Broadcloth or dress goods bought from a store might be used for their best clothes. But for every day the farmer's wife would spin linen and woolen thread from flax grown on the farm and from sheep raised there, and would weave the cloth and make the skirts and dresses herself (Ref. 24).

Henry Pendleton's wife, Mary Taylor, remarried at the age of 54. The marriage is recorded (Ref. 25) as "Watkins, Edward Married Mary, widow of Henry Pendleton, Book D 22, Page 407."

Children of HENRY PENDLETON and MARY TAYLOR are:
15.   i.   JAMES[7] PENDLETON, b. 1702, King & Queen Co., VA; d. 1763, Culpeper Co., VA.
16.   ii.   PHILIP PENDLETON, b. 1704, King & Queen Co., VA; d. 1778, VA.
17.   iii. ISABELLA PENDLETON, b. 1712, King & Queen Co., VA; d. 1790.
18.   iv.   NATHANIEL PENDLETON, b. 1715, King and Queen Co., Va.; d. 1793, Culpeper Co., VA.
19.   v.   MARY PENDLETON, b. 1717, King & Queen Co., VA; d. 1803, Madison Co., VA.
20.   vi.   JOHN PENDLETON, b. 1719, King & Queen Co., Va.; d. 1799, Hanover Co., VA.
       vii. EDMUND PENDLETON, b. Sep 09, 1721, Caroline Co., Va.; d. Oct 23, 1803, Richmond, Va.; m. (1) ELIZABETH ROY, Jan 21, 1740/41; d. Nov 17, 1742; m. (2) SARAH POLLARD, Jan 20, 1744/45; b. May 04, 1725; d. Feb 1815, Caroline Co., VA.

Edmund Pendleton (Fig. 6), a member of the seventh generation, remains the most famous descendant of the immigrant Philip Pendleton. He is the youngest son of Philip's eldest son Henry Pendleton. He had no children, dedicating his life to public service.

Figure 6 (from the National Archives). Edmund Pendleton was a friend of George Washington and a leader of the Virginia House of Burgesses in the years leading up to the American Revolution. Thomas Jefferson said of Edmund Pendleton, "Taken all in all he was the ablest man in debate I have ever met."

David John Mays (Ref. 10) wrote a detailed account of the life of Edmund Pendleton for those who wish to read more about this prominent Virginian. The following is Edmund's own biography. Completed on July 20, 1793, it was first published in the Richmond Enquirer, April 11, 1828.

I was born Sept. 9, 1721; my father died some time before. In Feb. 1734-'35 I was bound apprentice to Col. Benjamin Robinson, Clerk of Caroline Court. In 1737, I was made Clerk of the Vestry of St. Mary's Parish in Caroline; with the profits I purchased a few books, and read them very diligently. In 1740, I was made Clerk of Caroline Court Martial. In April, 1741,with my master's consent, I was licensed to practice Law, as an Attorney, being strictly examined by Mr. Barradall. Jan. 21, 1741, I was married to Betty, daughter of Mr. John Roy, against my friends' consent, as also my master's who, nevertheless, still continued his affection to me. My wife died Nov. 17, 1742. I was married a second time, the 20th of Jan. [1743], to Sarah, the daughter of Mr. Joseph Pollard, who was born on the 4th day of May 1725.

I practiced my profession with great approbation and success, more from my own good fortune, and the kind direction of providence, than my own merit; & in October, 1745, my reputation at the County Courts prompted to make an effort at the General Court, in which I continued, till 1774, when the dispute with Great Britain commenced.

In Nov. 1751, I was sworn a Justice of the Peace for Caroline, & continued to Nov. 1777. In Jan. 1752, I was elected a Burgess for Do. I was continued one of the representatives of Caroline without interruption until 1774, at which time I presided in Caroline Court, & was County Lieutenant. In June of that year, news arrived of the inimical designs of Parliament against the town of Boston; on which account the Assembly voted a fast and were dissolved by the Government. A number of members stayed in Williamsburg to keep the fast, when news arrived of the Boston Port Bill, when they collected and recommended to the people to choose members for Convention, to meet in August. I was chosen a member to that convention, who voted the utility of a General Congress of the States to meet in Philadelphia the first of Sept. I was chosen, and attended that Congress, and a second in May 1775. In Aug. 1775, I was appointed President of the Committee of Safety, and in Dec. following, President of the Convention, on the death of Mr. Randolph, and rechosen President of the new one in May, 1776. In Oct. 1776, I was elected to the chair of the House of Delegates who sat under the new Constitution. In March 1777, by a fall from a horse, I had my hip dislocated, & have been unable to walk ever since, except on crutches; however, the good people of Caroline the next month chose me as a delegate, in hopes of my recovery; but I could not attend in May session, and another speaker was appointed; in which, however, I was highly honoured, by all the candidates having promised to resign the chair, when I should come. I attended, on crutches, in the October session, but meant then to have leave of all public business and retire: but the General Court and Court of Chancery being established, I was prevailed on by some worthy members to consent to be nominated as a Chancery Judge, in which I was elected to the Presidency; and the whole by an unanimous vote.

In 1779, when the Court of Appeals was organized, and made to consist of the Judges of the General Court, Chancery and Admiralty, the Chancellors were to have the first rank, and of course I presided in that Court. In 1788, when a new arrangement was made of the Superior Courts, and that of Appeals, to consist of separate Judges, I retained my rank in that Court, and so may be considered as having been now 15 years at the head of the Judiciary Department. In 1788, when a State Convention was to meet to consider of a new proposed plan of federal Government, and all the officers of the State made eligible, my good old friends in Caroline again called me to their representation in Convention, and that respectable body to preside over them, indulging me with sitting in all my official duties, usually performed standing. Thus without any classical education

– without patrimony – without what is called the influence of Family Connection, and without solicitation, I have attained the highest offices in my Country.

I have often contemplated it a rare and extraordinary instance, and pathetically exclaimed, "Not unto me! Not unto me, O Lord, but unto thy name, be the praise." In his providence He was pleased to bestow on me a docile and unassuming mind, a retentive memory, a fondness for reading, a clear head, and upright heart, with a calm temper, benevolent to all; though particular in friendship with but few: And if I had uncommon merit in public business, it was that of superior diligence and attention.

Under the Regal Government I was a Whig in principle – considering it as designed for the good of society, and not for the aggrandizement of its officers, and influenced in my legislative and judicial character by that principle. When the dispute with Britain began, a redress of grievances, and not a revolution of Government was my wish: in this I was firm, but temperate; and whilst I was endeavoring to raise the spirits of the timid to a general united opposition, by stating to the uninformed the real merits of the dispute, I opposed and endeavored to moderate the violent and fiery, who were plunging us into rash measures, and had the happiness to find a majority of all the public bodies confirming my sentiments; which, I believe, was the corner stone of our success. Although I so long, and to so high a degree, experienced the favor of my country, I had always some enemies; few indeed, and I had the consolation to believe that their enmity was unprovoked, as I was ever unable to guess the cause, unless it was my refusing to go lengths with them, as their partizan.

Much of the Virginia Pendleton family chronology comes from Edmund Pendleton. In 1792 Edmund Pendleton wrote his family history on the blank pages between the Old and New Testaments of his family Bible. The following is taken from that history.

About the year 1674 Nathaniel Pendleton a Minister, and Philip Pendleton a school-master sons of Henry Pendleton of the city of Norwich, County of Norfolk in England, came from thence to Virginia in America.

Nathaniel died leaving no Issue, Philip went to England about 1680, returned to Virginia and, Philip intermarried with Isabella Hurt and died leaving issue three sons and four daughters, in November 1721. His two younger sons John and Philip severally married, died long ago and a considerable number of decendants from each are now living, but of them I can give no particular account. Elizabeth the eldest daughter intermarried with Samuel Clayton. Rachel the second with John Vass, Catherine the third with John Taylor and Isabella with Richard Thomas: Are dead and the posterity of each is numerous - but neither of these can I be particular.

Henry Pendleton the eldest son was born about 1683; In 1701 was married to Mary Taylor (daughter of James Taylor) who was born in 1688...so that he was 18 and she 13. He died in May 1721. She married a second husband Edward Watkins, whom she survived and died in 1770 aged 82.

James Pendleton eldest son of Henry, was born in 1702 , and died in 1762, leaving 4 children Henry, James, Philip and Anne , all married, now living and have issue. James and Anne are since dead. Philip Pendleton the second son died in 1778 leaving issue 5 daughters, all of whom married and have children, two are dead, three living, one since dead.

Nathaniel Pendleton, third son, was born in 1715 and is still living (1792) having children and grand children and great grand children. He died in 1794.

John Pendleton fourth son was born in 1719, and is still living (1792) having children grand children and great grand children. He died in 1799.

Edmund Pendleton fifth and youngest son was born in September 1721 (four months after the death of his father) was married in January 1741/2 to Elizabeth Roy, who in November following was delivered of a dead child and died in childbed. In June 1743 he was married to Sarah Pollard born in 1725 - both are now living and have never had a child. Her father Joseph Pollard was born in 1701 and died December 26th 1791, aged 90. Her mother still living aged 88. They lived together upwards of 68 years. She died July 27, 1794, aged 92. The said Edmund Pendleton [died] in Richmond whilst attending the court of appeals of which he was President on the 26th day of October 1803 in the 83rd year of his age.

The following is the will of Edmund Pendleton:

I, Edmund Pendleton of Edmundsbury in the County of Caroline, aged and infirm, but by divine favor tolerably free from bodily pain and of sound mind, do make this my will for settling my temporal concerns.

I give and devise the legal title and estate in a tract of land on west and reedy Creek, a branch of Holstein River the patent for which was granted in Virginia and confirmed by the Legislature of North Carolina, to my friend and relation Colonel John Taylor of Hazelwood (to whom I formerly sold an undivided moity thereof and received the purchase money) upon this trust and confidence, that he convey to the purchasers from my nephew Phillip Pendleton a tract of 500 acres, which I gave him out of my part, according to a survey thereof made by consent of James and Thomas Gaines in case the same is not already conveyed by virtue of my power of attorney for that purpose. And in trust to convey the land hereby devised, that is the residue according to the letter and spirit of two written agreements who, are jointly entered into respecting the same, the one with Messrs James and Thomas Gaines and the other with Mr. David Ross, taken together provided the said agreements are fulfilled on their parts, and my exors, receive the amount of John Ross's three bonds to me, or in case of failure to take such measures for the recovery of the money due to both of our joint expense as he my judge best. If he should die before the trust is fully executed, I empower any one of my executors, with the approbation of the others and of Colonel Taylor's executors, to make the like conveyances or take the other necessary measures.

I give to Edmund Pendleton Junr. son of my nephew Edmund a tract of land he is now in possession of, to begin at the mouth of a gut in Morocosic Creek a little above Samuel's Bridge running up the gut to the road, and along the road to my dwelling house to a corner, I mean to mark these. If not done to come two hundred and fifty yards from his cleared ground on the road thence North 40 degrees East to and across the _____ branch up the edge of the branch to his father's line along that line (to be so adjusted as to strike the branch to which I permitted my nephew to tend, including part of the land purchased of Col. John Taylor but made no conveyance and hereby confirm to him, to Morocosic Creek and down the creek to beginning. I also confirm my former gift of Mulatto J___ now in his possession.

In like manner I confirm to John Johnson of Newberry the gift of a girl Eddie now has in his possession.

I subject all my real estate to the payment of my debts if necessary but not to be sold during the life of my wife, unless by her consent and my Executors shall find it necessary to save my other estate for her, in that case I recommend a sale to be of New Gate plantation including the land below the road bounds of young Edmund's land to the road which leads over the bridge below my old mill and along that road to its nearest approach to the corner between that plantation and Capt. Jones and along the several lines to the creek and up the creek to the beginning, which I think will make a valuable settlement and sell well.

I give to my beloved wife the said New Gate plantation and all my other land in Caroline, all my slaves, stock and household goods, my chariot and harness, kitchen furniture, new goods, provisions and liquors in the house and such books as she shall choose, all which i give her the use of during her natural life, at her death I give the residue of my land except New Gate plantation above described, my great nephew John Pendleton of Newbury and his heirs, the slaves and other personal estate not consumed in the use to be equally divided between my nephew Edmund and his six children who are married, my faithful servant Nero to choose his master of them.

My New Gate plantation if not necessary to be sold I give to my nephew at the death of my wife, to hold during his life and at his death to his son John Pendleton and his heirs, but in that event I give no more of my land on the North East side of the road than shall lie southwest of a straight line to be run from young Edmund's corner, on that road to Dixon's line where it crosses the road above, and the residue of my land on the north east side of the said line I give to my great nephew Edmund Pendleton Junr. and his heirs who I hope will not think me partial to his brother for they share equally in my affection. I contemplate his equal provision from his father's land finally and only anticipated that for his brother on account of his more forward and growing family.

Out of my Crop of Grain growing or in the house at the time of my death, my wife is to have as much alloted her as will serve her family til another crop is made, the surplus only to be sold if any.

All the residue of my estate of what nature so ever, I give to my nephew Edmund Pendleton who knows my intention as to his father's mortgages and will act therein according.

My very numerous and respectable collateral relations share my affection and regard but are pretermitted in sharing my small fortune from justice to my nephew who being adopted by me when a child has a filial claim upon me which would have been injurious of me to disappoint.

I give to my friend Dr. William Baynham five guineas to buy a ring or such other memorial of me as he shall chuse, and to Col. John Taylor my gold headed cane present me by Dr. Baynham.

Of this will I appoint and request my said nephew Edmund Pendleton, his two sons John and Edmund, and my said relation and friend John Taylor to be executors assuredly confiding in their contributing all in their power to the happiness of my beloved wife who has been and is an affectionate aunt as well as a tender wife, revoking all former wills.

I have to this written my own hand to save the necessity of witnesses affixed my hand and seal, May the 19th, 1799.
Edmund Pendleton (SEAL)
At a court held for Caroline County of Tuesday, the 13th day of December, 1803.

This writing purporting to be the last will and testament of Edmund Pendleton without a subscribing witness thereto was presented to the Court and the Court from an inspection thereof was of opinion that the said will was wholly written by the said Pendleton. Ordered that the will be admitted to record.
Teste: William Nelson, C.C.C.

The will of Sarah (Pollard) Pendleton, Edmund's second wife is dated Jan. 1, 1811 and was proved in Caroline Co., February 1815.

9. ELIZABETH[6] PENDLETON *(PHILIP[5], HENRY[4], HENRY[3], GEORGE[2], GEORGE[1])* was born 1685 in Old Rappahannock Co., Virginia, and died 1761 in Essex Co., Virginia. She married SAMUEL CLAYTON 1705, son of SAMUEL CLAYTON. He was born 1689 in Gloucester Co., VA, and died 1735 in Essex Co., Virginia.

Children of ELIZABETH PENDLETON and SAMUEL CLAYTON are:
  i. PHILIP[7] CLAYTON, b. 1705, VA; d. 1786, Culpeper Co., VA; m. ANN COLEMAN.
    Philip Clayton was a Major in the Revolutionary War.

  ii. JOHN CLAYTON, b. Abt. 1710, VA; m. FARGESON.
  iii. III SAMUEL CLAYTON, b. 1715, VA; d. 1784.
21. iv. ELIZABETH CLAYTON, b. Abt. 1716, VA; d. Bef. 1793.
  v. LUCY CLAYTON, b. Abt. 1718, VA; d. May 16, 1763; m. WILLIAM WILLIAMS.
  vi. GEORGE CLAYTON, b. Oct 05, 1720, VA; d. Jun 09, 1765.

10. ISABELLA[6] PENDLETON *(PHILIP[5], HENRY[4], HENRY[3], GEORGE[2], GEORGE[1])* was born Abt. 1688 in Old Rappahannock Co., VA, and died Aft. 1748 in VA. She married RICHARD THOMAS, son of JOHN THOMAS and ELIZABETH? He was born Abt. 1680, and died Dec 03, 1748 in Drysdale Parish, Caroline Co., VA.

Children of ISABELLA PENDLETON and RICHARD THOMAS are:
  i. JOSEPH[7] THOMAS, b. 1722.
  ii. JAMES THOMAS, b. 1725.
  iii. MARY PENDLETON THOMAS, b. 1726; m. THOMAS BARBOUR, Dec 18, 1771; b. 1736.
  iv. RICHARD THOMAS, b. 1728; m. MILDRED TAYLOR.
  v. CATHERINE THOMAS, b. 1730; m. AMBROSE BARBOUR.

11. JOHN[6] PENDLETON *(PHILIP[5], HENRY[4], HENRY[3], GEORGE[2], GEORGE[1])* was born 1691 in Old Rappahannock Co., VA, and died 1776 in VA. He married MARY TINSLEY 1719. She was born 1703.

The only record available of this John Pendleton other than Edmund Pendleton's family history is the Virginia Tax Records, Quit Rent Roll for the Year 1715, Essex Co., VA where John Pendleton is listed with 200 acres.

John and his younger brother Philip Jr. are said to have removed from St. Stephen's Parish, the middle of three parishes in King and Queen County, and lived on the east slope of Tobacco Row Mountain in what is now Amherst County, VA. John and Philip are reputedly buried in the old Pendleton graveyard near Tobacco Row, but the graves are not marked (Ref. 1). There is no disputing the fact that John's son William lived in that area but this William is listed in the 1764 Culpeper County Rent rolls. It was, therefore, some time after 1764 that William removed to Amherst County where he died in 1779 and left a will. The property of William's heirs was established in 1783 and described in 1796 as on the south branch of Harris Creek which is near Tobacco Row Mountain, Amherst Co. It is thus feasible that John Pendleton spent his elder years with his son William in Amherst Co.

There has been some confusion as to the parentage of certain children of the third generation of Virginia Pendletons in the New World. Early research has erroneously assigned at least two third generation Pendletons (Henry and Mary of Spotsylvania) to Philip Pendleton Jr. (Refs. 1 to 3). However, a book of devotions printed about 1742 and owned by Henry Pendleton of Spotsylvania has several significant entries. In one place appears the note, "Henry Pendleton, his book, June 19, 1789." Another entry reads "Henry Pendleton, son of John Pendleton and Mary, his wife, was born the 19th of February 1723." To this has been added, "died the 6th of April 1818." This book of devotions establishes John Pendleton (1691-1776) who married Mary Tinsley, as the father of Henry Pendleton of Spotsylvania County (Ref. 5). The book of Henry Pendleton can be found in the Virginia Historical Archives. Earlier work summarized by Gottschalk and Nicklin (Ref. 3) clearly established Mary Pendleton as the sister of Henry Pendleton and thus it would follow that she is also a daughter of John Pendleton. In addition, Green in his narrative of settlers in Culpeper Co. (Ref. 1) identifies William Pendleton of Culpeper and Amherst Counties as the son of this John Pendleton.

Children of JOHN PENDLETON and MARY TINSLEY are:
22.   i.   WILLIAM[7] PENDLETON, b. 1720, Essex Co., VA; d. 1779, Amherst Co., VA.
23.   ii.   MARY PENDLETON, b. 1722, Essex Co., VA.
24.   iii. HENRY PENDLETON, b. Feb 19, 1723/24, Essex Co., VA; d. Apr 06, 1818, Spotsylvania Co., VA.

12. RACHEL[6] PENDLETON *(PHILIP[5], HENRY[4], HENRY[3], GEORGE[2], GEORGE[1])* was born Abt. 1693 in Essex Co., VA. She married JOHN VASS, son of VINCENT VASS. He was born Abt. 1683 in VA, and died 1755 in Essex Co., VA.
John Vass is listed in the Essex Co. Quit Rent Rolls of 1715 with 490 acres.

Children of RACHEL PENDLETON and JOHN VASS are:
      i.   PHILIP VINCENT[7] VASS, b. 1720.
      ii.   JOHN VASS, JR., b. King and Queen Co., VA.

iii. HENRY VASS.
iv. REUBEN VASS.

13. PHILIP[6] PENDLETON, JR. *(PHILIP[5], HENRY[4], HENRY[3], GEORGE[2], GEORGE[1])* was born 1695 in Essex Co., VA, and died 1753 in VA. He married ELIZABETH POLLARD 1717 in VA, daughter of ROBERT POLLARD and ELIZABETH BAYLOR. She was born 1700 in King & Queen Co., Va., and died 1751 in VA.

As previously noted, Philip Jr. along with his older brother John, are said to have removed from King and Queen Co., and lived on the east slope of "Tobacco Row Mountain" in what is now Amherst Co., VA. Of considerable interest in this regard is a record found "At a Court Continued for Albemarle County, January 24, 1745/46: Phillip May makes oath that Phillip Pendleton owes him L10/3 on account." Amherst Co. was later formed from Albemarle Co. in 1761. The Philip Pendleton in the Albemarle record could be Philip Jr. but seems more likely to be his son who married Spice Freeland (who tellingly was born in King and Queen Co.). The younger Philip Pendleton died about 1770 but Spice Freeland Pendleton and their children can be found later in the records of Cumberland and Buckingham Counties east of Amherst County.

Children of PHILIP PENDLETON and ELIZABETH POLLARD are:
      i. SARAH[7] PENDLETON, b. 1720, VA; m. JOSEPH THOMAS.
25.   ii. BENJAMIN PENDLETON, b. 1726, VA; d. Jan 07, 1798, King & Queen Co., VA.
26.   iii. PHILIP PENDLETON, b. Bef. 1728, VA; d. Abt. 1770, VA.
      iv. EDMUND PENDLETON, b. 1730, VA; d. 1779.
         This may be the Edmund Pendleton listed in "A Merchants Account Book - Thomas Hamilton's Cargo, 1750-51, King & Queen Co., VA" (Ref. 26).

      v. JOHN PENDLETON, b. 1734, VA.
27.   vi. PRISCILLA PENDLETON, b. Abt. 1736, VA.

14. CATHERINE[6] PENDLETON *(PHILIP[5], HENRY[4], HENRY[3], GEORGE[2], GEORGE[1])* was born 1699 in Essex Co., VA, and died Jul 26, 1774. She married JOHN TAYLOR Feb. 14, 1716, son of JAMES TAYLOR and MARY GREGORY. He was born Nov. 18, 1696, and died Mar. 22, 1780.

Children of CATHERINE PENDLETON and JOHN TAYLOR are:
      i. MARY[7] TAYLOR, b. May 30, 1718; d. Sep 13, 1757; m. JOSEPH PENN, Feb 03, 1734/35, Caroline Co., VA; b. Nov 17, 1717, King & Queen Co., VA; d. 1773, Spotsylvania Co., VA.
      ii. CATHERINE TAYLOR, b. Dec 30, 1719; d. 1774; m. MOSES PENN, Jul 04, 1739; b. 1712; d. Nov 04, 1759.
      iii. ANN TAYLOR, b. May 10, 1721.
      iv. EDMUND TAYLOR, b. May 12, 1723; d. 1808, Granville Co., NC; m. ANNIE LEWIS; b. 1733.
      v. ISABELLA TAYLOR, b. Jun 26, 1725; d. 1786; m. SAMUEL HOPKINS, Jan 25, 1749/50; b. 1725; d. 1796.

vi. JOHN TAYLOR, b. Jul 17, 1727; d. Oct 26, 1787; m. LUCY LYNNE.

vii. JAMES TAYLOR, b. Sep 07, 1729; d. 1756; m. ANNE POLLARD.

viii. PHILIP TAYLOR, b. Feb 17, 1731/32; d. 1765; m. MARY WALKER.

ix. ELIZABETH TAYLOR, b. Jul 09, 1735; m. (1) WILLIAM BULLOCK; m. (2) JAMES LEWIS, CAPT., Dec 25, 1752; b. 1726; d. May 21, 1764.

x. WILLIAM TAYLOR, b. Dec 19, 1736; d. 1803; m. ELIZABETH ANDERSON.

xi. JOSEPH TAYLOR, b. Feb 19, 1741/42; m. FRANCES ANDERSON, Apr 07, 1763; b. 1743.

Generation No. 7 – Late Colonial Virginia

The seventh generation consists of the grandchildren of the immigrant Philip Pendleton and Isabella Hurt. The time period is from about 1727, when James Pendleton, Philip's eldest grandchild first married in Lancaster Co., VA, to 1818 the year Philip's longest lived grandson, Henry Pendleton, died in Spotsylvania Co., VA. This generation includes the jurist Edmund Pendleton who, because he had no known offspring, is included once as a child of Henry Pendleton in the sixth generation (see page 19 for Edmund's life history). The seventh generation Pendletons like the sixth spent their entire lives within Virginia (Fig. 6).

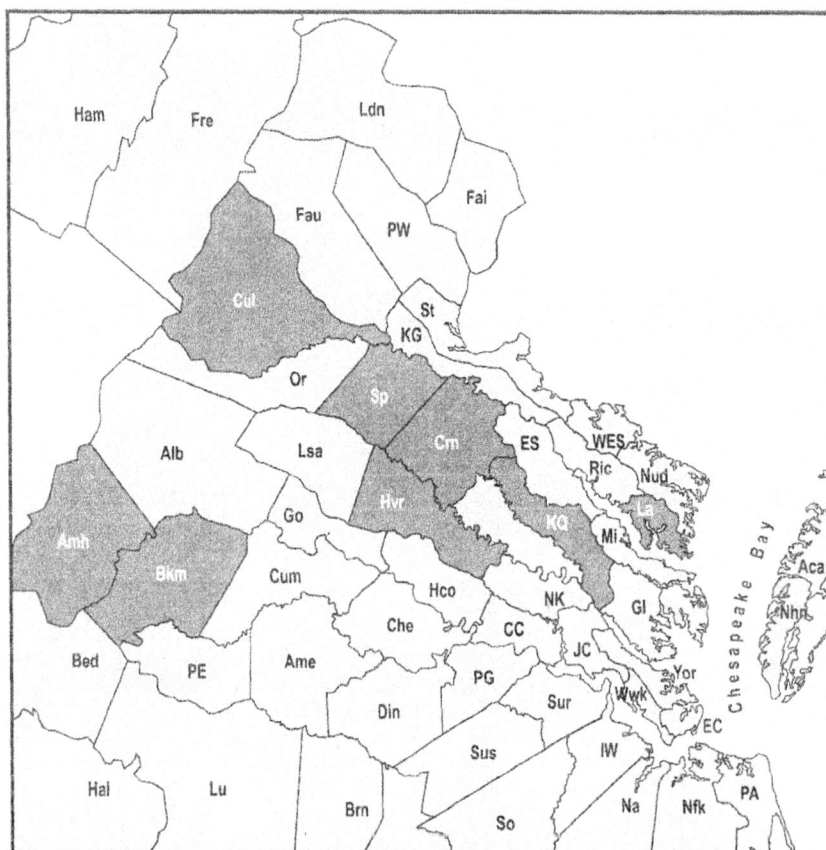

Figure 6. Virginia Counties in 1761. The children of Henry resided primarily in Culpeper (Cul) but also in Hanover (Hvr), Lancaster (La), and Caroline (Crn). The known children of John lived in Spotsylvania (Sp) and Amherst (Amh). The known children of Philip lived in King & Queen (KQ) and Buckingham (Bkm).

Early in the eighteenth century, the tidewater area was owned mainly by larger planters but the piedmont area west to the mountains was made up for the most part of smaller farms. Most of the Pendleton seventh generation moved west from their parents' tidewater farms in Essex and King and Queen Counties out to Culpeper, Lancaster,

Hanover, Caroline, Spotsylvania, Amherst, and Buckingham Counties. By 1749 the frontier of Virginia had moved upward from the fall line of its rivers to the crest of the Blue Ridge and thence across the Valley to the crest of the Alleghenies. Because it was easier to penetrate rivers than forests, English colonists pushed their way upland west along the James, the Roanoke, the Rappahannock, and the Potomac while Scottish-Irish, Germans and other immigrants moved south up the Shenandoah River Valley (Ref. 27).

A central aspect of life in early Virginia was slavery. The number of slaves in Virginia grew rapidly after the turn of the century and by 1763 about 60,000 blacks made up about half the state's population. The magnificent tidewater estates of the "gentry," the elegant plantation homes, and the society of the ruling class were all based on slave labor. The yeoman tobacco farmer had little chance to compete (Ref. 12).

One result of the spread of slavery over a wider and wider area of the tobacco economy, beyond the tidewater, was to give increasing political power to the smaller plantation owners which included many of the seventh generation Pendletons. These gentlemen had now entered the slaveholding aristocracy, and were competing for prestige with the group of great landowners who had dominated the scene in the seventeenth and early eighteenth centuries. Since the right to vote was restricted to free holders, the House of Burgesses became more and more to be made up of a landed slave-owning class. Whereas the council, appointed by the British government, had previously been the legislative branch that wielded the greater power, the House of Burgesses now replaced it as the center of political potency (Ref. 20). It was in this House of Burgesses that Edmund Pendleton, was to become one of the architects of the American Revolution. His brother John was also a member of the House of Burgesses. In fact, Edmund, James, Nathaniel, and John all sons of Henry were each prominent members of Virginia society as sheriffs, justices, and Anglican Church vestrymen. No doubt, their prestige and positions of authority reflected their continued association with the Anglican Church. This association was not the case for other members of the Pendleton family in Virginia.

In the middle of the 18th century, there were significant changes in the practice of religion by the Virginia Pendletons that reflected the changes in the Virginia population as a whole. The immigrant Reverend Nathaniel Pendleton was an Anglican minister and his brother, Philip Pendleton, Sr. no doubt shared his religious beliefs. The descendants of Philip's son Henry, most notably Judge Edmund Pendleton, continued to be closely associated with the Church of England. But others severed their ties with the Anglicans. For example, Henry Pendleton, Sr., Philip's grandson, was a devout Baptist. Changes in the family religion occurred throughout Virginia in the mid 1700s during and after the "Great Awakening."

By 1750 the established English Anglican Church, although still dominate in the tidewater, was challenged in the piedmont and the western frontier by the "new-light" Anglicans resulting from the "Great Awakening," and the incoming Scotch-Irish Presbyterians, the German Lutherans, Reformed Church, and Quakers. These newcomers were encouraged to settle in the mountains and great valley to the west. But the Baptists were a different story. "Regular" Baptists had been living quietly in the community for years until "Separate" Baptists from outside of Virginia arrived. The separate Baptists managed an important coup when they won over Samuel Harris of Hanover, a former

Anglican vestryman who had served in the House of Burgesses. Harris became a Baptist minister in 1760 and was a significant factor in the spectacular growth of the denomination from that year until the outbreak of the Revolution. Henry Pendleton, Sr. and his sons Henry, Jr. and Phillip became important members of this newly influential group noted for their fiery sermons, courage in the face of persecution, and as crusaders for religious freedom. These attributes were in stark contrast to the staid, conservative tidewater Anglicans (Ref. 12) and in contrast to the continued institution of slavery among the Baptists. But indeed, without slaves one could not effectively compete with the established plantations in the tobacco economy!

On November 20, 1767, Upper Spotsylvania Baptist Church was organized with twenty-five members, making it the first Baptist Church between the James and Rappahanock Rivers (Ref. 28). Lewis Craig was the first pastor. Now called Craig's Baptist Church, it still exists today on Rt. 608 near the Orange County line. Mine Road, with Henry Pendleton, Jr. as pastor, was the seventh Baptist church erected in the county in 1791.

Much has been written about the turning away of the citizenry from the Anglican Church. Certainly a spirit of independence pervaded the religious as well as the political life at the time of the Revolution. Perhaps the Established Church with its conformity to canons enforced by civil law was too closely associated with British imperialism. Whatever the reasons, Spotsylvanians by the hundreds turned to the dissenting denominations such as the Baptists and Methodists (Ref. 29).

The French-Indian war directly or indirectly effected the lives of many Virginia Pendletons – especially those near the frontier. Virginia's charter gave the colony the lands not only west, but also northwest of the tidewater and piedmont areas all the way to the Pacific! This claim brought the colony into conflict with France, which claimed much of the same territory. Hostilities began in earnest in 1755 when England decided to send regulars to drive out the French. Major General Braddock's troops suffered a major defeat leaving him dead on the Wilderness Road and the frontier area vulnerable to Indian attack. Families were massacred, outposts were raided and pioneers crowded back across the mountains (Ref. 24). By 1759, however, the French were defeated and the frontier was open once again for colonial expansion. A Philip Pendleton was given a Warrant for Land in Kentucky for Service in the French and Indian War. This was apparently Philip Pendleton III (bef. 1728- abt. 1770), son of Philip Pendleton, Jr. (1695 - 1753) and Elizabeth Pollard and grandson of Philip Pendleton, the emigrant.

The seventh generation Pendletons were too old to serve in the Revolutionary Army that was formed after the Declaration of Independence in 1776. However, Edmund Pendleton (1721-1803) played a central role as Speaker of the House of Burgesses. His exploits are summarized in his own words beginning on page 19. Others who contributed to the cause include Nathaniel Pendleton (1716-1793) who continued to serve as a Culpeper Co. Justice and furnished at frequent intervals, supplies for the use of the Army; John Pendleton (1719-1799) who was chosen for the Hanover Co. Committee of Safety in 1775; Henry Pendleton (1723/24-1818) who supplied beef to the Revolutionary Army; and Benjamin Pendleton (1726-1798) who was chosen for the King and Queen Co. Committee of Safety in 1774.

Generation No. 7

15. JAMES[7] PENDLETON *(HENRY[6], PHILIP[5], HENRY[4], HENRY[3], GEORGE[2], GEORGE[1])* was born 1702 in King & Queen Co., VA, and died 1763 in Culpeper Co., VA. He married (1) MARY LYELL TAYLOR Jan 08, 1727/28 in Lancaster Co., VA. She was a resident of Christ Church Parish, Lancaster Co. He married (2) ELIZABETH Abt. 1730 in VA. She died Sep 1769 in Culpeper Co., VA.

Perhaps the earliest record of this James Pendleton is in a Spotsylvania deed dated Aug 29, 1727 (Ref. 30). "James Taylor of Drysdale Par., King and Queen Co., surveyor, to Richard Thomas of the same par. And county, overseer. 5 shill., 1200a. Of land—part of pat. Granted ad. Taylor July 1, in St. Geo. Par., Spts. Co.; Witnesses: John Taylor, William Tayloe, James Pendleton; Rec. Novr. 7, 1727." Martha Taylor, wife of James Taylor, released her dower right to the above property to Richard Thomas by her attorney, John Waller. The marriage of James Pendleton and Mary Taylor is recorded (Ref. 31) as "January 8, 1727–8, Jas. Pendleton of Drysdale Par., King and Queen Co., and Mary Lyell, widow."

James was again a witness in 1742 (Ref. 32). "Daniel Brown of St. Mark's Par., Orange Co., to Thomas Brown of Par. And county afsd. £40 curr. Tract of land whereon sd. Daniel formerly lived, in St. Geo. Par., Spts. Co.—on S. side Pike Run, and part of a tract purchased by sd. Daniel of Larkin Chew, Decd., and part of a tract granted sd. Chew, June 4, 1722. Jas. Pendleton, Phillip Clayton, John Nalle, John Parks. July 6, 1742."

James Pendleton was a Justice of Orange Co. in May 1743. In 1757 he was a vestryman of St. Mark's Parish, Culpeper Co., and a Lay Reader. In 1758 he was High Sheriff of Culpeper Co. A will for James Pendleton of Culpeper Co. was dated 17 Dec 1762, and probated 17 Feb 1763 (Ref. 33).

Children of JAMES PENDLETON and ELIZABETH are:
28.   i.   HENRY[8] PENDLETON, b. 1733, VA; d. 1798, Culpeper Co., Virginia.
29.   ii.   JR. JAMES PENDLETON, b. 1735, Culpeper Co., VA; d. Dec 1793, Culpeper Co., VA.
30.   iii. ANNE PENDLETON, b. Abt. 1740; d. Feb 1815, Caroline Co., VA.
31.   iv.   PHILIP PENDLETON, b. Abt. 1741, Caroline Co., VA; d. Nov 01, 1793, Pittsylvania Co., VA.

16. PHILIP[7] PENDLETON *(HENRY[6], PHILIP[5], HENRY[4], HENRY[3], GEORGE[2], GEORGE[1])* was born 1704, VA and died 1778, VA. He married MARTHA RUFFIN.
Early genealogies (Refs. 1 and 2) attributed 14 children to Philip Pendleton and Martha Ruffin but this is disputed by Gottschalk and Nicklin (Ref. 3). And except for Jemima Pendleton no additional evidence is found for even the 5 children listed below (from Ref. 3).

It may be this Philip Pendleton who is mentioned in an Essex Co. deed of 14 Jul 1768 (Ref. 34) that includes articles of agreement between Constance Bond and William

Bond (her son) before her upcoming re-marriage to Phillip Pendleton. For her dower, he gives her one negro woman named Sarah, one negro girl named Chide, one black leather trunk, one small red trunk, and her side saddle. This Philip Pendleton is said to have lived in Lancaster Co., where they removed after this marriage.

Children of PHILIP PENDLETON and MARTHA RUFFIN are:
     i.   MARY[8] PENDLETON.
     ii. MARTHA PENDLETON.
     iii. MILDRED PENDLETON.
     iv. JUDITH PENDLETON.
32.   v. JEMIMA PENDLETON.

17. ISABELLA[7] PENDLETON *(HENRY[6], PHILIP[5], HENRY[4], HENRY[3], GEORGE[2], GEORGE[1])* was born 1712, King & Queen Co., VA, and died 1790, VA. She married WILLIAM GAINES, son of RICHARD GAINES and DOROTHY KELLEY. He was born 1704 in VA, and died 1792 in Culpeper Co., VA.

Isbell (sic) Pendleton and Elizabeth Penn were the Godmothers and James Pendleton the Godfather of Frances Madison who was born March 6, 1726 and baptized April 9. Frances Madison was an Aunt of President James Madison (Ref. 35). Isabella Pendleton was the grandmother of Gen. Edmund P. Gaines, Commander Fort Erie in the War of 1812 and the officer who arrested Aaron Burr on charges of treason.

Children of ISABELLA PENDLETON and WILLIAM GAINES are:
     i.   RICHARD[8] GAINES, b. Abt. 1728.
     ii. HENRY GAINES, b. Abt. 1730.
     iii. BENJAMIN GAINES, b. Abt. 1732; m. ELIZABETH BOTTS.
     iv. ROBERT GAINES, b. Abt. 1734.
     v. FRANCES GAINES, b. Abt. 1735.
     vi. THOMAS GAINES, b. Abt. 1738.
     vii. ANNE GAINES, b. Abt. 1742.
     viii. JAMES GAINES, b. Abt. 1742.
     ix. PHILIP GAINES, b. Abt. 1745.
     x. ISABELLA GAINES, b. Abt. 1750.

18. NATHANIEL[7] PENDLETON *(HENRY[6], PHILIP[5], HENRY[4], HENRY[3], GEORGE[2], GEORGE[1])* was born 1715 in King and Queen Co., Va., and died 1793 in Culpeper Co., VA. He married ELIZABETH CLAYTON Oct 14, 1745 in Essex Co., VA, daughter of SAMUEL CLAYTON and ELIZABETH PENDLETON. She was born Abt. 1716, and died Bef. 1793.

Nathaniel Pendleton is listed in the 1741 Essex County Tax Rolls (Ref. 36). He married his cousin, Elizabeth Clayton, widow of Joseph Anderson (who died in Essex County in 1735) and daughter of Samuel Clayton and Elizabeth Pendleton. The will of her father Samuel Clayton (Ref. 37) names his wife Elizabeth, eldest son Philip, sons George, Samuel and John; and daughters Elizabeth Anderson and Lucy Clayton. Nathaniel's marriage is listed as (Ref. 25) "Anderson, Elizabeth Administratrix of Joseph, married Nathaniel Pendleton, Book: O 13, Page: 254." Nathaniel and his wife later sold property in Essex Co. on Apr 21, 1752 (Ref. 38).

> Nathaniel Pendleton and Betty his wife of So. Farnham parish sell Robt Spilsby Coleman of Drysdale parish, King and Queen Co., for L 180., 200 acres, part of 1563 acres granted on 20 April 1687 to Edwin Thacker and by him sold to James Taylor of King and Queen Co, and by said Taylor devised to his daughter Mary who since intermarried with Edward Watkins and by Edward and Mary Watkins conveyed to Philip and John Pendleton [brothers of Nathaniel] by Deed of Gift recorded in Essex Court 19 Oct 1742. Philip and Jno Pendleton conveyed the land to Nathaniel Pendleton (party to this) by Lease and Release. Justice of the Peace, Culpeper Co.

Nathaniel Pendleton was High Sheriff of Culpeper County, Virginia and Chief Magistrate in 1765 and as such was the first to sign the Protest against the Stamp Act. This Protest, which is in his own handwriting, was signed by the sixteen Justices of the Peace of Culpeper County. He was prominent in St. Mark's Parish and was one of the founders of the town of Fairfax (now Culpeper). From 1762 to 1765 he was a Gentleman Justice. On 21 July 1763 with Ambrose Powell and Thomas Scott, he was ordered by the County Court to the Governor of Virginia as a "fit person for the office of Sheriff." On 15 December, 1763, as Nathaniel Pendleton, Gent., he was ordered paid "account for chairs for the county." During the Revolution he continued to serve as a Justice and furnished at frequent intervals, supplies for the use of the Army. His home was called "Redwood" and there descendants still reside in Culpeper County, VA. Both he and his brother James and later his nephew James Pendleton, Jr., were Clerks of the Vestry and Lay Readers of St. Mark's Parish.

Nathaniel Pendleton's will was recorded September 9, 1793 in Berkeley Co., VA abbreviated as "Dev.: Nat., Wm., Philip, sons; Mary Williams, Eliz. Tutt, Susannah Wilson, dau." His will was probated on 19 September 1793, Berkeley County, Virginia. A copy of it was filed in Deed Book Y., page 94, Culpeper County, as part of an "indenture made, Sept. 13, 1831, between William Pendleton executor of the last will and testament of Nathaniel Pendleton, deceased of the County of Berkeley and State of Virginia of the one part and Francis Ferguson of the County of Culpeper --- of the other part." Nathaniel is buried in Culpeper Cemetery, Culpeper, VA (Ref. 39).

Elizabeth Clayton was the executor of her first husband's estate (Ref. 40) "at a Court held for Essex County at Tappa' on the 16th day August 1743." This account was examined by the Court and allowed and then Elizabeth Pendleton the "Executrix of the last Will and Testam't of the sd Joseph Anderson dec'ed made Oath that the said account was Just and true." In the will book account the recorded expenses date from 1734 on.

Children of NATHANIEL PENDLETON and ELIZABETH CLAYTON are:

   i. MARY[8] PENDLETON, b. Abt. 1746; m. JOHN WILLIAMS.
33. ii. WILLIAM PENDLETON, b. Jan 13, 1748/49, Essex Co., Va.; d. Mar 31, 1817, Berkeley Co., VA.
   iii. HENRY PENDLETON, b. 1750, Culpeper Co., VA; d. Jan 10, 1789, Greenville, SC.

Henry Pendleton, having settled in South Carolina, was elected, April 27, 1776 one of the five new circuit judges for that state. When the British overran the state he joined the patriot forces and fought at Eutaw. Henry is listed in the 1778 South Carolina census, Charleston District. He resumed his judgeship in 1782 and was one of three judges appointed to revise the laws of the state in 1785. He originated the County Court act of South Carolina. He also served in the House of Representatives and in 1788 he was a member of the Constitutional Convention. Pendleton County, South Carolina was named for him (Ref. 41). He apparently died without issue. Additional biographical information can be found at the Virginia Historical Society (Ref. 42).

34.   iv.   PHILIP PENDLETON, b. 1752, VA; d. Dec 1801, Martinsburg, VA.

35.   v.   ELIZABETH PENDLETON, b. Abt. 1754.

36.   vi.   JR. NATHANIEL PENDLETON, JR., b. 1756, Culpeper Co., VA; d. Oct 20, 1821, Hyde Park, NY.

       vii.   SUSANNAH PENDLETON, b. Abt. 1760; m. JAMES WILSON, Feb 11, 1781, Berkeley Co., VA.

           James and Susannah Pendleton Wilson both died at Martinsburg, Berkeley Co., VA. Their daughter Nancy Wilson was born June 16,1783 at Berkeley Co. She died at Fayette Co., Ohio March 3,1870. On January 17,1802 Nancy married Isaac Smith (Smyth(e) Smit). Isaac was born June 16,1780 Berkeley Co. He died May 3,1853 at Fayette Co., Ohio. Isaac is the son of Alexander Smythe (b. abt. 1742 d. abt.1801) and his first wife(unknown). Alexander's father was Rev. William Smith (b.1716 in Holland) (Ref. 43).

19. MARY[7] PENDLETON (*HENRY*[6], *PHILIP*[5], *HENRY*[4], *HENRY*[3], *GEORGE*[2], *GEORGE*[1]) was born 1717, and died 1803 in Madison Co., VA. She married JAMES GAINES 1734 in VA, son of RICHARD GAINES and DOROTHY KELLEY. He was born 1710, and died 1786 in Culpeper Co., VA.

    Members of the Gaines family are found of record in Virginia within the first fifty years of its existence as a colony. James Gaines resided in Culpeper Co., where his will, made May 24, 1781, was probated March 20, 1786 (Ref. 44).

Children of MARY PENDLETON and JAMES GAINES are:

       i.   CATHERINE[8] GAINES, b. 1735.

      ii.   HENRY GAINES, b. 1737.

     iii.   JAMES GAINES, b. 1739.

     iv.   MARY GAINES, b. 1741.

      v.   RICHARD EDWARD GAINES, b. 1743.

     vi.   EDMUND GAINES, b. 1745.

    vii.   JOSEPH GAINES, b. 1747.

   viii.   WILLIAM GAINES, b. 1749.

     ix.   FRANCIS GAINES, b. 1752.

      x.   THOMAS GAINES, b. 1754.

xi.   ISABELLA GAINES, b. 1759.
xii.   SARAH GAINES, b. Aft. 1759.

20. JOHN[7] PENDLETON *(HENRY[6], PHILIP[5], HENRY[4], HENRY[3], GEORGE[2], GEORGE[1])* was born 1719 in King & Queen Co., Va., and died 1799 in Hanover Co., VA. He married (1) PHOEBE JAMES 1743. He married (2) SARAH MADISON 1761. She died Aft. 1815 in Hanover Co., VA?

John Pendleton was a member of the Orange Co., VA militia as an ensign in 1757. He was a member of the House of Burgesses in 1765; Sheriff of King & Queen Co. in 1766, and Justice from 1765 to 1769. He was the recipient of a Virginia Land Grant: "John Pendleton, 5 June 1765, Orange Co., 943 ac. on the south side of the SW Mountain Rd. adjoining land of Nathaniel Claiborne, Pat. 36, pg. 729."

He moved to Hanover Co. in 1770 where he was a member of that county's Committee of Safety in 1775. John Pendleton was too old for active service but in 1775 was appointed by a convention of Delegates at Richmond to sign part of the large issue of Treasury notes. He was also a member of the House of Delegates in 1779. John is listed along with his son James in numerous lists of Hanover County Taxpayers, Saint Paul's Parish from 1782 to 1798. In the listing of 1799 - 1803 John Pendleton's estate and one adult are included. A biographical sketch of John Pendleton (Ref. 45) is listed in The Virginia Historical Society Catalog. The following is the will of John Pendleton:

In the name of God, Amen. I John Pendleton of Hanover County, aged and infirm, but in mind and memory as perfect as usual, do make this my last Will and Testament. Imprimis, I give unto Sarah, my beloved wife, all the Tea and Coffee ware, the Silver Tea Spoons and Tongs, to her and her heirs forever. I also lend to her, my beloved wife, for and during her natural life one old negro woman named Esther, her two sons named Dick and Gabriel, and her two daughters Milley and Esther and their children, and a negro boy named Gilbert.
Item: I lend to my said wife, one half of all my Household, Kitchen, Dairy and meat-house furniture, six silver tablespoons, two horses, her choice, one yoke of oxen and cart, six other cattle, eight sheep, all the stock of hos, half of the plantation tools, six books, her choice, Fort barrels of Corn, and the Wheat this is put up for house use; with all the wool and cotton spinning wheels and cards; five Cyder Casks, and the remainder of my land and plantation I now live on, supposed to be about three hundred acres, for and during her natual life, and in lieu of Dower, and at her death, my will and desire is that the land together with all the other property lent to my beloved wife should be sold upon a credit of twelve months and the monies arising from such sale to be disposed of in the following manner, to wit:
Item: I give to my son Edmund, my silver cap, to him and his heirs forever.
Item: I give to my son John six silver tablespoons, to him and his heirs forever.
Item: I give to each of my daughters, Elizabeth and Mary, five pounds to them and their heirs forever.
Item: I give to my younger children, Henry, Sarah, James, Lucy and Thomas sixty pounds each to them and their heirs forever, under the following restrictions, towit, the land my son James is now in possession of, shall be valued by Edmund Taylor, John Thornton, and Thomas Price, and whatever sum the same may be valued at he my said son James must accountable for to my Executors, after giving him credit for the sixty pounds legacy. And it is my will and intention that all the legacys and bequests arising to

my daughter Lucy, under this my last will, should remain in the hands and under the control of my son Henry as Truste: for the maintainance of her my said Daughter Lucy and her children, and at her death to be equally divided among all her children, to them and their heirs forever; my intention in being thus particular as to the legacies intended for my Daughter Lucy is to prevent her husband, Robert Sydnor having any control.

Item: My will and desire is that the land my son James is to have and enjoy under this my will should be laid off in the following manner. Beginning at a beach on the river bank, running a nearly South East course by a line of marked trees, to a poplar in the branch near his spring, thence direct to a three-bodied oak on the west side of the path that leads to Mr. Madison's, thence along that path as it now stands to Beach Creek, thence up the Creek to Mr. Austin Morris's corner, thence along said Morris's line to the river; supposed to contain one hundred and fifty acres, to him and his heirs forever.

And in case my friends Edmund Taylor, John Thornton and Thomas Price, or either of them, die or refuse to perform the requisites herein required, then and in that case, it is my will and dsire that my Executors hereafter named shall name one person, my son James, a second, and they too, a third person to act with them in order to ascertain the value of the land devised to my son James.

Item: I give and bequeath to my son Thomas, immediately upon my death one feather bed and furniture to him and his heirs forever.

Item: All the rest and residue of my Estate, my will and desire is that my Executors hereinafter named, or either of them shall advertize and sell upon a credit of twelve months, requiring bond, with good security. And after the payment of all my just debts and legacys the residue to be equally divided among all my children to them and their heris forever, excepting my Daughter Lucy's part, and that my will is should be hel in Trust by my son Henry for the benefit of herself and Children as before directed and at her death to be divided in the same manner as before directed agreeable to the Act of Distribution.

And whereas my intention in this my last will is to place my five youngest Children precisely upon the same footing, it may not be improper to suggest in this place that there may be found after my decease accompts exhibited against them respectively which accompts it is my will and desire shall be considered as so much advanced. And in order to explain to my first children the motives governing me in making a difference between them and the last, it may not be thought improper to state that the greater part of the small patrimony came with the mother of the latter.

Lastly I do appoint my sons Edmund and Henry, and my son in law Thruston James, executors of this my last will and Testament, hereby revoking all others hitherto made. In witness whereof I have hereunto set my hand and affixed my seal this fourth day of January one thousand seven hundred and ninety nine."

John Pendleton
Signed and published in presence of us. Thom Price, Thaddeus Capron, Wm Lawrence, John Crenshaw, Wm Carmeron, Samuel Lawrence, Henry Madison

At a Court of Monthly Sessions held for Hanover County at the Court House, on Wednesday the 18th of September 1799 This last will and Testament of John Pendleton, deceased was proved by the oaths of Samuel Lawrence, Henry Madison and John Crenshaw witnesses thereto and is ordered to be recorded.
Teste: William Pollard, C.H.C.

Phebe (James) Pendleton, John's wife, was named in the will of Joseph Temple (1762), King William Co., VA as a witness to signature on 20 December, 1744.

Children of JOHN PENDLETON and PHOEBE JAMES are:

37.   i.   EDMUND[8] PENDLETON, b. Feb 04, 1743/44, VA; d. Jul 04, 1827, Caroline Co., VA.

38.   ii.   JR. JOHN PENDLETON, b. Abt. 1750, VA; d. Aug 1806, Richmond, VA?

      iii. ELIZABETH PENDLETON, b. Sep 1750, King and Queen Co., VA; d. Mar 25, 1831, Lynchburg, VA; m. WILLIAM PETERS MARTIN, REV., Feb 04, 1768, King and Queen Co., VA; b. Jun 01, 1745, King William Co., VA; d. Oct 30, 1829, Lynchburg, VA.

39.   iv. MARY JEAN PENDLETON, b. 1756, VA; d. Aft. 1800.

Children of JOHN PENDLETON and SARAH MADISON are:

40.   v.   HENRY[8] PENDLETON, b. Dec 04, 1762, King & Queen Co., Va.; d. Nov 11, 1822, Louisa Co., VA.

      vi. SARAH PENDLETON, m. THURSTON JAMES?

     vii. JAMES PENDLETON, b. Abt. 1770.

          This is the James Pendleton included in various lists of Hanover County Taxpayers, Saint Paul's Parish, with his father John Pendleton.

    viii. LUCY PENDLETON, m. ROBERT SYDNOR.

    ix. THOMAS PENDLETON.

21. ELIZABETH[7] CLAYTON (*ELIZABETH[6] PENDLETON, PHILIP[5], HENRY[4], HENRY[3], GEORGE[2], GEORGE[1]*) was born Abt. 1716, and died Bef. 1793. She married (1) JOSEPH ANDERSON Abt. 1733. He died 1735. She married (2) NATHANIEL PENDLETON Oct 14, 1745 in Essex Co., VA, son of HENRY PENDLETON and MARY TAYLOR. He was born 1715 in King and Queen Co., Va., and died 1793 in Culpeper Co., VA.

      See Nathaniel Pendleton (**18**) for notes on Elizabeth Clayton and for the Children of Nathaniel and Elizabeth Pendleton Clayton.

Child of ELIZABETH CLAYTON and JOSEPH ANDERSON is:

      i. CATHERINE[8] ANDERSON, b. Abt. 1734.

22. WILLIAM[7] PENDLETON (*JOHN[6], PHILIP[5], HENRY[4], HENRY[3], GEORGE[2], GEORGE[1]*) was born 1720 in Essex Co., VA, and died 1779 in Amherst Co., VA. He married ELIZABETH TINSLEY Abt. 1748 in VA, daughter of EDWARD TINSLEY. She died Aft. 1785.

      William Pendleton, apparently the eldest son of John Pendleton and Mary Tinsley, was likely born in Essex Co. or possibly King and Queen Co., VA where his grandfather, Philip Pendleton died in 1721. As stated in his will, he lived in Culpeper Co. before venturing southwest to Amherst County. He married his cousin, Elizabeth Tinsley, around the year 1748. The 1764 Rent Rolls for Culpeper Co. include a Will Pendleton. Much of what is known of William Pendleton comes from his will (Ref. 46):

> In the Name of God, Amen, I William Pendleton of Amherst County and Parish of _____ being weak in Body but perfect mind and memory and knowing that it is appoints for all _____ to d___make and _____this my last Will and Testament. In

manner and form following. I _____ that all my ____debts and funeral chargers be paid
____ _____. Item: I lend to my beloved Wife Elizabeth Pendleton the land and
plantation whereon I now live with all my stocks of all kinds and household furniture to
continue her during life or Widowhood and no longer and after her marriage or Death to
be Equally Divided between my Beloved Chitren Benjamin Pendleton, James Pendleton,
Edmund Pendleton, Richard Pendleton, Mary Pendleton, John Pendleton, Reubin
Pendleton, William Pendleton, Sarah Pendleton, Franka Pendleton, Isaac Pendleton, Betta
Pendleton, to them and their Heirs forever. Item what I have _____Benjamin Pendleton
before this Day to go in his part which is a Cow and Calf three pounds ten shillings a colt
forty shillings and ten shillings worth of _____, also James Pendleton has had a horse at
seven pounds to go in his part also Edmund Pendleton has had a mare at four pounds ten
shillings to go in his part, Item I give to James Pendleton fifty acres of land whereon he
now lives_____my upper line to him and his heirs forever the said fifty acres of land to
be valued immediately after my death without improvements and such valuation to go in
his part of the estate when divided. Also I request that my wife may give those of my
chitren that has had nothing as they come of Age a Cow and Calf and a Sow and Pigg if
she can Spare them, Like wise I do give unto Richard Vernal of Culpeper County one
Track of land whereon I formerly lived on the Waters of Smith Tun to him the __Vernal
and his heirs forever, Lastly I do appoint my Beloved Wife—Elizabeth Pendleton my
Executrix and my Beloved Sons James Pendleton and Edmund Pendleton my whole and
late Executors of this my last Will and Testament hereby Revoking and Disannulling all
other Testaments and Wills by me and Confirming this and no other to be my last Will
and Testament. In Witness where of I have ____to set my hand and seal this second Day
of January one Thousand Seven hundred and Seventy four.
Signed Sealed of -----------   William Pendleton (seal)
In the presence of John Tinsley, Isaac Tinsley, William (x) Whitten and Ambrose
Rucker

At a Court held for Amherst County the first Day of November 1779. This Last Will and
Testament of William Pendleton dec'd was this day presented in Court by Elizabeth
Pendleton the Executrix and James Pendleton one of the Executors here in named who
made oath there to according to Law and was proved by the oath of Ambrose Rucker and
Isaac Tinsley two the Witnesses and_____ to be _____ and the said Executors with
Ambrose Rucker and Isaac Tinsley their Securities acknowledge Bona in the penalty of
four Thousand pounds with the Conditions required by Law.
     Test. Edmd. ____Clk

     Additional information on the heirs of William is provided by James Wood
Esquire, Governor the Commonwealth of Virginia:

     To all to whom these Presents shall come Greeting Know ye that by virtue of a Land
office Treasury Warrant number fifteen thousand one hundred and seventynine issued the
twenty eight day of February one thousand seven hundred and eighty three, there is
Granted by the said Commonwealth unto Benjamin, James, Edmund, Richard, Mary,
John, Reuben, William, Sarah, Franky, Isaac and Betta Pendleton children and heirs of
William Pendleton deceased... a certain tract or parcel of Land Containing Sixty four
Acres by survey bearing date the seventh day of March one thousand seven hundred and
ninety six, Lying and being in the County of Amherst on the south branch of Harris's
Creek and is bounded as followsth to Wit Beginning at the Hickory corner own an
Ambrose Rucker (prob. the brother-in-law of William) and running thence with Ruckers
lines south eighty six degrees West Twenty two poles to pointers North sixty one degrees

West twenty eight poles to pointers North seventy eight degrees West fifty seven poles to a chestnut oak North eleven degrees West thirty five poles to a Chesnut North forty seven degrees East seventy two poles to a Chesnut oak North eighty two degrees East sixty seven to a spanish oak South seventy six degrees East seventy poles to pointers corner to William Pendleton deceased and with his line south seventeen degrees West twelve poles to a chestnut oak sapling south forty one degrees East fifty poles to a red oak south seventy five degrees West seventy eight poles to the beginning with its Appen__ancese to have and to hold the said tract or parcel of Sand with its Appen---nances to the said Benjamin, James, Edmund, Richard, Mary, John, Ruben, William, Sara, Franka, Isaac and Betta Pendleton and their heirs forever. In witness where of the said James Wood Esquire Governor of the Commonwealth of Virginia hath hereonto set his hand and caused the ___ ___ of the said Commonwealth to be affixed at Richmond on the Eleventh day of December in the year of our Lord one thousand seven hundred and ninety seven and of the Commonwealth the twenty second."

James Wood

Children of WILLIAM PENDLETON and ELIZABETH TINSLEY are:

41.   i.   BENJAMIN[8] PENDLETON, b. Abt. 1749, VA; d. Aft. 1815, Scott Co., VA.

42.   ii.   JAMES·PENDLETON, b. Apr 03, 1750, VA; d. Jul 02, 1832, Amherst Co., VA.

43.   iii.   EDMUND PENDLETON, b. 1754, VA; d. 1830, TN.

44.   iv.   REUBEN PENDLETON, b. 1755, VA; d. Nov 14, 1825, Amherst Co., VA.

45.   v.   RICHARD PENDLETON, b. 1760, VA; d. May 20, 1829, Amherst Co., VA.

46.   vi.   JOHN PENDLETON, b. 1760, Amherst Co., VA?; d. 1830, Lincoln Co., KY.

47.   vii.   ISAAC PENDLETON, b. Abt. 1761, VA; d. Aft. 1860, Trimble Co., KY.

48.   viii.   MARY PENDLETON, b. Abt. 1763.

49.   ix.   FRANCES PENDLETON, b. Abt. 1765.

        x.   WILLIAM PENDLETON, b. Abt. 1772, VA; d. Oct 1828, Amherst Co., VA; m. PATSY COX, Jun 08, 1794, Amherst Co., VA; b. 1770; d. Abt. 1857.

This is the William Pendleton in the 1810 and 1820 (as Will) Amherst County, VA census records. The 1810 census indicates that this William had no children. And Patsy Cox is apparently the Patsy Pendleton who married Reuben Baldock on July 14, 1829 in Amherst County. This Patsy Pendleton is in the 1850 Census as age 70 and living with Tabby A. (Tabitha A. Baldock) and Wiatt Cox. Tabby A is Tabitha Ann, the daughter of Elizabeth Pendleton Baldock and Reueben Baldock. Tabby married Wiatt Cox in 1840 in Amherst County (Ref. 47).

        xi.   SARAH PENDLETON, b. 1773; m. JOHN MAHONE, Oct 13, 1794, Amherst Co., VA.

Their marriage is recorded (Ref. 48) as "Mehone, John, bachelor, and Sally Pendleton, spinster, October 13, 1794. Richard Pendleton, surety. Consent of her [father?], Richard Pendleton, who testifies that she is 21 years of age." This Richard Pendleton is apparently her brother; a reexamination of the original document, if available, could clarify this issue.

50.   xii.   ELIZABETH "BETSY" PENDLETON, b. Abt. 1774, VA; d. Bef. 1829.

xiii. MARGARET PENDLETON, b. 1779; m. JAMES MILES, Nov 11, 1796, Amherst Co., VA.

23. MARY[7] PENDLETON *(JOHN[6], PHILIP[5], HENRY[4], HENRY[3], GEORGE[2], GEORGE[1])* was born 1722 in Essex Co., VA and died after 1765 in VA. She married EDMUND WALLER Oct 18, 1740 in Spotsylvania Co., VA, son of JOHN WALLER and DOROTHY KING. He was born 1713, and died 1771 in Culpeper Co., VA.

Edmund Waller and Mary Pendleton are included in a listing of early Spotsylvania Co. marriage licenses (Ref. 49). Edmund Waller and Mary, his wife, of St. George Parish, Spotsylvania Co. are included numerous times in the Spotsylvania Deed Books from May 1742 to June 1765.

Children of MARY PENDLETON and EDMUND WALLER are:

i. JOHN[8] WALLER, b. Dec 23, 1741, Spotsylvania Co., VA; d. Jul 4, 1802, Greenwood Co., SC; m. ELIZABETH CURTIS; b. Abt. 1742.

John Waller received a deed of gift (Ref. 50) from his grandfather, Rice Curtis Sr., Gent. of Spotsylvania Co., of "200 a. in Spts. Co., 47 a. of which the sd. Curtis bought of Larkin Chew, Gent., etc. Witnesses, Jane x Curtis, W. Buckner, Vincent Vass, Joseph Hern-don, James Colquhoun, John Benger, Thos. Bartlett. Recd. Augt. 1, 1763." He is also included in a deed of May 9, 1763, "from Rice Curtis of St. Geo. Par., Spts. Co., Gent., to John Waller, junr. Deed of Gift. Negro children, etc. Recd. Augt. 1, 1763."

ii. MARY WALLER, b. 1743; m. WILLIAM WIGGLESWORTH.

The following Spotsylvania Co. deed (Ref. 51) confirms this marriage: "Jany. 24, 1761. Edmund Waller of Spts. Co. and Mary, his wife, to their daughter, Mary, and William Wiglesworth, her husband. Deed of Gift. 200 a. in Spts. Co. Wm. Woodroof, Alice x Hicks. May 4, 1761."

iii. WILLIAM EDMUND WALLER, b. 1747; d. Aug 11, 1830; m. MILDRED SMITH.

William Edmund Waller served as a private in the Revolutionary War.

iv. BENJAMIN WALLER, b. 1749, Spotsylvania Co., VA; d. Jul 31, 1835, Prospect Hill, Spotsylvania Co., VA.

v. LEONARD JAMES WALLER, b. 1754; d. 1826; m. (1) FRANCES ROBINSON; m. (2) AGNES CHILES, 1779.

vi. DOROTHY JEMIMA WALLER, b. 1758, Spotsylvania Co., VA; d. Jan 12, 1838, Covington Co., KY; m. BENJAMIN STEPHENS, Apr 1775, Spotsylvania Co., VA.

vii. NANCY WALLER, b. Abt. 1759; m. GEORGE MASON.

24. HENRY[7] PENDLETON *(JOHN[6], PHILIP[5], HENRY[4], HENRY[3], GEORGE[2], GEORGE[1])* was born Feb 19, 1723/24 in Essex Co., VA, and died Apr 06, 1818 in Spotsylvania Co., VA. He married MARTHA CURTIS Jan 18, 1746/47 in Spotsylvania, Co., VA, daughter of RICE CURTIS and MARTHA THACKER. She was born Nov 15, 1729 in VA, and died Aug 18, 1794 in Spotsylvania Co., VA.

Like his older siblings William and Mary, Henry Pendleton was born in Essex County, VA. On Dec. 6, 1743, as Henry Pendleton, Gentleman, he was commissioned as Lieutenant of Foot under Captain Edmund Waller, his brother-in-law (husband of his older sister, Mary). Between 1742 and 1767 Henry Pendleton is included in a number of Spotsylvania Deed Book entries. In 1782 Henry was granted a certificate for supplies (beef) furnished for the use of the Continental Army (Ref. 3).

In the 1787 Census of Virginia, Personal Property Tax - List "B" for Spotsylvania Co., Henry Pendleton is listed with his sons Henry, Jr., John, Philip, and Rice. He and his sons owned 13 Blacks, 12 Horses, mares, colts & mules, and 22 Cattle. Obviously, Henry Pendleton, Sr. was a slave owner and probably of at least moderate wealth. The listed property of his sons was, for the most part, in direct proportion to the order of their birth. Rice Pendleton and his older brother Curtis (apparently without taxable property and not in the 1787 tax list) immigrated to Kentucky not long after this census.

About 1791 Henry Pendleton, Sr. was ordained to the care of the Mine Road Baptist Church, about nine miles west of Spotsylvania Court House. His oldest son, Henry Pendleton, Jr., was the first pastor of this church. In 1810, his fifth child, Phillip Pendleton, was the pastor (Ref. 29).

The Mine Road Baptist Church with an adjacent cemetery was organized in 1791 and is the third oldest Baptist Church in Spotsylvania County. The first sanctuary stood about ¼ mile south of the present site near Margo and was known as Pendleton's meetinghouse (Ref. 52). Semple in his "History of the Baptists in Virginia," says that Henry Pendleton, Sr., "father of the preacher" [the "preacher" is his son Philip Pendleton] was himself a preacher in another sense. He preaches by a godly and pious conversation. He is now [1810] a venerable old man of about four score years of age (Ref. 29)."

Children of HENRY PENDLETON and MARTHA CURTIS are:
51.   i. HENRY[8] PENDLETON, JR., b. Sep 30, 1748, King William Co., VA; d. Nov 28, 1801, Spotsylvania Co., VA.
      ii. MARY PENDLETON, b. Oct 28, 1750, King William Co., VA; d. Mar 4, 1774, Spotsylvania Co., VA.
      iii. CURTIS PENDLETON, b. Mar 3, 1753, Spotsylvania Co., VA; d. Jan 6, 1758, Spotsylvania Co., VA.
52.   iv. JOHN PENDLETON, b. Nov 25, 1755, Spotsylvania Co., VA; d. 1828, Spotsylvania Co., VA.
53.   v. PHILIP PENDLETON, b. Apr 6, 1758, Spotsylvania Co., VA; d. Abt. 1843, Spotsylvania Co., VA.
54.   vi. MARTHA PENDLETON, b. Aug 7, 1760, Spotsylvania Co., VA; d. 1824, MO.
55.   vii. CURTIS PENDLETON, b. May 9, 1763, Spotsylvania Co., VA; d. Jan 19, 1836, Todd Co., KY.
56.   viii. RICE PENDLETON, SR., b. Sep 9, 1765, Spotsylvania Co., VA; d. Dec 1823, Bath County, KY.
57.   ix. FRANCES PENDLETON, b. Jan 19, 1767, Spotsylvania Co., VA; d. Apr 1808, Clark Co., KY.

58. x. ROBERT PENDLETON, b. Apr 29, 1771, Spotsylvania Co., VA; d. 1845, Spotsylvania Co., VA?
    xi. THOMAS PENDLETON, b. Jan 16, 1780, Spotsylvania Co., VA; d. May 4, 1782, Spotsylvania Co., VA.

25. BENJAMIN[7] PENDLETON *(PHILIP[6], PHILIP[5], HENRY[4], HENRY[3], GEORGE[2], GEORGE[1])* was born 1726 in VA, and died Jan 07, 1798 in King & Queen Co., VA. He married MARY MACON Sep 30, 1750 in Orange Co., VA, daughter of JOHN MACON and ANNE HUNT. She was born 1725 in Caroline Co., VA?, and died Oct 1801.

    Benjamin Pendleton qualified as Attorney, Feb. 11, 1745 in Augusta Co., VA (Ref. 53). Benjamin also had a "License Issued for taverns, 1749-55." Benjamin Pendleton, Gentleman, was commissioned to be Captain of Foot, and took the oath Sept. 4, 1753. Benjamin Pendleton, Esquire, was Major of the Militia in Spotsylvania County with a commission dated Apr. 29, 1756 (Ref. 54). John Thornton's letter in 1757 to Governor Dinwiddie charged Alexander Spotswood with ignoring many gentlemen in the county "of good Estates" for commissions in the militia, while appointing men of lesser character and standing. In particular he cited the appointments of Aaron Bledsoe, Thomas Estis and Benjamin Pendleton. However, Benjamin was later chosen for the King and Queen County Committee of Safety, December 1774.

Children of BENJAMIN PENDLETON and MARY MACON are:
    i. ELIZABETH[8] PENDLETON, b. Jun 18, 1751, VA; d. Jul 30, 1751.
59. ii. PHILIP PENDLETON, b. Aug 02, 1752, VA; d. Jul 31, 1804, King & Queen Co., VA.
60. iii. JAMES PENDLETON, b. Aug 13, 1754, VA; d. Mar 06, 1815, King & Queen Co., VA.
    iv. SARAH PENDLETON, b. Aug 12, 1756, VA; d. Mar 17, 1774, King and Queen Co., VA.
    v. MARY PENDLETON, b. Mar 21, 1758, VA; d. 1830; m. BENJAMIN HOOMES.
    vi. CATHERINE "CATY" PENDLETON, b. Dec 10, 1759, VA; d. Aug 20, 1793; m. COURTNEY.
    vii. BENJAMIN PENDLETON, b. Sep 16, 1761, VA; d. Feb 06, 1762.
    viii. PRISCILLA PENDLETON, b. Mar 14, 1763, VA.
        This may be the Priscilla Pendleton of Richmond, VA who married William Holderby. He came to what is now Cabell County, VA at the beginning of the nineteenth century and died October 10, 1812. Their first son, James, was born in 1782.

61. ix. ANNE MACON PENDLETON, b. Jan 24, 1766, VA.

26. PHILIP[7] PENDLETON *(PHILIP[6], PHILIP[5], HENRY[4], HENRY[3], GEORGE[2], GEORGE[1])* was born Bef. 1728 in VA, and died Abt. 1770 in VA. He married (1) MARTHA. He married (2) SPICE FREELAND Abt. 1750 in VA, daughter of JAMES FREELAND and PRISCILLA. She was born Abt. 1730 in King and Queen Co., VA, and died Abt. 1804 in Buckingham Co., VA?

This is likely the Philip Pendleton mentioned "At a Court Continued for Albemarle County, January 24, 1745/46: Phillip May makes oath that Phillip Pendleton owes him L10/3 on account." And it is likely this Philip Pendleton who was granted 1,000 acres on the upper side [of] milly's river, at its confluence with the Ohio for service in the Colonial War of 1754 (Ref. 55). If these records do pertain to this Philip Pendleton he was both an early settler in Albemarle County and a veteran of the French and Indian War.

Spice Freeland Pendleton is listed in a 1790 Buckingham Co. land grant for 64 acres (Ref. 56). And on May 15, 1794 it was announced in a local newspaper (Ref. 57) that "William, Rob't, dec'd, Mace Freeland and Spice Pendleton will present a petition to exclude Elizabeth Jones from the act entitled 'An act to vest the estate of Robert Williams equally among Mace Freeland, Spice Pendleton, Elizabeth Jones and their heirs.'"

Child of PHILIP PENDLETON and MARTHA is:
    i. ELIZABETH[8] PENDLETON, m. MACE FREELAND; d. Aft. 1794.

Children of PHILIP PENDLETON and SPICE FREELAND are:
    ii. DAUGHTER1[8] PENDLETON.
    iii. DAUGHTER2 PENDLETON, m. WILSON.
    iv. JOHN PENDLETON, b. Buckingham Co., Va.; d. Aft. 1787, Buckingham Co., VA?
        This is the John Pendleton listed with his brothers Benjamin, Mace, and Micajah in the 1782-1787 Buckingham Co. tax lists and may be the John Pendleton, Sr. listed in the 1820 Buckingham Co., VA census (over 45 years old).

    v. JUDITH PENDLETON, m. JOHN CABELL.
62. vi. BENJAMIN PENDLETON, b. Aug 03, 1751, VA; d. Abt. 1835, Warren Co., KY?
63. vii. JAMES PENDLETON, b. Abt. 1754, Buckingham Co., Va.; d. Abt. 1803, Buckingham Co., VA.
64. viii. MACE PENDLETON, b. 1754, Buckingham Co., Va.; d. Buckingham Co., VA.
65. ix. MICAJAH PENDLETON, b. 1758, Buckingham Co., Va.; d. Feb 09, 1844, Nelson Co., VA.
    x. MILDRED PENDLETON, b. Abt. 1762; d. Jun 19, 1857, Bent Creek, VA; m. JOHN BASKERVILLE.
        John Baskerville was a Revolutionary War Soldier.

    xi. MINA PENDLETON, b. Abt. 1765, VA; m. GILES DAVIDSON; b. Abt. 1762; d. Jun 1848, Amherst Co., VA.
        Giles Davidson is listed in the 1810 through 1840 Amherst Co., VA census records. In 6th of July, 1833 Giles Davidson age 71 swore on oath in court supporting Micajah Pendleton as a Revolutionary War soldier. In 1840 he is listed in the census as between the ages of 70 and 80. In the household

is a female also aged between 70 and 80. This is apparently his wife Mina Pendleton. Giles was the son of David Davidson and Mary of Buckingham County, VA. Per his will, Giles Davidson also had a son named Joseph P. (Pendleton?) Davidson. Giles Davidson died in 1848 at the age of 86 per a 25 Jun, 1848 obit in the Richmond Whig (Ref. 58).

27. PRISCILLA[7] PENDLETON *(PHILIP[6], PHILIP[5], HENRY[4], HENRY[3], GEORGE[2], GEORGE[1])* was born Abt. 1736 in VA. She married WILLIAM HARWOOD, CAPT. He was born 1734, and died Sep 16, 1773 in King & Queen Co., VA. Children of PRISCILLA PENDLETON and WILLIAM HARWOOD are:

  i.   CHRISTOPHER[8] HARWOOD, d. 1793; m. MARGARET ROANE.
  ii. ELIZABETH HARWOOD, m. ROBERT POLLARD.
  iii. WILLIAM HARWOOD, b. 1758; d. Aug 16, 1789, King & Queen Co., VA.

Generation No. 8 – Independence

The eighth generation consists of the great grandchildren of the immigrant Philip Pendleton and Isabella Hurt. The time period is from about 1754, when Henry Pendleton, Philip's eldest great grandson turned 21 in Culpeper Co., VA, to about 1860 when his great grandson, Isaac Pendleton, died in Trimble Co., KY at about 100 years old, just before the Civil War. Significant members of the eighth generation who had no known children and are thus listed as children of seventh generation Pendletons include Henry Pendleton (1750-1789) and William Pendleton (1772-1828) whose histories can be found on pages 32 and 38, respectively.

At least 17 members of this Pendleton generation were soldiers in the Revolutionary War. And after the war, a number of these soldiers joined other Virginians in the pioneer movement west beyond the Blue Ridge mountains and Shenandoah Valley into present day West Virginia and Kentucky. In 1803 the United States territory if not its population had expanded almost across the continent with the Louisiana Purchase. Of the 39 known households of this eighth generation, 27 apparently remained in Virginia, 2 moved to what would become West Virginia, 7 removed to Kentucky, and one each moved to New York, North Carolina, and South Carolina (Fig. 7).

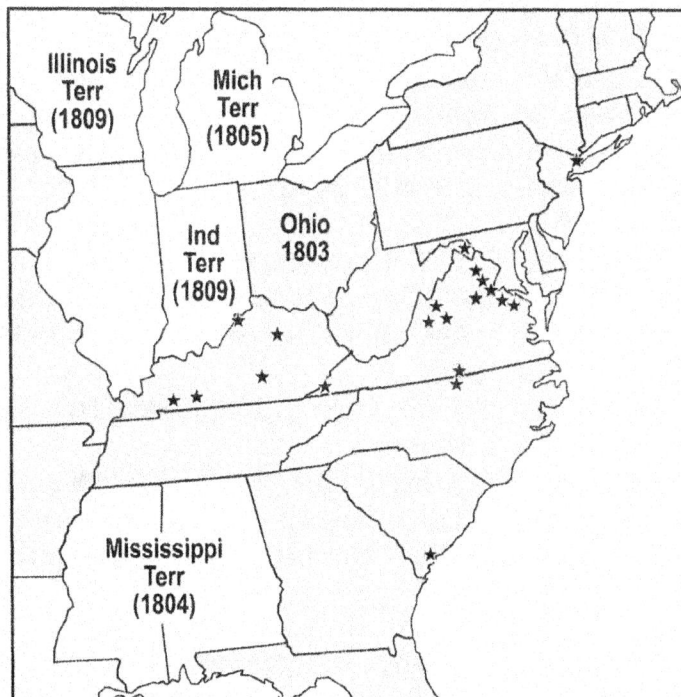

Figure 7. The Eastern United States in 1810 (Compiled by H.G. Stoll, Hammond, Inc., 1967; rev. U.S. Geological Survey, 1970). The approximate locations of each county in which the great grandchildren of Philip lived are indicated.

28. HENRY⁸ PENDLETON *(JAMES⁷, HENRY⁶, PHILIP⁵, HENRY⁴, HENRY³, GEORGE², GEORGE¹)* was born 1733 in VA, and died 1798 in Culpeper Co., Virginia. He married ANNE THOMAS. She was from Orange Co., VA, and died 1804.

Henry Pendleton is included in the Will of Jeremiah Sims (Ref. 59) "of the County of Culpeper being sick and weak. I do constitute and appoint my beloved wife, Agatha Sims, executrix, and my loving friends Edward Sims, John Nalle, Junr. and Henry Pendleton, executors, 24 March, 1768." Henry was a gentleman justice of Culpeper Co. and also a captain in the Revolutionary War. He was a member of the House of Burgesses and Committee of Safety of Culpeper Co., and of the Conventions of 1775 and 1776. On July 4, 1774, as Henry Pendleton, Esq., he was moderator at a meeting of the Freeholders and inhabitants of Culpeper Co., who met "to consider the most effectual methods to preserve the rights and liberties of America." The old Pendleton place in Culpeper Co., an historical structure, was apparently the home of this Henry Pendleton. It was built in 1775 and is located 8 miles north of Culpeper Courthouse, Virginia (Ref. 60).

Children of HENRY PENDLETON and ANNE THOMAS are:
      i.   CATHERINE⁹ PENDLETON m. RICHARD WILLIAMSON.

           This is likely the Catherine Pendleton in the 1800 Culpeper Co., VA Tax List. She later was married to Richard Williamson according to his will in Culpeper naming "wife Catherine, Brothers; Henry and Edward Pendleton. Cousin; Nancy Brown wife of William Brown, uncle; James Pendleton and nephew David Williamson. Sister in Scotland." Witnesses were Samuel Ferguson Jr. and Henry Pendleton Jr.

      ii. ELIZABETH PENDLETON, m. JAMES THOMAS, 1781.
     iii. FRANCES PENDLETON, m. (1) JOHN BROWNING, May 29, 1799, Culpeper Co., VA; b. Abt. 1766, Culpeper Co., VA; d. 1800; m. (2) WILLIAM WARD, 1802.
     iv. JOANNA PENDLETON, d. 1838; m. JESSE SMITH, Sep 30, 1796, Culpeper Co., VA; d. 1833.
66.   v. JR. HENRY PENDLETON, b. 1764, VA; d. 1848, Hardin Co., KY?
67.   vi. EDWARD PENDLETON, b. Aug 12, 1770; d. Feb 13, 1803.
68.   vii. EDMUND PENDLETON, b. Nov 01, 1776, VA; d. Sep 10, 1820, Winchester, VA.

29. JR. JAMES⁸ PENDLETON *(JAMES⁷, HENRY⁶, PHILIP⁵, HENRY⁴, HENRY³, GEORGE², GEORGE¹)* was born 1735 in Culpeper Co., VA, and died Dec 1793 in Culpeper Co., VA. He married CATHERINE BOWIE 1763 in VA, daughter of JOHN BOWIE and JUDITH CATLETT. She was born 1747, and died 1795 in VA.

James Pendleton Jr. was a member of the House of Burgesses from Culpeper Co., Justice of that county in 1762-4, High Sheriff in 1762, as well as Churchwarden, 1766-9, and 1776-7. He was one of the Culpeper Minute Men and later a Colonel of the Culpeper

Militia in the Revolutionary War. On May 21, 1763, he succeeded his brother, Henry, as Surveyor of the Roads. From 1782 to 1788 he was a member of the House of Delegates.

Children of JAMES PENDLETON and CATHERINE BOWIE are:

69.   i.   JOHN[9] PENDLETON, b. 1766, Culpeper Co., VA; d. 1807.
70.   ii.   MARGARET PENDLETON, b. 1769, VA; d. Nelson Co., KY.
71.   iii.   CATHERINE BOWIE PENDLETON, b. Abt. 1771, VA; d. 1818.
72.   iv.   THOMAS PENDLETON, b. Nov 26, 1773, VA; d. Nov 26, 1823, Culpeper Co., VA.
      v.   JAMES BOWIE PENDLETON, b. Abt. 1775, VA; d. Aft. 1800.
          James B. Pendleton is listed in the 1800 Culpeper Co. Tax List.

73.   vi.   WILLIAM PENDLETON, b. Jan 25, 1779, VA; d. 1824, Culpeper Co., VA?
74.   vii.   ELIZABETH COLEMAN PENDLETON, b. Abt. 1781, VA; d. Aft. 1830, Hardin Co., KY?
      viii.   CATLETT PENDLETON, b. 1783, VA; d. Mar 11, 1824, Culpeper Co., VA? Catlett is included in the Culpeper Co., VA 1810 census apparently with a wife but with no children. He was a Sergeant, Virginia Militia, 5th regiment, Cocke's Detachment, of Culpeper Co., War of 1812.

      ix.   NANCY "ANN" PENDLETON, b. 1785, VA; m. (1) VALENTINE JOHNSON, COL., Jun 08, 1806, Orange Co., VA; b. Jul 20, 1765, Orange Co., VA; d. Jun 18, 1848, Orange Co., VA; m. (2) WILLIAM C. BROWN; b. Abt. 1782, VA.
          William (age 68) and Nancy (age 65?) Brown are listed in the 1850 Culpeper Co., VA census, pg. 235.

30. ANNE[8] PENDLETON *(JAMES[7], HENRY[6], PHILIP[5], HENRY[4], HENRY[3], GEORGE[2], GEORGE[1])* was born Abt. 1740, and died Feb 1815 in Caroline Co., VA. She married JAMES TAYLOR 1765, son of GEORGE TAYLOR and RACHEL GIBSON. He was born 1738, and died Sep 03, 1807.

Children of ANNE PENDLETON and JAMES TAYLOR are:

75.   i.   ELIZABETH[9] TAYLOR, b. Abt. 1766; d. 1838, Nelson Co., KY.
      ii.   JAMES TAYLOR, b. Abt. 1767.
      iii.   NATHANIEL TAYLOR, b. Abt. 1769.
      iv.   ANN PENDLETON TAYLOR, b. 1779; d. 1809; m. THOMAS CRUTCHFIELD; d. 1810.
      v.   JOHN GIBSON TAYLOR, b. 1786; d. 1829; m. ELIZABETH LEE TAYLOR; b. 1792; d. 1845.
      vi.   MARY TAYLOR, b. Abt. 1787; m. RICHARD BARBOUR.

31. PHILIP[8] PENDLETON *(JAMES[7], HENRY[6], PHILIP[5], HENRY[4], HENRY[3], GEORGE[2], GEORGE[1])* was born Abt. 1741 in Caroline Co., VA, and died Nov 01, 1793 in Pittsylvania Co., VA. He married MARTHA AWBREY 1766 in VA, daughter of

CHANDLER AWBREY and ELIZABETH SORRELL. She was born Abt. 1747 in Westmoreland Co., VA?, and died Aft. Dec 1785 in VA.

This Philip served as a soldier in the Revolutionary War. He resigned as Lay Reader in 1780 and moved from St. Mark's Parish, Culpeper Co., where he had been Clerk of the Vestry in 1771, to Pittsylvania Co., where his name appears on the Tax List for 1785. It is evidently this Philip Pendleton mentioned in several Court Records in Pittsylvania Co. under less than favorable circumstances - although it is not clear why Sarah Pendleton is not included as this Philip's daughter in the various genealogical studies of this family.

Virginia against Philip Pendleton (transcribed by Janet Ariciu):

"Sept Court 1785: The complaint of Martha this wife of Philip Pendleton and the Recognizance of this said Philip for his appearance here for reasons appearing to the court is ordered to Dismissed."

"Sept Court 1785: Pendleton vs. Pendleton. Robert Williams Gent. Deputy Attorney for the Commonwealth comes into Court in given the Court now where to understand and be inform for and on behalf of Sarah Pendleton daughter of Philip Pendleton that the said Philip hath lately at three different time committed a Rape on the body of his said Sarah Where inform this ordered that the Sheriff with the Posey of the county do take the said Philip Pendleton into his Custody and him safety keep until he shall be thense discharge by due course of Law."

"Sept Court 1785: Pendleton. The said Philip Pendleton was lend he the Bar in Custody of Abraham Shelton Sherif of this County to where custody for the cause aforesaid he was committed and Robert Williams Gent. States Attorney protested against proceeding on his Examination alloying That no witness have appeared on behalf of the commonwealth. Where upon it was demanded of this said Philip Pendleton whether guilty or not guilty of the fat wherewith he stands charged. Answer not guilty and no witness appearing on be half of the Common Wealth ordered that he be acquitted and discharged out of custody Sign Wm Witcher Gent."

"Nov Court 1785 Corbin vs. Pendleton for the peace. Rawley Corbin comes into Court and craved the peace of Philip Pendleton and took the oath by law presided Whereupon it is order that the said Philip Pendleton be in custody of the Sherif until he fined sufficient security for his good behavior that some the said Philip Pendleton together with I monies Maid and Beverly Willard his Securilerie? And acknowledged themselves severally inedible the common wealth of Virginia That is to say the said Philip Pendleton in the sum of Thirty pounds and his said securities in the sum of fifteen pounds each to be levied if their several and respective goods and Chattles, Lands and Tenements to the use of behavior and keep the peace towards all the citizens of these Common Wealth and especially the said Rawley Corbin for one whole year and a day."

"Dec. 1785: Commonwealth vs. Pendleton. Ordered that the Sheif with the posie of this County do take Philip Pendleton into his custody and him safely keep until he shall find sufficient Securities for his good behavior (that is to say) the said Philip Pendleton on the sum of five hundred pounds and his securities in two hundred and fifty pounds each."

"Dec. 1785 Pendleton vs. Pendleton. Martha Pendleton Complainant Against } In Chanery for Alimony Philip Pendleton Defendant. Ordered that the defendant pay unto the Complainant five pounds immediately and the like sum at the end of three months successively for her supposed unto this matter shall be fully heard and determined in Equity and if is further Order that a summon be issued to compell the defendant to answer allowing to the payer of the bill."

Children of PHILIP PENDLETON and MARTHA AWBREY are:

    i. HENRY[9] PENDLETON.
    ii. JOSEPH PENDLETON.
    iii. MARTHA PENDLETON, m. WATSON.
    iv. PHILIP PENDLETON.

        This may be the Philip Pendleton in the 1810 Bedford Co., VA census (pg 478) listed with a wife and one child and again in the 1820 Bedford Co. census. If so, it was this Philip Pendleton referred to in the "Marriage Agreement For The Marriage Of Patsey Preast And Phillip Pendleton:"

           Know all men by these presents that we, Phillip Pendleton and Thomas Preas are held firmly bound unto Wm. A. Cabele esq. governor or chief magistrate of the commonwealth of Virginia to the true payment which bind myself, my heirs and our seals dated this 14th day of March 1807. The condition of this above obligation is such that whereas there is marriage shortly intended to be had and solemnized between the above bound, Phillip Pendleton and Patsey Preast. Now of these shall be unlawful cause to obstruct the said marriage then the above obligation to be void else to remain in full force and virtue. Teste Phillip Pendleton (S) Thomas Preas (S)The Clerk of Bedford will be pleased to issue license for Philip Pendleton to be married to my daughter Patsey Preast. Teste Margaret Preas Thomas Preas."
           March 13, 1807 Mace Hanes

    v. ROBERT PENDLETON.
76.   vi. ELIZABETH PENDLETON, b. 1765, Culpeper Co., VA; d. 1804, Pittsylvania Co., VA.
    vii. GABRIEL PENDLETON, b. Abt. 1767; m. MARGARET WILLIAMS, May 16, 1786, Augusta Co., VA.

        Gabriel Pendleton was an executor of a will in Augusta Co. (Ref. 61): "Joseph Burk vs. Gabriel Pendleton Court Case. Augusta, 22d November, 1791. Joseph Henderson's will--To wife, Sarah, 26th April, 1791; executors include Gabriel Pendleton, Augusta Co., VA."

77.   viii. JAMES PENDLETON, b. Abt. 1768, VA; d. 1841, Bullitt Co. KY.
78.   ix. REBECCA PENDLETON, b. Abt. 1775, VA.
79.   x. COLEMAN PENDLETON, b. Aug 04, 1780, Culpeper Co., Va.; d. May 31, 1862, Tallapoosa Co., AL.

32. JEMIMA[8] PENDLETON *(PHILIP[7], HENRY[6], PHILIP[5], HENRY[4], HENRY[3], GEORGE[2], GEORGE[1])* She married RICHARD GAINES. He was born 1731, and died 1805, Culpeper Co., VA.

Children of JEMIMA PENDLETON and RICHARD GAINES are:
    i.   NANCY ANN[9] GAINES, d. Clark Co, VA; m. CRISTOPHER CRIGLER.
    ii. JUDITH GAINES, m. THOMAS CHANCELLOR.

33. WILLIAM[8] PENDLETON *(NATHANIEL[7], HENRY[6], PHILIP[5], HENRY[4], HENRY[3], GEORGE[2], GEORGE[1])* was born Jan 13, 1748/49 in Essex Co., Va., and died Mar 31, 1817 in Berkeley Co., VA. He married (1) ELIZABETH FARGESON Apr 19, 1770 in VA, daughter of BENJAMIN FARGESON and SARAH ANNE. She was born Oct 10, 1753, and died Aug 15, 1799 in VA. He married (2) ELIZABETH DANIELS 1806. She was born Feb 02, 1748/49, and died Aug 06, 1808.

William Pendleton was a Culpeper Co. Minute Man during the Revolution. He was also a Lay Reader in St. Mark's Parish and furnished supplies to the Army during the Revolution. In 1778 he was a Gentleman Trustee for the establishment of the town of Martinsburg, Berkeley Co., VA. This is apparently the William Pendleton in the 1800 Culpeper Co. Tax List and the 1810 Berkeley Co., VA census. On Jan. 23, 1810, he was commissioned a Justice of Berkeley Co. by Gov. John Tyler, afterwards U.S. President. William Pendleton "for a number of years during the almost entire destitution of ministers, acted as a lay reader in Martinsburg and at the church in Hedgesville, the latter having been built chiefly by himself and Mr. Raleigh Colston" (Ref. 2).

Thomas Jefferson, on August 26, 1776, wrote the following to William Pendleton on requirements for voting (Ref. 62) indicating that voting for the Virginia house of representatives should be open to rich and poor alike.

> Now as to the representative house, which ought to be so constructed as to answer that character truly: I was for extending the rights of suffrage (or in other words the rights of a citizen) to all who had a permanent intention of living in the country. Take what circumstances you please as evidence for this, either the having resided a certain time, or having a family, or having property, any or all of them. Whoever intends to live in a country must wish the country well, and has a natural right of assisting in the preservation of it.

The Will of William Pendleton was recorded April 14, 1817 in Berkeley Co., VA and summarized as: "Dev.: Sarah Wigginton, Mary Orrick, Lucy Ferguson, Betty Cunningham, Ann Porterfield, Eleanor Walker, Emily, dau.; Nat., Benj., Wm.; others."

Children of WILLIAM PENDLETON and ELIZABETH FARGESON are:
80.   i.   MARY[9] PENDLETON, b. Mar 04, 1771, VA; d. Apr 15, 1838.
81.   ii. LUCY CLAYTON PENDLETON, b. Feb 20, 1773, Culpeper Co., VA; d. 1838, Sangoman Co., IL.
82.   iii. SARAH ANNE "SALLY" PENDLETON, b. Dec 17, 1774, Of Berkeley Co.; d. Aug 21, 1804, Frederick Co., VA.
83.   iv. NATHANIEL PENDLETON, b. Dec 26, 1777, VA; d. 1842, Warren Co., MO.
        v.   ELIZABETH PENDLETON, b. Jun 21, 1779; d. Nov 12, 1822, Jefferson Co., VA; m. JOHN CUNNINGHAM, Dec 22, 1800, Berkeley Co., VA.
84.   vi. BENJAMIN PENDLETON, b. Nov 19, 1781, Culpeper Co., VA; d. Mar 14, 1853, Hancock, MD.

vii. JOHN PENDLETON, b. 1782, VA; d. 1782, infancy.

viii. ANNE FARGESON PENDLETON, b. Sep 15, 1783, VA; m. JOHN PORTERFIELD, Mar 27, 1802, Berkeley Co., VA.

ix. SUSANNAH WILSON PENDLETON, b. May 10, 1786, VA; d. Aug 22, 1789.

85. x. WILLIAM PENDLETON, b. Aug 25, 1789, VA; d. Aug 01, 1855, Martinsburg, VA.

86. xi. FRANCES COLEMAN PENDLETON, b. Apr 01, 1792; d. Apr 08, 1864.

87. xii. ELEANOR PENDLETON, b. Nov 12, 1794; d. 1850.

xiii. EMILY PENDLETON, b. Sep 21, 1798, VA; d. Aug 27, 1845; m. PEACHY DYER, Dec 08, 1819, Pendleton Co., VA; b. Abt. 1796; d. 1835.

34. PHILIP[8] PENDLETON *(NATHANIEL[7], HENRY[6], PHILIP[5], HENRY[4], HENRY[3], GEORGE[2], GEORGE[1])* was born 1752 in VA, and died Dec 1801 in Martinsburg, VA. He married AGNES "PEGGY" PATTERSON 1773 in VA, daughter of ANGUS PATTERSON and LYDIA CHAPLINE. She died Aft. Jan 1802.

Colonel Philip Pendleton was the son of Nathaniel Pendleton of Culpepper County, Virginia. He removed to Berkeley County, Virginia, near Martinsburg, where he was admitted to the bar in 1772. From 1777 to 1781 he was an officer of the Berkeley County militia, and its representative in the state assembly of 1779 (Ref. 63). He was a Colonel (appointed April 3, 1777) of the Berkeley Co. Militia during the Revolutionary War. He was also Gentleman Justice of that county and one of the trustees of the town of Martinsburg in October 1778. From 1776 to 1777 and from 1785 to 1789 he represented Berkeley Co. in the House of Delegates.

It was apparently this Philip Pendleton who was granted 2,900 acres in Fayette Co., KY along the Licking River in 1785 and 1786 for service in the Revolutionary War (Ref. 64) and as relinquishing 2,000 acres in Jefferson Co., OH in1792 (Ref. 65). The Philip Pendleton listed in the Mason Co., KY 1800 Census is likely either this Philip or his son Philip Clayton Pendleton. "The first church built in Martinsburg, and which stood in the suburbs of the town, was erected chiefly at the cost and under the superintendence of Mr. Philip Pendleton, father of the present Mr. P. Pendleton of that place. He was a zealous Churchman, and so far as we know and believe, a good Christian" (Ref. 2).

His will was recorded January 25, 1802 in Berkeley Co., VA and summarized as: Dev.: Agnes, wife; Elizabeth Hunter, Nancy C. Kennedy, Sarah, Maria, dau.; Philip, James, Edmond (land on Potomac), Henry (lot Hancacktown, MD, son; Dan., slave; witness Nicholas Orrick.

Children of PHILIP PENDLETON and AGNES PATTERSON are:

88. i. ELIZABETH[9] PENDLETON, b. 1774, VA; d. 1822.

89. ii. ANNE "NANCY" CLAYTON PENDLETON, b. 1778, VA; d. Sep 13, 1854.

90. iii. PHILIP CLAYTON PENDLETON, b. Nov 24, 1779, Berkeley Co., VA; d. Apr 03, 1863, Berkeley Co., VA?

91. iv. SARAH PENDLETON, b. Jun 18, 1785, VA; d. Mar 13, 1855, Jefferson Co., VA?

92. v. EDMUND PENDLETON, b. 1790, VA; d. Aug 12, 1823.
93. vi. MARIA W. PENDLETON, b. Abt. 1795, VA.
    vii. WILLIAM HENRY PENDLETON, b. Abt. 1799, Martinsburg, VA; d. Sep
         1837, Harrisburg, TX.
             The following appeared in the Virginia Free Press, Nov. 30, 1837:
         "William Pendleton died at Harrisburg, TX in September last, in his 38th
         year, late of the Texan Army and formerly of Martinsburg, VA (now WV)."

   viii. JAMES PENDLETON, b. VA; d. without issue.
             This may be the James Pendleton listed in the 1800 Mason Co., KY
         census (with Philip Pendleton, either his brother or father).

35. ELIZABETH[8] PENDLETON *(NATHANIEL[7], HENRY[6], PHILIP[5], HENRY[4],
HENRY[3], GEORGE[2], GEORGE[1])* was born Abt. 1754. She married BENJAMIN TUTT.
He was born 1750 in VA, and died 1817.

Child of ELIZABETH PENDLETON and BENJAMIN TUTT is:
    i. CHARLES PENDLETON[9] TUTT, m. ANN MASON BONNYCASTLE.

36. NATHANIEL[8] PENDLETON, JR. *(NATHANIEL[7], HENRY[6], PHILIP[5], HENRY[4],
HENRY[3], GEORGE[2], GEORGE[1])* was born 1756 in Culpeper Co., VA, and died Oct 20,
1821 in Hyde Park, NY. He married SUSAN BARD Oct 04, 1785 in Savannah, GA,
daughter of JOHN BARD and SUSANNA VALLEAU. She was born Bet. 1755 - 1765.
        Nathaniel was the nephew of Edmund Pendleton and cousin of John Penn. He
entered the revolutionary army at nineteen years of age. He was taken prisoner at Fort
Washington, 16th November, 1776 and exchanged, 18th October, 1776. He was
promoted to Major and was Aide-de-Camp to General [Nathaniel] Greene, from
November 1780 to the end of the war. By the act of 29th October, 1781, it was
"Resolved, that Major-General Greene be desired to present the thanks of Congress to
Captain Pendleton, his Aide-de-Camp, in testimony of his particular activity and good
conduct during the whole action at Eutaw Springs, South Carolina."

        This is apparently the Nathaniel Pendleton who received a land grant of 4,666
acres in Kentucky for service during the Revolutionary War. He was a district judge and
Delegate to Continental Congress from Georgia, 1789. He is listed in the Georgia Tax
Index, Chatham Co., Savannah, 1793 and 1798. He was a Judge of U.S. District Court D.
VA, 1789-1796 and County Judge in 1821 the year of his death. He served as a second to
Alexander Hamilton in Hamilton's duel with Aaron Burr On July 11, 1804. Nathaniel
died in Hyde Park, N.Y., October 20, 1821 with interment at St. James' Churchyard,
Hyde Park, N.Y. (Refs. 41, 63, and 66).

Children of NATHANIEL PENDLETON and SUSAN BARD are:
    i. EDMUND HENRY[9] PENDLETON, b. 1786, GA; d. Feb 25, 1862, Hyde
        Park, Dutchess Co., NY; m. FRANCES MARIA JONES, Jan 09, 1811; b.
        Abt. 1792, NY; d. Aft. 1860, Hyde Park, NY?

Edmund Henry Pendleton was a NY State court judge and a U.S. Representative from New York's 5th District, 1831-1833. Internment is at St. James' Churchyard, Hyde Park, N.Y.

94.   ii. NATHANIEL GREENE PENDLETON, b. Aug 25, 1793, Savannah, GA; d. Jun 15, 1861, Cincinnati, OH.
      iii. JOHN BARD PENDLETON, b. 1795; d. Feb 02, 1830, St. Marks'-in-the-Bouwerie, NYC.
           A John B. Pendleton is listed in the Athens, Clarke Co., GA census of 1826. John B. Pendleton was promoted to First Lieutenant, 2nd U.S. Infantry, Sept. 17, 1828.

95.   iv. ANNA PIERCE PENDLETON, b. 1796; d. Dec 26, 1883.
96.   v.   JAMES M. PENDLETON, M.D., b. 1799; d. Jan 11, 1832, NYC.

37. EDMUND[8] PENDLETON *(JOHN[7], HENRY[6], PHILIP[5], HENRY[4], HENRY[3], GEORGE[2], GEORGE[1])* was born Feb 04, 1743/44 in VA, and died Jul 04, 1827 in Caroline Co., VA. He married MILDRED POLLARD Aug 16, 1764 in Goochland Co., VA, daughter of JOSEPH POLLARD and PRISCILLA HOLMES. She was born May 11, 1747 in Goochland, VA, and died Jul 04, 1827 in Caroline Co., VA.

He was called Edmund, Jr. in deference to his famous uncle, the Jurist Edmund Pendleton. In 1763 he graduated from William & Mary College. During the Revolution he was a Captain of the Caroline Co. Militia and later held the rank of Colonel.

Children of EDMUND PENDLETON and MILDRED POLLARD are:
97.   i.   JOHN[9] PENDLETON, b. Jun 22, 1765, Caroline Co., VA; d. Oct 1814, Caroline Co., VA.
      ii. FRANCES PENDLETON, b. Sep 18, 1767; d. Oct 20, 1831, VA; m. ROBERT TAYLOR, 1784; b. Apr 29, 1763.
      iii. EDMUND PENDLETON, b. Abt. 1770; d. infancy.
98.   iv. MILDRED PENDLETON, b. 1773, Caroline Co., VA.
99.   v.   EDMUND PENDLETON, b. Apr 18, 1774, VA; d. Jan 23, 1847, Hanover Co., VA.
      vi. ELIZABETH PENDLETON, b. Oct 24, 1776; m. REUBEN TURNER, Jun 17, 1793; b. Of Caroline Co.
100. vii. SARAH PENDLETON, b. 1781; d. 1815.
      viii. LUCY PENDLETON, b. Abt. 1785; m. THOMAS RICHARDS, Feb 07, 1805, Caroline Co., VA.

38. JR. JOHN[8] PENDLETON *(JOHN[7], HENRY[6], PHILIP[5], HENRY[4], HENRY[3], GEORGE[2], GEORGE[1])* was born Abt. 1750 in VA, and died Aug 1806 in Richmond, VA? He married MARY Abt. 1781. She died Nov 06, 1784 in Hanover Co., VA.

This is apparently the John Pendleton who lived in Richmond and the John Pendleton, nephew of Edmund, who secured (by his uncle's influence) the position of escheator whereby he received a commission in the sale of forfeited estates of expelled merchants. These merchants were expelled because they did not vow loyalty to the commonwealth. John grew wealthy from these commissions (Ref. 67).

There is a certificate dated 6 August 1795 stating that John Pendleton was justice of the peace in Henrico County, Virginia, signed by James Wood, lieutenant governor of Virginia (Ref. 68). And it was this John Pendleton, Esq. whose death notice appeared in the Virginia Gazette on Weds., Aug 13, 1806 [died last Saturday].

Mrs. Mary Pendleton appeared in the Virginia gazette, and weekly advertiser entry of Saturday, November 6, 1784 (p. 3, c. 1): "Died- Lately, at Clifton, Hanover County, Mrs. Mary Pendleton, spouse of Mr. John Pendleton, of this city."

Children of JOHN PENDLETON and MARY are:
- i. MARY[9] PENDLETON.

  It was apparently this Mary Pendleton whose marriage was announced in the VA Gazette & General Advertiser, 26 Nov., 1799: "Sheppard, Nathaniel mar. Miss Polly Pendleton on Thurs eve. last, both of Richmond."

- ii. III JOHN PENDLETON.
- 101. iii. ELIZABETH SMITH PENDLETON, b. Aug 12, 1782; d. Aug 09, 1861.

39. MARY JEAN[8] PENDLETON (*JOHN[7], HENRY[6], PHILIP[5], HENRY[4], HENRY[3], GEORGE[2], GEORGE[1]*) was born 1756 in VA, and died Aft. 1800. She married THOMAS HARRISON Abt. 1776 in Caswell Co., NC? He was born 1747 in Goochland Co., VA, and died 1799 in Caswell Co., NC.

Children of MARY PENDLETON and THOMAS HARRISON are:
- i. JOHN PENDLETON[9] HARRISON, b. Abt. 1778, Caswell Co., NC.
- ii. WILLIAM HARRISON, b. Abt. 1780, Caswell Co., NC.
- iii. JEAN HARRISON, b. Abt. 1782, Caswell Co., NC.
- iv. ROBERT HARRISON, b. Abt. 1784, Caswell Co., NC.
- v. ANDREW HARRISON, b. Abt. 1786, Caswell Co., NC.
- vi. MILDRED HARRISON, b. Abt. 1788, Caswell Co., NC.
- vii. PATSY HARRISON, b. Abt. 1790, Caswell Co., NC.

40. HENRY[8] PENDLETON (*JOHN[7], HENRY[6], PHILIP[5], HENRY[4], HENRY[3], GEORGE[2], GEORGE[1]*) was born Dec 04, 1762 in King & Queen Co., Va., and died Nov 11, 1822 in Louisa Co., VA. He married (1) ALCEY ANNE WINSTON Oct 27, 1785 in Louisa Co., VA, daughter of JOHN WINSTON and ALICE BICKERTON. She was born Aug 03, 1769, and died Jan 08, 1813 in Louisa Co., VA. He married (2) MARY (OVERTON) BURNLEY Apr 05, 1815. She was born 1780 in Culpeper Co., VA.

Henry Pendleton served in the Revolution in the Hanover Co. Militia. In 1799 he qualified as an Ensign in that County. From 1804 to 1806 he was a member of the House of Delegates from Louisa Co., VA. He was overseer of the poor of Louisa Co and is listed in the 1810 and 1820 Louisa Co., VA census records. He lived at Greenbay on North East Creek until, in 1818, he purchased the "Cuckoo" property. He is buried at the cemetery at Cuckoo (Ref . 69).

Children of HENRY PENDLETON and ALCEY WINSTON are:

102.   i.   EDMUND[9] PENDLETON, b. Oct 24, 1786, VA; d. Dec 12, 1838, Louisa Co., VA.

103.   ii.   JOHN BICKERTON PENDLETON, b. Feb 16, 1788, VA; d. Jun 06, 1840, Pickens Co., AL.

      iii.   HENRY PENDLETON, b. Nov 25, 1789, VA; d. Mar 11, 1801, VA.

104.   iv.   MATILDA WINSTON PENDLETON, b. Jan 15, 1792, VA; d. Jul 23, 1840.

105.   v.   SARAH "SALLY" MADISON PENDLETON, b. Oct 06, 1793, VA; d. 1827.

106.   vi.   BARBARA OVERTON PENDLETON, b. Jun 04, 1795, VA; d. Mar 23, 1855.

107.   vii.   JOSEPH WINSTON PENDLETON, b. Jul 31, 1797, VA; d. 1881, Whitehall, Louisa Co., VA.

      viii.   LUCY ANNE PENDLETON, b. Apr 14, 1799, VA; d. 1835, Albemarle Co., VA?; m. JOHN VOWLES, Sep 10, 1823, Albemarle Co., VA; b. Abt. 1797, England; d. Aft. 1850, Albemarle Co., VA?

      ix.   CATHERINE "KITTY" ROBERTSON PENDLETON, b. Feb 01, 1801, VA; d. Mar 19, 1839; m. JR. FRANCIS JOHNSON, DR., Dec 02, 1823, Louisa Co., VA.

      x.   MARTHA TODD PENDLETON, b. Apr 24, 1803, VA; d. 1831, Louisa Co., VA?; m. JAMES M. TRICE, CAPT., Nov 27, 1830, Louisa Co., VA; b. Abt. 1804, VA; d. Aft. 1860, Louisa Co., VA?

108.   xi.   THOMAS MADISON PENDLETON, b. Nov 09, 1804, Louisa Co., VA; d. Mar 04, 1835.

      xii.   MARY PENDLETON, b. Jul 22, 1806, Louisa Co., VA; d. Sep 30, 1806.

109.   xiii.   WILLIAM JAMES PENDLETON, b. May 31, 1809, Louisa Co., VA; d. Jan 07, 1872.

      xiv.   ALICE WINSTON PENDLETON, b. Jan 07, 1813, Louisa Co., VA; d. Sep 14, 1828.

Child of HENRY PENDLETON and MARY BURNLEY is:

110.   xv.   FRANCES SAMUELLA[9] PENDLETON, b. Sep 07, 1816, VA; d. Feb 06, 1856, Albemarle Co., VA?

41. BENJAMIN[8] PENDLETON *(WILLIAM[7], JOHN[6], PHILIP[5], HENRY[4], HENRY[3], GEORGE[2], GEORGE[1])* was born Abt. 1749 in VA, and died Aft. 1815 in Scott Co., VA. He married (1) FRANCES BALL CARTER. She was born 1741. He married (2) SARAH CARTER.

There is considerable debate concerning the descendants of William Pendleton of Amherst including this Benjamin, William's eldest son. Perhaps this is due to the location of this line of Pendletons – out on the western frontier. In any case, this is the Benjamin Pendleton listed with Edmund Pendleton, his brother, in the 1787 Russell Co., VA Personal Property Tax List, 2nd District with 1 horse and 3 cattle. Not long after this date, tragedy struck the family in the form of an Indian raid (Ref. 70).

> ...The most daring and crafty of these Chickamauga bushwhackers was Bob Benge, the son of an Indian trader named John Benge, who married a niece of the Old Tassel, and spent his life in the nation. His first enterprise in this quarter was undertaken in the

summer of 1791. Notwithstanding the treaty of July 2nd, on August 23rd he startled the settlements in the neighborhood of Moccasin Gap, or Clinch Mountain, by a sudden and unexpected assault on the house of the McDowells and Pendletons. Mrs. William McDowell and Frances Pendleton, the seventeen-year-old daughter of Benjamin Pendleton, were killed and scalped; Reuben Pendleton was wounded, and Mrs. Pendleton and a boy of eight years of age were carried into captivity. Three days later, in the same neighborhood, his party appeared at the house of Elisha Farris, about eight o'clock in the morning, killed and scalped his wife, and Mrs. Livingston and her three-year-old child, and mortally wounded Mr. Farris. His daughter, Nancy Farris, a girl about nineteen years of age, they carried off a prisoner,16. After this bloody raid they made good their escape, without discovery and without punishment.

As can be seen by the birth dates of Benjamin's children below, there is still some confusion as to the marriage dates of Benjamin and Frances and Sarah Carter and which children belong to which Carter wife or even whether or not Benjamin married twice. In any case, Benjamin is listed in a Virginia Land Grant of 11 Dec 1797 for 64 acres on the south branch of Harris Creek, Amherst Co. (Ref. 71). And on November 31, 1806 he transferred 40 acres on the south side of the Clinch River, Virginia to his son John (Reverend John Pendleton, 1792-1861). In 1811 there is a deed book reference to Benjamin Pendleton's new tract of 226 acres on the Rocky Spring Branch of the Clinch (Ref. 72).

It appears certain that this Benjamin, the son of William, spent his elder years in southeast Virginia. It must be noted that this Benjamin is often confused with the Benjamin Pendleton who spent his latter days in Warren Co., KY. However, that Benjamin is surely the son of Philip of Buckingham Co., VA.

A Sarah Pendleton is listed in the 1810 Census records for Russell Co., VA. Widows were sometimes listed as heads of households but it is not known if this is Sarah Carter Pendleton, Benjamin's second wife.

Children of BENJAMIN PENDLETON and FRANCES CARTER are:
- i. ELIZABETH[9] PENDLETON, b. Abt. 1773, VA; d. Apr 02, 1852, Morgan Co., KY; m. LEVI SWANSON.
- ii. FRANCES PENDLETON, b. 1774, VA; d. Aug 23, 1791, Indian attack at Mocassin Gap/Clinch River, Scott Co., VA.
- 111. iii. REUBEN PENDLETON, b. Abt. 1777, VA; d. Mar 03, 1860, Rye Cove, Scott Co., VA.
- 112. iv. JAMES A. PENDLETON, b. 1779, VA; d. 1848, Scott Co., VA?
- 113. v. MARY "POLLY" PENDLETON, b. Abt. 1787, Russell Co., VA; d. Jul 04, 1852, Morgan Co., KY.

Child of BENJAMIN PENDLETON and SARAH CARTER is:
- 114. vi. JOHN[9] PENDLETON, b. Abt. 1788, Russell Co., VA; d. Oct 11, 1861, Collin Co., TX.

42. JAMES[8] PENDLETON *(WILLIAM[7], JOHN[6], PHILIP[5], HENRY[4], HENRY[3], GEORGE[2], GEORGE[1])* was born Apr 03, 1750 in VA, and died Jul 02, 1832 in Amherst Co., VA. He married SARAH ELIZABETH RUCKER 1769, daughter of JOHN RUCKER and ELEANOR WARREN. She was born Jul 25, 1750 in Amherst Co., Va., and died Oct 16, 1825.

This James Pendleton was a Captain in the Revolutionary War. He served with the VA troops as a captain, Feb 7, 1777; he was at Valley Forge, June 3, 1778, and in camp near Chester, PA, July 9, 1779. He was promoted to brevet major during the war. In addition, he was an Episcopalian Vestryman from 1779 in Amherst Co. (Ref. 73). He maintained a plantation in Amherst County called "New Inventions" (Ref. 74).

Child of JAMES PENDLETON and SARAH RUCKER is:
115.   i.   ELIZABETH[9] PENDLETON, b. Dec 19, 1787; d. May 17, 1839.

43. EDMUND[8] PENDLETON *(WILLIAM[7], JOHN[6], PHILIP[5], HENRY[4], HENRY[3], GEORGE[2], GEORGE[1])* was born 1754 in VA, and died 1830 in TN. He married MARGARET.

Edmund Pendleton was a revolutionary soldier as shown by the Petitions of Amherst Co. of May 17, 1777. Edmund Pendleton is included in a list of soldiers asking for reimbursement for expenses caused by sickness. This is likely the Edmund Pendleton listed with Benjamin, his brother, in the 1787 Russell Co., VA Tax List and the Edmund Pendleton listed in 1799 with 281 acres on the Clinch River and Cove Creek, Russell Co. adjoining Thomas Carter land grants (Ref. 75).

Edmund is included in the Stony Creek Baptist Church Minute Books 1801 – 1811, Fort Blackmore, Scott County, Virginia:

> Church meeting held at Stony Creek. February the 21 day 1803. Brother Giles Lea acknowledged his fault for drinking too much and was restored. Received by letter Brother Hutchens and T.R. Abbel. Application by Br. Edmond Pendleton for a letter of dismission for him and his wife. Some objection being made in the church against it, we have appointed a committee: Br. Wilson, Br. Cock, Br. Brickey and Br. Leath to make a inquisition of the cause. We agree Sister Pendleton have a letter of dismission.

Children of EDMUND PENDLETON and MARGARET are:
           i.   SARAH[9] PENDLETON, m. ? WALLACE.
          ii.   LEWIS PENDLETON.
                    The David Walker family listed in the 1850 census of Greene Co., MO. were from KY; they had a Lewis Pendleton, age 85, living with them.

         iii.   JAMES PENDLETON.
116.   iv.   JOHN PENDLETON, b. 1777, VA; d. Aug 1860, Cannon Co. TN.
117.   v.   BENJAMIN PENDLETON, b. 1784, Russell Co., VA; d. 1856, Christian Co., MO.

44. REUBEN[8] PENDLETON *(WILLIAM[7], JOHN[6], PHILIP[5], HENRY[4], HENRY[3], GEORGE[2], GEORGE[1])* was born 1755 in VA, and died Nov 14, 1825 in Amherst Co.,

VA. He married FRANCES MARIA ANNA GARLAND 1785, daughter of WILLIAM GARLAND and ANNE SHEPHERD. She was born 1763, and died 1843.

Reuben Pendleton was a Private in Capt. William Tucker's Co. of Militia from Amherst. He was discharged 26 Mar, 1781 as a Corporal, with his brother Richard. He reenlisted and was a Minute Man of Amherst Co. and served with Lafayette; later he was at Yorktown, Oct 19, 1781. This is apparently the Reuben Pendleton in the 1810 Augusta Co., VA census and the 1820 Amherst Co. census.

Children of REUBEN PENDLETON and FRANCES GARLAND are:

      i. FRANCES GARLAND[9] PENDLETON, m. JOSEPH STAPLES, Jul 11, 1833.

     ii. MARTHA ANNE PENDLETON, m. (1) STOWELL; m. (2) ZACHARIAH LUCAS, Sep 01, 1834, Amherst Co., VA.

118. iii. NANCY PENDLETON.

     iv. POLLY PENDLETON, m. (1) ELIAS WELLS; m. (2) JOHN SEAY, Sep 13, 1830; m. (3) NOWLIN, Aft. 1831.

     v. SAMUEL PENDLETON, m. SARAH SPENCER.

119. vi. JANE GARLAND PENDLETON, b. Abt. 1787, VA; d. Abt. 1822, Nelson Co., VA.

120. vii. WILLIAM GARLAND PENDLETON, b. Apr 02, 1788, VA; d. Feb 1839, Lynchburg, VA.

   viii. SOPHIA PENDLETON, b. Abt. 1792, VA; d. Aft. 1850, Appomatox Co., VA?; m. (1) GEORGE POWELL, Nov 19, 1809, Amherst Co., VA; d. 1819; m. (2) FLEMING CASHWELL, Jul 02, 1815, Amherst Co., VA; b. Abt. 1794, VA; d. Aft. 1850 Appomatox Co., VA?

         Sophia's first marriage was announced on Dec. 16, 1809 (Ref. 76) as "Powell, Mr. George, Married to Miss Sophia Pendleton, second daughter of Reubin Pendleton, Esq., all of Amherst Co. On 19th ult." Fleming and Sophia Cashwell are listed in the 1850 Appomatox Co., VA census roles, pg. 194.

121. ix. JAMES SHEPHERD PENDLETON, b. Abt. 1795, VA; d. 1851, CA.

122. x. MICAJAH PENDLETON, b. 1796, VA; d. Oct 1861, Botetourt Co., VA?

123. xi. ELIZABETH JANE PENDLETON, b. 1802; d. 1860.

    xii. HARRIET PENDLETON, b. Abt. 1808.

   xiii. ADELAIDE PENDLETON, b. Abt. 1814.

45. RICHARD[8] PENDLETON (*WILLIAM[7], JOHN[6], PHILIP[5], HENRY[4], HENRY[3], GEORGE[2], GEORGE[1]*) was born 1760 in VA, and died May 20, 1829 in Amherst Co., VA. He married MARY TINSLEY Jan 04, 1784 in Culpeper Co., VA, daughter of WILLIAM TINSLEY. She was born 1764, and died 1844 in Nelson Co., VA.

Richard Pendleton enlisted in Amherst Co. as private or non-commissioned officer of the cavalry under Lt. William Penn in the early part of the Revolutionary War and marched north with Lt. Penn. He was in the battles of Brandywine, Germantown, and Monmouth in Capt. Spotswood Dandridge's company. He served 2 years and 9 months and took the smallpox while in service, marks of which were apparent to the day of his death. He also served as Cpl in Capt. William Tucker's Co. of Militia from Amherst and was discharged 26 Mar, 1781 along with his brother Reuben. Richard Pendleton is named in the pension application of John Webster as having enlisted in 1776 at the same time as he did (Ref. 77).

Richard Pendleton is listed in at least three Virginia Land Grants, one being 4 acres on the south branch of Harris's Creek, Amherst Co. on 12 June 1797. This Richard Pendleton appeared in the 1810 Augusta Co., VA census and the 1820 Amherst Co. census.

There's a pension application for Richard Pendleton, filed from Nelson Co, VA, 20 Aug 1844, by Mary Pendleton, 82, widow of Richard who died 20 May 1829, saying they were married 4 Jan 1784 in Culpeper Co, VA, by Rev. Herdsman. His service is outlined by various "witness" statements, and Reuben Pendleton is named as his brother. Abraham Tinsley is named as brother to Mary. James Tinsley is named as son of William Tinsley. William Tinsley of Madison Co, VA, stated he was executor of his father's will and that he had paid to Richard Pendleton, Mary's share of his estate.

Children of RICHARD PENDLETON and MARY TINSLEY are:
   i.   BETTIE[9] PENDLETON b. abt 1788, VA; m. AMBROSE LUCAS, Jan 25, 1806, Amherst Co., VA; b. Bet. 1780 - 1790.
        Ambrose Lucas is listed in the 1840 Amherst Co., VA census. Elizabeth Lucas (62) is listed in the 1850 Amherst Co., VA census along with Lucinda (30), Henry (28), and Sarah Ann (19) presumably her children.

   ii. LUCY PENDLETON, b. Bet. 1790 - 1800, VA; m. WESLEY E. CHRISTIAN, Jul 30, 1821, Amherst Co., VA; b. Bet. 1790 - 1800.
        Westley L. Christian and presumably Lucy (30 to 40 years old) are listed in the 1830 Amherst Co., VA census. Five children under 10 years old are listed. Wesley E. Christian is listed in the 1840 Amherst Co., VA census with 7 children under 20 years old and a female (another wife?) aged 30 to 40 years.

   iii. PAULINE PENDLETON.
   iv. POLLY PENDLETON.
   v.   REUBEN PENDLETON, m. MARTHA COX.
        This could be the Martha Pendleton (60) listed in the 1850 Bedford Co., VA census.

124. vi. SARAH PENDLETON, b. Mar 06, 1792, Nelson Co., VA; d. Jun 17, 1876, Amherst Co., VA.
      vii. HENRY T. PENDLETON, b. Bet. 1790 - 1800, VA; m. SARAH ANN REESE, Jun 1830; of Charlotte Co., VA.
           The following agreement recorded in Amherst Co. (Ref. 78) was between brothers Henry T. and William Pendleton regarding property of their uncle, William Pendleton, Sr. (1772- 1828): "Agreement 30 Sept. 1829 between Wm Pendleton of County of Amherst & Henry T. Pendleton. The interest

that said Wm Pendleton is entitled to receive ---real & personal Property---belonging to the late Wm Pendleton Sr. Deceased as heir of Richard Pendleton dec. recorded 1 Oct. 1829."

125. viii. JAMES PENDLETON, b. 1793, VA; d. 1851, Warren Co., MO.
126. ix. WILLIAM PENDLETON, b. Abt. 1800, Amherst Co., VA; d. Abt. 1838, Osage Co., MO.
      x. JR. RICHARD PENDLETON, b. 1803.

46. JOHN[8] PENDLETON *(WILLIAM[7], JOHN[6], PHILIP[5], HENRY[4], HENRY[3], GEORGE[2], GEORGE[1])* was born 1760 in Amherst Co., VA?, and died 1830 in Lincoln Co., KY. He married SARAH BANKS Jan 24, 1786 in Amherst Co., VA, daughter of LINN BANKS and SARAH PROCTOR. She was born 1766 in Amherst Co., VA, and died Aug 15, 1859 in Garrard Co., KY.

This John Pendleton was a soldier in the Revolutionary War (Ref. 73). He is apparently the John Pendleton in the 1782-1787 Botetourt Co., VA tax list; the 1800 Garrard Co., KY list, and the Lincoln Co., KY 1810 and 1820 census records.

Children of JOHN PENDLETON and SARAH BANKS are (Refs. 79 and 80):
127. i. MALINDA[9] PENDLETON, b. Dec 28, 1787, VA; d. Aug 18, 1870, Pendleton Co., KY.
      ii. REUBEN PENDLETON, b. 1790, Amherst Co., VA.
          This is likely the Reuben Pendleton listed in the 1812 Muster Rolls, Private, 5th and 6th Regiments, Virginia Militia. And it is likely this Reuben who married Malinda Jane Hays on 5 January 1824 (Ref. 81).

      iii. JR. JOHN F. PENDLETON, b. 1792; d. 1860, Jackson Co., MO?; m. ABIGAIL WINFREY, Jun 26, 1816, Adair Co., KY.
      iv. TINSLEY PENDLETON, b. Abt. 1794; d. Aft. 1850, Lincoln Co., KY.
          Tinsley Pendleton is listed in the 1830 Lincoln Co. census. He is also listed as a laborer, age 56, in the 1850 Lincoln Co., KY census in the household of Elijah Bailey.

128. v. LUCY PENDLETON, b. Abt. 1795; d. Aug 14, 1858, Lincoln Co., KY.
129. vi. MICAJAH PENDLETON, b. 1800, VA; d. 1878, Independence, MO.
      vii. DAUGHTER PENDLETON, b. Bet. 1800 - 1810.
      viii. DAUGHTER PENDLETON, b. Bet. 1800 - 1810; m. WILLIS.
130. ix. RICHARD PENDLETON, b. Abt. 1807; d. 1833, Henry Co., KY.
131. x. JAMES PENDLETON, b. Abt. 1808, KY; d. Aft. 1880, Independence, MO.

47. ISAAC[8] PENDLETON *(WILLIAM[7], JOHN[6], PHILIP[5], HENRY[4], HENRY[3], GEORGE[2], GEORGE[1])* was born Abt. 1761 in VA, and died Aft. 1860 in Trimble Co., KY. He married NANCY A. HARDWICK Feb 16, 1795 in Amherst Co., VA. She died Bef. 1850.

Isaac Pendleton is listed in the 1810 and 1830 Henry Co., KY census records. Isaac is listed in the Trimble Co., KY census of 1850 (age 90) in the household of William Peak (the father of his daughter-in-law).

Children of ISAAC PENDLETON and NANCY HARDWICK are (Ref. 82):

     i. PLEASANT H.[9] PENDLETON, b. Abt. 1800, VA; m. PRUDENCE ANN BROWN, Jan 05, 1835, Henry Co., KY; b. Abt. 1816, KY.

       Pleasant Pendleton is listed in the 1840 Trimble Co. census near Isaac, Lindsey, Robert K., and Welles Pendleton.

132.   ii. ROBERT HARDWICK PENDLETON, b. Dec 25, 1802, Lynchburg, VA; d. Dec 1889, Trimble Co., KY.

133.   iii. LINDSEY PENDLETON, b. Abt. 1805, VA; d. Aft. 1870, Henry Co., KY?

134.   iv. ISAAC T. PENDLETON, b. Abt. 1811, Mill Creek, Henry Co., KY; d. Aft. 1860, Henry Co., KY?

135.   v. FRANCES PENDLETON, b. Abt. 1813, KY; d. Aft. 1880, Trimble Co., KY?

136.   vi. WILLIS M. PENDLETON, b. Abt. 1813, Mill Creek, Henry Co., KY; d. Aft. 1860, MO?

     vii. ELIZA PENDLETON, b. Abt. 1816; m. JOHN O. HEAD, Mar 03, 1828, Trimble Co., KY; b. Abt. 1816, Trimble Co., KY.

     viii. PRUDENCE PENDLETON, b. Abt. 1818; m. CHARLES MEDCALF, Sep 03, 1844, Trimble Co., KY; b. Abt. 1818, Trimble Co., KY.

48. MARY[8] PENDLETON *(WILLIAM[7], JOHN[6], PHILIP[5], HENRY[4], HENRY[3], GEORGE[2], GEORGE[1])* was born Abt. 1763. She married JEREMIAH WHITTEN. He died 1800.

Children of MARY PENDLETON and JEREMIAH WHITTEN are:

     i. NANCY ELIZABETH[9] WHITTEN, m. JAMES FRANKLIN, 1802.

     ii. TABITHA WHITTEN, m. EDMUND BOLES, Abt. 1806.

49. FRANCES[8] PENDLETON *(WILLIAM[7], JOHN[6], PHILIP[5], HENRY[4], HENRY[3], GEORGE[2], GEORGE[1])* was born Abt. 1765. She married JABEZ CAMDEN Mar 13, 1801 in Amherst Co., VA, son of WILLIAM CAMDEN and SYBIL DENT. He was born Abt. 1770.

   Surety and witness to the marriage of Frances Pendleton and Jabez Camden included James Pendleton and S. Garland (Ref. 83).

Children of FRANCES PENDLETON and JABEZ CAMDEN are:

     i. JORDAN P.[9] CAMDEN, b. 1793.

     ii. BLUFORD CAMDEN, b. 1808.

50. ELIZABETH "BETSY"[8] PENDLETON *(WILLIAM[7], JOHN[6], PHILIP[5], HENRY[4], HENRY[3], GEORGE[2], GEORGE[1])* was born Abt. 1774 in VA, and died Bef. 1829. She married REUBEN BALDOCK Sep 09, 1793 in Amherst Co., VA, son of LEVI BALDOCK. He was born 1767 in VA, and died Mar 1838 in Amherst Co., VA.

Reuben Baldock later married Martha Jane "Patsy" Pendleton July 14, 1829. It seems likely that this is Patsy Cox Pendleton, wife of William Pendleton (brother of this Elizabeth Pendleton) who died October 1828. Patsy Pendleton appears in the Amherst Co. 1850 Census as living with Tabby A. and Wiatt Cox. Her age is 70 making her date of birth about 1780. She died abt June 6, 1851 (when her estate was submitted for inventory in Amherst County, VA).

Children of ELIZABETH PENDLETON and REUBEN BALDOCK are:

    i.   MARY ANNA "POLLY"[9] BALDOCK, b. 1795, Lincoln Co., KY; d. Feb 01, 1851, Casey Co., KY; m. RICHARD LEE SMITH.

    ii.   LEVI BALDOCK, b. 1797, Lincoln Co., KY; d. Bef. 1860, Gentry Co., MO?; m. RACHAEL SAPP, Jul 24, 1819, Casey Co., KY; b. 1800, KY.

    iii.   PENDLETON BALDOCK, b. 1801, Lincoln Co., KY; d. Aft. 1860; m. ELIZABETH ELDER, Bef. May 31, 1834, KY.

    iv.   JOHN W. BALDOCK, b. Mar 27, 1802, Lincoln Co., KY; d. Mar 19, 1890, Casey Co., KY; m. AGRA PINA CHRISTENSON, Jul 24, 1825, Casey Co., KY; b. 1803; d. 1891, Casey Co., KY.

    v.   WILLIAM BALDOCK, b. Abt. 1806, Lincoln Co., KY; d. Feb 1842, VA; m. ELIZABETH A. PADGETT, Nov 20, 1833, Amherst Co., VA; b. 1813; d. Aft. 1860.

    vi.   RICHARD BALDOCK, b. 1808, Lincoln Co., KY; d. Sep 1860; m. LOUISA, Abt. 1829, Casey Co., KY.

    vii.   GEORGE BALDOCK, b. Abt. 1811, Lincoln Co., KY.

    viii.   TABITHA ANN "TABBY A" BALDOCK, b. Abt. 1815, Lincoln Co., KY; d. Aft. 1850, Amherst Co., VA?; m. WIATT COX, Aug 06, 1840, Amherst Co., VA; b. Abt. 1810; d. Aft. 1850, Amherst Co., VA?.

    ix.   MALE BALDOCK, b. Abt. 1817, Lincoln Co., KY; d. In infancy.

    x.   NANCY S. BALDOCK, b. Abt. 1818, Lincoln Co., KY; d. Aft. 1860, Amherst Co., VA?; m. JOHN MATTHEW WILLS, Jun 25, 1838, Amherst Co., VA; b. Abt. 1816; d. Aft. 1860.

51. HENRY[8] PENDLETON, JR. *(HENRY[7], JOHN[6], PHILIP[5], HENRY[4], HENRY[3], GEORGE[2], GEORGE[1])* was born Sep 30, 1748 in King William Co., VA, and died Nov 28, 1801 in Spotsylvania Co., VA. He married ANNE KNIGHT Jan 4, 1773, daughter of EPHRAIM KNIGHT. She was born Sep 10, 1753.

    Henry Pendleton, Jr. held property in Spotsylvania Co. in 1777 (Ref. 84):

Lydia x Arnold of Spts. Co. and Wm. Arnold and Susannah, his wife, of Louisa Co. to Henry Pendleton, jr., of Spts. Co. £30 curr. 50 a. in Berkeley Par., Spts. Co., whereon Wm. Arnold, Decd., lived, and devised by him to his son, Wm., etc. Witnesses, Jno. Daniel, Thos. Coleman, jr.; Wm. Phillips, Wm. Pain, Wm. Trigg. Novr. 20, 1777.

    Henry Pendleton served as a private in the Revolutionary War in Capt. Bartlett's Company from Nov 14, 1776. An original letter written by him, dated Oct. 2, 1780 at Guilford Court House, NC, was in the possession of his descendant, Mrs. Lila Pendleton Proctor (1850 - 1932) of Warren Co., KY. He was the first Pastor of Mine Road Baptist

Church serving from 1791 to his death in1801. The Mine Road [Baptist Church] was described in 1810 (Ref. 29) as

> ...a small church taken off from Wallers in 1791. Mr. Henry Pendleton [Sr.] was ordained to the care of the church at the time of the constitution. From first to last this church has rather dragged on heavily, having had no revival, or none to any extent. Their present number is now less than at their first constitution. They have, however, some useful members, among whom is Mr. Henry Pendleton, Sr., father of the preacher, and himself a preacher in another sense. He preaches by a pious walk and godly conversation. He is now a venerable old man, of about four-score years of age. Henry Pendleton [Jr.], their first pastor, was, until a few years before his death, considered a very pious and rational man. He had fallen into the Arminian system, to which he adhered in all its branches; but being viewed as a pious man, was held in estimation. Strange to tell, in 1800, he put an end to his own existence by shooting himself. His conduct for some length of time previous to this fatal extent indicated some degree of melancholy insanity. To this state of mind charity requires us to ascribe an act so unpardonable, if perpetrated by one not in a state of sanity. Elder Philip Pendleton is their present pastor.

Children of HENRY PENDLETON and ANNE KNIGHT are:

137. i. BENJAMIN[9] PENDLETON, b. Abt. 1774, Spotsylvania Co., VA; d. Aft. 1830, Spotsylvania Co., VA?
138. ii. MARY "POLLY" PENDLETON, b. 1775, Spotsylvania Co., VA; d. 1844, Todd Co., KY.
139. iii. HENRY PENDLETON, b. 1778, Spotsylvania Co., VA; d. Jan 9, 1873, Spotsylvania Co., VA.
140. iv. JOHN PENDLETON, b. Apr 21, 1780, Spotsylvania Co., VA; d. Jan 26, 1838, Christian Co., KY.

52. JOHN[8] PENDLETON (*HENRY[7], JOHN[6], PHILIP[5], HENRY[4], HENRY[3], GEORGE[2], GEORGE[1]*) was born Nov 25, 1755 in Spotsylvania Co., VA, and died 1828 in Spotsylvania Co., VA. He married SALLY ALSOP Jan 1788 in VA. She was born Bef. 1765, and died Bef. 1820 in Spotsylvania Co., VA?

John Pendleton was a private in the Revolutionary War (Ref. 73). He became the guardian of Nancy Atherton in 1790 (Ref. 85): "March 2, 1790. Edwd. Herndon, Lewis Holloday and Wm. Bronaugh, Overseers of the Poor, Dist. No. 2, Spts. Co., do bind Nancy Atherton, daughter of Joseph Atherton, to John Pendleton, etc. Witnesses, Jno. Minor, A. Buchanan. March 4, 1790." It is this John Pendleton who is listed with 6 children and 4 slaves in the 1810 VA census, Spotsylvania Co. His will was proved in Spotsylvania Co. in 1828:

> I John Pendleton of the County of Spotsylvania being in perfect health and sound memory do make and ordain this as my last will and testament that is to say in the first place it is my desire that all my just debts may be paid and then that my son Chesley shall for the services he hath rendered to me in looking over my business as an overseer shall be allowed Seaventy [sic] Dollars a year including the year one thousand eight hundred and twenty three as long as he shall continue with me Also it is my desire that my Daughter Fanney shall be allowed Fifteen Dollars a year for her attendance to my house business including the year one thousand eight hundred and twenty three as long as she

shall continue with me. And then it is my desire that whatever may appear to remain after the above mentioned shall be equally divided among all my children whose names are as follows to wit it is my desire that Betsey and her heirs shall have one seavent [sic] part. Also it is my desire that Rice and his heirs shall have one seaventh [sic] part, also it is my desire] that Nancy and her heirs shall have one seaventh [sic] [part.] Also it is my desire that Salley and her heirs shall have one seaventh [sic] part. Also it is my desire that John and his heirs shall have one seaventh [sic] part. Also it is my desire that Fanney and her heirs shall have one seaventh [sic] part. Also it is my desire that Chesley and his heirs shall have one seaventh [sic] part. And I do constitute and appoint my sons Rice and Chesley Executors to this my last will and testament revoking all other wills heretofore by me made as witness my hand and seal this sixteenth day of June one thousand Eighteen hundred and twenty seaven [sic]."
/s/ John Pendleton [Seal]In presents of/s/ Samuel Alsop/s/ J M. Anderson

At a Court held for Spotsylvania County the 1st day of September 1828. The last will and testament of John Pendleton deceased was proved by the oaths of Samuel Alsop and John M. Anderson witnesses thereto and ordered to be recorded

Teste R. L. Stevenson, C. C. At a Court held for Spotsylvania County the 6th day of October 1828 On the motion of Rice Pendleton and Chesley Pendleton Executors named in the last will and testament of John Pendleton deceased who made oaths thereto and together with Willis Landrum and James Alsop their securities entered into and acknowledged a bond in the penalty of $6000 conditioned as the law directs Certificate is granted them for obtaining a probate of said will in due form.

Teste R. L. Stevenson, C. C.
Recorded liber M folio 298

Children of JOHN PENDLETON and SALLY ALSOP are:
141.   i.   ELIZABETH "BETSY"[9] PENDLETON, b. Jul 29, 1789, Spotsylvania Co., VA; d. Jul 20, 1873, Adair Co., KY.
        ii.   CURTIS PENDLETON, b. Abt. 1790, VA; d. 1814.
              It was probably this Curtis Pendleton who is listed in the 1810 VA census, Spotsylvania Co. and the Curtis Pendleton, Corporal, listed in the 16th Regiment (Wallers) Virginia Militia, War of 1812 Muster Rolls.

142.   iii. RICE PENDLETON, b. 1790, VA; d. 1836, Spotsylvania Co., VA?
        iv.   NANCY PENDLETON, b. Abt. 1792, VA; m. MARTIN HICKS, Sep 24, 1817, Spotsylvania Co., VA.
143.   v.   SALLY PENDLETON, b. Abt. 1795, VA.
144.   vi.   JOHN PENDLETON, b. 1797, VA; d. 1834, Adair Co., KY.
        vii. CHESLEY THACKER PENDLETON, b. Abt. 1802, VA; d. 1831.
145.   viii. FRANCES PENDLETON, b. Abt. 1805, VA; d. Aft. 1850, Spotsylvania Co., VA?

53. PHILIP[8] PENDLETON (*HENRY[7], JOHN[6], PHILIP[5], HENRY[4], HENRY[3], GEORGE[2], GEORGE[1]*) was born Apr 6, 1758 in Spotsylvania Co., VA, and died Abt. 1843 in Spotsylvania Co., VA. He married MILDRED THOMAS Feb 28, 1788 in Spotsylvania Co., VA, daughter of JOHN THOMAS and MARY. She was born Bet. 1760 - 1765 in VA, and died Bet. 1830 - 1840 in Spotsylvania Co., VA?

Philip Pendleton served in the Revolutionary War (Ref. 86):

Octr. 1, 1832. Philip Pendleton of Spts. Co., aged 74 years. Enlisted in Continental Army, 1775, with Capt. George Stubblefield as a minute man for 12 mos.; the sd. Stubblefield enlisting in the regular army, he was then under Capt. Francis Taliaferro, under whom he marched to Hampton. The commanding officer was Maj. Buchannan. Having served in that tour he went as volunteer under Capt. J. Craig to Wms'burg and was out about 50 days. In next tour went as militia man under Capt. Harry Stubblefield, after which he served under Capt. Francis Coleman, and they were under Maj. McWilliams and Hardyman, a little before the close of the war, after which he went with a band of prisoners under Capt. Thomas Croutcher to Nolings Ferry. Was born April 6, 1758, in Spts. Co., where he has always lived.

Philip was the Pastor of Mine Road Baptist Church from 1800 to 1843 taking the place of his brother Henry (Ref. 87). He is included in a list of Early Ministers of Orange Co., VA as "Philip Pendleton, 1813, Aug 28 (Baptist) Desenting Minister oath of allegiance." The 1810 Spotsylvania census shows 9 whites and 10 slaves in the Philip Pendleton household. Philip is also listed in the 1820 and 1830 Spotsylvania Co., VA census records. He owned land in Spotsylvania Co., VA (Ref. 88). P. Pendleton is listed in the 1840 Census of Pensioners (Revolutionary or Military Service) in Berkeley Parish, Spotsylvania Co., VA., age 79; head of family: Phil. Pendleton.

Children of PHILIP PENDLETON and MILDRED THOMAS are:

    i.   PATSY C.T.[9] PENDLETON.

    ii. POLLY PENDLETON, m. WILLIAM DAVIS.

146.   iii. ROBERT YATES PENDLETON, b. Sep 23, 1792, VA; d. May 1, 1867, Christian Co., KY.

147.   iv. ELIZABETH PENDLETON, b. Abt. 1794, VA; d. Abt. 1844, Spotsylvania Co., VA?

148.   v. LUCINDA PENDLETON, b. Abt. 1796, VA; d. Aft. 1850, Spotsylvania Co., VA?

    vi. MILDRED THOMAS PENDLETON, b. Abt. 1797, VA; m. SAMUEL LEE; b. Abt. 1790, VA.

        Sam (60) and Mildred Lee (53) are listed in the 1850 Spotsylvania Co., VA census, Eastern District, in the household next to Jackson Pendleton.

149.   vii. HULDAH PENDLETON, b. Abt. 1810, VA; d. Aft. 1860, Spotsylvania Co., VA?

54. MARTHA[8] PENDLETON *(HENRY[7], JOHN[6], PHILIP[5], HENRY[4], HENRY[3], GEORGE[2], GEORGE[1])* was born Aug 7, 1760 in Spotsylvania Co., VA, and died 1824 in MO. She married MASSEY THOMAS, JR. Dec 1786, son of MASSEY THOMAS and MARY PRICE. He was born Abt. 1747, and died in Woodford Co., KY.

Massey Thomas deeded slaves to his sisters in 1787 (Ref. 89): "Massey Thomas of Spots. Co. to his three sisters, Mildred, Peggy and Molly Thomas. Deed of Gift. Slaves. No witnesses." Massey Thomas is listed in the 1800 Ohio Co., KY census. Martha Thomas is listed as head of the household in the 1810 Clark Co., KY census.

Children of MARTHA PENDLETON and MASSEY THOMAS are (Ref. 90):
  i. FRANCES TAYLOR[9] THOMAS, b. 1788, VA; m. EDWARD LEWIS, Oct 22, 1809, Clark Co., KY.
  ii. PHILADELPHIA PENDLETON THOMAS, b. 1789, VA; d. May 31, 1832; m. JAMES DAMREL, Sep 20, 1812, Clark Co., KY.
  iii. SALLIE MINOR THOMAS, b. 1791, VA.
  iv. THOMAS GRANVILLE THOMAS, b. 1792.
  v. VIRGINIA CURTIS THOMAS, b. 1794, VA.
  vi. JOHN PRICE THOMAS, b. 1796.
  vii. MARTHA CURTIS THOMAS, b. 1798, VA.

55. CURTIS[8] PENDLETON *(HENRY[7], JOHN[6], PHILIP[5], HENRY[4], HENRY[3], GEORGE[2], GEORGE[1])* was born May 9, 1763 in Spotsylvania Co., VA, and died Jan 19, 1836 in Todd Co., KY. He married NANCY WILSON Dec 1785. She was born 1767 in VA, and died Aft. 1843 in Todd Co., KY.

Curtis Pendleton, like his older brothers Henry, John, and Philip, served (as a private) in the Revolutionary War from Spotsylvania. Evidently, his service ended in October 1781. He is included in the first Clark Co., KY tax list in 1792 with his brother Rice Pendleton. Curtis is listed with his younger brother Rice Pendleton and a John Pendleton, probably his nephew, in the 1794 tax list dated June 10 for Clark County. In the 1810 Clark Co. census Curtis has 5 sons and 2 daughters listed. He was a witness to the will of William Bullock in Clark Co., KY dated 10 May 1813 (Ref. 91). Curtis Pendleton and his family had removed to Todd Co., KY by the 1820 census. His eldest son, Edmund, and eldest daughter, Pamelia, however, remained in Clark Co. Curtis was one of the early immigrants of Todd County and was the progenitor of the Pendleton family there. Curtis was still living in 1825 when the estate of his father, Henry Pendleton, Sr. was settled. Curtis is also found in the 1830 Todd Co. census with 3 children remaining in the household, 2 sons and a daughter; the older children having left the household to establish their own.

Nancy Pendleton applied for a Revolutionary War pension on Nov 11, 1843 (age 74) in Todd Co., KY. She is listed in the 1850 Todd Co. census.

Children of CURTIS PENDLETON and NANCY WILSON are (Ref. 92):
150.   i. PAMELIA[9] PENDLETON, b. Abt. 1786, VA; d. Aft. 1850, Todd Co., KY?
151.   ii. EDMUND PENDLETON, b. Oct 2, 1788, VA; d. Aug 22, 1877, Clark Co., KY.
152. iii. JOHN PENDLETON, b. Abt. 1790, VA; d. Aft. 1850, Todd Co., KY?
      iv. NANCY PENDLETON, b. 1794, Clark Co., KY; m. THOMAS WADE, Apr 30, 1810, Clark Co., KY.
         A Nancy Wade (56) is listed in the 1850 Montgomery Co., KY census in the household of Pamelia Coons (30), likely her daughter and next to the household of Robert Wade (37), likely her son.

      v. MARY "POLLY" PENDLETON, b. 1796, Clark Co., KY; m. (1) BERKLEY DAWSON, Nov 11, 1816, Clark Co., KY; m. (2) WILLIAM JOHNSON, Abt. 1818.

Her first marriage was recorded as (Ref. 93) "Dawson, Berkley, and Polly Pendleton, daughter Curtis Pendleton (consent); surety, John Pendleton 1816 Nov 11."

153.   vi.   LUCINDA PENDLETON, b. 1797, Clark Co., KY; d. Abt. 1830, KY.

      vii.   JAMES PENDLETON, b. Abt. 1800, Clark Co., KY; d. Aft. 1830, Todd Co., KY?; m. MARTHA BAKER FRAZER, Jan 30, 1822, Todd Co., KY; b. Jan 11, 1807, KY.

           James Pendleton is listed in the 1830 Todd Co. census with his wife, 3 sons and a daughter.

154.   viii.   WILLIAM CURTIS PENDLETON, b. Abt. 1803, Clark Co., KY; d. Todd Co., KY?

155.   ix.   THOMAS W. PENDLETON, b. Apr 3, 1806, Clark Co., KY; d. Jul 15, 1870, Muhlenberg Co., KY.

56. RICE[8] PENDLETON, SR. *(HENRY[7], JOHN[6], PHILIP[5], HENRY[4], HENRY[3], GEORGE[2], GEORGE[1])* was born Sep 9, 1765 in Spotsylvania Co., VA, and died Dec 1823 in Bath County, KY. He married ELIZABETH QUISENBERRY Nov 3, 1788 in Orange Co., VA, daughter of GEORGE QUISENBERRY and JANE DANIEL. She was born Abt. 1770 in Orange Co., VA, and died Abt. 1844 in Clark Co., KY?

      Rice Pendleton, Sr. and his brother Curtis were among the earliest settlers of Clark Co., KY immigrating to Kentucky from Virginia in 1790 or 1791. Rice is included in a list of insolvents or delinquent taxpayers (reason: removed) of Spotsylvania County (Ref. 94). The list was completed on 6 Dec. 1788. This indicates that Rice had already left Spotsylvania by that time and may have already been on his way to Kentucky. Rice and Curtis followed their two pioneering brothers-in-law, James (in 1783) and John Quisenberry (in 1788). Rice and Curtis were joined in Clark County by John Pendleton. This John is likely Rice's nephew, the son of Henry Pendleton, Jr. This John later immigrated to Christian County, KY and was the progenitor of the Pendleton branch there. Other members of the Henry Pendleton family immigrating to Clark Co. Kentucky included Martha Pendleton Thomas and Frances Pendleton Arnold. Rice and Elizabeth Quisenberry Pendleton's first two children were born in 1790 and 1791 apparently just after their journeys along the Wilderness Trail from Virginia to Kentucky. In the 1795 Clark Co. tax lists, Rice, Curtis, and John are listed; the Curtis property was along Howard Creek. In the 1800 Clark Co. census, derived from Tax Lists, Curtis, Rice, and John Pendleton are again included.

      Most pioneers in Clark Co. passed through nearby Ft. Boonesborough in Madison Co., KY before establishing permanent settlement in Clark Co. across the Kentucky River. James Quisenberry was for some time a member of the Garrison at Fort Boonesborough under Daniel Boone (Ref. 95). Among the early settlers of Clark Co. was a group of forty Baptist families led by Capt. William Bush, who settled on lower Howard's Creek in 1785. In 1793 the group erected the Old Stone Meeting House that still exists. The main road to Boonesborough from Lexington was down Lower Howard's Creek (Ref. 96). Both Rice and Curtis Pendleton were members of this community. By 1815, Rice Pendleton owned property several miles northeast of the Old Stone Church and adjacent to the junction of Four Mile Creek and Lower Howards Creek near the frontier town of Winchester (Ref. 97).

In the 1810 Clark County Census, the only Pendleton heads of households included are Curtis and Rice. In the 1820 Kentucky census Rice and his eldest son Thacker show up in nearby Bath County.

The estate settlement of Rice Pendleton, Sr. was recorded in the Bath Co. December 19, 1823 (Refs. 98 and 99):

This inventory and appraisement of the Estate of Rice Pendleton, Dec., was returned approved and ordered to be recorded. Whereupon the same is truly recorded in my office as the law directs, William M. Luddith." Included as receiving at least one of over 100 items total were his sons Thacker, Rice, Preston, Prestley, his wife Elizabeth, his brother Curtis Pendleton, and his son-in-laws Thomas Hicks, Samuel Evins (sic), and Peter Bashaw. Elizabeth Quisenberry Pendleton was allotted the widow's part:

1 Bay horse & Roan Mare	$66.25
2 pairs (gears?) & pot	$3.00
2 ploughs & 1 griddle	$4.37 ½
2 beds and 2 wheels	$39.87 ½
1 pot trammele & hows & shovel	$1.75
1 table & 20 (geese?)	$5.00
4 chairs-1 chest & 3 blade stacks	$6.00
Wool & cotton cards, 4 sheep choice	$4.75
3 head cattle	$18.50
30 bls corn & sows & pigs	$27.50
Sundries	$6.25
	$175.00

The right of dower was administered February 15, 1825 at the house of Rice Pendleton, Dec. in Bath Co. (Ref. 100). Elizabeth Pendleton was assigned twenty acres one half & 33 poles of land including the building and part of the orchard along Salt Lick Creek. The drawing and description gives every indication of being the land that eventually came into the possession of their youngest son Thrashley Pendleton. Elizabeth was also assigned one negro man named Isaac at $500; $350 as her part of the personal estate; and a balance due of $86.58 from the legatees.

In an 1825 Spotsylvania Co., VA estate settlement of Henry Pendleton, his heirs Rice Pendleton, Philip Pendleton, Martha Thomas, Curtis Pendleton, Frances Arnold, and Robert Pendleton are named. The settlement due Rice was likely distributed to his heirs.

Elizabeth Quesinberry Pendleton is descended from Thomas Questenbury who emigrated to Virginia from England in 1624 (Ref. 95). Elizabeth Pendleton is listed in the 1830 Clark Co. census along with one male under 5 and one female under 30. The female was likely her daughter Jane who did not marry until 1833. The male could have been her youngest son Thrashley although he was about 15 in 1830.

Children of RICE PENDLETON and ELIZABETH QUISENBERRY are (Ref. 101):

156.   i.   SALLY[9] PENDLETON, b. Jun 21, 1790, KY; d. Jan 30, 1877, Clark Co., KY.

157.   ii.   THACKER PENDLETON, b. 1791, Clark County, KY?; d. Abt. 1864, Bath Co., KY.

158.   iii.   RICE PENDLETON, JR., b. 1792, Clark Co., KY; d. Jan 17, 1867, Clark Co., KY.

      iv.   ELIZABETH "BETSY" PENDLETON, b. Abt. 1795, Clark County, KY; d. Aft. 1830; m. THOMAS HICKS, Sep 30, 1816, Clark Co., KY; b. Bet. 1790 - 1800.

          In September, 1830 Thomas Hicks signed a statement concerning payments made to him from 1825 to 1827 as guardian of Champney Pendleton, Elizabeth's younger brother (Ref. 101). Thomas is listed in the 1830 Bath Co. census with his wife and 3 children. He may be the Thomas Hicks (aged 40-50) in the 1840 Hardin Co. census, pg. 27 and in the 1850 Montgomery Co. census, District 2, pg 78 with wife Martha (33) and apparent step son, Mark Alexander (9).

159.   v.   FRANCES "FANNY" PENDLETON, b. Mar 17, 1797, Clark County, KY; d. Mar 5, 1882, Waynesville, IL.

160.   vi.   MARTHA "PATSY" PENDLETON, b. Abt. 1800, Clark Co., KY; d. Abt. 1865, Bath Co., KY.

161.   vii.   PRESLEY PENDLETON, b. Jan 13, 1803, Clark County, KY; d. Sep 17, 1894, Ralls Co., MO.

162.   viii.   PRESTON PENDLETON, b. Nov 14, 1804, Clark County, KY; d. Aug 16, 1870, Waynesville, IL.

163.   ix.   LUCY E. PENDLETON, b. Jul 8, 1805, Clark County, KY; d. Jan 24, 1860, Lincoln Co., IL.

      x.   JANE PENDLETON, b. Abt. 1808, Clark County, KY; d. Aug 5, 1855, Lincoln, Logan Co., IL; m. ROBERT P. BOGGS, Aug 31, 1833, Clark Co., KY; b. Abt. 1806, KY; d. Aft. 1880, De Witt Co., IL?

          Jane Pendleton is buried with her husband at the Union Cemetery, Lincoln Co., IL. Jane was the first of three wives of Robert Boggs and apparently had no children (Ref. 101).

164.   xi.   CHAMPNEY PENDLETON, b. Dec 6, 1812, Clark Co., KY; d. Jan 23, 1857, Baker's Prairie, OR.

165.   xii.   THRASHLEY PENDLETON, b. 1815, Clark Co., KY; d. Abt. 1896, Bath Co., KY.

57. FRANCES[8] PENDLETON *(HENRY[7], JOHN[6], PHILIP[5], HENRY[4], HENRY[3], GEORGE[2], GEORGE[1])* was born Jan 19, 1767 in Spotsylvania Co., VA, and died Apr 1808 in Clark Co., KY. She married JOHN ARNOLD Sep 11, 1788. He was born Bet. 1760 - 1766 in VA, and died Aft. 1840 in Clark Co., KY?

    John Arnold is included in the 1788 Tax List, Fayette Co., KY with a James and a Nicholas Arnold. He is found in the 1810 Clark Co. census along with Rice Arnold. John and Frances apparently had many children although only Rice Arnold is listed.

Child of FRANCES PENDLETON and JOHN ARNOLD is:
  i. RICE W.⁹ ARNOLD, b. Abt. 1790, KY; m. SARAH RYAN, Jan 15, 1807, Clark Co., KY.

58. ROBERT⁸ PENDLETON (*HENRY⁷, JOHN⁶, PHILIP⁵, HENRY⁴, HENRY³, GEORGE², GEORGE¹*) was born Apr 29, 1771 in Spotsylvania Co., VA, and died 1845 in Spotsylvania Co., VA? He married ELIZABETH BURRUS Feb 2, 1797 in Orange Co., VA, daughter of EDMUND BURRUS and MARY PERRY. She was born Abt. 1781 in VA, and died Aft. 1851 in Spotsylvania Co., VA?

  Robert Pendleton was a witness to a Spotsylvania County deed on April 4, 1796 (Ref. 102):

> John x Fagg of Berkeley Par., Spots. Co. to his son, Joel Fagg, of same county and parish. Deed of Gift. 150 a. in Berkeley Par., Spots. Co., whereon he now lives, remainder of a tract purchased by sd. John Fagg of David Pulliam, after deducting 100 a. by him given to his son, Wm. Fagg, etc., etc. Witnesses, Nathaniel Pulliam, Moses x Wheeler, Robert x Pendleton. April 5, 1796.

  The 1810 Spotsylvania census shows 9 whites and 4 slaves in the Robert Pendleton household. He is also listed in the 1820, 1830, and 1840 census records for Spotsylvania. Robert and Elizabeth's children, Edmund, Elizabeth, Jackson, Robert, and Susan are listed in a court case, Fredericksburg, Spotsylvania Co. on 10 Oct., 1851.

  The will of Elizabeth Burrus Pendleton's mother was recorded in Spotsylvania Co.:

> Be it known to all men, that I Mary Burras [Elizabeth's mother] of the County of Spotsylvania having bought a negro girl by the name of Lucy with my own money that I had of my Father's Estates after my Husband's Death, this girl I bought of Joshua Long, who gave me a bill of sale for her and her increase. Now be it understood that whereas I live with Robert Pendleton Who Married my Daughter Betsy who are now both living. And are both a like tender of me in my old age, it is my desire that after my death Robert Pendleton and my Daughter Betsy shall have the above mentioned Lucy and her increase And that after their Deaths the said Lucy and her increase Shall then be equally divided amongst the Heirs of my Daughter Betsy that is any Grand Children for Ever.
> Witness my Hand and Seal this 19th day of November one Thousand Eight hundred and Seaven [sic].   Mary Burras [Seal]

> [Her mark]Teste; s/s Philip Pendletons/s John Pendletons/s Benj. Massey
> At a Court held for Spotsylvania County the 5th day of January 1829 The last Will and testament of Mary Burras deceased was proved by the oaths of Philip Pendleton and Benjamin Massey two of the witnesses thereto and ordered to be recorded. Teste R. L. Stevenson, C. C. Recorded liber M folio 334

  The 1850 Spotsylvania Co., VA census includes Elizabeth as well as her daughters Susan and Elizabeth, her son Robert, and two grandchildren, Martha and George.

Children of ROBERT PENDLETON and ELIZABETH BURRUS are:
  i. MARY ANN⁹ PENDLETON.

A Mary Ann Pendleton married Rueben Sorrell on Dec. 24, 1821; this Mary Ann's sister, Frances, m. Benjamin Sorrell.

      ii. MARTHA "PATSY" CURTIS PENDLETON, b. Abt. 1800, VA; d. 1847; m. ROBERT DUVAL, Dec 11, 1817, Spotsylvania Co., VA; b. Abt. 1781; d. 1830, Spotsylvania Co., VA?.

166.   iii. EDMUND B. PENDLETON, b. 1805, VA; d. 1856, Spotsylvania Co., VA?

      iv. SUSAN PENDLETON, b. Abt. 1808, VA; d. Sep 17, 1892, Spotsylvania Co., VA?

Susan Pendleton and her sister Elizabeth are listed in the Robert Pendleton household in the 1860 Spotsylvania Co., VA census

167.   v. JACKSON PENDLETON, b. Apr 4, 1810, VA; d. Jan 18, 1894, Spotsylvania Co., VA?

      vi. ELIZABETH PENDLETON, b. 1813, VA; d. May 1880, Livingston, Spotsylvania Co., VA.

Betsy Pendleton is included in the mortality list of the 1880 census: "Livingston, Spotsylvania, VA as female, white, single, b. in Virginia, age 73, month of death May, cause Dyspepsy."

168.   vii. FRANCES PENDLETON, b. Abt. 1814, Spotsylvania Co., VA; d. Abt. 1856, St. Louis Co., MO.

169.   viii. ROBERT PENDLETON, b. Mar 15, 1813, VA; d. Dec 9, 1892, Spotsylvania Co., VA.

170.   ix. LOUISA BURRUS PENDLETON, b. Abt. 1820, VA.

59. PHILIP[8] PENDLETON (*BENJAMIN*[7], *PHILIP*[6], *PHILIP*[5], *HENRY*[4], *HENRY*[3], *GEORGE*[2], *GEORGE*[1]) was born Aug 02, 1752 in VA, and died Jul 31, 1804 in King & Queen Co., VA. He married (1) MARTHA HOOMES 1777, daughter of BENJAMIN HOOMES. He married (2) MARY ANNE FLEET 1784, daughter of WILLIAM FLEET and SUSANNAH WALKER. She was born Jan 22, 1759, and died Sep 04, 1820 in King & Queen Co., VA.

This Philip Pendleton is included in the public record as early as 1774 (Ref. 103).

A petition of Philip Pendleton and James Myler, inspectors of Walkerton Warehouses in K&Q Co. was presented to the House and read: setting forth, that some time in the year 1774, one of the warehouses of the said inspection was broke open, and a hogshead of tobacco, weighing 1080 pounds neat, solen thereout, for which they have been obliged to pay 71. 0s. 4d. and praying to be reimbursed by the publick.

Philip Pendleton is the first recorded owner of Green Mount Estate, also called Pickle House - according to tradition it was the property of the Pickle family. Philip was probably living here at the time of the Revolution. He is known to have been an inspector of tobacco at Walkerton in 1774, and in 1776 was licensed to run an ordinary at Todd's, then a thriving village at the head of navigation on the Mattaponi. He served in the militia (as a colonel) before 1793, was a Justice of Peace in 1800, and in 1801 was certified as county sheriff. In 1804, an advertisement for claims on the estate of "Col

Philip Pendleton, decd." appeared. The house is near the junction of Hwy 360 and Hwy 721 (Ref. 104). The obituary of Philip Pendleton appeared in the Richmond Enquirer on August 8, 1804. His place of residence at time of death was King and Queen Co., VA (Ref. 105).

Philip's widow is likely the Mary Ann Pendleton in the 1810 King & Queen Co., VA census. The obituary of Mary Ann Pendleton appeared in the Richmond Enquirer on September 29, 1820. Her place of residence at time of death was King and Queen Co., VA (Ref. 105).

Children of PHILIP PENDLETON and MARTHA HOOMES are:
- i. JAMES[9] PENDLETON, b. 1778.

   The newspaper Daily Richmond Whig had the following entry on Saturday, March 12, 1831: "Married - In Caroline County, on March 8, by Elder T.M. Henley, Capt. William Harrison, to Miss Martha A. Pendleton, only child of Dr. James Pendleton, dec'd, of King & Queen County" (Ref. 105).

171.   ii. BENJAMIN PENDLETON, b. 1780, VA; d. Bef. 1828, King William Co., VA?

Children of PHILIP PENDLETON and MARY FLEET are:
172.   iii. PHILIP BAYLOR[9] PENDLETON, b. 1778, VA; d. 1836, King & Queen Co., VA?
- iv. WILLIAM FLEET PENDLETON, b. 1785, VA; d. Sep 11, 1860, Washington DC.

   William F. Pendleton was born in Virginia. He entered the army as ensign of the 20th infantry in June 1812 and rose to the rank of 1st lieutenant in May 1814. He resigned in December 1816, and held the office of member of executive council of Virginia for 14 years (Ref. 106). He is listed in the 1850 King and Queen Co., VA census in the household of his brother, George M. Pendleton.

173.   v. ROBERT M. PENDLETON, b. Abt. 1787, VA; d. Aft. 1840, King and Queen Co., VA?
174.   vi. MARY ANNE PENDLETON, b. Abt. 1789, VA.
175.   vii. GEORGE MACON PENDLETON, b. 1790, VA; d. Jul 30, 1866, King & Queen Co., VA?
- viii. MARY PENDLETON, b. Abt. 1792, VA; m THOMAS W. TODD.
- ix. WALKER PENDLETON, b. Abt. 1794, VA.

60. JAMES[8] PENDLETON *(BENJAMIN[7], PHILIP[6], PHILIP[5], HENRY[4], HENRY[3], GEORGE[2], GEORGE[1])* was born Aug 13, 1754 in VA, and died Mar 06, 1815 in King & Queen Co., VA. He married ELIZABETH PEACHEY PHILBROOK Sep 08, 1785 in Essex Co., VA, daughter of SAMUEL PEACHEY and ELIZABETH WEBB. She was born 1763, and died 1847 in King and Queen Co., VA.

This James Pendleton was apparently a Captain in the Revolutionary. War. He enlisted as an Ensign, Seventh Virginia, on February 7, 1776. He was promoted to Second Lieutenant on April 26, 1776 and to Captain First Continental (Virginia) Artillery, February 7, 1777. He was in service until October, 1778. His marriage to Elizabeth Peachey is included in Reference 25.

The will of Elizabeth Peachey Pendleton dated 31 August 1847, of King and Queen Co., is included in the personal papers of Waddill, Roland, 1915-1975. The will book containing this document is no longer extant.

Children of JAMES PENDLETON and ELIZABETH PHILBROOK are:

176.   i.   ELIZA^9 PENDLETON, b. Sep 02, 1786, VA.

      ii.   MARY MACON PENDLETON, b. Oct 13, 1788, VA; d. Bef. 1860, King & Queen Co., VA?; m. (1) PHILIP GATEWOOD, Apr 05, 1804, King & Queen Co., VA; b. 1774; m. (2) WILLIAM BOULWARE, Oct 25, 1832; b. Abt. 1809, VA; d. 1870, King & Queen Co., VA?

           Mary Pendleton's second marriage was announced in the Richmond Enquirer: "Married on the 25th inst. (Oct. 1832) by the Rev. Wm. Hill, Professor William Boulware of the Columbian College, D.C. to Mrs. Mary M. Gatewood of Traveller's Rest, King and Queen County. Note: Nee Mary Macon Pendleton (born 13 Oct. 1788), daughter of Captain James and Elizabeth (Peachey) Pendleton; she had married 1st Philip Gatewood of 'Traveller's Rest.' She was exactly twice the age of her second husband." William Boulware (farmer) and Mary M. are listed in the 1850 King & Queen Co., VA census.

           Philip Gatewood, Mary Pendleton's first husband, is included in the 1810 King & Queen Co., VA census. William Boulware, her second husband, is listed singly in the 1860 King & Queen Co., VA census.

177.   iii.   ANN MARIA "NANCY" PENDLETON, b. Apr 11, 1791, VA; d. Jul 01, 1828, King and Queen Co., VA.

      iv.   CHARLOTTE PENDLETON, b. May 20, 1793, VA; d. Aug 22, 1793.

      v.   JOHN PENDLETON, b. Dec 16, 1794, VA; d. May 23, 1795.

      vi.   JAMES PENDLETON, b. Apr 20, 1796, VA; d. Apr 30, 1796.

      vii.   MARTHA PENDLETON, b. Nov 18, 1799, VA; d. Dec 02, 1799.

      viii.   DAUGHTER PENDLETON, b. Sep 14, 1801, VA; d. Sep 15, 1801.

61. ANNE MACON^8 PENDLETON *(BENJAMIN^7, PHILIP^6, PHILIP^5, HENRY^4, HENRY^3, GEORGE^2, GEORGE^1)* was born Jan 24, 1766 in VA. She married (1) WILLIAM HARWOOD, CAPT. He was born 1734, and died Sep 16, 1773 in King & Queen Co., VA. She married (2) MORDICAI COOKE. He was born Bef. 1775, and died 1823 in Gloucester Co., VA?

      Mordecai Cooke is listed in the 1820 Gloucester Co., VA census.

Child of ANNE PENDLETON and WILLIAM HARWOOD is:

      i.   MARIA PENDLETON^9 HARWOOD.

62. BENJAMIN[8] PENDLETON *(PHILIP[7], PHILIP[6], PHILIP[5], HENRY[4], HENRY[3], GEORGE[2], GEORGE[1])* was born Aug 03, 1751 in VA, and died Abt. 1835 in Warren Co., KY? He married JANE COLEMAN daughter of SAMUEL COLEMAN and NANCY WRIGHT. Jane apparently died before 1803.

Benjamin is included in 1782-87 and 1800 Buckingham Co. Tax Lists. Benjamin Pendleton of Buckingham Co. was among 500 petitioners in 1785 to petition the State of Virginia against the levying of an assessment on the people to support the ministry. Benjamin deposed at Peachey Franklin's in New Glasgow, VA in 1816 that he knew George Hilton 40 years (Ref. 107).

It is likely this Benjamin Pendleton (over 45) who is included in the 1820 Butler Co., KY census. Two Benjamin Pendletons (apparently this Benjamin and his son) are included in the 1830 Warren Co., KY census along with a Rebecca Pendleton in Butler Co. The Kentucky Pension Roll of 1835, Warren Co. lists Benjamin Pendleton, "Virginia Militia, private, $40 Annual Allowance, $120.00 Amount Received, May 6, 1833 Pension Started, Age 83."

The Last Will and Testament of Samuel Coleman, At a court held for Buckingham County, Virginia, July 11, 1803 indicates Jane Coleman as the wife of Benjamin:

> ..I give unto my daughter Liza Coleman, fifty pounds cash, and after the death of my wife Elizabeth Coleman, my wish is that the Negroes, namely Tom, Charles, Bartley, Dick, Nan, Rose, Chloe, Patty, Judea, Anaca, Jane, Aggy, and Dafney, and their increase to be divided equally amongst my children, namely, George Coleman, Sally Pendleton, Wife of Mace Pendleton, Mary Pendleton, Francis Harris, Wife of Robert Harris, Betsey Coleman, Ann Mourning Coleman & My Grandchildren Benjamin Pendleton had by? my daughter Jane to come in as one Legatee, and all my stock of every kind with all my household furniture after the death of my wife I give to my children that is to possess my Negroes.

Children of BENJAMIN PENDLETON and JANE COLEMAN? are:

178. i.   SALLY[9] PENDLETON, b. Abt. 1780, Buckingham Co., VA; d. Bef. 1849, Smith Co., TN?
179. ii. BENJAMIN PENDLETON, b. Abt. 1800, VA; d. Aft. 1860, Wayne Co., IL?
      iii. MAHALY PENDLETON, m. MOSES BOYCE, Sep 27, 1821, Warren Co., KY.

63. JAMES[8] PENDLETON *(PHILIP[7], PHILIP[6], PHILIP[5], HENRY[4], HENRY[3], GEORGE[2], GEORGE[1])* was born Abt. 1754 in Buckingham Co., Va., and died Abt. 1803 in Buckingham Co., VA. He married MARY ANN PHIPPS Abt. 1771, daughter of ROBERT PHIPPS. She was born Abt. 1755 in Albemarle Co., VA.

This James Pendleton is included in the 1800 Buckingham Co. Tax List.

Child of JAMES PENDLETON and MARY PHIPPS is:

180. i.   JOHN[9] PENDLETON, b. 1787, Buckingham Co., VA; d. Aft. 1860, Lawrence Co., MO.

64. MACE[8] **PENDLETON** *(PHILIP*[7]*, PHILIP*[6]*, PHILIP*[5]*, HENRY*[4]*, HENRY*[3]*, GEORGE*[2]*, GEORGE*[1]*)* was born 1754 in Buckingham Co., Va., and died Aft. 1803 in Buckingham Co., VA. He married SALLY COLEMAN Abt. 1780, daughter of SAMUEL COLEMAN and NANCY WRIGHT. She was born 1763 in Buckingham Co., VA, and died Abt. 1820 in Buckingham Co., VA.

Mace Pendleton is included in the VA Land Grants (Ref. 108): "13 May 1793, Buckingham Co., 50a. adjoining Allens and George Helton." Mace and Sally Pendleton are included in the 1800 Buckingham Co. Tax List as well as in the will of her father Samuel Coleman in 1803.

Child of MACE PENDLETON and SALLY COLEMAN is:

181.   i.   MACE COLEMAN[9] PENDLETON, b. Abt. 1804, VA; d. Aft. 1850, Rowan Co., NC?

65. MICAJAH[8] **PENDLETON** *(PHILIP*[7]*, PHILIP*[6]*, PHILIP*[5]*, HENRY*[4]*, HENRY*[3]*, GEORGE*[2]*, GEORGE*[1]*)* was born 1758 in Buckingham Co., Va., and died Feb 09, 1844 in Nelson Co., VA. He married (1) MISS BRECKINRIDGE Abt. 1780. He married (2) MARY CABELL HORSLEY Dec 16, 1799 in Amherst Co., VA, daughter of WILLIAM HORSLEY and MARTHA MEGGINSON. She was born Abt. 1783 in VA, and died Aft. 1850 in Nelson Co., VA?

Much of the information on Micajah Pendleton was obtained from papers on file in the pension claim S.8915, based on his military service. Micajah Pendleton states in his papers that he was born in 1758 in the county of Buckingham, Virginia. While Micajah Pendleton was a resident of Buckingham he enlisted and served as a private with the Virginia troops as follows: From the winter of 1778 or 1779 he served three months under Captain William Duiguid and Colonel Taylor, being discharged in March. From January 10, 1781, until April 9, 1781, under Captain Charles Patterson. From June, 1781, until September 18, 1781, under Captain Robert Cary. After the Revolutionary War he moved to that part of Amherst Co., VA that became Nelson Co., VA.

A prominent Methodist and temperance reformer; before the year 1800, he circulated a temperance pledge; his theory of reform extended to the exclusion of wine and cider, differing from whiskey only in strength (Ref. 106). He is listed as a property owner in Amherst Co. in 1810 (Ref. 109): "31 Aug, 1810; Reuben Gatewood & wife Elizabeth, Frances Hall & wife Elizabeth sold 1 1/2 acres to Lewis Lane -- adjoining Micajah Pendleton, Wm. B. Gooch, Robt Coleman."

At age 76, he is listed in the 1835 pension roles of Nelson Co., VA: "Annual Allowance $80.00; Amount Received $240.00; Pension Started January 9, 1834." In his file there is a letter dated Feb. 7, 1839 from the Treasury Department, Second Comptroller's Office. This letter states he was a Pensioner on the Roll of the Richmond, Virginia, agency at the rate of Thirty Dollars per annum, under the law of the 7th June, 1832, has been paid at this Department, from the 4th of Sept, 1837 to the 4th of March, 1838. Rev Micajah Pendleton, 82, made a statement 8 Apr 1840, in support of the pension application of James Dillard. At age 85, Micajah deposed on 21 Dec 1843.

Child of MICAJAH PENDLETON and MISS BRECKINRIDGE is:

182.   i.   JOSEPH[9] PENDLETON, b. 1781, Buckingham Co., Va.; d. Sep 15, 1839, Schuyler Co., IL while visiting son.

Children of MICAJAH PENDLETON and MARY HORSLEY are:

       ii.   EDMUND[9] PENDLETON.

183.   iii.   LETITIA BRECKINRIDGE PENDLETON.

       iv.   JOSEPH PENDLETON, b. Abt. 1799; d. Sep 27, 1825, Nelson Co., VA.

       v.   MARTHA M. PENDLETON, b. Abt. 1801; d. aft. 1850, Nelson Co., VA?
          Martha M. Pendleton is listed in the 1850 Nelson Co., VA census with Isabella? Horsley and Priscilla? Garland. In the adjacent household is her brother Robert N. Pendleton (36), Mary (28), and Jane (2).

184.   vi.   EDNA PENDLETON, b. Abt. 1805, VA; d. Bet. 1840 - 1850, VA.

185.   vii.   MARY ELIZABETH PENDLETON, b. 1812; d. 1904.

186.   viii.   ROBERT N. PENDLETON, b. Abt. 1814, VA; d. Aft. 1870, Amherst, VA?

Generation No. 9 – Western Expansion

The ninth generation consists of the great great grandchildren of the immigrant Philip Pendleton and Isabella Hurt. The time period is from about 1796, when Henry Pendleton Jr., the first born of this generation, married his cousin Elizabeth Coleman Pendleton, to about 1904 when the last of this generation, Mary Elizabeth Pendleton Emett, died at age 92. Significant members of the eighth generation who had no known children and are thus listed as children of seventh generation Pendletons include Edmund Henry Pendleton (1786-1862) and William Fleet Pendleton (1785-1860) whose histories can be found on pages 50 and 71, respectively.

By 1850 the United States had acquired most of its current territory. Less than half of the approximately 120 known households of the ninth Pendleton generation remained in Virginia; and about half of those leaving Virginia spent their lives in Kentucky. Missouri and Illinois were other favored destinations (Fig. 8). It was typically the sons of pioneers who continued to venture west.

A few of this generation fought in the War of 1812 but for the most part it was a time of peace and increasing prosperity along with western expansion. Many of this generation, however, lived to witness the devastation of the Civil War.

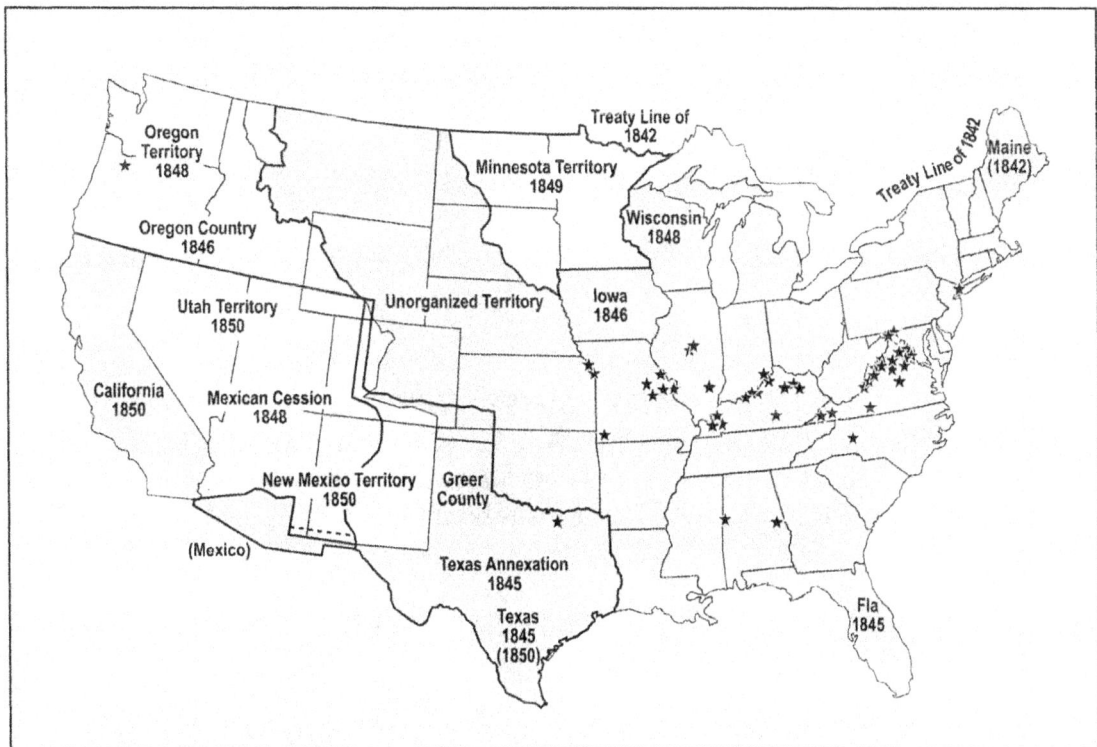

Figure 8. The United States in 1850 (Compiled by H.G. Stoll, Hammond, Inc., 1967; rev. U.S. Geological Survey, 1970). The approximate locations of each county in which the great great grandchildren of Philip lived are indicated.

66. JR. HENRY[9] PENDLETON *(HENRY[8], JAMES[7], HENRY[6], PHILIP[5], HENRY[4], HENRY[3], GEORGE[2], GEORGE[1])* was born 1764 in Culpeper Co., VA, and died 1848 in Hardin Co., KY? He married ELIZABETH COLEMAN PENDLETON Mar 05, 1796 in VA, daughter of JAMES PENDLETON and CATHERINE BOWIE. She was born Abt. 1781 in VA, and died Aft. 1830 in Hardin Co., KY?

This Henry Pendleton is listed in the VA District Court Records of 1805 as a defendant along with his father (dec'd). The Plaintiff listed is Bogle Somerville & Co. and the deponent is Alexander F. Rose. The case dealt with a Tobacco account at Dixon's Warehouse in 1772-1774 apparently in Culpeper. Henry is listed in the Culpeper Co. 1800, 1810, and 1820 census records. He removed to Hardin Co., KY abt. 1824 where he appears in the Hardin Co. census records of 1830 and 1840.

Children of HENRY PENDLETON and ELIZABETH PENDLETON are:

     i.   EDWIN H.[10] PENDLETON, d. 1884; m. ? SPRAGUE.

        An Edwin Pendleton (72; b. VA) is listed in the 1880 Schuyler Co., IL census along with Mary (68; b. KY), Christopher (25; b. IL), and Edward (23; b. IL).

187.   ii.   CATHERINE ANNE PENDLETON, b. 1799, Culpeper Co., Va.; d. 1875, Meade Co, KY.

188.   iii. MARIANNE PENDLETON, b. Bet. 1800 - 1810, VA.

189.   iv. JAMES HENRY PENDLETON, b. 1806, VA; d. 1861, Hardin Co., KY?

190.   v.   THOMAS CATLETT PENDLETON, b. Abt. 1811, VA; d. Aft. 1860, Hardin Co., KY?

     vi. ELIZABETH PENDLETON, b. Bet. 1815 - 1820; m. DANIEL VAN METER.

191.   vii. MARGARET ELLEN PENDLETON, b. May 04, 1820, VA; d. Apr 24, 1889, Hardin Co., KY.

192. viii. JOANNA PENDLETON, b. Abt. 1824, KY; d. Aft. 1880, Hardin Co., KY?

67. EDWARD[9] PENDLETON *(HENRY[8], JAMES[7], HENRY[6], PHILIP[5], HENRY[4], HENRY[3], GEORGE[2], GEORGE[1])* was born Aug 12, 1770, and died Feb 13, 1803. He married SARAH STROTHER Oct 28, 1794 in Culpeper Co., VA, daughter of JOSEPH STROTHER and NANCY STEWARD. She was born Oct 28, 1776, and died May 27, 1832.

Child of EDWARD PENDLETON and SARAH STROTHER is:

     i.   ANNE STROTHER[10] PENDLETON.

68. EDMUND[9] PENDLETON *(HENRY[8], JAMES[7], HENRY[6], PHILIP[5], HENRY[4], HENRY[3], GEORGE[2], GEORGE[1])* was born Nov 01, 1776 in VA, and died Sep 10, 1820 in Winchester, Frederick Co., VA. He married ELIZABETH WARD Feb 10, 1800 in Culpeper Co., VA. She was born Jun 18, 1784, and died Feb 05, 1875.

This is the Edmund Pendleton in the 1810 Culpeper Co., VA census. His obituary appeared September 22, 1820 in the Central Gazette: "Capt. Edmund Pendleton on Sunday 10, Winchester, Va, in the 44th year of age - He was long a respectable inhabitant of that town, and has left a wife and large family."

Children of EDMUND PENDLETON and ELIZABETH WARD are:

193.   i.   MARY ANNE[10] PENDLETON, b. Nov 16, 1800, VA; d. Mar 14, 1879, Culpeper Co., VA.

        ii.   CATHERINE PENDLETON, b. Oct 30, 1801, VA; d. Aug 01, 1803.

      iii.   EDWARD HENRY PENDLETON, b. May 24, 1803, Culpeper Co., VA; d. Oct 08, 1858, Washington, DC; m. JACQUELINE EMILY MILLS, Sep 17, 1833, Washington, DC; b. 1814; d. Apr 17, 1859, VA.

            Edward Pendleton is listed in the 1840 and 1843 Washington DC census records.

      iv.   HELEN MARIA PENDLETON, b. Nov 01, 1805, VA; d. Dec 05, 1874.

       v.   WILLIAM WARD PENDLETON, b. Dec 22, 1806, VA; d. youth.

      vi.   DANIEL WARD PENDLETON, b. Sep 20, 1808, VA; d. Oct 16, 1827.

194. vii.   THORNTON PRESLEY COCKE PENDLETON, b. Apr 28, 1810, VA; d. 1884, Clarke Co., VA?

195. viii.   ELIZABETH WARD PENDLETON, b. Jan 04, 1812, VA; d. Mar 10, 1899, Baltimore, MD.

196.   ix.   ROBERT WARD PENDLETON, b. Jul 16, 1814, VA; d. Apr 17, 1861, Baltimore, MD?

197.   x.   PHILIP PETER PENDLETON, b. Dec 17, 1816, VA; d. Dec 09, 1877, Baltimore, MD.

198.   xi.   GEORGE WASHINGTON PENDLETON, b. Feb 17, 1819, VA; d. 1858.

69. JOHN[9] PENDLETON *(JAMES[8], JAMES[7], HENRY[6], PHILIP[5], HENRY[4], HENRY[3], GEORGE[2], GEORGE[1])* was born 1766 in Culpeper Co., VA, and died 1807. He married ELIZABETH TAYLOR Nov 09, 1785 in Orange Co., VA, daughter of JAMES TAYLOR and ANNE PENDLETON. She was born Abt. 1766, and died 1838 in Nelson Co., KY.

John Pendleton, apparently in preparation for a move to Kentucky, placed the following advertisement in The Virginia Herald, February 18, 1800; 4:1:

For sale, Between 5 and 6 hundred acres of land, lying on the river Rappahannock, at Eastham's ford in the county of Culpeper, on the main road leading from Culpeper court-house to Fauquier court-house, 10 miles from the former and 14 from the latter; 40 miles from the town of Fredericksburg, and 60 from the City of Washington and Alexandria. - This tract embraces a variety of soils, suitable to the production of tobacco, corn, wheat, rye, grass, &c. -About 150 acres are cleared, of which two thirds are low grounds -The whole enclosed by good fences, and in good arable order. The building improvements consist of a dwelling house almost new, 38 by 18 feet, three rooms, a passage, and a closet below, two rooms, an entry, and a closet above, with 4 fire places; a very good dairy, smoke house, and kitchen; and a large framed barn 40 by 20 feet, covered with pine shingles. The grounds on which the houses stand is very elevated and commands a beautiful prospect. The whole extent of this tract is intersected by runs, and watered by lasting springs. -Further particulars will be communicated by the subscriber who lives on the premises.

Elizabeth Taylor Pendleton is included in an abstract of her father's will in Jefferson Co., KY (Ref. 110): "Taylor, James; in good health; Sep 3, 1807 - June 13, 1808; son Jas. to have land where he lives; son John Gibson Taylor to have land where I live, 460 acres; Nathaniel P., under age, my son, to be educated, to have negroes and 600 lbs.; dau Elizabeth to have land; dau. Ann P. Crutchfield to have 50 acres." The will of Elizabeth Taylor Pendleton was probated Feb. 12, 1838 in Nelson Co., KY.

Children of JOHN PENDLETON and ELIZABETH TAYLOR are:

      i.   JAMES TAYLOR[10] PENDLETON, b. Jan 25, 1786, VA; d. Aft. 1820, Jefferson Co., KY?; m. HARRIET CASTLEMAN, Jun 27, 1815, Shelby Co., KY; b. 1798, KY; d. 1848.

           A James T. Pendleton is included in the 1812 Muster Rolls, Kentucky Volunteers, Dudley's Mounted Batt'n and 9th Regiment (Simrall's) Mounted. The marriage of James T. Pendleton is recorded in the Marriage Bonds for Shelby County, Kentucky 1792-1800. This is the James Pendleton listed in the 1820 Jefferson Co., KY census.

      ii. CATHERINE ANNE BOWIE PENDLETON, b. Mar 02, 1788, VA; d. Aug 18, 1852, Franklin Co., KY?; m. (1) ROBERT KEMP; m. (2) BURR HARRISON, DR., 1817.

199.   iii. JOHN TAYLOR PENDLETON, b. May 09, 1790, VA; d. Jun 22, 1855, Frankfort, KY.

200.   iv. THOMAS CLAYTON PENDLETON, b. 1792, VA; d. 1840, Jefferson Co., KY?

70. MARGARET[9] PENDLETON *(JAMES[8], JAMES[7], HENRY[6], PHILIP[5], HENRY[4], HENRY[3], GEORGE[2], GEORGE[1])* was born 1769 in VA, and died in Nelson Co., KY. She married (1) ROBERT SLAUGHTER 1783, son of JAMES SLAUGHTER and SUSAN CLAYTON. He was born 1762, and died 1803. She married (2) JOHN LIGHTFOOT Aug 31, 1809, son of GOODRICH LIGHTFOOT and SUSANNA SLAUGHTER. He was born Mar 19, 1758 in VA, and died 1811 in Nelson Co., KY. She married (3) JOSHUA MORRIS, REV. Aft. 1810. He was born Abt. 1753 in VA, and died Sep 24, 1840 in Nelson Co., KY.

Children of MARGARET PENDLETON and ROBERT SLAUGHTER are:

      i.   MARGARET BOWIE[10] SLAUGHTER.

      ii. ANN SLAUGHTER.

Child of MARGARET PENDLETON and JOHN LIGHTFOOT is:

      iii. PENDLETON GOODRICH[10] LIGHTFOOT, b. Jul 08, 1810, Nelson Co., KY; d. 1834, Daviess Co., KY.

71. CATHERINE BOWIE^9 PENDLETON *(JAMES^8, JAMES^7, HENRY^6, PHILIP^5, HENRY^4, HENRY^3, GEORGE^2, GEORGE^1)* was born Abt. 1771 in VA, and died 1818. She married ARCHIBALD TUTT Nov 10, 1789. He died 1827.

Child of CATHERINE PENDLETON and ARCHIBALD TUTT is:
    i.   WILLIAM PENDLETON^{10} TUTT, b. 1807; d. 1851.

72. THOMAS^9 PENDLETON *(JAMES^8, JAMES^7, HENRY^6, PHILIP^5, HENRY^4, HENRY^3, GEORGE^2, GEORGE^1)* was born Nov 26, 1773 in VA, and died Nov 26, 1823 in Culpeper Co., VA. He married JANE FARMER Jan 29, 1794 in Culpeper Co., VA. She was born Dec 02, 1775 in Fredericksburg, VA, and died Dec 31, 1845 in Culpeper Co., VA?

    This is the Thomas Pendleton in the 1800, 1810, and 1820 Culpeper Co. census records. He is found in the Spotsylvania Court Records as a defendant in the Citation Jeffries vs. Brown, 1802 in Culpeper. The suit involved a slave, Edmund, property of William C. Brown. Jane Pendleton is the head of the household in the 1830 Culpeper Co., VA census.

Children of THOMAS PENDLETON and JANE FARMER are:
      i.   WILLIAM C.^{10} PENDLETON, b. Apr 01, 1795, VA; d. Feb 07, 1815.
     ii.   MARY PENDLETON, b. Sep 27, 1796, VA; d. Feb 22, 1797, VA.
201. iii.   ANNE TAYLOR PENDLETON, b. Dec 30, 1797, VA; d. Oct 13, 1857.
202. iv.   JAMES PENDLETON, b. Dec 23, 1799, Culpepper Co., VA; d. Sep 25, 1885, VA.
203.   v.   ELIZABETH COLEMAN PENDLETON, b. Nov 17, 1801, VA.
204. vi.   DANIEL FARMER PENDLETON, b. Oct 10, 1803, Culpepper Co., VA?; d. 1887, Marion Co., MO.
205. vii. GEORGE WASHINGTON PENDLETON, b. Feb 24, 1804, VA; d. Oct 16, 1858, Madison Co., VA?
206. viii. JOHN BOWIE PENDLETON, b. Aug 01, 1805, Culpeper Co., VA; d. Dec 24, 1885, Monroe Co., MO.
     ix.   CATHERINE BOWIE PENDLETON, b. Jun 08, 1807, VA; m. PHILIP SNAP MENEFEE, Jun 23, 1829; b. Oct 08, 1803; d. Apr 19, 1876, Mt. Pleasant, Iowa, Richmond Cem.
      x.   ALEXANDER PENDLETON, b. Jul 10, 1809, VA; d. Apr 16, 1881, Culpeper Co., VA?; m. JEMIMA; b. Abt. 1822, VA; d. Oct 18, 1872, Culpeper Co., VA.
           George Washington Pendleton's sons Thomas G. (15) and William E. are listed in the household of his brother, Alexander Pendleton in the 1850 Culpeper Co., VA census. Alexander (farmer) and Jemima Pendleton are listed in the 1860 Culpeper Co., VA census. Jemima Pendleton is included in the Culpeper County, Virginia Listing of Deaths, 1854 - 1879: "Jemima Pendleton, White Female; 18 Oct 1872, Years: 50, Cause: Consumption."

73. WILLIAM[9] PENDLETON *(JAMES[8], JAMES[7], HENRY[6], PHILIP[5], HENRY[4], HENRY[3], GEORGE[2], GEORGE[1])* was born Jan 25, 1779 in VA, and died 1824 in Culpeper Co., VA? He married NANCY STROTHER Jun 04, 1799 in Faquier Co., VA, daughter of JOHN STROTHER and HELEN PIPER. She was born Nov 20, 1784 in VA, and died 1819.

This is apparently the William Pendleton in the 1810 and 1820 Culpeper Co., VA census records. He is included in a listing of The Mutual Assurance Society of Virginia: Policy, William Pendleton; Culpeper County, 1816; Value, 3000; Property, Rock Mills.

Children of WILLIAM PENDLETON and NANCY STROTHER are:

   i. PEGGY STROTHER CATLETT[10] PENDLETON, b. Apr 19, 1800.
   ii. JOHN STROTHER PENDLETON, b. Mar 01, 1802, Culpeper Co., VA; d. Nov 19, 1868, Culpeper Co., VA; m. LUCY ANNE WILLIAMS, Dec 02, 1824, Orange Co., VA; b. Abt. 1804, VA; d. Jun 22, 1872, Culpeper Co., VA.

   John Strother Pendleton,, a Representative from Virginia was born near Culpeper, Culpeper County, Va., March 1, 1802. He pursued preparatory studies, studied law, and was admitted to the bar in 1824. He practiced law in Culpeper County before he became a member of the State house of delegates 1830-1833 and 1836-1839. The Virginia Historical Society Catalog lists a Speech of Mr. Pendleton of Rappahannock, on the election of a United States senator, delivered in the House of delegates, on the 15th February, 1839 in support of William Cabell Rive.

   He was Chargé d'Affaires to Chile 1841-1844 and elected as a Whig to the Twenty-ninth and Thirtieth Congresses (March 4, 1845-March 3, 1849). He is listed in the 1850 Culpeper Co., VA census as a Lawyer. No children are listed. He then became the Chargé d'Affaires to the Argentine Confederation 1851-1854; empowered jointly with Robert C. Schenck, American Minister to Brazil, April 27, 1852, to negotiate a treaty of commerce with Paraguay and Uruguay. He retired from political life and engaged in farming in his later years. He died near Culpeper, Va., November 19, 1868 and is interred in the family burying ground, "Redwood," Culpeper, Va. (Ref. 111).

   iii. JAMES BOWIE PENDLETON, b. Feb 03, 1804.
207. iv. JAMES FRENCH PENDLETON, b. Jul 01, 1805, VA; d. Sep 12, 1878, Smyth Co., VA?
208.   v. ALBERT GALLATIN PENDLETON, b. Jun 30, 1807, Of Culpeper, VA; d. Jun 19, 1875, Giles Co., VA?
      vi. EDMUND PENDLETON, b. 1808.
     vii. WILLIAM PENDLETON, b. Feb 05, 1810.
           This may be the William Pendleton who married Catherine Davis Oct 17, 1835, in Giles Co., VA.

    viii. FRENCH STROTHER PENDLETON, b. Aug 01, 1812; d. Feb 06, 1831, VA.
      ix. ADDISON PENDLETON, b. Oct 05, 1813.
       x. HELEN ANNE CATLETT PENDLETON, b. Dec 28, 1815.

74. ELIZABETH COLEMAN⁹ PENDLETON *(JAMES⁸, JAMES⁷, HENRY⁶, PHILIP⁵, HENRY⁴, HENRY³, GEORGE², GEORGE¹)* was born Abt. 1781 in VA, and died Aft. 1830 in Hardin Co., KY? She married JR. HENRY PENDLETON Mar 05, 1796 in VA, son of HENRY PENDLETON and ANNE THOMAS. He was born 1764 in VA, and died 1848 in Hardin Co., KY?

Elizabeth's children are listed above under **(66)** Henry Pendleton, her cousin.

75. ELIZABETH⁹ TAYLOR *(ANNE⁸ PENDLETON, JAMES⁷, HENRY⁶, PHILIP⁵, HENRY⁴, HENRY³, GEORGE², GEORGE¹)* was born Abt. 1766, and died 1838 in Nelson Co., KY. She married JOHN PENDLETON Nov 09, 1785 in Orange Co., VA, son of JAMES PENDLETON and CATHERINE BOWIE. He was born 1766 in Culpeper Co., VA, and died 1807.

Elizabeth Taylor's children are listed above under **(69)** John Pendleton, her cousin.

76. ELIZABETH⁹ PENDLETON *(PHILIP⁸, JAMES⁷, HENRY⁶, PHILIP⁵, HENRY⁴, HENRY³, GEORGE², GEORGE¹)* was born 1765 in Culpeper Co., VA, and died 1804 in Pittsylvania Co., VA. She married DAVID JAMES MOTLEY Aug 17, 1785 in Pittsylvania Co., VA, son of JOSEPH MOTLEY and MARTHA ELLINGTON. He was born Abt. 1753 in Amelia Co., VA, and died Mar 1826 in Pittsylvania Co., VA.

Children of ELIZABETH PENDLETON and DAVID MOTLEY are:
    i. SAMUEL C.¹⁰ MOTLEY, b. Dec 19, 1800; d. Apr 10, 1876.
    ii. WILLIAM DAVID MOTLEY.
    iii. JAMES COLEMAN MOTLEY, b. Abt. 1788; d. Abt. 1887, Near Anniston, AL.

77. JAMES⁹ PENDLETON *(PHILIP⁸, JAMES⁷, HENRY⁶, PHILIP⁵, HENRY⁴, HENRY³, GEORGE², GEORGE¹)* was born Abt. 1768 in VA, and died 1841 in Bullitt Co. KY. He married SARAH BELL Feb 07, 1788 in Staunton, Augusta Co., VA, daughter of JAMES BELL. She was born Abt. 1769 in Staunton, VA?, and died in KY.
    James Pendleton gave witness and surety on September 1, 1790 for the marriage of Isaac Scott and Nancy Bell, daughter of James Bell (consent) in Augusta Co., VA. He is listed in two court cases in Virginia: "James Pendleton vs. William Rice--Debt. Augusta, 10th May, 1790;" and "William Wallace vs. Robert Bell, James Bell, and James Pendleton - Debt Writ, Augusta, 1794" (Ref. 61). James and Sarah Pendleton are listed as legatees in Nelson Co., KY in the early 1800's (Ref. 112): "Bell, James Aug 6, 1801 Nov 1805 Wife: Ester; Children Ester Evans, Dorcas Bell, Jenny, Eliz., Robert, Thomas, Samuel, James. Legatees: James and Sarah (dau. Samuel) Pendleton, Mary Moon, Nancy Scott (Isaac Scott), Ex: John Bidford, Wit. John Young, Francis Davis."

This is apparently the James Pendleton in the 1800 Mason Co., KY, 1810 Campbell Co., KY, and 1820 Nelson Co., KY census records. It is also the James Pendleton listed with his son James C. Pendleton in the 1830 Bullitt Co. and 1840 Breckinridge Co. census records.

The will of James Pendleton, was recorded in 1841 in Bullitt Co., KY (Ref. 113):

In the name of God Amen. I James Pendleton of the County of Bullitt and Commonwealth of Kentucky being of sound mind and memory But knowing the uncertainty of all things here below Do constitute and ordain this to be my last will and Testament In manner and Form hereafter mentioned revoking all other wills concerning my worldly property heretofore by me made To all intents and purposes.

Item: I give and bequeath all my worldly property which it hath pleased almighty God to bestow on his unprofitable servant unto my four youngest children Towit: Margaret, Malinda Pendleton, Her Mother, Edmund Gaines, Minerva Jane And William Clayton.

Item: I have given all my other children, eleven in number long since all that I was able or intended to give them. In witnesse whereof I have hereto set my hand and seal this seventh day of January 1841.

I intended to mention the said property above mentioned to be given divided at lawfull age or day of marriage so as to assist the other small property by remaining in one stock? And lastly I constitute and appoint my son James Coleman Pendleton and my friend Noah Summers my Executors and my wife Rebecca Pendleton Executrix, Revoking all other wills by me heretofore made. In witness whereof I have hereunto set my hand seal the day and year above written."
(signed) James Pendleton
Recorded 17 Nov, 1841 Bullitt Co. KY Court; James C. Pendleton; Mary A. M. Hite; David H. Pendleton; Joseph S. Hite.

Children of JAMES PENDLETON and SARAH BELL are:

    i.   ROBERT[10] PENDLETON, b. Abt. 1789.

        This may be the Robert Pendleton who married Esther Bell, dau. of Robert Bell, Aug 21, 1817 (Ref. 114).

    ii.   ALFRED PENDLETON, b. Abt. 1790.

    iii.   SINGLETON PENDLETON, b. Abt. 1791.

209.   iv.   JAMES COLEMAN PENDLETON, b. 1793, VA; d. Feb 22, 1855, Bullitt Co., KY?

    v.   JOSEPH PENDLETON, b. Abt. 1795.

    vi.   DAVID H. PENDLETON, b. Abt. 1797.

    vii.   PATSY AWBRY PENDLETON, b. Mar 01, 1798; d. May 15, 1830; m. STEPHEN LEWIS HITE, Jan 24, 1822, Bullitt Co., KY; b. 1799; d. 1828.

    viii.   DORCAS PENDLETON, b. Abt. 1800.

    ix.   MARGARET MALINDA PENDLETON, b. Abt. 1802.

    x.   EDMUND GAINES PENDLETON, b. Abt. 1804.

    xi.   MINERVA JANE PENDLETON, b. Abt. 1806.

    xii.   WILLIAM CLAYTON PENDLETON, b. Abt. 1808.

    xiii.   HARRIETT PENDLETON.

78. REBECCA[9] PENDLETON *(PHILIP[8], JAMES[7], HENRY[6], PHILIP[5], HENRY[4], HENRY[3], GEORGE[2], GEORGE[1])* was born Abt. 1775 in VA. She married WILLIAM MONKERS Feb 25, 1795 in Washington Co., VA. He was born 1754 in Pittsylvania Co., VA, and died Sep 15, 1854 in Platte Co., MO.

Children of REBECCA PENDLETON and WILLIAM MONKERS are:

    i. MARTHA MARY[10] MONKERS, b. Jan 06, 1796, Washington Co., VA; d. Oct 12, 1863, Clay Co., MO; m. ANDREW BAKER BALDWIN, Jul 12, 1812; b. 1796.

    ii. MARY MONKERS, b. 1797, Washington Co., VA; m. JOHN THOMPSON, Jun 28, 1818, Howard Co., MO.

    iii. BENJAMIN FRANKLIN MONKERS, b. Apr 17, 1799, Campbell Co., TN; d. Apr 17, 1885, Marion Co., OR; m. MARY POLLY CROWLEY, Jul 12, 1818, Howard Co., MO; b. Oct 01, 1802, Campbell Co., TN; d. Mar 07, 1888, Marion Co., OR.

    iv. MATILDA MONKERS, b. 1806, Campbell Co., TN; d. Jan 1892, Buchanan Co., MO; m. BLUFORD STANTON, Jan 18, 1827, MO; b. Jan 1805, KY; d. Mar 04, 1865, Jefferson Co., AL.

    v. HANNAH MONKERS, b. 1807, Campbell Co., TN.

    vi. WILLIAM COLUMBUS MONKERS, b. Mar 10, 1810, Campbell Co., TN; d. Jul 18, 1877, Cherokee Co., TX; m. (1) MINERVA MCKNIGHT; m. (2) MARGARET COULTER, 1831, Washington Co., AR; b. Abt. 1811, TN; d. Jun 10, 1863, Cherokee Co., TX.

    vii. JANE MONKERS, b. 1811, Campbell Co., TN; m. (1) JOSEPH BLANTON, Aug 27, 1833, Jackson Co., MO; d. 1844; m. (2) SAMUEL ABNER HACKWORTH, Abt. 1847, MO.

    viii. ABSALOM MONKERS, b. Apr 10, 1815, Campbell Co., TN; d. Sep 15, 1894; m. (1) ELIZABETH CROCKETT, Mar 18, 1836, Clay Co., MO; d. Bef. 1845; m. (2) MARTHA ANN GEE, Apr 08, 1845.

    ix. JOHN MONKERS, b. 1818, MO; m. VIRGINIA WASHINGTON?

79. COLEMAN[9] PENDLETON *(PHILIP[8], JAMES[7], HENRY[6], PHILIP[5], HENRY[4], HENRY[3], GEORGE[2], GEORGE[1])* was born Aug 04, 1780 in Culpeper Co., Va., and died May 31, 1862 in Tallapoosa Co., AL. He married MARTHA GILBERT Jun 06, 1808 in Putnam Co., GA, daughter of BENJAMIN GILBERT and HANNAH BUTLER. She was born May 31, 1789 in Hancock Co., GA, and died Aug 06, 1874 in Tallapoosa Co., AL.

    Coleman Pendleton is listed in the 1824 Putnam Co., GA Tax List and the 1850 Harris Co., GA, Dowdell's District, census, as well as the 1860 census, Chambers Co., AL. A biographical sketch (Ref. 115) of Coleman is included in the Virginia Historical Society Catalog.

Children of COLEMAN PENDLETON and MARTHA GILBERT are:

210.   i. LOUISA EMILY[10] PENDLETON, b. 1809, GA; d. May 10, 1881, Chambers Co., AL.

211.   ii. WILLIAM ROBERT PENDLETON, b. Mar 09, 1811, Putnam Co., GA; d. Jul 07, 1841, Baker Co., GA.

212.   iii. PHILIP COLEMAN PENDLETON, b. Nov 17, 1812, Eatonville, GA; d. Jun 19, 1869, Valdosta, GA.

213.   iv. EDMUND MONROE PENDLETON, b. Mar 19, 1815, Eatonton, GA; d. Jan 26, 1884, Atlanta, GA.

80. MARY[9] PENDLETON *(WILLIAM[8], NATHANIEL[7], HENRY[6], PHILIP[5], HENRY[4], HENRY[3], GEORGE[2], GEORGE[1])* was born Mar 04, 1771 in VA, and died Apr 15, 1838. She married NICHOLAS ORRICK Feb 03, 1788. He was born Apr 05, 1759, and died Jul 09, 1822.

   The Honorable NICHOLAS ORRICK, of Berkeley and Morgan Counties, West Virginia, was the sixth born of Capt. Nicholas and Hannah (Cromwell) Orrick, of Baltimore County, MD. He served as Justice and High Sheriff of Berkeley County (Ref. 116). He was a witness for the will of Philip Pendleton, his wife's uncle, on January 25, 1802 in Berkeley Co., VA.

Children of MARY PENDLETON and NICHOLAS ORRICK are (Ref. 116):

   i. WILLIAM PENDLETON ORRICK, b. Apr 24, 1789; d. 1860.
   ii. JAMES ORRICK, b. Oct. 4 1791; d. 1804.
   iii. CROMWELL ORRICK, b. 1793.
   iv. ELIZABETH ORRICK, Oct 20, 1795; d. 1847; She married EDWARD ALLEN GIBBS, b. 1807, Campbell Co., TN.
   v. MARY ANN ORRICK, b. Oct 4, 1797; d. 1851; She married EBEN CLOUGH.
   vi. BENJAMIN ORRICK, b. Mar 25, 1800.
   vii. SUSANNAH PENDLETON ORRICK, b. Nov 25, 1802; d. 1869; She married JOHN B.TAYLOR.
   viii. JOHN ORRICK, b. Jan 12, 1805; d. Jul 4, 1874; He married URILLA STONEBRAKER, Sep 22, 1833.

81. LUCY CLAYTON[9] PENDLETON *(WILLIAM[8], NATHANIEL[7], HENRY[6], PHILIP[5], HENRY[4], HENRY[3], GEORGE[2], GEORGE[1])* was born Feb 20, 1773 in Culpeper Co., VA, and died 1838 in Sangoman Co., IL. She married BENJAMIN FERGESON 1791 in Culpeper Co., VA. He was born Jun 15, 1756 in MD, and died 1830 in VA.

   The following account is from a history of Illinois pioneers (Ref. 117).

   Mrs. Lucy Ferguson was born about 1767 in Culpepper county, Va. Her maiden name was Pendleton. She was married there in 1791 to Benjamin Ferguson, who was also a native of Virginia. They had fifteen children born in Virginia, and Mr. F. died there. The mother, with five children, moved to Sangamon county, arriving in the fall of 1836, about three miles east of Rochester. Just before she left Virginia, Mrs. Ferguson was enumerating her descendants: there were seventy-five then.

   WILLIAM H., born February, 1798, married in Virginia in 1818 to Lucy Broadux. They came to Illinois with their mother. Mrs. Lucy Ferguson died in the fall of 1871, and Wm. H. died March, 1873, leaving four children, three of whom are now married.

   LUCY C., born in Virginia, was married there in 1832 to Isaac Haines. He was a Methodist preacher. They came west with their mother. He died in 1838. She died in 1850, leaving two children, one of whom, WILLIAM C., married, and lives one mile south of Taylorville. LUCY A. married J. Clark, and resides opposite Cairo, in Missouri.

   ELLEN, born in 1812, married in Sangamon county in 1838 to Daniel Johnson. They have one child, ELIAS, who married, and resides on the farm with his father, four miles east of Rochester. Mrs. Ellen Johnson died about 1841.

   PHILIP C., born June, 1815, in Virginia, married there in 1836 to Mary Haines. They have five children living. They all reside in Kansas but one, EZEKIEL, who married a

Miss Kelly, and lives near Taylorville. Philip C. Ferguson was a physician, and died from lockjaw in 1862. His widow resides near Wathena, Kan.

JAMES, born March 11, 1817, married in Sangamon county March 21, 1838, to Mary J. Young, who was born in 1824, in Trigg county, Ky. They have four children.

MARTHA J., born Jan. 16, 1840, in Sangamon county, married Oct. 25, 1860, in Christian county, to Archibald Sattley. CLARA A., born April 24, 1842, married Feb. 15, 1862, in Christian county, to Charles E. Sattley. ALBERT L., born Jan. 31, 1849, and ADA M., reside with their father. James Ferguson came to Sangamon county with his mother, and engaged in farming; has been for twelve years justice of the peace at Stonington, and assisted in organizing the first Sunday school there, and has been superintendent ever since. Mrs. Mary J. Ferguson died Oct. 20, 1875.

Mrs. Lucy Ferguson died in the autumn of 1838, on the farm where they settled in 1836

Children of LUCY PENDLETON and BENJAMIN FERGESON are:
   i. LUCY C.[10] FERGESON, b. VA; d. 1850, IL; m. ISAAC HAINES, VA; d. 1838, IL.
   ii. WILLIAM H. FERGESON, b. Feb 1798; d. Mar 1873; m. LUCY BROADUX; d. 1871.
   iii. BENJAMIN PENDLETON FERGESON, b. 1802; d. 1864; m. EDNA AMISS, 1825; b. 1806; d. 1845.
   iv. ELLEN FERGESON, b. 1812; d. Abt. 1841; m. DANIEL JOHNSON, 1838, Sangamon Co., IL.
   v. PHILIP C. FERGESON, b. Jun 1815, VA; m. MARY HAINES, 1836, VA.
   vi. JAMES FERGESON, b. Mar 11, 1817, VA; m. MARY J. YOUNG, Mar 21, 1838, Sangamon Co., IL; b. 1824, Trigg Co., KY; d. Oct 20, 1875.

82. SARAH ANNE "SALLY"[9] PENDLETON *(WILLIAM[8], NATHANIEL[7], HENRY[6], PHILIP[5], HENRY[4], HENRY[3], GEORGE[2], GEORGE[1])* was born Dec 17, 1774 in Berkeley Co., and died Aug 21, 1804 in Frederick Co., VA. She married JAMES WIGGINTON, CAPT. May 19, 1796. He was born 1766 in Of Culpeper Co., and died 1847.

Children of SARAH PENDLETON and JAMES WIGGINTON are:
   i. WILLIAM PENDLETON[10] WIGGINTON.
   ii. JAMES BOTTS WIGGINTON, b. Abt. 1800; d. 1847, Lewis Co., MO; m. SARAH ANN SETTLE.

83. NATHANIEL[9] PENDLETON *(WILLIAM[8], NATHANIEL[7], HENRY[6], PHILIP[5], HENRY[4], HENRY[3], GEORGE[2], GEORGE[1])* was born Dec 26, 1777 in VA, and died 1842 in Warren Co., MO. He married HANNAH CUNNINGHAM. She was born Abt. 1780, and died Aft. 1840 in Warren Co., MO?

This is the Nathaniel Pendleton in the 1810 and 1820 Pendleton Co., VA (now WV) census records and who represented Pendleton Co. in the House of Delegates 1805-6 and 1813-1815. He left Pendleton Co. by 1829 and lived in Ohio, later moving to Missouri. He is listed in a land transaction in Bath Co., VA in 1829: "Lodge Land Surveys: A Series Indenture, dated 7 Aug 1829, Nathaniel Pendleton & Hannah, his wife to Robert Corley, a parcel on Jackson R. in Bath Co., known as the Burrus tract" (Ref. 26). Nathaniel, his wife and 3 children are listed in the 1830 St. Charles Co., MO census.

In 1836 a railroad convention was held in St. Louis, MO composed of delegates from various MO counties. Nathaniel Pendleton was a delegate from Warren County, MO. Hannah Pendleton is listed in the 1840 Warren Co., MO census, Camp Branch.

Children of NATHANIEL PENDLETON and HANNAH CUNNINGHAM are:

        i.   ELIZABETH "PHOEBE" ANN[10] PENDLETON, m. ROBERT L. ALLEN, Oct 09, 1838, MO.

                Robert L. Allen was first married to Anna Pendleton, by whom he had five children. After her death he married Louisa B. Harnett and they had three children. Mr. Allen was county judge of Warren County for some time, and represented that county in the Legislature two years. (Ref. 118)

       ii.   HENRY PENDLETON.
      iii.   JOHN W. PENDLETON, b. Culpepper Co., VA; d. 1842, Dawson Massacre, TX.

                A company of 53 men from Fayette Co., TX was enlisted by Captain Dawson to repel Mexican invaders not long after the battle of the Alamo, San Antonio, TX. The 36 Texans, including John Pendleton, who died at the battle site of what is now Fort Sam Houston, were buried in shallow graves in the mesquite thicket where they fell (Ref. 119).

      iv.   NATHANIEL PENDLETON.
       v.   PHILIP PENDLETON.
      vi.   WILLIAM PENDLETON.
214. vii.   JAMES C. PENDLETON, b. 1806, VA; d. Aft. 1860, TX?
     viii.   BENJAMIN PENDLETON, b. Abt. 1810.
      ix.   JESSE PENDLETON, b. Abt. 1812.

                This is likely the Jesse Pendleton (35), carpenter, in the 1850 Calhoun Co., TX census, La Vaca City. His spouse listed as Leuthy? and the children are listed as Westly Loone (12), Allen Loone (9), Sarah Loone, and Agnes Pendleton (1); also listed is Benjamin Pendleton (40), carpenter. This Jesse and Benjamin were born in MO. In addition, Jesse C. and John W. Pendleton are listed in the 1839 and 1840 Fayette Co., TX tax lists. Jesse Pendleton is listed as a patentee, in the following Texas Land Title Abstract: "Fannin District; Grayson County; Certificate 56; 29 Nov 1845; 160 Acres."

84. BENJAMIN[9] PENDLETON *(WILLIAM[8], NATHANIEL[7], HENRY[6], PHILIP[5], HENRY[4], HENRY[3], GEORGE[2], GEORGE[1])* was born Nov 19, 1781 in Culpeper Co., VA, and died Mar 14, 1853 in Hancock, MD. He married (1) ELIZABETH STROTHER Oct 31, 1805 in Jefferson Co., VA, daughter of BENJAMIN STROTHER and CATHERINE PRICE. She was born Jan 23, 1784 in Jefferson, VA, and died Nov 12, 1822 in "Locust Grove," Jefferson Co., VA. He married (2) AGATHA BULLOCK YANCEY Apr 19, 1825 in Culpeper Co., Va., daughter of RICHARD YANCEY and JUDITH FIELD. She was born Abt. 1790 in Culpeper Co., VA, and died 1827 in Culpeper Co., VA. He married (3) MARY WIGGINTON Aft. 1827. He married (4) HARRIET STEVENS Aft.

1827. She was born Dec 24, 1788, and died Apr 23, 1850. He married (5) RACHEL THOMAS Aft. 1827.

This is apparently the Benjamin Pendleton in the 1810 and 1830 Berkeley Co. and 1820 Jefferson Co., VA census records.

Children of BENJAMIN PENDLETON and ELIZABETH STROTHER are:
215.   i.   CATHERINE THORNTON[10] PENDLETON, b. Aug 03, 1806, "Locust Grove," VA; d. Aug 11, 1874, New Castle, PA.
        ii.   BENJAMIN STROTHER PENDLETON, b. Feb 24, 1808.
216.   iii. JAMES WILLIAM PENDLETON, b. Sep 07, 1809, VA; d. Abt. 1845, Franklin Co., AR?

85. WILLIAM[9] PENDLETON *(WILLIAM[8], NATHANIEL[7], HENRY[6], PHILIP[5], HENRY[4], HENRY[3], GEORGE[2], GEORGE[1])* was born Aug 25, 1789 in VA, and died Aug 01, 1855 in Martinsburg, VA. He married (1) HANNAH BRADY Feb 15, 1806 in Berkeley Co., VA. He married (2) SUSAN SNODGRASS Feb 19, 1811 in Berkeley Co., VA, daughter of STEPHEN SNODGRASS and ELIZABETH VERDIER. She was born Jun 18, 1790, and died Mar 25, 1834 in Berkeley Co., VA? He married (3) MRS. ELIZABETH A. ROBINSON Jun 22, 1840 in Berkeley Co., VA. She was born Dec 26, 1802 in MD, and died 1869.

William Pendleton is included in the 1820 Berkeley County Census and is listed as a farmer, age 61, 8th district, Berkeley Co. 1850 census. The following is on his tombstone: "In Memory of William Pendleton died Augt. 1st, 1855; Aged 65 years, 11 mo. & 6 days. 'Asleep in Jesus, blessed sleep, From which none ever wake to weep.'"

The following is on Susan Snodgrass Pendleton's tombstone: "To the memory of Susan Pendleton this humble monument is placed as a tribute of gratitude for her maternal care and love; she was a kind mother and a devoted wife; she died in the faith of Christ and in the communion of the Episcopal Church; she was born June 18th, 1790 and died March 25th, 1834."

Children of WILLIAM PENDLETON and SUSAN SNODGRASS are:
217.   i.   ANNE ELIZA[10] PENDLETON, b. Feb 22, 1812, Berkeley Co., VA; d. Jan 17, 1884, Culpeper Co., VA?
        ii.   SUSAN VERDIER SHEPHERD PENDLETON, b. Oct 15, 1813, Berkeley Co., VA; d. Mar 25, 1888, Cumberland, MD?; m. JAMES CAMPBELL ORRICK, Feb 19, 1835, Berkeley Co., VA; b. Oct 10, 1807, VA; d. Jul 17, 1891, Cumberland, MD?
        iii. ELEANOR PENDLETON, b. Aug 01, 1815, Berkeley Co., VA; d. 1844; m. NATHANIEL PENDLETON CAMPBELL, Aug 25, 1841, Berkeley Co., VA; b. Dec 19, 1819; d. Sep 28, 1878.
218.   iv. WILLIAM HENRY PENDLETON, b. Sep 30, 1817, Berkeley Co., VA; d. Mar 08, 1873, Fauquier Co., VA.
        v.   NATHANIEL PENDLETON, b. Jul 13, 1820, Berkeley Co., VA; d. Sep 01, 1824.
219.   vi. ROBERT SHEPHERD PENDLETON, b. Mar 20, 1824, Berkeley Co., VA; d. 1880.

vii.   PHILIP EDMUND PENDLETON, b. Jun 11, 1827, Berkeley Co., VA; d. Jan 22, 1830.

220.   viii.   STEPHEN JAMES PENDLETON, b. Apr 03, 1831, Berkeley Co., VA; d. Jul 01, 1862, Battle of Malvern Hill.

86. FRANCES COLEMAN[9] PENDLETON *(WILLIAM[8], NATHANIEL[7], HENRY[6], PHILIP[5], HENRY[4], HENRY[3], GEORGE[2], GEORGE[1])* was born Apr 01, 1792, and died Apr 08, 1864. She married WILLIAM CAMPBELL Mar 05, 1811 in Berkeley Co., VA, son of JAMES CAMPBELL and SARA CAMPBELL. He was born 1784.

Child of FRANCES PENDLETON and WILLIAM CAMPBELL is:
   i.   LEMUEL[10] CAMPBELL, b. 1826; d. 1907; m. ISABELLA MCKOWN, 1847; b. 1816; d. 1888.

87. ELEANOR[9] PENDLETON *(WILLIAM[8], NATHANIEL[7], HENRY[6], PHILIP[5], HENRY[4], HENRY[3], GEORGE[2], GEORGE[1])* was born Nov 12, 1794, and died 1850. She married (1) JAMES WALKER Sep 26, 1814 in Berkeley Co., VA. She married (2) JOHN MAXWELL 1825. He was born 1800, and died 1857.

Child of ELEANOR PENDLETON and JOHN MAXWELL is:
   i.   AMELIA[10] MAXWELL, b. 1838; m. WILLIAM G. STRATTON; b. 1820; d. 1885.

88. ELIZABETH[9] PENDLETON *(PHILIP[8], NATHANIEL[7], HENRY[6], PHILIP[5], HENRY[4], HENRY[3], GEORGE[2], GEORGE[1])* was born 1774 in VA, and died 1822. She married DAVID HUNTER Nov 19, 1791 in Berkeley Co., VA. He was born 1761, and died 1829.

   David Hunter and his father-in-law Philip Pendleton are included in a lawsuit Marshall vs. Hunter in Berkeley Co. filed 22 June, 1799 (Ref. 61):

   Fairfax had set aside 800 acres for himself which he contemplated giving to a certain _____ Beal (?), but Beal removed out of Berkeley (Frederick). Fairfax devised it to Denny Martin, who conveyed to James M. and John Marshall and others by deed recorded in General Court. The Commonwealth confirmed to purchasers the lands set apart by Lord Fairfax to his own use. Philip Pendleton and David Hunter are in possession of the tract by a treasury warrant, and the parties leave the controversy to the Court.

Children of ELIZABETH PENDLETON and DAVID HUNTER are:
   i.   NANCY[10] HUNTER.
   ii.   EDMUND PENDLETON HUNTER, b. 1809.

89. ANNE "NANCY" CLAYTON[9] PENDLETON *(PHILIP[8], NATHANIEL[7], HENRY[6], PHILIP[5], HENRY[4], HENRY[3], GEORGE[2], GEORGE[1])* was born 1778 in VA, and died Sep 13, 1854. She married JOHN KENNEDY Oct 02, 1794 in Berkeley Co., VA. He was born 1769, and died 1836.

Children of ANNE PENDLETON and JOHN KENNEDY are:
    i.   JOHN PENDLETON[10] KENNEDY, b. Oct 25, 1795; d. Aug 18, 1870.
    ii. ANDREW KENNEDY.
    iii. PHILIP P. KENNEDY.
    iv. ANTHONY KENNEDY, m. SARAH STEPHENA DANDRIDGE; b. Nov 07, 1811; d. Oct 25, 1846.

90. PHILIP CLAYTON[9] PENDLETON (*PHILIP*[8], *NATHANIEL*[7], *HENRY*[6], *PHILIP*[5], *HENRY*[4], *HENRY*[3], *GEORGE*[2], *GEORGE*[1]) was born Nov 24, 1779 in Berkeley Co., VA, and died Apr 03, 1863 in Berkeley Co., VA? He married SARAH ANN BOYD Nov 25, 1813 in Berkeley Co., VA. She was born Mar 29, 1797 in VA, and died Jul 16, 1868 in Berkeley Co., VA?

        Philip Clayton Pendleton was appointed a Federal Judge by President John Quincy Adams. He represented Berkeley Co. in the House of Delegates from 1805 to 1810 and was a county commissioner. Philip C. Pendleton was listed in the 1812 Muster Rolls as a Paymaster, 4th Regiment (Boyd's) Virginia Militia. He is listed in the 1820, 1830, and 1840 Berkeley Co. census records. He is listed in the 1850 Berkeley Co. Census, Martinsburg, age 70, as a Counselor; value of property $53,000. The Virginia Historical Society Catalog listings include a biographical sketch of Philip C. Pendleton (Ref. 120).

Children of PHILIP PENDLETON and SARAH BOYD are:
221.   i.   JR. PHILIP CLAYTON[10] PENDLETON, b. Aug 29, 1814, Berkeley Co., VA; d. Oct 08, 1899.
222.   ii. EDMUND BOYD PENDLETON, b. Nov 27, 1816, Berkeley Co., VA; d. Mar 26, 1880, Frederick Co., VA?
223.   iii. ELISHA BOYD PENDLETON, b. Jan 13, 1820, Berkeley Co., VA; d. Jul 12, 1902, Morgan Co., WV?

91. SARAH[9] PENDLETON (*PHILIP*[8], *NATHANIEL*[7], *HENRY*[6], *PHILIP*[5], *HENRY*[4], *HENRY*[3], *GEORGE*[2], *GEORGE*[1]) was born Jun 18, 1785 in VA, and died Mar 13, 1855 in Jefferson Co., VA? She married ADAM STEPHEN DANDRIDGE Jan 01, 1805 in Berkeley Co., VA, son of ALEXANDER SPOTSWOOD DANDRIDGE. He was born Dec 05, 1782, and died 1821 in Martinsburg, VA.

Children of SARAH PENDLETON and ADAM DANDRIDGE are:
    i.   MARY EVALINA[10] DANDRIDGE, m. R. M. T. HUNT.
    ii. ANN SPOTSWOOD DANDRIDGE, b. Oct 19, 1806; d. infancy.
    iii. SARAH STEPHENA DANDRIDGE, b. Nov 07, 1811; d. Oct 25, 1846; m. ANTHONY KENNEDY.
    iv. ANN SPOTSWOOD DANDRIDGE, b. Jun 18, 1813; m. T. E. BUCHANAN.
    v. JR. ADAM STEPHEN DANDRIDGE, b. Dec 13, 1814, VA; d. Jan 04, 1894; m. SERENA CATHERINE PENDLETON Feb 21, 1837, Winchester, VA, dau. EDMUND PENDLETON and SERENA PURNELL; b. Jun 09, 1816, MD; d. Sep 02, 1889.

    vi.   PHILIP PENDLETON DANDRIDGE, b. Oct 02, 1817; m. (1) MRS. MARY
          ELIZABETH (TAYLOR) BLISS; m. (2) CAROLYN GOLDBOROUGH.
    vii. ALEXANDER SPOTSWOOD DANDRIDGE, DR., b. Nov 19, 1819,
          Jefferson Co., VA; d. Apr 28, 1889; m. MARTHA ELIZA PENDLETON
          May 04, 1843, Hamilton Co., OH; dau. NATHANIEL PENDLETON and
          JANE HUNT; b. Dec 30, 1823, OH; d. Aft. 1880 in Hamilton Co., OH?

92. EDMUND[9] PENDLETON *(PHILIP[8], NATHANIEL[7], HENRY[6], PHILIP[5], HENRY[4], HENRY[3], GEORGE[2], GEORGE[1])* was born 1790 in VA, and died Aug 12, 1823. He married SERENA CATHERINE PURNELL Mar 23, 1811.

Children of EDMUND PENDLETON and SERENA PURNELL are:
        i.   ISAAC PURNELL[10] PENDLETON, d. without issue.
224.   ii. SERENA CATHERINE PENDLETON, b. Jun 09, 1816, MD; d. Sep 02,
          1889.

93. MARIA W.[9] PENDLETON *(PHILIP[8], NATHANIEL[7], HENRY[6], PHILIP[5], HENRY[4], HENRY[3], GEORGE[2], GEORGE[1])* was born Abt. 1795 in VA. She married JOHN ROGERS COOKE Nov 18, 1813 in Berkeley Co., VA. He was born 1788, and died Dec 10, 1854 in Richmond, VA.

      John Rogers Cooke,, jurist, was born in St. George, Bermuda, in 1788; son of Dr. Stephen and Catherine (Esten) Cooke. He attended William and Mary College, Va., 1806-09, and the College of New Jersey, 1816-11. He then studied law and practiced at the Virginia bar for forty-five years. He served in the defence of the coast in 1812 and was a member of the Virginia house of delegates, 1812-14. With John Marshall, James Madison, John Randolph and Benjamin W. Lee, he was a delegate to the reform convention of 1829-30, which framed the state constitution. He was married to Maria, daughter of Philip Pendleton of Berkeley county. Their three sons, Philip, Henry, and Edward St. George, became honored citizens of Virginia. He died in Richmond, Va., Dec. 10, 1854. (Ref. 121).

Children of MARIA PENDLETON and JOHN COOKE are:
        i.   PHILIP PENDLETON[10] COOKE, b. Oct 26, 1816, Martinsburg, VA; d. Jan
          20, 1850, Clark Co., VA; m. ANN CORBIN TAYLOR BURWELL, 1837,
          Clark Co., VA.
       ii. EDMUND PENDLETON COOKE, b. Abt. 1824; d. Feb 14, 1840,
          Charleston, VA.
      iii. SALLIE DANDRIDGE COOKE, b. Mar 18, 1828; d. Dec 14, 1887; m.
          ROBERT R. DUVAL, Jun 06, 1849, Richmond, Henrico Co., VA.
      iv. JOHN ESTEN COOKE, b. Nov 30, 1830, Winchester, VA; m. MARY
          FRANCES PAGE, Sep 18, 1867.

94. NATHANIEL GREENE[9] PENDLETON *(NATHANIEL[8], NATHANIEL[7], HENRY[6], PHILIP[5], HENRY[4], HENRY[3], GEORGE[2], GEORGE[1])* was born Aug 25, 1793 in Savannah, GA, and died Jun 15, 1861 in Cincinnati, OH. He married (1) JANE FRANCES HUNT 1820, daughter of JESSE HUNT. She was born 1802, and died 1839.

He married (2) ANNE JAMES May 12, 1841. She was born Feb 21, 1810 in OH, and died Feb 07, 1891.

Nathaniel Greene Pendleton was born in Savannah, Ga., August 25, 1793. He moved to New York City with his parents where he was graduated from Columbia College in 1813. Nathaniel studied law and was admitted to the bar. He served in the War of 1812 and moved to Cincinnati, Ohio, in 1818 where he practiced law. He was a member of the State senate 1825-1829 and was elected as a Whig to the Twenty-seventh Congress (March 4, 1841-March 3, 1843). Nathaniel is listed in the Ohio census records of 1830 and 1840, Cincinnati, First Ward. He declined to be a candidate for renomination in 1842 and resumed the practice of law. He died in Cincinnati, Ohio, June 16, 1861 and is interred in Spring Grove Cemetery (Ref. 111).

Children of NATHANIEL PENDLETON and JANE HUNT are:

225.   i.   SUSAN LOUISA[10] PENDLETON, b. Feb 23, 1821, Cincinnati, OH; d. Feb 06, 1877, Cincinnati, OH.

226.   ii.   MARTHA ELIZA PENDLETON, b. Dec 30, 1823, OH; d. Aft. 1880, Hamilton Co., OH?

227.   iii.   GEORGE HUNT PENDLETON, b. Jul 19, 1825, Cincinnati, OH; d. Nov 24, 1889, Brussels, Belgium.

228.   iv.   ELIOTT HUNT PENDLETON, b. Dec 19, 1828, OH; d. Oct 14, 1892, Cincinnati, OH?

229.   v.   ANNA PIERCE PENDLETON, b. Dec 27, 1830, OH; d. Dec 29, 1887, Brooklyn, NY?

        vi.   NATHANIEL PENDLETON, b. Apr 01, 1834, OH; d. Nov 01, 1862.

Children of NATHANIEL PENDLETON and ANNE JAMES are:

        vii.   CHARLOTTE[10] PENDLETON, b. 1842, Washington DC; d. Nov 21, 1921, Washington DC?

            Miss Charlotte Pendleton was a member of The National Society of the Daughters of the American Revolution. Charlotte Pendleton (78), single, is listed in the 1920 Washington DC census, Hampshire Ave.

230.   viii.   EDMUND HENRY PENDLETON, b. Jun 22, 1843, OH; d. Mar 14, 1910.

95. ANNA PIERCE[9] PENDLETON *(NATHANIEL[8], NATHANIEL[7], HENRY[6], PHILIP[5], HENRY[4], HENRY[3], GEORGE[2], GEORGE[1])* was born 1796, and died Dec 26, 1883. She married ARCHIBALD ROGERS May 08, 1821. He was born 1791, and died 1850.

Children of ANNA PENDLETON and ARCHIBALD ROGERS are:

        i.   NATHANIEL PENDLETON[10] ROGERS, b. Apr 29, 1822; m. EMILY MOULTON, 1847.

        ii.   EDMUND PENDLETON ROGERS, b. Jul 31, 1827; d. Feb 10, 1895; m. VIRGINIA HOLT DUMMER, May 24, 1851.

        iii.   PHILIP CLAYTON ROGERS, b. Aug 13, 1829.

        iv.   SUSAN BARD ROGERS, b. Nov 04, 1834; m. HERMAN T. LIVINGSTON, Nov 04, 1834.

96. JAMES M.[9] PENDLETON, M.D. *(NATHANIEL[8], NATHANIEL[7], HENRY[6], PHILIP[5], HENRY[4], HENRY[3], GEORGE[2], GEORGE[1])* was born 1799, and died Jan 11, 1832 in NYC. He married MARGARET JONES Jan 27, 1825, daughter of JOSHUA JONES.

Child of JAMES PENDLETON and MARGARET JONES is:

     i. JAMES M. JONES[10] PENDLETON, b. Abt. 1831, NY; d. Bet. 1860 - 1870, NYC, NY?; m. GERTRUDE JAMES, Oct 16, 1850, NYC, NY; b. Abt. 1831, NY; d. NYC, NY?;.

        James M. Pendleton (gentleman) and Gertrude Pendleton are listed in the 1860 NYC census.

97. JOHN[9] PENDLETON *(EDMUND[8], JOHN[7], HENRY[6], PHILIP[5], HENRY[4], HENRY[3], GEORGE[2], GEORGE[1])* was born Jun 22, 1765 in Caroline Co., VA, and died Oct 1814 in Caroline Co., VA. He married NANCY "ANNE" LEWIS Sep 20, 1789 in Williamsburg, VA, daughter of JOHN LEWIS and BETTY. She was born Dec 06, 1766 in Richmond, VA, and died Aft. 1830 in Caroline Co., VA?

     On Jan. 14, 1808, John Pendleton made bond as Clerk of Caroline Co., VA with the jurist Edmund Pendleton as his security. John Pendleton served as Clerk of Court of Caroline County from 1799 to 1814. His son John Lewis Pendleton succeeded him as Clerk. There were 18 persons in John's household according to the 1810 Caroline Co. census.

Children of JOHN PENDLETON and NANCY LEWIS are:

231.   i. JOHN LEWIS[10] PENDLETON, b. Jul 07, 1790, Caroline Co., VA; d. 1869, Caroline Co., VA?

232. ii. EDMUND ALLEN PENDLETON, b. 1791, VA; d. 1883, Augusta, GA?

233. iii. ELIZABETH ALLEN PENDLETON, b. 1793, VA; d. 1865, Caroline Co., VA?

     iv. MARY ANNE PENDLETON, b. 1795, VA.

234. v. EVELINA MILDRED PENDLETON, b. 1797, VA; d. 1864.

235. vi. WILLIAM ARMISTEAD PENDLETON, b. 1801, VA; d. Jul 22, 1854, Campbell Co., KY?

     vii. CHARLES LEWIS PENDLETON, b. 1803, VA; d. Mar 06, 1835, Richmond City, VA; m. SARAH ANNE TOMPKINS, May 29, 1828, Richmond, Henrico Co., VA; b. Bet. 1800 - 1810, Of Richmond, VA.

        The marriage of Charles Lewis Pendleton is listed in the Annals of Henrico Parish Marriages. He is buried in Shockoe Hill Cemetery, Richmond City, VA.

236. viii. ROBERT TAYLOR PENDLETON, b. Jul 08, 1805, Caroline Co., VA; d. Abt. 1840, Caroline Co., VA.

     ix. BENJAMIN FRANKLIN PENDLETON, b. 1806, VA; d. 1826.

237. x. NATHANIEL PHILIP HENRY PENDLETON, b. Feb 12, 1809, VA; d. Jul 13, 1877, Port Royal, Caroline Co., VA.

98. MILDRED[9] PENDLETON *(EDMUND[8], JOHN[7], HENRY[6], PHILIP[5], HENRY[4], HENRY[3], GEORGE[2], GEORGE[1])* was born 1773 in Caroline Co., VA. She married THOMAS MANN PAGE 1798, son of JOHN PAGE and JANE BYRD. He was born 1773 in VA, and died 1834 in Cumberland Co., VA.

Child of MILDRED PENDLETON and THOMAS PAGE is:
    i. ROBERT THOMAS[10] PAGE, b. 1805, VA.

99. EDMUND[9] PENDLETON *(EDMUND[8], JOHN[7], HENRY[6], PHILIP[5], HENRY[4], HENRY[3], GEORGE[2], GEORGE[1])* was born Apr 18, 1774 in VA, and died Jan 23, 1847 in Hanover Co., VA. He married (1) JANE BURWELL PAGE Aug 23, 1794, daughter of JOHN PAGE and BETTY BURWELL. She was born 1774, and died 1796. He married (2) LUCY NELSON May 16, 1798 in York Co., VA, daughter of HUGH NELSON and JUDITH PAGE. She was born 1776 in VA, and died 1848 in Caroline Co., VA?

    This is apparently the Edmund Pendleton in the 1810 through 1840 Caroline Co., VA census records. His funeral is recorded in St. Martin's Parish Register: "Edmund Pendleton 73; January 25, 1847; Hanover Co., VA."

Child of EDMUND PENDLETON and JANE PAGE is:
238.   i. ELIZABETH PAGE[10] PENDLETON, b. 1795; d. Apr 1839.

Children of EDMUND PENDLETON and LUCY NELSON are:
239.   ii. HUGH NELSON[10] PENDLETON, b. Apr 13, 1800, VA; d. May 27, 1875, Jefferson Co., WV?
240.   iii. MILDRED PENDLETON, b. Mar 21, 1802, VA; d. 1892, Augusta, GA?
241.   iv. JUDITH PAGE PENDLETON, b. Dec 08, 1803, Caroline Co., VA; d. Jul 1834, Caroline Co., VA.
242.   v. FRANCIS WALKER PENDLETON, DR., b. Dec 07, 1808, Caroline Co., VA; d. 1865, Richmond Co., VA.
243.   vi. WILLIAM NELSON PENDLETON, REV., b. Dec 26, 1809, Richmond, VA; d. Jan 15, 1883, Lexington, Rockbridge Co., VA.
    vii. ROBERT CARTER PENDLETON, b. Sep 14, 1812, VA; d. Apr 28, 1836, Uniontown, PA.
244.   viii. JAMES LAWRENCE PENDLETON, b. 1814, VA; d. Dec 20, 1851, Richmond, VA.
245.   ix. GUERDON HUNTINGDON PENDLETON, b. Apr 07, 1817, Caroline Co., VA; d. Jan 30, 1878, Wythe Co., VA?
    x. EDMUND PENDLETON.

100. SARAH[9] PENDLETON *(EDMUND[8], JOHN[7], HENRY[6], PHILIP[5], HENRY[4], HENRY[3], GEORGE[2], GEORGE[1])* was born 1781, and died 1815. She married DANIEL TURNER Feb 05, 1796.

Children of SARAH PENDLETON and DANIEL TURNER are:
    i. GEORGE PENDLETON[10] TURNER.

246.   ii.   SARAH FRANCES TURNER, b. 1810, Caroline Co., VA; d. Aft. 1860, Richmond Co., VA?

247.   iii. ANNE MADISON TURNER, b. Dec 18, 1811, VA; d. Apr 11, 1892, Port Royal, Caroline Co., VA.

101. ELIZABETH SMITH[9] PENDLETON *(JOHN[8], JOHN[7], HENRY[6], PHILIP[5], HENRY[4], HENRY[3], GEORGE[2], GEORGE[1])* was born Aug 12, 1782, and died Aug 09, 1861. She married SPOTSWOOD LIPSCOMB Jul 06, 1799.

Child of ELIZABETH PENDLETON and SPOTSWOOD LIPSCOMB is:
     i.   CAROLINE[10] LIPSCOMB, b. 1815; d. 1878; m. DR. MILO SMITH; b. 1807; d. 1869, Chatanooga, TN.

102. EDMUND[9] PENDLETON *(HENRY[8], JOHN[7], HENRY[6], PHILIP[5], HENRY[4], HENRY[3], GEORGE[2], GEORGE[1])* was born Oct 24, 1786 in VA, and died Dec 12, 1838 in Louisa Co., VA. He married UNITY YANCY KIMBROUGH Feb 10, 1808 in Louisa Co., VA, daughter of CAPT. JOSEPH KIMBROUGH and ELIZABETH YANCEY. She was born Nov 28, 1787 in VA, and died Dec 23, 1866 in Louisa Co., VA.

The following is from a history of Louisa County (Ref. 69):

Edmund was born at Greenbay, on North East Creek, VA. He was a very prosperous man, and at his death left a large estate. He was a colonel and a member of the county militia, where he received his title. He fought as a captain in the War of 1812 with the Louisa county militia. Later he was a Colonel in the Mexican War. Edmund is listed in the 1810, 1820, and 1830 Louisa Co., VA census records. He is buried in the cemetery close by 'Cuckoo.'

Unity Pendleton is listed in the 1860 Louisa Co., VA census, Fredericks Hall.

Children of EDMUND PENDLETON and UNITY KIMBROUGH are:
248.   i.   MADISON[10] PENDLETON, DR., b. Jan 09, 1809, VA; d. May 18, 1872, Louisa Co., VA.

249.   ii.   JOSEPH KIMBROUGH PENDLETON, b. Dec 05, 1810, VA; d. 1883, Louisa Co, VA?

250.   iii. ELIZABETH KIMBROUGH PENDLETON, b. Jan 09, 1813, VA; d. Dec 1830, Louisa Co., VA.

        iv.   ALCEY ANNE WINSTON PENDLETON, b. Aug 27, 1815, VA; d. Oct 21, 1816.

251.   v.   WILLIAM KIMBROUGH PENDLETON, b. Sep 08, 1817, Yanceyville, VA; d. Sep 01, 1899, Bethany, WV.

252.   vi.   PHILIP BARBOUR PENDLETON, b. Dec 13, 1819, VA; d. Mar 16, 1907, Louisa Co., VA?

        vii. SARAH LOUISA PENDLETON, b. Mar 17, 1822, VA; d. Apr 04, 1844, Louisa Co., VA.

        viii. HENRY PENDLETON, b. Jul 15, 1824, VA; d. Apr 17, 1845.

103. JOHN BICKERTON[9] PENDLETON *(HENRY[8], JOHN[7], HENRY[6], PHILIP[5], HENRY[4], HENRY[3], GEORGE[2], GEORGE[1])* was born Feb 16, 1788 in VA, and died Jun 06, 1840 in Pickens Co., AL. He married ELIZABETH ANN PAULETTE, daughter of RICHARD PAULETTE and CATHERINE SMITH. She was born Abt. 1800 in GA, and died Aft. 1860 in Walker Co., AL?

Eliza A. Pendleton (50) is listed as head of household in the 1850 Franklin Co., AL census.

Children of JOHN PENDLETON and ELIZABETH PAULETTE are:

253. i. MARY OVERTON[10] PENDLETON, b. Aug 05, 1820, AL; d. Aft. 1860, Abeville, SC?
254. ii. HENRY PENDLETON, b. Oct 03, 1822, Pickens Co., AL; d. Jan 13, 1897.
      iii. MARTHA E. PENDLETON, b. Abt. 1833.
      iv. WILLIAM T.W. PENDLETON, b. Abt. 1837.

104. MATILDA WINSTON[9] PENDLETON *(HENRY[8], JOHN[7], HENRY[6], PHILIP[5], HENRY[4], HENRY[3], GEORGE[2], GEORGE[1])* was born Jan 15, 1792 in VA, and died Jul 23, 1840. She married PETER STRACHAN BARRETT Jun 04, 1810 in Louisa Co., VA. He was born 1785, and died 1850.

Children of MATILDA PENDLETON and PETER BARRETT are:

      i. ALEXANDER BUCHANAN[10] BARRETT, b. Mar 18, 1811.
      ii. JOHN BARRETT.
      iii. WILLIAM BARRETT.

105. SARAH "SALLY" MADISON[9] PENDLETON *(HENRY[8], JOHN[7], HENRY[6], PHILIP[5], HENRY[4], HENRY[3], GEORGE[2], GEORGE[1])* was born Oct 06, 1793 in VA, and died 1827. She married PHILIP BICKERTON WINSTON Dec 05, 1811 in Louisa Co., VA. He was born 1786, and died 1853.

Child of SARAH PENDLETON and PHILIP WINSTON is:

      i. WILLIAM OVERTON[10] WINSTON, b. 1812; d. Mar 21, 1862, Richmond, VA; m. SARAH ANN GREGORY; b. Dec 09, 1823; d. Mar 28, 1901, Richmond, VA.

106. BARBARA OVERTON[9] PENDLETON *(HENRY[8], JOHN[7], HENRY[6], PHILIP[5], HENRY[4], HENRY[3], GEORGE[2], GEORGE[1])* was born Jun 04, 1795 in VA, and died Mar 23, 1855. She married WILLIAM BARRETT PHILLIPS Mar 19, 1816 in Louisa Co., VA, son of RICHARD PHILLIPS and ELIZABETH WADDY. He was born Sep 10, 1788 in Louisa Co., VA.

Children of BARBARA PENDLETON and WILLIAM PHILLIPS are:

      i. RICHARD SAMUEL[10] PHILLIPS, b. Abt. 1817.
      ii. ELIZABETH PHILLIPS, b. Abt. 1819.
      iii. MARTHA PENDLETON PHILLIPS, b. Abt. 1821.

107. JOSEPH WINSTON⁹ PENDLETON *(HENRY⁸, JOHN⁷, HENRY⁶, PHILIP⁵, HENRY⁴, HENRY³, GEORGE², GEORGE¹)* was born Jul 31, 1797 in VA, and died 1881 in Whitehall, Louisa Co., VA. He married (1) ELIZABETH MINOR GOODWIN May 15, 1820 in Louisa Co., VA, daughter of HARWOOD GOODWIN and SARAH MINOR. She was born Mar 1800 in VA, and died 1851. He married (2) MARY G. P. She was born Abt. 1816 in VA.

   Joseph Pendleton was an ordained minister of the Baptist Church, 1837. He studied medicine at the Univ. of Maryland where he graduated in 1844. Joseph is listed as a farmer in the 1850 Louisa Co., VA census.

Children of JOSEPH PENDLETON and ELIZABETH GOODWIN are:
     i.   JOHN HARDIN¹⁰ PENDLETON, d. young.
     ii.   SARAH LEWIS PENDLETON, d. young.
255. iii. JOSEPH HENRY PENDLETON, b. 1827, VA; d. 1881, Brooke Co., WV?
256. iv. JOHN OVERTON PENDLETON, b. 1829, VA; d. Aft. 1880, Albemarle Co., VA?
257. v. MARY BURNLEY PENDLETON, b. 1833, VA; d. 1903.
258. vi. ELIZABETH HENLY PENDLETON, b. 1836, VA; d. 1871, Louisa Co., VA?
     vii. LUCY CATHERINE PENDLETON, b. 1838, VA; m. (1) GEORGE W. K. BAYLOR; m. (2) ROBERT KIMBROUGH, DR.

108. THOMAS MADISON⁹ PENDLETON *(HENRY⁸, JOHN⁷, HENRY⁶, PHILIP⁵, HENRY⁴, HENRY³, GEORGE², GEORGE¹)* was born Nov 09, 1804 in Louisa Co., VA, and died Mar 04, 1835. He married LOUISA ANNE JACKSON Apr 24, 1827 in Louisa Co., VA, daughter of ELISHA JACKSON. She was born Abt. 1808 in VA, and died Aft. 1850 in Cumberland Co., VA?

   Louisa A. Pendleton is in the household of Elisha Jackson (62) in the 1850 Cumberland Co., VA census.

Children of THOMAS PENDLETON and LOUISA JACKSON are:
     i.   WILLIAM JAMES¹⁰ PENDLETON.
     ii.   VICTORIA J. PENDLETON, b. Nov 09, 1830, Louisa Co., VA; d. Nov 09, 1830, Louisa Co., VA.
259. iii. ELISHA HENRY PENDLETON, b. Abt. 1835, VA.

109. WILLIAM JAMES⁹ PENDLETON *(HENRY⁸, JOHN⁷, HENRY⁶, PHILIP⁵, HENRY⁴, HENRY³, GEORGE², GEORGE¹)* was born May 31, 1809 in Louisa Co., VA, and died Jan 07, 1872. He married CATHERINE MARY HARRIS Dec 12, 1831 in Louisa Co., VA, daughter of FREDERICK HARRIS and CATHERINE SMITH. She was born 1812 in VA, and died 1864.

   A deed of trust in the year 1835, of William H. W. Luke to Dr. Henry Curtis for the benefit of Frederick Harris (executor of David Bullock) for 158 acres in Hanover County, Virginia bears affidavits of Frederick Harris, George Harris, Dr. William James Pendleton, Benjamin Pollard, and Philip Bickerton Winston (Ref. 122). William is listed as a Physician in the 1850 Louisa Co., VA census.

Children of WILLIAM PENDLETON and CATHERINE HARRIS are:
260.   i.   DAVID HARRIS[10] PENDLETON, DR., b. 1832, Louisa Co., VA; d. Mar 05, 1859, Louisa Co., VA.
        ii. FREDERICK HARRY PENDLETON, b. 1836, Louisa Co., VA; d. Jan 17, 1894.
             This is likely the F. H. Pendleton (manager, 23) listed in the 1860 Henderson Co., KY census in the household of merchant, Alexander B. Barrett.

261.   iii. JULIANA PENDLETON, b. May 13, 1839, Louisa Co., VA; d. May 12, 1926, Cuckoo, Louisa Co., VA?
        iv. ALICE WINSTON PENDLETON, b. 1843, Louisa Co., VA; d. 1877; m. WALLER OVERTON, 1860; b. Nov 17, 1838, Fayette Co., KY; d. Aft. 1887.
             The following account is from a history of Kentucky (Ref. 123).

             Waller Overton, cashier of the German National Bank, of Newport, Ky., is a native of Fayette County, Ky., and was born November 17, 1838, a son of Dabney Caw and Eliza (Harris) Overton, who were natives, respectively, of Fayette County, Ky., and Louisa County, Va. Walter Overton, the grandfather of our subject, settled near Lexington, Ky, very early in the history of the State. The family is of English and Welsh origin. Dabney C. Overton was a graduate of both law and medicine, but was a farmer by occupation. He took a great interest in his son's education, who was reared on the farm, but who, after a four-years' course at Bethany College, West Virginia, graduated at that institution. He served in the Confederate Army as adjutant of the Second Kentucky Battalion Cavalry, all through the war. He settled in Newport in 1868, and in 1882 assisted in organizing the German National Bank, successor to James Taylor & Sons, of which bank Samuel Show is president and Mr. Overton is cashier. The bank has a capital of $100,000, with $22,000 surplus, and an average deposit of $350,000. In 1870 he married Miss Alice Winston Pendleton, of Louisa County, Va., who died in 1877. Mr. Overton is a Royal Arch Mason, and a gentleman of rare business attainments.

110. FRANCES SAMUELLA[9] PENDLETON (*HENRY[8], JOHN[7], HENRY[6], PHILIP[5], HENRY[4], HENRY[3], GEORGE[2], GEORGE[1]*) was born Sep 07, 1816 in VA, and died Feb 06, 1856 in Albemarle Co., VA? She married WILLIAM WHITE TOMPKINS May 24, 1837 in Albemarle Co., VA. He was born Abt. 1815 in VA, and died Aft. 1860 in Orange Co., VA?

Children of FRANCES PENDLETON and WILLIAM TOMPKINS are:
        i.   HENRY P.[10] TOMPKINS, b. Abt. 1838, VA.
        ii. ALEXANDER C. TOMPKINS, b. Abt. 1839, VA.
        iii. JOHN C. TOMPKINS, b. Abt. 1842, VA.
        iv. JOSEPH B. TOMPKINS, b. 1850, VA.

111. REUBEN[9] PENDLETON *(BENJAMIN[8], WILLIAM[7], JOHN[6], PHILIP[5], HENRY[4], HENRY[3], GEORGE[2], GEORGE[1])* was born Abt. 1777 in VA, and died Mar 03, 1860 in Rye Cove, Scott Co., VA. He married (1) PATIENCE GUTHRIE, daughter of DANIEL GUTHRIE and JANE NASH? She was born Abt. 1780, and died Abt. 1840 in Scott Co., VA. He married (2) RACHEL MORRIS Nov 14, 1840 in Scott Co., VA. She was born Abt. 1779 in VA, and died Jun 1860 in Scott Co., VA.

Reuben Pendleton is listed in the 1810 Russell Co., VA census and the 1820, 1830, and 1840 Scott Co. Census records. In the 1850 Scott Co., VA census he is listed at age 72 and with no occupation; Rachael Pendleton (72) is included in his household. The following is from the 1860 Mortality Schedule Scott Co., VA: "Pendleton, Rachel, Age 61, White, Born in VA, died in June, Occupation: Spinster, Disease: Old Age, Days ill: 15."

Children of REUBEN PENDLETON and PATIENCE GUTHRIE are (Ref. 124):
262.   i.   FRANCES[10] PENDLETON, b. Sep 25, 1804, Rye Cove, Scott Co., VA; d. Aug 16, 1852.
263.   ii.   IRA NASH PENDLETON, b. 1805, Scott Co., VA; d. Abt. 1850.
264.   iii. SAMUEL GUTHRIE PENDLETON, b. 1807; d. Jan 09, 1837, Scott Co., VA.
265.   iv.   REBECCA PENDLETON, b. 1812, VA.
        v.   ELISHA PENDLETON, b. 1815.
              This is likely the Elisha Pendleton (32) in the 1850 Hawkins Co., District 7, TN census with wife Alice (32) and children Enoch (4), and Creed (3).

266.   vi.   ENOCH PENDLETON, b. 1815, Scott Co., VA.
        vii. JAMES PENDLETON, b. 1817.

112. JAMES A.[9] PENDLETON *(BENJAMIN[8], WILLIAM[7], JOHN[6], PHILIP[5], HENRY[4], HENRY[3], GEORGE[2], GEORGE[1])* was born 1779 in VA, and died 1848 in Scott Co., VA? He married POLLY CONN Abt. 1800. She was born Bet. 1780 - 1785.

Like his brother Reuben, James Pendleton is listed in the 1810 Russell Co., VA and 1820, 1830 and 1840 Scott Co., VA census records.

Children of JAMES PENDLETON and POLLY CONN are (Ref. 125):
267.   i.   SARAH "SALLY"[10] PENDLETON, b. 1801, VA; d. Aft. 1850.
268.   ii.   JOHN L. PENDLETON, b. 1802, Russell Co., VA; d. May 17, 1868, Scott Co., VA.
269.   iii. JEMIMA PENDLETON, b. 1804, VA; d. Aft. 1870, Scott Co., VA?
270.   iv.   MARY "MOLLY" PENDLETON, b. 1810, VA; d. Feb 26, 1903, Scott Co., VA.
271.   v.   JAMES A. PENDLETON, JR., b. Abt. 1816, VA; d. 1880.
        vi.   ALICE PENDLETON.
        vii. IVY PENDLETON.
        viii. ROBERT PENDLETON.

113. MARY "POLLY"[9] PENDLETON *(BENJAMIN[8], WILLIAM[7], JOHN[6], PHILIP[5], HENRY[4], HENRY[3], GEORGE[2], GEORGE[1])* was born Abt. 1787 in Russell Co., VA, and died Jul 04, 1852 in Morgan Co., KY. She married JESSE WILSON CONN. He was born 1788 in VA, and died Abt. 1868 in Morgan Co., KY.

Children of MARY PENDLETON and JESSE CONN are (Ref. 126):

    i. MARGARET[10] CONN, b. Abt. 1807, VA; m. JACOB MOSLEY, May 19, 1822, Scott Co., VA.

    ii. JOHN CONN, b. 1808, Russell Co., VA; d. Jackson Co., OH?; m. (1) URSULA CARTER, Nov 22, 1824, Scott Co., VA; b. Abt. 1810, Russell Co., VA; d. Abt. 1852, Morgan Co., KY; m. (2) RACHEL MELISSA BRYANT, Dec 22, 1853, Morgan Co., KY.

    iii. CYNTHIA CONN, b. 1812, Russell Co., VA; d. Aft. 1880, Elliott Co., KY; m. GEORGE WASHINGTON CARTER, Jun 07, 1829, Scott Co., VA; b. Dec 08, 1807, VA; d. Aft. Apr 09, 1885, KY.

    iv. SAMUEL CONN, b. 1812; m. ORISSAVILLA FOWLER.

    v. JAMES CONN, b. Abt. 1814, VA; m. (1) SARAH; m. (2) KESIAH REBECCA LANE, Mar 05, 1835, Scott Co., VA; b. Abt. 1819, VA.

    vi. CATHERINE CONN, b. 1817, Scott Co., VA; d. 1880, KY; m. DAVID LANE, Abt. 1835, Scott Co., VA; b. 1813, Scott Co., VA; d. 1880.

    vii. REUBEN HARRISON CONN, b. 1819, VA; d. Bef. 1900, KY; m. ELIZABETH ROSE, Abt. 1845, VA; b. Mar 1823, VA; d. Aft. 1900, KY.

    viii. JESSE WILSON CONN, JR., b. Jan 1822, VA; d. Aft. 1900, Elliott Co., KY; m. EMERINE HUNTER, Apr 03, 1850, Morgan Co., KY; b. Jan 1822, KY; d. Aft. 1900, Elliott Co., KY.

    ix. JOSIAH CONN, b. 1825, Scott Co., VA; d. Aft. 1900, Elliott Co., KY; m. (1) FRANCES BARNETT, Oct 23, 1853, Morgan Co., KY; b. 1823, VA; m. (2) JULIEANN WEBB, Feb 25, 1858, Morgan Co., KY; b. Abt. 1837, KY.

    x. LUCINDA CONN, b. 1825, Scott Co., VA; m. WILLIAM J. JENKINS; b. 1820, VA.

    xi. ANDREW JACKSON CONN, b. Abt. 1836, VA; d. Aft. 1910; m. (1) SARAH JANE FLANNERY, Mar 28, 1861, Morgan Co., KY; b. Abt. 1838, Morgan Co., KY; m. (2) ROSA ELLEN GOODMAN, Abt. 1875, KY; b. Mar 1858, KY; d. Aft. 1910.

    xii. ELIZABETH CONN, b. Abt. 1838, Scott Co., VA; m. WILLIAM MORGAN BARNETT, Apr 02, 1855, Morgan Co., KY; b. Abt. 1833, Russell Co., VA.

114. JOHN[9] PENDLETON *(BENJAMIN[8], WILLIAM[7], JOHN[6], PHILIP[5], HENRY[4], HENRY[3], GEORGE[2], GEORGE[1])* was born Abt. 1788 in Russell Co., VA, and died Oct 11, 1861 in Collin Co., TX. He married JEMIMA KILGORE, daughter of WILLIAM KILGORE and VIRGINIA JANE OSBORNE. She was born Sep 14, 1794 in VA, and died May 28, 1868 in Collin Co., TX?

    Like his brothers Reuben and James, John Pendleton is listed in the 1810 Russell Co., VA and the 1820, 1830 and 1840 Scott Co. census records. In 1850 he is listed as age 52 in the Lee Co., VA census along with Jemima (50) and their youngest 7 children. He is included in the 1860 Collins Co. census, Farmersville P.O., a year before his death.

Children of JOHN PENDLETON and JEMIMA KILGORE are (Refs. 127 and 128):

272. i. MALINDA A.[10] PENDLETON, b. Dec 21, 1810, VA; d. Sep 10, 1861.

273. ii. WILLIAM GAINES PENDLETON, b. 1813, VA; d. May 11, 1875, TX.

274. iii. HIRAM KILGORE PENDLETON, b. Feb 16, 1815, Scott Co., VA; d. Nov 01, 1888, Scott Co., VA.

275. iv. IVY TAYLOR PENDLETON, b. 1817, VA; d. Aft. 1880, Owsley Co., KY?

276. v. ISAAC NEWTON PENDLETON, b. 1819, VA; d. Aft. 1880, Jack Co., TX?

277. vi. JANE PENDLETON, b. 1821, VA; d. 1879, Scott Co., VA?

278. vii. JOHN CRAIG PENDLETON, b. Jul 27, 1826, VA; d. Dec 22, 1910, Collin Co., TX?

279. viii. ELIZA PENDLETON, b. 1829, VA; d. 1897.

280. ix. ANDREW JACKSON PENDLETON, b. Sep 19, 1832, VA; d. Feb 02, 1900, Scott Co., VA?

281. x. ALLISON OSBORN PENDLETON, b. Oct 25, 1832, Rye Cove, Scott Co., VA; d. Nov 10, 1914, Coryell Co., TX.

282. xi. MINERVA JEMIMA PENDLETON, b. 1835, Scott Co., VA; d. Mar 01, 1907.

xii. SARAH ELIZABETH PENDLETON, b. 1837, Scott Co., VA; d. Dec 26, 1886, Lander (Fremont), WY; m. ANDREW JOSEPH GAYLOR, Oct 12, 1867; b. 1848, TX.

283. xiii. MELVIN C. PENDLETON, b. 1840, VA.

115. ELIZABETH[9] PENDLETON (*JAMES[8], WILLIAM[7], JOHN[6], PHILIP[5], HENRY[4], HENRY[3], GEORGE[2], GEORGE[1]*) was born Dec 19, 1787, and died May 17, 1839. She married WILLIAM MCDANIEL Jan 26, 1801 in Amherst Co., VA, son of JOHN MCDANIEL and MARGARET RUCKER. He was born Feb 22, 1774, and died Jun 19, 1857.

Children of ELIZABETH PENDLETON and WILLIAM MCDANIEL are:

i. SALLY RUCKER[10] MCDANIEL, b. Jul 06, 1802; d. Oct 03, 1827; m. JOHN MEYERS, Oct 16, 1817.

ii. MARGARET MCDANIEL, b. Oct 26, 1804; d. Oct 01, 1820.

iii. KATHERINE MCDANIEL, b. Mar 27, 1807; m. NATHAN GLENN.

iv. JAMES PENDLETON MCDANIEL, b. Jun 19, 1809; d. Jul 28, 1877; m. MARY GLENN, 1832.

v. ELIZABETH MCDANIEL, b. May 30, 1811; m. L. OGDEN.

vi. JOHN RUCKER MCDANIEL, b. Jan 02, 1813; m. ELIZABETH THURMAN, 1837.

vii. JANE MCDANIEL, b. Feb 29, 1816; d. May 17, 1871.

viii. WILLIAM MCDANIEL, b. Sep 03, 1817; m. MARY THURMAN.

ix. LINDSAY MCDANIEL, b. Jul 25, 1819; m. MARTHA GLENN.

x. MARY ANNE MCDANIEL, b. Feb 22, 1821; d. died young.

xi. PHILIP B. MCDANIEL, b. May 10, 1824.

xii. SOPHIE BURRUS MCDANIEL, b. May 04, 1827; d. Feb 15, 1889; m. HARDWAY TURNER, 1848; b. 1819; d. 1887.

xiii. EDWARD JACKSON MCDANIEL, b. Mar 14, 1829; d. Oct 05, 1832.

116. JOHN^9 PENDLETON *(EDMUND^8, WILLIAM^7, JOHN^6, PHILIP^5, HENRY^4, HENRY^3, GEORGE^2, GEORGE^1)* was born 1777 in VA, and died Aug 1860 in Cannon Co. TN. He married RACHEL LUCAS Feb 04, 1813. She was born Dec 10, 1796 in NC, and died Aft. 1860 in Cannon Co. TN?

"In May, 1836, John Pendleton and 25 others, all bearing commissions as justices, met at the house of Henry d. McBroom, which was the old hotel, in Woodbury, for the purpose of organizing the [Cannon] county court" (Ref. 129). In the 1850, Cannon Co. census he is listed as a farmer (72) along with Rachel (55), Sarah, William, and Edmund H. The following entry is found in the TN Mortality Schedule of Aug 1860: "John Pendleton, Cannon Co., TN, 75, Male, Fever, Farmer." Rachel, Sarah, E. H. (Edmund) and Mary Pendleton are listed in the 1860 Cannon Co., TN census.

Children of JOHN PENDLETON and RACHEL LUCAS are (Ref. 130):

284.   i.   MARY LUCAS^{10} PENDLETON, b. Feb 13, 1814, TN; d. Aft. 1870, De Kalb Co., TN?
285.   ii.   JAMES LUCAS PENDLETON, b. Dec 23, 1815, TN; d. Aft. 1860.
286.   iii.   MARGARET PENDLETON, b. May 26, 1817, TN.
287.   iv.   ELIZABETH PENDLETON, b. Mar 28, 1819, Cannon Co., TN.
        v.   SARAH PENDLETON, b. Oct 21, 1821, Cannon Co., TN; d. Aft. 1860, Cannon Co., TN?
288.   vi.   SAMUEL L. PENDLETON, b. Sep 07, 1822, Warren Co., TN; d. 1900, Hill Co., TX.
289.   vii.   BENJAMIN PENDLETON, b. Jan 14, 1824, TN.
290.   viii.   JOHN F. PENDLETON, b. May 27, 1826, TN; d. Aft. 1870, Cannon Co., TN?
        ix.   LORENE PENDLETON, b. Jul 04, 1828, TN.
        x.   MALINDA PENDLETON, b. Mar 10, 1830, TN; m. CHARLES WEST, Oct 07, 1848, Cannon Co., TN.
291.   xi.   WILLIAM G. PENDLETON, b. Jul 15, 1832, Cannon Co., TN; d. Abt. 1920, Coffee Co., TN.
        xii.   EDMUND H. PENDLETON, b. Nov 19, 1835, TN; m. MARY; b. Abt. 1843, TN.

117. BENJAMIN^9 PENDLETON *(EDMUND^8, WILLIAM^7, JOHN^6, PHILIP^5, HENRY^4, HENRY^3, GEORGE^2, GEORGE^1)* was born 1784 in Russell Co., VA, and died 1856 in Christian Co., MO. He married ANN (ELKINS) BROWN Abt. 1814, daughter of GABRIEL ELKINS and STACY DILLARD. She was born Abt. 1795 in NC?, and died Aft. 1860 in Christian Co., MO?

Benjamin Pendleton served in a regiment commanded by Col. Stephen Copeland and in the company led by Captain William Douglass, one of the Tennessee units that participated in the War of 1812. He is found in the 1840 Cannon Co., TN census along with his brother, John. He moved to Missouri about 1851. Letters of Administrations were issued on 5 December 1856 to Thomas Pendleton for the estate of Benjamin Pendleton. Bond was given by Thomas D. Pendleton, A.A. Pendleton and C. Roberts in Greene Co., MO (Ref. 131).

Children of BENJAMIN PENDLETON and ANN BROWN are (Ref. 130):

292.   i.   EDMUND[10] PENDLETON, b. May 23, 1815, Cannon Co., TN; d. Mar 11, 1868, TX.

293.   ii.   THOMAS DILLARD PENDLETON, b. 1819, TN; d. Oct 13, 1862, On the Mississippi between AR and MO.

294.   iii.   ANDREW JACKSON PENDLETON, b. Mar 04, 1821, TN; d. Mar 07, 1910, Christian Co., MO?

      iv.   BENJAMIN D. PENDLETON, b. Sep 26, 1822, TN; d. Aug 13, 1863, TN.

          B. Pendleton (28), born in TN, is included in the 1850 census, Precinct 1, Cass Co., TX in the household of an Inn Keeper. This is surely the Benjamin Pendleton buried in the Leeville Graveyard, Wilson Co., TN along with Mrs. Gelie Pendleton, Sept. 5, 1836-June 7, 1917, presumably his wife.

295.   v.   STACY CAROLINE PENDLETON, b. Abt. 1825, TN; d. 1853, Christian Co., MO.

296.   vi.   JOSEPH PENDLETON, b. Abt. 1827, TN; d. Aft. 1880, Gonzales, TX?

297.   vii.   MARY JANE PENDLETON, b. Jan 10, 1828, TN; d. Dec 31, 1906, Christian Co., MO.

      viii.   KATHERINE PENDLETON, b. 1831, TN; m. GEORGE M. DARDEN, Cannon Co., TN?; b. 1831, TN.

298.   ix.   DILLARD PENDLETON, b. 1834, TN; d. Mar 22, 1885.

118. NANCY[9] PENDLETON (*REUBEN[8], WILLIAM[7], JOHN[6], PHILIP[5], HENRY[4], HENRY[3], GEORGE[2], GEORGE[1]*) She married JAMES WARE, CAPT. Dec 13, 1800 in Amherst Co., VA.

Children of NANCY PENDLETON and JAMES WARE are:

      i.   JAMES D.[10] WARE, d. Feb 1854, Hinds Co., MS.

          The will of James D. Ware of Hinds County, MS., was signed by him on Nov. 18, 1853 and probated Feb. 1854: "To Dr. M. [Micajah] Pendleton's two daughters, Susan and Sarah, living in Rockbridge County, Va., I bequeath a debt me from their father of $1000, it being a draft Dr. Pendleton drew on me. This amount I desire him to pay the two girls without interest in the lifetime of the Doctor, if he should feel able to do so; if not, to be paid them from his estate after his death."

      ii.   M. PENDLETON WARE.

      iii.   WILLIAM A. WARE.

      iv.   A. H. WARE.

      v.   GARLAND P. WARE.

      vi.   K. S. WARE.

      vii.   MARY WARE, m. EUBANKS.

      viii.   ANN WARE, m. PEEBLES.

      ix.   JOHN D. WARE.

      x.   MANSFIELD WARE.

119. JANE GARLAND[9] PENDLETON *(REUBEN[8], WILLIAM[7], JOHN[6], PHILIP[5], HENRY[4], HENRY[3], GEORGE[2], GEORGE[1])* was born Abt. 1787 in VA, and died Abt. 1822 in Nelson Co., VA. She married (1) BENJAMIN POWELL Oct 28, 1811 in Nelson Co., VA, son of BENJAMIN POWELL and JANE COOPER. He was born Abt. 1785 in Nelson Co., VA, and died Aug 15, 1822 in Nelson Co., VA. She married (2) CORNELIUS CROW Jun 17, 1822 in Amherst Co., VA.

Children of JANE PENDLETON and BENJAMIN POWELL are (Ref. 132):

     i. FREDERICK GROVER[10] POWELL, b. Abt. 1812, Nelson Co., VA; m. LOUISA SANDERS; b. Abt. 1828.

     ii. JANE POWELL, b. Abt. 1814, Nelson Co., VA; d. Abt. 1822, Nelson Co., VA.

120. WILLIAM GARLAND[9] PENDLETON *(REUBEN[8], WILLIAM[7], JOHN[6], PHILIP[5], HENRY[4], HENRY[3], GEORGE[2], GEORGE[1])* was born Apr 02, 1788 in VA, and died Feb 1839 in Lynchburg, VA. He married MARY GLENN ALEXANDER Dec 23, 1813 in Campbell Co., VA, daughter of ROBERT ALEXANDER and NANCY AUSTIN. She was born Oct 03, 1793 in Campbell Co., VA?, and died Jan 19, 1871 in Richmond, VA?

William G. Pendleton is listed in the 1810 Henrico Co., VA census, Richmond City. William G. Pendleton, Richmond, is listed May 14, 1834 with 1,325 acres along the Virginia? watercourse (Ref. 133). He served as Proctor of the University of Virginia during the 1830's. His obituary appeared in the Lynchburg Virginian and Richmond Whig on Feb. 8, 1839: "Died on Friday at the Washington Hotel in Lynchburg, William G. Pendleton in his 52nd year. A lawyer, he served as Register in the Land Office and afterwards Clerk of the Old Chancery Court in Richmond." Mary Pendleton (77) is listed in the 1870 Richmond, VA census in the household of her son, Stephen.

Children of WILLIAM PENDLETON and MARY ALEXANDER are:

299.   i. FRANCES ANN[10] PENDLETON, b. Nov 03, 1814, VA; d. Aft. 1880, Henry Co., VA?

     ii. CHARLOTTE ADELAIDE SMITH PENDLETON, b. Jan 20, 1817, VA; d. Aug 20, 1817.

300.   iii. ALEXANDER GARLAND PENDLETON, b. Mar 27, 1819, VA; d. Feb 16, 1865, Montgomery Co., MD?

301.   iv. MARY JANE PENDLETON, b. May 30, 1821, VA; d. Aft. 1870, NJ?

     v. ALGERNON SYDNEY PENDLETON, b. Oct 06, 1823, VA; d. Oct 17, 1824.

     vi. CHARLOTTE AUSTIN PENDLETON, b. Oct 06, 1825, VA; d. Aft. 1880, Henry Co., VA?

       Charlotte Pendleton is listed in the 1860 census in the household of Robert (physician) and Frances Read, her sister. Charlotte Pendleton (41; teacher) is listed in the 1870 Horse Pasture, Henry Co., VA census.

302.   vii. STEPHEN TAYLOR PENDLETON, b. Oct 18, 1828, VA; d. 1915, Richmond, VA?

303.   viii. WILLIAM DOUGLAS PENDLETON, b. Dec 13, 1831, VA.

121. JAMES SHEPHERD[9] PENDLETON *(REUBEN[8], WILLIAM[7], JOHN[6], PHILIP[5], HENRY[4], HENRY[3], GEORGE[2], GEORGE[1])* was born Abt. 1795 in VA, and died 1851 in CA. He married CATHERINE ALDRIDGE Nov 30, 1815. She was born 1802 in Amherst Co., VA, and died 1838.

James S. Pendleton was an ensign in the War of 1812 from Amherst Co. He is said to have moved to California later. A James S. Pendleton, however, is listed in the 1820 through 1840 Amherst Co., VA census records.

Children of JAMES PENDLETON and CATHERINE ALDRIDGE are:

304.　　i.　ROBERT ALDRIDGE[10] PENDLETON, b. 1818, VA; d. 1892, Amherst, VA?

　　　ii.　ANNA MARIA PENDLETON, b. 1820; d. 1843.

305.　　iii.　WILLIAM GARLAND PENDLETON, b. Jun 22, 1820, VA; d. Jun 22, 1874, Union Co., AR?

　　　iv.　ADELAIDE PENDLETON, b. 1822, VA; d. Aft. 1880, Lynchburg, VA?
　　　　　Adelaide Pendleton is listed in the Robert A. Coghill (28) household in the1850 Amherst Co., VA census along with Jane Aldridge (64) ($10,000) and in the William Rose household (with her sister Eliza Pendleton Rose) in the 1860 census, Amherst Co., VA.

306.　　v.　JAMES SHEPHERD PENDLETON, b. 1823, New Glasgow, VA; d. 1877, Lynchburg, VA.

307.　　vi.　ELIZA JANE PENDLETON, b. Abt. 1827, VA; d. Aft. 1880, Lynchburg, VA?

122. MICAJAH[9] PENDLETON *(REUBEN[8], WILLIAM[7], JOHN[6], PHILIP[5], HENRY[4], HENRY[3], GEORGE[2], GEORGE[1])* was born 1796 in VA, and died Oct 1861 in Botetourt Co., VA? He married (1) LOUISA JANE DAVIS Sep 20, 1822 in Amherst Co., VA, daughter of JAMES DAVIS and SALLIE DUDLEY RAGLAND. She was born Dec 20, 1806 in Amherst Co., VA, and died Sep 02, 1840 in Amherst Co., VA. He married (2) MARY ANNE CARPER Apr 25, 1844 in Botetourt Co., VA, daughter of BENJAMIN CARPER. She was born Dec 12, 1821 in Botetourt Co., VA?, and died 1890 in Floyd Co., VA?

Micajah Pendleton is included in the 1830 Amherst Co., VA census as well as the 1840 Botetourt Co., VA census. He is listed as a physician, age 55, in the 1850 Botetourt Co., 8th district, census along with Mary A., age 28, his second wife, and his children Susan (17), Sarah (15), and William (4). This family is also listed in the 1860 Botetourt Co., VA census. The Virginia Historical Society Catalog lists the following Rare Book: "Constitution and by-laws of Micajah Pendleton Division, no. 410: Sons of Temperance, instituted at Elk Union Church, Amherst, February 8th, 1851" published in Lynchburg.

Mary Anne is listed in a Virginia Land Grant: "Mary Ann Pendleton, 1 Sep, 1856 Botetourt Co. 220 acres. Grants 112, p. 770."

Children of MICAJAH PENDLETON and LOUISA DAVIS are:

308.　　i.　EDMUND[10] PENDLETON, b. Sep 29, 1823, Amherst Co., VA; d. Jun 26, 1899, Lexington, Rockbridge Co., VA.

309.　ii.　ANNE GARLAND PENDLETON, b. Sep 15, 1826, VA; d. Dec 31, 1905, Botetourt Co., VA.

310.　iii.　JAMES DUDLEY PENDLETON, b. 1829, VA; d. 1907, Powhatan Co., VA?

　　　iv.　SUSAN FRANCES PENDLETON, b. 1832, VA; d. Aft. 1880, Rockbridge Co., VA?

　　　　　Susan Pendleton is listed in the household of her sister, Anne G. Brugh (farmer), in the 1860 Botetourt Co., VA census. Susan and her sister Sarah (Sally) both of Rockbridge Co., VA are included in the will of their uncle James Ware.

311.　v.　SALLY DUDLEY RAGLAND PENDLETON, b. Mar 18, 1834, Botetourt Co., VA; d. Feb 16, 1918.

Children of MICAJAH PENDLETON and MARY CARPER are:

312.　vi.　WILLIAM F.[10] PENDLETON, b. Mar 1847, VA; d. 1916, Floyd Co., VA?

　　　vii.　CHARLES B. PENDLETON, b. Aft. 1850, VA; d. young.

313.　viii.　ELIZABETH PENDLETON, b. Mar 30, 1853, VA; d. Apr 04, 1889.

314.　ix.　WALTER PENDLETON, b. Mar 07, 1855, Botetourt Co., VA; d. Mar 16, 1921, Havana, Cuba.

　　　x.　LOUISA PENDLETON, b. Abt. 1857, VA; m. ZACHARY TAYLOR DORVINS.

123. ELIZABETH JANE[9] PENDLETON *(REUBEN[8], WILLIAM[7], JOHN[6], PHILIP[5], HENRY[4], HENRY[3], GEORGE[2], GEORGE[1])* was born 1802, and died 1860. She married WILLIAM WALLER SCOTT Feb 25, 1819 in Amherst Co., VA, son of WILLIAM SCOTT and ANN JONES. He was born 1795, and died 1874.

"Walter Scott was married on Thursday evening, 25 Feb 1819, to the amiable Miss Eliza Pendleton of Amherst County" (Ref. 134). Mrs. Elizabeth Pendleton Scott Clark, granddaughter of William and Elizabeth Pendleton Scott was a member of The National Society of the Daughters of the American Revolution (Volume 39, page 114).

Children of ELIZABETH PENDLETON and WILLIAM SCOTT are:

　　　i.　FRANCES ANN[10] SCOTT, m. GEORGE DAMERON, Nov 24, 1852.

　　　ii.　HUGH ROY SCOTT, m. (1) JANE CARY HARRISON; m. (2) ANNA MARAGARET SCOTT.

　　　iii.　MARY CAMDEN SCOTT, m. C.C. WINGFIELD.

　　　iv.　WILLIAM PRESTON SCOTT, b. Abt. 1820; m. FRANCES J. TINSLEY, Feb 22, 1848, Amherst Co., VA.

　　　v.　JAMES PENDLETON SCOTT, b. 1826; m. JENNIE KIRKPATRICK.

　　　vi.　ROBERT GARLAND SCOTT, b. Nov 29, 1830, VA; d. Dec 14, 1909, VA; m. (1) IDA ETHEL BAILEY; m. (2) SARAH SHELTON, Nov 30, 1859, VA; b. Aug 15, 1844, VA; d. Nov 05, 1883, VA.

　　　vii.　EDWARD WALLER SCOTT, b. Nov 16, 1848, Amherst Co., VA; d. Mar 26, 1900; m. IDA GERTRUDE FLETCHER, Dec 16, 1874.

124. SARAH[9] PENDLETON *(RICHARD[8], WILLIAM[7], JOHN[6], PHILIP[5], HENRY[4], HENRY[3], GEORGE[2], GEORGE[1])* was born Mar 06, 1792 in Nelson Co., VA, and died Jun 17, 1876 in Amherst Co., VA. She married GEORGE JONES Mar 16, 1816 in Amherst Co., VA.

Sarah Jones is listed in the Nelson Co., VA Death Register: "Jones, Sarah, white, female, died June 17, 1876, Amherst Co., Old Age, age 84 years, 3 months, and 11 days; parents: Richard & Mary Pendleton, b. Nelson Co., Married." Mrs. Annie Pendleton Shepherd Darragh, Gr.-granddaughter of George Jones and Sarah Pendleton, his wife, is included as a member of The National Society of the Daughters of the American Revolution (Volume 42, page 49).

Child of SARAH PENDLETON and GEORGE JONES is:
    i.   PAULINE[10] JONES, m. SHELTON WRIGHT.

125. JAMES[9] PENDLETON *(RICHARD[8], WILLIAM[7], JOHN[6], PHILIP[5], HENRY[4], HENRY[3], GEORGE[2], GEORGE[1])* was born 1793 in VA, and died 1851 in Warren Co., MO. He married FRANCES NARCISSA "NANCY" SHARP Oct 28, 1816 in Campbell Co., VA. She was born Abt. 1799 in VA, and died Aft. 1850 in Warren Co., MO?

James Pendleton and Nancy Sharp settled in Warren Co., MO in 1833. James C. Pendleton is listed in Missouri Land Patents in Warren Co. dated May 1, 1833 and Jan 1, 1846. He is found in the 1840 Warren Co., MO census, Hickary, p. 166.

Children of JAMES PENDLETON and FRANCES SHARP are (Ref. 135):
315.   i.   ROBERT H.[10] PENDLETON, b. Nov 01, 1817, VA; d. Bef. 1870, Warren Co., MO.
    ii. FRANCES PENDLETON, b. Abt. 1820; m. CHARLES C. ALLEN.
        Charles C. [Allen] married Fanny Pendleton and they had but two children (Ref. 118).

316.   iii. LUCY JANE PENDLETON, b. Abt. 1822, VA.
    iv. PATRICK W. PENDLETON, b. Abt. 1824, VA.
        Patrick W. Pendleton, tobacconist, is listed in the 1850 St. Charles Co., MO census, pg. 90.

317.   v. JAMES LEWIS PENDLETON, b. Dec 1828, VA; d. Aft. 1900, Warren Co., MO?
    vi. SUSAN B. PENDLETON, b. Abt. 1829, VA; m. GEORGE A. KENNER, Nov 19, 1850, Warren Co., MO; b. Abt. 1818, VA; d. Aft. 1860, Warren Co., MO?
        G.A. Kenner, hotel keeper, is listed in the 1860 Warren Co., MO census.

    vii. ELIZABETH H. PENDLETON, b. Abt. 1831, VA; m. TINSLEY.
318. viii. GEORGE W. PENDLETON, b. Abt. 1834, VA.
    ix. CAROLINE PENDLETON, b. Abt. 1836, VA.

126. WILLIAM[9] PENDLETON *(RICHARD[8], WILLIAM[7], JOHN[6], PHILIP[5], HENRY[4], HENRY[3], GEORGE[2], GEORGE[1])* was born Abt. 1800 in Amherst Co., VA, and died Abt. 1838 in Osage Co., MO. He married FLORENTINE S.D. ISBELL Jul 30, 1821 in Amherst Co., VA, daughter of ZACHARIAH ISBELL and SARAH DABNEY. She was born Abt. 1807 in Amherst Co., VA, and died Aug 07, 1856 in Osage Co., MO.

The following account is provided by a descendant (Ref. 136). However, the assertion that this William is the son of William and Pattsey Pendleton is likely a mistake. It is more likely that this William is the son of Richard and Mary Tinsley Pendleton.

William Jr., son of William and Pattsey, was born about 1800 in Virginia. On July 30, 1821 he married Florentine S.D. Isbell. This was in Amherst County, Virginia. The next reference to William and Florentine, is that their son, William said that they arrived in Missouri about 1836. With their four sons, William, Zachariah, George, Richard and daughter, Frances, they settled in Gasconade County, Missouri.

Frances was the oldest child, about fourteen at this time, and little Richard was only seven. This area to which they had come was rich farming land along the Osage River. The journey had stopped at Castle Rock, in what was then Gasconade County, Missouri. This was near the mouth of the Osage River, a little below Sugar Creek. A little village sprang up here. It was first called McKnight, later Isbell Station, or just Isbell. After the long trek from Virginia, William's family and the other pioneer families must have been pleased to settle here. No virgin land was left, so these settlers had to homestead the land; make improvements on it to establish permanent residence. Houses and barns needed to be built, field cleared and the coming year's crops to be planted to supply the staple of life.

William died within two years of his arrival in Missouri. He is thought to be buried at McKnight or Osage City. No marker can be found. His wife, the former Florentine Isbell, was only thirty-two years old, with five minor children in This "sort of wilderness", making it next to impossible to provide for them alone. No record of land registered in his name was found. Apparently this young family had not had time to establish a claim.

What was to become of William's family in Missouri? Luckily, Zachariah Isbell, Florentine's brother, came to their rescue. In the 1840 census of Osage County, Missouri, we find Zachariah and other family members living on adjoining farms, indicating they may have arrived about the same time, or as a group. Most likely they travelled by wagon caravan.

On May 6, 1839, Zachariah Isbell appeared at the county court held at Mt. Sterling, Gasconade County, Missouri, to apply for guardianship of the five "Pendleton infants." Records show that this was approved and ordered to be put on record. A bond of $600 was furnished by Davis S. Woody. Seems he did not bother to transfer this until the boys were coming to the age of maturity. It would now be necessary to 'touch all legal bases'

In the Amherst County, Va. will book, dated June 16, 1821, there is a guardian bond which reads: "Bond in sum of $10,000. William Pendleton will pay and deliver unto Florentine S.D. Isbell, orphan of Zach Isbell, deceased, when she shall obtain lawful age. She was then 13 or 14 years old."

Children of WILLIAM PENDLETON and FLORENTINE ISBELL are:
319.　　i.　WILLIAM[10] PENDLETON, b. Nov 1822, VA; d. Aft. 1900, Cole Co., MO?

320. ii. FRANCES PENDLETON, b. Abt. 1824, Amherst Co., VA; d. Feb 20, 1897, Maries Co., MO.

321. iii. ZACHARIAH PENDLETON, b. 1824, Amherst Co., VA; d. Aug 02, 1865, MO.

322. iv. GEORGE WASHINGTON PENDLETON, b. Oct 1825, Amherst Co., VA; d. Sep 30, 1908, Osage Co., MO.

323. v. JAMES RICHARD PENDLETON, b. 1828, Amherst Co., VA; d. Abt. 1860, MO.

127. MALINDA[9] PENDLETON (*JOHN[8], WILLIAM[7], JOHN[6], PHILIP[5], HENRY[4], HENRY[3], GEORGE[2], GEORGE[1]*) was born Dec 28, 1787 in VA, and died Aug 18, 1870 in Pendleton Co., KY. She married THOMAS SCOTT Jan 02, 1817 in Lincoln Co., KY. He was born Abt. 1785 in VA.

A Thomas and Malinda Scott are listed in the 1850 Lincoln Co., KY census.

Children of MALINDA PENDLETON and THOMAS SCOTT are:
   i. CATHERINE[10] SCOTT, b. 1825.
   ii. LUCY ANN SCOTT, b. 1827.

128. LUCY[9] PENDLETON (*JOHN[8], WILLIAM[7], JOHN[6], PHILIP[5], HENRY[4], HENRY[3], GEORGE[2], GEORGE[1]*) was born Abt. 1795, and died Aug 14, 1858 in Lincoln Co., KY. She married JAMES HIRAM PEPPLES Jul 09, 1819 in Lincoln Co., KY. He was born Abt. 1794 in Scotland, and died Oct 26, 1875 in Lincoln Co., KY.

Children of LUCY PENDLETON and JAMES PEPPLES are (Ref. 137):
   i. MALINDA[10] PEPPLES, b. Oct 14, 1821, Lincoln Co., KY; d. Apr 24, 1897, Lincoln Co., KY.
   ii. JOHN PEPPLES, b. 1823, Lincoln Co., KY; d. 1898, Lincoln Co., KY; m. MARTHA DUDDERAR, Jan 01, 1849, Lincoln Co., KY.
   iii. JAMES PEPPLES, b. 1826, Lincoln Co., KY; d. 1907, Lincoln Co., KY.
   iv. DAVID PEPPLES, b. Aug 13, 1829, Lincoln Co., KY; d. May 19, 1908, Stanford, Lincoln Co., KY; m. MARY FRANCES SCOTT, Dec 12, 1854, Stanford, Lincoln Co., KY.
   v. MARY ANN PEPPLES, b. Nov 04, 1830, Lincoln Co., KY; d. Sep 30, 1910, Lincoln Co., KY.

129. MICAJAH[9] PENDLETON (*JOHN[8], WILLIAM[7], JOHN[6], PHILIP[5], HENRY[4], HENRY[3], GEORGE[2], GEORGE[1]*) was born 1800 in VA, and died 1878 in Independence, MO. He married EMILY FLUORNOY Jan 08, 1824 in Mercer Co., KY, daughter of SAMUEL FLUORNOY and NANCY. She was born 1801 in KY, and died Aft. 1880 in Washington, Jackson Co., MO?

The marriage of Micajah Pendleton and Emily Fluorney is listed in the Marriage Records of Mercer County, Kentucky 1816-1830. The following is the estate settlement of Samuel Flornoy, his father-in-law, in the Mercer County, Kentucky Will Records Will Book:

Division of Land of, Heirs: Matthew Flornoy, James Flornoy, Abram Keel, and Nancy Keel, his wife; Stewart White and Amelia White, his wife, Martha Flornoy, Samuel Flornoy, Eli Hart and Cassandra Hart, his wife; Macajah Pendleton and Emily Pendleton, his wife; Simmons Fallis and Agnes Fallis, his wife; Carter Keel and Rachel Keel, his wife Comm.: G. H. Briscoe, D. Hart, Richard Huff, and Beverly Williams February 10, 1825.

Children of MICAJAH PENDLETON and EMILY FLUORNOY are:
      i.   FRANK[10] PENDLETON.
      ii. SALLY PENDLETON, m. SHORT.
324. iii. NANCY MARLIN PENDLETON, b. 1825, Stanford, KY; d. Nov 23, 1907, Kansas City, MO.
325. iv. THOMAS J. PENDLETON, b. Abt. 1830, KY.
326. v.   LEWIS E. PENDLETON, b. Abt. 1834, KY.
      vi. ARCHIBALD B. PENDLETON, b. Abt. 1842, KY.
          Archy B. Pendleton (farmhand) is listed in the household of William Beasley in the 1860 Garrard Co., KY census. An Archibald P. Pendleton served in the KY 3rd Cav. Co. E and in the KY Cav. 2nd Bn. (Dortch's) Co. A.

327. vii. EMILY J. PENDLETON, b. Abt. 1844, Lincoln Co., KY.

130. RICHARD[9] PENDLETON *(JOHN[8], WILLIAM[7], JOHN[6], PHILIP[5], HENRY[4], HENRY[3], GEORGE[2], GEORGE[1])* was born Abt. 1807, and died 1833 in Henry Co., KY. He married MARY ANN BERRY Apr 13, 1829 in Washington Co., KY, daughter of EDWARD BERRY and MARY BRAZELTON. She was born Abt. 1815 in Washington Co., KY, and died Abt. 1848 in Washington Co., KY.

     Richard is listed in the 1830 Washington Co., KY census adjacent to his brother Micajah Pendleton.

Children of RICHARD PENDLETON and MARY BERRY are:
328. i. JOHN EDWARD[10] PENDLETON, b. Sep 01, 1831, Washington Co., KY; d. Jan 01, 1897, Ohio Co., KY.
329. ii. NAOMI F. PENDLETON, b. Feb 28, 1833, KY; d. Jul 27, 1907, Bates Co., MO.

131. JAMES[9] PENDLETON *(JOHN[8], WILLIAM[7], JOHN[6], PHILIP[5], HENRY[4], HENRY[3], GEORGE[2], GEORGE[1])* was born Abt. 1808 in KY, and died Aft. 1880 in Independence, MO. He married NANCY. She was born Abt. 1813 in KY, and died Aft. 1860.

     James Pendleton, farmer, and family are listed in the 1850 Lincoln Co., KY census near his brother Micajah. James Pendleton (farmer) and family are also listed in the 1860 Jackson Co., MO census. This is likely the James Pendleton (73) in the 1880 Independence, MO census with Elizabeth (49).

Children of JAMES PENDLETON and NANCY are:
330. i. JOHN T.[10] PENDLETON, b. Abt. 1829, KY; d. Aft. 1880, Jackson Co., MO?

331. ii. LOGAN PENDLETON, b. Dec 30, 1830, Lincoln Co., KY; d. Mar 30, 1903, Jackson Co., MO.

332. iii. MICAJAH PENDLETON, b. Abt. 1834, KY; d. Aft. 1880, Independence, MO?

333. iv. ALFRED PENDLETON, b. Dec 23, 1836, KY; d. Dec 16, 1896, Kansas City, MO.

334. v. EBERLE PENDLETON, b. May 1839, KY; d. Aft. 1900, Jackson Co., MO?

    vi. WILLIAM PENDLETON, b. Jan 26, 1841, KY; d. Jan 26, 1914, Kansas City, MO; m. LAVINA B. CAMPBELL; b. Nov 27, 1843, MO; d. Feb 28, 1921, Kansas City, MO.

    vii. EMILY PENDLETON, b. Abt. 1843.

335. viii. JAMES CREW PENDLETON, b. Abt. 1845, KY; d. Aft. 1880, Jackson Co., MO?

336. ix. THOMAS J. PENDLETON, b. Abt. 1847, KY; d. Aft. 1920, Blue, Jackson Co., MO?

    x. RICHARD PENDLETON, b. 1850, KY.

    xi. TIMOTHY PENDLETON, b. Abt. 1855, KY.

132. ROBERT HARDWICK[9] PENDLETON (*ISAAC[8], WILLIAM[7], JOHN[6], PHILIP[5], HENRY[4], HENRY[3], GEORGE[2], GEORGE[1]*) was born Dec 25, 1802 in Lynchburg, VA, and died Dec 1889 in Trimble Co., KY. He married SARAH "SALLY" PEAK Mar 11, 1827 in Oldham Co., KY, daughter of WILLIAM PEAK and ELIZABETH FORTS. She was born Abt. 1812 in Oldham Co., KY, and died Abt. 1891 in Trimble Co., KY.

The following account is from an early history of Kentucky (Ref. 123).

Robert H. Pendleton is a native of the Old Dominion and was born near Lynchburg, August 12, 1802, the second of nine children born to Isaac and Nancy (Hardwick) Pendleton. He was brought to Kentucky in 1806, to Garrard County; was reared on a farm, and educated in the common schools. He began life a poor boy, and previous to the civil war was quite wealthy, but that struggle deprived him of by far the greater portion of his wealth. He still owns, however, 110 acres of fine land, well improved, on the Ohio River, near Milton, and is engaged in farming and stock raising. He married in 1827, Miss Sarah Peak, daughter of William and Elizabeth (Forts) Peak. To this union six children were born, three of whom are living: Christopher, Elizabeth, John R. and William A., Nancy and Robert. John R. served in the civil war on the Confederate side, and was killed at Mt. Sterling in 1865. Mr. Pendleton and family are members of the Christian Church. Politically he is a Democrat.

Robert is listed adjacent to his father, Isaac, in the 1830 Henry Co., KY census and in the 1840 Trimble Co. census (as Robert K.). In the 1850 Trimble Co. census, pg 434, District 1, he is listed as Pendleton, Robert H. (47), Farmer, along with Sarah (37) and their six children. He continued to be listed in the Trimble Co., KY census records through 1880.

Children of ROBERT PENDLETON and SARAH PEAK are:

    i. CHRISTOPHER[10] PENDLETON, b. 1827, KY; d. Aft. 1880, Trimble Co., KY?; m. AMERICA; b. Abt. 1846, KY.

Christopher Pendleton is listed as a school teacher in the 1850 Trimble Co., KY census in the household of Robert H. Pendleton. He is listed in the 1880 Trimble Co., KY census as a farmer, age 52, along with America, age 30.

 ii. ELIZABETH PENDLETON, b. 1830, KY; d. Aft. 1860, Trimble Co., KY?; m. AUGUST WILHELM MEWES, Dec 27, 1853, Trimble Co., KY; b. Aug 28, 1818, Germany; d. Aft. 1860, Trimble Co., KY?

 iii. JOHN R. PENDLETON, b. 1834, KY; d. 1865, Civil War at Mt. Sterling, KY.

  John R. Pendleton enlisted in the Confederate Army as a private on 10 Sep 1862, Trimble Co., KY and served in the KY 4th Cav., Co. A.

 iv. WILLIAM A. PENDLETON, b. 1838, KY.

  It was likely this William A. Pendleton who married Mary J. Taylor in 1859, Carroll Co., KY.

337. v. NANCY J. PENDLETON, b. 1840, KY; d. 1897, Trimble Co., KY.
338. vi. ROBERT HARDWICK PENDLETON, b. Oct 1848, Trimble Co., KY; d. Jun 21, 1921, Trimble Co., KY.

133. LINDSEY[9] PENDLETON (*ISAAC*[8], *WILLIAM*[7], *JOHN*[6], *PHILIP*[5], *HENRY*[4], *HENRY*[3], *GEORGE*[2], *GEORGE*[1]) was born Abt. 1805 in VA, and died Aft. 1870 in Henry Co., KY? He married MILDRED JACKSON Jan 15, 1834 in Henry Co., KY. She was born Abt. 1812 in KY, and died Aft. 1870 in Henry Co., KY?

 Lindsey is listed in the 1840 Trimble Co. census near Isaac Pendleton. He is also found in the 1850 Henry Co., KY census, District 1, pg. 387 as age 40, along with his wife, Mildred (37), and two children. Lindsey (farmer) and Mildred Pendleton are listed in the 1870 Port Royal, Henry Co., KY census.

Children of LINDSEY PENDLETON and MILDRED JACKSON are:
339. i. ROLAND L.[10] PENDLETON, b. Jan 1842, KY; d. Aft. 1900, Henry Co., KY?
340. ii. EMILY PENDLETON, b. 1844, KY; d. Aft. 1880, Henry Co., KY?

134. ISAAC T.[9] PENDLETON (*ISAAC*[8], *WILLIAM*[7], *JOHN*[6], *PHILIP*[5], *HENRY*[4], *HENRY*[3], *GEORGE*[2], *GEORGE*[1]) was born Abt. 1811 in Mill Creek, Henry Co., KY, and died Aft. 1860 in Henry Co., KY? He married DIANNA G. ROBBINS Oct 30, 1837 in Henry Co., KY, daughter of ABEL ROBBINS and MARY D. She was born Abt. 1811 in Mill Creek, Henry Co., KY, and died Aft. 1870 in Henry Co., KY?

 Isaac is listed in the 1850 Henry Co., KY census, District 1, pg 433 at age 38, along with his wife, Dianah (38), and his first six children. The family is again found in Henry Co., KY for the 1860 census.

 In the will of Abel Robbins it states "My daughter Dianah G. Pendleton is hereby charged with one hundred Dollars to bear interest from the 15th December 1855" (Ref.

138). Dinah (58), Felix (26) , Fulton (24), David (21), and Stephen (17) are listed in the 1870 Jericho, Henry Co., KY census.

Children of ISAAC PENDLETON and DIANNA ROBBINS are:
  i.   EVAN[10] PENDLETON, b. Abt. 1837, Mill Creek, Henry Co., KY.
  ii. WILLIAM PENDLETON, b. Abt. 1841, Mill Creek, Henry Co., KY.
  iii. FELIX PENDLETON, b. Abt. 1843, Mill Creek, Henry Co., KY.
       Felix Pendleton served as a private in the KY 9th Cavalry, CSA.

  iv. FULTON PENDLETON, b. Abt. 1845, Mill Creek, Henry Co., KY.
       Fulton Pendleton is listed in the 1870 Kansas Census, Atchison Co., pg 232, along with Carrie Pendleton.

  v.   TERESSA PENDLETON, b. Abt. 1846, Mill Creek, Henry Co., KY.
  vi. DAVID PENDLETON, b. Abt. 1849, Mill Creek, Henry Co., KY.
  vii. STEPHEN PENDLETON, b. Abt. 1853.

135. FRANCES[9] PENDLETON (*ISAAC[8], WILLIAM[7], JOHN[6], PHILIP[5], HENRY[4], HENRY[3], GEORGE[2], GEORGE[1]*) was born Abt. 1813 in KY, and died Aft. 1880 in Trimble Co., KY? She married WILLIAM M. PEAK Jan 30, 1841 in Trimble Co., KY. He was born Abt. 1815 in KY, and died Aft. 1880 in Trimble Co., KY?

Children of FRANCES PENDLETON and WILLIAM PEAK are:
  i.   ISAAC[10] PEAK, b. Abt. 1844, KY.
  ii. JOHN PEAK, b. Abt. 1846, KY; d. Aft. 1880.
  iii. NORMA PEAK, b. Abt. 1851, KY; m. JOHN C. ROGIN; b. Abt. 1833, PA.
  iv. WILLIAM PEAK, b. Abt. 1855, KY.

136. WILLIS M.[9] PENDLETON (*ISAAC[8], WILLIAM[7], JOHN[6], PHILIP[5], HENRY[4], HENRY[3], GEORGE[2], GEORGE[1]*) was born Abt. 1813 in Mill Creek, Henry Co., KY, and died Aft. 1860 in MO? He married (1) JULIANN LADD Dec 12, 1836 in Henry Co., KY, daughter of JAMES LADD and ELIZABETH HARDWICK. She was born 1815 in Mill Creek, Henry Co., KY, and died Nov 14, 1850 in Henry Co., KY. He married (2) MARTHA Abt. 1852. She was born Abt. 1825 in VA.
      This is probably the Welles Pendleton listed in the 1840 Trimble Co., KY census and the Willis M. Pendleton of Gentry, MO Listed in Missouri Land Patents, Daviess Co. on Nov 1, 1848. Willis Pendleton (farmer) and family are listed in the 1860 Daviess Co., MO census.

Children of WILLIS PENDLETON and JULIANN LADD are:
  i.   JAMES[10] PENDLETON, b. Abt. 1840, KY.
  ii. ROBERT PENDLETON, b. Abt. 1841, KY.
  iii. MARTHA PENDLETON, b. Abt. 1843, MO.
  iv. JOANNA PENDLETON, b. Abt. 1844, MO.
  v.   MARY PENDLETON, b. Abt. 1845, MO.

vi.   NANCY PENDLETON, b. Abt. 1847, MO.
vii. ISAAC PENDLETON, b. 1850, MO.

Children of WILLIS PENDLETON and MARTHA are:
viii. ELIZA[10] PENDLETON, b. Abt. 1855, MO.
ix.   EMILY PENDLETON, b. Abt. 1857, MO.
x.   SARAH PENDLETON, b. Abt. 1859, MO.

137. BENJAMIN[9] PENDLETON *(HENRY[8], HENRY[7], JOHN[6], PHILIP[5], HENRY[4], HENRY[3], GEORGE[2], GEORGE[1])* was born Abt. 1774 in Spotsylvania Co., VA, and died Aft. 1830 in Spotsylvania Co., VA? He married (1) ELIZABETH QUISENBERRY Jun 2, 1796 in Orange Co., VA. He married (2) REBECCA ARNOLD Mar 6, 1815 in Spotsylvania Co., VA, daughter of GEORGE ARNOLD and SARAH WHITE. She was born Abt. 1782 in Spotsylvania Co., VA.

This Benjamin Pendleton is listed in the 1810 Spotsylvania Co. census with a wife, 2 children and 4 slaves.

Children of BENJAMIN PENDLETON and ELIZABETH QUISENBERRY are:
341.   i.   WILLIAM M.[10] PENDLETON, b. Abt. 1797, Spotsylvania Co., VA; d. Sep 21, 1842, Clarke Co., AL.
342.   ii. JOHN T. PENDLETON, b. Abt. 1805, VA; d. Oct 28, 1878, Spotsylvania Co., VA?

Child of BENJAMIN PENDLETON and REBECCA ARNOLD is:
iii. ANNE[10] PENDLETON, b. Abt. 1815.

138. MARY "POLLY"[9] PENDLETON *(HENRY[8], HENRY[7], JOHN[6], PHILIP[5], HENRY[4], HENRY[3], GEORGE[2], GEORGE[1])* was born 1775 in Spotsylvania Co., VA, and died 1844 in Todd Co., KY. She married JOHN THOMAS DAVIS Nov 26, 1808 in Spotsylvania Co., VA. He was born Abt. 1768 in Spotsylvania Co., VA, and died May 1826 in Todd Co., KY.

The following is from the Todd Co. Will Book A. 1820 – 1826: "Davis, Thomas Mar 15 1826; wife: Mary Davis; Sarah Ann, Mary Elizabeth; ex. John Pendleton; wit: Benj. Downs, George Fristoes, William Burgess." John and Mary Pendleton Davis are buried in the Hall Family cemetery adjacent to Hwy 68 between Elkston and Fairview, Todd Co., KY.

Children of MARY PENDLETON and JOHN DAVIS are:
i.   SARAH A.[10] DAVIS, b. Oct 28, 1809, Spotsylvania Co., VA; d. Aft. 1884, Todd Co., KY; m. HENRY TANDY, Dec 16, 1824, Todd Co., KY; b. 1800, Spotsylvania Co., VA.
The following is from an early history of Todd County (Ref. 139).

Mrs. Sarah A. Tandy was born in Spotsylvania County, Va., October 28, 1809, where she was reared, and on the 16th of December, 1824, was married to Henry, son of Henry Tandy, of Orange County, Va., who was born in 1800; removed to Todd County, Ky., 1825, where he died in 1848.

To them were born: John H., Mary E. (Hall) and Oscar E. Subject's father, John Davis, was born in Virginia, died 1826, aged forty-eight years. His wife, Mary (Pendleton), was born in Virginia; died in 1844, age sixty-nine years. Their children are: Subject, as above, and Mary E., wife of Dr. N. M. Tandy, of Todd County. Mrs. Sara [sic] is engaged in farming, having 306 acres of good land on West Fork. She is a member of the Bethel Baptist Church.

ii. MARY ELIZABETH DAVIS, b. 1815; d. 1843; m. NATHANIEL MILLS TANDY; b. 1810, Christian Co., KY; d. 1881, Todd Co., KY.
The following is from the same early history of Todd County (Ref. 139).

John Davis Tandy. The subject of this sketch was born January 23, 1837 in Todd County, Ky. where he still retains his residence. His father, Nathaniel Mills Tandy, was born in 1810 in Christian County; he removed to Todd County, Ky. in 1834, where he died in 1881. He was the son of Mills Tandy who was born in Virginia in 1780; moved to Barren County in 1808 where he remained six months; moved to Christian County in 1809, and died in Christian County, Ky. in 1861. His father was Henry Tandy, of Virginia. Subject's mother, Mary E., daughter of John and Mary (Pendleton) Davis, was born in 1815 and died in 1843. To her and her husband, Nathaniel Mills Tandy, were born: Olivia (deceased) and our subject. To Nathaniel Mills Tandy and his second wife (Margaret J. Jesup), were born: Samuel R. Jesup M. and Charles E. Subject secured a good common education and is a general reader of standard books and current literature. He was married October 23, 1860, to Miss Catherine, daughter of Preston L. and Elizabeth A. (Jesup) Yancy, of Crittenden County., Ky., and this union has been blessed with: Preston E., Robert M., Mary D. and Clarence. Subject is by profession a farmer, owning 700 acres of good and valuable land, which is finely improved and in a high state of cultivation. He is prudently turning his attention largely to the growth of the grasses, thereby maintaining and improving the fertility of his already productive farm. He is enterprising, energetic and public spirited. He is an honored member of the Masonic fraternity, a Baptist and a Democrat.

139. HENRY[9] PENDLETON *(HENRY[8], HENRY[7], JOHN[6], PHILIP[5], HENRY[4], HENRY[3], GEORGE[2], GEORGE[1])* was born 1778 in Spotsylvania Co., VA, and died Jan 9, 1873 in Spotsylvania Co., VA. He married CATHERINE DUVAL 1806, daughter of WILLIAM DUVAL and AGNES S. She was born Abt. 1780, and died 1827 in Spotsylvania Co., VA?

In the 1810 Spotsylvania Co., VA census there were 4 whites and one slave in the Henry Pendleton household. Henry is also listed in the 1820 and 1830 Spotsylvania Co. census records. In the 1850 Spotsylvania Co. census Henry is listed at age 70. The value of his farm was $1825. Included in household were Lucy (30), Mary C. (18), Eugenia? (16), Maria (14), Virginia (11), and William (11), (twins?). These were Hugh Claiborne Pendleton's children.

In his will he advanced money to his daughter Agnes Ann P. Swan, and he left money to his son Hugh, to his daughter Lucy E. Pendleton [she apparently wasn't married at the time], and to his son, Edwin. To his daughter Lucy E. Pendleton he left his present residence "Spring Field" containing one hundred and thirteen acres. To his son Edwin Pendleton he left one hundred acres of land on the river Ta known as Johnsons. To his son Hugh C. he left the land on which he now resides (Ref. 140).

Children of HENRY PENDLETON and CATHERINE DUVAL are:
343.   i.   HUGH CLAIBORNE[10] PENDLETON, b. 1807, VA; d. 1873, "Old Pendleton Place," Spotsylvania Co., VA.
        ii. EDWIN PENDLETON, b. Abt. 1809, VA; d. Aft. 1870, Spotsylvania Co., VA?

           This is apparently the Edmond Pendleton (overseer, age 35) listed in the 1850 Spotsylvania Co., VA census with Eliza (40). An E. M. Pendleton (62; works on farm) is listed in the 1870 Berkeley, Spotsylvania Co., VA census in the household of Ann W. Coleman (70).

344.   iii. AGNES ANNE PENDLETON, b. Abt. 1812, VA; d. Aft. 1900, Madison Co., VA?
        iv. LUCY E. PENDLETON, b. Abt. 1817, VA; m. WILLIAM HOLLIDAY, Jan 1867.

           Lucy Holladay (55) is listed in the 1880 Berkley, Spotsylvania Co., VA census, pg. 324B with Maria (Jackson?) Pendleton (35), her niece.

140. JOHN[9] PENDLETON (*HENRY*[8], *HENRY*[7], *JOHN*[6], *PHILIP*[5], *HENRY*[4], *HENRY*[3], *GEORGE*[2], *GEORGE*[1]) was born Apr 21, 1780 in Spotsylvania Co., VA, and died Jan 26, 1838 in Christian Co., KY. He married FRANCES JACKSON THOMPSON Dec 23, 1806 in Spotsylvania Co., VA, daughter of WILLIAM THOMPSON and FRANCES MILLS. She was born Dec 29, 1784 in VA, and died Nov 4, 1863 in Christian Co., KY.

It is likely this John Pendleton who is listed with Rice and Curtis Pendleton (his uncles) in the 1795 Clark Co., KY tax list and the 1800 Clark Co. census. If so, he moved back to VA where he is listed in the 1810 Orange Co., VA census. He is subsequently listed in the 1820 and 1830 Christian Co., KY census records. His biography is provided in a history of Kentucky Baptists (Ref. 141).

John Pendleton emigrated from Spottsylvania (sic) county, Virginia, to Christian County, Kentucky, in 1812. He entered into the constitution of Bethel church, which he served long, both as clerk and deacon. He was a man of enlarged views, and was far in advance of the Baptists in Red River Association, of which he was a member about twelve years. He entered with his church into the constitution of Bethel Association, and was a very prominent member of that body, during what may be called its formative period, serving as clerk, a number of years. Being an earnest and enlightened advocate of missions and the support of the ministry, he contributed no small part in giving direction to the counsels of Bethel Association, in these matters. As a citizen, he occupied a prominent position in his county, which honored him with a seat in the State Legislature [State Representative from Christian County] in 1833. He died in 1833. [John Pendleton actually died in 1838, not 1833]. Among his children, were the distinguished J. M. Pendleton, D.D., William H. Pendleton, long a deacon of the church at Hopkinsville, and a most valuable church member, and Cyrus N. Pendleton, a prominent lawyer and politician of Christian County, and a member of Bethel church.

"The year 1838, opened inospicious, on the 25th January our beloved Bro. John Pendleton who had acted as Deacon and clerk nearly since the commencement of the church with fidelity fell asleep in the arms of Jesus" (Ref. 142).

The will of John Pendleton was recorded in Christian Co., KY (Ref. 143).

In the name of God amen, I John Pendleton of Christian County and State of Kentucky being of sound mind and disposing memory (for which I thank God) and calling to mind the uncertainty of human life and being desirous to dispose of all such worldly estate as it has pleased God to bless me with, I give and bequeath the same in manner following, that is to say,

1st I give to my son James M. Pendleton one negro boy named Henry one horse one cow and one bed and furniture to him and his heirs forever.

2nd I give to my son John T Pendleton one negro boy named Richard one horse one cow and one bed and furniture to him & his heirs forever.

3ly I give to my son William H Pendleton one negro boy named Robert, one horse one cow, and bed and furniture to him and his heirs forever.

4ly I give to my son Edmund W Pendleton, one negro boy named Spencer one horse, one cow, one bed and furniture, to him and his heirs forever.

5ly I give to my son Cyrus N Pendleton one negro named George, one horse one cow one bed and furniture to him and his heirs forever.

6ly I give to my daughter Mary Pendleton one negro girl named Betsy with her future increase, one horse one cow, one bed and furniture (all of which she has received) to her and her heirs forever.

7ly I give to my daughter Frances A Garnett one negro girl named Haney with her future increase, one horse one cow, one bed and furniture (all of which she has received) to her and her heirs forever.

8ly I give to my daughter Caroline Pendleton one negro girl named Resetta and her increase, one horse, one cow, one bed and furniture to her & her heirs forever.

9ly I give to my daughter Juliet T Pendleton one negro boy named Washington one horse, one cow, one bed and furniture to her & her heirs forever.

10ly I give to my daughter Emily L Pendleton one negro girl named Mary Jane, and her future increase one horse, one cow, one bed and furniture to her and her heirs forever.

If any of the negroes named above should die before they come into the posession of the respective legatees then, in that event, it is my desire that such legatee have assigned to him or her another negro of as nearly the same value as may be selected by my widow or any two disinterested neighbors, to be held by said legatee as before provided

All the legacies before mentioned to be paid over to the several legatees as they arrive at the age of 21 or when they marry.

11ly All the remainder of my negroes, after the above named bequests to gether with all the personal property of every description whatsoever I give and bequeath to my wife during her natural life, to be used for the support of herself and children during the time they live with her, provided they continue as heretofore to promote the welfare of the family or estate.

12ly As it respects my landed estate I wish my wife to select one of the tracts as the place of her residence, and that of the unmarried children, and the other tract to be divided among all the children or if more profitable to the legatees to sell said land and divide the proceeds equally among all the children.

13ly At the death of my wife it is my will & desire that the whole of the estate entrusted to my wife during her life, both real and personal be equally divided amongst all my children, or sold if thought most advantageous, and the proceeds equally divided, the

selling has reference to the land only, as to the negroes will admit of it. I should prefer them being valued by competent judges and then for each legatee to draw for his lot. Lastly I do hereby constitute and appoint my son James M Pendleton and John T. Pendleton Executor of this my last will and testament hereby revoking all other or former wills or testaments by me heretofore made. And as I am not, nor do I expect to be largely indebted hereafter, and as I have the utmost confidence in the integrity of my Executors, I request the Court to permit them to qualify without giving security. In witness whereof I have hereunto set my hand and affixed my seal the 14th day of November in the year 1837."
John Pendleton [Seal]

Declared to be the last will & testament of the above named John Pendleton in presence of us: Will Tandy; A Webber.
Commonwealth of Kentucky County of Christian to wit) I Abraham Stiles the Clerk of the County Court of Christian County aforesaid do certify that this last will of John Pendleton deceased was on this day produced in open court and proven to be the last will of the said deceased by the oath of Wm Tandy one of the subscribing witnesses in the manner required by law & was ordered to be recorded whereupon in pursuance of said order the said will together with the foregoing certificate hath been duly admitted to record in my office -- Given under my hand this 5th day of February 1838
Attest Abram Stiles C.C.C.C.

Frances Pendleton is listed as an original member of the Bethel Baptist Church, Jan. 22, 1814, Salubria Springs, Christian Co., KY (Ref. 142). She is listed as head of the household in the 1840 Christian Co. census. Frances J. Pendleton (65) is included in the 1850 Christian Co. census, 2nd District, pg 382, along with Julia T., Waller E. (farmer), Ann E., and Cyrus N. (student).

Children of JOHN PENDLETON and FRANCES THOMPSON are:
  i. MARY[10] PENDLETON, b. Jun 4, 1808, VA; d. Mar 14, 1847.
345. ii. FRANCES ANNE PENDLETON, b. Jan 30, 1810, Spotsylvania Co., VA; d. May 12, 1903, Christian Co., KY.
346. iii. JAMES MADISON PENDLETON, b. Nov 20, 1811, Spotsylvania Co., VA; d. Mar 4, 1891, TN?
347. iv. JOHN THOMPSON PENDLETON, b. Jun 19, 1815, Christian Co., KY; d. Aft. 1880, Nashville, TN?
348. v. CAROLINE AUGUSTA PENDLETON, b. Dec 8, 1816, KY; d. Oct 5, 1876, Paducah, KY.
  vi. JULIET THOMPSON PENDLETON, b. Dec 23, 1818, Christian Co., KY; d. Jan 2, 1884, Christian Co., KY.
      The following excerpt is from "Church Minutes Bethel Baptist Church, Christian Co., KY, dated Sat. before 4th Sunday March 1865: The church sat in conference, the regular modr presiding Previous minutes not being present, the reference to missions was taken up. After remarks from Eld. Hunt, on motion a committee of Sisters Juliet Pendleton and Jennie Vass, and Brethren W.W. Sergeant, E.W. Pendleton, J.B. Moody were appointed to take up collection for said object."

349. vii. WILLIAM HENRY PENDLETON, b. Dec 16, 1820, Christian Co., KY; d. Mar 3, 1863, Christian Co., KY.

350. viii. EDMUND WALLER PENDLETON, b. Dec 1, 1822, Christian Co., KY; d. Dec 4, 1870, Christian Co., KY?

351. ix. EMILY LOUISA PENDLETON, b. Oct 13, 1825, KY; d. Aft. 1870, Todd Co., KY?

352. x. CYRUS NEVILLE PENDLETON, b. Feb 19, 1831, Christian Co., KY; d. Aug 30, 1899, Christian Co., KY.

141. ELIZABETH "BETSY"[9] PENDLETON *(JOHN[8], HENRY[7], JOHN[6], PHILIP[5], HENRY[4], HENRY[3], GEORGE[2], GEORGE[1])* was born Jul 29, 1789 in Spotsylvania Co., VA, and died Jul 20, 1873 in Adair Co., KY. She married JOSEPH HICKS Jan 15, 1807 in Spotsylvania Co., VA. He was born Dec 23, 1785 in VA, and died Mar 22, 1843 in Adair Co., KY.

Children of ELIZABETH PENDLETON and JOSEPH HICKS are:
    i. MARY E.[10] HICKS, b. Nov 22, 1808, Spotsylvania Co., VA; m. MILTON YATES, Apr 17, 1826, Adair Co., KY.
    ii. SALLY ANN HICKS, b. Jan 11, 1811, Spotsylvania Co., VA; d. Apr 5, 1856, Adair Co., KY; m. LITTLETON FILLIMORE ESTES, Sep 27, 1834, Adair Co., KY.
    iii. WILLIAM SANFORD HICKS, b. Mar 3, 1812; m. JANE P. BEASLEY, May 5, 1836, Adair Co., KY.
    iv. ELIZABETH E. HICKS, b. Nov 5, 1813, Spotsylvania Co., VA; d. Oct 3, 1893, Adair Co., KY; m. JAMES MADISON BRAGG, Jan 25, 1833, Adair Co., KY.
    v. LOUISA HICKS, b. Sep 3, 1815, VA; d. Mar 6, 1898, Adair Co., KY; m. ROBERT M. WALKUP, Dec 17, 1840, Adair Co., KY.

142. RICE[9] PENDLETON *(JOHN[8], HENRY[7], JOHN[6], PHILIP[5], HENRY[4], HENRY[3], GEORGE[2], GEORGE[1])* was born 1790 in VA, and died 1836 in Spotsylvania Co., VA? He married AGNES ROBBINS Apr 24, 1817 in Spotsylvania Co., VA, daughter of JAMES ROBBINS and ELIZABETH. She was born Abt. 1790, and died 1834 in Spotsylvania Co., VA?
    This is probably the Rice Pendleton listed as overseer at Farmington, Hanover Co., VA (undated). He was a private in Capt. James Fox's Co., 16 Regiment (Wallers) of Virginia Militia, War of 1812. The Last Will and Testament of James Robbins, Nov 4, 1825 includes the following: "7thly I give and bequeath unto Rice Pendleton who maried my Daughter Agness Robbins one third part of all my Estate of every kind and description not before mentioned." Rice is listed in the 1830 Spotsylvania Co., VA census.

Children of RICE PENDLETON and AGNES ROBBINS are:
    i. JOHN JAMES[10] PENDLETON, b. Abt. 1819, Spotsylvania Co., VA?; d. Aug 28, 1831, Caroline Co., VA.

The obituary of John Pendleton appeared in the Virginia Herald, Aug 31, 1833: "Died at Mr. George Alsop's in Caroline Co., Aug 28, John James Pendleton, only son of _____ Pendleton in his 14th year."

353. ii. JANE AGNES PENDLETON, b. Abt. 1828, VA; d. Apr 2, 1874, Louisa Co., VA.
354. iii. MARY E. PENDLETON, b. Abt. 1829, VA.
355. iv. MALVINA RICE PENDLETON, b. 1834, VA; d. Apr 23, 1878.

143. SALLY[9] PENDLETON *(JOHN[8], HENRY[7], JOHN[6], PHILIP[5], HENRY[4], HENRY[3], GEORGE[2], GEORGE[1])* was born Abt. 1795 in VA. She married WILLIS LANDRUM Mar 26, 1817 in Spotsylvania Co., VA, son of WILLIAM LANDRUM and MARY HUBBARD. He was born Abt. 1797 in VA, and died Aft. 1860 in Spotsylvania Co., VA.

What remains of Willis' home in Spotsylvania is now part of the National Park Service (NPS). Portions of two chimneys of the Landrum House remain at the Spotsylvania Court House Battlefield. There is a brass marker describing the action that occurred there and a photo showing the house before its destruction. Willis Landrum's daughter Lucy gave an interview to the NPS in 1939 relating what she recalled of the battle that took place in May, 1864 (Ref. 144). Willis Landrum (farmer) and family are listed in the 1850 (pg. 421) and 1860 (pg. 365) Spotsylvania Co., VA census records.

Children of SALLY PENDLETON and WILLIS LANDRUM are:
  i. MARY F.[10] LANDRUM, b. Abt. 1829.
  ii. MARTHA A. LANDRUM, b. Abt. 1831.
  iii. CHARLES C. LANDRUM, b. Abt. 1832.
  iv. HENRY W. LANDRUM, b. Abt. 1834.

144. JOHN[9] PENDLETON *(JOHN[8], HENRY[7], JOHN[6], PHILIP[5], HENRY[4], HENRY[3], GEORGE[2], GEORGE[1])* was born 1797 in VA, and died 1834 in Adair Co., KY. He married MARY "POLLY" MARSHALL ESTES Dec 8, 1818 in Adair Co., KY, daughter of PETER ESTES and SALLY YATES. She was born 1801 in VA, and died Aft. 1850 in Adair Co., KY?

He is one of the two John Pendletons listed in the 1820 Adair Co. census and one of three listed in the 1830 Adair Co. census. Polly M. Pendleton is listed as head of household in the 1840 and 1850 Adair Co. census records.

Children of JOHN PENDLETON and MARY ESTES are (Ref. 145):
356. i. CHESLEY THACKER[10] PENDLETON, b. Mar 6, 1824, Adair Co., KY; d. Aft. 1900, Metcalfe Co., KY?
357. ii. ABNER J. PENDLETON, b. Mar 25, 1825, Adair Co., KY; d. Jan 25, 1879, Metcalfe Co., KY.
358. iii. JOHN HIRAM PENDLETON, b. Mar 25, 1825, Adair Co., KY; d. Abt. 1860, Adair Co., KY?
  iv. POLLY PENDLETON, b. Abt. 1832; m. S. HIRAMS.

145. FRANCES[9] PENDLETON *(JOHN[8], HENRY[7], JOHN[6], PHILIP[5], HENRY[4], HENRY[3], GEORGE[2], GEORGE[1])* was born Abt. 1805 in VA, and died Aft. 1850 in Spotsylvania Co., VA? She married JAMES H. HAWKINS Oct 2, 1829 in Spotsylvania Co., VA. He was born Abt. 1805 in VA, and died Aft. 1850 in Spotsylvania Co., VA?

James H. Hawkins (farmer) and family are listed in the 1850 Spotsylvania Co., VA census, pg. 379.

Children of FRANCES PENDLETON and JAMES HAWKINS are:

 i. JOHN T.[10] HAWKINS, b. Abt. 1830, VA.
 ii. LUCY HAWKINS, b. Abt. 1832, VA.
 iii. SALLY HAWKINS, b. Abt. 1833, VA.
 iv. ELIZA HAWKINS, b. Abt. 1834, VA.
 v. MARTHA HAWKINS, b. Abt. 1835, VA.
 vi. HULDAH HAWKINS, b. Abt. 1836.
 vii. FANNY HAWKINS, b. Abt. 1838, VA.
 viii. ALEX HAWKINS, b. Abt. 1842, VA.
 ix. CORDELIA HAWKINS, b. Abt. 1843, VA.
 x. ISABELLA HAWKINS, b. Abt. 1848, VA.

146. ROBERT YATES[9] PENDLETON *(PHILIP[8], HENRY[7], JOHN[6], PHILIP[5], HENRY[4], HENRY[3], GEORGE[2], GEORGE[1])* was born Sep 23, 1792 in VA, and died May 1, 1867 in Christian Co., KY. He married MARY RAY RAWLINGS Abt. 1818, daughter of JOHN RAWLINGS? She was born Abt. 1802 in MD, and died Oct 6, 1835.

Robert Y. Pendleton is listed in the VA Muster Roles, 1812 as a sub for Thomas Herndon, 16th Regiment (Waller's) Virginia Militia. Robert Y. Pendleton is also included in a listing of Christian Co., KY enlistees under Major Reuben Harrison (Ref. 146). Robert Y. Pendleton is subsequently listed in the 1820, 1830, 1850, and 1860 (Hopkinsville) Christian Co., KY census records.

Robert Yates was a member of the budding union movement of Kentucky (Ref. 147).

> The Brotherhood of the Union was founded in 1848 or 1849 by the novelist George Lippard. The organization survived right up to the present, though it reorganized in the twentieth century as the "Brotherhood of America." The surviving manuscript records mention that R.Y. Pendleton and Francis C. Cowarden were members of Circle No. 164 at Pembroke, Christian County, Kentucky near Hopkinsville. Notice of the circle and the names of those two members are on an undated composite manuscript that predated Lippard's death in February 1854, and likely refers to an organization from 1851-52. These unions clearly established an important organizational foundations for all sorts of labor and farmers' organizations that followed in the state's history.

Children of ROBERT PENDLETON and MARY RAWLINGS are:

  i. SON[10] PENDLETON, b. Abt. 1819, Christian Co., KY.
359. ii. JOHN HAMILTON PENDLETON, b. Abt. 1821, Christian Co., KY; d. 1858, Christian Co., KY?
360. iii. SARAH ANNE PENDLETON, b. Abt. 1825, Christian Co., KY; d. 1866, Christian Co., KY.

iv. ELEANOR PENDLETON, b. Bet. 1825 - 1830, Christian Co., KY.
361. v. ROBERT YATES PENDLETON, JR., b. Dec 1827, Christian Co., KY; d. Aft. 1900, Christian Co., KY.
vi. JOSEPH HENRY PENDLETON, b. Bet. 1830 - 1835, Christian Co., KY.

147. ELIZABETH[9] PENDLETON *(PHILIP[8], HENRY[7], JOHN[6], PHILIP[5], HENRY[4], HENRY[3], GEORGE[2], GEORGE[1])* was born Abt. 1794 in VA, and died Abt. 1844 in Spotsylvania Co., VA? She married BLAND GERRELL in VA. He was born Abt. 1790 in VA, and died Mar 25, 1855 in Spotsylvania Co., VA?

Bland Gerald (60) is listed in the 1850 Spotsylvania Co. census, Eastern District, page 400, along with Mary (45) and Mildred (30).

Children of ELIZABETH PENDLETON and BLAND GERRELL are:
362. i. JOSEPH HENRY[10] GERRELL, b. Abt. 1815, VA; d. Aft. 1855, VA?
ii. MILDRED THOMAS GERRELL, b. Abt. 1820, VA; d. Aft. 1850; m. PRITCHARD?
iii. LUCY ANN GERRELL, b. Abt. 1821; m. CARNAHAN?
iv. MARY ELIZABETH GERRELL, b. Abt. 1823; m. PITTS?
363. v. MARGARET HERNDON GERRELL, b. Abt. 1824, VA; d. Aft. 1860.
vi. EDMOND W. GERRELL, b. Abt. 1829.
vii. ROBERT YATES GERRELL, b. Nov 11, 1830, Spotsylvania Co., VA; d. Feb 22, 1912, Ballard Co., KY; m. TAMASIA ANN PEYTON, Nov 22, 1855, Spotsylvania Co., VA; b. May 2, 1835; d. Feb 2, 1905.
viii. WILLIAM JEFFERSON GERRELL, b. Abt. 1833.

148. LUCINDA[9] PENDLETON *(PHILIP[8], HENRY[7], JOHN[6], PHILIP[5], HENRY[4], HENRY[3], GEORGE[2], GEORGE[1])* was born Abt. 1796 in VA, and died Aft. 1850 in Spotsylvania Co., VA? She married WILLIAM LEWIS Dec 23, 1824 in Spotsylvania Co., VA. He was born Abt. 1796 in VA, and died Aft. 1850 in Spotsylvania Co., VA?

Her marriage is recorded in the Marriage Register 1793-1853, of Spotsylvania Co. William (54) and Lucinda Lewis (54) are listed in the 1850 census, Spotsylvania Co., VA, next to the Elizabeth (Burrus) Pendleton household.

Children of LUCINDA PENDLETON and WILLIAM LEWIS are:
i. HULDAH E.[10] LEWIS, b. Abt. 1830, VA.
ii. PHILIP PENDLETON LEWIS, b. Abt. 1832, VA; d. 1864.
iii. LUCINDA LEWIS, b. Abt. 1834, VA.
iv. MAHALA A. LEWIS, b. Abt. 1836, VA.

149. HULDAH[9] PENDLETON *(PHILIP[8], HENRY[7], JOHN[6], PHILIP[5], HENRY[4], HENRY[3], GEORGE[2], GEORGE[1])* was born Abt. 1810 in VA, and died Aft. 1860 in Spotsylvania Co., VA? She married BENJAMIN MASSEY. He was born Abt. 1799 in VA, and died Aft. 1860 in Spotsylvania Co., VA?

Benjamin Massey (farmer) and family are listed in the 1860 Spotsylvania Co., VA census, pg. 211.

Children of HULDAH PENDLETON and BENJAMIN MASSEY are:

    i.   JAMES[10] MASSEY, b. Abt. 1830, VA.

   ii. SILAS MASSEY, b. Abt. 1845, VA.

  iii. THOMAS MASSEY, b. Abt. 1847, VA.

150. PAMELIA[9] PENDLETON (*CURTIS[8], HENRY[7], JOHN[6], PHILIP[5], HENRY[4], HENRY[3], GEORGE[2], GEORGE[1]*) was born Abt. 1786 in VA, and died Aft. 1850 in Todd Co., KY? She married WILLIAM M. RICE May 31, 1803 in Clark Co., KY, son of JOHN RICE and MARY. He was born Bet. 1780 - 1790, and died Aft. 1830 in Todd Co., KY.

     William Rice is listed in the 1830 Todd Co., KY census, pg. 385. Parnela (sic) Rice (60) is listed as head of the household in the 1850 Todd Co., KY census, pg. 217.

Children of PAMELIA PENDLETON and WILLIAM RICE are:

    i.   EDMUND PENDLETON[10] RICE, b. Abt. 1804, KY; d. Jun 19, 1872, Crittenden Co., KY; m. ARELINA GORIN, Abt. 1840; b. Oct 21, 1809, Warren Co., KY.

         Edmund Rice lived in the Dycusburg area of Crittenden Co., KY per the 1860 census, land located near the Cumberland River, southern part of the county near Lyon and Livingston Counties. He died of pneumonia and his will recorded in Crittendon Co. His brother, Claborn Rice was his Executor. On the 1870 census, his wife was shown as head of household, had an Ella (18), Harvey Gray (28), and Emaline Tinsdale (10), also in the household (Ref. 148).

   ii. CYNTHIA RICE, b. 1806; m. JAMES MANSFIELD.

  iii. ANN NANCY RICE, b. 1810, KY; m. JOSIAH CARNEAL.

   iv. JOHN C. "JACK" RICE, b. 1813.

    v. WILLIAM CLAYBORNE RICE, b. Dec 15, 1818; d. 1872; m. (1) KNOTT, 1846; d. 1848; m. (2) SARAH GLENN, 1850.

   vi. LOUISA "LOU" RICE, b. Abt. 1820.

  vii. CLAYBORNE RICE, b. 1824; d. 1895; m. MARTHA WILSON.

 viii. CATHERINE RICE, m. JOHN D. GREY.

   ix. PAMELIA RICE, m. WILLIAM SHUREY.

151. EDMUND[9] PENDLETON (*CURTIS[8], HENRY[7], JOHN[6], PHILIP[5], HENRY[4], HENRY[3], GEORGE[2], GEORGE[1]*) was born Oct 2, 1788 in VA, and died Aug 22, 1877 in Clark Co., KY. He married RACHEL ALLEN Jan 4, 1814 in Clark Co., KY, daughter of THOMAS ALLEN. She was born Abt. 1799, and died Dec 5, 1844 in Clark Co., KY.

     Edmund Pendleton is listed in the 1812 Muster Rolls in the 2nd Regiment (Dannaldson's) Mounted, Kentucky Volunteers, 1st Sergeant. He served in the War of 1812 under Gov. Isaac Shelby. He is listed in the 1830 through 1870 Clark Co., KY census rolls. Edmund, along with his wife Rachael and sons Virgil and Thomas, are buried in family graveyard (Allen-Pendleton) at the S. Willis Van Meter farm on Van Meter Rd at the intersection of Bourbon, Clark, and Fayette Counties near Clintonville, KY (Ref. 149).

Surety for the marriage bond of Rachel Allen and Edmund Pendleton was provided by Thomas Allen, her father. The following was extracted from a Clark Co., KY will book (Ref. 150):

Name: Rachel Headrick. Rachel Headrick and Gibson Clark Headrick, children of John, My son My daughters, towit, Sally McConnell and Polly Allen To Rachel Pendleton, Jefferson Allen, Thomas B. Allen, Cyrus Allen, children of Thomas and Polly Allen To Milissa McConnell, Ovia McCracken McConnell, Isaac Perry McConnell, Archibald F. McConnell and Sally M. McConnell, children of Archibald and Sally McConnell To Rachel Pendleton If Cyrus McCracken Witnesses: William Barkley and James Barnes Written: 28 June 1816 Probated: July 1822.

Children of EDMUND PENDLETON and RACHEL ALLEN are (Ref. 151):

i. PAMELIA[10] PENDLETON, b. Jan 30, 1815, Clark Co., KY; d. Aug 1, 1847; m. ROBERT A. GIBNEY, DR., Apr 30, 1839, Clark Co., KY; b. Abt. 1817.

The following narrative (Ref. 152) indicates that Dr. R. A. Gibney remarried and that Virgil Pendleton Gibney is the son of Amanda Weagley Gibney. However, the name and date of birth suggest that Pamelia Pendleton could have been his mother.

Virgil Pendleton Gibney,, surgeon, was born in Jessamine county, Ky., Sept. 29, 1847; son of Robert A. and Amanda (Weagley) Gibney. He was graduated from Kentucky university, Lexington, A.B., 1833, A.M., 1872, and received his M.D. degree from the Bellevue Hospital medical college, New York city, in 1871. He was connected with the Hospital for ruptured and crippled, New York city, as resident junior assistant for a few months of 1871; as house surgeon, 1871-83; as assistant surgeon from January to May, 1884, and as surgeon-in-chief from 1887. He was one of the founders of the New York polyclinic in 1882 and occupied its chair of orthopedic surgery, 1882-95, resigning to accept the first chair of orthopedic surgery in the medical department of Columbia university (College of physicians and surgeons, N.Y.) He became consulting orthopedic surgeon to the Nursery and Child's hospital, New York city, in 1884; was president of the New York orthopedic society, 1885, and first president of the American orthopedic association, 1887. In 1876 he was elected a fellow of the New York academy of medicine and was chairman of the orthopedic section in 1886. He was made a member of several other medical societies, local and national. He published The Hip and its Diseases (1883); besides many contributions to medical periodicals." R.A. Gibney (33), physician, is found in the 1850 Jessamine Co., KY census with Amanda (26) and Virgil (2).

ii. CURTIS PENDLETON, b. Nov 23, 1816, Clark Co., KY; d. Abt. 1818, Clark Co., KY.

His nurse let him fall in a kettle of hot water (Ref. 151).

364. iii. MARY ALLEN PENDLETON, b. Sep 12, 1819, Clark Co., KY.

365. iv. VIRGIL M. PENDLETON, b. May 7, 1821, Clark Co., KY; d. Mar 23, 1863, Clark Co., KY.

v.   NANCY W. PENDLETON, b. Apr 20, 1823, KY; m. I. J. SPENCER, REV., Oct 19, 1846, Clark Co., KY.

vi.   THOMAS A. PENDLETON, b. 1825, KY; d. Jan 24, 1849, Clark Co., KY.

vii.   EDMUND PENDLETON, b. 1827, Clark Co., KY; d. Feb 9, 1878, Clark Co., KY.

An Edmund Pendleton (23) is listed in the household of Allen Baldwin, candle maker, in the 1850 Fayette Co., KY, District 2 census. Edmund Pendleton is buried in the Lexington Cemetery.

152. JOHN[9] PENDLETON *(CURTIS[8], HENRY[7], JOHN[6], PHILIP[5], HENRY[4], HENRY[3], GEORGE[2], GEORGE[1])* was born Abt. 1790 in VA, and died Aft. 1850 in Todd Co., KY? He married (1) PATSY RICHARDSON Dec 22, 1810 in Clark Co., KY. She was born Abt. 1790, and died Abt. 1815 in Todd Co., KY. He married (2) REBECCA REED Mar 14, 1819 in Christian Co., KY. He married (3) NANCY HILL Apr 6, 1824 in KY. He married (4) LUCY MILLER Bef. 1850. She was born Abt. 1790 in VA, and died Aft. 1850 in Todd Co., KY?

John Pendleton is listed near his father, Curtis, in the 1820 Todd Co. census. He is also listed in the 1830, 1840, and 1850 Todd Co., KY census records.

Children of JOHN PENDLETON and PATSY RICHARDSON are:
366.   i.   HARVEY B.[10] PENDLETON, b. 1811, KY; d. Aft. 1850, Todd Co., KY?
367.   ii.   NANCY C. PENDLETON, b. Abt. 1815, Todd Co., KY; d. Aft. 1884, Todd Co., KY?

Children of JOHN PENDLETON and REBECCA REED are:
368.   iii.   SARAH ANN[10] PENDLETON, b. Abt. 1820, KY.
369.   iv.   ELIZA REBECCA PENDLETON, b. Oct 19, 1822, Todd Co., KY; d. Aft. 1880.

153. LUCINDA[9] PENDLETON *(CURTIS[8], HENRY[7], JOHN[6], PHILIP[5], HENRY[4], HENRY[3], GEORGE[2], GEORGE[1])* was born 1797 in Clark Co., KY, and died Abt. 1830 in KY. She married JOHN GAY Dec 17, 1811 in Clark Co., KY, son of JAMES GAY and SARAH PATTON. He was born May 18, 1792 in Clark Co., KY, and died Aft. 1860 in Boone Co., MO?

Children of LUCINDA PENDLETON and JOHN GAY are:
i.   ELIZABETH[10] GAY, b. Abt. 1812, KY.
ii.   JAMES GAY, b. 1814, KY; d. 1876, IN?; m. DEBORAH CAMPBELL RIGGS, May 7, 1840, Boone Co., MO; b. Nov 5, 1821, Boone Co., MO; d. May 16, 1873, Audrain Co., MO.
iii.   MARY GAY, b. Abt. 1820, KY; m. WILLIAM LYNE, Oct 24, 1838, Boone Co., MO.
iv.   WILLIAM T. GAY, m. SALLY R. BASS, Feb 26, 1851, Boone Co., MO.
v.   JOHN DUNLAP GAY, b. Apr 14, 1824; d. Jan 19, 1911, Callaway Co., MO; m. MARY JANE; b. Apr 16, 1832; d. Jan 15, 1891, Callaway Co., MO.

vi. CURTIS P. MARTIN GAY, b. 1827, KY; m. CATHERINE HOLMES, Jan 31, 1850, Boone Co., MO; b. 1831, TN.

154. WILLIAM CURTIS⁹ PENDLETON *(CURTIS⁸, HENRY⁷, JOHN⁶, PHILIP⁵, HENRY⁴, HENRY³, GEORGE², GEORGE¹)* was born Abt. 1803 in Clark Co., KY, and died in Todd Co., KY? He married HARRIET MABEN FRAZER Jun 21, 1827 in KY, daughter of JOSEPH FRAZER and LOCKEY EWING. She was born Oct 8, 1811 in KY, and died Abt. 1885.

William Pendleton is listed in the 1830 Todd Co., KY census adjacent to John Pendleton, his brother.

Children of WILLIAM PENDLETON and HARRIET FRAZER are:

370. i. LUCINDA G.¹⁰ PENDLETON, b. 1829, KY; d. Muhlenberg Co., KY?
ii. NANCY RACHEL PENDLETON, b. Mar 31, 1834, KY.

A Nancy Pendleton (16) is in the household of J.C. Frazier, in the Todd Co, KY 1850 census. Apparently, this is her grandfather Joseph Coulton Frazier.

iii. JULIET ANN PENDLETON, b. Bet. 1828 - 1837.
iv. THOMAS H. PENDLETON, b. Bet. 1828 - 1837.

A Thomas K.? Pendleton is listed near the Presley Pendleton household in the 1850 Ralls Co., MO census, 73rd district.

155. THOMAS W.⁹ PENDLETON *(CURTIS⁸, HENRY⁷, JOHN⁶, PHILIP⁵, HENRY⁴, HENRY³, GEORGE², GEORGE¹)* was born Apr 3, 1806 in Clark Co., KY, and died Jul 15, 1870 in Muhlenberg Co., KY. He married ELIZA ANN MCQUARRY Abt. 1838 in KY. She was born Abt. 1820 in VA, and died Aft. 1900 in Daviess Co., KY?

Thomas Pendleton is listed in the 1840 Todd Co. (Todd City) census adjacent to his brother John Pendleton. Thomas W. Pendleton (farmer) is listed in the 1850 Muhlenberg Co., KY census, Subdivision 2, pg 259.

Children of THOMAS PENDLETON and ELIZA MCQUARRY are:

i. WILLIAM C.¹⁰ PENDLETON, b. 1840, KY.

A William C. Pendleton enlisted in the Confederate Army in Hopkinsville, KY as a private on 22 September 1861. He served in C Co. 9th Infantry Regiment and died of wounds at Shelbyville, TN on 15 Mar 1862 (estimated date of death).

ii. SARAH E. PENDLETON, b. 1843, KY.
iii. MARY E. PENDLETON, b. 1845, KY.
371. iv. FANNY R. PENDLETON, b. 1847, KY; d. Aft. 1900, Daviess Co., KY?
v. JAMES M. PENDLETON, b. 1850, KY.
vi. JOHN T. PENDLETON, b. 1853, KY.
vii. EDMUND J. PENDLETON, b. 1855, KY.
viii. NANCY W. PENDLETON, b. 1858, KY.
372. ix. ISAIAH PENDLETON, b. 1860, KY; d. Aft. 1910, Owensbero, KY?

x. THORNTON PENDLETON, b. Abt. 1863, KY; d. Aft. 1900, Daviess Co., KY?

156. SALLY[9] PENDLETON *(RICE[8], HENRY[7], JOHN[6], PHILIP[5], HENRY[4], HENRY[3], GEORGE[2], GEORGE[1])* was born Jun 21, 1790 in KY, and died Jan 30, 1877 in Clark Co., KY. She married DANIEL WADE Jun 21, 1812 in Clark Co., KY. He was born Sep 22, 1788 in Goochland Co., VA, and died Feb 1, 1877 in Clark Co., KY.

Sally Wade is listed in the 1850 Clark Co, KY census, age 60, with Daniel Wade (62), farmer, William Wade (37), farmer, and Susan Wade (17); value of farm $16,000. The household is adjacent to a John Evans, perhaps the brother of Samuel Evans (husband of Lucy Pendleton). Daniel and Sally Wade are buried in the Wade Cemetery, Mt. Sterling, KY.

Children of SALLY PENDLETON and DANIEL WADE are:
    i. WILLIAM[10] WADE, b. Apr 10, 1813, Clark Co., KY; d. May 17, 1898, Clark Co., KY.
        William Wade is buried in the Wade Cemetery, Mt. Sterling, KY.

    ii. LUCY WADE, b. Abt. 1815, Clark Co., KY.
    iii. DUDLEY WADE, b. Dec 4, 1817, Clark Co., KY; d. Dec 9, 1883, Clark Co., KY; m. ELIZA A.; b. Dec 8, 1818; d. Jan 18, 1897, Mt. Sterling, KY.
        Dudley and Eliza A. Wade are buried at the Wade's Cemetery, Mt. Sterling, KY.

    iv. EDMUND WADE, b. Abt. 1821, Clark Co., KY; m. SALLY ANN MORRIS.
    v. ELIZABETH WADE, b. Oct 18, 1822, Clark Co., KY; d. Aug 2, 1867, Clark Co., KY.
    vi. EVELINE WADE, b. Abt. 1824, Clark Co., KY.
    vii. SUSAN WADE, b. Abt. 1832, Clark Co., KY.

157. THACKER[9] PENDLETON *(RICE[8], HENRY[7], JOHN[6], PHILIP[5], HENRY[4], HENRY[3], GEORGE[2], GEORGE[1])* was born 1791 in Clark County, KY?, and died Abt. 1864 in Bath Co., KY. He married POLLY ROUNDTREE Oct 3, 1816 in Winchester, Clark Co., KY, daughter of JOHN ROWNTREE and LUCY GORDON. She was born Abt. 1794 in VA, and died Aft. 1864.

Thacker Pendleton is included with his father Rice Pendleton in the 1820 Bath Co., Owingsville census. In the 1830 census he is in Clark Co. Thacker (farmer) and family are in Bath Co. for the 1840 and 1850 census. The Thacker Pendleton Estate Settlement is recorded at the Bath County Court House, dated Dec 15, 1864. Rice Pendleton was his administrator. Settlements and Credits were dispersed to James Crouch & Wife, Ruben Young, Charles Gordon & Wife, William Gordon (Jordan?) & Wife, John P. Kerrick & Nephew, Rice Pendleton, Walter Kerrick Heirs, and John T. Maze.

Children of THACKER PENDLETON and POLLY ROUNDTREE are (Ref. 153):

373.   i. CLARISSA[10] PENDLETON, b. Aug 1817, KY; d. Jan 3, 1854, Bath Co., KY.

374.   ii. MARTHA PENDLETON, b. Abt. 1820, Bath Co., KY; d. Abt. 1840, Bath Co., KY.

375.   iii. MARY PENDLETON, b. Abt. 1823, KY; d. Aft. 1860, Bath Co., KY?

376.   iv. RICE PENDLETON, b. 1828, Clark Co., KY; d. Jan 5, 1902, Clark Co., KY.

         v. SARAH PENDLETON, b. Abt. 1831, Clark Co., KY; m. FRANKLIN SHOUSE, Apr 5, 1855, Bath Co., KY.

        vi. NANCY PENDLETON, b. Abt. 1834, Clark Co., KY.

158. RICE[9] PENDLETON, JR. *(RICE[8], HENRY[7], JOHN[6], PHILIP[5], HENRY[4], HENRY[3], GEORGE[2], GEORGE[1])* was born 1792 in Clark Co., KY, and died Jan 17, 1867 in Clark Co., KY. He married (1) ELIZABETH JUDY Nov 21, 1816 in Clark Co., KY, daughter of MARTIN JUDY and ELIZABETH JUDY. She was born 1785 in PA, and died Jan 27, 1844 in Clark Co., KY. He married (2) CATHERINE REGAN Abt. 1846. She was born Abt. 1797 in Clark Co., KY, and died Aug 19, 1861 in Clark Co., KY. He married (3) MRS. ELIZABETH MITCHELL Dec 10, 1861 in Montgomery Co., KY. She was born Abt. 1811 in Montgomery Co., KY, and died Aft. 1867.

Rice Pendleton is listed as a private in the 1812 Muster Rolls, in the 17th Regiment (Francesco's), Kentucky Militia. He is listed in the 1830, 1850, and 1860 Clark Co., KY census records. Rice Pendleton, Jr. apparently lived in Clark Co. his entire life; he was a farmer and owned land on Stoner Creek in northern Clark Co.

Elizabeth Judy Pendleton is the daughter of Martin Judy and Elizabeth Judy who were cousins. Their farm on Wades Mill Pike in Clark Co, KY still exists. Apparently, someone took gravestones from the farm to IL in the 1930's because of the cemetery's poor condition. However, Elizabeth's daughter Elizabeth Pendleton Hardman and Elizabeth's husband Rice Pendleton remain buried there (Ref. 154).

Children of RICE PENDLETON and ELIZABETH JUDY are:

377.   i. ELIZABETH[10] PENDLETON, b. Oct 26, 1817, Clark Co., KY; d. May 7, 1866, Clark Co., KY.

378.   ii. EMILY PENDLETON, b. Nov 7, 1819, Clark Co., KY; d. Aug 6, 1845, Clark Co., KY.

         iii. DULCINDA PENDLETON, b. Abt. 1821, Clark Co., KY.
              She apparently died young as only 4 children are listed in the 1830 Clark Co. census.

379.   iv. DAVID J. PENDLETON, b. Nov 1824, Clark County, KY; d. Oct 1, 1900, Clark County, KY.

380.   v. LUCY ANN PENDLETON, b. Aug 14, 1827, Clark Co., KY; d. Dec 22, 1854, Clark Co., KY.

159. FRANCES "FANNY"[9] PENDLETON *(RICE[8], HENRY[7], JOHN[6], PHILIP[5], HENRY[4], HENRY[3], GEORGE[2], GEORGE[1])* was born Mar 17, 1797 in Clark County, KY, and died Mar 5, 1882 in Waynesville, IL. She married PETER S. BASHAW Nov 16,

1819 in Bath Co., KY. He was born 1800 in Culpepper Co, VA, and died 1860 in Polk Co., AR.

Peter and Frances Bashaw were in Sangamon Co., IL by 1828. They may have settled there in the portion that was partitioned into Logan Co. in 1839. However, in 1842, Peter Bashaw paid taxes on 550 acres along the Licking River water course, Bath Co., KY for 18 horses; 26 cattle.; 4 children over age 7, but under age 17. Frances Pendleton Bashaw is buried in Evergreen Cemetery, Waynesville, IL (Ref. 155).

Peter Bashaw apparently left his wife in the 1840's in Missouri and took up with Eve, a half-Cherokee girl, the dau of Hugh Tibbetts who was born in Vermont. Hugh was a Trader with the Early Cherokees who settled in the area starting soon after 1800. Peter Bashaw had several children with Eve (Ref. 155).

Children of FRANCES PENDLETON and PETER BASHAW are:
  i. AUSTIN[10] BASHAW, b. 1820.
  ii. DAUGHTER1 BASHAW, b. 1822.
  iii. JANE? BASHAW, b. 1825, Bath County, KY; d. 1826.
  iv. CHESLEY BASHAW, b. Abt. 1826, Bath Co., KY.
        Chesley Bashaw (24) was in the household of his Aunt, Jane Pendleton Boggs, in the 1850 Logan Co., IL census.

  v. JAMES BASHAW, b. 1831, Sangamon Co., IL; d. 1860, AR.
        A James Bashaw, private, served in the 47th Illinois infantry, Co. K and the 86th, Co. H., Union Army.

  vi. DANIEL B. BASHAW, b. 1833, IL; d. Abt. 1860, AR.
  vii. GEORGE WASHINGTON BASHAW, b. 1836, Pulaski Co., MO; d. Dec 10, 1862, AR.
        A George Bashaw served in the 139th Illinois Infantry, Co. C, Union Army; discharged as a Sergeant Major.

160. MARTHA "PATSY"[9] PENDLETON (*RICE*[8], *HENRY*[7], *JOHN*[6], *PHILIP*[5], *HENRY*[4], *HENRY*[3], *GEORGE*[2], *GEORGE*[1]) was born Abt. 1800 in Clark Co., KY, and died Abt. 1865 in Bath Co., KY. She married JONATHAN CASSITY CROUCH Jan 24, 1820 in Bath Co., KY, son of JONATHON CROUCH and HANNAH WELLS. He was born Jan 13, 1801 in KY, and died 1889 in Bath Co., KY.

In the 1840s Jonathon Crouch and his wife Patsy were involved in several land transactions in Bath Co. mostly connected with the former Pendleton lands (Ref. 101).

Children of MARTHA PENDLETON and JONATHAN CROUCH are:
  i. CURTIS R.[10] CROUCH, b. 1821, KY; m. CAROLINE HYMER; b. Abt. 1826, KY.
        Curtis Crouch and family are listed in the 1850 Bath Co., KY census.

  ii. THOMAS CROUCH, b. Abt. 1822, KY; m. AMANDA MELVINA RICE, Apr 2, 1843, Bath Co., KY.

iii. ELIZABETH ANN CROUCH, b. 1824, Bath Co., KY; d. Abt. 1890, Bath Co., KY; m. JAMES PERGREM, Aug 31, 1843, Bath Co., KY; b. Jun 4, 1818, Montgomery Co., KY; d. Bath Co., KY;.

iv. JONATHON G. CROUCH, b. 1829; m. SARAH RICE, Jul 25, 1850, Bath Co., KY.

v. MARTHA JANE CROUCH, b. 1834; d. 1909; m. JAMES SILAS MOORE.

vi. THRASHLEY "DICK" CROUCH, b. 1834, KY; d. 1910; m. ELIZABETH SPENCER, Dec 21, 1862, Bath Co., KY; b. Abt. 1845.

vii. FOSTER CROUCH, b. 1836.

161. PRESLEY[9] PENDLETON *(RICE[8], HENRY[7], JOHN[6], PHILIP[5], HENRY[4], HENRY[3], GEORGE[2], GEORGE[1])* was born Jan 13, 1803 in Clark County, KY, and died Sep 17, 1894 in Ralls Co., MO. He married DULCINA JUDY Jul 13, 1828 in Clark Co., KY. She was born Oct 29, 1803 in KY, and died Jul 24, 1876 in Ralls Co., MO.

Presley is listed in the 1830 Ralls Co. census, Salt River Township. Presley purchased 360 acres in Township 55-N, Ralls Co., MO from the Bureau of Land Management Palmyra Office in 6 increments from Nov 10, 1830 to Jan 1, 1850.

Dulcina Judy was the daughter of either John Judy or Martin Judy, Jr. She was the granddaughter of Martin & Elizabeth (Judy) Judy. The will of Martin Judy Sr. is recorded in Winchester, Clark Co., KY (Ref. 156): "I give to my Grandaughter, Dulcinda Pendleton, one negro girl slave named Eleanor...also three negros, Jacob, Isaac, and Jerry be equally divided between by Grandchildren...The heirs of Polly Ely, Anna Maxwell....Will Probated October Court, 1831."

Children of PRESLEY PENDLETON and DULCINA JUDY are (Ref. 157) :

381. i. DEBORAH STEVENS[10] PENDLETON, b. 1829, KY; d. 1899.

ii. EDMUND PENDLETON, b. Abt. 1832, Ralls Co., MO.
This may be the Edmund P. Pendleton in the 1860 Snohomish Co., WA census.

382. iii. MARTIN J. PENDLETON, b. Mar 24, 1834, Ralls Co., MO; d. Dec 4, 1907, Monroe Co., MO?

383. iv. PRESLEY A. PENDLETON, b. Abt. 1836, Ralls Co., MO; d. Aft. 1880, Monroe Co., MO?

384. v. DAVID J. PENDLETON, b. Oct 29, 1837, Ralls Co., MO; d. Dec 7, 1888, Butteville, OR?

385. vi. WILLIAM RICE PENDLETON, b. May 20, 1840, Ralls Co., MO; d. Nov 30, 1880, Ralls Co., MO.

vii. SARAH D. PENDLETON, b. Abt. 1847, Ralls Co., MO.

162. PRESTON[9] PENDLETON *(RICE[8], HENRY[7], JOHN[6], PHILIP[5], HENRY[4], HENRY[3], GEORGE[2], GEORGE[1])* was born Nov 14, 1804 in Clark County, KY, and died Aug 16, 1870 in Waynesville, IL. He married REBECCA HURT Jul 29, 1829 in Clark Co., KY, daughter of JOSHUA HURT and SALLY DAVIS. She was born Aug 13, 1811 in TN, and died Jun 30, 1878 in Waynesville, IL.

Preston and Rebecca Pendleton left KY in 1829, apparently shortly after their marriage and settled in Chester Township of what is now Logan Co., IL. Preston purchased land in Illinois in Township "19N" on November 3, 1829, July 2, 1831, October 5, 1835, and March 22, 1836. Each purchase was for $125 and involved over 4,000 acres each. Preston is listed in the 1840 Logan Co. Census. Later they moved to Big Grove on Kickapoo Creek between Atlanta, IL and Waynesville, IL. The family is listed in the 1850 Waynesville, DeWitt Co., IL census (his occupation: Milling) and the 1860 Logan Co., census, pg. 68. Preston is buried with his wife in the Evergreen Cemetery, Waynesville, IL (Ref. 101).

Children of PRESTON PENDLETON and REBECCA HURT are (Ref. 158):

386.   i.   BERRYMAN H.[10] PENDLETON, b. Dec 20, 1830, Logan Co, IL; d. Apr 13, 1881, IL.

        ii.   PRESLEY PENDLETON, b. Feb 2, 1832, IL; d. Sep 8, 1863, Memphis, TN - Civil War.

                Presley Pendleton is listed in the 1860 Logan Co., IL census adjacent to a household with a Mary Pendleton (26 and born in OH, perhaps his wife?). Presley Pendleton enlisted in the Union Army as a private on 01 August 1862. He claimed Residence in Atlanta, Logan Co., IL. He served in the Illinois, E Company, 106th Infantry Regiment (Ref. 159). He died of disease in Memphis Hospital, TN.

        iii. ALFRED W. PENDLETON, b. Jan 13, 1835, Lincoln, Logan Co., IL; d. Nov 24, 1876, IL.

                Alfred Pendleton (laborer) is apparently listed twice in the 1860 Logan Co. census: in the household of Richard Hurt and in the household of Robert Dugan. Alfred W. Pendleton enlisted in the Union Army as a private on 6 August, 1862 and served for the state of Illinois. He claimed residence in Chicago. He enlisted in Battery A Company, 1st LA Regiment, IL. He mustered Out on 10 July 1865 (Ref. 159). A pension application for Alfred Pendleton was filed June 18, 1891; application no. 424089; class invalid.

387.   iv.   EDMUND PENDLETON, b. Jan 18, 1837, Lincoln, Logan Co., IL; d. Aft. 1880, Logan Co., IL or CA?

388.   v.   SAMUEL EVANS PENDLETON, b. Aug 20, 1839, Logan Co., IL; d. Aft. 1900, Dickinson Co., KS?

389.   vi.   CYNTHIA A. PENDLETON, b. Oct 29, 1843, Lincoln, Logan Co., IL; d. Aft. 1880, DeWitt Co, IL?

        vii. LOUISA J. PENDLETON, b. Aug 5, 1848, Lincoln, Logan Co., IL; d. Oct 17, 1869; m. CHARLES E. SAMPSON.

390. viii.   JOHN S. PENDLETON, b. Nov 18, 1849, Lincoln, Logan Co., IL; d. Mar 3, 1918, Clintonia Township, IL.

        ix.   ELISHA W. PENDLETON, b. Oct 10, 1852, IL; d. Nov 14, 1867, Waynesville, Dewitt Co., IL.

163. LUCY E.[9] PENDLETON *(RICE[8], HENRY[7], JOHN[6], PHILIP[5], HENRY[4], HENRY[3], GEORGE[2], GEORGE[1])* was born Jul 8, 1805 in Clark County, KY, and died Jan 24, 1860 in Lincoln Co., IL. She married SAMUEL EVANS Nov 27, 1820 in Bath Co., KY. He was born Feb 11, 1805, and died Mar 30, 1847 in Lincoln Co., IL.

Samuel and Lucy Pendleton Evans moved to Illinois in 1828 and settled in Chester Township, in present day Logan Co. Later they moved to Salt Creek where he was licensed to operate a ferry across that creek in 1829. On 1 March 1837, the General Assembly of Illinois passed a special bill to permit him to build a toll bridge across this creek, which he had completed by the 1840 presidential campaign. He was an enthusiastic Whig. Lucy was living with her son Preston Evans, a merchant, in the 1850 Logan Co., IL census. None of their children lived to have families of their own and all are buried near the old family cabin atop Salt Creek Hill in the Evans Reserve of Union Cemetery (Ref. 101).

Child of LUCY PENDLETON and SAMUEL EVANS is:

    i. PRESTON[10] EVANS, b. Abt. 1829, IL; m. ESTHER; b. Abt. 1833.

        A Preston Evans, corporal, served in the 57th Indiana Infantry, Co. H, Union Army.

164. CHAMPNEY[9] PENDLETON *(RICE[8], HENRY[7], JOHN[6], PHILIP[5], HENRY[4], HENRY[3], GEORGE[2], GEORGE[1])* was born Dec 6, 1812 in Clark Co., KY, and died Jan 23, 1857 in Baker's Prairie, OR. He married PHEBE MANN Jul 29, 1830 in Sangamon Co., IL, daughter of MICHAEL MANN and ELIZABETH. She was born Dec 31, 1814 in OH, and died May 14, 1882 in Clackamas Co., OR.

Champney was about 11 years old when his father, Rice Sr. died in 1823. His guardian until at least 1827 was Thomas Hicks, husband of Elizabeth Pendleton and apparently a final settlement was made of the guardianship in Bath Co. in 1830 (Ref. 160). There are records of a Champney Pendleton purchasing land in Corwin Township, probably in Sangamon Co., IL in 1828 and 1829 and in Mt. Pulaski Township in 1831. Because of the movement of several of his brothers and sisters to this locality about this time, it is believed that this is the Champney Pendleton who purchased the land (Ref. 101). Champney is listed in the 1840 Logan Co., IL Census with 5 children (3 boys and 2 girls). The Champney Pendleton family traveled from Illinois to Oregon along the Oregon Trail about 1845. Champney (farmer) and family are listed in the 1850 Oregon Territory, Clackamas Co. Census. Pendletons were associated with various land claims in Oregon in the 1850's. Champney was buried at the Pendleton cemetery which was located on Champion Pendleton's Donation Land Claim in Canby, OR. All remains in the cemetery were moved to Zion Memorial Cemetery in Nov. 1965. A residential development is now on the location of the old farm and cemetery. The Inscription on his grave reads: "Aged 44 yrs 1 mo 17 das." The grave inscription of Phebe Mann Pendleton reads: "Wife of C. Pendleton" (Ref. 161).

Children of CHAMPNEY PENDLETON and PHEBE MANN are:

    i. RICE[10] PENDLETON, b. 1831, IL; d. Aft. 1870, Lane Co., OR?

        Rice is listed in the 1870 Lane Co., OR census, Eugene Township.

ii. JOHN PENDLETON, b. 1832, IL.

John H. Pendleton served in the Union Army, 1st Regiment, Co. I, Oregon Infantry with his brother Francis M.

391. iii. MICHAEL PENDLETON, b. Jan 6, 1835, IL; d. May 21, 1923, Molalla, Clackamas Co., OR.

392. iv. HANNAH PENDLETON, b. Aug 1837, IL; d. Aft. 1920, Marion Co., OR?

393. v. FRANCIS M. PENDLETON, b. 1841, IL; d. Aft. 1880.

394. vi. ELIZABETH PENDLETON, b. 1843, IL.

395. vii. LUCY JANE PENDLETON, b. 1847, OR; d. 1890, Clackamas Co., OR.

viii. PRESTON PENDLETON, b. Oct 1849, OR; d. Dec 9, 1924, Marion Co., OR.

Preston Pendleton (farmer) is listed in the 1900 Clackamas Co., OR census, pg. 50a. (not married). His death is recorded in the Oregon Death Index, 1903-98, Certificate 841.

ix. SAMUEL R. T. PENDLETON, b. Mar 2, 1851, OR; d. Feb 28, 1871, Clackamas Co., OR.

165. THRASHLEY[9] PENDLETON *(RICE*[8]*, HENRY*[7]*, JOHN*[6]*, PHILIP*[5]*, HENRY*[4]*, HENRY*[3]*, GEORGE*[2]*, GEORGE*[1]*)* was born 1815 in Clark County, KY, and died Abt. 1896 in Bath Co., KY. He married ARTEMECIA MCCLAIN Mar 28, 1852 in Bath Co., KY, daughter of GEORGE MCCLAIN and ELIZABETH RICHARDSON. She was born Jan 15, 1835 in Bath Co., KY, and died Mar 14, 1916 in Bath Co., KY.

Thrashley was the youngest son of Rice Pendleton, Sr. and was about 8 years old when his father died. Thrashley was apparently left in the care of his brother-in-law and sister, Jonathon and Martha Pendleton Crouch. In 1826, not long after Rice's death, Jonathon Crouch acquired 51 acres of the 243 1/4-acre Pendleton tract in Bath Co., KY. In 1828 he obtained another 80 acres of the Pendleton lands on Salt Lick Creek (Ref. 101). Thrashley first appears in the records of Bath County (Ref. 162) on 28 September, 1840 when he paid $30 to purchase 20 acres of property. He is subsequently involved in a number of real estate transactions in the 1840's mainly involving the sale of land on Salt Lick Creek. The old Pendleton property, indicated on local maps by the label "Pendleton Branch," can be found today east of Olympia Springs on highway 211 about 2 miles north of the highway 36 junction.

Thrashley Pendleton (farmer) and family are listed in Bath County District, White Sulfur Precinct #5 (near the old Upper Salt Lick Church) in the 1860, 1870 and 1880 census records. Thrashley along with his sons Newton, Lafayette, and Tilford, along with a Samuel Pendleton (no known relation) are included in a list of voters in White Sulphur Precinct, No. 5, Aug. 13, 1883. A 'T. Pendleton' appears on both an 1875-76 and an 1884 Survey Map of the White Sulphur precinct near the Upper Salt Lick Church. Thrashley died before April 23, 1896 when his property (140 acres at his death) was divided among his heirs (Ref. 163).

The residence of Artemicia McClain Pendleton in the 1910 census was along Mud Lick Rd., Bath Co., KY near Salt Lick.

Children of THRASHLEY PENDLETON and ARTEMECIA MCCLAIN are:

    i.   LAFAYETTE[10] PENDLETON, b. Jan 26, 1854, Bath Co., KY; d. Aug 3, 1906, Bath Co., KY.

        Lafayette, Uncle "Laif," lived on the family farm along Salt Lick Creek his entire life. After the death of his father, Thrashley, he was considered the head of the household in the 1900 Census. He never married and is buried in Upper Salt Lick Cemetery, Rt. 211 Bath Co., KY.

396.   ii.   TILFORD PENDLETON, b. May 1855, Bath Co., KY; d. Aug 1, 1924, Salt Lick, KY.

    iii.   NEWTON PENDLETON, b. Sep 26, 1857, Bath Co., KY; d. Oct 11, 1928, Bath Co., KY.

        Newton Pendleton, Uncle "Newt," kept his money under his bed. The money was stolen and he grieved terribly over the loss (Ref. 164). He also died unmarried and is buried in Upper Salt Lick Cemetery.

397.   iv.   SARAH E. PENDLETON, b. May 26, 1860, Bath Co., KY; d. 1925, Bath Co., KY.

    v.   MARY ELIZA PENDLETON, b. Nov 23, 1863, Bath Co., KY; d. Apr 7, 1918, Salt Lick, KY.

        Mary also never married and lived on the family farm her entire life. Her Death Certificate contains the following:

        Housekeeper; Single; Birthplace, Bath County, Kentucky; Father, Threshley Pendleton; Maiden Name of Mother, Artie M. McClain; "I hereby certify that I attended the deceased from August 1917 to March 31, 1918, that I last saw her alive on March 31, 1918, and that death occurred on the date stated above at 1:45 AM." The cause of death, tuberculosis of lungs; Signed C.T. Jones MD of Salt Lick, April 7, 1918; Burial, Salt Lick Graveyard; Date of Burial, April 8, 1918; Undertaker, Razor of Salt Lick, Kentucky.

    vi.   WILLIAM PENDLETON, b. Sep 17, 1867, Bath Co., KY; d. Jun 13, 1907, Bath Co., KY.

    vii.   GEORGE PENDLETON, b. Sep 1870, Bath Co., KY; d. Dec 17, 1934, Bath Co., KY; m. ARABELLA CROUCH, Bef. 1920; b. 1884, KY; d. Aug 31, 1957, Bath Co., KY.

        George Pendleton married late in life and had no children. He apparently lost an eye. He is also buried in Upper Salt Lick Cemetery; grave unmarked (Ref. 164). On Feb 19, 1835, the property of George Pendleton, deceased, was appraised. On April 6, 1935, Arabella Pendleton, administered the estate of George Pendleton (total property $161.76); her balance of $61.01 was exempt from distribution (Ref. 160).

166. EDMUND B.[9] PENDLETON *(ROBERT[8], HENRY[7], JOHN[6], PHILIP[5], HENRY[4], HENRY[3], GEORGE[2], GEORGE[1])* was born 1805 in VA, and died 1856 in Spotsylvania

Co., VA? He married LUCY ELLEN LEWIS Jan 12, 1837 in Spotsylvania Co., VA, daughter of JOEL LEWIS, JR. She was born Abt. 1820 in VA.

Edmund Pendleton (farmer) and family are listed in the 1850 Spotsylvania Co. census.

Children of EDMUND PENDLETON and LUCY LEWIS are:

i. WILLIAM STAPLETON[10] PENDLETON, b. 1838, Spotsylvania Co., VA; d. Bef. 1889, Richmond, VA; m. (1) MARTHA ANN WILLOUGHBY; b. 1838; d. 1857; m. (2) LUCY DEMARIONY LAFONG, Apr 28, 1859, Fredericksburg, VA; b. Oct 1838; d. Aft. 1910, Richmond, VA?.

The marriage of William Pendleton was announced in the Fredericksburg, Virginia Newspaper, dated May 17, 1859: "On the 28th of April, at the residence of Mr. James T. Smith, in this city by; the Rev. Mr. Pritchett, Mr. W.M.S. Pendleton, of Spotsylvania, to Miss Demariony L. LaFong, of Fredericksburg." He lived in Richmond, VA and was a conductor on the Richmond & Fredericksburg Railroad. The Richmond, Virginia City Directories, 1889-90 includes Lucy D Pendleton, widow of William S. at 826 Grace, W. Richmond, VA.

398. ii. ROBERT LEWIS PENDLETON, b. Aug 1843, Spotsylvania Co., VA; d. 1906, Spotsylvania Co., VA?

iii. ELIZABETH FANNY PENDLETON, b. 1848, Spotsylvania Co., VA; m. CHARLES TURNER, Dec 1872.

iv. MARY ELIZA PENDLETON, b. 1850, Spotsylvania Co., VA.

v. JOEL HENRY PENDLETON, b. 1856, Spotsylvania Co., VA.

167. JACKSON[9] PENDLETON (*ROBERT[8], HENRY[7], JOHN[6], PHILIP[5], HENRY[4], HENRY[3], GEORGE[2], GEORGE[1]*) was born Apr 4, 1810 in VA, and died Jan 18, 1894 in Spotsylvania Co., VA? He married (1) MARIA E. DUERSON Dec 24, 1835 in Spotsylvania Co., VA. She was born Abt. 1815 in VA, and died Apr 4, 1864. He married (2) DULCIE B. She was born Abt. 1835 in VA.

Jackson Pendleton (farmer) is listed in Spotsylvania Co., VA census records from 1840 to 1880. He is included in The Fredericksburg News (VA) in a court case on Oct 10, 1851 along with Robert and Edmund his brothers, Susan his sister, and Elizabeth Pendleton, his mother.

Children of JACKSON PENDLETON and MARIA DUERSON are:

i. MARY JANE[10] PENDLETON, b. Oct 31, 1842, VA; d. Mar 3, 1928, Spotsylvania Co., VA; m. LUCIUS M. ESTES, Dec 5, 1865; b. Abt. 1838, VA; d. Bef. 1910.

Mary Jane Pendleton is listed in the 1920 Orange Co., VA census with her sister, Edmonia.

ii. ELIZABETH "BETTIE" E. PENDLETON, b. Mar 22, 1845, VA; m. J. MATTHEW JOHNSON, Jan 1, 1872.

iii. MARTHA ANNE PENDLETON, b. Mar 4, 1847, VA; d. May 24, 1911.

iv. MARIA JACKSON PENDLETON, b. Mar 17, 1851, VA; d. Sep 15, 1890.

v. JOHN THOMAS PENDLETON, b. Mar 17, 1853, VA; d. Jul 20, 1915, Spotsylvania Co., VA?

John Pendleton (farmer) and his sisters Edmonia and Virginia are listed in the 1900 Spotsylvania Co., VA census, pg. 268a. All are single. They are joined by Mary Pendleton Estes, their sister, in the 1910 Spotsylvania Co., VA census.

vi. EDMONIA PENDLETON, b. Sep 7, 1855, VA; d. Dec 27, 1938, Orange Co., VA?

Edmonia Pendleton (single; farmer) is listed in the 1920 Gordon Township, Orange Co., VA census, pg. 6B.

vii. WILLIAM JACKSON PENDLETON, b. Jun 11, 1857, VA; d. Mar 13, 1881.

168. FRANCES[9] PENDLETON *(ROBERT[8], HENRY[7], JOHN[6], PHILIP[5], HENRY[4], HENRY[3], GEORGE[2], GEORGE[1])* was born Abt. 1814 in Spotsylvania Co., VA, and died Abt. 1856 in St. Louis Co., MO. She married WILLIAM EATHERTON Jan 28, 1830 in Spotsylvania Co., VA, son of BENJAMIN EATHERTON. He was born Abt. 1807 in Spotsylvania Co., VA, and died Jul 27, 1891 in St. Louis Co., MO.

William and Frances Eatherton moved to Gasconade Co., MO in 1839. William Eatherton purchased property in 1845 where the current Lake Chesterfield Apartments, south of Manchester Road in Wildwood, MO, is located. During construction of the apartments in 1998, a small family cemetery was discovered near the property (Ref. 165).

Children of FRANCES PENDLETON and WILLIAM EATHERTON are:

i. JAMES ROBERT[10] EATHERTON, b. May 10, 1830, VA; d. Apr 28, 1901, MO; m. MARTHA JANE BALL, Sep 22, 1852, St. Louis, MO; b. Mar 30, 1834, MO; d. Dec 19, 1902, St. Louis Co., MO.

"With Messrs. Eicherman and Woolsey of St. Louis, James Robert Eatherton erected a splendid mill at Orrville at a cost of $32,000. It burned down in 1868. James Eatherton owned the Captain Tyler Farm. He married the daughter of James Ball" (Ref. 166).

ii. JOHN BENJAMIN EATHERTON, b. May 10, 1833, VA; d. Jun 20, 1899, St. Louis Co., MO; m. SARAH LOUISE BOCOCH, Abt. 1860; b. May 1, 1833, VA; d. Jul 7, 1897, St. Louis Co., MO.

iii. WILLIAM EATHERTON, b. Dec 26, 1835, VA; d. Sep 20, 1892, St. Louis Co., MO; m. MARY JANE WILCOX, Apr 17, 1862, St. Louis Co., MO.

William Eatherton, private, served in the 3rd MO Infantry, Co. C, CSA.

iv. ELIZABETH EATHERTON, b. Abt. 1837, VA.

v. ALBERT G. EATHERTON, b. Abt. 1839, VA.

vi. SUSANNA EATHERTON, b. Abt. 1840, MO.

vii. LOUISA EATHERTON, b. Abt. 1844, MO.

viii. GEORGE L. EATHERTON, b. 1845, MO; d. 1915, St. Louis Co., MO; m. LOUISA E. WARFIELD, May 1870, St. Louis, MO; b. May 6, 1850; d. Jan 28, 1893, St. Louis Co., MO.

George L. Eatherton, private, served in the 4th MO Cavalry, Co. H, CSA.

ix. EDWARD T. EATHERTON, b. Abt. 1846, MO.
x. VIRGINIA EATHERTON, b. Mar 1848, MO; d. Feb 20, 1920; m. G. LOUIS STRECKER, Apr 8, 1869, St. Louis Co., MO; b. 1842, Louisville, KY; d. 1923, St. Louis Co., MO.
xi. THOMAS B. EATHERTON, b. Abt. 1851, MO.
xii. EDMOND EATHERTON, b. Abt. 1853, MO.
xiii. EMILY EATHERTON, b. Abt. 1856, MO.

169. ROBERT^9 PENDLETON *(ROBERT^8, HENRY^7, JOHN^6, PHILIP^5, HENRY^4, HENRY^3, GEORGE^2, GEORGE^1)* was born Mar 15, 1813 in VA, and died Dec 9, 1892 in Spotsylvania Co., VA. He married MARTHA ANNE ELIZABETH KELSO Dec 7, 1847 in Spotsylvania Co., VA, daughter of JAMES KELSO and ELIZABETH. She was born May 26, 1820 in VA, and died Jun 11, 1875 in Spotsylvania Co., VA.

Robert Pendleton is listed as manager in the 1850 Spotsylvania Co., VA census (age 35); also listed are his mother Elizabeth (69), farmer c/o?, his sisters, Susan (40) and Elizabeth (37), his wife, Martha, and his son, George (2). Robert Pendleton (farmer) and family are listed in the 1870 Livingston, Spotsylvania Co., VA census.

Children of ROBERT PENDLETON and MARTHA KELSO are:
399. i. GEORGE ALLEN^{10} PENDLETON, b. Oct 18, 1848, VA; d. Feb 6, 1912, Spotsylvania Co., VA.
400. ii. ROBERT JAMES PENDLETON, b. Jul 30, 1851, VA; d. Feb 18, 1927, Spotsylvania Co., VA.
iii. MARY ELIZABETH PENDLETON, b. May 30, 1855, VA; d. Aft. 1870, (young).
iv. SUSAN FRANCES PENDLETON, b. Jul 27, 1858, VA; d. Aft. 1910, Spotsylvania Co., VA?; m. ALVIN TEMPLE SMITH, Oct 16, 1901; b. Abt. 1855, VA; d. Aft. 1910, Spotsylvania Co., VA?

Alvin T. Smith (farmer) and family are listed in the 1910 Spotsylvania Co., VA census. Eugene A. Smith (21) is apparently a son of his first wife.

v. MARTHA JANE PENDLETON, b. Aug 27, 1861, VA; d. Jun 30, 1863.

170. LOUISA BURRUS^9 PENDLETON *(ROBERT^8, HENRY^7, JOHN^6, PHILIP^5, HENRY^4, HENRY^3, GEORGE^2, GEORGE^1)* was born Abt. 1820 in VA. She married JOSEPH HENRY GERRELL Dec 3, 1840, son of BLAND GERRELL and ELIZABETH PENDLETON. He was born Abt. 1815 in VA, and died Aft. 1855 in VA?

Children of LOUISA PENDLETON and JOSEPH GERRELL are:
i. MARY E.^{10} GERRELL, b. Sep 11, 1841.

ii. ROBERT HENRY GERRELL, b. Dec 14, 1843, Spotsylvania Co., VA; d. Jan 20, 1907, Spotsylvania Co., VA?; m. SARAH ANN JOHNSON, Oct 19, 1865; d. Jan 1, 1907, Spotsylvania Co., VA?

iii. LOUISA A. GERRELL, b. Jan 18, 1846.

iv. JOHN BLAND GERRELL, b. May 2, 1848; d. Jan 19, 1912.

v. MARGARET F. GERRELL, b. Oct 26, 1850.

vi. JOSEPHINE GERRELL, b. Nov 14, 1857.

vii. SUSAN ALICE GERRELL, b. May 21, 1863.

171. BENJAMIN[9] PENDLETON *(PHILIP[8], BENJAMIN[7], PHILIP[6], PHILIP[5], HENRY[4], HENRY[3], GEORGE[2], GEORGE[1])* was born 1780 in VA, and died Bef. 1828 in King William Co., VA? He married CATHERINE GATEWOOD Apr 06, 1804 in King & Queen Co., VA. She was born 1783 in VA, and died Aft. 1850 in King and Queen Co., VA?

Benjamin Pendleton is listed in the 1810 and 1820 King William Co., VA census records. Catherine Pendleton (67) is listed in the household of William (70) and Frances (65) Massoc in the 1850 King and Queen Co., VA census.

Children of BENJAMIN PENDLETON and CATHERINE GATEWOOD are:

401. i. JOSEPH HOLMES[10] PENDLETON, b. Dec 19, 1809, Of King and Queen Co., VA; d. 1848, VA.

402. ii. PRISCILLA PENDLETON, b. Jan 13, 1813, VA.

iii. ALICE PENDLETON, b. Bet. 1815 - 1820, VA; m. ? BAYLOR.

172. PHILIP BAYLOR[9] PENDLETON *(PHILIP[8], BENJAMIN[7], PHILIP[6], PHILIP[5], HENRY[4], HENRY[3], GEORGE[2], GEORGE[1])* was born 1778 in VA, and died 1836 in King & Queen Co., VA? He married (1) MARY WOOD Oct 16, 1810 in Essex Co., VA. He married (2) REBECCA WOOD. She was born Abt. 1800 in VA, and died Aft. 1860 in King & Queen Co., VA?

The marriage of Philip Pendleton and Polly (Mary) Wood is recorded in Reference 25. Philip B. Pendleton is listed in the 1812 Muster Rolls, Corporal, 6th Regiment (Read Jr.'s), Virginia Militia. Philip B. Pendleton was involved in the first Church building of the first Disciples of Christ (Smyrna Church) in Powcan, King & Queen Co. in 1832. He was against the sale of liquor. He is listed in the 1830 King William Co., VA census. Philip B. Pendleton of Virginia married Miss Rebecca Wood of Lexington, KY on Dec. 19, 1838 (Ref. 167).

Rebecca Pendleton (50) is listed in 1850 King and Queen Co., VA census with Africa Smith (30; female) near the household of George M. Pendleton. She is also listed in the King and Queen Co. 1860 census.

Children of PHILIP PENDLETON and MARY WOOD are:

i. MARY CATHERINE[10] PENDLETON, m. DR. WILLIAM B. TODD.
    Dr. William B. Todd (40) is listed in the 1850 King & Queen Co., VA census, St. Stephens Parish, along with Julia (30) and William V. Robin (15).

ii. PATTIE PENDLETON, d. young.

403.   iii.   JAMES PENDLETON, b. Abt. 1821, King and Queen Co., VA; d. Richmond, Henrico Co., VA?

404.   iv.   ROBINETTE PENDLETON, b. Jun 21, 1822, VA; d. Dec 09, 1905, King and Queen Co., VA?

405.   v.   JR. PHILIP BAYLOR PENDLETON, b. Abt. 1826, King and Queen Co., VA; d. Abt. 1860, King and Queen Co., VA.

173. ROBERT M.[9] PENDLETON (*PHILIP[8], BENJAMIN[7], PHILIP[6], PHILIP[5], HENRY[4], HENRY[3], GEORGE[2], GEORGE[1]*) was born Abt. 1787 in VA, and died Aft. 1840 in King and Queen Co., VA? He married (1) MISS DESHAZO. He married (2) ELIZABETH CAMPBELL Apr 09, 1812 in King and Queen Co., VA, daughter of WHITAKER CAMPBELL and MARTHA DESHAZO. She was born Abt. 1795 in VA, and died Aft. 1860 in Kenton Co., KY?

R. M. Pendleton is listed in the 1840 King & Queen Co., VA census.

Child of ROBERT PENDLETON and ELIZABETH CAMPBELL is:
   i.   MARY C.[10] PENDLETON, b. Abt. 1815.

174. MARY ANNE[9] PENDLETON (*PHILIP[8], BENJAMIN[7], PHILIP[6], PHILIP[5], HENRY[4], HENRY[3], GEORGE[2], GEORGE[1]*) was born Abt. 1789 in VA. She married JOHN PHILIP DUVAL, DR. Nov 04, 1819 in King & Queen Co., VA, son of WILLIAM DUVAL. He was born May 21, 1795 in Gloucester Co., VA.

Child of MARY PENDLETON and JOHN DUVAL is:
   i.   MARY ANNE[10] DUVAL.

175. GEORGE MACON[9] PENDLETON (*PHILIP[8], BENJAMIN[7], PHILIP[6], PHILIP[5], HENRY[4], HENRY[3], GEORGE[2], GEORGE[1]*) was born 1790 in VA, and died Jul 30, 1866 in King & Queen Co., VA? He married KATHERINE LIPSCOMB Nov 06, 1816 in VA. She was born 1799 in VA, and died 1874 in King & Queen Co., VA?

George M. Pendleton is included in the 1812 Muster Rolls, 52nd Regiment (Christian's) Virginia Militia. George M. Pendleton is listed in the 1820 and 1830 King William Co., VA census records and the 1840 King and Queen Co. census. He appears as a farmer in the 1850 King and Queen Co., VA census (age 58), value of farm $6,000; also listed are Catherine (52), Benjamin F. (15), Ella (9), and his brother William F. Pendleton (62).

Children of GEORGE PENDLETON and KATHERINE LIPSCOMB are:
406.   i.   ADELINE[10] PENDLETON, b. Oct 26, 1817, King & Queen Co., VA; d. Aug 27, 1908, Mount Lebanon, LA.

407.   ii.   WILLIAM HENRY PENDLETON, b. Oct 15, 1819, King William Co., VA; d. Oct 25, 1895, Downey, CA.

408.   iii.   GEORGE MACON PENDLETON, b. Dec 27, 1825, VA; d. Mar 27, 1907, Union Co., AR.

409.   iv.   CATHERINE ANNE PENDLETON, b. Dec 1827, VA; d. Aft. 1900, King & Queen Co., VA?

410. v. MARIA LOUISA PENDLETON, b. Abt. 1829, VA; d. Aft. 1860, King & Queen Co., VA?

411. vi. JOHN BAYLOR PENDLETON, b. Sep 1831, VA; d. Abt. 1901, Dinwiddie Co., VA?

412. vii. BENJAMIN FLEET PENDLETON, b. 1835, King and Queen Co., VA; d. 1862, Civil War.

viii. POMPEY PENDLETON, b. Abt. 1837, King and Queen Co., VA; d. infancy.

ix. EDMUND PENDLETON, b. Jul 23, 1839, King and Queen Co., VA; d. infancy.

413. x. ELLA PENDLETON, b. Abt. 1841, King and Queen Co., VA; d. 1933, Newton, King and Queen Co., VA?

176. ELIZA[9] PENDLETON *(JAMES[8], BENJAMIN[7], PHILIP[6], PHILIP[5], HENRY[4], HENRY[3], GEORGE[2], GEORGE[1])* was born Sep 02, 1786 in VA. She married (1) JAMES MUSCOE GARNETT Dec 22, 1806. He was born 1784, and died Mar 10, 1807 in Essex Co., VA. She married (2) THOMAS W. TODD Dec 01, 1808.

Children of ELIZA PENDLETON and THOMAS TODD are:
  i. JAMES BERNARD[10] TODD, b. Sep 28, 1809; d. Mar 17, 1813.
  ii. ELIZABETH ELLEN TODD, b. Jan 05, 1813; d. May 08, 1860; m. JOHN K. GARNETT, Jun 16, 1831.
  iii. FRANCES ANNE TODD, b. Mar 03, 1816; d. Dec 23, 1861; m. THOMAS WILLIAM LOWEY FAUNTLEROY, Jun 16, 1832.
  iv. MARY PEACHEY TODD, b. Jan 11, 1819; d. Nov 13, 1862; m. GEORGE WILLIAM POLLARD, DR., Jun 15, 1837, King & Queen Co., VA.

177. ANN MARIA "NANCY"[9] PENDLETON *(JAMES[8], BENJAMIN[7], PHILIP[6], PHILIP[5], HENRY[4], HENRY[3], GEORGE[2], GEORGE[1])* was born Apr 11, 1791 in VA, and died Jul 01, 1828 in King and Queen Co., VA. She married REUBEN MERIWETHER GARNETT, COL. Dec 22, 1812 in King and Queen Co., VA. He was born 1777, and died 1847.

Children of ANN PENDLETON and REUBEN GARNETT are:
  i. MARY SUSAN[10] GARNETT, m. BENJAMIN F. DEW.
  ii. JOHN MUSCOE GARNETT, b. 1819; d. 1855; m. ANNE ELIZABETH HANCOCK, 1845; b. 1823; d. 1892.

178. SALLY[9] PENDLETON *(BENJAMIN[8], PHILIP[7], PHILIP[6], PHILIP[5], HENRY[4], HENRY[3], GEORGE[2], GEORGE[1])* was born Abt. 1780 in Buckingham Co., VA, and died Bef. 1849 in Smith Co., TN? She married JAMES PARIS Oct 24, 1800 in Prince Edward Co., VA, son of JAMES PARIS and ELIZABETH. He was born Abt. 1782 in Prince Edward Co., VA, and died Abt. 1848 in Smith Co., TN?

Children of SALLY PENDLETON and JAMES PARIS are (Ref. 168):

     i.   BENJAMIN[10] PARIS, b. Abt. 1801, VA; d. Bet. 1870 - 1880, Crittenden Co., KY; m. JANE, Abt. 1825, Smith Co., TN; b. Abt. 1803, SC; d. Bet. 1870 - 1880, Crittenden Co., KY.

    ii. JAMES LEONARD PARIS, b. May 01, 1803, Prince Edward Co., VA; d. Apr 13, 1862, Crittenden Co., KY; m. JULIA A. HUGHES, Abt. 1824, Buckingham Co., VA; b. Abt. 1805, Buckingham Co., VA; d. Bet. 1850 - 1860, Crittenden Co., KY.

   iii. OBADIAH PARIS, b. Mar 19, 1805, Prince Edward Co., VA; d. Mar 08, 1870, Crittenden Co., KY; m. MARTHA ELLISON, Abt. 1823, Smith Co., TN; b. Jun 29, 1805, Green Co., KY; d. Jul 04, 1879, Crittenden Co., KY.

   iv. MARTHA N. PARIS, b. Abt. 1807, Prince Edward Co., VA; m. (1) LEANDER HUGHES, Abt. 1832, Smith Co., TN; b. Bet. 1770 - 1780, Cumberland Co., VA; d. 1836, Smith Co., TN; m. (2) REUBEN BAIRD, Abt. 1842, Smith Co., TN; b. Bet. 1800 - 1805; d. Aug 1849, Smith Co., TN.

    v. ELIZABETH PARIS, b. Abt. 1808, Prince Edward Co., VA; d. Bet. 1850 - 1857, Smith Co., TN; m. EPHRAIM AGEE, Bet. 1825 - 1828, Smith Co., TN; b. Abt. 1808, Smith Co., TN; d. Abt. 1860, Smith Co., TN.

   vi. UNK. PARIS, b. Abt. 1810.

  vii. UNK. PARIS, b. Bet. 1810 - 1820.

 viii. PLEASANT PARIS, b. Abt. 1813, Prince Edward Co., VA; d. Nov 23, 1864, Eddysville, KY; m. NANCY JANE PARIS, Dec 25, 1834, Smith Co., TN; b. Abt. 1816, Smith Co., TN.

   ix. SARAH J. PARIS, b. Abt. 1816, Prince Edward Co., VA; d. Abt. 1851, Crittenden Co., KY; m. LITTLE BERRY ALLISON, Abt. 1835, Smith Co., TN; b. Apr 30, 1817, Smith Co., TN; d. Aug 08, 1867, Crittenden Co., KY.

    x. NANCY L. PARIS, b. Abt. 1820, Smith Co., TN; m. FRANCES MARION SMART; b. Abt. 1819, Wilson Co., TN.

   xi. WILLIAM PARIS, b. Oct 11, 1821, Smith Co., TN; d. Feb 26, 1888, Smith Co., TN; m. TRANQUILLA J. TWIGG; b. Sep 17, 1820, TN; d. Smith Co., TN;.

  xii. DELILAH PARIS, b. Aug 08, 1824, Smith Co., TN; d. Feb 20, 1904, Smith Co., TN; m. JEREMIAH H. BAIRD, Jan 19, 1843, Smith Co., TN; b. Feb 02, 1824, Smith Co., TN; d. Feb 10, 1898, Smith Co., TN.

179. BENJAMIN[9] PENDLETON (*BENJAMIN[8], PHILIP[7], PHILIP[6], PHILIP[5], HENRY[4], HENRY[3], GEORGE[2], GEORGE[1]*) was born Abt. 1800 in VA, and died Aft. 1860 in Wayne Co., IL? He married PHOEBE DONAHO Jan 14, 1824 in Warren Co., KY. She was born Abt. 1803 in KY, and died Aft. 1860 in Wayne Co., IL?

    Benjamin Pendleton was granted 12 Acres, June 15, 1841, in Warren Co., KY with no watercourse (Ref. 169). Benjamin Pendleton (farmer) and his wife Phoebe are listed in the 1860 Wayne Co., IL census.

Children of BENJAMIN PENDLETON and PHOEBE DONAHO are:
    i.   W. L.[10] PENDLETON, b. Abt. 1827, KY.
         W.L. Pendleton (carpenter) is listed in the 1860 Wayne Co., IL census in the household of Andrew Jackson, coach maker.

414.   ii. JAMES B. PENDLETON, b. Abt. 1829, KY.

180. JOHN[9] PENDLETON *(JAMES[8], PHILIP[7], PHILIP[6], PHILIP[5], HENRY[4], HENRY[3], GEORGE[2], GEORGE[1])* was born 1787 in Buckingham Co., VA, and died Aft. 1860 in Lawrence Co., MO. He married MARY DOSS Abt. 1811 in Buckingham Co., VA. She was born 1790 in VA, and died May 27, 1874 in Buck Prairie, Lawrence Co., MO.
      This is apparently the John Pendleton, Jr. listed in the 1820 Buckingham Co., VA census. He moved to KY and later to MO. John and Mary Pendleton are listed in the 1860 Lawrence Co., MO census along with Sarah Pendleton Dunning and her children.

Children of JOHN PENDLETON and MARY DOSS are (Ref. 170):
      i. NANCY PHIPPS[10] PENDLETON, b. Abt. 1813, Buckingham Co., VA.
415.   ii. ELIZABETH JENKINS PENDLETON, b. May 28, 1816, Buckingham Co., VA; d. Feb 12, 1903, Mt. Vernon, Lawrence, MO.
416.   iii. WILLIAM MONROE PENDLETON, b. 1821, VA; d. 1909, MO?
417.   iv. JOHN PENDLETON, b. 1824, Buckingham Co., VA; d. Nov 11, 1897, Lawrence Co., MO.
      v. POLLY PENDLETON, b. Abt. 1825; m. HENRY CAMPLINE, Feb 12, 1846, Caldwell Co., KY.
     vi. JAMES T. PENDLETON, b. 1829, KY; m. MARY A. STACY, Aug 19, 1852, Lawrence Co., MO.
         A James T. Pendleton enlisted in Williamport, TN on 9 Dec., 1862 as Private in CSA; served in A Co., 15th Cav. Reg., KY

418. vii. SARAH JANE PENDLETON, b. 1835, Caldwell Co., KY; d. Aft. 1880, Aurora, Lawrence Co., MO.

181. MACE COLEMAN[9] PENDLETON *(MACE[8], PHILIP[7], PHILIP[6], PHILIP[5], HENRY[4], HENRY[3], GEORGE[2], GEORGE[1])* was born Abt. 1804 in VA, and died Aft. 1850 in Rowan Co., NC? He married SUSAN BALLINGER Apr 12, 1825 in VA, daughter of HENRY BALLINGER. She was born 1811 in Of Lynchburg, VA, and died Aft. 1850.
      Mace Pendleton is listed in the 1830 Pittsylvania Co., VA census. He is listed as a printer in the Salisbury, Rowan Co., 1850 NC Census.

Children of MACE PENDLETON and SUSAN BALLINGER are:
    i.   RICHARD B.[10] PENDLETON, b. Abt. 1828; m. MARY A.
         Richard B. Pendleton is listed as a printer in the Salisbury, Rowan Co., 1850 NC Census; household adjacent to Mace Pendleton.

    ii. HAMILTON J. PENDLETON, b. 1835, Danville, VA. d. Mar 1, 1863.

Hamilton J. Pendleton served in the NC 7th Infantry, Company F as Sgt., CSA; he enlisted 13 June, 1861 (age 26) in Rowan Co., NC. He was wounded in action and captured 14 March 1862, New Bern, North Carolina.

    iii.   MACE C. PENDLETON, b. Abt. 1839.

182. JOSEPH[9] PENDLETON *(MICAJAH[8], PHILIP[7], PHILIP[6], PHILIP[5], HENRY[4], HENRY[3], GEORGE[2], GEORGE[1])* was born 1781 in Buckingham Co., Va., and died Sep 15, 1839 in Schuyler Co., IL while visiting son. He married (1) ELIZABETH RILEY Nov 06, 1801 in Washington Co., VA. He married (2) LUCY.

This Joseph Pendleton was an itinerant Methodist preacher and a school teacher. And is apparently the Joseph Pendleton listed in the 1810 Washington Co., VA census indicating 5 children. Joseph is also listed in the 1820 and 1830 Washington Co., VA census records.

Children of JOSEPH PENDLETON and ELIZABETH RILEY are:
    i.   AXLEY[10] PENDLETON, d. young.
    ii.   HEZEKIAH PENDLETON, d. Schuyler Co., IL.
    iii.   JOHN PENDLETON.
    iv.   JOSEPH PENDLETON.
        It is probably this Joseph's obituary published in the Lynchburg Virginian on Thurs. Sep 29, 1825: "Died on Sep 27, in Nelson Co., Joseph Pendleton, son of Micajah Pendleton, in his 16th year [this should probably be son of Joseph, Sr. and grandson of Micajah]."

    v.   LUCY PENDLETON, m. ? FERGUSON.
    vi.   WILLIAM JAMES PENDLETON, m. KATIE DAVIS.
        A William G.O Pendleton married Catherine Davis on 17 October 1835 in Giles Co. (Ref. 81).

    vii.   ELIZABETH PENDLETON, b. 1802; m. ? BOWMAN.
419. viii.   LUCINDA PENDLETON, b. 1803.
420.   ix.   PHILIP HARPER PENDLETON, b. Abt. 1810; d. Bef. 1850, Niagara Falls, NY.
421.   x.   JAMES VANCE PENDLETON, b. Feb 28, 1816, Chilhowie, VA; d. Apr 1870, Giles Co., VA?

183. LETITIA BRECKINRIDGE[9] PENDLETON *(MICAJAH[8], PHILIP[7], PHILIP[6], PHILIP[5], HENRY[4], HENRY[3], GEORGE[2], GEORGE[1])* She married HUDSON MARTIN GARLAND Oct 14, 1828 in Nelson Co., VA, son of JAMES GARLAND and ANN WINGFIELD. He was born 1770 in Hanover Co., VA, and died Aft. 1830 in Amherst Co., VA?

Hudson Garland was a Captain in the War of 1812. Hudson M. Garland is listed in the 1830 Amherst Co., VA census.

Children of LETITIA PENDLETON and HUDSON GARLAND are:
     i.   JAMES[10] GARLAND.
    ii.   JOHN GARLAND.

184. EDNA[9] PENDLETON *(MICAJAH[8], PHILIP[7], PHILIP[6], PHILIP[5], HENRY[4], HENRY[3], GEORGE[2], GEORGE[1])* was born Abt. 1805 in VA, and died Bet. 1840 - 1850 in VA. She married DABNEY PHILIP GOOCH Jul 12, 1827 in Nelson Co., VA. He was born 1796 in Amherst Co., VA, and died Abt. 1861 in Henrico Co., VA.

Children of EDNA PENDLETON and DABNEY GOOCH are (Ref.171):
      i.   MALE[10] GOOCH, b. Bet. 1828 - 1830.
     ii.   MARY GOOCH, b. Abt. 1834.
    iii.   ELIZABETH GOOCH, b. Abt. 1835.
    iv.   FLEMING GOOCH, b. Jul 1837.
     v.   JULIA GOOCH, b. Abt. 1839; m. WILLIAM PIERCE.

185. MARY ELIZABETH[9] PENDLETON *(MICAJAH[8], PHILIP[7], PHILIP[6], PHILIP[5], HENRY[4], HENRY[3], GEORGE[2], GEORGE[1])* was born 1812, and died 1904. She married THOMAS TRUXTON EMETT Dec 07, 1839 in Nelson Co., VA. He was born 1805, and died 1899.

Child of MARY PENDLETON and THOMAS EMETT is:
     i.   PENDLETON[10] EMETT, b. 1841; d. 1911; m. REBECCA ALICE PRINGLE.

186. ROBERT N.[9] PENDLETON *(MICAJAH[8], PHILIP[7], PHILIP[6], PHILIP[5], HENRY[4], HENRY[3], GEORGE[2], GEORGE[1])* was born Abt. 1814 in VA, and died Aft. 1870 in Amherst, VA? He married MARY ELIZABETH TALIAFERRO Jan 19, 1841 in Amherst Co., VA. She was born Abt. 1822 in VA.

    Robert Pendleton and family are listed in the 1850 Nelson Co., VA census adjacent to the household of his sister, Martha M. Pendleton. A Robert N. (farmer) and Mildred A. Pendleton are listed in the 1860 and 1870 Amherst Co., VA Census records.

Child of ROBERT PENDLETON and MARY TALIAFERRO is:
     i.   JANE R.[10] PENDLETON, b. Abt. 1848, VA.

Generation No. 10 – Civil War

The tenth generation consists of the great (3) grandchildren of the immigrant Philip Pendleton and Isabella Hurt. The time period is from about 1816, when Catherine Anne Pendleton, the first born of this generation, married in Culpeper, VA, to about 1933 when the last of this generation, Ella Pendleton Crump, died at age 92. Significant members of the tenth generation who had no known children and are thus listed as children of ninth generation Pendletons include John Strother Pendleton (1802-1868), John W. Pendleton (-1842), and William Stapleton Pendleton (1838 - bef. 1889) whose histories can be found on pages 79, 85, and 133, respectively.

It was primarily this tenth and the following eleventh generations who fought in the Civil War - most for the South. Almost without exception, those Pendleton men who resided in Virginia and were not too old or young saw action in the battlefields for the South. A great many from Kentucky, Missouri, Illinois, Tennessee and other states volunteered as well for both the South and the North. A few Pendleton men rose to prominence during the war; many lost their lives. Still, the migration into new states and territories continued both before and after the war. In all, This tenth generation set up at least 235 households in at least 21 states. The proportion that remained in Virginia continued to decline to about 33% of the total. Just over 21% were in Kentucky and about 15% in Missouri. Other predominant states included Texas, West Virginia, and Tennessee. Very few ventured north into Yankee territory. The movement of the Pendleton line continued to reflect the greater migration pattern of English Americans with roots in Virginia.

Generation No. 10

187. CATHERINE ANNE[10] PENDLETON *(HENRY[9], HENRY[8], JAMES[7], HENRY[6], PHILIP[5], HENRY[4], HENRY[3], GEORGE[2], GEORGE[1])* was born 1799 in Culpeper Co., Va., and died 1875 in Meade Co, KY. She married JAMES S. LEWIS Dec 19, 1816 in Culpeper Co., VA. He was born Jul 11, 1793 in Culpeper Co., Va., and died Sep 1842 in Meade Co, KY.

Children of CATHERINE PENDLETON and JAMES LEWIS are:
- i. MARY JANE[11] LEWIS, m. STEPHEN E. BERRY, Oct 18, 1836.
- ii. WILLIAM HENRY LEWIS.
- iii. ELIZABETH C. LEWIS, b. Dec 07, 1822.
- iv. JOHN A. LEWIS, b. Aug 14, 1824, Culpeper Co., VA; d. Jun 30, 1895, Meade Co., KY; m. NANCY S. BERRY, Oct 30, 1848, Meade Co., KY.
- v. CATHERINE ANN LEWIS, b. Mar 05, 1829, Meade Co., KY; d. Feb 04, 1872; m. WILLIAM T. BERRY, Apr 26, 1849, Meade Co., KY.

vi. MARTHA H. LEWIS, b. Jul 23, 1833, Meade Co., KY; d. Jan 02, 1919, Meade Co., KY; m. (1) VARDEMAN BLAND, Oct 10, 1849, Meade Co., KY; m. (2) CYRUS B. HOBBS, Aug 19, 1890, Meade Co., KY.

vii. JAMES B. LEWIS, b. Sep 01, 1835, Meade Co., KY; m. BARBARA WHITELY, Dec 20, 1855, Meade Co., KY.

viii. ROBERT C. LEWIS, b. 1838, Meade Co., KY.

ix. DELIA MARIA LEWIS, b. 1841, Meade Co., KY; m. WILLIAM W. NELSON; b. Sep 09, 1861, Meade Co., KY.

x. FRANCES ELLEN LEWIS, b. Apr 1842, Meade Co., KY; d. 1923, Hardin Co., KY; m. JOHN THOMAS WILLIAMS, Oct 30, 1861, Meade Co., KY.

188. MARIANNE[10] PENDLETON *(HENRY[9], HENRY[8], JAMES[7], HENRY[6], PHILIP[5], HENRY[4], HENRY[3], GEORGE[2], GEORGE[1])* was born Bet. 1800 - 1810 in VA. She married AARON COFFMAN May 23, 1830, son of ABRAHAM COFFMAN and MARGARET TRIPLETT. He was born Bet. 1800 - 1810.

Aaron Coffman is listed in the 1830 Hardin Co., KY census.

Children of MARIANNE PENDLETON and AARON COFFMAN are:
i. ABRAHAM[11] COFFMAN, b. Abt. 1831, Hardin Co., KY.
ii. HENRY PENDLETON COFFMAN, b. Abt. 1833, Hardin Co., KY; m. SALLY; b. Abt. 1833, KY.
Henry and Sally Coffman are listed in the 1850 Hardin Co., KY census.

189. JAMES HENRY[10] PENDLETON *(HENRY[9], HENRY[8], JAMES[7], HENRY[6], PHILIP[5], HENRY[4], HENRY[3], GEORGE[2], GEORGE[1])* was born 1806 in VA, and died 1861 in Hardin Co., KY? He married (1) MARGARET TARPLEY. She was born Abt. 1814, and died Bef. 1840 in Hardin Co., KY? He married (2) MARGARET GOODLET Aft. 1840. She was born Abt. 1815 in KY, and died Aft. 1880 in Hardin Co., KY?

James H. Pendleton is listed in the 1830 through 1860 Hardin Co., KY census records. In 1830 he is listed near Henry Pendleton. This may be the Major James H. Pendleton, 23rd Virginia Infantry CSA.

Children of JAMES PENDLETON and MARGARET TARPLEY are:
i. WILLIAM[11] PENDLETON, b. Abt. 1829, KY; m. KITTY; b. Abt. 1831, KY.
William Pendleton (21) and Kitty (19) are included in the William Tarpley household of the 1850 Hardin Co., KY census.

ii. KATHERINE PENDLETON, b. Abt. 1832.
iii. EDWIN? PENDLETON.

190. THOMAS CATLETT[10] PENDLETON *(HENRY[9], HENRY[8], JAMES[7], HENRY[6], PHILIP[5], HENRY[4], HENRY[3], GEORGE[2], GEORGE[1])* was born Abt. 1811 in VA, and died Aft. 1860 in Hardin Co., KY? He married MARY BROWN 1832 in Hardin Co., KY. She was born Abt. 1811 in KY, and died Aft. 1870 in Hardin Co., KY?

This is likely the Thomas Pendleton listed in the 1840 Meade Co., KY census. Thomas Pendleton (farmer) is listed in the 1850 Hardin Co., KY census, pg 371, District

3. Mary C. Pendleton (61), John (22; works on farm), and Thomas (19) are listed in the 1870 Allison's Precinct, Hardin Co., KY census.

Children of THOMAS PENDLETON and MARY BROWN are:
    i. ELIZA A.[11] PENDLETON, b. Abt. 1833.
    ii. MARY PENDLETON, b. Abt. 1835.
    iii. ELIZABETH PENDLETON, b. Dec 1837, Colesburg, Hardin Co., KY.
        Elizabeth Pendleton is listed in the "Families of St. Clare Catholic Church in Colesburg, KY." She was baptized Dec 10, 1837; her sponsors were Matilda Mattingly and her parents, Thomas and Mary Pendleton.

422.   iv. JAMES PENDLETON, b. Abt. 1840, KY.
       v. LORADA PENDLETON, b. Abt. 1843.
423.   vi. WILLIAM E. PENDLETON, b. Abt. 1846, KY; d. Aft. 1880, Hardin Co., KY?
424.   vii. JOHN THOMAS PENDLETON, b. Jul 19, 1848, KY; d. Apr 08, 1922, Hardin Co., KY.

191. MARGARET ELLEN[10] PENDLETON *(HENRY[9], HENRY[8], JAMES[7], HENRY[6], PHILIP[5], HENRY[4], HENRY[3], GEORGE[2], GEORGE[1])* was born May 04, 1820 in VA, and died Apr 24, 1889 in Hardin Co., KY. She married ALFRED J. BERRY. He was born Feb 16, 1815 in Washington Co, KY, and died Jul 28, 1872 in Hardin Co., KY.

Children of MARGARET PENDLETON and ALFRED BERRY are:
    i. WILLIAM HENRY[11] BERRY, b. Abt. 1840.
    ii. FRANCES BERRY, b. Abt. 1842.
    iii. JOANNA BERRY, b. Abt. 1843.
    iv. JAMES H. BERRY, b. Abt. 1846.
    v. LUCY E. BERRY, b. Aft. 1850.
    vi. PEGGY M. BERRY, b. Aft. 1850.

192. JOANNA[10] PENDLETON *(HENRY[9], HENRY[8], JAMES[7], HENRY[6], PHILIP[5], HENRY[4], HENRY[3], GEORGE[2], GEORGE[1])* was born Abt. 1824 in KY, and died Aft. 1880 in Hardin Co., KY? She married EZEKIEL R. COWHERD Bef. 1850. He was born Abt. 1824 in IN, and died Aft. 1880 in Hardin Co., KY?
    Ezekiel (26) and Joanna Cowherd (24) are listed in the 1850 Hardin Co., KY census, District 3 near the household of her sister Margaret Pendleton Berry. The family is listed in the 1860, 1870, and 1880 Hardin Co. census as well.

Children of JOANNA PENDLETON and EZEKIEL COWHERD are:
    i. ELIZABETH J.[11] COWHERD, b. Dec 1859, KY.
    ii. JOHN H. COWHERD, b. Abt. 1869, KY.

193. MARY ANNE[10] PENDLETON *(EDMUND[9], HENRY[8], JAMES[7], HENRY[6], PHILIP[5], HENRY[4], HENRY[3], GEORGE[2], GEORGE[1])* was born Nov 16, 1800 in VA, and died Mar 14, 1879 in Culpeper Co., VA. She married WILLIAM T. FOUSHEE Jul 30,

1831 in VA, son of CHARLES FOUSHEE and LUCY CRUTCHER. He was born 1794 in VA, and died Aug 15, 1839 in Culpeper Co., VA.

Mary A. Foushee is buried in the Latham grave plot in the Fairview Cemetery in Culpeper, Virginia (Ref. 172).

Child of MARY PENDLETON and WILLIAM FOUSHEE is:
    i. ELIZABETH W.[11] FOUSHEE, b. Jul 02, 1833; d. Mar 11, 1917; m. FAYETTE MAUZY LATHAM, Feb 06, 1854, Culpepper Co., VA.

194. THORNTON PRESLEY COCKE[10] PENDLETON *(EDMUND[9], HENRY[8], JAMES[7], HENRY[6], PHILIP[5], HENRY[4], HENRY[3], GEORGE[2], GEORGE[1])* was born Apr 28, 1810 in VA, and died 1884 in Clarke Co., VA? He married EMILY JANE RICHARDSON Jan 26, 1836 in Frederick Co., VA, daughter of JOHN RICHARDSON. She was born Abt. 1821 in VA, and died Aft. 1870 in Clarke Co., VA?

Thornton P. Pendleton served as Captain, Quartermaster, CSA. Thornton (farmer) and family are listed in the 1860 and 1870 Clarke Co., VA census records, pgs. 645 and 426, respectively.

Children of THORNTON PENDLETON and EMILY RICHARDSON are:
    i. ELIZABETH[11] PENDLETON, b. Abt. 1837, VA.
    ii. JOHN PENDLETON, b. Abt. 1840, VA.
425.   iii. HELEN N. PENDLETON, b. 1841, VA; d. 1912, MD?
    iv. EDMUND PENDLETON, b. Abt. 1844, VA; d. 1865.
        Edmund Pendleton was a Lieutenant, C.S.A.; killed in action.

    v. EMMA PENDLETON, b. Abt. 1844, VA; d. Jan 10, 1910.
    vi. PHILIP PENDLETON, b. Abt. 1847, VA.
        Philip is listed as a lawyer in the 1870 Clarke Co., VA census in the household of his father.

    vii. SOPHIA PENDLETON, b. Abt. 1851, VA.
    viii. VIRGINIA PENDLETON, b. Abt. 1854, VA; d. Apr 02, 1875; m. CHARLES HARVEY.
    ix. CHARLOTTE T. PENDLETON, b. Abt. 1859, VA; d. Aft. 1920, Washington DC?; m. MORDECAI JOHN PLUMMER, Dec 19, 1883, Prince Georges Co., MD.
        Charlotte Plummer (widow) is listed in the 1920 Washington DC census.

    x. ROBERT PENDLETON, b. Abt. 1861, VA; m. SOPHIA RUST.

195. ELIZABETH WARD[10] PENDLETON *(EDMUND[9], HENRY[8], JAMES[7], HENRY[6], PHILIP[5], HENRY[4], HENRY[3], GEORGE[2], GEORGE[1])* was born Jan 04, 1812 in VA, and died Mar 10, 1899 in Baltimore, MD. She married ELLIS BARCROFT LONG Nov 13, 1833 in Baltimore, MD, son of JOHN LONG and HENRIETTA CHRISMAW. He was born Jun 21, 1807 in Stevensburg, VA, and died Aug 06, 1876 in Baltimore, MD.

Children of ELIZABETH PENDLETON and ELLIS LONG are (Ref. 173):
    i.   EDWARD PENDLETON[11] LONG, b. Sep 13, 1834, Baltimore, MD; d. 1878.
   ii.   VIRGINIA HENRIETTA LONG, b. May 05, 1836; d. Mar 13, 1840.
  iii.   JOHN RICARDS LONG, b. Nov 02, 1837.
   iv.   GERTRUDE SUMMERVILLE LONG, b. Aug 10, 1839; d. Jan 23, 1928, Culpeper Co., VA; m. GEORGE M. WILLIAMS.
    v.   ELLIS B. LONG, b. Jul 16, 1841; d. Feb 12, 1842.
   vi.   HELEN MARY LONG, b. Apr 11, 1848.

196. ROBERT WARD[10] PENDLETON (*EDMUND[9], HENRY[8], JAMES[7], HENRY[6], PHILIP[5], HENRY[4], HENRY[3], GEORGE[2], GEORGE[1]*) was born Jul 16, 1814 in VA, and died Apr 17, 1861 in Baltimore, MD? He married SOPHIA JULIA CHAFFEE May 02, 1837. She was born Abt. 1819 in VA, and died Aft. 1870 in Baltimore, MD?

Children of ROBERT PENDLETON and SOPHIA CHAFFEE are:
    i.   EDMUND[11] PENDLETON, b. Jun 18, 1841, MD; d. Aft. 1900, Chicago, IL?; m. VIRGINIA YOST, Jun 23, 1869; b. Abt. 1840, MD; d. Aft. 1900, Chicago, IL?
       Edmund Pendleton (retired at 45) and Virginia Pendleton (40) are listed in the 1880 Chicago census, pg. 55A.

   ii.   MATILDA CHAFFEE PENDLETON, b. 1842, MD; d. 1886, Baltimore, MD?
  iii.   GRACE PENDLETON, b. 1847; d. 1872.
426.   iv.   SOPHIA ELIZABETH PENDLETON, b. Apr 09, 1850, Baltimore, MD; d. 1906, Philadelphia, PA?
    v.   ALBERT RANDOLPH PENDLETON, b. 1853, MD; d. 1906, Baltimore, MD?; m. MRS. FLORENCE HARDEN.
       Albert and Matilda (his sister) are listed in the 1880 Baltimore, MD census, pg. 147D.

197. PHILIP PETER[10] PENDLETON (*EDMUND[9], HENRY[8], JAMES[7], HENRY[6], PHILIP[5], HENRY[4], HENRY[3], GEORGE[2], GEORGE[1]*) was born Dec 17, 1816 in VA, and died Dec 09, 1877 in Baltimore, MD. He married MARY JANE LECHE 1843. She was born 1820 in MD, and died 1896 in Baltimore, MD?

      Mary J. Pendleton and family are listed in the 1880 Baltimore, MD census, pg. 386C.

Children of PHILIP PENDLETON and MARY LECHE are:
427.   i.   DAVID ELLIS[11] PENDLETON, b. 1844, MD; d. Apr 07, 1900.
   ii.   ELIZABETH WARD PENDLETON, b. 1848, Baltimore, MD.
       Miss Elizabeth Ward Pendleton was a member of The National Society of the Daughters of the American Revolution (Volume 93, page 79).

  iii.   PHILIP PENDLETON, b. 1852; d. 1865.

428.   iv.   NATHAN SMITH PENDLETON, b. 1856, MD; d. Aft. 1920, Baltimore, MD?

198. GEORGE WASHINGTON[10] PENDLETON *(EDMUND[9], HENRY[8], JAMES[7], HENRY[6], PHILIP[5], HENRY[4], HENRY[3], GEORGE[2], GEORGE[1])* was born Feb 17, 1819 in VA, and died 1858. He married VIRENDA ALETHEA GAINES Apr 23, 1846 in Chicot Co., AR. She was born Abt. 1826 in KY, and died 1903.

This may be the George W. Pendleton listed as a Marshal in the 1850 Madison Co., VA census (age 34); a George W. Pendleton signed the census record as Assistant Marshal, Eastern VA.

Children of GEORGE PENDLETON and VIRENDA GAINES are:
          i.   WILLIAM[11] PENDLETON, b. Abt. 1848, AR.
429.   ii.   ALETHEA EARLY PENDLETON, b. 1850, AR; d. Aft. 1930, Hot Springs, AR?

199. JOHN TAYLOR[10] PENDLETON *(JOHN[9], JAMES[8], JAMES[7], HENRY[6], PHILIP[5], HENRY[4], HENRY[3], GEORGE[2], GEORGE[1])* was born May 09, 1790 in VA, and died Jun 22, 1855 in Frankfort, KY. He married ELIZABETH MORRIS Oct 02, 1821 in Franklin Co., KY. She was born Dec 08, 1803 in KY, and died Feb 14, 1830 in Franklin Co., KY.

John T. Pendleton is a witness in the will of John Savary, recorded in Bourbon Co., KY, Nov 8, 1814. The property of John T. Pendleton in Frankfort, Franklin Co., KY was recorded in several court entries from 1819 to 1823 (Ref. 174). John T. Pendleton and Elizabeth are listed in the 1829/30 Franklin Co., KY, tax lists in Frankfort. John Pendleton is listed in the 1840 Franklin Co. census and again in 1850, District 2, pg. 74 (as a clerk).

Children of JOHN PENDLETON and ELIZABETH MORRIS are:
430.   i.   JOHN MORRIS[11] PENDLETON, b. Mar 08, 1823, KY; d. Aft. 1900, Montgomery Co., TN?
         ii.   ANNE MORRIS PENDLETON, b. Jun 15, 1826, KY; d. Apr 25, 1859.
               Anne Pendleton is in the household of John Morris in the 1850 Census, Franklin Co., KY, District 1, pg 6.

431.   iii. ELIZABETH W. PENDLETON, b. Feb 22, 1828, KY; d. Aft. 1880, Frankfort, KY?
432.   iv.   CATHERINE E.T. PENDLETON, b. Feb 04, 1830, KY; d. Oct 27, 1882, Paducah, KY?

200. THOMAS CLAYTON[10] PENDLETON *(JOHN[9], JAMES[8], JAMES[7], HENRY[6], PHILIP[5], HENRY[4], HENRY[3], GEORGE[2], GEORGE[1])* was born 1792 in VA, and died 1840 in Jefferson Co., KY? He married ELIZABETH JANUARY TAYLOR Mar 27, 1817 in KY. She was born 1799, and died 1832.

This is apparently the Thomas Pendleton listed in 1820 Franklin Co., KY census, and the 1830 and 1840 Jefferson Co. census records.

Children of THOMAS PENDLETON and ELIZABETH TAYLOR are:
433.   i.   ELIZABETH[11] PENDLETON, b. Abt. 1818, KY; d. Aft. 1860, Jefferson Co.,
             KY?
        ii. JOHN GIBSON PENDLETON, b. Abt. 1820, KY; d. Aft. 1860, Oldham Co.,
             KY?; m. NANCY E. GRANT; b. Abt. 1825, KY.
                 John Pendleton is listed in the 1850 Oldham Co., KY census, District 1,
             pg. 152 as a carpenter.

434.   iii. GEORGE TAYLOR PENDLETON, b. Dec 18, 1823, KY; d. Jan 25, 1883,
             Cooper Co., MO.
435.   iv. MARY ELEANOR PENDLETON, b. Abt. 1824, KY; d. Aug 20, 1853,
             Mercer Co., KY?
436.   v.   REBECCA PENDLETON, b. Feb 25, 1830, KY; d. Aft. 1880, Oldham Co.,
             KY?

201. ANNE TAYLOR[10] PENDLETON *(THOMAS[9], JAMES[8], JAMES[7], HENRY[6],
PHILIP[5], HENRY[4], HENRY[3], GEORGE[2], GEORGE[1])* was born Dec 30, 1797 in VA, and
died Oct 13, 1857. She married JOHN MENEFEE Jan 11, 1816 in Chesterfield Co., VA,
son of JONAS N. MENEFEE. He was born 1792, and died 1847.

Child of ANNE PENDLETON and JOHN MENEFEE is:
        i.   ROBERT PHILIP[11] MENEFEE, b. Apr 13, 1833, Marion Co., MO; d. Aft.
             1900, Bozeman, MT?
                 The following account was recorded by the Society of Montana Pioneers
             (Ref. 175):

                 Robert Philip Menefee, son of John and Ann Taylor (Pendleton)
                 Menefee; born in Marion Co., MO, April 13, 1833; Place of departure for
                 Montana, Salt Lake City, Utah; Route traveled, up Malad Valley, Sublette's
                 cutoff, Portneuf River to Snake River Valley; Arrived at Horse Prairie, June
                 20th, and at Gold Creek, July 15, 1862; Occupation, farmer; Residence,
                 Bozeman.

202. JAMES[10] PENDLETON *(THOMAS[9], JAMES[8], JAMES[7], HENRY[6], PHILIP[5],
HENRY[4], HENRY[3], GEORGE[2], GEORGE[1])* was born Dec 23, 1799 in Culpepper Co.,
VA, and died Sep 25, 1885 in VA. He married SUSAN M. CONNER Nov 24, 1825 in
VA, daughter of URIEL CONNER and NANCY NALLE. She was born Abt. 1805 in
VA, and died Aft. 1870 in Culpeper Co., VA?
        James Pendleton is listed in the 1830, 1840, and 1850 Culpeper Co. census
records. He is listed as a Constable in the 1850 census. Susan Pendleton (farmer) is
listed as the head of the household in the 1860 Culpeper Co., VA census. Susan M. (65)
and Henry C. (27) Pendleton are listed in the 1870 Culpeper Co., VA census, pg. 46,
Catalpa Township.

Children of JAMES PENDLETON and SUSAN CONNER are (Ref. 176):
        i.   FRANCES E.[11] PENDLETON, b. Apr 24, 1832; d. Sep 09, 1833.

437.   ii.   JAMES FRENCH PENDLETON, b. Jul 09, 1834, Culpeper Co., VA; d. Jun 15, 1918, Ryan, OK.
      iii.   EDMUND P. PENDLETON, b. Jul 15, 1837, Culpeper Co., VA?; d. Apr 02, 1863.

      Edmund Pendleton enlisted in 1862 and served in the 1st Virginia Infantry, Kemper's Brigade, Pickett's Division; he died in 1863.

438.   iv.   HENRY CLAY PENDLETON, b. Oct 22, 1842, VA; d. May 19, 1913, Culpeper Co., VA.

203. ELIZABETH COLEMAN[10] PENDLETON *(THOMAS[9], JAMES[8], JAMES[7], HENRY[6], PHILIP[5], HENRY[4], HENRY[3], GEORGE[2], GEORGE[1])* was born Nov 17, 1801 in VA. She married WILLIAM HAINES Nov 17, 1830.

A William (35) and Elizabeth (44) Haines are listed in the 1850 Henrico Co., VA census, pg 411, Richmond City along with William H. (11) and Emery (4).

Child of ELIZABETH PENDLETON and WILLIAM HAINES is:
      i.   ANN TAYLOR[11] HAINES, b. 1831, Rappahanock Co., VA; d. Oct 10, 1901; m. LEWIS CORBIN GAUNT, Sep 09, 1852; b. 1817; d. 1888.

204. DANIEL FARMER[10] PENDLETON *(THOMAS[9], JAMES[8], JAMES[7], HENRY[6], PHILIP[5], HENRY[4], HENRY[3], GEORGE[2], GEORGE[1])* was born Oct 10, 1803 in Culpepper Co., VA?, and died 1887 in Marion Co., MO. He married PHOEBE SIMS Apr 17, 1834 in Rappahannock Co., VA. She died 1840 in MO.

Daniel Pendleton is listed in the 1840 Ralls Co., MO census. Daniel F. Pendleton (house joiner) is listed without his children in the 1850 Marion Co. census, Miller township. A Daniel Pendleton married Elizabeth Brown in Marion Co., MO on Dec 27, 1864 (Ref. 177).

Children of DANIEL PENDLETON and PHOEBE SIMS are:
      i.   WILLIAM GIDEON[11] PENDLETON, b. Feb 14, 1835, MO; d. Aft. 1900, Daviess Co., MO?; m. MARIA T., Abt. 1860; b. Sep 1834, MO; d. Sep 18, 1914, MT.

      William G. and Maria T. Pendleton are listed in the 1900 Daviess Co., MO census, pg. 203. The death of Maria T. Pendleton (79) is recorded in Reference 178.

      ii.   MARGARET JANE PENDLETON, b. Nov 08, 1836, MO; d. Nov 05, 1915; m. GEORGE WILLIAM SANDUSKY, Nov 07, 1854, Linn Co., MO; b. Aug 22, 1834; d. May 12, 1896.
      iii.   THOMAS B. PENDLETON, b. Abt. 1840.

205. GEORGE WASHINGTON[10] PENDLETON *(THOMAS[9], JAMES[8], JAMES[7], HENRY[6], PHILIP[5], HENRY[4], HENRY[3], GEORGE[2], GEORGE[1])* was born Feb 24, 1804 in VA, and died Oct 16, 1858 in Madison Co., VA? He married (1) LUCY C. SLAUGHTER Oct 30, 1834. She was born Bet. 1810 - 1920, and died Bef. 1850 in

Madison Co., VA? He married (2) MARY A. BLEDSOE Jul 18, 1850. She was born 1832 in VA, and died 1862.

George Pendleton is listed in the 1840 Madison Co., VA census and in the 1850 Madison Co. census, age 34, in the household of Hiram Carver as Marshall. George's children, Ann E. Pendleton (13) and John C. Pendleton (8), are listed in the 1850 Madison Co. census along with a Daniel B. Slaughter (25), laborer (George's brother-in-law?) in the household of William Robson. His sons Thomas G. (15) and William E. (12) are listed in the household of his brother, Alexander Pendleton in the 1850 Culpeper Co., VA census. A Frances Pendleton (10), apparently his daughter, is listed in the household of William Armstrong of Rappahanock Co., VA.

Children of GEORGE PENDLETON and LUCY SLAUGHTER are:

    i.   THOMAS GALEN[11] PENDLETON, b. Oct 22, 1835, VA; d. 1910, Monroe Co., MO?; m. SARAH CATHERINE PENDLETON, Oct 06, 1856; b. Feb 22, 1838, MO.

       Thomas (day laborer) and Sarah Pendleton are listed in the 1900 Monroe Co., MO census, pg. 127.

439.   ii.   ANNE ELIZABETH PENDLETON, b. Jul 06, 1837, VA; d. 1877, Clinton Co., MO?

    iii. WILLIAM EDMUND PENDLETON, b. Oct 27, 1838, VA.

       William E. Pendleton served as a private in the VA 7th Infantry, Companies H and E, C.S.A.

    iv. FRANCES JANE PENDLETON, b. Sep 13, 1840, VA.

    v.   JOHN CALHOUN PENDLETON, b. Apr 02, 1842, VA.

       John Calhoun Pendleton is said to have been a soldier in the Civil War, C.S.A.

Children of GEORGE PENDLETON and MARY BLEDSOE are:

    vi. HENRY CLAY[11] PENDLETON, b. Aug 25, 1851, VA; d. Jul 05, 1857.

    vii. LAURA PENDLETON, b. Mar 15, 1855, VA; d. May 10, 1855.

440. viii. WASHINGTON WINTER PENDLETON, b. Apr 05, 1858, VA; d. Aft. 1920, Richmond, VA?

206. JOHN BOWIE[10] PENDLETON (*THOMAS[9], JAMES[8], JAMES[7], HENRY[6], PHILIP[5], HENRY[4], HENRY[3], GEORGE[2], GEORGE[1]*) was born Aug 01, 1805 in Culpeper Co., VA, and died Dec 24, 1885 in Monroe Co., MO. He married ELIZABETH ANNE ODELL Nov 01, 1831 in Culpepper Co., VA, daughter of JEREMIAH ODELL and POLLY MENEFEE. She was born Aug 22, 1812 in Sperryville, VA, and died Jun 18, 1873 in Monroe Co., MO.

John Pendleton, his wife Elizabeth Ann and the family slaves moved from Culpeper Co., Virginia to Hannibal, MO in 1831 and remained there until 1838 when they moved to their country estate in Monroe County, Missouri. They remained on this country estate until their deaths (Ref. 179). John Pendleton is listed in the Missouri Land Patents for Monroe Co. on Apr 1, 1839, Jun 1, 1848, and Sep 1, 1856.

Children of JOHN PENDLETON and ELIZABETH ODELL are:

i. JAMES H.[11] PENDLETON, b. 1832, MO; d. 1833, Hannibal, MO.
441. ii. ALBERT FRENCH PENDLETON, b. Apr 22, 1835, MO; d. 1912, Monroe Co., MO.
iii. SARAH CATHERINE PENDLETON, b. Feb 22, 1838, MO; m. THOMAS GALEN PENDLETON, Oct 06, 1856; b. Oct 22, 1835, VA; d. 1910, Monroe Co., MO?
442. iv. ARTHUR MENEFEE PENDLETON, b. Dec 28, 1840, Monroe Co., MO; d. Feb 03, 1915, Chandlerville, IL?
v. WILLIAM PENDLETON, b. 1842; d. 1842.
443. vi. RICHARD J. PENDLETON, b. Mar 06, 1845, MO; d. Aft. 1900, Monroe Co., MO?
vii. ANNE ELIZA PENDLETON, b. 1848; d. 1875.
viii. MARY VIRGINIA PENDLETON, b. 1855; d. 1875.
ix. JOHN MCNUTT PENDLETON, b. 1861, MO; d. 1861, MO.

207. JAMES FRENCH[10] PENDLETON *(WILLIAM[9], JAMES[8], JAMES[7], HENRY[6], PHILIP[5], HENRY[4], HENRY[3], GEORGE[2], GEORGE[1])* was born Jul 01, 1805 in VA, and died Sep 12, 1878 in Smyth Co., VA? He married NARCISSA POSTON CECIL Sep 03, 1829. She was born Jun 15, 1815 in VA, and died Apr 23, 1887 in Smyth Co., VA?

James Pendleton is listed in the Smyth Co. Tax List of 1838. James F. Pendleton (Smyth Co.) is included in an 1846 list of Virginia School Commissioners. He was the First clerk of Smyth Co., VA and is listed as a clerk in the 1850 Smyth Co. census. He served as such for 27 years. He was a Member of the Virginia Convention of 1850-1 and a member of the House of Delegates 1843-4, 1845-6, 1849-50, 1855-6, 1865-6, and 1866-7. James F. Pendleton (farmer) and family are listed in the 1870 Fairfield, Henrico Co., VA census.

Children of JAMES PENDLETON and NARCISSA CECIL are:

i. SAMUEL CECIL[11] PENDLETON, b. May 19, 1834, VA; d. Aug 28, 1854.
444. ii. ALBERT GALLATIN PENDLETON, b. Feb 20, 1836, Smyth Co., VA; d. Mar 02, 1901, Roanoke, VA.
445. iii. JOHN STROTHER PENDLETON, b. Oct 14, 1838, VA; d. Aug 14, 1917, Albemarle Co., VA?
iv. JAMES FRENCH PENDLETON, b. Oct 24, 1843, VA; d. Feb 02, 1883, Smyth Co., VA?

James French Pendleton was a physician and surgeon. He is listed with his mother, Narcissa, and brother, E.P. in the 1880 Wythe Co., VA census.

446. v. WILLIAM CECIL PENDLETON, b. Jan 16, 1847, Smyth Co., VA; d. May 05, 1941, Bluefield, Tazewell Co., VA.
447. vi. EDMUND PIPER PENDLETON, b. Mar 11, 1855, Smyth Co., VA?; d. Aft. 1900, Fort Worth, TX?

208. ALBERT GALLATIN[10] PENDLETON *(WILLIAM[9], JAMES[8], JAMES[7], HENRY[6], PHILIP[5], HENRY[4], HENRY[3], GEORGE[2], GEORGE[1])* was born Jun 30, 1807 of

Culpeper, VA, and died Jun 19, 1875 in Giles Co., VA? He married ELVINA CHAPMAN Apr 20, 1831 in Giles Co., VA. She was born Apr 30, 1811 in VA, and died Aug 18, 1868 in Pearisburg, VA.

A number of Giles and Mercer Co., VA deeds involved Albert G. Pendleton. He was licensed in 1860 to practice in the courts of Virginia, the First Circuit Superior Court. Albert G. Pendleton (lawyer) and family are listed in the 1860 Giles Co., VA census. He is buried in a cemetery near Ripplemead, Giles Co., VA along with Elvina and Alberta Pendleton (Ref. 180).

Children of ALBERT PENDLETON and ELVINA CHAPMAN are:
- i. HENLEY CHAPMAN[11] PENDLETON, b. May 19, 1846, VA.
- 448. ii. NANCY STROTHER PENDLETON, b. Nov 11, 1847, VA; d. Aug 25, 1925.
- 449. iii. SARAH ELIZABETH STROTHER PENDLETON, b. Jul 08, 1850, VA.
- 450. iv. ALBERTA FRANKLIN PENDLETON, b. Jan 31, 1856, VA; d. Jul 28, 1902, Wythe Co., VA.

209. JAMES COLEMAN[10] PENDLETON (*JAMES[9], PHILIP[8], JAMES[7], HENRY[6], PHILIP[5], HENRY[4], HENRY[3], GEORGE[2], GEORGE[1]*) was born 1793 in VA, and died Feb 22, 1855 in Bullitt Co., KY? He married SUSAN Abt. 1815. She was born Abt. 1793 in VA, and died Aft. 1860 in Bullitt Co., KY?

This is likely the James C. Pendleton in the 1830 Butler Co., KY census and the James C. Pendleton listed in a Jury of 5 Oct 1848 in Bullitt Co., KY Circuit Court. J.C. Pendleton (farmer) and family are included in the Bullitt Co. 1850 census, pg 168.

Children of JAMES PENDLETON and SUSAN are:
- i. ALBERT[11] PENDLETON.
- ii. HANNAH PENDLETON.
- iii. JAMES P. PENDLETON.
- iv. JOHN PENDLETON.
- 451. v. MARY JANE PENDLETON, b. Abt. 1827, KY.
- 452. vi. DAVID H. PENDLETON, b. Dec 24, 1828, KY; d. Aug 10, 1905, Bullitt Co., KY.
- 453. vii. WILLIAM D. PENDLETON, b. Oct 30, 1830, KY; d. Feb 14, 1920, Bullitt Co., KY.
- viii. SUSAN AWBREY PENDLETON, b. Abt. 1838, KY; m. ABRAHAM V. BREWER, Feb 07, 1856, Bullitt Co., KY.

210. LOUISA EMILY[10] PENDLETON (*COLEMAN[9], PHILIP[8], JAMES[7], HENRY[6], PHILIP[5], HENRY[4], HENRY[3], GEORGE[2], GEORGE[1]*) was born 1809 in GA, and died May 10, 1881 in Chambers Co., AL. She married JOHN JOSEPH OLIVER Dec 04, 1828 in Butts Co., GA, son of FLORENCE OLIVER and SUSSANA CLARK. He was born Abt. 1810 in GA, and died Jul 15, 1881 in Chambers Co., AL.

John J. (farmer) and Louisa E. Oliver are included in the 1850 census, Harrison County, GA.

Children of LOUISA PENDLETON and JOHN OLIVER are (Ref. 181):

    i. PENDLETON[11] OLIVER, b. Abt. 1830, GA.

    ii. WILLIAM H. OLIVER, b. Abt. 1832, GA; d. Aug 23, 1864, Civil War, Harrisonburg, VA; m. SERENA ALLEN, Jun 13, 1854, Tallapoosa Co., GA; b. Abt. 1835, GA; d. Bef. 1870, Tallapoosa Co., GA.

    iii. MARTHA A. E. OLIVER, b. Abt. 1834, GA; m. LASHLEY ODEN.

    iv. JOSEPH CALEB OLIVER, b. Jul 12, 1840, GA; m. MARTHA DEMARIS BIBBY.

    v. PHILIP OLIVER, b. Abt. 1843.

    vi. EMILY AUBRA OLIVER, b. Abt. 1844, GA; m. BARTLEY COLLINS BIBBY; b. Oct 02, 1830, GA.

    vii. WINTON SALEM OLIVER, b. Abt. 1847.

    viii. SAMANTHA OLIVER, b. Aug 10, 1849, GA.

    ix. MONROE ALONZA OLIVER, b. 1854.

211. WILLIAM ROBERT[10] PENDLETON (*COLEMAN[9], PHILIP[8], JAMES[7], HENRY[6], PHILIP[5], HENRY[4], HENRY[3], GEORGE[2], GEORGE[1]*) was born Mar 09, 1811 in Putnam Co., GA, and died Jul 07, 1841 in Baker Co., GA. He married MARION C. JORDAN Apr 02, 1835 in Madison Co., GA, daughter of THOMAS JORDAN and PRISCILLA APPLEWHITE. She was born 1818 in Oglethorpe Co., GA, and died 1892 in GA.

    Mary C. Pendleton married Johnson Maley, Mar 24, 1844 in Madison Co., GA.

Children of WILLIAM PENDLETON and MARION JORDAN are:

454.   i. EMILY JANE[11] PENDLETON, b. Apr 27, 1836, GA; d. Jul 05, 1887, Gainesville, GA.

455.   ii. MARTHA ANNA PRISCILLA PENDLETON, b. Aug 13, 1837, GA; d. Aug 18, 1880, Hart Co., GA.

    iii. PHILIP COLEMAN PENDLETON, b. Dec 17, 1838, GA; d. 1840, GA.

    iv. MARY LOUISA PENDLETON, b. Oct 09, 1840, GA; d. Jul 09, 1841, GA.

212. PHILIP COLEMAN[10] PENDLETON (*COLEMAN[9], PHILIP[8], JAMES[7], HENRY[6], PHILIP[5], HENRY[4], HENRY[3], GEORGE[2], GEORGE[1]*) was born Nov 17, 1812 in Eatonville, GA, and died Jun 19, 1869 in Valdosta, GA. He married CATHERINE SARAH MELISSA TEBEAU Nov 23, 1841 in Chatham Co., GA, daughter of FREDERICK EDMUND TEBEAU and HULDA LEWIS. She was born May 28, 1822 in Savannah, GA, and died May 12, 1889 in Valdosta, GA.

    Philip C. Pendleton (47), farmer, is listed in the 1860 Ware Co., GA census, Waresboro P.O., pg 152; value of real property $6,000. He served in the Army during the Indian Wars in Florida. He was a Major, 50th Georgia Regiment, C.S.A.; he enlisted in GA on 22 Mar, 1862 (age 50) as a Major. In 1867 he established the "Southern Georgia Times" and published this paper until his death. His obituary is listed in the Southern Christian Advocate Obituaries, 1867-78: "Philip Coleman Pendleton was born in Eatonton, Ga., Nov. 17th 1812, and died near Valdosta, June 19th 1869. While residing in Savannah, he married Miss Catherine S. M. Tebeau, who survives."

Children of PHILIP PENDLETON and CATHERINE TEBEAU are:

        i.   EDMUND TEBEAU[11] PENDLETON, b. Apr 06, 1843, GA; d. Oct 01, 1846.

456.   ii. WILLIAM FREDERICK PENDLETON, b. Mar 25, 1845, Savannah, GA; d. Nov 05, 1927, Bryn Athyn, PA.

      iii. JAMES AUBREY PENDLETON, b. Dec 02, 1846, GA; d. Oct 18, 1881.

      iv. PHILIP COLEMAN PENDLETON, b. Jul 25, 1848, GA; d. Sep 10, 1870.

457.   v. CHARLES RITTENHOUSE PENDLETON, b. Jun 26, 1850, Effingham Co., GA; d. Jan 16, 1914, Bibb Co., GA.

      vi. EMILY TEBEAU PENDLETON, b. Dec 30, 1852, GA; d. 1919.

458.   vii. ALEXANDER SHAW PENDLETON, b. Mar 17, 1855, Sandersville, VA; d. Apr 13, 1925, Valdosta, GA.

     viii. MARY ZELLA PENDLETON, b. Jun 29, 1857, GA; d. Mar 16, 1932, Bryn Athyn, PA?

      ix. LOUIS BEAUREGARD PENDLETON, b. Apr 21, 1861, GA; d. 1939, Bryn Athyn, PA?

          Louis B. Pendleton is a novelist of Philadelphia; and the author of "Bewitched, and Other Stories," "In the Wire Grass," a novel of Southern Georgia, "King Tom and the Runaways," a juvenile tale, "The Wedding Garment," a Tale of the Life to Come, "The Sons of Ham," "Corona of the Nantahalas," and "In the Okefenokee," a juvenile tale (Ref. 41). Louis Pendleton (editor) is listed in the 1900 Bibb Co., GA census, pg. 76 in the household of his brother, Charles R. Pendleton. Louis (authorship and journalism) and his sister, M. Zella, are listed in the 1920 Bryn Athyn, PA census near their sister Luella Pendleton Caldwell. The Virginia Historical Society Catalog lists "The question of state sovereignty," by Louis Pendleton, in the South Atlantic quarterly. Durham, NC. v.7 (1908), p. 23-41.

459.   x. NATHANIEL DANDRIDGE PENDLETON, b. Feb 19, 1865, Valdosta, GA; d. 1937, Bryn Athyn, PA.

213. EDMUND MONROE[10] PENDLETON (*COLEMAN*[9], *PHILIP*[8], *JAMES*[7], *HENRY*[6], *PHILIP*[5], *HENRY*[4], *HENRY*[3], *GEORGE*[2], *GEORGE*[1]) was born Mar 19, 1815 in Eatonton, GA, and died Jan 26, 1884 in Atlanta, GA. He married SARAH JANE THOMAS Nov 27, 1838 in Hancock Co., GA. She was born Mar 22, 1818, and died Jul 10, 1892 in Atlanta, GA.

      Edmund Pendleton was a noted surgeon and chemist according to his biography (Ref. 182).

      Edmund Monroe Pendleton, chemist, was graduated at the Medical college of the state of South Carolina in 1837, and then practised his profession in Warrenton and Sparta, Georgia, for many years. On the organization of Oglethorpe medical college, Savannah, he was elected professor of surgery, but declined the appointment on account of his health. He then turned his attention to agriculture, was the originator of the Pendleton formulas for fertilizers, which have long been successfully used, and was the first to employ animal matter and cotton-seed meal in the manufacture of fertilizers. Dr. Pendleton was the first to develop the fact that phosphoric acid and nitrogen are the two plant-constituents that are first exhausted from soils by cereals and cotton-culture. In 1872-'7 he held the chair of agriculture and horticulture in the University of Georgia. In the latter year failing health forced him to retire, and he moved to Atlanta, Georgia, where with his son, William M. Pendleton, he founded the Pendleton guano company, of which he was elected chemical director, a place that he held until his death. He contributed to various periodicals in both prose and verse, and his "Scientific Agriculture" (New York, 1874) was extensively used as a text-book in colleges and other institutions of learning

E.M. Pendleton is listed in the 1860 Hancock Co., GA census. Edmund's wife, Sarah Jane Thomas Pendleton is buried at the Historic Oakland Cemetery, Atlanta, GA (Ref. 183).

Children of EDMUND PENDLETON and SARAH THOMAS are:
    i. MARY LOUISE[11] PENDLETON, b. Sep 03, 1839; d. Dec 15, 1839.
    ii. ADELINE MARIAN PENDLETON, b. Oct 17, 1840; d. Sep 28, 1841.
    iii. ELIZA ANNE PENDLETON, b. Nov 09, 1841; d. Oct 01, 1842.
    iv. EMILY AUGUSTA PENDLETON, b. Dec 26, 1842; d. Oct 26, 1843.
    v. EDMUND MONROE PENDLETON, b. Jun 22, 1845; d. Mar 13, 1861.
460. vi. PHILIP THOMAS PENDLETON, b. Dec 13, 1847, GA; d. Feb 20, 1892, Richmond Co., GA?
461. vii. WILLIAM MICAJAH PENDLETON, b. Aug 29, 1849, GA; d. Feb 24, 1915, Atlanta, GA.
462. viii. SUSAN FRANCINA PENDLETON, b. Jul 24, 1851, GA; d. Aft. 1900, Atlanta, GA?
463. ix. JAMES COLEMAN PENDLETON, b. May 28, 1853, GA; d. Aug 20, 1929, Fulton Co., GA.
    x. FRANCIS RITTENHOUSE PENDLETON, b. Aug 25, 1854; d. Sep 28, 1855.
    xi. NATHANIEL AUBREY PENDLETON, b. Feb 12, 1856; d. May 12, 1857.

214. JAMES C.[10] PENDLETON *(NATHANIEL*[9]*, WILLIAM*[8]*, NATHANIEL*[7]*, HENRY*[6]*, PHILIP*[5]*, HENRY*[4]*, HENRY*[3]*, GEORGE*[2]*, GEORGE*[1]*)* was born 1806 in VA, and died Aft. 1860 in TX? He married (1) UNKNOWN. She was born in KY. He married (2) EVALINE ROGERS Jun 02, 1846 in Mason Co., KY. She was born Abt. 1813 in OH, and died Aft. 1880 in Hopkins Co., TX?

The marriage of James C. Pendleton and Evaline Rogers is included in the Marriage Records of Mason County, Kentucky 1845-1855 Volume V. James C. is listed in the 1850 Warren Co., MO census index, 99th District. James C. migrated with his family to Hopkins Co., TX in 1854 and settled near a small community named Dike (Ref. 184). James C. Pendleton is listed in the Hopkins Co., TX, Tarrant P.O., 1860 census along with an M. C. Pendleton.

Evaline Pendleton is listed in the 1870 Hopkins Co. census, White Oak Precinct along with Nat. Pendleton, her stepson.

Children of JAMES PENDLETON and UNKNOWN are:
464.   i. DIADAMIA HANNAH[11] PENDLETON, b. Abt. 1836, MO; d. Nov 22, 1928, Hopkins Co., TX.

465.   ii.   NATHANIEL C. PENDLETON, b. Nov 1837, MO; d. Nov 21, 1906, Hopkins Co., TX.

Children of JAMES PENDLETON and EVALINE ROGERS are:
iii.   ELIZABETH C.[11] PENDLETON, b. Dec 01, 1848, Warren Co., MO; d. May 17, 1854, Hopkins Co., TX.
iv.   ANNE E. PENDLETON, b. 1849, MO.

215. CATHERINE THORNTON[10] PENDLETON (*BENJAMIN[9], WILLIAM[8], NATHANIEL[7], HENRY[6], PHILIP[5], HENRY[4], HENRY[3], GEORGE[2], GEORGE[1]*) was born Aug 03, 1806 in "Locust Grove," VA, and died Aug 11, 1874 in New Castle, PA. She married JOHN BAILEY NICKLIN I Mar 23, 1830. He was born Feb 23, 1803, and died Oct 21, 1891.

Children of CATHERINE PENDLETON and JOHN NICKLIN are:
i.   BENJAMIN STROTHER[11] NICKLIN, b. Oct 08, 1831; d. Aug 17, 1873; m. SARAH WHITE HERSEY, Oct 25, 1853.
ii.   ELIZABETH CATHARINE NICKLIN, b. Nov 29, 1833; d. Sep 10, 1910; m. ESPY CONNELY, Jan 16, 1857.
iii.   MARTHA VIRGINIA NICKLIN, b. Mar 09, 1836; d. May 22, 1838.
iv.   MARY MARSHALL NICKLIN, b. Jan 19, 1838; d. May 29, 1921; m. JOHN NELSON EMERY, Mar 15, 1865.
v.   SAMUEL CHURCH NICKLIN, b. Feb 18, 1840; d. Sep 29, 1911; m. HARRIET UTLEY, Sep 07, 1865.
vi.   II JOHN BAILEY NICKLIN, b. Aug 05, 1843, Allegheny City, PA; d. May 06, 1919, Chattanooga, TN.
vii.   LUCY CRANE NICKLIN, b. Apr 28, 1846; d. Oct 02, 1846.
viii.   LAURA PENDLETON NICKLIN, b. Sep 05, 1848; d. Apr 10, 1872; m. CHARLES B. ANSART, DR., 1871.
ix.   WILLIAM FULLER NICKLIN, b. Mar 11, 1853; d. Feb 18, 1858.

216. JAMES WILLIAM[10] PENDLETON (*BENJAMIN[9], WILLIAM[8], NATHANIEL[7], HENRY[6], PHILIP[5], HENRY[4], HENRY[3], GEORGE[2], GEORGE[1]*) was born Sep 07, 1809 in VA, and died Abt. 1845 in Franklin Co., AR. He married MARGARETTA CATHERINE HUMRICKHOUSE Sep 05, 1840 in Ozark, Ark, daughter of ALBERT HUMRICKHOUSE and ELIZABETH WEIS. She was born Aug 30, 1818 in Shepherdstown, VA, and died Aft. 1870 in Shepherdstown, WV?

J.W. Pendleton was the county clerk of Franklin Co., AR from 1838 to 1844. In March 1838 the County business began in Ozark in a log, doorless, windowless school-house. Mr. Pendleton was the deputy. Pendleton & Crain, R.D. & O.B. Alston had general stores (Ref. 185). His sons, Ben and Albert Pendleton, were in the household of H.F. and Margaret White in the 1850 Arkansas census, town of Ozark, 6 December.

Children of JAMES PENDLETON and MARGARETTA HUMRICKHOUSE are:
466.   i.   BENJAMIN STROTHER[11] PENDLETON, b. Mar 28, 1842, Ozark, Ark; d. Jan 19, 1931, Jefferson Co., WV?

ii. JAMES ALBERT PENDLETON, b. May 08, 1844, Ozark, Ark; d. Aug 30, 1862, Battle of Manassas.

      James Albert Pendleton served as a courier to Stonewall Jackson during the Civil War. Albert was killed in the first Battle of Manassas, being in Stonewall Jackson's Brigade (Ref. 186).

217. ANNE ELIZA[10] PENDLETON *(WILLIAM[9], WILLIAM[8], NATHANIEL[7], HENRY[6], PHILIP[5], HENRY[4], HENRY[3], GEORGE[2], GEORGE[1])* was born Feb 22, 1812 in Berkeley Co., VA, and died Jan 17, 1884 in Culpeper Co., VA? She married AMOS WILLIAMSON Jul 16, 1840 in Berkeley Co., VA. He was born Abt. 1802 in VA, and died Aft. 1870 in Berkeley Co., WV?

Children of ANNE PENDLETON and AMOS WILLIAMSON are:
    i. SAMUEL[11] WILLIAMSON, b. Abt. 1841, VA.
    ii. SUSAN WILLIAMSON, b. Abt. 1844, VA.
    iii. BENJAMIN WILLIAMSON, b. Abt. 1845, VA.
    iv. ROBERT WILLIAMSON, b. Abt. 1847, VA.
    v. AMOS WILLIAMSON, b. Abt. 1849, VA.
    vi. EDMOND WILLIAMSON, b. Abt. 1851, VA.
    vii. ANNIE WILLIAMSON, b. Abt. 1851, VA.

218. WILLIAM HENRY[10] PENDLETON *(WILLIAM[9], WILLIAM[8], NATHANIEL[7], HENRY[6], PHILIP[5], HENRY[4], HENRY[3], GEORGE[2], GEORGE[1])* was born Sep 30, 1817 in Berkeley Co., VA, and died Mar 08, 1873 in Fauquier Co., VA. He married HENRIETTA RANDOLPH May 09, 1850 in Clark Co., VA, daughter of PHILLIP GRIMES RANDOLPH and MARY O'NEALE. She was born May 09, 1827 in Washington DC, and died May 19, 1894 in Fauquier Co., VA.

      William Pendleton of Berkeley Co. was included in an 1846 list of Virginia School Commissioners (Ref. 187). He was an eloquent Episcopalean preacher, and an indefatigable worker with parishes in Fauquier, Roanoke, and Bedford counties. The Reverend W. H. (35) and Henrietta (25) Pendleton are listed in the 1850 Fauquier Co. census, 9th district. W.H. Pendleton (ministry) and family are listed in the 1870 Forest, Bedford Co., VA census. His home, "The Grove," built of stone about 1825, is located 1.4 miles south of Delaplane, Virginia on Route 55 (Ref. 188). Biographical sketches of William H. Pendleton as well as his wife, Henrietta Randolph Pendleton, are included in the Virginia Historical Society archives.

Children of WILLIAM PENDLETON and HENRIETTA RANDOLPH are:
    i. LUCY WELFORD RANDOLPH[11] PENDLETON, b. Jun 26, 1851, VA; d. Jul 10, 1926.
    ii. SUSAN SPARROW PENDLETON, b. Apr 09, 1853, Fauquier Co., VA; d. Jan 26, 1936.
    iii. MARY RANDOLPH PENDLETON, b. Oct 05, 1854, VA; d. Nov 29, 1856.
    iv. PHILIP RANDOLPH PENDLETON, b. Jan 04, 1858, VA; d. Apr 15, 1875.
    v. HENRIETTA GRYMES PENDLETON, b. Mar 10, 1860, VA; d. Sep 17, 1925.

467. vi. ELLEN SHEPHERD PENDLETON, b. Mar 21, 1862, VA; d. May 19, 1894.

468. vii. GARNETT PEYTON PENDLETON, b. Oct 08, 1864, VA; d. May 15, 1939.

469. viii. WILLIAM HENRY KINKLE PENDLETON, b. Jan 17, 1867, Bedford Co., VA; d. Aft. 1920, Spartanburg, SC?

ix. ROBERT CARTER PENDLETON, b. Feb 02, 1870, Bedford Co., VA; d. Feb 15, 1891.

A biographical sketch of Robert Carter Pendleton is included in The Virginia Historical Society archives (Ref. 189).

219. ROBERT SHEPHERD[10] PENDLETON *(WILLIAM[9], WILLIAM[8], NATHANIEL[7], HENRY[6], PHILIP[5], HENRY[4], HENRY[3], GEORGE[2], GEORGE[1])* was born Mar 20, 1824 in Berkeley Co., VA, and died 1880. He married MARY ANNE PFEIFFER Dec 03, 1846. She was born Abt. 1826 in VA.

Robert S. Pendleton is listed as a merchant, age 26, in 1850 Berkeley Co. Census, Martinsburg.

Children of ROBERT PENDLETON and MARY PFEIFFER are:

i. MARY M.[11] PENDLETON, b. 1848.

470. ii. WILLIAM HENRY PENDLETON, b. Jan 1850, VA; d. Aft. 1880, New Brunswick, NJ?

471. iii. JAMES PHILIP BOSMAN PENDLETON, b. Aft. 1850; d. Schenectady, NY?

iv. ROBERT EDMUND PENDLETON, b. Aft. 1850; d. Jun 05, 1921.

220. STEPHEN JAMES[10] PENDLETON *(WILLIAM[9], WILLIAM[8], NATHANIEL[7], HENRY[6], PHILIP[5], HENRY[4], HENRY[3], GEORGE[2], GEORGE[1])* was born Apr 03, 1831 in Berkeley Co., VA, and died Jul 01, 1862 in Battle of Malvern Hill. He married EMMA H. TAYLOR Jul 08, 1852 in Williamsburg, VA. She was born Abt. 1834 in Williamsburg, VA.

Stephen J. Pendleton began publishing the VA weekly, Abingdon Democrat, in 1856; it ceased publication in 1861. Stephen J. Pendleton, private, served in the 3rd Virginia Infantry, Local Defense, Company F.

Emma H. Pendleton (40) is listed in the 1880 Williamsburg, James City Co., VA census along with Robert L. Pendleton (8).

Children of STEPHEN PENDLETON and EMMA TAYLOR are:

i. EMMA[11] PENDLETON, b. VA?

ii. CLAUDIA L. PENDLETON, b. Feb 01, 1856, Williamsburg, VA.
Claudia Pendleton is listed in the household of her aunt, Susan Pendleton Orrick, in the 1880 Cumberland, MD census.

472. iii. WILLIAM HENRY PENDLETON, b. 1858, Williamsburg, VA; d. 1915, Lawrence, Douglas Co., KS?

221. JR. PHILIP CLAYTON[10] PENDLETON *(PHILIP CLAYTON[9], PHILIP[8], NATHANIEL[7], HENRY[6], PHILIP[5], HENRY[4], HENRY[3], GEORGE[2], GEORGE[1])* was born

Aug 29, 1814 in Berkeley Co., VA, and died Oct 08, 1899. He married VIRGINIA M. TUTT Jun 14, 1838 in Loudon Co., VA. She was born Sep 26, 1818 in VA, and died Dec 23, 1895.

Philip C. Pendleton is listed in 1850 and 1860 Berkeley Co. WV census, Martinsburg.

Children of PHILIP PENDLETON and VIRGINIA TUTT are:
473.   i.   PHILIP CLAYTON[11] PENDLETON, b. Apr 16, 1839, VA; d. MD.
474.   ii.   EDMUND PENDLETON, b. Nov 27, 1840, VA; d. Aft. 1900, Morgan Co., WV?
        iii. EDWARD GRAY PENDLETON, b. Jan 24, 1844; m. REBECCA TUTT.
        iv.   CHARLES MASON PENDLETON, b. Dec 28, 1848, VA.
            Charles M. Pendleton (32) is in the household of Henry Willard in the 1880, Bath, Morgan Co., WV census.

222. EDMUND BOYD[10] PENDLETON (*PHILIP CLAYTON[9], PHILIP[8], NATHANIEL[7], HENRY[6], PHILIP[5], HENRY[4], HENRY[3], GEORGE[2], GEORGE[1]*) was born Nov 27, 1816 in Berkeley Co., VA, and died Mar 26, 1880 in Frederick Co., VA? He married CHARLOTTE RAMSEY ROBINSON Dec 14, 1847, daughter of ALEXANDER ROBINSON and ANGELICA KAUFMAN PEALE. She was born Jun 14, 1819 in Baltimore, MD, and died Apr 24, 1886.

Edmund Pendleton is listed as a Lawyer, age 33, in the 1850 Berkeley Co. Census, Martinsburg; value of property $4,000. He was a delegate from Berkeley Co. to the Virginia secession convention of 1861. He voted no in both the Apr 4, 1861 and Apr 17, 1861 ballots. Edmund Pendleton (lawyer) and family are listed in the 1870 Winchester, Frederick Co., VA census. He is the author of a report to the Ways and Means Committee, U.S. Congress, Feb 12, 1875 (Ref. 190).

Sarah Miriam Peale painted the wedding portrait in 1847 of Charlotte Ramsay Robinson, a grand daughter of Charles Wilson Peale, to commemorate her marriage to Judge Edmund Pendleton. The subject is an attractive, well-dressed woman with gleaming eyes (Ref. 191).

Children of EDMUND PENDLETON and CHARLOTTE ROBINSON are:
        i.   ALEXANDER ROBINSON[11] PENDLETON, b. Sep 27, 1848, Berkeley, VA; d. Aft. 1900, Frederick Co., VA?; m. SARAH GOLDSBOROUGH (DANDRIDGE) BOYD; b. Abt. 1852, Berkeley, VA; d. Bef. 1880.
            Alexander Robinson Pendleton is listed in the 1880 Stonewall, Frederick Co., VA census with his mother Charlotte Ramsey. He is listed as a lawyer in the 1900 Stonewall, Frederick Co., VA census, pg. 107, with two servants. "Selma, the palatial home of Alexander R. Pendleton, Esq., a retired member of the Winchester Bar, located on the lofty eminence just East of Hawthorn, occupies the site of Senator James M. Mason's old home Selma. The old mansion was destroyed during the War by Federal troops, because of Mr.

Mason's mission abroad as representative of the Confederate States Government, to secure recognition of the Confederacy" (Ref. 192).

ii. PHILIP CLAYTON PENDLETON, b. Nov 26, 1850, VA; d. 1863.

223. ELISHA BOYD[10] PENDLETON *(PHILIP CLAYTON[9], PHILIP[8], NATHANIEL[7], HENRY[6], PHILIP[5], HENRY[4], HENRY[3], GEORGE[2], GEORGE[1])* was born Jan 13, 1820 in Berkeley Co., VA, and died Jul 12, 1902 in Morgan Co., WV? He married MARIA LUCINDA TUTT Nov 25, 1843 in Washington DC. She was born Sep 26, 1821 in VA, and died Aug 14, 1887.

Elisha B. Pendleton is included in an 1841 listing of Virginia Students Of Medicine At The University Of Maryland. Elisha is listed in the 1850 Berkeley Co. census, age 30, as a physician in the household of his father.

Children of ELISHA PENDLETON and MARIA TUTT are:
475.   i. CHARLES HENRY[11] PENDLETON, b. Jan 21, 1845, VA; d. Jul 13, 1914, Morgan Co., WV?
      ii. SALLIE B. PENDLETON, b. 1847, VA; m. EUGENE VAN RENNSALAER; b. NY?
476.   iii. NATHANIEL SPOTSWOOD DANDRIDGE PENDLETON, b. Nov 09, 1851, VA; d. Jan 11, 1931, Morgan Co., WV?

224. SERENA CATHERINE[10] PENDLETON *(EDMUND[9], PHILIP[8], NATHANIEL[7], HENRY[6], PHILIP[5], HENRY[4], HENRY[3], GEORGE[2], GEORGE[1])* was born Jun 09, 1816 in MD, and died Sep 02, 1889. She married JR. ADAM STEPHEN DANDRIDGE Feb 21, 1837 in Winchester, VA, son of ADAM DANDRIDGE and SARAH PENDLETON. He was born Dec 13, 1814 in VA, and died Jan 04, 1894.

Children of SERENA PENDLETON and ADAM DANDRIDGE are:
      i. SERENA C.[11] DANDRIDGE, b. Abt. 1838, VA.
     ii. SARAH P. DANDRIDGE, b. Abt. 1839, VA.
   iii. EDMUND P. DANDRIDGE, b. Abt. 1841, VA.
   iv. SAMUEL P. DANDRIDGE, b. Abt. 1843, VA.
    v. MARY R. DANDRIDGE, b. Abt. 1846, VA.
   vi. PHILIP P. DANDRIDGE, b. Abt. 1848, VA.
  vii. ALEXANDER S. DANDRIDGE, b. Abt. 1849, VA.

225. SUSAN LOUISA[10] PENDLETON *(NATHANIEL GREENE[9], NATHANIEL[8], NATHANIEL[7], HENRY[6], PHILIP[5], HENRY[4], HENRY[3], GEORGE[2], GEORGE[1])* was born Feb 23, 1821 in Cincinnati, OH, and died Feb 06, 1877 in Cincinnati, OH. She married ROBERT BONNER BOWLER Oct 20, 1842 in Cincinnati, OH. He died Bef. 1870 in Cincinnati, OH?

Children of SUSAN PENDLETON and ROBERT BOWLER are (Ref. 193):
      i. NATHANIEL PENDLETON[11] BOWLER, b. Sep 20, 1843, Cincinnati, OH; d. Jul 15, 1845, Cincinnati, OH.

ii. GEORGE PENDLETON BOWLER, b. Feb 22, 1846, Cincinnati, OH; d. Mar 23, 1878, Paris, France; m. MAY WILLIAMSON, Oct 15, 1867, Paris, France.

iii. JESSE HUNT BOWLER, b. Jul 31, 1848, Cincinnati, OH; d. May 28, 1850, Cincinnati, OH.

iv. JANE HUNT BOWLER, b. Abt. 1850, Cincinnati, OH; d. Apr 02, 1856, Cincinnati, OH.

v. ROBERT BONNER BOWLER, b. Jan 17, 1856, Cincinnati, OH; d. Sep 16, 1902, Cincinnati, OH; m. ALICE BERNARD WILLIAMSON, Aug 08, 1877, London, England.

vi. LOUISA FOOTE BOWLER, b. Mar 27, 1861, Cincinnati, OH; m. JOHN CALLENDAR LIVINGSTON, Feb 17, 1890, Berlin, Germany.

226. MARTHA ELIZA[10] PENDLETON *(NATHANIEL GREENE[9], NATHANIEL[8], NATHANIEL[7], HENRY[6], PHILIP[5], HENRY[4], HENRY[3], GEORGE[2], GEORGE[1])* was born Dec 30, 1823 in OH, and died Aft. 1880 in Hamilton Co., OH? She married ALEXANDER SPOTSWOOD DANDRIDGE, DR. May 04, 1843 in Hamilton Co., OH, son of ADAM DANDRIDGE and SARAH PENDLETON. He was born Nov 19, 1819 in Jefferson Co., VA, and died Apr 28, 1889.

Children of MARTHA PENDLETON and ALEXANDER DANDRIDGE are:
i. MARTHA[11] DANDRIDGE.
ii. SARAH KENNEDY DANDRIDGE.
iii. SUSAN BOWLER DANDRIDGE.
iv. JANE P. DANDRIDGE, b. Abt. 1845, OH.
v. NATHANIEL PENDLETON DANDRIDGE, b. Abt. 1846, OH.
vi. ALEXANDER SPOTSWOOD DANDRIDGE, b. Abt. 1851, OH.
vii. ALICE K. DANDRIDGE, b. Abt. 1856, OH.
viii. MARY EVALINA DANDRIDGE, b. Abt. 1860, OH.

227. GEORGE HUNT[10] PENDLETON *(NATHANIEL GREENE[9], NATHANIEL[8], NATHANIEL[7], HENRY[6], PHILIP[5], HENRY[4], HENRY[3], GEORGE[2], GEORGE[1])* was born Jul 19, 1825 in Cincinnati, OH, and died Nov 24, 1889 in Brussels, Belgium. He married MARY ALICIA LLOYD NEVINS KEY Jun 02, 1846 in Washington DC, daughter of FRANCIS SCOTT KEY and MARY TAYLOE LLOYD. She was born 1823 in MD, and died May 20, 1886.

George Hunt Pendleton was probably the most widely known descendant of Philip Pendleton in the 19th century. His biography was written a number of times; the following is a condensed version (Ref. 111).

George Hunt Pendleton pursued an academic course in the schools of Cincinnati [Cincinnati College] and attended Heidelberg University, Germany where he studied law. He was admitted to the bar in 1847 and commenced practice in Cincinnati, OH. He was a member of the State senate 1854-1856 and an unsuccessful candidate for election in 1854 to the Thirty-fourth Congress. He was elected as a Democrat to the Thirty-fifth and to the three succeeding Congresses (March 4, 1857-March 3, 1865). He was an unsuccessful candidate for reelection in 1864 to the Thirty-ninth Congress. George H.

was one of the managers appointed by the House of Representatives in 1862 to conduct the impeachment proceedings against West H. Humphreys, United States judge for the several districts of Tennessee. George Hunt Pendleton was the Democratic candidate for Vice President on the ticket headed by George B. McClellan in 1864. He was again an unsuccessful candidate for election in 1866 to the Fortieth Congress. George was a delegate to the Loyalist Convention at Philadelphia in 1866 and unsuccessful Democratic candidate for Governor of Ohio in 1869. Pendleton, OR was named after him in 1868. He was president of the Kentucky Central Railroad 1869-1879. He was then elected as a Democrat to the United States Senate and served from March 4, 1879, to March 3, 1885 but was an unsuccessful candidate for renomination. George introduced the civil service reform bill, known as the Pendleton Act. He was appointed Envoy Extraordinary and Minister Plenipotentiary to Germany on March 23, 1885, and served until his death in Brussels, Belgium, November 24, 1889. He is buried in Spring Grove Cemetery, Cincinnati, Ohio

Children of GEORGE PENDLETON and MARY KEY are:
477. i. FRANCIS KEY[11] PENDLETON, b. Jan 03, 1850, Cincinnati, OH; d. Jul 26, 1930, New York, NY.
ii. MARY LLOYD PENDLETON, b. Mar 26, 1852, OH; d. Jul 30, 1929, New York City; m. HON. JOHN RUTLEDGE ABNEY, Nov 21, 1896, Washington DC; b. Jan 11, 1850, Edgefield, SC; d. Aft. 1910, New York City?

John R. Abney (60) is listed in the 1910 Manhattan, NY census.

478. iii. JANE FRANCES PENDLETON, b. Apr 22, 1860, Washington DC; d. Aft. 1920, Washington DC?

228. ELIOTT HUNT[10] PENDLETON (*NATHANIEL GREENE[9], NATHANIEL[8], NATHANIEL[7], HENRY[6], PHILIP[5], HENRY[4], HENRY[3], GEORGE[2], GEORGE[1]*) was born Dec 19, 1828 in OH, and died Oct 14, 1892 in Cincinnati, OH? He married EMMA GAYLORD. She was born Abt. 1830 in PA, and died Aft. 1880.

Children of ELIOTT PENDLETON and EMMA GAYLORD are:
i. ANNA PIERCE[11] PENDLETON, d. young.
ii. EMMA GAYLORD PENDLETON, d. young.
479. iii. LUCY GAYLORD PENDLETON, b. Dec 1850, OH; d. Aft. 1910, Ambrose Co., OH?
iv. THOMAS GAYLORD PENDLETON, b. 1856, OH; d. 1876.
480. v. JR. ELIOTT HUNT PENDLETON, b. Dec 08, 1859, OH; d. Jul 10, 1926, Cincinnati, OH?
481. vi. NATHANIEL GREENE PENDLETON, b. Abt. 1862, OH; d. Aft. 1910, NJ?
vii. ANGELINE GAYLORD PENDLETON, b. Abt. 1865, OH.
viii. GEORGE HUNT PENDLETON, b. 1867, OH; d. 1869.
ix. SUSAN BOWLER PENDLETON, b. Abt. 1868, OH.

229. ANNA PIERCE[10] PENDLETON (*NATHANIEL GREENE[9], NATHANIEL[8], NATHANIEL[7], HENRY[6], PHILIP[5], HENRY[4], HENRY[3], GEORGE[2], GEORGE[1]*) was born Dec 27, 1830 in OH, and died Dec 29, 1887 in Brooklyn, NY? She married NOAH

HUNT SCHENCK, REV. Nov 14, 1850, son of PETER SCHENCK and SARAH VAN KIRK. He was born Jun 30, 1825 in Pennington, NJ, and died Jan 04, 1885 in Brooklyn, NY.

Children of ANNA PENDLETON and NOAH SCHENCK are (Ref. 194):
- i. SUSAN BOWLER[11] SCHENCK, b. Abt. 1853.
- ii. NATHANIEL SCHENCK, b. Abt. 1855.
- iii. GRACE FITZ RANDOLPH SCHENCK, b. Abt. 1857.
- iv. SPOTSWOOD DANDRIDGE SCHENCK, b. Abt. 1857.
- v. IDA SUTPHIN SCHENCK, b. Abt. 1860, IL.
- vi. JOHN BARD SCHENCK, b. Abt. 1861.
- vii. ERNEST WHARTON SCHENCK, b. Abt. 1863, MD.
- viii. PENDLETON SCHENCK, b. Abt. 1864, MD.
- ix. GEORGE ELLIOT PENDLETON SCHENCK, b. Abt. 1868, France.
- x. DORSEY NOAH SCHENCK, b. Abt. 1870, NY.
- xi. ANN PENDLETON SCHENCK, b. Abt. 1874, NY.

230. EDMUND HENRY[10] PENDLETON (*NATHANIEL GREENE[9], NATHANIEL[8], NATHANIEL[7], HENRY[6], PHILIP[5], HENRY[4], HENRY[3], GEORGE[2], GEORGE[1]*) was born Jun 22, 1843 in OH, and died Mar 14, 1910. He married CORNELIA MARCY Apr 28, 1864, daughter of WILLIAM LEARNED MARCY.

In 1861 Edmund Henry Pendleton was appointed Second Lieutenant of Company E, 4th NY Artillery. Commissioning papers signed by Abraham Lincoln in 1862 promoted Edmund Pendleton to the rank of 1st Lieutenant in the 3rd Regiment of Artillery (the commission was effective in 1961). He received a brevat promotion to captain after the battle of Williamsburg (Ref. 195). In 1863-64 he was Aide de Camp to General Edmund de Russy. He was an author of several books, president of the Cincinnati Exposition of Arts and Industries, and President of the Cincinnati Music Festival, 1880-2. Edmund H. Pendleton is buried in the Arlington National Cemetery.

Child of EDMUND PENDLETON and CORNELIA MARCY is:
482.   i. WILLIAM LEARNED MARCY[11] PENDLETON, b. Feb 19, 1865, NY.

231. JOHN LEWIS[10] PENDLETON (*JOHN[9], EDMUND[8], JOHN[7], HENRY[6], PHILIP[5], HENRY[4], HENRY[3], GEORGE[2], GEORGE[1]*) was born Jul 07, 1790 in Caroline Co., VA, and died 1869 in Caroline Co., VA? He married ELIZABETH BANKHEAD MAGRUDER May 26, 1820 in Port Royal, Caroline Co., Va. She was born Bet. 1790 - 1800, and died Feb 02, 1842 in Bowling Green, Caroline Co., VA.

John L. Pendleton was the clerk of Caroline Co. Court from 1814 to 1845. He is listed in the 1850 Caroline Co., VA census as Caroline County Clerk.

Children of JOHN PENDLETON and ELIZABETH MAGRUDER are:
- i. JR. JOHN LEWIS[11] PENDLETON.
- ii. GEORGE ALLEN PENDLETON, b. 1823, Bowling Green, Caroline Co., VA; d. Mar 05, 1871, San Diego, CA; m. CLARA EMILY FINN, 1865, San

Diego, CA; b. Jun 05, 1848, Cape Girardeau, MO; d. Jun 07, 1912, La Jolla, CA.

George A. Pendleton is listed in the 1860 and 1870 San Diego Co., CA census, San Diego Township. Throughout the first few years of county government, most of the county offices and records were maintained by the officials in their own homes at Old Town. George A. Pendleton, County Clerk and Recorder from 1857 to 1871, had his office in a room of his home, about 200 yards southwest of the Plaza. Still standing at the end of Harney Street, close to the Santa Fe tracks, this old house was built in 1852 by Don Juan Bandini for his daughter. Captain Pendleton acquired it in the 60's (Ref. 196).

483.   iii.   WILLIAM ARMISTEAD PENDLETON, b. 1825, VA; d. 1870, St. Louis, MO?
484.   iv.   EUGENE BEAUHARNAIS PENDLETON, b. 1828, Caroline Co., VA; d. 1901, Rapides Parish, LA?
      v.   JULIEN PENDLETON, b. 1828, VA; d. 1840.
     vi.   THOMAS MAGRUDER PENDLETON, b. 1832, VA.
   vii.   ALLEN BOWIE PENDLETON, b. 1835, VA; d. 1900, St. Louis, MO.
        Allan Bowie Pendleton is a great great-grandson of Patrick Henry, Governor of Virginia (Ref. 197). He is buried in St. Louis; the cemetery address is 4004 Lindell (Ref. 198).

  viii.   ELIZA PENDLETON.
   ix.   HENRY PENDLETON, b. Abt. 1838, VA.

232. EDMUND ALLEN[10] PENDLETON (*JOHN*[9], *EDMUND*[8], *JOHN*[7], *HENRY*[6], *PHILIP*[5], *HENRY*[4], *HENRY*[3], *GEORGE*[2], *GEORGE*[1]) was born 1791 in VA, and died 1883 in Augusta, GA? He married MILDRED PENDLETON Nov 14, 1825 in Caroline Co., VA, daughter of EDMUND PENDLETON and LUCY NELSON. She was born Mar 21, 1802 in VA, and died 1892 in Augusta, GA?

Edmund Pendleton is listed in the 1850 Hanover Co., VA census as a farmer, Western District. Edmund and family are listed in the 1860 census, Richmond, VA.

Children of EDMUND PENDLETON and MILDRED PENDLETON are:
      i.   EDMUND LEWIS[11] PENDLETON, b. Jan 28, 1827, VA; m. CALISTA E. NORTON, Oct 24, 1850.
485.   ii.   WILLIAM PENDLETON, b. Jun 21, 1828, VA; d. Aft. 1900, Augusta, GA?
    iii.   JOHN PENDLETON, b. Mar 15, 1834, Caroline Co., VA; d. Aft. 1880, Augusta, GA?
486.   iv.   HUGH PENDLETON, b. Mar 15, 1834, Caroline Co., VA; d. May 04, 1902, Hamilton Co., TN?
     v.   JUDITH PAGE PENDLETON, b. 1836, VA; d. 1863, Richmond, VA?; m. RICHARD B. WILLIAMS, Apr 1859, Richmond, VA; b. Abt. 1816, VA; d. Aft. 1860, Richmond, VA?

According to the Richmond Enquirer (semiweekly), the place of residence at the time of the marriage of J.P. Pendleton and R. B. Williams was Richmond, Virginia.

487.   vi. ARMISTEAD FRANKLIN PENDLETON, b. Sep 25, 1838, VA; d. Aft. 1900, Richmond Co., GA?

       vii. ANNE ELIZABETH PENDLETON, b. 1844, VA; d. 1930.

233. ELIZABETH ALLEN[10] PENDLETON *(JOHN[9], EDMUND[8], JOHN[7], HENRY[6], PHILIP[5], HENRY[4], HENRY[3], GEORGE[2], GEORGE[1])* was born 1793 in VA, and died 1865 in Caroline Co., VA? She married WILLIAM GRAY. He was born Abt. 1789 in VA, and died Aft. 1850 in Caroline Co., VA?

Children of ELIZABETH PENDLETON and WILLIAM GRAY are:

     i. ISABELLA[11] GRAY, b. Abt. 1828, VA.

    ii. EVALINA GRAY, b. Abt. 1830, VA.

   iii. ANN L. GRAY, b. Abt. 1831, VA.

234. EVELINA MILDRED[10] PENDLETON *(JOHN[9], EDMUND[8], JOHN[7], HENRY[6], PHILIP[5], HENRY[4], HENRY[3], GEORGE[2], GEORGE[1])* was born 1797 in VA, and died 1864. She married SAMUEL COLEMAN DICKINSON, DR. Jan 08, 1818 in Caroline Co., Va., son of DAVID DICKINSON and ANN COLEMAN. He was born Oct 06, 1787.

Child of EVELINA PENDLETON and SAMUEL DICKINSON is:

     i. WILLIAM FESTUS[11] DICKINSON, b. Jul 07, 1823; d. Jul 13, 1908, Gallion, AL; m. JULIA M., Jan 11, 1849, Laurel Grove, VA.

235. WILLIAM ARMISTEAD[10] PENDLETON *(JOHN[9], EDMUND[8], JOHN[7], HENRY[6], PHILIP[5], HENRY[4], HENRY[3], GEORGE[2], GEORGE[1])* was born 1801 in VA, and died Jul 22, 1854 in Campbell Co., KY? He married FRANCES MARY PERRY May 26, 1839 in Campbell Co., KY. She was born Abt. 1810 in KY, and died Aft. 1870 in Campbell Co., KY?

William A. Pendleton performed marriages in Campbell Co., KY, 1835, 36, and 37 and in Kenton Co., KY in 1842. He is listed in the 1840 Kenton Co., KY census.

Children of WILLIAM PENDLETON and FRANCES PERRY are:

     i. CHARLES LEWIS[11] PENDLETON, b. Apr 19, 1840; d. Aug 05, 1841.

    ii. ROBERTA LEWIS PENDLETON, b. Mar 19, 1843; d. Nov 04, 1875; m. ? WHITTEN.

488.   iii. JR. WILLIAM ARMISTEAD PENDLETON, b. May 11, 1844, KY; d. Jan 06, 1882, Campbell Co., KY?

    iv. FRANCES I.C. PENDLETON, b. 1846; d. Jul 01, 1849.

    v. ANNA E. PENDLETON, b. 1851; d. Apr 16, 1868.

236. ROBERT TAYLOR[10] PENDLETON *(JOHN[9], EDMUND[8], JOHN[7], HENRY[6], PHILIP[5], HENRY[4], HENRY[3], GEORGE[2], GEORGE[1])* was born Jul 08, 1805 in Caroline Co., VA, and died Abt. 1840 in Caroline Co., VA. He married JUDITH ALLEN HOOMES Feb 05, 1829 in Bowling Green, Caroline Co., VA, daughter of RICHARD HOOMES. She was born Mar 09, 1812 in Bowling Green, Caroline Co., VA, and died Jul 20, 1856 in Caroline Co., VA.

The marriage of Robert Pendleton was announced Wednesday, February 11, 1829 in the Virginia Herald (Fredericksburg, Va.): "Married- At the Bowling Green, on Thursday, February 5, by Rev. Edward C. McGuire, Robert T. Pendleton, to Miss Judith A. Hoomes, daughter of the late Richard Hoomes" (Ref.105). Robert T. Pendleton performed marriages in Kenton Co., KY in 1842-3.

Judith Pendleton is listed in the 1850 Caroline Co., VA census in the household of Hannah Gatewood (61).

Children of ROBERT PENDLETON and JUDITH HOOMES are:
489.   i.   ROBERT LEWIS[11] PENDLETON, b. Jan 24, 1830, Caroline Co., VA; d. Dec 12, 1880, Baltimore, MD.
       ii. HANNAH B. PENDLETON, b. 1837.

237. NATHANIEL PHILIP HENRY[10] PENDLETON *(JOHN[9], EDMUND[8], JOHN[7], HENRY[6], PHILIP[5], HENRY[4], HENRY[3], GEORGE[2], GEORGE[1])* was born Feb 12, 1809 in VA, and died Jul 13, 1877 in Port Royal, Caroline Co., VA. He married ANNE MADISON TURNER Dec 27, 1838 in Caroline Co., VA, daughter of DANIEL TURNER and SARAH PENDLETON. She was born Dec 18, 1811 in VA, and died Apr 11, 1892 in Port Royal, Caroline Co., VA.

Nathaniel Pendleton is Listed as a clerk in the 1850 Carolina Co., VA Census and as a merchant in 1860. Nathaniel is buried at "Hazelwood" west of Port Royal, VA.

Children of NATHANIEL PENDLETON and ANNE TURNER are:
490.   i.   HENRIETTA[11] PENDLETON, b. Dec 23, 1840, VA; d. Oct 11, 1919.
491.   ii. SARAH ANNE PENDLETON, b. Feb 22, 1842, VA; d. Nov 27, 1930, Elizabeth City, NJ?
      iii. WILLIAM LEWIS PENDLETON, b. 1848, VA; d. Apr 25, 1851, VA.

238. ELIZABETH PAGE[10] PENDLETON *(EDMUND[9], EDMUND[8], JOHN[7], HENRY[6], PHILIP[5], HENRY[4], HENRY[3], GEORGE[2], GEORGE[1])* was born 1795, and died Apr 1839. She married JOHN CARTER SUTTON Jan 28, 1817 in Caroline Co., VA. He was born 1782.

Children of ELIZABETH PENDLETON and JOHN SUTTON are:
       i.   EDMUND PENDLETON[11] SUTTON.
      ii. WILLIAM CARTER SUTTON.
     iii. HUGH CARTER SUTTON.
     iv. NORBORNNE E. SUTTON.
      v. JOHN CARTER SUTTON.
     vi. ROBERT W. SUTTON.

vii. PATRICK H. SUTTON.
viii. SARAH JANE SUTTON.
 ix. LUCY CARTER SUTTON.
  x. ANNE LEWIS SUTTON.
 xi. BETTY BURWELL SUTTON.

239. HUGH NELSON[10] PENDLETON (*EDMUND*[9], *EDMUND*[8], *JOHN*[7], *HENRY*[6], *PHILIP*[5], *HENRY*[4], *HENRY*[3], *GEORGE*[2], *GEORGE*[1]) was born Apr 13, 1800 in VA, and died May 27, 1875 in Jefferson Co., WV? He married (1) LUCY R. NELSON Mar 12, 1829 in Hanover Co., VA, daughter of ROBERT NELSON, JUDGE. She was born 1804, and died May 20, 1837 in Hanover Co., VA. He married (2) ELIZABETH DIGGES May 08, 1839 in Louisa Co., VA, daughter of DUDLEY DIGGES and ALICE PAGE. She was born Jan 11, 1814 in VA, and died Oct 22, 1876.

Hugh Pendleton was educated at William and Mary College where he graduated in 1818. He practiced law in Caroline, Richmond, and Louisa Counties. He reportedly moved to Clarke Co. in 1846 and built his home "Westwood" there. However, he is listed as a farmer (age 51) in the 1850 Jefferson Co., VA census; value of farm $15,000.

Lucy R. Nelson Pendleton's tombstone is enscribed with "Lucy, wife of Hugh N. Pendleton; Granddaughter of Govs. Thos. Nelson and John Page and only child of Judge Robert Nelson; On the 20th of May 1837 At the age of 33 years and a few days, her spirit returned unto him who gave it" (Ref. 199). Her funeral is recorded in St. Martins Parish Register: "Mrs. Lucy Pendleton, 30; May 22, 1837; Hanover Co., VA."

Child of HUGH PENDLETON and LUCY NELSON is:
492. i. JULIA NELSON[11] PENDLETON, b. Jan 21, 1830, VA; d. Jul 23, 1865.

Children of HUGH PENDLETON and ELIZABETH DIGGES are:
493. ii. DUDLEY DIGGES[11] PENDLETON, b. Mar 02, 1840, Jefferson Co., VA; d. Aug 25, 1886, Shepherdstown, WV?
494. iii. ROBERT NELSON PENDLETON, b. Feb 04, 1843, Jefferson Co., VA; d. Jun 22, 1905.
      iv. KENNETH MURRAY PENDLETON, b. 1845, VA; d. Jun 20, 1846, Hanover Co., VA.
          Kenneth Pendleton is buried at Fork Church Cemetery, Hanover Co., VA.

240. MILDRED[10] PENDLETON (*EDMUND*[9], *EDMUND*[8], *JOHN*[7], *HENRY*[6], *PHILIP*[5], *HENRY*[4], *HENRY*[3], *GEORGE*[2], *GEORGE*[1]) was born Mar 21, 1802 in VA, and died 1892 in Augusta, GA? She married EDMUND ALLEN PENDLETON Nov 14, 1825 in Caroline Co., VA, son of JOHN PENDLETON and NANCY LEWIS. He was born 1791 in VA, and died 1883 in Augusta, GA?

The children of Mildred Pendleton are listed above under (**232**) Edmund Allen Pendleton, her cousin.

241. JUDITH PAGE[10] PENDLETON (*EDMUND*[9], *EDMUND*[8], *JOHN*[7], *HENRY*[6], *PHILIP*[5], *HENRY*[4], *HENRY*[3], *GEORGE*[2], *GEORGE*[1]) was born Dec 08, 1803 in Caroline

Co., VA, and died Jul 1834 in Caroline Co., VA. She married ROBERT H. HARRISON Jun 06, 1826 in Caroline Co., VA.

Children of JUDITH PENDLETON and ROBERT HARRISON are:
    i. WILLIAM L.[11] HARRISON, m. LAURA A. LUMPKIN.
    ii. MARY F. HARRISON, m. JAMES E. WILLIAMS, DR.

242. FRANCIS WALKER[10] PENDLETON, DR. (*EDMUND*[9], *EDMUND*[8], *JOHN*[7], *HENRY*[6], *PHILIP*[5], *HENRY*[4], *HENRY*[3], *GEORGE*[2], *GEORGE*[1]) was born Dec 07, 1808 in Caroline Co., VA, and died 1865 in Richmond Co., VA. He married SARAH FRANCES TURNER Jan 27, 1833 in Caroline Co., VA, daughter of DANIEL TURNER and SARAH PENDLETON. She was born 1810 in Caroline Co., VA, and died Aft. 1860 in Richmond Co., VA?

    Francis Pendleton can be found in the 1840 census, Richmond, VA. F. W. Pendleton (Richmond) is included in an 1846 list of Virginia School Commissioners. He is listed as a doctor in the Richmond, VA 1850 census. He was a Clerk of Richmond Co. and a Justice of the Peace.

Children of FRANCIS PENDLETON and SARAH TURNER are:
    i. ROBERT CARTER[11] PENDLETON, b. 1836, Richmond Co., VA; d. Sep 07, 1852, Warsaw, Richmond Co, VA.

        A Robert Pendleton (age 14) is listed in 1850 Richmond Co., VA census, Farnham Parish, as a student in the establishment of Catherine D. Brittendese. His obituary is published in the Richmond Whig (Sep 17, 1852): "died on Sep 7, at Warsaw, Richmond Co., in his 17th year, Robert Carter Pendleton, only son of Dr. F.W. Pendleton."

    ii. ANN "NANNIE" F. PENDLETON, b. 1841, Richmond Co., VA.
495. iii. MILDRED EDMONIA PENDLETON, b. 1843, Richmond Co., VA.

243. WILLIAM NELSON[10] PENDLETON, REV. (*EDMUND*[9], *EDMUND*[8], *JOHN*[7], *HENRY*[6], *PHILIP*[5], *HENRY*[4], *HENRY*[3], *GEORGE*[2], *GEORGE*[1]) was born Dec 26, 1809 in Richmond, VA, and died Jan 15, 1883 in Lexington, Rockbridge Co., VA. He married ANZOLETTE PAGE Jul 15, 1831 in VA, daughter of FRANCIS PAGE and SUSANNAH NELSON. She was born 1807 in of Hanover Co., VA, and died Jan 15, 1884 in Lexington, VA?

    The following is from just one of many biographies of William Nelson Pendleton (Ref. 200).

    William Nelson Pendleton graduated in 1830 from the United States Military Academy, where he formed a close friendship with Robert E. Lee and Jefferson Davis. He was for a year an instructor at West Point, then as second lieutenant served with the artillery at Fort Hamilton, New York, until 1833, when he resigned. He was a professor at Bristol (Pennsylvania) College, and then at Delaware College. In 1837 he took orders in the Episcopal church, and received the degree of D. D. In 1861 he became captain of a Lexington company, and soon was commissioned captain of artillery, C. S. A. He commanded the Rockbridge artillery until shortly before the battle of Manassas, when he was promoted to colonel and made chief of artillery to Gen. J. E. Johnston. It is told that in the battle, when he brought his artillery into action, he said, with solemn reverence, "Lord, have mercy on their souls!" He continued under Johnston, was promoted to brigadier-general, and after Lee came into command of the army, served under him in the same capacity to the end of the war. Under him the artillery rendered excellent service at Gettysburg. With Gens. Longstreet and Gordon he arranged the details of the surrender at Appomattox. After the war he resumed his clerical duties at Latimer Parish, Lexington where R. E. Lee served on his vestry.

The Family, professional and military correspondence of William N. Pendleton, cover his opinions on slavery. These include slaves building Confederate fortifications (1861); thoughts of slaves on possible Yankee victory (1862); instructions on handling rebellious slaves (1863); the postwar situation with African Americans (1865); and justifications of the institution of slavery using passages from the Bible (1880). The collection also includes an Annual Report of the Pennsylvania Colonization Society, which transported blacks who wanted to return to Africa to Liberia (1881) (Ref. 201).

His only son, Col. "Sandie" Pendleton, was a member of Gen. Jackson's staff, and was mortally wounded at the battle of Fisher's Hill, Winchester.

Children of WILLIAM PENDLETON and ANZOLETTE PAGE are:

496. i.   SUSAN[11] PENDLETON, b. Dec 10, 1831, VA; d. Dec 10, 1911, Lexington, VA.
      ii. MARY NELSON PENDLETON, b. Abt. 1833, VA; d. Mar 19, 1918, Lexington, VA.
      iii. ROSE PAGE PENDLETON, b. Abt. 1835, VA; d. Feb 24, 1910, Lexington, VA.

      Rose Page Pendleton wrote "General David Hunter's sack of Lexington, Virginia, June 10-14, 1864" (Ref. 202).

497. iv. ALEXANDER SWIFT "SANDY" PENDLETON, b. Sep 28, 1840, Of Richmond, Henrico Co., VA; d. Sep 22, 1864, Battle of Fisher's Hill.
      v.   NANCY PAGE PENDLETON, b. Abt. 1842, VA; d. 1901.
      vi. HUGHELLA PENDLETON, b. Abt. 1844, Lexington, VA; d. Mar 08, 1919; m. EDWARD MILES GADSDEN, Feb 12, 1885, Rockbridge Co., VA; b. Dec 28, 1859; d. Mar 31, 1900.

244. JAMES LAWRENCE[10] PENDLETON (*EDMUND*[9], *EDMUND*[8], *JOHN*[7], *HENRY*[6], *PHILIP*[5], *HENRY*[4], *HENRY*[3], *GEORGE*[2], *GEORGE*[1]) was born 1814 in VA, and died Dec 20, 1851 in Richmond, VA. He married ANNALETHIA CARTER Mar 02, 1840 in Henrico Co., VA, daughter of SAMUEL S. CARTER. She was born Abt. 1823 in VA, and died 1881 in Elizabeth, NJ?

Anna L. Pendleton listed in 1860 Henrico Co., VA census, Richmond.

Children of JAMES PENDLETON and ANNALETHIA CARTER are:

498. i.   SAMUEL HEISLER[11] PENDLETON, b. Jan 27, 1841, VA; d. Sep 27, 1918, Elizabeth City, NJ?
      ii. THOMAS HUGH PENDLETON, b. 1843, VA; d. Jul 03, 1863, Gettysburg.

iii. MARTHA CARTER PENDLETON, b. Abt. 1848, VA; m. JOSEPH M. FURQUEREAU, 1871.

499. iv. WILLIAM J. PENDLETON, b. Abt. 1850, VA.

v. EMMA WALKER PENDLETON, b. Abt. 1852, VA; m. ROBERT C. LITTLE, Sep 18, 1882, VA; b. of Columbus, GA.

Mrs. Emma Walker Pendleton Little was a member of The National Society of the Daughters of the American Revolution (Volume 49, page 178). She was Gr-granddaughter of Hugh Nelson and Judith Page, his wife. Colonel Hugh Nelson (1750-1800) commanded the Virginia forces at Yorktown during the revolution.

245. GUERDON HUNTINGDON[10] PENDLETON *(EDMUND[9], EDMUND[8], JOHN[7], HENRY[6], PHILIP[5], HENRY[4], HENRY[3], GEORGE[2], GEORGE[1])* was born Apr 07, 1817 in Caroline Co., VA, and died Jan 30, 1878 in Wythe Co., VA? He married JANE BYRD PAGE May 11, 1854, daughter of MANN RANDOLPH PAGE. She was born Jul 23, 1832 in VA, and died Jun 16, 1906 in Wytheville, VA?

Guerdon Pendleton is listed as a farmer in the 1850 Jefferson Co., WV census (age 33), unmarried; value of farm $6520.

Children of GUERDON PENDLETON and JANE PAGE are:

i. MARY[11] PENDLETON, b. 1855; d. 1864.

500. ii. EDMUND PENDLETON, b. May 22, 1856, of Wytheville, VA; d. 1935.

501. iii. MANN RANDOLPH PAGE PENDLETON, b. Mar 01, 1858, VA; d. Jul 06, 1922, Wytheville, Wythe Co., VA?

iv. LUCY W. PENDLETON, b. Abt. 1860; d. young.

v. HUGH PENDLETON, d. infancy.

vi. MARGARET PENDLETON, d. infancy-twin of Hugh.

502. vii. JULIA NELSON PENDLETON, b. Apr 20, 1865, WV; d. Aft. 1920, Wytheville, VA?

503. viii. MILDRED LOUISE PENDLETON, b. May 22, 1867, Wytheville, VA; d. Mar 25, 1944, Charlotte, NC.

504. ix. JANE BYRD PENDLETON, b. Jun 26, 1869, Jefferson Co., WV; d. Aft. 1910, Wythe Co., VA?

505. x. FRANCES LAWRENCE PENDLETON, b. Apr 15, 1873, Wytheville, VA; d. Aft. 1920, Wytheville, VA?

246. SARAH FRANCES[10] TURNER *(SARAH[9] PENDLETON, EDMUND[8], JOHN[7], HENRY[6], PHILIP[5], HENRY[4], HENRY[3], GEORGE[2], GEORGE[1])* was born 1810 in Caroline Co., VA, and died Aft. 1860 in Richmond Co., VA? She married FRANCIS WALKER PENDLETON, DR. Jan 27, 1833 in Caroline Co., VA, son of EDMUND PENDLETON and LUCY NELSON. He was born Dec 07, 1808 in Caroline Co., VA, and died 1865 in Richmond Co., VA.

The children of Sarah Turner are listed above under (**242**) Francis Walker Pendleton, Dr., her cousin.

247. ANNE MADISON[10] TURNER *(SARAH[9] PENDLETON, EDMUND[8], JOHN[7], HENRY[6], PHILIP[5], HENRY[4], HENRY[3], GEORGE[2], GEORGE[1])* was born Dec 18, 1811 in VA, and died Apr 11, 1892 in Port Royal, Caroline Co., VA. She married NATHANIEL PHILIP HENRY PENDLETON Dec 27, 1838 in Caroline Co., VA, son of JOHN PENDLETON and NANCY LEWIS. He was born Feb 12, 1809 in VA, and died Jul 13, 1877 in Port Royal, Caroline Co., VA.

The children of Anne Turner are listed above under **(237)** Nathaniel Philip Henry Pendleton, her cousin.

248. MADISON[10] PENDLETON, DR. *(EDMUND[9], HENRY[8], JOHN[7], HENRY[6], PHILIP[5], HENRY[4], HENRY[3], GEORGE[2], GEORGE[1])* was born Jan 09, 1809 in VA, and died May 18, 1872 in Louisa Co., VA. He married ELIZABETH KIMBROUGH BARRETT Dec 17, 1829 in Louisa Co., VA. She was born Aug 27, 1807 in VA, and died May 27, 1898.

  Madison Pendleton is listed as a physician in the 1850 Louisa Co., VA census; value of property $7200.

Children of MADISON PENDLETON and ELIZABETH BARRETT are:

506.	i.	JOHN BARRETT[11] PENDLETON, b. Oct 21, 1830, Louisa Co., VA; d. Jul 10, 1861, killed while in C.S.A.
507.	ii.	EDMUND STRACHAN PENDLETON, b. May 09, 1833, Louisa Co., VA; d. Dec 27, 1909, Iron Gate, Louisa Co., VA.
508.	iii.	CHARLES KIMBROUGH PENDLETON, b. Nov 30, 1835, Louisa Co., VA; d. Feb 10, 1918, Ashland, VA.
509.	iv.	WILLIAM BARRETT PENDLETON, b. Feb 12, 1838, Louisa Co., VA; d. Jan 17, 1914, Louisa Co., VA.
	v.	JOSEPH MADISON PENDLETON, b. Feb 03, 1840; d. Apr 30, 1843.
	vi.	PHILIP HENRY PENDLETON, b. Apr 04, 1842, Louisa Co., VA; d. May 12, 1864, killed at Bloody Angle, Spotsylvania Co., Civil War.

  Philip H. Pendleton served in the VA Light Artillery, Carrington's Co., CSA.

249. JOSEPH KIMBROUGH[10] PENDLETON *(EDMUND[9], HENRY[8], JOHN[7], HENRY[6], PHILIP[5], HENRY[4], HENRY[3], GEORGE[2], GEORGE[1])* was born Dec 05, 1810 in VA, and died 1883 in Louisa Co, VA? He married CHARLOTTE REBECCA HARRIS Oct 03, 1836 in Louisa Co., VA, daughter of FREDERICK HARRIS and CATHERINE SMITH. She was born 1816 in VA, and died Aft. 1870.

  Joseph Pendleton is listed as a lawyer in the 1850 Louisa Co., VA census; value of property $9270. He was a Member of the House of Delegates 1850-2, and 1855-6 from Louisa Co., VA.

Children of JOSEPH PENDLETON and CHARLOTTE HARRIS are:

	i.	LEWIS L. SMITH[11] PENDLETON, DR., b. Jul 1837, Louisa Co., VA; d. Aft. 1910, Louisa Co., VA?; m. ANNE TERRELL KEAN, Abt. 1873; b. Apr 1848, VA; d. Aft. 1920, Cuckoo, Louisa Co., VA?

Lewis Pendleton (farmer) and wife are listed in the 1900 Louisa Co., VA census, pg. 25. They had no children. Anne T. Pendleton (73, farm manager) is listed in the 1920 Cuckoo, Louisa Co., VA census, pg. 6B.

ii. JANE CLAYBROOKE PENDLETON, b. 1841, Louisa Co., VA; d. 1870; m. JR. JOHN HUNTER, Feb 13, 1866, Louisa Co., VA; b. Jan 1838, Louisa Co., VA; d. Jul 1909.
iii. HENRY PENDLETON, b. 1849, Louisa Co., VA; d. 1896.

250. ELIZABETH KIMBROUGH[10] PENDLETON *(EDMUND[9], HENRY[8], JOHN[7], HENRY[6], PHILIP[5], HENRY[4], HENRY[3], GEORGE[2], GEORGE[1])* was born Jan 09, 1813 in VA, and died Dec 1830 in Louisa Co., VA. She married WILLIAM THOMPSON GOODWIN Mar 08, 1830 in Louisa Co., VA. He was born 1807, and died 1833.

Child of ELIZABETH PENDLETON and WILLIAM GOODWIN is:
i. EDMUND PENDLETON[11] GOODWIN, b. 1830; d. 1869; m. LUCY ANN CHILES; b. 1834; d. 1906.

251. WILLIAM KIMBROUGH[10] PENDLETON *(EDMUND[9], HENRY[8], JOHN[7], HENRY[6], PHILIP[5], HENRY[4], HENRY[3], GEORGE[2], GEORGE[1])* was born Sep 08, 1817 in Yanceyville, VA, and died Sep 01, 1899 in Bethany, WV. He married (1) LAVINIA M. CAMPBELL Oct 1840 in Louisa Co., VA. She was born 1817, and died 1846. He married (2) CLARINDA CAMPBELL Jul 1848 in VA. She was born 1822, and died Jan 10, 1851. He married (3) CATHERINE HUNTINGTON KING Sep 19, 1855, daughter of LEICESTER KING and JULIAN HUNTINGTON. She was born Jul 08, 1832 in Warren Co., OH, and died Jan 17, 1907 in Augusta, GA.

William K. Pendleton's biography was published in 1902 (Ref. 203).

William K. Pendleton attended the Univ. of Virginia and was admitted to the Virginia Bar in 1840. He accepted the Chair of Natural Philosophy at Bethany College in October 1841. He is listed as Professor, age 32, in the 1850 Brooke Co. census and is included again in the 1860 Brooke Co. census. From 1866 to 1884 he was President of the college. He was elected as a Senatorial Representative to the West Virginia Constitutional Convention of 1872.

On November 21, 2003 it was announced that Pendleton Heights, a Bethany College landmark, was to be restored with the support of $220,000 in federal funds. William Pendleton and his wife, Lavinia Campbell, constructed the house 162 years ago on farmland adjacent to the college. According to historical documents cited by the college, the basement of Pendleton Heights provided refuge to slaves traveling the Underground Railroad to Pennsylvania.

Child of WILLIAM PENDLETON and LAVINIA CAMPBELL is:
i. CAMPBELLINA[11] PENDLETON, b. 1841; d. 1919.

Child of WILLIAM PENDLETON and CLARINDA CAMPBELL is:
510. ii. WILLIAM CAMPBELL[11] PENDLETON, b. May 03, 1849, Bethany, Brooke Co., VA; d. Oct 07, 1922, Trumbull Co., OH?

Children of WILLIAM PENDLETON and CATHERINE KING are:

511.   iii.   CLARINDA HUNTINGTON[11] PENDLETON, b. Aug 26, 1856, WV; d. Apr 27, 1943, Atlanta, GA.
512.   iv.   HUNTINGTON KING PENDLETON, b. Sep 07, 1861, WV.
513.   v.   PHILIP YANCEY PENDLETON, b. Sep 25, 1863, WV; d. Feb 01, 1930.
514.   vi.   WINSTON KENT PENDLETON, b. Oct 24, 1869, Bethany, WV; d. Eustis, FL?
515.   vii.   DWIGHT LYMAN PENDLETON, b. Oct 14, 1871, WV; d. Feb 12, 1955, Clark Co, KY- Winchester Cemetery.

252. PHILIP BARBOUR[10] PENDLETON *(EDMUND[9], HENRY[8], JOHN[7], HENRY[6], PHILIP[5], HENRY[4], HENRY[3], GEORGE[2], GEORGE[1])* was born Dec 13, 1819 in VA, and died Mar 16, 1907 in Louisa Co., VA? He married JANE KIMBROUGH HOLLIDAY Dec 14, 1847 in Louisa Co., VA. She was born Oct 12, 1827 in Louisa Co., VA, and died Aug 13, 1915 in Richmond, VA.

Philip Pendleton is listed as a physician in the 1850 Louisa Co., VA census; others in the household include Mrs. W. Pendleton (63), Jane K. (22), Madison (1), and Ed. P. Goodwin (2), student. The value of property listed was $9800 (Mrs. Pendleton) and $6700 (P.B. Pendleton). Philip graduated from Jefferson Medical College at Philadelphia. He was an elder of historic Gilboa Church of which he became pastor in 1874.

Children of PHILIP PENDLETON and JANE HOLLIDAY are:

      i.   MADISON HENRY[11] PENDLETON, b. May 22, 1849, Louisa Co., VA; d. 1927, Richmond, VA?; m. E. MILDRED DAVIS, Feb 05, 1878; b. Abt. 1850, VA.

             Madison Pendleton whose occupation is listed as "lab" is included in the Richmond, Virginia City Directories, 1889-90 at 921 Williams, Richmond, VA.

516.   ii.   EUGENE B. PENDLETON, DR., b. Jun 22, 1851, VA; d. Sep 09, 1927, Cuckoo, Louisa Co., VA?
517.   iii.   SALLY LOUISE PENDLETON, b. Feb 04, 1853, VA; d. Jul 15, 1932.
518.   iv.   JOSEPH KIMBROUGH PENDLETON, b. Feb 11, 1855, VA.
519.   v.   WILLIAM "WILLIE" WALLER PENDLETON, b. Sep 26, 1856, Louisa Co., VA; d. Aft. 1920, Clifton Forge, VA?
      vi.   ELLA KIMBROUGH PENDLETON, b. Mar 03, 1860, VA; m. DANIEL STEPHENS MCCARTHY, Feb 23, 1881.
520.   vii.   ELIZABETH YANCEY PENDLETON, b. Jan 12, 1862, VA; d. Bef. 1920.
521.   viii.   PHILIP BARBOUR PENDLETON, b. Jun 23, 1868, VA; d. Jun 05, 1908.

253. MARY OVERTON[10] PENDLETON *(JOHN BICKERTON[9], HENRY[8], JOHN[7], HENRY[6], PHILIP[5], HENRY[4], HENRY[3], GEORGE[2], GEORGE[1])* was born Aug 05, 1820 in AL, and died Aft. 1860 in Abeville, SC? She married WILLIAM W. WALLER Jul 24, 1834. He was born Jun 02, 1813 in SC, and died Aft. 1860 in Abeville, SC?

Children of MARY PENDLETON and WILLIAM WALLER are:
  i. SARA ELIZA BROWN[11] WALLER, b. Apr 16, 1841.
  ii. MARY AMELIA WALLER, b. Oct 11, 1843, AL.
  iii. THOMAS PENDLETON WALLER, b. Aug 04, 1845, AL.
  iv. ANN ELIZABETH WALLER, b. May 03, 1847, AL.
  v. FRANCES J. WALLER, b. Jan 03, 1849.
  vi. JOHN HENRY WALLER, b. Feb 03, 1851, SC.
  vii. WILLIAM S. WALLER, b. Mar 25, 1853, SC.
  viii. ANNE E. WALLER, b. Abt. 1855, SC.
  ix. SARAH WALLER, b. Abt. 1857, SC.

254. HENRY[10] PENDLETON *(JOHN BICKERTON[9], HENRY[8], JOHN[7], HENRY[6], PHILIP[5], HENRY[4], HENRY[3], GEORGE[2], GEORGE[1])* was born Oct 03, 1822 in Pickens Co., AL, and died Jan 13, 1897. He married NANCY DORENDA KEASLER Dec 22, 1870, daughter of SAMUEL KEASLER and ESTHER ALEXANDER. She was born Sep 10, 1843 in Pickens Co., AL, and died May 10, 1925.

Henry Pendleton is listed as a farmer in the 1880 Pickens Co., AL census.

Child of HENRY PENDLETON and NANCY KEASLER is:
522. i. ERNEST COPELAND[11] PENDLETON, b. Feb 24, 1877, Pickens Co., AL;
         d. Feb 05, 1941.

255. JOSEPH HENRY[10] PENDLETON *(JOSEPH WINSTON[9], HENRY[8], JOHN[7], HENRY[6], PHILIP[5], HENRY[4], HENRY[3], GEORGE[2], GEORGE[1])* was born 1827 in VA, and died 1881 in Brooke Co., WV? He married MARGARET CAMPBELL EWING 1848. She was born 1829 in OH, and died Aft. 1870 in Brooke Co., WV?

Major Joseph H. Pendleton was an attorney-at-law and a member of House of Delegates, VA, 1863-65. He was brevetted Lieut. Colonel, C.S.A. and was a staff member of Quartermaster Dept. J.H. Pendleton (23) and M.C. (21) are listed in the 1850 Brooke Co. census. It appears the term Attorney was written over the term Lawyer for his occupation. J. H (lawyer) and M. C. Pendleton and family are listed in the Brooke Co., WV census in 1870.

Children of JOSEPH PENDLETON and MARGARET EWING are:
  i. JOSEPH M.[11] PENDLETON, b. 1849, VA.
  ii. JOHN OVERTON PENDLETON, b. Jul 04, 1851, Wellsburg, Brooke Co.,
      VA; d. Dec 24, 1916, Wheeling, WV.
      John Overton Pendleton's biography was recorded because of his
      Congressional service (Ref. 111).

      John Overton Pendleton moved with his parents to Wheeling, Va. (now
      West Virginia), in 1851. He attended Aspen Hill Academy, Louisa County,
      Va., 1865-1869, and Bethany College, West Virginia, 1869-1871. He
      studied law and was admitted to the bar and commenced practice in
      Wheeling, W. Va., in 1874. He was an unsuccessful Democratic candidate
      for State senator in 1886 and presented credentials as a Democratic Member-
      elect to the Fifty-first Congress where he served from March 4, 1889, to

February 26, 1890. He was succeeded by George W. Atkinson, who contested the election. John Pendleton was elected as a Democrat to the Fifty-second and Fifty-third Congresses (March 4, 1891-March 3, 1895) but was an unsuccessful candidate for renomination in 1894. He resumed the practice of law in Wheeling, W. Va., and died there December 24, 1916; interment in Greenwood Cemetery

     iii. HENRY H. PENDLETON, b. 1853, VA.
          Henry Pendleton was Consul to Southampton, England, 1887-89 and Assistant Attorney General, WV.

     iv. ELIZABETH WINSTON PENDLETON, b. 1855.
523.   v. IDA EWING PENDLETON, b. 1858, VA.
524.   vi. VIRGINIA CAMPBELL PENDLETON, b. 1861, VA.
     vii. MARGARET JOSEPHINE PENDLETON, b. 1866, WV; d. Aft. 1910, Nicholas Co., WV?; m. GEORGE S. HUGHES, Abt. 1885; b. Abt. 1861, WV; d. Aft. 1910, Nicholas Co., WV?

256. JOHN OVERTON[10] PENDLETON (*JOSEPH WINSTON*[9], *HENRY*[8], *JOHN*[7], *HENRY*[6], *PHILIP*[5], *HENRY*[4], *HENRY*[3], *GEORGE*[2], *GEORGE*[1]) was born 1829 in VA, and died Aft. 1880 in Albemarle Co., VA? He married ANNE LEWIS HARRIS Sep 13, 1851 in Albemarle Co., VA, daughter of JOHN HARRIS and BARBARA TERRELL. She was born 1835 in VA, and died Aft. 1880 in Albemarle Co., VA?

    John O. Pendleton served in the CSA during the Civil War. He is listed in the 1880 Albemarle Co., VA census, Scottsville.

Children of JOHN PENDLETON and ANNE HARRIS are:
     i. SARAH[11] PENDLETON, b. 1852, VA.
525.   ii. JOHN O. H. PENDLETON, b. Feb 1861, VA; d. Aft. 1910, Albemarle Co., VA?
     iii. BARBARA ELIZABETH PENDLETON, b. 1864, VA; m. JOHN MOORMAN, 1890.

257. MARY BURNLEY[10] PENDLETON (*JOSEPH WINSTON*[9], *HENRY*[8], *JOHN*[7], *HENRY*[6], *PHILIP*[5], *HENRY*[4], *HENRY*[3], *GEORGE*[2], *GEORGE*[1]) was born 1833 in VA, and died 1903. She married CHARLES JOSEPH KEMPER. He was born 1829 in VA, and died 1901 in Brooke Co., WV?

    Charles Kemper (physician) and family are listed in the 1880 Brooke Co., WV census, pg. 21B.

Children of MARY PENDLETON and CHARLES KEMPER are:
     i. CHARLES PENDLETON[11] KEMPER, b. Sep 17, 1858, Rockingham Co., VA.
     ii. GEORGE WHITFIELD KEMPER, b. Abt. 1870; d. 1921; m. LYDIA BELLE MYERS.

iii. MATTHEW FONTAINE MAURY KEMPER, b. Abt. 1873, VA; m.
      ESTELLE WHITNEY.
iv. GRAHAM HAWES KEMPER, b. Abt. 1877, WV.

258. ELIZABETH HENLY[10] PENDLETON *(JOSEPH WINSTON[9], HENRY[8], JOHN[7], HENRY[6], PHILIP[5], HENRY[4], HENRY[3], GEORGE[2], GEORGE[1])* was born 1836 in VA, and died 1871 in Louisa Co., VA? She married JOHN B. ANDERSON, DR. Dec 12, 1854 in Louisa Co., VA. He was born Abt. 1826 in VA, and died Aft. 1870 in Louisa Co., VA?

John Anderson (physician; farmer) and family are listed in the 1870 Louisa Co., VA census.

Children of ELIZABETH PENDLETON and JOHN ANDERSON are:
i. LIZZIE W.[11] ANDERSON, b. Abt. 1856.
ii. MATTIE W. ANDERSON, b. Abt. 1857.

259. ELISHA HENRY[10] PENDLETON *(THOMAS MADISON[9], HENRY[8], JOHN[7], HENRY[6], PHILIP[5], HENRY[4], HENRY[3], GEORGE[2], GEORGE[1])* was born Abt. 1835 in VA. He married LUCY DANDRIDGE Jan 18, 1869 in Richmond, VA, daughter of BOLLING DANDRIDGE and ELIZABETH BOWLES. She was born in VA.

Elisha H. is listed in the 1850 Henrico Co., VA census, Richmond City, age 18, as a clerk in the household of Samuel Pulliam. Elisha H. Pendleton (age 24) enlisted in the Confederate Army as private on 23 Apr 1861, Cumberland Co., VA. He served in the VA 18th Infantry, Company E as Ordnance Sgt. The dates of his muster cards suggest he was at Antietam and Gettysburg. An article written by a veteran of his unit, "The Black Eagle Rifles" indicates that unit fought in these battles.

Children of ELISHA PENDLETON and LUCY DANDRIDGE are:
i. ADA E.[11] PENDLETON.
ii. LOUISA A. PENDLETON.
526. iii. ELIZABETH B. PENDLETON, b. Jul 28, 1872, VA; d. 1957, WV.
527. iv. CHARLES WILLIAM PENDLETON, b. May 26, 1878, VA; d. Jul 20, 1970, WV?

260. DAVID HARRIS[10] PENDLETON, DR. *(WILLIAM JAMES[9], HENRY[8], JOHN[7], HENRY[6], PHILIP[5], HENRY[4], HENRY[3], GEORGE[2], GEORGE[1])* was born 1832 in Louisa Co., VA, and died Mar 05, 1859 in Louisa Co., VA. He married JULIANA HUNTER Dec 05, 1855 in Louisa Co., VA, daughter of JOHN HUNTER. She was born 1836 in Louisa Co., VA, and died 1910.

Children of DAVID PENDLETON and JULIANA HUNTER are:
i. CHARLES POTTIE[11] PENDLETON, b. Abt. 1856; d. infancy.
528. ii. JOHN HUNTER PENDLETON, b. Jan 22, 1858, VA; d. Aug 01, 1940, Rockbridge, VA?

261. JULIANA[10] PENDLETON *(WILLIAM JAMES[9], HENRY[8], JOHN[7], HENRY[6], PHILIP[5], HENRY[4], HENRY[3], GEORGE[2], GEORGE[1])* was born May 13, 1839 in Louisa Co., VA, and died May 12, 1926 in Cuckoo, Louisa Co., VA? She married (1) THOMAS WILLIAM MEREDITH Mar 13, 1860. He was born Abt. 1837 in VA. She married (2) WILLIAM BARRETT PENDLETON May 03, 1870 in Louisa Co., VA, son of MADISON PENDLETON and ELIZABETH BARRETT. He was born Feb 12, 1838 in Louisa Co., VA, and died Jan 17, 1914 in Louisa Co., VA.

Child of JULIANA PENDLETON and THOMAS MEREDITH is:
    i.   KATE W.[11] MEREDITH, b. Mar 1865, VA.

Children of JULIANA PENDLETON and WILLIAM PENDLETON are:
529.   ii.   PHILIP HENRY[11] PENDLETON, b. May 05, 1871, VA; d. Nov 26, 1916, Fayette Co., PA?
530.   iii. ALICE OVERTON PENDLETON, b. Mar 06, 1873.
      iv. JULIA MADISON PENDLETON, b. Sep 24, 1875; d. Mar 27, 1878.
       v. ELIZABETH KIMBROUGH PENDLETON, b. Dec 20, 1877; d. Jan 02, 1897.
531.   vi. WILLIAM BARRETT PENDLETON, b. Feb 12, 1880, VA; d. Nov 1969, VA.

262. FRANCES[10] PENDLETON *(REUBEN[9], BENJAMIN[8], WILLIAM[7], JOHN[6], PHILIP[5], HENRY[4], HENRY[3], GEORGE[2], GEORGE[1])* was born Sep 25, 1804 in Rye Cove, Scott Co., VA, and died Aug 16, 1852. She married WILLIAM T. HORTON May 15, 1827 in Scott Co., VA. He was born Jun 25, 1807 in Russell Co., VA, and died Mar 31, 1869 in Rye Cove, Scott Co., VA.

Children of FRANCES PENDLETON and WILLIAM HORTON are (Ref. 204):
    i.   ALBY C.[11] HORTON, m. THOMAS MITCHELL, Jan 20, 1853.
    ii. JAMES HARVEY HORTON, b. Mar 04, 1828, VA; d. Jun 15, 1904; m. AMANDA C. KILGORE; b. Jun 19, 1824.
   iii. ELIZA HORTON, b. Oct 27, 1829; d. Aug 01, 1907; m. JAMES B. CARTER.
   iv. SAMUEL P. HORTON, b. Feb 10, 1831, VA; d. Jul 31, 1852; m. MARY COLLIER, Jan 27, 1849.
    v. JEMIMA C. HORTON, b. Mar 31, 1833, VA; d. Apr 07, 1836, VA.
   vi. WILLIAM A. HORTON, b. Nov 02, 1834, Scott Co., VA; d. Oct 27, 1922, OK; m. ELIZABETH A. CARTER, Jul 08, 1852; b. Mar 24, 1835, Scott Co., VA; d. Apr 04, 1893, Clinchport, VA.
  vii. ENOCH HORTON, b. Apr 25, 1840, VA; d. Dec 22, 1863; m. SALLIE CARTER, May 12, 1859; b. 1841.
 viii. REBECCA R. HORTON, b. May 10, 1844, VA; d. Dec 07, 1867; m. JAMES P. FRAZER, Dec 23, 1858.

263. IRA NASH[10] PENDLETON *(REUBEN[9], BENJAMIN[8], WILLIAM[7], JOHN[6], PHILIP[5], HENRY[4], HENRY[3], GEORGE[2], GEORGE[1])* was born 1805 in Scott Co., VA, and died Abt. 1850. He married ROSAMOND TAYLOR May 07, 1830 in Scott Co., VA, daughter of JAMES TAYLOR and SARA CARTER. She was born in VA.

Children of IRA PENDLETON and ROSAMOND TAYLOR are (Ref. 205):

532.   i.   JAMES TRIGG[11] PENDLETON, b. Nov 15, 1827, Lee Co., VA; d. Dec 18, 1880, Johnson Co., KY.

533.   ii. DULCENA PENDLETON, b. Abt. 1830, VA; d. Abt. 1915, Scott Co., VA?

       iii. ROSANNAH PENDLETON, b. Abt. 1836; m. GEORGE WASHINGTON PRIDEMORE; b. Sep 16, 1842, Kyles Ford, KY; d. Jun 13, 1923, Lee Co., VA.

            G. W. Pridemore apparently later married Rosannah's younger sister Rosamond in 1866.

534.   iv. SAMUEL G. PENDLETON, b. Apr 29, 1840, Scott Co., VA; d. 1907, Johnson Co., KY?

535.   v.   SARAH T. PENDLETON, b. Abt. 1841, VA; d. Aft. 1880, Scott Co., VA?

       vi. JOSEPHINE PENDLETON, b. 1844; d. 1872; m. FRANCIS ASBERRY MANESS, Feb 28, 1872, Scott Co., VA; b. 1845, Scott Co., VA; d. Abt. 1900, Lee Co., VA.

536.   vii. ROSAMOND PENDLETON, b. Dec 28, 1846, VA; d. Mar 12, 1924, Lee Co., VA.

264. SAMUEL GUTHRIE[10] PENDLETON *(REUBEN[9], BENJAMIN[8], WILLIAM[7], JOHN[6], PHILIP[5], HENRY[4], HENRY[3], GEORGE[2], GEORGE[1])* was born 1807, and died Jan 09, 1837 in Scott Co., VA. He married REBECCA SPENCER Jul 25, 1826, daughter of JAMES SPENCER and ELIZABETH BOLTON. She was born Abt. 1800 in VA, and died Mar 31, 1837 in Scott Co., VA.

       Samuel Pendleton is listed in the 1830 Scott Co., VA census. He is named in a VA Land Grant for Scott Co., 1 Aug 1835: 16 ac. on south of Clinch River, Grant no. 85, pg 76. The Scott Co. VA Will Book 4, p.89-94, provides an accounting of the disposition of the estate of Samuel Guthrie Pendleton(1807-1837) to his heirs. It states that "There are 5 heirs, viz. Bluford (sic), Ira N, Jas M, W.S, & James Taylor & Martha his wife." Ira N. Pendleton (1805-1848), Samuel's older brother was the administrator of Samuel's estate & guardian of the above heirs. After Ira's death in 1848, his co-administrators continued administration of Sam's estate until a final accounting was made to the court in 1855 & the estate was split 5 ways among the heirs. Samuels wife, Rebecca Spencer, died about the same time as Samuel. Robert P. Spencer, her brother is listed as administrator of her estate & after Ira N's death is listed as guardian of the same heirs noted above (Ref. 124).

Children of SAMUEL PENDLETON and REBECCA SPENCER are:

537.   i.   MARTHA JANE[11] PENDLETON, b. 1827, Scott Co., VA; d. 1906, Scott Co., VA.

538.   ii. IRA NASH PENDLETON, b. Jun 16, 1828, VA; d. Feb 26, 1918, Washington Co., VA?

iii. JAMES M. PENDLETON, b. Jul 17, 1830, Scott Co., VA; d. Nov 03, 1856, Scott Co., VA.

539. iv. WILLIAM SAMUEL PENDLETON, b. Apr 1834, Scott Co., VA; d. 1905, Hancock Co., TN.

v. JOHN QUINLAN PENDLETON, b. 1835.

vi. ROSAMINE PENDLETON, b. 1836.

265. REBECCA[10] PENDLETON *(REUBEN[9], BENJAMIN[8], WILLIAM[7], JOHN[6], PHILIP[5], HENRY[4], HENRY[3], GEORGE[2], GEORGE[1])* was born 1812 in VA. She married JAMES B. COCKE Mar 10, 1832 in Scott Co., VA. He was born May 13, 1808 in Scott Co., VA, and died Nov 26, 1887 in Scott Co., VA.

Children of REBECCA PENDLETON and JAMES COCKE are:

i. ENOCH[11] COCKE, b. Abt. 1834.

ii. ELISHA COCKE, b. Abt. 1835.

iii. ELIZAH COCKE, b. Abt. 1838.

iv. DAVID COCKE, b. Abt. 1840.

v. ROBERT COCKE, b. Abt. 1842.

vi. NANCY COCKE, b. Abt. 1844.

vii. WILLIAM COCKE, b. Abt. 1846.

viii. JAMES COCKE, b. Abt. 1849.

266. ENOCH[10] PENDLETON *(REUBEN[9], BENJAMIN[8], WILLIAM[7], JOHN[6], PHILIP[5], HENRY[4], HENRY[3], GEORGE[2], GEORGE[1])* was born 1815 in Scott Co., VA. He married (1) SARENA? He married (2) MARGARET KIMBLER Apr 16, 1849 in Scott Co., VA, daughter of GEORGE KIMBLER and MARY ESTEP. She was born Abt. 1816, and died Abt. 1850 in Scott Co., VA?

Enoch is listed as a farmer in the 1850 Scott Co., VA census (wife not listed); value of farm $1500.

Children of ENOCH PENDLETON and SARENA? are:

i. SARENA[11] PENDLETON, b. Abt. 1839.

ii. DINAH PENDLETON, b. Abt. 1843.

iii. PATIENCE PENDLETON, b. Abt. 1845.

iv. EMILY PENDLETON, b. Abt. 1847.

An Emily Pendleton married William P. Good, 1863 in Scott County, VA (Ref. 206).

267. SARAH "SALLY"[10] PENDLETON *(JAMES A.[9], BENJAMIN[8], WILLIAM[7], JOHN[6], PHILIP[5], HENRY[4], HENRY[3], GEORGE[2], GEORGE[1])* was born 1801 in VA, and died Aft. 1850. She married GEORGE STANDLEY Feb 22, 1823 in Scott Co., VA, son of RICHARD STANDLEY and AGNES MARTIN. He was born Abt. 1801 in Franklin Co., VA, and died Aft. 1855 in Franklin Co., VA.

The George and Sarah Standley family is listed in the 1850 Scott Co., VA census.

Children of SARAH PENDLETON and GEORGE STANDLEY are:
    i.   JOHN[11] STANDLEY, b. Abt. 1832.
    ii. MARY J. STANDLEY, b. Abt. 1834.
    iii. GRANVILLE H. STANDLEY, b. Abt. 1836.
    iv. MATILDA STANDLEY, b. Abt. 1838.
    v. SARAH STANDLEY, b. Abt. 1840.

268. JOHN L.[10] PENDLETON (*JAMES A.[9], BENJAMIN[8], WILLIAM[7], JOHN[6], PHILIP[5], HENRY[4], HENRY[3], GEORGE[2], GEORGE[1]*) was born 1802 in Russell Co., VA, and died May 17, 1868 in Scott Co., VA. He married MARY "POLLY" HILL Jun 01, 1829 in Scott Co., VA. She was born 1812 in VA, and died Aft. 1870 in Scott Co., VA?

    John Pendleton is listed in the 1830 and 1840 Scott Co., VA census. John L. Pendleton and James Ambrose are named in a VA Land Grant: Scott Co., 40 ac on south of Clinch River on the bluff, 10 Sep., 1836. John L. Pendleton (farmer) and family are listed in the 1860 Scott Co., VA census.

Children of JOHN PENDLETON and MARY HILL are:
    i. ISABELLA V.[11] PENDLETON, b. 1830; d. Jan 11, 1859.
        Isabella never married and died of fever.

540.   ii. MALINDA PENDLETON, b. Jan 09, 1832, Scott Co., VA; d. Jan 24, 1889, Scott Co., VA.

541.   iii. JOSEPH DOUGLAS PENDLETON, b. 1835, VA; d. May 17, 1871, Scott Co., VA?

542.   iv. JOHN EMERSON PENDLETON, b. Sep 09, 1836, VA; d. Jan 10, 1903, Scott Co., VA?

    v. LILBOURN H. PENDLETON, b. 1838, VA; d. Dec 16, 1864, Camp Douglas, IL.

        Lilbourn H. Pendleton was a Confederate Soldier in the Civil War, Company C, 64th VA Mounted Infantry, private, and 21st VA infantry, Company D, sergeant. He died of small pox as a prisoner of war at Camp Douglas, Illinois and is buried in the Oakwood Cemetery, Chicago.

543.   vi. JAMES F. PENDLETON, b. May 07, 1841, Scott Co., VA; d. Aug 16, 1916, Letcher Co., KY.

544.   vii. SAMUEL DAVID PENDLETON, b. Jul 29, 1844, VA; d. Nov 17, 1911, Scott Co., VA?

545.   viii. ROBERT KENNUS PENDLETON, b. Jun 1846, VA; d. Jan 15, 1913, Scott Co., VA?

546.   ix. WILLIAM DANIEL E. PENDLETON, b. Apr 28, 1850, VA; d. Dec 24, 1912, Scott Co., VA?

269. JEMIMA[10] PENDLETON (*JAMES A.[9], BENJAMIN[8], WILLIAM[7], JOHN[6], PHILIP[5], HENRY[4], HENRY[3], GEORGE[2], GEORGE[1]*) was born 1804 in VA, and died Aft. 1870 in Scott Co., VA? She married EDWARD HILL. He was born Abt. 1790 in VA, and died Aft. 1870 in Scott Co., VA?

Children of JEMIMA PENDLETON and EDWARD HILL are:

      i.   JAMES[11] HILL, b. Abt. 1828.
     ii.   POLLY HILL, b. Abt. 1833, VA.
    iii.   ROBERT HILL, b. Abt. 1834, VA.
     iv.   JOHN HILL, b. Abt. 1836, VA.
      v.   HIRAM HILL, b. Abt. 1838, VA.
     vi.   MARTIN HILL, b. Abt. 1840, VA.
    vii.   ELIZABETH HILL, b. Abt. 1842, VA.
   viii.   JEMIMA HILL, b. Abt. 1844, VA.
     ix.   MARGARET HILL, b. Abt. 1848, VA.

270. MARY "MOLLY"[10] PENDLETON (*JAMES A.[9], BENJAMIN[8], WILLIAM[7], JOHN[6], PHILIP[5], HENRY[4], HENRY[3], GEORGE[2], GEORGE[1]*) was born 1810 in VA, and died Feb 26, 1903 in Scott Co., VA. She married MEADOW BOATRIGHT Sep 17, 1828 in Scott Co., VA. He was born Jul 19, 1796 in Cumberland Co., VA, and died Dec 24, 1876 in Scott Co., VA.

Children of MARY PENDLETON and MEADOW BOATRIGHT are (Ref. 207):

      i.   JAMES B.[11] BOATRIGHT, b. Abt. 1829, VA.
     ii.   ELIZABETH J. BOATRIGHT, b. Abt. 1834, VA.
    iii.   SARAH J. BOATRIGHT, b. Abt. 1836, VA.
     iv.   GRANVILLE HENDERSON BOATRIGHT, b. Jul 10, 1838, Scott Co., VA.
      v.   JOHN M. BOATRIGHT, b. Abt. 1838, VA.
     vi.   LEWIS C. BOATRIGHT, b. Abt. 1842, VA.
    vii.   LOUISA BOATRIGHT, b. Abt. 1844, VA.
   viii.   JONAS BOATRIGHT, b. Abt. 1847, VA.

271. JAMES A.[10] PENDLETON, JR. (*JAMES A.[9], BENJAMIN[8], WILLIAM[7], JOHN[6], PHILIP[5], HENRY[4], HENRY[3], GEORGE[2], GEORGE[1]*) was born Abt. 1816 in VA, and died 1880. He married PHOEBE FLANARY Jan 12, 1838 in Scott Co., VA. She was born Abt. 1820 in VA.

James Pendleton and family are listed in 1850 Scott Co., VA census as follows: James (34), Jemima (10), Phebe (30), Louisa (8), Robert (4), Ira (2), and Rosannah (1/12, b. June 1950).

Children of JAMES PENDLETON and PHOEBE FLANARY are (Ref. 208):

547.   i.   JEMIMA[11] PENDLETON, b. Abt. 1840, VA.
       ii.   LOUISA PENDLETON, b. Abt. 1842, VA; m. (1) THOMAS T. DINGUS; b. Abt. 1838; m. (2) LAFAYETTE F. STARNES; b. Abt. 1847.
548.   iii.   ROBERT PENDLETON, b. Feb 1845, VA; d. Aft. 1900, Scott Co., VA?
549.   iv.   IRA M. PENDLETON, b. Feb 10, 1848, VA; d. Jun 19, 1894, Scott Co., VA.
       v.   ROSANNAH PENDLETON, b. Jun, 1850.
      vi.   LUCINDA PENDLETON, b. Abt. 1854; m. L. MONROE QUILLEN; b. Abt. 1852.
550.   vii.   SARAH S. PENDLETON, b. Abt. 1856, VA.
551. viii.   ELBERT M. PENDLETON, b. Feb 1859, VA; d. Aft. 1920, Scott Co., VA?

ix. MARTHA A. PENDLETON, b. Abt. 1861.
x. JOHN H. PENDLETON, b. Abt. 1865, VA.

272. MALINDA A.[10] PENDLETON *(JOHN[9], BENJAMIN[8], WILLIAM[7], JOHN[6], PHILIP[5], HENRY[4], HENRY[3], GEORGE[2], GEORGE[1])* was born Dec 21, 1810 in VA, and died Sep 10, 1861. She married DANIEL PRICE Jul 12, 1831 in Scott Co., VA.

Children of MALINDA PENDLETON and DANIEL PRICE are:
i. WILLIAM H.[11] PRICE, b. 1832.
ii. LOUISA M. PRICE, b. 1835; d. 1864; m. W. R. MCNUTT.
iii. EMILY I. PRICE, b. 1838; d. Infancy.
iv. SARAH C. PRICE, b. 1840; m. COLSTON.
v. HARRIETT PRICE, b. 1843; m. CURRAN M. ROGERS.
vi. JOHN E. PRICE, b. 1846.
vii. JAMES D. PRICE, b. 1849.

273. WILLIAM GAINES[10] PENDLETON *(JOHN[9], BENJAMIN[8], WILLIAM[7], JOHN[6], PHILIP[5], HENRY[4], HENRY[3], GEORGE[2], GEORGE[1])* was born 1813 in VA, and died May 11, 1875 in TX. He married (1) CHARLOTTE BELL COUPLAND Oct 11, 1842 in Knox Co., TN, daughter of CHARLES COUPLAND and ELIZABETH ROBINSON. She was born 1817 in TN, and died 1857. He married (2) RHODA DAY CHANDLER May 21, 1865, daughter of JOSEPH DAY and SOPHIA DUNN. She was born Abt. 1838 in VA, and died Aft. 1920 in Waco, TX?
    William Pendleton is listed as a School Teacher in the 1850 Knox Co. census, 15th subdivision. Rhoda Pendleton is listed in the 1880 Collins Co., TX census, E.D. 21, 119, and in the 1920 Waco, TX census with her daughter, Cordelia Pendleton Curtis and son-in-law, Frank A. Curtis.

Children of WILLIAM PENDLETON and CHARLOTTE COUPLAND are:
552.   i. ELDRIDGE HOWARD[11] PENDLETON, b. Aug 02, 1843, TN; d. 1906, Collin Co., TX?
ii. JOHN BELL PENDLETON, b. 1846, TN; d. 1876.
        A John B. Pendleton, private, served in the 2nd Texas Cavalry, Co. B.

iii. WILLIAM PENDLETON, d. Infancy.

Children of WILLIAM PENDLETON and RHODA CHANDLER are:
553. iv. HENRY[11] PENDLETON, b. 1866; d. 1894.
554.   v. PARALEE PENDLETON, b. 1870; d. Dec 29, 1919, Cherokee Co., AL.
555. vi. JOSEPH DAY PENDLETON, b. Aug 1869, TX; d. Aft. 1920, Van Zandt Co., TX?
556. vii. CORDELIA PENDLETON, b. 1873, TX; d. Aft. 1920, Waco, TX?
viii. EMMETT PENDLETON, b. 1875, TX; d. 1883.

274. HIRAM KILGORE[10] PENDLETON *(JOHN[9], BENJAMIN[8], WILLIAM[7], JOHN[6], PHILIP[5], HENRY[4], HENRY[3], GEORGE[2], GEORGE[1])* was born Feb 16, 1815 in Scott

Co., VA, and died Nov 01, 1888 in Scott Co., VA. He married ELIZA JANE RICHMOND Oct 03, 1843 in Scott Co., VA. She was born Jul 1824 in VA, and died Aft. 1900 in Sullivan Co., TN?

Hiram Pendleton and family are listed in the 1850 Scott Co., VA census.

Children of HIRAM PENDLETON and ELIZA RICHMOND are:
557. i. WILLIAM MARION[11] PENDLETON, b. Jul 1844, VA; d. 1921, Scott Co., VA.
558. ii. JOHN W. PENDLETON, b. 1847, VA.
559. iii. SARAH HELEN PENDLETON, b. 1849, VA; d. 1872.
560. iv. THOMAS CLINTON PENDLETON, b. Abt. 1852, VA.
561. v. BENJAMIN FRANKLIN PENDLETON, b. Mar 1854, VA; d. Aft. 1920, Sullivan Co., TN?
562. vi. JEMIMA JANE PENDLETON, b. 1856, VA; d. Aft. 1920, Russell Co., VA?
      vii. GEORGE WASHINGTON PENDLETON, b. 1859, VA; m. (1) COX; m. (2) MELISSA A. MOORE.
            This is apparently the G.W. Pendleton, farmer, listed in the 1900 Scott Co., VA census, pg. 289 along with M.A. Pendleton and Moore stepchildren.

563. viii. ROBERT MELVIN PENDLETON, b. Apr 1861, VA; d. Aft. 1930, Sullivan Co., TN?
       ix. MINERVA PENDLETON, b. 1868, VA; m. J. B. PECTOL.
        x. MARY ELIZABETH "MOLLIE" PENDLETON, b. Jul 1871, VA; m. LEWIS MELVIN TYNER, Aft. 1900; b. Sep 1870, Kansas City, MO; d. Apr 14, 1921, TN.

275. IVY TAYLOR[10] PENDLETON (*JOHN[9], BENJAMIN[8], WILLIAM[7], JOHN[6], PHILIP[5], HENRY[4], HENRY[3], GEORGE[2], GEORGE[1]*) was born 1817 in VA, and died Aft. 1880 in Owsley Co., KY? He married PHEBE FLANARY. She was born 1825 in VA, and died Bef. 1880 in Owsley Co., KY?

Ivy Pendleton is listed as Ira Pendleton in the 1850 Lee Co., VA census as farmer (age 30); others listed are Phebe (25), Rebecca J. (5), Eliza E. (3), and William T. (1). Ivey T. Pendleton is listed in a Land grant in KY County Court Records, pg. 1590: 4 acres, 2/15/1861, Owsley Co., Mill Rock Br. In 1880 Ivey T. Pendleton is listed in the Buck Creek, Owsley Co., KY census as a farmer, age 60, along with George (21), Elizabeth (18), and Mary J. (16), George's wife. In 1885 he lived in Booneville, KY (Ref. 209).

Children of IVY PENDLETON and PHEBE FLANARY are:
564. i. REBECCA JANE[11] PENDLETON, b. 1845, VA; d. Aft. 1900, Owsley Co., KY?
565. ii. ELIZABETH E. PENDLETON, b. Abt. 1848, VA.
566. iii. EMILY PENDLETON, b. Abt. 1849, VA.
      iv. WILLIAM F. PENDLETON, b. 1849.
       v. TOM PENDLETON, b. Aft. 1850.
            Tom Pendleton died at the age of 16.

567.   vi.   CATHERINE PENDLETON, b. Dec 04, 1851, VA; d. Sep 16, 1887, Owsley Co., KY.

568.   vii.   GEORGE W. PENDLETON, b. Apr 30, 1859, KY; d. Sep 17, 1931, Owsley Co., KY.

      viii.   MARY E. PENDLETON, b. Abt. 1862, KY.

276. ISAAC NEWTON[10] PENDLETON *(JOHN[9], BENJAMIN[8], WILLIAM[7], JOHN[6], PHILIP[5], HENRY[4], HENRY[3], GEORGE[2], GEORGE[1])* was born 1819 in VA, and died Aft. 1880 in Jack Co., TX? He married (1) MARY. She was born 1828 in VA. He married (2) LUCY SHIFTLETT Feb 26, 1874 in Hunt Co., TX. She was born Abt. 1856 in GA.

      According to W.C. Pendleton, Isaac's first wife, Mary, was killed by desperados (Ref. 128). Newton Pendleton and family are listed in the 1870 Hunt Co., TX census, District 2.

Children of ISAAC PENDLETON and MARY are:
      i.   WILLIAM[11] PENDLETON, b. Abt. 1846.
     ii.   JEMIMA J. PENDLETON, b. Abt. 1849.
    iii.   JAMES PENDLETON, b. Abt. 1853.
    iv.   JOHN PENDLETON, b. Abt. 1857.
     v.   ELIZABETH PENDLETON, b. Abt. 1860.
    vi.   ROBERT PENDLETON, b. Abt. 1862.
   vii.   FLORENCE V. PENDLETON, b. Abt. 1865.
  viii.   ALICE PENDLETON, b. Abt. 1867.

277. JANE[10] PENDLETON *(JOHN[9], BENJAMIN[8], WILLIAM[7], JOHN[6], PHILIP[5], HENRY[4], HENRY[3], GEORGE[2], GEORGE[1])* was born 1821 in VA, and died 1879 in Scott Co., VA? She married JOHN DUNCAN Jun 05, 1844 in Scott Co., VA. He was born Abt. 1812 in VA, and died Aft. 1860 in Scott Co., VA?

Children of JANE PENDLETON and JOHN DUNCAN are:
      i.   SARAH E.[11] DUNCAN, b. Abt. 1845; m. JAMES B. RICHMOND.
     ii.   NANCY J. DUNCAN, b. Abt. 1847; m. TAYLOR.
    iii.   ELIZA DUNCAN, b. Mar 1850; m. CLAUDE DRAPER.
    iv.   AMANDA C. DUNCAN, b. Abt. 1853; m. CLAUDE DRAPER.
     v.   MARY A. DUNCAN, b. Abt. 1856.
    vi.   SUSAN M. DUNCAN, b. Abt. 1859.

278. JOHN CRAIG[10] PENDLETON *(JOHN[9], BENJAMIN[8], WILLIAM[7], JOHN[6], PHILIP[5], HENRY[4], HENRY[3], GEORGE[2], GEORGE[1])* was born Jul 27, 1826 in VA, and died Dec 22, 1910 in Collin Co., TX? He married MARTHA ANN ASBURY Oct 11, 1860 in Hunt Co., TX, daughter of JESSE ASBURY and MARY SPRATLING. She was born Jan 12, 1842 in IL, and died Mar 09, 1885 in Collin Co., TX?

      This is apparently the John C. Pendleton, farmer, listed in the 1850 Scott Co., VA census. Craig Pendleton is listed in the 1870 Collins Co., TX census, Farmersville. John

C. Pendleton and his youngest 3 sons are listed in the 1900 Collin Co., TX census, pg. 179a.

Children of JOHN PENDLETON and MARTHA ASBURY are:
569.   i.   MARY JANE[11] PENDLETON, b. Aug 1861, Fannin Co., TX; d. Jun 17, 1939.
570.   ii.   JEMIMA ELIZABETH PENDLETON, b. Feb 1862, TX; d. 1905, Choctaw Nation, OK?
571.   iii. MARTHA ADELINE PENDLETON, b. 1865, TX; d. Aft. 1920, Hunt Co., TX?
572.   iv. ANGINETTA VIRGINIA PENDLETON, b. 1867, TX; d. Aft. 1910, Custer Co., OK?
573.   v.   JOHN ASBURY PENDLETON, b. Mar 1868, TX; d. Aft. 1920, Collin Co., TX?
574.   vi. ALICE NORA PENDLETON, b. Feb 1871, TX; d. Fannin Co., TX?
        vii. AMANDA PENDLETON, b. 1872, TX; d. 1900; m. PERCY GIBSON.
       viii. ROSETTA VICTORIA PENDLETON, b. 1874; m. F. E. ROGERS, Dec 30, 1891, Hunt Co., TX.
        ix. CHARLES ELDRIDGE PENDLETON, b. 1876, TX; d. 1879.
575.   x.   WILLIAM CRAIG PENDLETON, b. 1879, TX; d. Sep 20, 1965, Collin Co., TX.
576.   xi. LUTHER DOUGLAS PENDLETON, b. Dec 05, 1881, TX; d. Feb 15, 1975, Lubbock, TX.
577.   xii. ELMER WENDELL PENDLETON, b. Dec 12, 1884, TX.

279. ELIZA[10] PENDLETON *(JOHN[9], BENJAMIN[8], WILLIAM[7], JOHN[6], PHILIP[5], HENRY[4], HENRY[3], GEORGE[2], GEORGE[1])* was born 1829 in VA, and died 1897. She married (1) MONROE W. LEGG Sep 18, 1850 in Lee Co., VA. He was born 1826 in VA, and died Aft. 1860 in Collin Co., TX? She married (2) ELIJAH W. HENDRIX Jan 23, 1866.

    M. W. Legg (farmer) and family are listed in the 1860 Collin Co., TX census.

Children of ELIZA PENDLETON and MONROE LEGG are:
      i.   JOHN CRAIG[11] LEGG, b. Abt. 1853, VA.
      ii. WILLIAM HUSTON LEGG, b. Abt. 1854, VA.
      iii. MARGARET D. LEGG, b. Abt. 1856, VA.
      iv. JAMES M. LEGG, b. Abt. 1857, TX.

Child of ELIZA PENDLETON and ELIJAH HENDRIX is:
      v.   ELIZA[11] HENDRIX, m. W. M. SOUTH.

280. ANDREW JACKSON[10] PENDLETON *(JOHN[9], BENJAMIN[8], WILLIAM[7], JOHN[6], PHILIP[5], HENRY[4], HENRY[3], GEORGE[2], GEORGE[1])* was born Sep 19, 1832 in VA, and died Feb 02, 1900 in Scott Co., VA? He married SARA 'SALLY' TAYLOR Mar 20, 1865 in Scott Co., VA, daughter of RAD TAYLOR. She was born 1849 in VA.

Andrew Pendleton is listed in 1860 Scott Co., VA census, Estillville. Andrew J. Pendleton, private, served in the VA 37th Infantry Company D, CSA. He wrote the following letter concerning his kin to Mr. C. H. Pendleton [Charles Henry Pendleton of Berkeley Co, WV] from Rye Cove, Scott Co., VA on Nov. 12, 1885.

Dear Sir.
I received your letter Enquiring about the Kin. I am a son of John Pendleton, who moved from here to Farmersville, Tex. in 1857. Benjamin Pendleton and Edman [Edmund] Pendleton Died 10 miles from here about 30 years ago. Reuben Pendleton Died here about 25 years ago. They all came here from Amherst Co., near Lynchburgh, Va. Any other Information you Require I will cheerfully Furnish on Application.
Yours Respectfully, A. J. Pendleton

Children of ANDREW PENDLETON and SARA TAYLOR are:

      i.   CALLIE D.[11] PENDLETON, b. Jan 31, 1867, VA; d. Jan 14, 1916; m. FRED PENDERGAST.

     ii.   MOLLIE E. PENDLETON, b. Nov 14, 1868, VA; m. SMITH.

578. iii. JAMES MARION PENDLETON, b. Oct 04, 1870, VA.

    iv. MELVIN C. PENDLETON, b. Nov 18, 1872, VA.

     v. JOHN PENDLETON, b. Mar 27, 1875, VA.

    vi. NANNIE ERNESTINE PENDLETON, b. Mar 19, 1876, VA; d. Sep 22, 1948; m. MALCOLM MEYERS.

579. vii. BONNIE LAURA PENDLETON, b. Jul 11, 1878, VA; d. Feb 26, 1948.

  viii. KATHERYN PENDLETON, b. Dec 12, 1880, VA; d. Jan 02, 1946; m. ALBERT MONTGOMERY.

    ix. WILLIAM DUDLEY PENDLETON, b. Mar 15, 1883, VA; d. Mar 07, 1924, Gainesville, TX?; m. CORDELIA PENDERGAST, May 13, 1905; b. Abt. 1885, VA.

       William Dudley Pendleton registered for the World War I Draft in Cooke Co., TX (Ref. 210).

     x. TOY RAY PENDLETON, b. Mar 22, 1885, VA; d. Mar 13, 1943; m. MARY E. MORIARTY, Oct 1905.

    xi. EUGENE PENDLETON.

   xii. BESSIE MAY PENDLETON, b. Aug 23, 1888, VA; d. Nov 17, 1956; m. WYLIE ENIS.

  xiii. ELDRIDGE HOWARD PENDLETON, b. Nov 23, 1890, VA; d. Nov 17, 1939; m. CHLOE SUSIE ALLEN.

       Like his brother William, Eldridge Pendleton registered for the World War I Draft in Cooke Co., TX (Ref. 210).

281. ALLISON OSBORN[10] PENDLETON (*JOHN*[9], *BENJAMIN*[8], *WILLIAM*[7], *JOHN*[6], *PHILIP*[5], *HENRY*[4], *HENRY*[3], *GEORGE*[2], *GEORGE*[1]) was born Oct 25, 1832 in Rye Cove, Scott Co., VA, and died Nov 10, 1914 in Coryell Co., TX. He married REBECCA ANN LAWSON Jan 15, 1856 in Scott Co., VA, daughter of WILLIAM LAWSON and LIZA. She was born Jul 12, 1835 in Rye Cove, Scott Co., VA, and died Apr 15, 1925 in Coryell Co., TX.

In the fall of 1858 Allison Pendleton came to Collin County, Texas with his family including his mother, father, and nine siblings. They made the trip by wagon train in 64 days. Many Pendleton descendants settled around Farmersville in Collin County. An old Pendleton Cemetery is located just east of Farmersville on land once owned by the Pendleton family. John, Jemima, and many other family members are buried there (Ref. 211).

Allison O. Pendleton served in the TX Cav. Martin's Regt., Co. F, CSA. He enlisted in the Confederate Army under Captain J. K. Bumpass and fought the four years of the war. He is listed in the 1860 and 1870 Collin Co. TX census, Farmersville and the 1880 Montague Co. census, E.D. 124. Allison O. Pendleton (farmer) and family are listed in the 1900 Coryell Co., TX census, pg. 10a.

Children of ALLISON PENDLETON and REBECCA LAWSON are (Ref. 212):
  i. ELIZA JANE[11] PENDLETON, b. Nov 13, 1856, Scott Co., VA; d. Nov 14, 1889.
580. ii. HIRAM KILGORE PENDLETON, b. Mar 10, 1859, Collin Co., TX; d. Oct 06, 1938, Erath Co., TX.
581. iii. PATTON MONROE PENDLETON, b. Jul 19, 1864, Collin Co., TX; d. Jan 15, 1957, Erath Co., TX.
582. iv. HARVEY ELDRIDGE PENDLETON, b. Jan 29, 1870, Gainesville, TX; d. Apr 29, 1942, Breckinridge, TX.
  v. RHODA MELISSA PENDLETON, b. Nov 17, 1877, TX.

282. MINERVA JEMIMA[10] PENDLETON (*JOHN[9], BENJAMIN[8], WILLIAM[7], JOHN[6], PHILIP[5], HENRY[4], HENRY[3], GEORGE[2], GEORGE[1]*) was born 1835 in Scott Co., VA, and died Mar 01, 1907. She married (1) LEVI HOWELL Feb 20, 1860 in Collin Co., TX, son of ASKINS HOWELL and SUSANNAH TIPTON. He was born 1835 in Marion Co., IL, and died Abt. 1861. She married (2) JOSEPH RICE BUCHANAN Feb 05, 1866. He was born 1830 in IL, and died 1885 in Fannin Co., TX?

Child of MINERVA PENDLETON and LEVI HOWELL is:
  i. GINNY JEMIMA[11] HOWELL, b. Jul 26, 1861.

Children of MINERVA PENDLETON and JOSEPH BUCHANAN are:
  ii. LENORA G.[11] BUCHANAN, b. 1866, TX; m. J. W. SUMMER, Jan 24, 1889; b. 1850; d. 1938.
  iii. ROBERT LEE BUCHANAN, b. 1868, TX; m. GEORGIA EDWARDS, Jul 22, 1890.
  iv. GENETIA BUCHANAN, b. 1870, TX; m. T. M. LATTIMORE, Oct 16, 1890.
  v. LAFAYETTE DOUGLAS BUCHANAN, b. Jan 27, 1873, TX; d. May 06, 1951; m. LEONA TINSLEY DAVIS, Mar 01, 1896; b. Oct 16, 1870; d. Jun 29, 1941.
  vi. FLOYD PETER BUCHANAN, b. 1876, TX; m. SUSIE MCCALLISTER, Aug 05, 1892.

283. MELVIN C.^{10} PENDLETON *(JOHN^9, BENJAMIN^8, WILLIAM^7, JOHN^6, PHILIP^5, HENRY^4, HENRY^3, GEORGE^2, GEORGE^1)* was born 1840 in VA. He married (1) MARY E. DAVIS Jan 19, 1866. He married (2) NARCISSUS M. BRUMMETT Sep 17, 1867.

      Melvin Pendleton served in the TX 16th Cavalry, Company E, CSA. He is listed in the 1860 Collin Co., TX census, Farmersville P.O.

Children of MELVIN PENDLETON and NARCISSUS BRUMMETT are:
583.   i.   SARAH BELLE^{11} PENDLETON.
584.   ii.   ANDREW J. "JACK" PENDLETON, b. Sep 1868, MO.

284. MARY LUCAS^{10} PENDLETON *(JOHN^9, EDMUND^8, WILLIAM^7, JOHN^6, PHILIP^5, HENRY^4, HENRY^3, GEORGE^2, GEORGE^1)* was born Feb 13, 1814 in TN, and died Aft. 1870 in De Kalb Co., TN? She married GABRIEL MURPHY ELKINS. He was born Abt. 1815 in TN, and died Aft. 1860 in De Kalb Co., TN?

Children of MARY PENDLETON and GABRIEL ELKINS are:
    i.   JOHN M.^{11} ELKINS, b. Abt. 1840, TN.
    ii.   JULIAN RACHEL ELKINS, b. Abt. 1842, TN.
   iii.   MELINDA F. ELKINS, b. Abt. 1843, TN.
   iv.   ELIZABETH T. ELKINS, b. Abt. 1845, TN.
    v.   ANGELINE A. ELKINS, b. Abt. 1846, TN.
   vi.   MARY M. ELKINS, b. Abt. 1847, TN.
  vii.   LUCY V. ELKINS, b. Abt. 1849, TN.
 viii.   MATILDA C. ELKINS, b. Abt. 1849, TN.
   ix.   JAMES ELKINS, b. Abt. 1852, TN.
    x.   GEORGE W. ELKINS, b. Abt. 1855, TN.
   xi.   TABITHA E. ELKINS, b. Abt. 1858, TN.

285. JAMES LUCAS^{10} PENDLETON *(JOHN^9, EDMUND^8, WILLIAM^7, JOHN^6, PHILIP^5, HENRY^4, HENRY^3, GEORGE^2, GEORGE^1)* was born Dec 23, 1815 in TN, and died Aft. 1860. He married ISABEL ALLEN Aug 22, 1835. She was born Abt. 1815 in TN, and died Aft. 1860.

      James L. Pendleton is listed in 1850 Cannon Co. Census, 5th District, as a farmer; value of farm $200.

Children of JAMES PENDLETON and ISABEL ALLEN are:
585.   i.   SAMUEL D.^{11} PENDLETON, b. Jun 10, 1836, TN; d. Bef. 1900, Izard Co., AR?

     ii.   MARY JANE PENDLETON, b. Sep 27, 1838, TN; d. Aft. 1900, Izard Co., AR?
   iii.   DERINDA M. PENDLETON, b. Aug 14, 1840.
   iv.   RACHEL A. PENDLETON, b. Abt. 1843.
    v.   WILLIAM TITUS PENDLETON, b. Feb 06, 1846.

286. MARGARET[10] PENDLETON *(JOHN[9], EDMUND[8], WILLIAM[7], JOHN[6], PHILIP[5], HENRY[4], HENRY[3], GEORGE[2], GEORGE[1])* was born May 26, 1817 in TN. She married DAVID WALKER.

Child of MARGARET PENDLETON and DAVID WALKER is:
    i.   ANDREW JACKSON[11] WALKER, b. Abt. 1834, TN.

287. ELIZABETH[10] PENDLETON *(JOHN[9], EDMUND[8], WILLIAM[7], JOHN[6], PHILIP[5], HENRY[4], HENRY[3], GEORGE[2], GEORGE[1])* was born Mar 28, 1819 in Cannon Co., TN. She married HENRY ELAM Oct 24, 1840 in Cannon Co. TN, son of REUBEN ELAM and SARAH VANCE. He was born Abt. 1820 in Cannon Co. TN.

Children of ELIZABETH PENDLETON and HENRY ELAM are (Ref. 213):
    i.   SARAH A.[11] ELAM, b. Mar 1842.
   ii.   CAROLINE ELAM, b. 1844; m. MARTIN V. WOODS.
  iii.   MARY ANN ELAM, b. Dec 16, 1845, TN; d. Aug 26, 1913, Grandview, TX; m. JOHN LEE WILSON, May 25, 1866; b. Apr 15, 1847, TN; d. 1928, Irene, TX.
   iv.   MARGARET ELAM, b. 1856.
    v.   JACQUELINE ELAM, b. Abt. 1860, TN; m. ROBERT SHELLY KIRBY, Oct 09, 1879, TN; b. Mar 09, 1849; d. Mar 21, 1927, TN.

288. SAMUEL L.[10] PENDLETON *(JOHN[9], EDMUND[8], WILLIAM[7], JOHN[6], PHILIP[5], HENRY[4], HENRY[3], GEORGE[2], GEORGE[1])* was born Sep 07, 1822 in Warren Co., TN, and died 1900 in Hill Co., TX. He married (1) MARY THOMAS Dec 21, 1842 in Cannon Co., TN. She was born Abt. 1823 in TN, and died Aft. 1870. He married (2) NANCY C. Dec 20, 1877. She was born Feb 1856 in TN.
    The following narrative is from the Cannon County Marriage Book 1 Entry 336 Pg 57: Samuel Pendleton to Miss Mary Thomas. "I solemnized between the parties named in the within License on the 21st day of December 1842. By me, Martin L. Prater Justice of the Peace, Cannon County." Samuel is listed as a farmer in the 1850 Cannon Co. census, 2nd District; value of farm $300. Samuel L. Pendleton and Nancy C. are listed in the 1900 Hill Co., TX census, pg. 182.

Children of SAMUEL PENDLETON and MARY THOMAS are (Ref. 130):
          i.   JAMES[11] PENDLETON, b. Abt. 1844, TN.
         ii.   ELIZABETH PENDLETON, b. Abt. 1846, TN; m. HAILEY.
586. iii.   JOHN L. PENDLETON, b. Feb 01, 1848, Cannon Co., TN; d. Mar 24, 1930, Cannon Co., TN.
         iv.   RACHEL PENDLETON, b. Abt. 1849, TN.
587.   v.   WILLIAM GREEN PENDLETON, b. Oct 16, 1853, Woodbury, Cannon Co., TN; d. Nov 11, 1927, Hill Co., TX.
         vi.   MARY T. PENDLETON, b. 1857, TN.

289. BENJAMIN[10] PENDLETON *(JOHN[9], EDMUND[8], WILLIAM[7], JOHN[6], PHILIP[5], HENRY[4], HENRY[3], GEORGE[2], GEORGE[1])* was born Jan 14, 1824 in TN. He married

ALISA MCADOO Jan 26, 1848 in Cannon Co., TN, daughter of WILLIAM MCADOO and JANE. She was born Abt. 1824 in TN.

Child of BENJAMIN PENDLETON and ALISA MCADOO is:
    i.   OLLY[11] PENDLETON, b. 1850.

290. JOHN F.[10] PENDLETON (*JOHN[9], EDMUND[8], WILLIAM[7], JOHN[6], PHILIP[5], HENRY[4], HENRY[3], GEORGE[2], GEORGE[1]*) was born May 27, 1826 in TN, and died Aft. 1870 in Cannon Co., TN? He married LUCINDA WEST Aug 09, 1847 in Cannon Co., TN. She was born Abt. 1827 in TN, and died Aft. 1880 in Warren Co., TN?

    John Pendleton is listed as a farmer in the 1850 Cannon Co., TN census; no children. John Pendleton (shoemaker) and family are listed in the 1860 Cannon Co., TN census. A John F. Pendleton, private, served in the 2nd (Woodword's) KY Cavalry, Company A and the 1st (Helm's) KY Cavalry, Company G.

Children of JOHN PENDLETON and LUCINDA WEST are:
    i.   SARAH[11] PENDLETON, b. Abt. 1852, TN.
    ii. JOHN F. PENDLETON, b. Abt. 1854, TN; m. MATILDA; b. Abt. 1855, TN.

291. WILLIAM G.[10] PENDLETON (*JOHN[9], EDMUND[8], WILLIAM[7], JOHN[6], PHILIP[5], HENRY[4], HENRY[3], GEORGE[2], GEORGE[1]*) was born Jul 15, 1832 in Cannon Co., TN, and died Abt. 1920 in Coffee Co., TN. He married SARAH MALISSA MUNSEY Jun 10, 1855 in Coffee Co., TN. She was born Sep 1835 in Coffee Co., TN, and died Aug 01, 1917 in Coffee Co., TN.

    William Pendleton (farmer) and wife are listed in the 1900 Coffee Co., TN census, pg. 219a.

Children of WILLIAM PENDLETON and SARAH MUNSEY are:
          i.   ELIZABETH[11] PENDLETON, b. 1856, Coffee Co., TN; m. SULLIVAN.
    588. ii. EDMOND HARRIS PENDLETON, b. Sep 23, 1858, Cannon Co., TN; d. Aug 22, 1952, Birmingham, AL.
    589. iii. WILLIAM SEAMOR PENDLETON, b. May 1867, TN; d. Aft. 1930, Warren Co., TN?

292. EDMUND[10] PENDLETON (*BENJAMIN[9], EDMUND[8], WILLIAM[7], JOHN[6], PHILIP[5], HENRY[4], HENRY[3], GEORGE[2], GEORGE[1]*) was born May 23, 1815 in Cannon Co., TN, and died Mar 11, 1868 in TX. He married SARAH SMARTT Aug 16, 1842 in TN, daughter of WILLIAM SMARTT and MARGARET COLVILLE. She was born Jun 23, 1823 in TN, and died Dec 10, 1891 in Belton, TX.

    Edmund Pendleton is listed as a merchant in the 1850 Warren Co., TN census, 8th civil district; value of property $2,200.

Children of EDMUND PENDLETON and SARAH SMARTT are:
    i.   MARGARET ANNA[11] PENDLETON, b. Jun 29, 1843, TN; d. Apr 11, 1864; m. ROBERT SLAUGHTER, Dec 18, 1861.

590.   ii.   GEORGE CASSETY PENDLETON, b. Apr 23, 1845, Coffee Co., TN; d. Jan 19, 1913, Temple, Bell Co., TX.

591.   iii.   WILLIAM SMARTT PENDLETON, b. Feb 06, 1848, TN; d. Aft. 1900, Fort Worth, TX?

592.   iv.   EDMUND GAINES PENDLETON, b. Sep 28, 1852, TN; d. Nov 19, 1931, Sherman Co., TX?

       v.   ALICE PENDLETON, b. Apr 04, 1855; m. WILLIAM POMPEY BLACKBURN, Dec 17, 1876.

593.   vi.   OCTAVIA PENDLETON, b. Jan 1858, TX; d. Jul 03, 1947, Fort Worth, TX.

594.   vii.   DAVID RAMSEY PENDLETON, b. Feb 06, 1861, TX; d. Aft. 1910, Bell Co., TX?

293. THOMAS DILLARD[10] PENDLETON (*BENJAMIN[9], EDMUND[8], WILLIAM[7], JOHN[6], PHILIP[5], HENRY[4], HENRY[3], GEORGE[2], GEORGE[1]*) was born 1819 in TN, and died Oct 13, 1862 in On the Mississippi between AR and MO. He married (1) UNKNOWN. He married (2) ELIZABETH MELTON Aug 05, 1849 in Cannon Co., TN, daughter of JACOB MELTON and LUCY MATTHEWS. She was born 1824 in TN, and died Feb 08, 1905 in Christian Co., MO.

     Thomas D. Pendleton is named in Missouri Land Patents, Christian Co. on May 15, 1857 and Jun 1, 1859. Thomas Pendleton and family are listed in the 1860 Christian Co., MO census. He enlisted into Company F the 20 August 1861 in Rolla, Missouri as 1st Sergeant and mustered into service the 14th October 1861 at St. Louis, Missouri. His record shows a height of 5'9" with black hair, blue eyes and a fair complexion. He was promoted to 2nd lieutenant on the 13 December 1861 to fill the vacancy by the absence of 2nd lieutenant Henry Sullivan who was in Southwest Missouri and was captured by the enemy. Thomas was slightly wounded at the battle of Pea Ridge, Arkansas, Mar 1862. In May 1862 he was a recruiting officer in Batesville, Arkansas. He died 13 Oct, 1862 aboard the steamer "Edward Walsh" while it was running on the Mississippi River from Helena, Arkansas to Sulphur Springs, Missouri. The cause of death was chronic diarrhea (Ref. 214). Elizabeth Melton Pendleton, widow of Thomas D. Pendleton received a widow's pension: Thomas D. Pendleton, [1st sergeant] Company F, 24th MO Infantry, May 13, 18??, Application No. 213A3, Certificate No. 90555.

Children of THOMAS PENDLETON and UNKNOWN are:

595.   i.   ANDREW A.[11] PENDLETON, b. 1844, Cannon Co., TN; d. Hill Co., TX?

      ii.   NANCY PENDLETON, b. 1848, Cannon Co., TN.

294. ANDREW JACKSON[10] PENDLETON (*BENJAMIN[9], EDMUND[8], WILLIAM[7], JOHN[6], PHILIP[5], HENRY[4], HENRY[3], GEORGE[2], GEORGE[1]*) was born Mar 04, 1821 in TN, and died Mar 07, 1910 in Christian Co., MO? He married (1) LYDIA E. BROWN Dec 31, 1854 in Green Co., MO. She was born Jan 31, 1831 in NC, and died May 14, 1888 in Christian Co., MO? He married (2) MARTHA F. EDWARDS Jan 27, 1889 in Christian Co., MO. She was born May 07, 1846 in MO, and died Jan 14, 1913.

     A.J. (farmer) and Martha Pendleton are listed in the 1900 Christian Co., MO census, pg. 107.

Child of ANDREW PENDLETON and LYDIA BROWN is:
     i.   LUNDA JANE[11] PENDLETON, b. Oct 14, 1855, Christian Co., MO; d. Aug 10, 1928; m. JULIAN HERNDON, Jan 03, 1877, Christian Co., MO.

295. STACY CAROLINE[10] PENDLETON *(BENJAMIN[9], EDMUND[8], WILLIAM[7], JOHN[6], PHILIP[5], HENRY[4], HENRY[3], GEORGE[2], GEORGE[1])* was born Abt. 1825 in TN, and died 1853 in Christian Co., MO. She married BENJAMIN ALLEN STONE Jul 17, 1845 in Cannon Co., TN. He was born Feb 22, 1822 in Warren Co., TN, and died Apr 23, 1896 in MO.

     Benjamin Stone along with other families including the Pendletons settled in the area which came to be known as Parch Corn Hollar in Christian Co., MO. It is believed that the families from TN brought the name with them from TN. There was a creek called Parch Corn Branch in Cannon Co., TN where the Stone and Pendleton families had lived. Benjamin Stone had been the Deputy Sheriff in Cannon Co., TN (Ref. 215).

Children of STACY PENDLETON and BENJAMIN STONE are:
     i.   MARGARET ANN[11] STONE, b. Sep 20, 1846, Cannon Co., TN.
     ii. ROBERT BROWN STONE, b. Oct 15, 1848.
     iii. JOHN EDWARD STONE, b. Dec 05, 1850.
     iv. DILLARD STONE, b. Mar 06, 1853; d. 1853, Christian Co., MO.

296. JOSEPH[10] PENDLETON *(BENJAMIN[9], EDMUND[8], WILLIAM[7], JOHN[6], PHILIP[5], HENRY[4], HENRY[3], GEORGE[2], GEORGE[1])* was born Abt. 1827 in TN, and died Aft. 1880 in Gonzales, TX? He married MALISSA N. 1848 in TN. She was born 1823 in TN, and died Aft. 1880 in Gonzales Co., TX?

     Joseph Pendleton and family are listed in the 1850 Cannon Co. Census , Page 50. Joseph Pendleton is also listed in the 1860 and 1880 Gonzales Co. census, Town of Gonzales.

Child of JOSEPH PENDLETON and MALISSA N. is:
     i.   ELIZABETH[11] PENDLETON, b. 1849, Cannon Co., TN?

297. MARY JANE[10] PENDLETON *(BENJAMIN[9], EDMUND[8], WILLIAM[7], JOHN[6], PHILIP[5], HENRY[4], HENRY[3], GEORGE[2], GEORGE[1])* was born Jan 10, 1828 in TN, and died Dec 31, 1906 in Christian Co., MO. She married (1) JAMES MATTISON MELTON Jul 10, 1845 in Cannon Co., TN, son of JACOB MELTON and LUCY MATTHEWS. He was born Jan 21, 1821 in Warren Co., TN, and died Dec 01, 1872 in Christian Co., MO. She married (2) THOMAS J. MELTON Mar 13, 1902 in Christian Co., MO.

Children of MARY PENDLETON and JAMES MELTON are (Ref. 216):
     i.   EDMUND PENDLETON[11] MELTON, b. Dec 26, 1846; d. Mar 29, 1929, Christian Co., MO.
     ii. OCTAVIA MELTON, b. Aug 23, 1849, TN; d. Jun 17, 1927, Christian Co., MO.

iii. ANCEL MARION MELTON, b. Dec 15, 1854, Christian Co., MO; d. Feb 15, 1941, Christian Co., MO.
iv. JAMES A. MELTON, b. Abt. 1856, Christian Co., MO.
v. LUCY ANN MELTON, b. Jan 04, 1861.
vi. BENJAMIN MELTON, b. Jun 16, 1863, Christian Co., MO.
vii. THOMAS DILLARD MELTON, b. Sep 01, 1865, TN.
viii. JOSEPH E. MELTON, b. May 31, 1869, Christian Co., MO; d. Mar 04, 1962.
ix. JOHN DELBERT MELTON, b. Feb 08, 1872; d. Aft. 1950, Ontario, CA.

298. DILLARD[10] PENDLETON *(BENJAMIN[9], EDMUND[8], WILLIAM[7], JOHN[6], PHILIP[5], HENRY[4], HENRY[3], GEORGE[2], GEORGE[1])* was born 1834 in TN, and died Mar 22, 1885. He married ELIZABETH WALKER Sep 21, 1853 in Greene Co., MO. She was born 1837 in TN.

Dillard Pendleton and family are listed in the 1860 Finley, Christian Co., MO census.

Children of DILLARD PENDLETON and ELIZABETH WALKER are:
i. THOMAS C.[11] PENDLETON, b. 1855, MO.
ii. JOSEPH PENDLETON, b. 1857, Greene Co., MO; d. Gonzales Co., TX.
596. iii. JOHN BENJAMIN PENDLETON, b. Jul 1858, Christian Co., MO; d. Aug 11, 1928, Caldwell Co., TX.
597. iv. STACY A. PENDLETON, b. 1866, Christian Co., MO; d. Nov 01, 1888, Gonzales Co., TX.
v. GEORGE W. PENDLETON, b. Nov 25, 1869, TX; d. Apr 03, 1947, Caldwell Co., TX.

G.W. Pendleton is in the household of his uncle Joseph Pendleton in the 1880 Gonzales Co., TX census.

vi. WILLIAM WALKER PENDLETON, b. Dec 25, 1872, TX; d. Jul 09, 1927, Austin, Travis Co., TX; m. WILLIE EUGENIA THREADGILL, Dec 25, 1907, Caldwell Co., TX; b. Nov 22, 1879, Smithville, TX; d. Apr 02, 1916, Smithville, TX.

William Pendleton is listed in the 1880 Gonzales Co., TX census in the household of his sister and brother-in-law, E. S. Carlos.

299. FRANCES ANN[10] PENDLETON *(WILLIAM GARLAND[9], REUBEN[8], WILLIAM[7], JOHN[6], PHILIP[5], HENRY[4], HENRY[3], GEORGE[2], GEORGE[1])* was born Nov 03, 1814 in VA, and died Aft. 1880 in Henry Co., VA? She married M.D. ROBERT A. READ Nov 05, 1834 in Albemarle Co., VA. He was born 1813 in VA, and died Aft. 1880 in Henry Co., VA?

Children of FRANCES PENDLETON and ROBERT READ are:
i. JOHN[11] READ, b. Abt. 1850, VA.
ii. LAVINA READ, b. Abt. 1852, VA.
iii. EDWARD READ, b. Abt. 1854, VA.

iv. TAYLOR READ, b. Abt. 1856, VA.
v. JANETTE READ, b. Abt. 1858, VA.

300. ALEXANDER GARLAND[10] PENDLETON *(WILLIAM GARLAND[9], REUBEN[8], WILLIAM[7], JOHN[6], PHILIP[5], HENRY[4], HENRY[3], GEORGE[2], GEORGE[1])* was born Mar 27, 1819 in VA, and died Feb 16, 1865 in Montgomery Co., MD? He married SELINA CHRISTIANA DICKSON Sep 25, 1840 in Norfolk, VA, daughter of JOHN DICKSON and SELINA WHITE. She was born Abt. 1822 in Norfolk, VA, and died Jun 24, 1885 in Montgomery Co., MD?

Alexander Pendleton, Professor of Mathematics, and family are listed in the 1860 Montgomery Co., MD census.

Children of ALEXANDER PENDLETON and SELINA DICKSON are:
598. i. SELINA DICKSON[11] PENDLETON, b. Abt. 1844, VA; d. Aft. 1910, Montgomery Co., MD?
599. ii. ROSE B. PENDLETON, b. Abt. 1846, VA.
600. iii. EDWIN CONWAY PENDLETON, b. May 27, 1847, Richmond, VA; d. Sep 28, 1919, Philadelphia, PA -U.S. Naval Hosp.
iv. FRANCES RUCKER PENDLETON, b. Abt. 1850, Wash DC; m. NATHANIEL MANSON READ.
601. v. ALEXANDER GREENHEW PENDLETON, b. Abt. 1852, Wash DC; d. Aft. 1900, Gila Co., AZ?
vi. WILLIAM GARLAND PENDLETON, b. Abt. 1855, Wash DC.
vii. DOUGLAS PENDLETON, b. Abt. 1857, Wash DC; d. Aft. 1880.
Douglas Pendleton (24; model maker) is listed as a boarder in the 1880 Washington DC census.
viii. MARY LOUISE PENDLETON.

301. MARY JANE[10] PENDLETON *(WILLIAM GARLAND[9], REUBEN[8], WILLIAM[7], JOHN[6], PHILIP[5], HENRY[4], HENRY[3], GEORGE[2], GEORGE[1])* was born May 30, 1821 in VA, and died Aft. 1870 in NJ? She married JOHN HIGHTOWER Jun 04, 1840 in Pendleton Co., VA (now WV). He was born Abt. 1813 in NC, and died Abt. 1850 in Cole Co., MO.

"John and Mary Jane Pendleton Hightower were living in Cole/Moniteau County, MO in 1843 where John apparently died in 1850. However, John Hightower (tobacconist) and family are listed in the 1850 Moniteau Co., MO census. After his death, she petitioned the court for money from John's estate for traveling money back to her family in VA. She is in the 1860 Richmond, VA census with her mother, Mrs. G. Pendleton. A letter from Mary Jane was written in 1868 from Bergen, Bergen County, NJ. Mary Jane and her two sons were living together in the 1870 Jersey City, Hudson census; her son John was 24, listed as a 'reporter;' her son Edward (she called him by his middle name Taylor) was a bank cashier" (Ref. 217).

Children of MARY PENDLETON and JOHN HIGHTOWER are:
i. JOHN ALEXANDER[11] HIGHTOWER, b. Abt. 1844, MO.
ii. EDWARD TAYLOR HIGHTOWER, b. Abt. 1847, MO.

302. STEPHEN TAYLOR[10] PENDLETON *(WILLIAM GARLAND[9], REUBEN[8], WILLIAM[7], JOHN[6], PHILIP[5], HENRY[4], HENRY[3], GEORGE[2], GEORGE[1])* was born Oct 18, 1828 in VA, and died 1915 in Richmond, VA? He married CAROLINE (DUDLEY) READ 1856. She was born Abt. 1832 in VA.

Stephen Pendleton, age 21, is listed in the Brunswick Co., Northern District 1850 census at a school; he was unmarried at that time. Stephen Pendleton (teacher) and family are listed in the 1870 Richmond, VA census. Stephen T. Pendleton is included in the Richmond, Virginia City Directories, 1889-90 as a principal, Central Public School, with an address of 1201 Clay, E. Richmond VA. The personal papers of Stephen Taylor Pendleton are at the Virginia Historical Society, Richmond, VA.

Children of STEPHEN PENDLETON and CAROLINE READ are:
- i. BALDWIN ALEXANDER[11] PENDLETON, b. Dec 05, 1856, Richmond, VA; d. Aft. 1920, Richmond, VA; m. JANE ALLISON BUCHANAN, Apr 11, 1887.
  Baldwin Alexander Pendleton is included in the Presbyterian Ministerial Directory 1898: "Ordination, May 1886, City, Lookout Mountain, Birth City, Richmond." Baldwin A. Pendleton (63; Presbyterian Minister) is listed in the 1920 Richmond, VA census with his sister-in-law Mary A. Pendleton (62).

- ii. EDWIN TAYLOR PENDLETON, b. 1859, Richmond, VA.
- iii. WEBSTER PENDLETON, b. 1860, Richmond, VA?
- iv. FRANK SAMPSON PENDLETON, b. 1862, VA.
- v. JESSIE READ PENDLETON, b. 1866, VA; d. 1932, Richmond, VA?
  Miss Jesse R. Pendleton, teacher, is included in the Richmond, Virginia City Directories, 1889-90. Her address is listed as 124th N. Richmond, VA.

- vi. FRANCES G. PENDLETON, b. 1870, VA.
- vii. LEE POWELL PENDLETON, b. 1872, VA; d. 1878.
- viii. WILLIAM GARLAND PENDLETON, b. 1875, VA; d. 1876.
- ix. CAROLINE CABELL PENDLETON, b. 1878, VA.

303. WILLIAM DOUGLAS[10] PENDLETON *(WILLIAM GARLAND[9], REUBEN[8], WILLIAM[7], JOHN[6], PHILIP[5], HENRY[4], HENRY[3], GEORGE[2], GEORGE[1])* was born Dec 13, 1831 in VA. He married CLARA DRUFORD PAIGE Aug 09, 1864. She was born Aug 16, 1837.

Children of WILLIAM PENDLETON and CLARA PAIGE are:
- i. ALEXANDER GARLAND[11] PENDLETON, b. Jul 16, 1865; d. Jul 22, 1866.
- ii. BLANCHE CLARA PENDLETON, b. Mar 14, 1869; d. Jul 25, 1869.
- iii. CLARA PENDLETON, b. 1871.
- iv. CLARA ALEXANDER PENDLETON, b. Feb 01, 1872.
- v. WILLIAM PENDLETON, b. Jan 13, 1878; d. Jul 22, 1878.
- vi. DOUGLAS SCHLEY PENDLETON, b. Oct 12, 1879.

304. ROBERT ALDRIDGE^{10} PENDLETON (*JAMES SHEPHERD^9, REUBEN^8, WILLIAM^7, JOHN^6, PHILIP^5, HENRY^4, HENRY^3, GEORGE^2, GEORGE^1*) was born 1818 in VA, and died 1892 in Amherst, VA? He married (1) LOUISA E. PIERCE May 20, 1839. She was born Abt. 1820 in VA, and died Aft. 1860 in Amherst Co., VA? He married (2) MRS. ANNIE S. GILLIAM Jul 17, 1866. She was born Jul 25, 1834 in VA, and died Jan 11, 1921.

Robert Pendleton is listed in the 1840 Amherst Co., VA census and as a school master in the 1850 Amherst Co., VA census. Robert A. Pendleton (Circuit Court Clerk) and family are listed in the 1860 and 1870 Amherst, Amherst Co., VA census records. He is buried in the "Winton" Graveyard, Amherst Co. (Ref. 218).

Children of ROBERT PENDLETON and LOUISA PIERCE are:
602.　　i.　WILLIAM ADDISON^{11} PENDLETON, b. Aug 1840, VA; d. Aft. 1920, Amherst Co., VA?
　　　ii.　SALLY PENDLETON, b. 1842.
　　　iii.　JAMES PENDLETON, b. 1844.
　　　iv.　JACOB PENDLETON, b. 1846.
　　　v.　ROBERT ALDRIDGE PENDLETON, b. 1847, VA; d. 1911.
　　　　　A biographical sketch of Robert Pendleton (Ref. 219) is listed in the Virginia Historical Society Catalog.

　　　vi.　ANNA MARIA PENDLETON, b. 1848.
　　　vii.　MILLIE PENDLETON, b. Abt. 1850.
　　viii.　OLLIE PENDLETON, b. Abt. 1854.
　　　ix.　JACOB PENDLETON, b. Abt. 1856.
　　　x.　NELLIE PENDLETON, b. Abt. 1860.

Children of ROBERT PENDLETON and MRS. GILLIAM are:
603.　　xi.　RICHARD S.^{11} PENDLETON, b. Apr 1867, VA; d. Aft. 1920, Lynchburg, VA?
　　　xii.　MARY ELIZA PENDLETON, b. 1870, VA; m. ELDRED MYERS.
　　xiii.　ROBERTA ELLIS PENDLETON, b. 1873; m. ROBERT HARRISON.
　　xiv.　LUCY VIRGINIA PENDLETON, b. 1877; m. (1) ERNEST YALE BURCH; m. (2) ROBERT SHRADER.

305. WILLIAM GARLAND^{10} PENDLETON (*JAMES SHEPHERD^9, REUBEN^8, WILLIAM^7, JOHN^6, PHILIP^5, HENRY^4, HENRY^3, GEORGE^2, GEORGE^1*) was born Jun 22, 1820 in VA, and died Jun 22, 1874 in Union Co., AR? He married MRS. DRUCILLA JOHNSTON DOTY SMITH Jul 03, 1855 in Union Co., AR. She was born Mar 19, 1828 in TN, and died Mar 23, 1900.

William G. Pendleton is listed in the 1860 and 1870 Union Co. census records, Jackson township.

Children of WILLIAM PENDLETON and MRS. SMITH are:
604.　　i.　ANNA CATREN^{11} PENDLETON, b. Jun 22, 1856, AR; d. Sep 10, 1910, Union Co., AR?

ii. WILLIAM GARLAND PENDLETON, b. Aug 12, 1858, AR; d. Aft. 1900, Union Co., AR?; m. MRS. SALLIE CARMICHAEL GRACE.

William Pendleton (farmer) is listed in the 1900 Union Co., AR census, pg. 171.

iii. EMMETTE HARGRAVE PENDLETON, b. Jul 18, 1860, AR; d. Apr 27, 1877.

605. iv. HERBERT GEORGE PENDLETON, b. Dec 31, 1863, AR; d. Jan 27, 1950, Union Co., AR.

v. KATE MAY PENDLETON, b. May 10, 1869, AR; d. Apr 24, 1886.

306. JAMES SHEPHERD[10] PENDLETON (*JAMES SHEPHERD*[9], *REUBEN*[8], *WILLIAM*[7], *JOHN*[6], *PHILIP*[5], *HENRY*[4], *HENRY*[3], *GEORGE*[2], *GEORGE*[1]) was born 1823 in New Glasgow, VA, and died 1877 in Lynchburg, VA. He married LUCY ANN MILLS 1853. She was born Abt. 1835 in VA, and died Aft. 1880 in Lynchburg, VA?

A James Pendleton (26) is listed in the 1850 Appomattox, VA Census in household 333 (a hotel). James Shepherd Pendleton is included in the Virginia Military Institute Class of 1844 Roster: "James Shepherd Pendleton and Catharine Aldridge [parents]; non-graduate; Civil War Captain & Commissary, 30th Infantry, Company D, CSA; physician and farmer." James S. (37; farmer), Lucy A. (27) Pendleton and family are listed in the 1860 Amherst Co., VA census.

Children of JAMES PENDLETON and LUCY MILLS are:

606. i. LELIA A.[11] PENDLETON, b. Abt. 1854, VA.

ii. JAMES WALTER PENDLETON, b. 1855; d. infancy.

James Walter Pendleton is buried in the "Winton" Graveyard, Amherst Co. He is the son of Dr. J. S. Pendleton who bought the "Brick House" after the death of David Shepherd Garland, his great uncle (Ref. 218).

iii. ROBERT ALDRICH PENDLETON, b. Abt. 1859; d. infancy.

Robert A. C. Pendleton is buried in the "Winton" Graveyard (Ref. 218).

607. iv. LUCIE SHEPHERD PENDLETON, b. Abt. 1864, VA; d. Aft. 1920, Lynchburg, VA?

v. CHARLES DIX PENDLETON, b. Abt. 1866, VA; m. SALLIE MORRIS; b. Cohutta Springs, GA.

Mrs. Sally Gardner Morris Pendleton was a member of The National Society of the Daughters of the American Revolution (Volume 90, page 44). She is a descendant of Brig. General John Sevier and of Maj. John McDowel.

307. ELIZA JANE[10] PENDLETON (*JAMES SHEPHERD*[9], *REUBEN*[8], *WILLIAM*[7], *JOHN*[6], *PHILIP*[5], *HENRY*[4], *HENRY*[3], *GEORGE*[2], *GEORGE*[1]) was born Abt. 1827 in VA, and died Aft. 1880 in Lynchburg, VA? She married WILLIAM H. ROSE Apr 07, 1846 in Amherst Co., VA. He was born Abt. 1815 in VA, and died Aft. 1880 in Lynchburg, VA?

William H. Rose and family are listed in the 1880 census, Lynchburg, VA, pg. 365A. Included is his sister-in-law, Frances A. (Adelaide?) Pendleton (age 58).

Children of ELIZA PENDLETON and WILLIAM ROSE are:
  i.   WILLIAM[11] ROSE, b. Abt. 1852.
  ii. ANNAH ROSE, b. Abt. 1853.
  iii. JAMES ROSE, b. Abt. 1855.
  iv. LESLEY W. ROSE, b. Abt. 1858.
  v.   ROBERT P. ROSE, b. Abt. 1864.

308. EDMUND[10] PENDLETON (*MICAJAH[9], REUBEN[8], WILLIAM[7], JOHN[6], PHILIP[5], HENRY[4], HENRY[3], GEORGE[2], GEORGE[1]*) was born Sep 29, 1823 in Amherst Co., VA, and died Jun 26, 1899 in Lexington, Rockbridge Co., VA. He married CORNELIA MORGAN Feb 13, 1845 in Cincinnati, OH, daughter of EPHRAIM MORGAN and CHARLOTTE ANTHONY. She was born Apr 16, 1824 in Cincinnati, OH, and died Mar 26, 1894 in Rockbridge Co., VA?

Edmund Pendleton is included in the Virginia Military Institute Class of 1842 Roster: "Parents, Micajah Pendleton and Louisa Jane Davis; graduate; Civil War - 3rd and 15th Louisiana Infantry." Edmund Pendleton followed the profession of law for many years. He was a member of the Virginia Senate, sessions of 1869-71, and took up his residence in Rockbridge County, in 1879. In 1884 he was practicing law in Lexington, where he had his residence and post office address (Ref. 220).

Children of EDMUND PENDLETON and CORNELIA MORGAN are:
  i.   WILLIAM WOOD[11] PENDLETON, b. Dec 24, 1845; d. 1870.
       William Wood Pendleton served in the Confederate Army in the Washington Artillery from New Orleans. He is included in the Roster of VMI New Market Cadets Class of 1867. A biographical sketch of William Wood Pendleton (Ref. 219) is included in the Virginia Historical Society Catalog.

608. ii. ELIZABETH CHILES PENDLETON, b. Mar 08, 1849, VA; d. Oct 16, 1929, Rockbridge, VA?
609. iii. EPHRAIM MORGAN PENDLETON, b. Aug 25, 1857, VA; d. Feb 16, 1919.

309. ANNE GARLAND[10] PENDLETON (*MICAJAH[9], REUBEN[8], WILLIAM[7], JOHN[6], PHILIP[5], HENRY[4], HENRY[3], GEORGE[2], GEORGE[1]*) was born Sep 15, 1826 in VA, and died Dec 31, 1905 in Botetourt Co., VA. She married LEWIS BRUGH Aug 23, 1847 in Botetourt Co., VA, son of DANIEL BRUGH and CATHERINE PAINTER. He was born Jul 14, 1818 in Botetourt Co., VA, and died Oct 09, 1856 in Baltimore, MD.

Children of ANNE PENDLETON and LEWIS BRUGH are (Ref. 221):
  i.   CORNELIA PENDLETON[11] BRUGH, b. Dec 19, 1848; d. Jul 30, 1869, Darien, GA; m. WILLIAM C. CLARK, Feb 21, 1867.
  ii. LOUISA JANE DAVIS BRUGH, b. Apr 16, 1850; d. Nov 30, 1930, Wichita, KS; m. RICHARD COGDELL, Jun 03, 1870, Faircastle, VA.

iii. VIRGINIA GROVE BRUGH, b. Sep 27, 1851; d. 1886, Wichita, KS; m. MATTHEW BOWES, Dec 05, 1882.

iv. ALICE DUDLEY BRUGH, b. Feb 11, 1853; d. Jun 22, 1933; m. JOSEPH DAKIN, Nov 26, 1874.

v. NANCY LEWIS BRUGH, b. Jul 19, 1856; d. Dec 04, 1899, Wichita, KS; m. GEORGE W. KELLY, 1878.

310. JAMES DUDLEY[10] PENDLETON *(MICAJAH[9], REUBEN[8], WILLIAM[7], JOHN[6], PHILIP[5], HENRY[4], HENRY[3], GEORGE[2], GEORGE[1])* was born 1829 in VA, and died 1907 in Powhatan Co., VA? He married CLARA PULLIAM ROCK Abt. 1853, daughter of ROCK and S. A. She was born Aug 1834 in VA, and died Aft. 1910 in Bedford Co., VA?

James Dudley Pendleton was an Officer of the Virginia Senate and a Medical Doctor. James and family are listed in the 1880 Gardensville, Orange Co., VA census. J.D. Pendleton (farmer) and family are listed in the 1900 Powhatan Co., VA census, pg. 5. His home, a two-story, frame building built in 1845 in Powhatan Co., is on the historical register list (Ref. 222). A biographical sketch of James Dudley Pendleton (Ref. 45) is listed in the Virginia Historical Society Catalog.

Children of JAMES PENDLETON and CLARA ROCK are:
    i. WILLIE D.[11] PENDLETON, b. 1855, VA; d. Aft. 1920, Bedford Co., VA?; m. JOHN MORTON SPEECE, Dec 19, 1891, VA; b. Sep 02, 1859, VA; d. Aft. 1910, Bedford Co., VA?

610. ii. EDMUND PENDLETON, b. Nov 30, 1862, VA; d. Jun 08, 1927, Powhatan Co., VA?

311. SALLY DUDLEY RAGLAND[10] PENDLETON *(MICAJAH[9], REUBEN[8], WILLIAM[7], JOHN[6], PHILIP[5], HENRY[4], HENRY[3], GEORGE[2], GEORGE[1])* was born Mar 18, 1834 in Botetourt Co., VA, and died Feb 16, 1918. She married (1) GEORGE W. JOHNSON 1859. He was born Abt. 1832 in VA, and died 1861. She married (2) JOHN FULTON TOMPKINS Jun 05, 1867 in Botetourt Co., VA. He was born May 15, 1830 in Albemarle Co., VA, and died Aft. 1880 in Rockbridge Co., VA?

George W. Johnson (hotel keeper) and Sally are listed in the 1860 Lexington, Rockbridge Co., VA census.

Children of SALLY PENDLETON and JOHN TOMPKINS are:
    i. EDMUND PENDLETON[11] TOMPKINS, b. Abt. 1869, VA.
    ii. SALLY LOUISA TOMPKINS, b. Abt. 1871, VA; m. WILLIAM MORTON MCNUTT.
    iii. GEORGE JOHN TOMPKINS, b. Abt. 1873, VA.
    iv. BERTIE LEE TOMPKINS, b. Abt. 1876, VA.

312. WILLIAM F.[10] PENDLETON *(MICAJAH[9], REUBEN[8], WILLIAM[7], JOHN[6], PHILIP[5], HENRY[4], HENRY[3], GEORGE[2], GEORGE[1])* was born Mar 1847 in VA, and died 1916 in Floyd Co., VA? He married (1) ELIZA HARMAN 1876. She was born 1859 in VA, and died 1887. He married (2) BIRDIE HARRISON PENN Abt. 1892. She was born Nov 1867 in VA, and died Aft. 1920 in Floyd Co., VA?

A William F. Pendleton enlisted in Virginia, 18 August, 1861 as a Private in B Company, 4th Infantry Regiment. He was discharged for disability on 23 October 1861 (for chronic diarrhea). William F. Pendleton (druggist) and family are listed in the 1880 Floyd Co., VA census, pg. 339A. Also listed are his mother, Mary A. Pendleton (60) and his sister, Elizabeth Pendleton (26). William F. Pendleton (druggist) and family are listed in the 1900 Floyd Co., VA census, pg. 47a.

Children of WILLIAM PENDLETON and ELIZA HARMAN are:

        i.   LILLIAN[11] PENDLETON, b. Dec 1876, VA; d. Aft. 1930, Floyd Co., VA?; m. JOHN H. CRAVEN, 1915; b. Abt. 1880, MA; d. Aft. 1930, Floyd Co., VA?

611.   ii.   MARY PEARL PENDLETON, b. Nov 1879, VA; d. Aft. 1910, Roanoke Co., VA?

612.   iii.   WILLIAM HARMON PENDLETON, b. Oct 08, 1881, VA; d. 1928, Washington DC?

613.   iv.   EDMUND MICAJAH PENDLETON, b. May 1883, VA.

        v.   FRANK PENDLETON, b. 1885, VA; d. 1911.
            This may be the Frank M. Pendleton (b. Oct 1886) in the household of William Harman in the 1900 Floyd Co., VA census, pg. 104.

Children of WILLIAM PENDLETON and BIRDIE PENN are:

      vi.   HAILES JANNEY[11] PENDLETON, b. Nov 15, 1892; d. Aug 08, 1911.

     vii.   ELIZABETH PENN PENDLETON, b. Aug 12, 1894; d. Jul 1974, Richmond, VA; m. ANDREW LEWIS MICOU, Sep 14, 1916.

    viii. MARY SPENCER PENDLETON, b. Feb 09, 1896; m. LUTHER HUNT DAVIS, Feb 08, 1929.

313. ELIZABETH[10] PENDLETON (*MICAJAH*[9], *REUBEN*[8], *WILLIAM*[7], *JOHN*[6], *PHILIP*[5], *HENRY*[4], *HENRY*[3], *GEORGE*[2], *GEORGE*[1]) was born Mar 30, 1853 in VA, and died Apr 04, 1889. She married JOSEPH T. JETT Aug 26, 1880. He was born Dec 12, 1835, and died Apr 04, 1898.

Children of ELIZABETH PENDLETON and JOSEPH JETT are:

        i.   SAMUEL GRIGGS[11] JETT, b. May 31, 1881; m. VIRGINIA HARMON HOWARD, Jun 01, 1905.

       ii.   EDGAR MANTLEBERT JETT, b. May 17, 1883; m. SUE LAMBERT, Oct 03, 1905.

      iii.   WALTER CLEVELAND JETT, b. Feb 01, 1885; m. MAUDE GRIMM, Nov 18, 1909.

      iv.   LOUISE PENDLETON JETT, b. Dec 19, 1887; m. ZEBULON VANCE JOHNSON, Dec 12, 1908.

       v.   ELIZABETH PENDLETON JETT, b. Mar 28, 1889; d. Jul 04, 1889.

314. WALTER[10] PENDLETON (*MICAJAH*[9], *REUBEN*[8], *WILLIAM*[7], *JOHN*[6], *PHILIP*[5], *HENRY*[4], *HENRY*[3], *GEORGE*[2], *GEORGE*[1]) was born Mar 07, 1855 in Botetourt Co., VA, and died Mar 16, 1921 in Havana, Cuba. He married (1) NELLIE MCMATH Apr 26, 1886. She was born in of Foster, Bracken Co., KY, and died Jun 29, 1892 in Spencer, Roane Co., WV. He married (2) PEARL MONROE Jan 29, 1895, daughter of W. W. MONROE, DR. She was born Abt. 1873 in of Parkersburg, WV, and died Oct 23, 1911 in Spencer, Roane Co., WV.

According to his biography (Ref. 223) written just after his death, Walter Pendleton was a southern gentleman of the "old school."

The late Hon. Walter Pendleton earned distinction in law and politics and worthily upheld the traditions of one of the oldest and most prominent families in the South. Walter Pendleton was a descendant of the English family of that name, the line of which is traced back into the Plantagenet era of early English history. The Pendletons were established in Virginia about 1674, and since then the family has produced many leaders in public affairs, and in every war of the nation there has been a Pendleton of high official rank engaged, including even the World war. Walter Pendleton was born at Buchanan, in Botetourt County, Virginia, March 7, 1856, a son of Dr. Micajah Pendleton, a prominent physician of that state and a descendant of Edmund Pendleton, president of the Continental Congress that framed the Declaration of Independence and the first president of the Supreme Court of Appeals of Virginia. [Edmund was actually the cousin of Walter's great grandfather, William Pendleton]. Walter Pendleton was reared and educated in old Virginia. He was admitted to the bar in that state in 1876, and practiced his profession at Hillsville in Carroll County until his removal to Spencer in 1882. He was a prominent leader in the democratic party in West Virginia and was democratic nominee for Congress in 1896, participating in a campaign in a republican district and when the strength of the republican party was at its high tide. He was defeated by only a small majority. In 1908 he was nominated by his party for judge of the Supreme Court of Appeals of West Virginia, and again was defeated, though running thousands of votes ahead of his ticket. He was a member of the Methodist Episcopal Church, South, and was affiliated with Moriah Lodge No. 38, F. and A. M., Spencer Chapter No. 42, Royal Arch Masons, and Parkersburg Lodge No. 198, Benevolent and Protective Order of Elks. Walter Pendleton died at Havana, Cuba, March 16, 1921. His death brought profound sorrow to his many old friends and associates in Roane County, where he had practiced law almost forty years. He began his professional career in West Virginia practically among strangers, went through a period of considerable hardship while struggling for recognition, but for a number of years before his death was regarded as the foremost representative of the local bar. A professional friend characterized his career as follows: "Walter Pendleton was a lawyer of the old school. The strongest advocate found in him a worthy opponent and one who always played the game fairly. His manner was courteous, his logic convincing, his sincerity was apparent. He believed that his client was entitled to the best that was in him and he rendered it without stint or measure, but he did not seek undue advantage or stoop to the plane of a shyster at any time. Coming as he did from the old State of Virginia and with a family whose name adorns the pages of her history, a fact of which he was always proud, he ever exhibited the traits of the 'Virginia gentleman' but not with haughtiness or seclusion. He understood the struggle of the young and inexperienced practitioner at the bar because he himself had passed through the same, and he deemed it a pleasure to extend to such a one the glad hand of assistance. He reached a ripe age, yet he never permitted his spirit to grow old. He was happiest when he was surrounded with his younger companions, which we believe was the secret of his heart staying young." The first wife of Walter Pendleton was Nellie McMath, a native of Foster, Kentucky, who died at Spencer in 1892, survived by two sons, Daniel and

Dudley. Walter Pendleton afterward married Miss Pearl Monroe, a native of Parkersburg, who died at Spencer in 1911. Her father was the late Dr. W. W. Monroe, one of the prominent dentists of Parkersburg.

Mrs. Pearl Monroe Pendleton was a member of The National Society of the Daughters of the American Revolution (Volume 48, page 207). She is the great great granddaughter of Andrew Monroe and Mary Dailey, his wife. Andrew Monroe (1760-1847) served as a private in Capt. William Bentley's company, Third Virginia regiment, commanded by Col. John Neville.

Children of WALTER PENDLETON and NELLIE MCMATH are:
   i. DANIEL MICAJAH[11] PENDLETON, b. Apr 06, 1887, Spencer, Roane Co., WV; d. Aft. 1920, Parkersburg, WV?; m. EDNA MORFORD, 1915, Parkersburg, Wood Co., WV; b. Abt. 1894, Green Co., PA; d. Aft. 1920.
   Daniel M Pendleton registered for the WWI draft in Roane Co., WV (Ref. 210). Daniel and Edna Pendleton are listed in the 1920 Roane Co., WV census. Daniel's biography can be found adjacent to his father's (Ref. 223).

   Daniel Pendleton is a prominent lawyer of Spencer, also publisher and proprietor of the Roane County Reporter, and bears a name that has had honorable associations in the bar of Roane County forty years. Daniel Pendleton is liberally educated, beginning in the public schools of Spencer, later graduating from the Parkersburg High School and receiving his law degree from the University of West Virginia at Morgantown. He practiced law at Spencer until 1910, and for the following five years was an active member of the Oklahoma bar at Ada. In 1915 he returned to Spencer, and was associated with his father until the latter's death. Among other interests represented by him he is attorney for the Baltimore & Ohio Railway Company. Mr. Pendleton in 1918 acquired the ownership of the Roane County Reporter, the official democratic paper of this section of West Virginia, and . a journal of great influence and prestige. This paper was established in 1878 as The Bulletin, was later sold to a stock company and finally became the Roane County Reporter in 1911. Mr. Pendleton is chairman of the Democratic County Committee of Roane County. He is president of the Spencer Independent District Board of Education. He is a Rotarian and a member of the Methodist Episcopal Church, South, of Moriah Lodge No. 38, A. F. and A. M., Spencer Chapter No. 42, R. A. M., West Virginia Consistory No. 1 of the Scottish Rite at Wheeling, Nemesis Temple of the Mystic Shrine at Parkersburg, Spencer Lodge No. 55, Knights of Pythias, and Parkersburg Lodge No. 198, Benevolent and Protective Order of Elks. Mr. Pendleton is a stockholder in the Roane County Bank and in the Spencer Water & Ice Company, and has a considerable amount of property, including his home, one of the best residences in the city, his office building on Church Street, the Telephone Exchange Building, and he owns a farm near Ada, Oklahoma, and coal lands in Illinois. During the war Mr. Pendleton was active in all war work in Roane County, and especially exerted himself in publicity work during the various Liberty Loan campaigns. In 1915, at Parkersburg, Mr. Pendleton married Miss Edna Morford, who was born at Morford in Greene County, Pennsylvania, and finished her education in the Wheeling High School. Her father, George L.

Morford, was born in Greene County, Pennsylvania, in 1863, was a teacher there during his early life, and in 1895 established a home and business at Spencer. In 1897 he removed to Parkersburg, and since 1908 has been active in business at Wheeling. He is a democrat and a Baptist. The mother of Mrs. Pendleton was Minnie Miller, a native of Greene County, Pennsylvania.

   ii.   JAMES DUDLEY PENDLETON, b. Jul 17, 1889, WV.
        James Dudley Pendleton registered for the World War I draft in Roane Co., WV (Ref. 210).

   iii.   NELLIE HELEN PENDLETON, b. Jun 23, 1892, WV; d. Sep 04, 1892, WV.

Child of WALTER PENDLETON and PEARL MONROE is:
   iv.   WATSON MONROE[11] PENDLETON, b. Jul 18, 1898; d. Sep 24, 1898.

315. ROBERT H.[10] PENDLETON *(JAMES[9], RICHARD[8], WILLIAM[7], JOHN[6], PHILIP[5], HENRY[4], HENRY[3], GEORGE[2], GEORGE[1])* was born Nov 01, 1817 in VA, and died Bef. 1870 in Warren Co., MO. He married MARTHA PRATT Feb 21, 1839 in Warren Co., MO, daughter of THOMAS PRATT. She was born Jan 26, 1824 in Culpeper Co., VA, and died Dec 13, 1904 in Lincoln Co., MO.

     Robert H. Pendleton moved with his parents from VA to Warren Co., MO in the early 1830's. He is found in the 1840 Warren Co. census, Hickary, p. 167. Robert Pendleton is listed in Missouri Land Patents, Warren Co. on Apr 10, 1843 and Aug 1, 1853. Robert H. Pendleton and family are listed in the 1860 Warren Co., MO census.

Children of ROBERT PENDLETON and MARTHA PRATT are:
   i.   HENRY T.[11] PENDLETON, b. Mar 15, 1840, MO; d. Feb 04, 1891, St. Louis, MO.
        Henry T. Pendleton, [owner of] flour and saw mill, is listed in the Missouri State Gazetteer and Business Directory for 1881-82, Wentzville, St. Charles, Co., MO. Henry T. Pendleton is listed in the St. Louis City Death Records, 1850-1908: 04 Feb 1891, 3134 Brantner Pl.

   ii.   SUSAN ANN PENDLETON, b. Jun 29, 1841, MO.
   iii.   JAMES S. PENDLETON, b. Jan 20, 1843, MO.
        A James S. Pendleton (born in MO; age 36) is listed in the 1880 Tulare Co., CA census.

   iv.   SARAH ELLEN PENDLETON, b. Sep 26, 1844, MO; m. DOGGETT.
614.   v.   WILCHER LEWIS PENDLETON, b. Sep 09, 1847, Wright City, MO; d. Nov 24, 1923, Whittier, CA.
   vi.   ROBERT M. PENDLETON, b. Abt. 1849, MO.
615.   vii.   CORNELIA PENDLETON, b. Dec 18, 1850, MO.
   viii.   EDMUND PENDLETON, b. Dec 03, 1853; d. Feb 09, 1925, Lincoln Co., MO.
   ix.   GEORGE W. PENDLETON, b. Dec 22, 1855.
   x.   FANNIE PENDLETON, b. Aug 05, 1858; m. PERKINS.

616.   xi.   LAFAYETTE PENDLETON, b. Apr 09, 1861, MO; d. Aft. 1920, Lincoln Co., MO?

316. LUCY JANE[10] PENDLETON (*JAMES[9], RICHARD[8], WILLIAM[7], JOHN[6], PHILIP[5], HENRY[4], HENRY[3], GEORGE[2], GEORGE[1]*) was born Abt. 1822 in VA. She married WILLIAM A. KABLER Sep 19, 1844 in Warren Co., MO. He was born Abt. 1822 in VA.

     "Rev. Nicholas C. Kabler, of Campbell Co., VA., was a son of Rev. Nicholas Kabler, of the same county. He married Sarah Golden, of Virginia, and settled in Warren Co., MO., in 1830. He was a Methodist minister, and traveled with Rev. Andrew Monroe for a number of years. His children were--Ellen, Simeon, William A., Lucy, Anna, Parks and Charles. Ellen married William McMurtry, of Callaway county. Simeon and Lucy died in Virginia. William A. married Lucy J. Pendleton, of Warren County, whose father and mother, James Pendleton and Nancy Sharp, settled in that county in 1833" (Ref. 118).

Child of LUCY PENDLETON and WILLIAM KABLER is:
     i.   ROBERT[11] KABLER, b. Abt. 1846.

317. JAMES LEWIS[10] PENDLETON (*JAMES[9], RICHARD[8], WILLIAM[7], JOHN[6], PHILIP[5], HENRY[4], HENRY[3], GEORGE[2], GEORGE[1]*) was born Dec 1828 in VA, and died Aft. 1900 in Warren Co., MO? He married (1) UNKNOWN. He married (2) MRS. FANNIE MARTIN Abt. 1874. She was born Sep 1841 in MO, and died Aft. 1900.

     Lewis Pendleton (tobacconist) is listed in the 1860 Warren Co., MO census. James L. Pendleton (gardener) and family are listed in the 1900 Warren Co., MO census, pg. 94.

Child of JAMES PENDLETON and UNKNOWN is:
617.   i.   JENNIE[11] PENDLETON, b. Jul 1867, IL.

Children of JAMES PENDLETON and MRS. MARTIN are:
     ii.   LUCY[11] PENDLETON, b. 1877, MO.
     iii.   IANTHA PENDLETON, b. Jul 1879, MO.

318. GEORGE W.[10] PENDLETON (*JAMES[9], RICHARD[8], WILLIAM[7], JOHN[6], PHILIP[5], HENRY[4], HENRY[3], GEORGE[2], GEORGE[1]*) was born Abt. 1834 in VA. He married SUSANA. She was born Abt. 1836 in IL.

     George W. Pendleton (carpenter) and family are listed in the 1860 Warren Co., MO census.

Child of GEORGE PENDLETON and SUSAN A. is:
     i.   VICTORIA[11] PENDLETON, b. 1859, MO.

319. WILLIAM[10] PENDLETON (*WILLIAM[9], RICHARD[8], WILLIAM[7], JOHN[6], PHILIP[5], HENRY[4], HENRY[3], GEORGE[2], GEORGE[1]*) was born Nov 1822 in VA, and died Aft. 1900 in Cole Co., MO? He married (1) SARAH LURTON Abt. 1846. She was born Abt. 1832, and died Abt. 1856 in MO. He married (2) MARTHA ANN BALLANGEE Sep 11, 1856 in Miller Co., MO. She was born Nov 1833 in Wayne Co., IN, and died Aft. 1900 in Cole Co., MO?

This is likely the William Pendleton named in the Missouri Land Patent, Osage Co. on Dec 1, 1848. William Pendleton and family are listed in the 1860 Osage, Miller Co., MO census.

Children of WILLIAM PENDLETON and SARAH LURTON are:
618.   i.   ANDREW DAVIS[11] PENDLETON, b. Jan 1847, MO; d. Aft. 1910, Miller Co., MO?
       ii. HENRY PENDLETON, b. Abt. 1849.
619.   iii. OWEN R. PENDLETON, b. Sep 1855, MO.

Children of WILLIAM PENDLETON and MARTHA BALLANGEE are:
620.   iv. CHARLES WESLEY[11] PENDLETON, b. Feb 08, 1859, Cole Co., MO; d. Mar 16, 1935, Jefferson City, MO.
621.   v.   JOSEPH M. PENDLETON, b. Nov 20, 1861, Miller Co., MO.
622.   vi. JOHN E. PENDLETON, b. Sep 1863, MO; d. Aft. 1910, Miller Co., MO?
       vii. GEORGE WILSON PENDLETON, b. Apr 04, 1865, MO.
       viii. WILLIAM S. PENDLETON, b. Jan 06, 1867, MO.
623.   ix. THOMAS E. PENDLETON, b. Jul 02, 1869, MO; d. Aft. 1920, Cole Co., MO?

320. FRANCES[10] PENDLETON *(WILLIAM[9], RICHARD[8], WILLIAM[7], JOHN[6], PHILIP[5], HENRY[4], HENRY[3], GEORGE[2], GEORGE[1])* was born Abt. 1824 in Amherst Co., VA, and died Feb 20, 1897 in Maries Co., MO. She married LEWIS G. WILES Feb 05, 1846 in Osage Co., MO. He was born 1822 in TN, and died 1888 in Maries Co., MO?

Children of FRANCES PENDLETON and LEWIS WILES are:
       i.   THOMAS A.[11] WILES, b. Abt. 1857, MO; m. MARY; b. Abt. 1860, MO.
       ii. EMILY WILES, b. Abt. 1860, MO.

321. ZACHARIAH[10] PENDLETON *(WILLIAM[9], RICHARD[8], WILLIAM[7], JOHN[6], PHILIP[5], HENRY[4], HENRY[3], GEORGE[2], GEORGE[1])* was born 1824 in Amherst Co., VA, and died Aug 02, 1865 in MO. He married (1) BARBARA ANN BARNHART Aug 23, 1849 in Osage Co., MO. She was born Abt. 1830 in Green Co., TN, and died Apr 14, 1858. He married (2) MARY E. BARNHART Nov 05, 1858. She was born 1837 in TN.

Zachariah Pendleton is named in Missouri Land Patents, Osage Co. on Apr 1, 1843, Jan15, 1856, and Apr 2, 1860. He is included in the 1850 MO census, Osage Co., Washington township. Zachariah Pendleton served in the Confederate Arkansas Calvary, Crabtree's (46th) guerrilla regiment and was discharged Oct 1, 1862. He is buried in Jefferson Barracks National Cemetery, MO.

Children of ZACHARIAH PENDLETON and BARBARA BARNHART are:

624.   i.   WILLIAM HOOVER[11] PENDLETON, b. Oct 03, 1850, MO; d. Jun 15, 1917, Maries Co., MO?

        ii.   FRANCES EMILINE PENDLETON, b. Jun 02, 1852, Osage Co., MO; d. Sep 02, 1854, MO.

625.   iii.   JAMES RICHARD PENDLETON, b. Dec 24, 1854, Osage Co., MO; d. Sep 14, 1903, Cooper Co., MO.

Children of ZACHARIAH PENDLETON and MARY BARNHART are:

        iv.   SARAH JANE[11] PENDLETON, b. Oct 13, 1859, Maries Co., MO; d. May 20, 1876, Meta, MO; m. DAVID BARNHART.

626.   v.   GEORGE PINCKNEY PENDLETON, b. Aug 21, 1861, Maries Co., MO; d. Bef. 1920, Maries Co., MO?

627.   vi.   MARTHA ELIZABETH PENDLETON, b. Feb 07, 1863, Maries Co., MO; d. Nov 27, 1939, Jefferson City, MO.

322. GEORGE WASHINGTON[10] PENDLETON (*WILLIAM[9], RICHARD[8], WILLIAM[7], JOHN[6], PHILIP[5], HENRY[4], HENRY[3], GEORGE[2], GEORGE[1]*) was born Oct 1825 in Amherst Co., VA, and died Sep 30, 1908 in Osage Co., MO. He married ELIZABETH GREEN, daughter of AZARIAH GREEN and SALLY COBB. She was born Mar 18, 1830 in KY, and died Nov 30, 1924 in MO.

      George Washington Pendleton came to Missouri with his parents and siblings in the early 1830's. George W. Pendleton is named in Missouri Land Patents, Osage Co. on Mar 30, 1849, and Maries Co. on May 1, 1854, Jan 15, 1856, Apr 2, 1857, and Jun 1, 1859. He is listed in the 1850 Osage Co. census index, Washington Township. George Pendleton (farmer) and wife are listed in the 1900 Maries Co., MO census, pg. 8a.

Children of GEORGE PENDLETON and ELIZABETH GREEN are:

        i.   SARAH[11] PENDLETON, b. Abt. 1849.

628.   ii.   AZARIAH B. PENDLETON, b. May 07, 1850, Meta, MO; d. Sep 14, 1888, Maries Co., MO.

        iii.   ANNA PENDLETON, b. Abt. 1851, Osage Co., MO.

629.   iv.   WILLIAM E. PENDLETON, b. Feb 09, 1854, Maries Co., MO; d. Dec 10, 1905, Meta, MO.

630.   v.   ZACHARIAH PENDLETON, b. Jan 18, 1856, Meta, MO; d. Sep 01, 1934, Clinton, MO.

631.   vi.   JAMES HENRY PENDLETON, b. Oct 12, 1859, Meta, MO; d. Dec 13, 1931, Maries Co., MO.

632.   vii.   JOHN RILEY PENDLETON, b. Jul 14, 1860, Meta, MO; d. Aft. 1920, Maries Co., MO?

633.   viii.   SARAH E. PENDLETON, b. May 23, 1862, Meta, MO; d. Apr 01, 1929, Meta, MO.

634.   ix.   GEORGE W. PENDLETON, b. Mar 25, 1864, Meta, MO; d. Abt. 1937, Meta, MO.

635.   x.   CORDELIA PENDLETON, b. Apr 03, 1868, Meta, MO; d. Jun 15, 1944, Maries Co., MO.

323. JAMES RICHARD[10] PENDLETON *(WILLIAM[9], RICHARD[8], WILLIAM[7], JOHN[6], PHILIP[5], HENRY[4], HENRY[3], GEORGE[2], GEORGE[1])* was born 1828 in Amherst Co., VA, and died Abt. 1860 in MO. He married SARAH JANE BARNHART 1850 in MO, daughter of MATTHIAS BARNHART and ELIZABETH SEATON. She was born 1831 in TN, and died 1902.

Children of JAMES PENDLETON and SARAH BARNHART are (Ref. 224):
636.   i.   JAMES H.[11] PENDLETON, b. Aug 15, 1855, Osage Co., MO; d. Dec 15, 1944, Boone Township, Meta Co., MO.
     ii.   M. ELIZABETH PENDLETON, b. Abt. 1857.
    iii.   PERMELIA FRANCISCA PENDLETON, b. Jan 13, 1859, Boone Township, Meta Co., MO; d. Dec 13, 1915, Boone Township, Meta Co., MO.

324. NANCY MARLIN[10] PENDLETON *(MICAJAH[9], JOHN[8], WILLIAM[7], JOHN[6], PHILIP[5], HENRY[4], HENRY[3], GEORGE[2], GEORGE[1])* was born 1825 in Stanford, KY, and died Nov 23, 1907 in Kansas City, MO. She married WILLIAM EDWARD SHANKS Dec 14, 1842 in Lincoln Co., KY. He was born Abt. 1823 in Stanford, KY, and died Sep 1860 in Jackson Co., MO.

Children of NANCY PENDLETON and WILLIAM SHANKS are (Ref. 225):
     i.   SARAH BELLE[11] SHANKS, b. 1845, KY; d. Dec 11, 1860; m. LEANDER CARUTH (LEE) MILLER, DR.
    ii.   DAVID SHANKS, b. Abt. 1846, KY.
   iii.   FRANCIS M. SHANKS, b. 1849, MO; d. Mar 02, 1936; m. CARRIE HEARD, 1893.
   iv.   WILLIAM EDWARD SHANKS, b. Jul 16, 1855, Independence, MO; d. Jan 02, 1938, Webster, FL; m. JESSIE EDITH KIMMONS, 1882, Kansas City, MO.
    v.   EMMA SHANKS, b. Abt. 1857, MO.
   vi.   MACK RICHARD SHANKS, b. Dec 25, 1860, MO; m. BERTHA FROLMES.

325. THOMAS J.[10] PENDLETON *(MICAJAH[9], JOHN[8], WILLIAM[7], JOHN[6], PHILIP[5], HENRY[4], HENRY[3], GEORGE[2], GEORGE[1])* was born Abt. 1830 in KY. He married ELIZA A. She was born Abt. 1840 in MO.
    Thomas J. and Lewis E. Pendleton (both carpenters) and their families are in adjacent households in the 1860 Jackson Co., MO census.

Child of THOMAS PENDLETON and ELIZA A. is:
     i.   MARY E.[11] PENDLETON, b. 1860.

326. LEWIS E.[10] PENDLETON *(MICAJAH[9], JOHN[8], WILLIAM[7], JOHN[6], PHILIP[5], HENRY[4], HENRY[3], GEORGE[2], GEORGE[1])* was born Abt. 1834 in KY. He married MARY A. She was born Abt. 1843 in KY.

Children of LEWIS PENDLETON and MARY A. are:
    i. SUSAN E.[11] PENDLETON, b. Abt. 1858, MO.
    ii. ANN M. PENDLETON, b. 1860.

327. EMILY J.[10] PENDLETON *(MICAJAH[9], JOHN[8], WILLIAM[7], JOHN[6], PHILIP[5], HENRY[4], HENRY[3], GEORGE[2], GEORGE[1])* was born Abt. 1844 in Lincoln Co., KY. She married RUFUS HUDSON. He was born Abt. 1830 in AL, and died Aft. 1880 in Jackson Co., MO?

Children of EMILY PENDLETON and RUFUS HUDSON are:
    i. MARY E.[11] HUDSON, b. Abt. 1862, MO.
    ii. FANNIE HUDSON, b. Abt. 1863, MO.
    iii. EMMA HUDSON, b. Abt. 1865, MO.

328. JOHN EDWARD[10] PENDLETON *(RICHARD[9], JOHN[8], WILLIAM[7], JOHN[6], PHILIP[5], HENRY[4], HENRY[3], GEORGE[2], GEORGE[1])* was born Sep 01, 1831 in Washington Co., KY, and died Jan 01, 1897 in Ohio Co., KY. He married (1) MARGARET NALLE Mar 01, 1855 in KY, daughter of JOHN NALLE and EMILY HENDERSON. She was born Jan 19, 1836 in KY, and died Jul 06, 1869 in Ohio Co., KY. He married (2) IDA NALLE 1870, daughter of JOHN NALLE and EMILY HENDERSON. She was born 1851, and died 1905.

    John E. Pendleton and family are listed in the 1860 Hartford, Ohio Co., KY census. He served in the Ninth Mounted Infantry unit of the KY "Orphan Brigade," Confederate States Army. He enlisted as a surgeon on 6 Oct 1861, in Russellville, KY. He is buried in Oakwood Cemetery, Hartford, Ohio Co., KY (Ref. 80).

Children of JOHN PENDLETON and MARGARET NALLE are:
637.   i. LAURA[11] PENDLETON, b. Abt. 1856, KY.
638.   ii. MARY PENDLETON, b. Feb 13, 1858, KY; d. Dec 19, 1919, Ohio Co., KY.
       iii. CHARLES M. PENDLETON, b. 1860, KY; d. Miami, FL?
          Charles M. Pendleton is listed as a lawyer in the 1880 census, Hartford, Ohio Co., KY in the household of John E. Pendleton. A Charles M. Pendleton (59), real estate agent and wife Mary (54), both born in KY, are listed in the 1920 Dade Co., Miami, FL census.

       iv. JOHN E. PENDLETON, b. Abt. 1861, KY.
639.   v. EUGENE BANKS PENDLETON, b. Feb 1866, KY; d. Apr 09, 1930, Daviess Co., KY.

Child of JOHN PENDLETON and IDA NALLE is:
    vi. TULA D.[11] PENDLETON, b. Abt. 1873, Hartford, KY; m. HOLMES CUMMINS.
         Mrs. Tula Pendleton Cummins was a member of The National Society of the Daughters of the American Revolution (Volume 106, page 175).

329. NAOMI F.[10] PENDLETON *(RICHARD[9], JOHN[8], WILLIAM[7], JOHN[6], PHILIP[5], HENRY[4], HENRY[3], GEORGE[2], GEORGE[1])* was born Feb 28, 1833 in KY, and died Jul 27, 1907 in Bates Co., MO. She married HENRY C. ALLIN, DR. May 04, 1852. He was born Feb 10, 1825 in Harrodsburg, KY, and died 1905.

The marriage of Henry Allin and Naomi Pendleton is recorded in Reference 226. Henry Allin (physician) and family are listed in the 1860 Mackville, KY census.

Children of NAOMI PENDLETON and HENRY ALLIN are:

 i. MARY[11] ALLIN, b. Abt. 1854, KY; m. THOMAS JEFFERSON SMITH, 1882; b. 1849.
 ii. ANNA ALLIN, b. Abt. 1856, KY.
 iii. MARGARET PENDLETON ALLIN, b. Abt. 1858, KY; m. W. R. CURRY.
  Mrs. Margaret Pendleton Allin Curry was a member of The National Society of the Daughters of the American Revolution (Volume 115, page 245).

330. JOHN T.[10] PENDLETON *(JAMES[9], JOHN[8], WILLIAM[7], JOHN[6], PHILIP[5], HENRY[4], HENRY[3], GEORGE[2], GEORGE[1])* was born Abt. 1829 in KY, and died Aft. 1880 in Jackson Co., MO? He married MARGARET BRUNETTE WILSON Oct 12, 1859 in Jackson Co., MO. She was born Abt. 1833 in TN, and died Aft. 1880 in Jackson Co., MO?

John T. and family are listed in the 1880 Blue, Jackson Co., MO census, pg. 93D. A John T. Pendleton, coal agent, is listed in Missouri State Gazetteer and Business Directory for 1881-82, Part K. This may be the John Pendleton (91; uncle) in the household of Roy Helms, 1920 census, Polk, Sullivan Co., MO

Children of JOHN PENDLETON and MARGARET WILSON are:

 i. G. W.[11] PENDLETON, b. Abt. 1861, MO.
 ii. H. H. PENDLETON, b. Abt. 1865.
 iii. S.T. PENDLETON, b. Abt. 1867.
 iv. JESSIE PENDLETON, b. Abt. 1872.

331. LOGAN[10] PENDLETON *(JAMES[9], JOHN[8], WILLIAM[7], JOHN[6], PHILIP[5], HENRY[4], HENRY[3], GEORGE[2], GEORGE[1])* was born Dec 30, 1830 in Lincoln Co., KY, and died Mar 30, 1903 in Jackson Co., MO. He married SERENA MATILDA BROOKING Jun 19, 1862 in Jackson Co., MO, daughter of ALVAN BROOKING and PERMILIA. She was born Feb 01, 1834 in KY, and died May 26, 1904 in Jackson Co., MO.

"The children of his [Alvan Brooking's] first marriage [to Permelia] numbered eight, and of that number, five grew to maturity. Their names are as follows: John, Mary, Wallace, Americus, Robert, Julia, Henry C., and Serena M. All have passed away [by 1896] except the two youngest. Serena M. is the wife of Logan Pendleton, of this township, and has ten children" (Ref. 227).

Children of LOGAN PENDLETON and SERENA BROOKING are (Ref. 228):

 i. LILLIE[11] PENDLETON, b. 1864.

ii. ROBERT PENDLETON, b. 1866.

iii. EDWARD PENDLETON, b. 1868.

iv. MADALINE PENDLETON, b. 1869.

v. ALEX PENDLETON.

vi. ELVIRA PENDLETON.

vii. MARCUS PENDLETON.

332. MICAJAH[10] PENDLETON *(JAMES[9], JOHN[8], WILLIAM[7], JOHN[6], PHILIP[5], HENRY[4], HENRY[3], GEORGE[2], GEORGE[1])* was born Abt. 1834 in KY, and died Aft. 1880 in Independence, MO? He married SARAH C. She was born Abt. 1837 in KY.

Children of MICAJAH PENDLETON and SARAH C. are:

i. JAMES H.[11] PENDLETON, b. Abt. 1858, KY.

ii. ANDREW PENDLETON, b. Abt. 1861, KY.

iii. STELLA PENDLETON, b. Abt. 1866, MO.

iv. LULU PENDLETON, b. Abt. 1871, MO.

333. ALFRED[10] PENDLETON *(JAMES[9], JOHN[8], WILLIAM[7], JOHN[6], PHILIP[5], HENRY[4], HENRY[3], GEORGE[2], GEORGE[1])* was born Dec 23, 1836 in KY, and died Dec 16, 1896 in Kansas City, MO. He married PERMELIA A. She was born Aug 15, 1842 in MO, and died Apr 28, 1910 in Kansas City, MO.

An Alfred L. Pendleton served in the Union 13th KY Infantry Company H. Both Alfred and Permelia A. Pendleton are buried at Brooking Cemetery, Kansas City, MO (Ref. 229).

Children of ALFRED PENDLETON and PERMELIA A. are:

640.   i. THOMAS R.[11] PENDLETON, b. Jul 1865, MO; d. 1932, Kansas City, MO.

ii. HENRY PENDLETON, b. Abt. 1866, MO.

iii. MARY PENDLETON, b. Abt. 1870, MO.

iv. FANNIE PENDLETON, b. Abt. 1876, MO.

334. EBERLE[10] PENDLETON *(JAMES[9], JOHN[8], WILLIAM[7], JOHN[6], PHILIP[5], HENRY[4], HENRY[3], GEORGE[2], GEORGE[1])* was born May 1839 in KY, and died Aft. 1900 in Jackson Co., MO? He married MARY N. IRWIN Nov 29, 1864 in Jackson Co., MO, daughter of WILLIAM IRWIN and PRISCILLA SULLIVAN. She was born Dec 1836 in White Co., TN, and died Aft. 1900 in Jackson Co., MO?

Children of EBERLE PENDLETON and MARY IRWIN are (Ref. 230):

i. JAMES LEE[11] PENDLETON, b. Abt. 1866, MO; m. LETTIE, 1891, Jackson Co., MO; b. Dec 1864, IN.

641.   ii. CLAUDE L. PENDLETON, b. Aug 1869, MO; d. Aft. 1920, Jackson Co., MO?

iii. GEORGE EBLEY PENDLETON, b. Dec 1870, MO.

iv. ALFRED I. PENDLETON, b. Apr 1872, MO; d. Aft. 1920; m. LULA N.; b. Abt. 1887, MO.

Alfred I. Pendleton (huckster) and family are listed in the 1920 Kansas City, MO census.
- v. MARTHA E. PENDLETON, b. Dec 1876, MO.
- vi. EVERETT S. PENDLETON, b. Nov 1879, MO.

335. JAMES CREW[10] PENDLETON (*JAMES[9], JOHN[8], WILLIAM[7], JOHN[6], PHILIP[5], HENRY[4], HENRY[3], GEORGE[2], GEORGE[1]*) was born Abt. 1845 in KY, and died Aft. 1880 in Jackson Co., MO? He married LAURA HENLEY May 22, 1867 in Jackson Co., MO, daughter of ELIZABETH. She was born Abt. 1848 in KY, and died Aft. 1880 in Jackson Co., MO?

Child of JAMES PENDLETON and LAURA HENLEY is:
- i. MILLIE[11] PENDLETON, b. Abt. 1869, MO.

336. THOMAS J.[10] PENDLETON (*JAMES[9], JOHN[8], WILLIAM[7], JOHN[6], PHILIP[5], HENRY[4], HENRY[3], GEORGE[2], GEORGE[1]*) was born Abt. 1847 in KY, and died Aft. 1920 in Blue, Jackson Co., MO? He married NANCY. She was born Abt. 1857 in MO, and died Bef. 1920 in Jackson Co., MO?

Thomas J. Pendleton, wife Nancy, and brothers Richard and Timothy, are listed in the 1880 Blue, Jackson Co., MO census, pg 75A. Thomas (stillman; oil refinery) and Roland Pendleton (auctioneer) are listed in the 1920 Blue, Jackson Co., MO census.

Child of THOMAS PENDLETON and NANCY is:
- i. ROLAND[11] PENDLETON, b. Abt. 1894, MO.

337. NANCY J.[10] PENDLETON (*ROBERT HARDWICK[9], ISAAC[8], WILLIAM[7], JOHN[6], PHILIP[5], HENRY[4], HENRY[3], GEORGE[2], GEORGE[1]*) was born 1840 in KY, and died 1897 in Trimble Co., KY. She married JOSEPH FOREST BUTLER 1859 in KY, son of JOHN BUTLER and FRANCES J. FARLEY. He was born Feb 14, 1842 in Trimble Co., KY, and died Apr 15, 1914 in Trimble Co., KY.

The biography of Nancy Pendleton's husband was recorded in an early history of Kentucky (Ref.123).

Joseph F. Butler was the fourth of eleven children born to John F. and Frances J. (Farley) Butler. John F. was born in Kentucky and died in 1860; his widow died in 1873. Subject's grandparents were natives of Virginia, moved to Kentucky at an early date, and settled in Trimble County. His grandfather served in the war of 1812, and was killed at a battle in Vincennes, Ind. Joseph F. has followed farming and fruit growing, and owns a fine farm of 147 acres, well improved. In 1864 he enlisted in the Federal service under Col. H. M. Buckley, Fifty-fourth Kentucky Mounted Infantry, Company B, Capt. Robert Young. He served until the close of the war, and received an honorable discharge. In 1859 he was united in marriage with Miss Nancy J. Pendleton, daughter of Robert H. and Sallie (Peak) Pendleton. Mr. Pendleton was a native of Virginia, but moved to Kentucky in 1799, and settled in Trimble County. Eight children were born to Mr. and Mrs. Butler: Benjamin F., Sallie, Mary, Charley, Joseph, Ella, John and Mark C. Mr. Butler is a zealous member of the Christian Church. Politically he is a Democrat.

Joseph Butler and family are listed in the 1880 census, Trimble Co., KY, pg. 447C.

Children of NANCY PENDLETON and JOSEPH BUTLER are (Ref. 231):

  i. BENJAMIN FRANKLIN[11] BUTLER, b. Feb 26, 1860, Trimble Co., KY; d. Abt. 1927, Trimble Co., KY; m. MARY BROOK TROUT; b. Apr 07, 1874, Trimble Co., KY.
  ii. SARAH "SALLIE" BUTLER, b. Mar 1863, Trimble Co., KY.
  iii. MARY ELIZABETH BUTLER, b. Feb 06, 1867, Gentry Co., MO; d. Mar 16, 1948, Trimble Co., KY.
  iv. CHARLES BUTLER, b. 1870, Trimble Co., KY; d. Feb 13, 1923, Trimble Co., KY.
  v. JOSEPH FOSTER BUTLER, b. Mar 23, 1874, Trimble Co., KY; d. Oct 23, 1954, Trimble Co., KY; m. BESSIE BELL HUDSON, Nov 10, 1916; b. Apr 20, 1890.
  vi. ELY BUTLER, b. Feb 07, 1877, KY.
  vii. JOHN ROBERT BUTLER, b. Abt. 1878, Trimble Co., KY.
  viii. MARK COLLIS BUTLER, b. Jun 09, 1882, Trimble Co., KY; d. Oct 05, 1972, Trimble Co., KY; m. MINNIE BASKET SNYDER, Jul 28, 1914.

338. ROBERT HARDWICK[10] PENDLETON (*ROBERT HARDWICK⁹, ISAAC⁸, WILLIAM⁷, JOHN⁶, PHILIP⁵, HENRY⁴, HENRY³, GEORGE², GEORGE¹*) was born Oct 1848 in Trimble Co., KY, and died Jun 21, 1921 in Trimble Co., KY. He married AMANDAH M. Abt. 1875 in Oldham Co., KY. She was born Jan 1851 in IN, and died Aug 30, 1915 in Trimble Co., KY.

Robert Pendleton (farmer) and family are listed in the 1900 Trimble Co., KY census, pg. 225.

Children of ROBERT PENDLETON and AMANDAH M. are:

  i. SALLIE[11] PENDLETON, b. Abt. 1877, Trimble Co., KY.
  ii. MARY PENDLETON, b. Apr 1879, Trimble Co., KY.
  iii. ROBERT HARDWICK PENDLETON, b. Oct 29, 1880, Trimble Co., KY; m. SARAH ELIZABETH.

  The WWI draft card of Robert Hardwick Pendleton lists his residence as Milton, Trimble Co., KY, and occupation as farming (Ref. 210).

  iv. STELLA PENDLETON, b. Nov 1884, KY.
  v. ADDIE PENDLETON, b. Sep 1886, KY.
  vi. BENJAMIN FRANKLIN PENDLETON, b. Mar 02, 1888, Milton, Trimble Co., KY.

  The WWI draft card of Benjamin Franklin Pendleton lists his residence as Milton, Trimble Co., KY, and occupation as farming (Ref. 210). Ben H. Pendleton (1889-1963) and Edna Pendleton (1896-) are buried in Lile Cemetery, Gallatin, Daviess Co., MO (Ref. 232).

  vii. RENNIE HURLEY PENDLETON, b. Nov 07, 1892, Milton, Trimble Co., KY.

  The WWI draft card of Rennie Hurley Pendleton lists his residence as Milton, Trimble Co., KY, and occupation as farming (Ref. 210).

339. ROLAND L.^{10} PENDLETON (*LINDSEY^9, ISAAC^8, WILLIAM^7, JOHN^6, PHILIP^5, HENRY^4, HENRY^3, GEORGE^2, GEORGE^1*) was born Jan 1842 in KY, and died Aft. 1900 in Henry Co., KY? He married BAMBDRY? Abt. 1895. She was born Jan 1866 in KY.

    The family of Roland Pendleton (60), farmer, is listed in the 1900 Henry Co., KY census, pg. 319.

Children of ROLAND PENDLETON and BAMBDRY? are:
    i.   BEULA^{11} PENDLETON, b. Dec 1896, KY.
    ii. MAHETTA PENDLETON, b. Oct 1899, KY.

340. EMILY^{10} PENDLETON (*LINDSEY^9, ISAAC^8, WILLIAM^7, JOHN^6, PHILIP^5, HENRY^4, HENRY^3, GEORGE^2, GEORGE^1*) was born 1844 in KY, and died Aft. 1880 in Henry Co., KY? She married JOHN W. CHILTON Apr 03, 1865 in Henry Co., KY. He was born Abt. 1842 in KY.

    John W. Chilton and family are listed in the 1880 Port Royal, Henry Co., KY census, pg. 83C.

Children of EMILY PENDLETON and JOHN CHILTON are:
    i.   MILDRED^{11} CHILTON, b. Abt. 1866, KY.
    ii.   JAMES L. CHILTON, b. Abt. 1868, KY.
    iii. ISAAC CHILTON, b. Abt. 1870, KY.
    iv. LEVI CHILTON, b. Abt. 1872, KY.
    v.   EMILY CHILTON, b. Abt. 1875.
    vi. WILLIAM T. CHILTON, b. Abt. 1877, KY.
    vii. CALLUS CHILTON, b. Abt. 1879, KY.

341. WILLIAM M.^{10} PENDLETON (*BENJAMIN^9, HENRY^8, HENRY^7, JOHN^6, PHILIP^5, HENRY^4, HENRY^3, GEORGE^2, GEORGE^1*) was born Abt. 1797 in Spotsylvania Co., VA, and died Sep 21, 1842 in Clarke Co., AL. He married MARTHA E. CHRISTMAS Dec 10, 1832 in Clarke Co., AL. She was born 1800 in SC, and died Aft. 1850 in Clarke Co., AL?

    The marriage of William Pendleton and Martha Christmas is recorded in Reference 233. William is listed in the 1840 Clarke Co., AL census. William M. Pendleton was a founder of the Pendleton Academy, and a teacher of high classical attainments (Ref. 234). His obituary was published in The Chicago Historical Society, page 318: "William M Pendleton died near Coffeeville, Clarke co., Ala., Sept. 21, 1842 in his 45th year." Alabama Land Records lists William M. Pendleton in reference to property in St. Stephens township with a date of March 1, 1843. Old St. Stephens is now an historical park. M. E. Pendleton (William's wife) and children are listed in the 1850 Clarke Co., AL census in the household of Felix Christmas.

Children of WILLIAM PENDLETON and MARTHA CHRISTMAS are:
    i.   OCTAVIUS M.^{11} PENDLETON, b. Abt. 1834, Clarke Co., AL.
         Octavius M. Pendleton (27, Teacher, P.S.) is listed in the 1860 Clarke Co., AL census, Grove Hill P.O., pg. 564.

ii. JULIA A. PENDLETON, b. Abt. 1836, Clarke Co., AL; m. THOMAS A. COX, Jan 12, 1855, Clarke Co., AL.

342. JOHN T.[10] PENDLETON *(BENJAMIN[9], HENRY[8], HENRY[7], JOHN[6], PHILIP[5], HENRY[4], HENRY[3], GEORGE[2], GEORGE[1])* was born Abt. 1805 in VA, and died Oct 28, 1878 in Spotsylvania Co., VA? He married HULDAH LEWIS Feb 10, 1831 in Spotsylvania Co., VA, daughter of TRUEMAN LEWIS. She was born Abt. 1803 in VA, and died Aft. 1880 in Spotsylvania Co., VA?

There is a Spotsylvania Co. deed, 2 February 1847, of John T. Pendleton and William R. Powell (executors of Philip Pendleton) to William Lewis (d. 1863) for 171 acres in Spotsylvania County, Virginia. The deed bears affidavits of Stapleton Crutchfield (1808-1859), Claiborne Duvall, and Marshall Johnson of Fredericksburg, VA, cousin of Edmund B. Pendleton. John T. Pendleton (farmer) and family are listed in the 1870 Cortland, Spotsylvania Co., VA census.

Children of JOHN PENDLETON and HULDAH LEWIS are:
   i. MARY ELIZABETH "BETTY"[11] PENDLETON, b. Abt. 1832, VA; m. THOMAS L. DUERSON; b. Abt. 1829, VA.

   Thomas L. Duerson, sergeant, served in the 9th VA Cavalry, Company E., Confederate Army. Thomas L. and Mary E. Duerson are listed in the 1870 Cortland, Spotsylvania Co., VA census. Included in the household is Lilla A. Pendleton (9) who is apparently the daughter of William M. Pendleton and Anne Arnold. Thomas and Mary Duerson are listed in the 1880 census, Spotsylvania Co., VA, pg. 345B.

642. ii. WILLIAM M. PENDLETON, b. 1833, VA; d. Aft. 1870, Spotsylvania Co., VA?
   iii. MARTHA A. PENDLETON, b. Abt. 1835, VA; d. Aft. 1860, Spotsylvania Co., VA?
   iv. JAMES L. PENDLETON, b. 1836, VA; d. Abt. 1864, Civil War; m. BETTIE L. JONES; d. Aft. 1900, Spotsylvania Co., VA?

   James L. Pendleton (farmer) is listed in the 1860 Spotsylvania Co. census in the household of his brother, William M. Pendleton, pg. 354. He was apparently not yet married. He died in prison during the Civil War. Bettie L. Pendleton is listed in the VA Confederate Pension Rolls in 1888 and 1900, Spotsylvania Co., VA.

643. v. JOHN HAMILTON PENDLETON, b. 1838, VA; d. Aft. 1920, Spotsylvania Co., VA?
644. vi. LAWRENCE BATAILLE PENDLETON, b. Aug 11, 1840, Westmoreland, VA; d. Dec 1903, Spotsylvania Co., VA.

343. HUGH CLAIBORNE[10] PENDLETON *(HENRY[9], HENRY[8], HENRY[7], JOHN[6], PHILIP[5], HENRY[4], HENRY[3], GEORGE[2], GEORGE[1])* was born 1807 in VA, and died 1873 in "Old Pendleton Place," Spotsylvania Co., VA. He married (1) MARY ANN SWAN Jan 5, 1830 in Spotsylvania Co., VA, daughter of ROBERT SWAN and MARY

RICKETTS. She was born Bet. 1810 - 1815 in VA, and died Abt. 1839 in Spotsylvania Co., VA? He married (2) MELVINA CARNAHAN Jan 15, 1848, daughter of JOSEPH CARNAHAN and NANCY GIBSON. She was born 1821 in Spotsylvania Co., VA, and died Feb 26, 1883 in Orange Co., VA. He married (3) JOSEPHINE. She was born Abt. 1833 in VA.

Hugh Pendleton, farmer (age 40), is listed in the 1850 Spotsylvania Co., VA census adjacent to the household of his father, Henry Pendleton. Hugh's children were listed with Henry. Also listed were Maryann (28), Asa (0) newborn?, and Nancy Carnahan (60), apparently Melvina's mother. Hugh Claiborne Pendleton died around the same time as his father. Evidently, the land stayed in the family until either Edwin or Lucy Pendleton died and then deed books in Spotsylvania indicate that James Alexander Swan (son of Agnes Ann Pendleton Swan) bought the land, cut off the timber and sold it (Ref. 140).

Children of HUGH PENDLETON and MARY SWAN are (Refs. 235 and 236):
    i.   MARY CATHERINE[11] PENDLETON, b. 1832.
          A Mary Catherine Pendleton (b.1834 in Caroline County, VA, d. abt. 1870 in Caroline County, VA) married William S. Flippo, 1857 in Spotsylvania Co., and is buried at Bethany Baptist, Caroline Co., VA. They had a child, Littleberry Terrell Flippo, b. Oct 4, 1858 in Central Point, Caroline County, VA (Ref. 237).

    ii. EUGENIA PENDLETON, b. 1834; d. young.
    iii. MARIA PENDLETON, b. 1836; d. young.
    iv. VIRGINIA PENDLETON, b. 1839.
    v. WILLIAM H. PENDLETON, b. 1839; d. 1862.

Children of HUGH PENDLETON and MELVINA CARNAHAN are:
    vi. ORIETTA[11] PENDLETON, b. 1848, VA.
645. vii. JOSEPH ALBERT PENDLETON, b. May 30, 1851, VA; d. Feb 15, 1933, Spotsylvania Co., VA.
646. viii. SALLIE A. PENDLETON, b. Sep 20, 1853, VA.
    ix. CHARLES EDWARD PENDLETON, b. Sep 11, 1855, VA; m. KITTY GOODWIN.
          Charles E. Pendleton is listed in court cases in Fredericksburg, VA, Feb 8, 1877, and Mar 12, 1877. He is mentioned in a local Fredericksburg newspaper, 12 Jun 1888, as a murderer 11 years ago, to go on trial in Sep, 1889, and finally seeking parole Feb 14, 1893.

    x. LUCY J. PENDLETON, b. 1857; d. young.
647. xi. JAMES MONROE PENDLETON, b. Dec 1861, VA; d. Aft. 1900.
648. xii. OSCAR L. PENDLETON, b. 1865, VA.

Child of HUGH PENDLETON and JOSEPHINE is:
    xiii. SUSAN[11] PENDLETON, b. 1868.

344. AGNES ANNE[10] PENDLETON *(HENRY[9], HENRY[8], HENRY[7], JOHN[6], PHILIP[5], HENRY[4], HENRY[3], GEORGE[2], GEORGE[1])* was born Abt. 1812 in VA, and died Aft. 1900 in Madison Co., VA? She married (1) BLOXAM HOWARD Jan 17, 1831 in Spotsylvania Co., VA. She married (2) CHARLES WILLIAM SWAN Abt. 1833 in MD, son of ROBERT SWAN and MARY RICKETTS. He was born Abt. 1808 in VA, and died Aft. 1860 in Madison Co., VA?

Susan Pendleton (69) is listed in the household of James H. Lohr, her son-in-law in the 1880 Rapidan, Madison Co., VA census, pg. 343A. Charles W. Swan (farmer) and family are listed in the 1850 and 1860 Madison Co., VA census records.

Children of AGNES PENDLETON and CHARLES SWAN are:

    i.   LUCY JANE[11] SWAN, b. Abt. 1835, VA; m. REUBEN L. LINDSAY.

   ii.   ROBERT HENRY SWAN, b. Feb 22, 1837, VA; m. ALMIRA DAWSON SWAN, Dec 28, 1858.

  iii.   JAMES ALEXANDER SWAN, b. Mar 8, 1839, VA; d. May 21, 1925, Culpeper Co., VA; m. ELIZA ELEN TUCKER, Dec 23, 1861.

   iv.   WILLIAM DUVAL SWAN, b. Mar 21, 1841, VA.

    v.   CORDELIA C. SWAN, b. 1843, VA.

   vi.   EMILY PENDLETON SWAN, b. Abt. 1845, VA.

  vii.   ANNIE WAYLAND SWAN, b. Sep 4, 1847, VA; d. Jun 19, 1926; m. JAMES HENRY LOHR; b. Abt. 1855, VA.

 viii.   CHARLES E. SWAN, b. 1850, Madison Co., VA.

345. FRANCES ANNE[10] PENDLETON *(JOHN[9], HENRY[8], HENRY[7], JOHN[6], PHILIP[5], HENRY[4], HENRY[3], GEORGE[2], GEORGE[1])* was born Jan 30, 1810 in Spotsylvania Co., VA, and died May 12, 1903 in Christian Co., KY. She married ELDREDGE BROCKMAN GARNETT Sep 23, 1834 in KY, son of JAMES GARNETT. He was born May 10, 1813 in Albemarle Co., VA, and died Aft. 1870 in Christian Co., KY?

Eldredge and Frances Garnett and family are listed in the 1850 Christian Co., KY census, District 2, pg. 379, and in the 1860 and 1870 census records, Hopkinsville, Christian Co., KY.

Children of FRANCES PENDLETON and ELDREDGE GARNETT are:

    i.   HELEN L.[11] GARNETT, b. Abt. 1835, KY; m. R. W. MOREHEAD, Feb 1863.

   ii.   VIRGIL A. GARNETT, b. Abt. 1837; d. Nov 16, 1899; m. MAGGIE THOMSON.

  iii.   WILLIAM W. GARNETT, b. Abt. 1838.

   iv.   JOHN P. GARNETT, b. Jan 16, 1841; m. (1) ROSA L. LACY; b. Jun 4, 1852, Christian Co., KY; d. Jun 8, 1890; m. (2) SUE M. TRIMBLE, Mar 4, 1891.

    v.   JAMES B. GARNETT, b. Jul 28, 1845, Christian Co., KY; m. VIRGINIA HEWELL, Oct 1877; d. Nov 30, 1878.

        The following account is from a History of Trigg County (Ref. 238).

        The Honorable James B. Garnett was born on July 28, 1845, near Pembroke, Christian County; he is the youngest of five children born to

Eldred and Frances A. (Pendleton) Garnett. The father was born in Albermarle [sic] County, Va., in 1813, and died on his farm in Christian County, Ky., in 1870. The mother was born in 1810 Orange County, Va., and is now living in Christian County. Our subject has three brothers in Christian County, two engaged in merchandising at Pembroke, the other in farming and teaching school. His sister is the wife of Rev. R. W. Morehead, of Princeton, Ky. In 1866 Mr. Garnett commenced the study of law at the Lebanon Law School, and graduated at this college of learning in the class of 1868. Immediately after he came to Cadiz and located here, and since that time has been actively engaged in the practice of his profession. In 1870 he was elected County Attorney and Commissioner for two years. In August, 1875, he was elected State Senator from the Third Senatorial District, which was composed of the counties of Trigg, Calloway, Lyon and Livingston. In 1880 he was elected Commonwealth's Attorney for the Second Judicial District, comprising the counties of Muhlenburg [sic], Christian, Hopkins, Trigg, Caldwell and Lyon, for the term of six years; this office he still honorably fills. Mr. Garnett was a delegate to the National Democratic Convention at Baltimore in 1872, and at St. Louis in 1876; he was married in October, 1877, to Miss Virginia Hewell, of Tuscaloosa, Ala. This lady died on November 30, 1878"

346. JAMES MADISON[10] PENDLETON (*JOHN*[9], *HENRY*[8], *HENRY*[7], *JOHN*[6], *PHILIP*[5], *HENRY*[4], *HENRY*[3], *GEORGE*[2], *GEORGE*[1]) was born Nov 20, 1811 in Spotsylvania Co., VA, and died Mar 4, 1891 in TN? He married CATHERINE STOCKTON GARNETT Mar 13, 1838, daughter of RICHARD GARNETT and THEODOSIA STOCKTON. She was born 1814 in KY, and died 1898.

"In 1823, two acres of land were bought on the road leading to Fairview, [Christian Co., KY], and the celebrated old brick house was erected and stood for more than sixty years. Rev. William Tandy served as pastor until his death in 1838. Other pastors were Jack Wilson, William Warfield, J. M. Pendleton, Reuben Ross and J. M. Bennett (Ref. 146). In November, 1833, Rev. Pendleton was ordained by Elders Ross, Warfield, Tandy and Rutherford. The life and works of this man of God are too well known to need mention in this connection. He is a man of splendid powers, highly cultivated, but lie is still serving his Master, and after he has been called hence will be time enough for those who know him to speak of his excellencies. In December, 1836, Elder Pendleton withdrew from this church, but he was requested to preach to the congregation as often as convenient (Ref. 239). James M. Pendleton is listed in the in 1840 Warren Co., KY census and in the1850 Warren Co., KY census as a Baptist preacher, District 1, pg. 35. James later was a Baptist clergyman of Upland, PA and the author of "Three Reasons Why I Am a Baptist," "Church Manual," "Christian Doctrines," "Distinctive Principles of Baptists," and "Atonement of Christ." He became professor of Theology at Union Univ., Murfreesboro, Rutherford Co., TN" (Ref. 240).

James M. Pendleton is in a list of applicants to the Southern Claims Commission, Rutherford Co., TN (1871-3) for property taken by the U.S. Govt. during the Civil War. A biographical sketch of James Madison Pendleton (Ref. 241) and his reminiscences (Ref. 242) are listed in the Virginia Historical Society Catalog.

Children of JAMES PENDLETON and CATHERINE GARNETT are:

  i.   LETITIA[11] PENDLETON, b. 1839, Warren Co., KY; d. 1917, Nashville,
       TN?; m. JAMES WATERS, 1860; b. Abt. 1836, TN; d. Aft. 1880.

       James and Letitia Waters are listed in the 1880 census, Davidson Co., TN,
       pg. 354D.

  ii. JOHN MALCOLM PENDLETON, b. 1841, Warren Co., KY; d. Oct 8, 1862,
       Confederate Army, killed in the battle of Perryville, KY.

       The following account is from the Military Annals of Tennessee
       Confederate (Ref. 243).

            Company B, in which John Malcolm Pendleton served, was enlisted in
       May, 1861, at Brownsville, TN. A large majority of the men were natives of
       Haywood County. With but few exceptions they were young men of good
       families and liberally educated. Of the many sad events of this battle [At
       Perryville, KY, on the 8th of October, 1862], this one is given: John M.
       Pendleton, possessing a brilliant mind and thorough education, a son of Dr.
       James M. Pendleton, Professor in Union University, joined Co. B at the
       opening of hostilities. Soon thereafter he was given a commission in the
       commissariat without seeking it. On reading Gen. Butler's famous order to
       his troops in New Orleans, Capt. Pendleton resigned his commission and
       went back to his company, saying, 'I will not stay in a bombproof department
       as long as this insult is flaunted in the face of the women of our Southland.'
       Poor fellow! While the regiment was supporting Carnes's battery just before
       the infantry became engaged, a shell from the enemy exploded just over
       Pendleton's head, and a piece of it crushed through his brain before he had an
       opportunity to fire his gun"

649. iii. FRANCES "FANNY" PENDLETON, b. 1843, Warren Co., KY; d. 1925.
      iv. LILA B. PENDLETON, b. Aug 25, 1850, Warren Co., KY; d. Nov 27, 1932,
           Warren Co., KY; m. BENJAMIN FRANKLIN PROCTOR, Nov 9, 1876,
           Upland, PA; b. Nov 26, 1849, Logan Co., KY; d. Nov 30, 1944, Christian
           Co., KY.

           Mrs. Lila Pendleton Proctor was a member of The National Society of the
           Daughters of the American Revolution (Volume 52, page 397). She is a Gr-
           grand daughter of Henry Pendleton, Jr., and Ann Knight, his wife. Henry
           Pendleton (1744-1800), served as a private, 1780, in the Virginia militia.
           B.F. Proctor, lawyer, and Lila are listed in the 1880 census, Bowling Green,
           KY, pg. 10C and the1910 Bowling Green census.

650. v.   GARNETT PENDLETON, b. 1855, KY; d. 1921, Upland, PA?

347. JOHN THOMPSON[10] PENDLETON (*JOHN*[9], *HENRY*[8], *HENRY*[7], *JOHN*[6],
PHILIP[5], *HENRY*[4], *HENRY*[3], *GEORGE*[2], *GEORGE*[1]) was born Jun 19, 1815 in Christian
Co., KY, and died Aft. 1880 in Nashville, TN? He married (1) JEANETT ERVIN. She
was born Abt. 1819 in Christian Co., KY. He married (2) AMELIA PINCKNEY WEBB
Jan 25, 1858 in Nashville, TN. She was born Abt. 1837 in VA, and died Aft. 1880 in
Nashville, TN?

This is apparently the John Pendleton listed near Frances J. Pendleton in the 1840 Christian Co. census. John Pendleton (druggist) and family are listed in the 1860 and 1880 Nashville, TN census records.

Child of JOHN PENDLETON and JEANETT ERVIN is:
    i.   HENRY ERVIN[11] PENDLETON, b. Aug 26, 1847, TN.

Child of JOHN PENDLETON and AMELIA WEBB is:
    ii. THERESA[11] PENDLETON, b. 1860, TN; m. J. B. DANIEL.

348. CAROLINE AUGUSTA[10] PENDLETON *(JOHN[9], HENRY[8], HENRY[7], JOHN[6], PHILIP[5], HENRY[4], HENRY[3], GEORGE[2], GEORGE[1])* was born Dec 8, 1816 in KY, and died Oct 5, 1876 in Paducah, KY. She married WILLIAM KAY Jul 10, 1845 in Christian Co., KY, son of JAMES KAY and SARAH WAGGENER. He was born Mar 27, 1807 in Culpeper Co., VA, and died Apr 15, 1881 in Lynnville, TN.
    The family of William and Caroline Kay is listed in the 1850 Christian Co., KY census.

Children of CAROLINE PENDLETON and WILLIAM KAY are:
    i.   JOHN FRANCIS[11] KAY, b. Jun 26, 1846, Christian Co., KY; d. Aug 28, 1846.
    ii.   JULIET PENDLETON KAY, b. Oct 1, 1847, Christian Co., KY; m. ELIJAH BROCKMAN RICHARDSON; b. Jul 17, 1840.
    iii. KATIE KAY, b. Jan 7, 1850, Christian Co., KY.
    iv.   CARRIE LEE KAY, b. May 9, 1852; d. Mar 13, 1930, Los Angeles, CA.
    v.   FANNIE THOMPSON KAY, b. May 7, 1860; m. RICHARD NEEL, Dec 18, 1878; b. Abt. 1854.

349. WILLIAM HENRY[10] PENDLETON *(JOHN[9], HENRY[8], HENRY[7], JOHN[6], PHILIP[5], HENRY[4], HENRY[3], GEORGE[2], GEORGE[1])* was born Dec 16, 1820 in Christian Co., KY, and died Mar 3, 1863 in Christian Co., KY. He married ISABELLA MAJORS. She was born Abt. 1825 in KY, and died Aft. 1880 in Atlanta, GA?
    William H. Pendleton is listed in the 1840 Christian Co., KY census and as a merchant in 1850 Christian Co., KY census, pg 375. There were frequent changes in the mercantile houses [of Hopkinsville, KY] and finally Richardson & Williams became proprietors of the leading store which in 1858 was sold to W. H. Pendleton, W. W. Garnett and E. G. Buck. As W. H. Pendleton & Company, they were running in 1861 and closed down when all of the members of the firm entered the Confederate Army (Ref. 146). W.H. Pendleton served in the KY 2nd (Woodward's) Cavalry, Company A, CSA. "With feelings of regret we have heard of the death of Bro. Wm. H. Pendleton, one of the Deacons of this church which was caused by drowning in Duck River about the 3rd of March, [1863]" March (Ref. 244). "William H. Pendleton's name will bring to the memory of those who knew him best one of the most active, earnest and faithful members of this church. A close Bible student. gifted in prayer and exhortation, and whether in the Sunday-school, in the prayer-meeting, or in the financial interests of the church, he was alike not only efficient but enthusiastic in his work. With many positive

elements of character, he was aggressive in his nature, and his heart was ever enlisted in the work of the Lord. A life of great usefulness was spread out before him, but the summons came, and he exchanged the toils of earth for a crown in heaven" (Ref. 239). The property of William Pendleton is mentioned in the 1871 description of the boundary of the original Hopkinsville School District No. 37, Christian Co., KY (Ref. 146).

Isabella Pendleton (55) and her daughter, Kate Pendleton (23) are listed in the 1880 Atlanta, GA census in the household of Theresa A. Kenny.

Children of WILLIAM PENDLETON and ISABELLA MAJORS are:
651. i. JOHN THOMAS[11] PENDLETON, b. Abt. 1845, Christian Co., KY; d. Oct 5, 1922, Atlanta, GA.
      ii. KATHERINE PENDLETON, b. Abt. 1856, Christian Co., KY.

350. EDMUND WALLER[10] PENDLETON *(JOHN[9], HENRY[8], HENRY[7], JOHN[6], PHILIP[5], HENRY[4], HENRY[3], GEORGE[2], GEORGE[1])* was born Dec 1, 1822 in Christian Co., KY, and died Dec 4, 1870 in Christian Co., KY? He married ANNE ELIZA BARCLAY 1846. She was born 1829 in KY, and died 1888 in Christian Co., KY?
      The following account is from the History of Christian County (Ref. 146).

A great many citizens from the surrounding country had collected to see the fight [Col. Johnson's Confederate regiment and Federal forces stationed at Russelville under Gen. McCook] or hear the news, and when Johnson's men came dashing through, and the head of the Federal column appeared, they also joined in the rout and made still greater confusion. The Federals followed as far as the country and then gave up the chase. Many citizens were captured and taken to Hopkinsville for trial. Among them were Jas. A. Radford, then an old man, and E. W. Pendleton. They were dismounted. Mr. Radlord was forced to get on a mule and Mr. Pendleton to mount behind him and ride to Hopkinsville"

E.W. Pendleton (farmer) and family are listed in the 1870 Christian Co., KY census, District 3.

Children of EDMUND PENDLETON and ANNE BARCLAY are:
652. i. PHILANDER BARCLAY[11] PENDLETON, b. Jul 4, 1852, Logan Co., KY; d. Aft. 1904, Christian Co., KY?
      ii. CAROLINE PENDLETON, b. Abt. 1863, Christian Co., KY; m. (1) HERSCHEL PORTER; m. (2) FRANK RICHARDSON, JUDGE, May 12, 1884, Christian Co., KY; b. 1861.
          Mrs. Carrie Pendleton Porter was a member of The National Society of the Daughters of the American Revolution (Volume 55, page 312).

653. iii. LOOLYE B. PENDLETON, b. Abt. 1867, Christian Co., KY; d. 1964, Clarksville, TN.

351. EMILY LOUISA[10] PENDLETON *(JOHN[9], HENRY[8], HENRY[7], JOHN[6], PHILIP[5], HENRY[4], HENRY[3], GEORGE[2], GEORGE[1])* was born Oct 13, 1825 in KY, and died Aft. 1870 in Todd Co., KY? She married BENJAMIN B. DOWNER Dec 20, 1847 in Todd

Co., KY, son of BENJAMIN DOWNER and ELIZABETH SLAUGHTER. He was born Aug 10, 1819 in Todd Co., KY, and died Aft. 1884.

Benjamin Downer and family are listed in the 1860 Todd Co., KY census, pg. 715 and in the 1870 Fairview, Todd Co., KY census. "James Waller Downer [his son], of Hopkinsville, was born in Todd County, Kentucky, on the 20th day of November, 1853. His father came from Virginia to Kentucky in 1811, and located in that county. Benjamin Downer followed farming in Todd County for many years, and was an influential and highly respected citizen of the community in which he lived. He married Emily L. Pendleton, whose people also came from Virginia, and located in Christian County, Kentucky, in the year 1812. Her brother, James M. Pendleton, D.D., a minister of the Baptist denomination, became a prominent divine, and was the author of a number of works on theological subjects" (Ref. 123).

Children of EMILY PENDLETON and BENJAMIN DOWNER are:
    i.   WILLIAM K.[11] DOWNER, b. 1848, KY.
   ii.   MARY "ADDIE" DOWNER, b. 1850, KY.
  iii.   FRANK N. DOWNER, b. Abt. 1852, KY.
  iv.   JAMES WALLER DOWNER, b. Nov 20, 1853, Todd Co., KY.
   v.   LIZZIE DOWNER, b. Abt. 1856, KY.
  vi.   JOHN P. DOWNER, b. Jan 28, 1858, Todd Co., KY; m. JENNIE KIRBY, Dec 23, 1884.

The biography of John Downer is included in an early history of Kentucky (Ref. 123).

> Prof. John P. Downer was born January 28, 1858, near Fairview, Todd Co., Ky., and is a son of Benjamin and Emily L. (Pendleton) Downer, who had born to them five sons and four daughters, of whom our subject is the sixth. The father was born in Todd County in 1819, as a leading farmer of that county and a member of the Methodist Episcopal Church. He was a son of Benjamin and Elizabeth (Slaughter) Downer, who came from Spottsylvania County, Va., and settled in Todd County about 1809. Elizabeth (Slaughter) Downer was a daughter of John S. Slaughter, who married Susan Brown in 1779 and reared thirteen children. John S. Slaughter was a son of John Slaughter, and he a son of Francis Slaughter, and he the son or grandson of a Welshman, who settled in Virginia in its early days. The mother of Prof. Downer was a daughter of John Pendleton, who came from Spottsylvania County, Va., in 1812, and settled in southern Kentucky; he was a teacher and surveyor. Prof. Downer was reared on a farm, and received a good common school education. At the age of eighteen he entered Cumberland University, at Lebanon, Tenn., from which he graduated in the spring of 1881 as A. B. In the fall of the same year he was engaged as assistant in Smith's Grove College under the management of Rev. R. W. Hooker. In 1882 he moved to Franklin and taught one term, when he returned to Smith's Grove, and with Prof. John O. Beck opened Smith's Grove College. In September, 1884, he took entire charge of the college and leased the buildings and grounds for a term of years. English, the sciences and the classics embrace the three courses of study in the college. There is also a musical department. The Professor is thorough and is one of the leading educators in the State. The college is located in a beautiful grove in the village surrounded by a beautiful

country, and for health is unsurpassed. December 23, 1884, the Professor was united in marriage with Jennie Kirby, daughter of David and Lydia (Bohannon) Kirby, Prof. Downer is a member of the Baptist and his wife of the Cumberland Presbyterian Church.

   vii.   CARRIE DOWNER, b. Abt. 1861, KY.
  viii.   EMILY L. DOWNER, b. Abt. 1864, KY.
   ix.   BENJAMIN R. DOWNER, b. Abt. 1867, KY.

352. CYRUS NEVILLE[10] PENDLETON *(JOHN[9], HENRY[8], HENRY[7], JOHN[6], PHILIP[5], HENRY[4], HENRY[3], GEORGE[2], GEORGE[1])* was born Feb 19, 1831 in Christian Co., KY, and died Aug 30, 1899 in Christian Co., KY. He married ELLA POPE GORIN Jun 26, 1860 in Logan Co., KY, daughter of JOHN GORIN and ELIZA WILSON. She was born Jul 5, 1835 in Russellville, Logan Co., KY, and died Aug 30, 1925 in Christian Co., KY.

C.N. Pendleton is listed in Logan Co. in "Lawyers in Kentucky, 1859." C.N. Pendleton served in the Confederate Army, 1st Regiment, Kentucky Cavalry (Helms'). Cyrus was elected State Senator in 1875 from Christian County. He is listed in the 1880 census, Pembroke, Christian Co., KY as a farmer. Of professional gentlemen, Pembroke, Christian Co. boasts three lawyers [in 1884], one of them an ex-State Senator, Hon. C. N. Pendleton (Ref. 245).

Children of CYRUS PENDLETON and ELLA GORIN are (Ref. 246):
           i.   JULIET[11] PENDLETON, b. Apr 4, 1861, KY; d. Feb 9, 1865.
654.   ii.   MARY FRANCES PENDLETON, b. May 26, 1863, KY.
          iii.   FLORENCE PENDLETON, b. Mar 15, 1866, KY; d. 1880.
655.   iv.   NEVILLE PENDLETON, b. Jan 3, 1869, Christian Co., KY; d. 1949, Albuquerque, NM.
           v.   GEORGE CYRUS PENDLETON, b. Feb 15, 1872, KY; d. 1887.
          vi.   EDWARD D. PENDLETON, b. Apr 5, 1875, KY; m. NETTIE VIRGINIA MORRIS; b. Abt. 1880.
656.   vii.   JAMES MONTAGUE PENDLETON, b. Aug 24, 1880, KY; d. Mar 10, 1942, Daviess Co., KY.

353. JANE AGNES[10] PENDLETON *(RICE[9], JOHN[8], HENRY[7], JOHN[6], PHILIP[5], HENRY[4], HENRY[3], GEORGE[2], GEORGE[1])* was born Abt. 1828 in VA, and died Apr 2, 1874 in Louisa Co., VA. She married JOHN CHEW CAMMACK Jan 18, 1844 in Spotsylvania Co., VA. He was born Sep 9, 1819 in VA, and died Dec 6, 1872 in Louisa Co., VA.

John and Jane Cammack are listed in the 1850 Spotsylvania Co. census, pg. 414, in the household of a physician. John C. Cammack and family are listed in the 1870 Louisa Co., VA census.

Children of JANE PENDLETON and JOHN CAMMACK are:
           i.   JOHN C.[11] CAMMACK, b. Abt. 1851.
          ii.   RICE P. CAMMACK, b. Abt. 1853.
         iii.   SAM CAMMACK, b. Abt. 1854.

354. MARY E.[10] PENDLETON *(RICE[9], JOHN[8], HENRY[7], JOHN[6], PHILIP[5], HENRY[4], HENRY[3], GEORGE[2], GEORGE[1])* was born Abt. 1829 in VA. She married GEORGE PHILIP GOODLOE Sep 25, 1845 in Spotsylvania Co., VA. He was born Abt. 1821 in VA, and died Aft. 1880.

Philip (29) and Mary (21) Goodloe are listed in the household of Elizabeth Goodloe (57), presumably his mother, in the 1850 Spotsylvania Co. census.

Child of MARY PENDLETON and GEORGE GOODLOE is:
  i. ELIZA[11] GOODLOE, b. Abt. 1849.

355. MALVINA RICE[10] PENDLETON *(RICE[9], JOHN[8], HENRY[7], JOHN[6], PHILIP[5], HENRY[4], HENRY[3], GEORGE[2], GEORGE[1])* was born 1834 in VA, and died Apr 23, 1878. She married WILLIAM FESTUS CHILES May 29, 1856 in VA. He was born 1830 in VA, and died 1877.

Notes for MALVINA RICE PENDLETON:
Malvina Pendleton (16) is listed in the household of Robert R. Taylor, Physician in the 1850 Goochland Co., VA census. Perhaps she was a nursing student. The marriage of W.R. Chiles and Malvina R. Pendleton, Spotsylvania, was announced in the Daily Express (Petersburg, VA) on May 31, 1856, page 2, column 4. She had 9 children; 5 died in infancy. William Festus Chiles was a farmer and merchant of Louisa Co., VA.

Children of MALVINA PENDLETON and WILLIAM CHILES are:
  i. ELMORE PENDLETON[11] CHILES, b. 1857, VA; d. 1934, Alleghany Co., VA?; m. EMMA J. LEMON; b. Abt. 1867, VA; d. Aft. 1910, Alleghany Co., VA?
  ii. NANNIE W. CHILES, b. 1859; d. 1892; m. GRAHAM ROBINSON.
  iii. MARY GEORGE CHILES.
  iv. EDGAR FESTUS CHILES.
  v. ROSA PENDLETON CHILES, b. Jan 28, 1866, Louisa Co., VA; d. Washington DC?
  vi. WALTER FESTUS CHILES.
  vii. JANE AGNES CHILES.
  viii. MABEL CLARE CHILES, b. 1875; d. 1927; m. I. D. BOYD; d. 1929.

356. CHESLEY THACKER[10] PENDLETON *(JOHN[9], JOHN[8], HENRY[7], JOHN[6], PHILIP[5], HENRY[4], HENRY[3], GEORGE[2], GEORGE[1])* was born Mar 6, 1824 in Adair Co., KY, and died Aft. 1900 in Metcalfe Co., KY? He married (1) ELIZA JANE PULLIAM Oct 13, 1842 in Adair Co., KY, daughter of A. C. PULLIAM. She was born Abt. 1826 in Barren Co., KY, and died Oct 6, 1858 in Adair Co., KY. He married (2) MARTHA J. JEFFRIES Jan 11, 1861 in Metcalfe Co., KY. She was born Abt. 1828 in KY, and died Aft. 1880.

Chesley Pendleton (farmer) and family are listed as in 1850 Adair Co., KY census, pg 507. Chelsey and Eliza J. Pendleton are listed as grantees of 25 acres along the E. Fk. Watercourse, Adair Co., as heirs of A.C. Pulliam. The survey date was Feb 11, 1857. C.T. Pendleton is also listed (with Browning, R. L.) in reference to 70 acres,

Metcalfe Co., E. Fk Little Barren Creek on Dec 29, 1868 (Ref. 247). Chesley is listed in the Adair Co. 1860 Census, 1st District, Columbia and as a farmer in the 1870 and 1880 Metcalfe Co., East Fork Precinct.

The U.S. Federal Census Mortality Schedule, 1860, Adair Co. lists Eliza J Pendleton: Cause of death, Typhoid Fever.

Children of CHESLEY PENDLETON and ELIZA PULLIAM are:
657.   i.   JOHN A.[11] PENDLETON, b. Oct 23, 1843, Adair Co., KY; d. May 17, 1892, Metcalfe Co., KY.
658.   ii. MARY ANN PENDLETON, b. 1845, Adair Co., KY; d. 1877, Metcalfe Co., KY.
659.   iii. JAMES H. PENDLETON, b. Mar 1848, Adair Co., KY; d. Apr 15, 1928, Adair Co., KY.
       iv. ELIZABETH J. PENDLETON, b. Abt. 1852, Adair Co., KY.
       v.   MARTHA J. PENDLETON, b. Abt. 1854, Adair Co., KY.
            "Benjamin F. Taylor married, on the 12th of October, 1873, Mattie Pendleton, of Metcalfe County, Ky.; to this union was born one son, James, October 12, 1877. He entered the University of Louisville, from which he graduated with honors, and took his degree of M. D. in 1878" (Ref. 123).

357. ABNER J.[10] PENDLETON (*JOHN[9], JOHN[8], HENRY[7], JOHN[6], PHILIP[5], HENRY[4], HENRY[3], GEORGE[2], GEORGE[1]*) was born Mar 25, 1825 in Adair Co., KY, and died Jan 25, 1879 in Metcalfe Co., KY. He married NANCY JANE STEPHENS Nov 2, 1845 in Adair Co., KY, daughter of ELIJAH STEPHENS and DIZA PARMLEY. She was born Mar 12, 1821 in Hopkins Co., MO, and died Feb 1, 1898 in Metcalfe Co., KY.

Abner Pendleton, farmer, is listed in the 1850, 1860, and 1870 Adair Co., KY census records. Abner is listed as grantee of 7 acres along the Little Barren River, Metcalfe Co., KY, Aug 27, 1869 (Ref. 248). Nancy Pendleton is listed as head of household in the 1880 census, Metcalfe Co., KY, with Alford A., John, Hiram, Sarah P., and Thomas.

Children of ABNER PENDLETON and NANCY STEPHENS are:
660.   i.   MARY JANE[11] PENDLETON, b. Nov 16, 1845, Adair Co., KY; d. May 6, 1935, Metcalfe Co., KY.
       ii.   LUCY B. PENDLETON, b. Abt. 1847, Adair Co., KY.
661.   iii. ELIZABETH ELLEN PENDLETON, b. Jul 1, 1848, Metcalfe Co., KY.
662.   iv.   ABNER J. PENDLETON, JR., b. Jan 1, 1853, Metcalfe Co., KY; d. Sep 27, 1904, Metcalfe Co., KY.
663.   v.   KIZZIAH PENDLETON, b. Feb 10, 1855, Metcalfe Co., KY; d. Jan 8, 1934, Metcalfe Co., KY.
664.   vi.   JOHN A. PENDLETON, b. Jun 1, 1857, Metcalfe Co., KY; d. Oct 30, 1944, Garrard Co., KY.
665.   vii. HIRAM PENDLETON, b. Nov 30, 1858, Metcalfe Co., KY; d. Dec 21, 1951, Cincinnati, OH.
       viii. RICE PENDLETON, b. Jun 1860, Adair Co., KY; d. Oct 1860, Adair Co., KY.

Rice Pendleton is listed in the U.S. Federal Census Adair Co., KY
Mortality Schedules, 1860: Age, 4/12; Cause of Death, Fits.

666.   ix.   SARAH PORTER PENDLETON, b. Feb 10, 1862, Metcalfe Co., KY; d. Dec 6, 1947, Metcalfe Co., KY.

667.   x.   THOMAS CHESLEY PENDLETON, b. Jun 9, 1865, Metcalfe Co., KY; d. Oct 7, 1908, Metcalfe Co., KY?

358. JOHN HIRAM[10] PENDLETON *(JOHN[9], JOHN[8], HENRY[7], JOHN[6], PHILIP[5], HENRY[4], HENRY[3], GEORGE[2], GEORGE[1])* was born Mar 25, 1825 in Adair Co., KY, and died Abt. 1860 in Adair Co., KY? He married SARAH FRANCES PULLIAM Nov 5, 1850 in Adair Co., KY, daughter of A. C. PULLIAM. She was born Abt. 1836 in Adair Co., KY, and died Aft. 1860.

John Pendleton is listed as a farmer in the 1850 Adair Co, KY census; living with Mary (54) presumably his mother. John Hiram Pendleton is listed as grantee of 220 acres along the East Fork, Little Barren River on May 26, 1852 and of 25 acres on Jul 8, 1857 (Ref. 247). Sarah Pendleton and family are listed in the 1860 Adair Co., KY census.

Children of JOHN PENDLETON and SARAH PULLIAM are (Ref. 249):
668.   i.   THEOPHILIS[11] PENDLETON, b. Abt. 1851, Adair Co., KY; d. Apr 8, 1922, Metcalfe Co., KY.
      ii.   ELLIS PENDLETON, b. Abt. 1853, Adair Co., KY.
      iii.   CURTIS PENDLETON, b. Abt. 1857, Adair Co., KY.
669.   iv.   SARAH FRANCES BECK PENDLETON, b. Nov 1, 1859, Adair Co., KY; d. Oct 18, 1946, Adair Co., KY.

359. JOHN HAMILTON[10] PENDLETON *(ROBERT YATES[9], PHILIP[8], HENRY[7], JOHN[6], PHILIP[5], HENRY[4], HENRY[3], GEORGE[2], GEORGE[1])* was born Abt. 1821 in Christian Co., KY, and died 1858 in Christian Co., KY? He married MARGARET HERNDON GERRELL Nov 20, 1844 in Caroline Co., VA, daughter of BLAND GERRELL and ELIZABETH PENDLETON. She was born Abt. 1824 in VA, and died Aft. 1860.

John H. Pendleton is listed as a farmer in the 1850 Christian Co., KY census, pg 372. "The Baptist Church was the offspring of one of the oldest churches in [Christian] county, the old Bethel church. In 1814 it became a sort of union church of the West Fork Church, and in 1816 became an independent body at Salubria Springs. John Pendleton served as clerk until his death in 1858" (Ref. 146). Margrit H. Pendleton (58), sister-in-law of Robert Yates Pendleton, Jr., is listed in Robert's household in the 1880 Christian Co., KY census.

Children of JOHN PENDLETON and MARGARET GERRELL are:
670.   i.   MARY ELLEN[11] PENDLETON, b. Abt. 1848; d. 1875, Christian Co., KY.
671.   ii.   ANNIE PENDLETON, b. Abt. 1851, KY.

360. SARAH ANNE[10] PENDLETON *(ROBERT YATES[9], PHILIP[8], HENRY[7], JOHN[6], PHILIP[5], HENRY[4], HENRY[3], GEORGE[2], GEORGE[1])* was born Abt. 1825 in Christian

Co., KY, and died 1866 in Christian Co., KY. She married ROBERT WILSON GARRETT, son of ISAAC GARRETT and JANE RADFORD. He was born 1821, and died 1898.

Child of SARAH PENDLETON and ROBERT GARRETT is:
    i. NANNIE AGEE[11] GARRETT.

361. ROBERT YATES[10] PENDLETON, JR. *(ROBERT YATES[9], PHILIP[8], HENRY[7], JOHN[6], PHILIP[5], HENRY[4], HENRY[3], GEORGE[2], GEORGE[1])* was born Dec 1827 in Christian Co., KY, and died Aft. 1900 in Christian Co., KY. He married HELEN SLAUGHTER May 15, 1865 in Vanderburgh Co., IN, daughter of ARMISTEAD G. SLAUGHTER and MARIA LOUISE YANCEY. She was born Aug 1844 in KY, and died Jan 20, 1922 in Christian Co., KY.

    The personal history of Robert Pendleton is included in Perrin's early Christian Co. biographies (Ref. 239).

    Robert Y. Pendleton, was born in Christian County, KY, December 7, 1828, and has continued to be a resident of the same to the present time. His father, Robert Y. Pendleton, Sr., was born in Spotsylvania County, VA, September 23, 1792 and came to Christian County, KY, previous to the war of 1812; but after one year returned to Virginia and entered the army, then returned to this county in 1815, and on December 24, 1816, was married to Miss Mary R., daughter of John Rawlins of Christian County, Ky. From this union sprang: John H,, Sarah A. (Garrett), Eleanor, Robert Y., our subject, and Joseph H. Subject's father died May 31, 1867; his mother, October 6, 1835. His grandfather, Philip Doderige Pendleton, was a noted Baptist minister in Virginia. Subject's vocation is that of a farmer, in which he has been successful, being at present the owner of 700 acres of land, most of which is valuable, and in a fine state of cultivation. On May 15, 1865, he was married to Hiss Helen, daughter of A. G. and Maria (Yancy) Slaughter, of Christian County. Armistead G. Slaughter was born in Virginia, and died at Hopkinsville, Ky., in May, 1874. To subject and wife were born two children, viz.: Robert Y., Jr., March 14, 1866, and John, October 6, 1868. Mr. Pendleton's educational advantages were such as the common schools of the country afforded in his youth, but he has improved his opportunities by reading the works of standard authors, and the current literature of the day. He is a member of the Pembroke Masonic Lodge, and in politics a Democrat.

    Robert is listed in the 1880 Pembroke, Christian Co., KY census as a farmer along with Hellen (sic), Robert Y. (14), John (11), and Margrit H., sister in law (58). Robert Y (farmer), Helen, and John H. (hardware salesman) are listed in the 1900 Christian Co., KY census, pg. 127a (Pembroke).

Children of ROBERT PENDLETON and HELEN SLAUGHTER are:
672.   i. ROBERT YATES[11] PENDLETON III, b. Mar 1866, Christian Co., KY; d. Apr 8, 1952, Christian Co., KY.
       ii. JOHN H. PENDLETON, b. Oct 6, 1868, Christian Co., KY; d. Aft. 1900, Christian Co., KY?
          John H. Pendleton is listed in Ferrell's High School Roster, '85-'86, Christian County.

362. JOSEPH HENRY[10] GERRELL *(ELIZABETH[9] PENDLETON, PHILIP[8], HENRY[7], JOHN[6], PHILIP[5], HENRY[4], HENRY[3], GEORGE[2], GEORGE[1])* was born Abt. 1815 in VA, and died Aft. 1855 in VA? He married LOUISA BURRUS PENDLETON Dec 3, 1840, daughter of ROBERT PENDLETON and ELIZABETH BURRUS. She was born Abt. 1820 in VA.

Children are listed above under (**170**) Louisa Burrus Pendleton.

363. MARGARET HERNDON[10] GERRELL *(ELIZABETH[9] PENDLETON, PHILIP[8], HENRY[7], JOHN[6], PHILIP[5], HENRY[4], HENRY[3], GEORGE[2], GEORGE[1])* was born Abt. 1824 in VA, and died Aft. 1860. She married JOHN HAMILTON PENDLETON Nov 20, 1844 in Caroline Co., VA, son of ROBERT PENDLETON and MARY RAWLINGS. He was born Abt. 1821 in Christian Co., KY, and died 1858 in Christian Co., KY?

Children are listed above under (**359**) John Hamilton Pendleton.

364. MARY ALLEN[10] PENDLETON *(EDMUND[9], CURTIS[8], HENRY[7], JOHN[6], PHILIP[5], HENRY[4], HENRY[3], GEORGE[2], GEORGE[1])* was born Sep 12, 1819 in Clark Co., KY. She married JOHN CUTRIGHT LARY Oct 3, 1850 in Clark Co., KY.
    Surety for the marriage of Mary Allen Pendleton was provided by Virgil M. Pendleton, her brother.

Children of MARY PENDLETON and JOHN LARY are:
    i.   ALLEN P.[11] LARY, b. Aug 17, 1856, Bourbon Co., KY.
   ii.   AMELIA LARY.
  iii.   JOHN CURTIS LARY.
   iv.   MARY LARY.

365. VIRGIL M.[10] PENDLETON *(EDMUND[9], CURTIS[8], HENRY[7], JOHN[6], PHILIP[5], HENRY[4], HENRY[3], GEORGE[2], GEORGE[1])* was born May 7, 1821 in Clark Co., KY, and died Mar 23, 1863 in Clark Co., KY. He married MARY JANE CHAMBERLAIN Mar 31, 1846, daughter of ELISHA CHAMBERLAIN. She was born Abt. 1830 in KY, and died Aft. 1860 in Des Moines, Iowa?
    Virgil M. Pendleton (lawyer) and family are listed in the 1860 Des Moines, Iowa census. Virgil M. Pendleton enlisted in the 1st Infantry, Company G, Confederate Army, as private on 01 Jun 1861, Owensboro, KY. He mustered out at Richmond, 14 May 1862. Virgil [W.] Pendleton enlisted as a Captain on 10 Sep, 1862, Burlington, IA. He was Captain of Company D, 8th KY Confederate Cavalry and died during the Civil War at Mt. Sterling, KY on 23 Mar 1863. He is buried in the Allen-Pendleton family grave yard in Clark Co., KY. He is said to have been wounded and then rescued by his cousin, David J. Pendleton, at the battle of Mt. Sterling, KY (Ref. 101).

Children of VIRGIL PENDLETON and MARY CHAMBERLAIN are:
    i.   WILLIAM[11] PENDLETON, b. 1850, KY.
   ii.   ELISHA CHAMBERLAIN PENDLETON, b. Abt. 1856, KY.

iii. IDA PENDLETON, b. Abt. 1858, Iowa.
iv. JEANNETTE PENDLETON.

366. HARVEY B.¹⁰ PENDLETON *(JOHN⁹, CURTIS⁸, HENRY⁷, JOHN⁶, PHILIP⁵, HENRY⁴, HENRY³, GEORGE², GEORGE¹)* was born 1811 in KY, and died Aft. 1850 in Todd Co., KY? He married LOUISA M. CARNALL, daughter of GEORGE CARNALL and BETSEY. She was born 1831 in VA.

Harvey Pendleton (farmer) and family are listed in the 1850 Todd Co., KY census, District 1, pg 233

Children of HARVEY PENDLETON and LOUISA CARNALL are:
i. MARTHA A.¹¹ PENDLETON, b. Abt. 1849, KY; d. Bef. 1884, KY.
673. ii. JAMES R. PENDLETON, b. Nov 20, 1850, Todd Co., KY; d. Oct 15, 1925, Todd Co., KY.
iii. CENARA PENDLETON, b. Aft. 1850; d. Bef. 1884.

367. NANCY C.¹⁰ PENDLETON *(JOHN⁹, CURTIS⁸, HENRY⁷, JOHN⁶, PHILIP⁵, HENRY⁴, HENRY³, GEORGE², GEORGE¹)* was born Abt. 1815 in Todd Co., KY, and died Aft. 1884 in Todd Co., KY? She married JAMES T. GRADY Nov 19, 1835 in Todd Co., KY, son of JESSE GRADY. He was born Abt. 1815 in Todd Co., KY, and died Aft. 1870 in Todd Co., KY?

Children of NANCY PENDLETON and JAMES GRADY are:
i. MARY E.¹¹ GRADY, b. Abt. 1836, KY.
ii. NANNIE C. GRADY, b. Abt. 1841, KY.
iii. SARAH F. GRADY, b. Abt. 1841, KY; m. ANDREW NEWTON MOORE, Mar 24, 1864, Todd Co., KY; b. Jun 2, 1840, Todd Co., KY; d. Aft. 1884.
iv. ROBERT R. GRADY, b. Sep 28, 1842, KY.
v. LUCY P. GRADY, b. Abt. 1844, KY.
vi. REBECCA GRADY, b. 1850, KY.

368. SARAH ANN¹⁰ PENDLETON *(JOHN⁹, CURTIS⁸, HENRY⁷, JOHN⁶, PHILIP⁵, HENRY⁴, HENRY³, GEORGE², GEORGE¹)* was born Abt. 1820 in KY. She married (1) WILLIAM GRADY Oct 6, 1842 in Todd Co., KY. She married (2) EDWARD HATSELL Bef. 1850. He was born Abt. 1823 in TN.

Children of SARAH PENDLETON and WILLIAM GRADY are:
i. REBECCA¹¹ GRADY, b. 1843, KY.
ii. JOHN GRADY, b. 1845, KY.

369. ELIZA REBECCA¹⁰ PENDLETON *(JOHN⁹, CURTIS⁸, HENRY⁷, JOHN⁶, PHILIP⁵, HENRY⁴, HENRY³, GEORGE², GEORGE¹)* was born Oct 19, 1822 in Todd Co., KY, and died Aft. 1880. She married REUBEN O. MANION Sep 2, 1842 in Todd Co., KY, son of JAMES MANION and JANE WINDERS? He was born 1823 in Todd Co., KY, and died Aft. 1884.

Children of ELIZA PENDLETON and REUBEN MANION are:
  i.   JAMES A.[11] MANION, b. Abt. 1842, KY.
  ii. JOHN A. MANION, b. Abt. 1844, KY.
  iii. MARY C. MANION, b. Abt. 1844, KY.
  iv. SALLIE ELIZABETH MANION, b. Oct 29, 1845, KY; d. Aft. 1884; m.
       BENJAMIN R. TAYLOR; b. Jun 4, 1837; d. Oct 26, 1879.
          "Mrs. Sallie Taylor was born in Todd Co, KY on Oct 29, 1845. Her father,
       Reuben O. Manion, was born in this county in 1828. He is the son of James
       Manion, a native of South Carolina, who lived until 1849. Subject's mother
       was Eliza R. Pendleton, born Oct 19, 1822, daughter of John & Rebecca
       (Reed) Pendleton of Todd Co, KY" (Ref. 250).

  v.   NANCY J. MANION, b. Jan 1850, Todd Co., KY.

370. LUCINDA G.[10] PENDLETON *(WILLIAM CURTIS[9], CURTIS[8], HENRY[7], JOHN[6], PHILIP[5], HENRY[4], HENRY[3], GEORGE[2], GEORGE[1])* was born 1829 in KY, and died in Muhlenberg Co., KY? She married JOHN A. MANSFIELD Aug 21, 1845 in Montgomery, KY. He was born Abt. 1825 in KY.

Children of LUCINDA PENDLETON and JOHN MANSFIELD are:
  i.   MARY E.[11] MANSFIELD, b. 1846.
  ii.   JAMES R. MANSFIELD, b. 1848.
  iii. THOMAS MANSFIELD, b. 1850.
  iv.   L. V. MANSFIELD, b. 1852.
  v.   BEN F. MANSFIELD, b. 1853.
  vi.   OLIVER A. MANSFIELD, b. Jul 1, 1855.
  vii. HENRY C. MANSFIELD, b. Abt. 1858.
  viii. NANNIE MANSFIELD, b. Abt. 1864.
  ix.   JOHN W. MANSFIELD, b. Abt. 1866.
  x.   ROBERT T. MANSFIELD, b. Abt. 1868.
  xi.   ELLER H. MANSFIELD, b. Abt. 1872.

371. FANNY R.[10] PENDLETON *(THOMAS W.[9], CURTIS[8], HENRY[7], JOHN[6], PHILIP[5], HENRY[4], HENRY[3], GEORGE[2], GEORGE[1])* was born 1847 in KY, and died Aft. 1900 in Daviess Co., KY? She married WOOD. He was born in Ireland.

Child of FANNY PENDLETON and WOOD is:
  i.   WALTER P.[11] WOOD, b. Abt. 1886, KY.

372. ISAIAH[10] PENDLETON *(THOMAS W.[9], CURTIS[8], HENRY[7], JOHN[6], PHILIP[5], HENRY[4], HENRY[3], GEORGE[2], GEORGE[1])* was born 1860 in KY, and died Aft. 1910 in Owensboro, KY? He married CLARA T. She was born Abt. 1864 in KY.
       Isaiah Pendleton (carpenter - construction) and family are listed in the 1910 Daviess Co., KY census, Owensboro.

Children of ISAIAH PENDLETON and CLARA T. are:
  i.   NANNIE LEE[11] PENDLETON, b. Abt. 1893, KY.
  ii. MILDRED F. PENDLETON, b. Abt. 1903, KY.

373. CLARISSA[10] PENDLETON (*THACKER*[9], *RICE*[8], *HENRY*[7], *JOHN*[6], *PHILIP*[5], *HENRY*[4], *HENRY*[3], *GEORGE*[2], *GEORGE*[1]) was born Aug 1817 in KY, and died Jan 3, 1854 in Bath Co., KY. She married WALTER K. KERRICK Jan 26, 1836 in Winchester, Clark Co., KY. He was born Feb 2, 1816 in Fayette Co., KY, and died Jan 9, 1896 in Harrison Co., KY.

Children of CLARISSA PENDLETON and WALTER KERRICK are:
  i.   MARY ANN[11] KERRICK, b. Mar 18, 1837, Bath Co., KY.
  ii.   THACKER KERRICK, b. Dec 20, 1838, Bath Co., KY; d. Feb 14, 1862, Civil War at Bardstown, Nelson Co., KY; m. PAULINE DANIELS, May 13, 1858, Bath Co., KY; b. Jan 1841, Bath Co., KY; d. May 26, 1929, Bath Co., KY.
  iii. MARTHA E. KERRICK, b. Dec 14, 1842, Bath Co., KY.
  iv.   WALTER J. KERRICK, b. Jan 2, 1843, Bath Co., KY; m. MARY JANE LEMMONS, Jan 4, 1864, Harrison Co., KY.
  v.   BIBARY KERRICK, b. Jan 2, 1845, Bath Co., KY.
  vi.   CLARISSA KERRICK, b. Aug 25, 1846, Bath Co., KY.
  vii. AARON KERRICK, b. Nov 1, 1848, Bath Co., KY.
  viii. PRESSLEY P. KERRICK, b. Jun 21, 1850, Bath Co., KY.
  ix.   ROBERT T. KERRICK, b. Dec 11, 1852, Bath Co., KY.

374. MARTHA[10] PENDLETON (*THACKER*[9], *RICE*[8], *HENRY*[7], *JOHN*[6], *PHILIP*[5], *HENRY*[4], *HENRY*[3], *GEORGE*[2], *GEORGE*[1]) was born Abt. 1820 in Bath Co., KY, and died Abt. 1840 in Bath Co., KY. She married THOMAS KERRICK Feb 8, 1836 in Bath Co., KY. He was born Abt. 1813, and died Aft. 1870 in Bath Co., KY?

Children of MARTHA PENDLETON and THOMAS KERRICK are:
  i.   JOHN PRESLEY[11] KERRICK, b. Abt. 1837, KY; d. 1919.
  ii. LUCY A. KERRICK, b. Abt. 1838, KY; d. Nov 20, 1856, Bath Co., KY; m. JOHN T. MAZE.

375. MARY[10] PENDLETON (*THACKER*[9], *RICE*[8], *HENRY*[7], *JOHN*[6], *PHILIP*[5], *HENRY*[4], *HENRY*[3], *GEORGE*[2], *GEORGE*[1]) was born Abt. 1823 in KY, and died Aft. 1860 in Bath Co., KY? She married JAMES CROUCH Feb 15, 1845 in Bath Co., KY. He was born Abt. 1815 in VA, and died Aft. 1860 in Bath Co., KY?
    James Crouch (farmer) and family are listed in the 1850 Bath Co., KY census, pg. 22 and in the 1860 Bath Co., KY census, pg. 206.

Children of MARY PENDLETON and JAMES CROUCH are:
  i.   JONATHON[11] CROUCH, b. Abt. 1845.
  ii.   SARAH MARGARET CROUCH, b. Abt. 1848.
  iii. RICE CROUCH, b. Abt. 1852.

iv. JOHN CROUCH, b. Abt. 1855.
v. ANDREW CROUCH, b. Abt. 1857.
vi. MARY CROUCH, b. Abt. 1859.

376. RICE[10] PENDLETON *(THACKER[9], RICE[8], HENRY[7], JOHN[6], PHILIP[5], HENRY[4], HENRY[3], GEORGE[2], GEORGE[1])* was born 1828 in Clark Co., KY, and died Jan 5, 1902 in Clark Co., KY. He married ELIZA JANE CROUCH Jan 24, 1848 in Bath Co., KY, daughter of ISAAC CROUCH and MARGARET MYERS. She was born 1830 in KY, and died Sep 25, 1899 in Clark Co., KY?

Rice Pendleton and family are listed in the 1860 Clark Co. census, district 1, pg. 20; in the 1870 Clark Co. census, pg 82/83, Blue Ball Pct; and in the 1880 Montgomery Co. census, Aaron's Run, Pct. 4.

Children of RICE PENDLETON and ELIZA CROUCH are:
  i. MARY M.[11] PENDLETON, b. Abt. 1849, KY.
674. ii. ISAAC THOMAS PENDLETON, b. 1849, Clark Co., KY; d. Jun 12, 1923, Fayette Co., KY.
  iii. SARAH PENDLETON, b. Abt. 1852, KY.
675. iv. THACKER V. PENDLETON, b. Dec 1, 1854, Bath Co., KY; d. Oct 1, 1936, Clark Co., KY.
676. v. JOHN RICE PENDLETON, b. Dec 1858, Clark Co., KY; d. Jun 10, 1923, Montgomery Co., KY.
677. vi. THOMAS JEFFERSON PENDLETON, b. Dec 12, 1860, Clark Co., KY; d. May 30, 1948, Fayette Co., KY.
  vii. MARTHA JANE "MATTIE" PENDLETON, b. Abt. 1866.
  viii. HANNAH PENDLETON, b. Abt. 1871.

377. ELIZABETH[10] PENDLETON *(RICE[9], RICE[8], HENRY[7], JOHN[6], PHILIP[5], HENRY[4], HENRY[3], GEORGE[2], GEORGE[1])* was born Oct 26, 1817 in Clark Co., KY, and died May 7, 1866 in Clark Co., KY. She married GEORGE E. HARDMAN Jan 11, 1836 in Clark Co., KY. He was born Jul 28, 1811 in VA, and died Dec 1, 1881 in Clark Co., KY.

Elizabeth Pendleton Hardman is buried in Pendleton Cemetery, Wades Mill, Clark Co., KY.

Children of ELIZABETH PENDLETON and GEORGE HARDMAN are:
  i. SARAH A.[11] HARDMAN, b. Abt. 1837, KY.
  ii. JOHN R. HARDMAN, b. Abt. 1839, KY.
    John R. Hardman, private, served in the 3rd Battalion Kentucky Mounted. Rifles, CSA.

  iii. ELIZABETH S. HARDMAN, b. Dec 3, 1840, KY; d. Dec 17, 1925, Clark Co., KY; m. PATTERSON.
  iv. DAVID P. HARDMAN, b. Jul 29, 1842, KY; d. Apr 11, 1918, Clark Co., KY; m. MARANDA BRANCH; b. Mar 14, 1849; d. Feb 19, 1905, Clark Co., KY.

David Hardman, private, served with his brother John, in the 3rd Battalion Kentucky Mounted Rifles, CSA.

     v.   LUCY C. HARDMAN, b. Sep 27, 1844, KY; d. Mar 22, 1875.
    vi.   NANCY HOOD HARDMAN, b. 1846, KY.
   vii.   ELIZA J. HARDMAN, b. 1848, KY; d. Apr 27, 1936, Clark Co., KY; m. GAYLORD WILLIS PALMETER; b. 1847; d. Jul 20, 1924, Clark Co., KY.
  viii.   GEORGE G. HARDMAN, b. Apr 24, 1855, KY; d. Dec 26, 1933, Clark Co., KY; m. LAURA J.; b. Nov 12, 1857; d. Jun 9, 1904.
   ix.   REZIN CONSTANT HARDMAN, b. May 16, 1858, Wades Mill, Clark Co., KY; d. Jul 3, 1911, Fayette Co., KY; m. EMMA GILLASPIE, Jan 3, 1876, Bourbon Co., KY; b. May 4, 1861; d. Sep 17, 1939, Clark Co., KY.

378. EMILY[10] PENDLETON *(RICE[9], RICE[8], HENRY[7], JOHN[6], PHILIP[5], HENRY[4], HENRY[3], GEORGE[2], GEORGE[1])* was born Nov 7, 1819 in Clark Co., KY, and died Aug 6, 1845 in Clark Co., KY. She married ROBERT SCOBEE Oct 20, 1836 in Clark Co., KY, son of ROBERT SCOBEE and ELIZABETH BROHARD. He was born Nov 29, 1816 in KY, and died Apr 26, 1882 in Clark Co., KY.

The Robert Scobee household was adjacent to the Rice Pendleton household in the 1850 Clark Co. census.

Children of EMILY PENDLETON and ROBERT SCOBEE are:
     i.   ELIZABETH ANN[11] SCOBEE, b. Dec 28, 1837, Clark Co., KY; m. H. J. BENTON, Jan 8, 1856.
    ii.   REZIN A. SCOBEE, b. Sep 9, 1839, Clark Co., KY; d. Nov 27, 1924, Clark Co., KY; m. (1) SARAH R. KING, Oct 31, 1861, Clark Co., KY?; b. Mar 26, 1844, Clark Co., KY; d. Jul 22, 1877, Clark Co., KY; m. (2) MOLLIE EVANS, Oct 30, 1883.

379. DAVID J.[10] PENDLETON *(RICE[9], RICE[8], HENRY[7], JOHN[6], PHILIP[5], HENRY[4], HENRY[3], GEORGE[2], GEORGE[1])* was born Nov 1824 in Clark County, KY, and died Oct 1, 1900 in Clark County, KY. He married ELIZABETH ANN LINDSAY Jul 13, 1846 in Clark Co., KY. She was born Sep 1826 in KY, and died 1920 in Clark Co., KY.

Surety for the marriage bond of David J. Pendleton and Elizabeth Lindsay was provided by Charles Lindsay. David J. Pendleton and family are listed in the 1850 and 1860 Clark Co. census records, District 1. D. J. Pendleton enlisted in the Confederate Army, Clark Co., KY as 1st Sgt. on 10 Sept. 1862. He served in the KY 8th Cavalry., Company D as 1st Sgt., CSA, and was discharged on 13 March, 1863. He was reportedly present at the Battle of Mt. Sterling, KY where he was captured while attempting to rescue his wounded cousin, Capt. Virgil Pendleton, who also served in the KY 8th Cavalry (Ref. 101). David J. Pendleton (Surveyor) is listed in the 1870 Clark Co. Census, pg 94, Winchester Pct. 114. He was the County Surveyor of Clark County for at least 17 years. From this line have descended three of the mayors of Winchester, KY (Ref. 101). He is buried in the Winchester, KY Cemetery along with his wife, Elizabeth Pendleton.

Children of DAVID PENDLETON and ELIZABETH LINDSAY are:
  i. JOHN T. JOHNSON[11] PENDLETON, b. 1847, Clark Co., KY; d. 1862, Clark Co., KY.
  ii. CHARLES LILBURN PENDLETON, b. 1849, Clark Co., KY; d. Jan 2, 1935, Lexington, KY.

> The Lexington local newspaper of January 4, 1935 announced that Charles L. Pendleton, 85, of Fontaine Road died at hospital on the 2nd. He is buried in Winchester Cemetery along with Annie B. Pendleton (1856 – 1940) and Annie Pendleton (1852 – 1946).

678. iii. FRANKLIN P. PENDLETON, b. Nov 1852, Clark Co., KY; d. 1946, Clark Co., KY.

380. LUCY ANN[10] PENDLETON (*RICE[9], RICE[8], HENRY[7], JOHN[6], PHILIP[5], HENRY[4], HENRY[3], GEORGE[2], GEORGE[1]*) was born Aug 14, 1827 in Clark Co., KY, and died Dec 22, 1854 in Clark Co., KY. She married ROBERT SCOBEE May 14, 1846 in Clark Co., KY, son of ROBERT SCOBEE and ELIZABETH BROHARD. He was born Nov 29, 1816 in KY, and died Apr 26, 1882 in Clark Co., KY.

This is the Robert Scobee who first married Emily Pendleton, Lucy's older sister.

Children of LUCY PENDLETON and ROBERT SCOBEE are:
  i. RICE PENDLETON[11] SCOBEE, b. Jun 23, 1847, Clark Co., KY; d. 1927, Clark Co., KY; m. MARTHA J. CHORN, Mar 13, 1868; b. 1854; d. 1919, Clark Co., KY.

> The biography of Rice Scobee is included in an early history of Kentucky (Ref. 123).

> Rice P. Scobee, a native of Clark County, Ky., was born June 23, 1847, and is a son of Robert and Lucy (Pendleton) SCOBEE. Robert SCOBEE, also a native of Clark County, was a farmer by occupation, a popular citizen of the community in which he lived, and died in April, 1882, a son of Robert SCOBEE, who was a farmer, distiller and miller. Mrs. Lucy Scobee was born in Clark County, and was a daughter of Rice PENDLETON. Rice P. SCOBEE was reared on his father's farm and educated at the common schools. In 1862 he enlisted in the Confederate army, in the company commanded by Capt. Bedford, under Col. Clay, but during the latter part of the war he was under Gen. Morgan. He received a gunshot wound at Cynthiana. Ky., was taken prisoner and confined at Camp Douglas for nine months. At the close of the war he returned to Clark County and resumed farming, in which occupation he is still engaged, and of late has been devoting considerable attention to breeding and raising Shorthorn cattle. March 13, 1868, he married Miss Martha CHORN, of Clark County, daughter of Josiah and M. (Thompson) CHORN. Five children have been born to this union, viz: James C., Rezin, Columbus, Robert and Nannie Lu. He and Mrs. Scobee are strict members of the Primitive Baptist Church, and Mr. Scobee owns 385 acres of fine farming land. Politically he is a Democrat.

ii. MARY C. "KATE" SCOBEE, b. Mar 25, 1849.
iii. EMMA AMELIA SCOBEE, b. Feb 25, 1851, Clark Co., KY; d. Feb 14, 1930, Marshall, Saline Co., MO.; m. J. W. BARNHILL.

    J. W. Barnhill and Emma Scobee are the parents Edgar Pendleton Barnhill (Nov 11,1881 - Sep 18, 1948) who is buried at Ridge Park Cemetery of Marshall, Saline County, MO.

iv. JAMES W. SCOBEE, b. Dec 24, 1852, Clark Co., KY; d. 1940, Clark Co., KY; m. SUSIE E.; b. 1856; d. 1912, Clark Co., KY.
v. ROBERT S. SCOBEE, b. Dec 10, 1854, Clark Co., KY; d. Jul 10, 1937, Winchester, Clark Co., KY; m. DEE BRATTON, Dec 14, 1876.

381. DEBORAH STEVENS[10] PENDLETON *(PRESLEY[9], RICE[8], HENRY[7], JOHN[6], PHILIP[5], HENRY[4], HENRY[3], GEORGE[2], GEORGE[1])* was born 1829 in KY, and died 1899. She married CLABOURNE K. MOSS. He was born 1822 in KY, and died Mar 1869 in Ralls Co., MO.

Claibourne Moss (farmer) and family are listed in the 1860 Ralls Co., MO census. The Will of Claiborn Moss (Ref. 251), probated Mar 8, 1969, Ralls Co., includes the following: "My wife, Deborah, P. A. Pendleton (Presley A.), Executors."

Children of DEBORAH PENDLETON and CLABOURNE MOSS are (Ref. 252):
i. ELIZA ALICE[11] MOSS, b. Abt. 1848, MO; m. TOM ELY.
ii. PRESLEY PENDLETON MOSS, b. 1849, Monroe City, MO.
iii. WILLIAM EDMOND MOSS, b. May 17, 1851, Ralls Co., MO; d. Jun 27, 1943, Marion City, MO; m. FANNIE OPHELIA DAVENPORT, Dec 18, 1877, Monroe City, MO.
iv. MARTHA MOSS, b. 1853, Monroe City, MO; m. TOM STEVENS.
v. JOHN J. MOSS, b. 1856, MO; d. 1857.
vi. DULCENA J. MOSS, b. 1858, Monroe City, MO; d. 1863, Monroe City, MO.
vii. CORDELIA MOSS, b. 1864, Monroe City, MO.

382. MARTIN J.[10] PENDLETON *(PRESLEY[9], RICE[8], HENRY[7], JOHN[6], PHILIP[5], HENRY[4], HENRY[3], GEORGE[2], GEORGE[1])* was born Mar 24, 1834 in Ralls Co., MO, and died Dec 4, 1907 in Monroe Co., MO? He married (1) LUCY A. She was born Abt. 1841 in MO, and died Aft. 1880. He married (2) NANCY ANN JAMES Abt. 1890, daughter of MOSES JAMES and SARAH CUMMINS. She was born Nov 1, 1843 in KY, and died Mar 7, 1921 in Marion Co., MO.

Martin Pendleton (farmer) and family are listed in the 1860 Saline, Ralls Co., MO census. Martin J. Pendleton (farmer) and his second wife are listed in the 1900 Monroe Co., MO census, pg. 130. Nancy A. Pendleton is listed in the 1910 and 1920 Marion Co., MO census records.

Children of MARTIN PENDLETON and LUCY A. are:
679.   i. JAMES WILLIAM[11] PENDLETON, b. Aug 8, 1855, Ralls Co., MO; d. Sep 7, 1897, Shannon Co., MO.

ii. EDMOND PENDLETON, b. Abt. 1859, Ralls Co., MO.
iii. DEBORAH A. PENDLETON, b. Abt. 1863, Ralls Co., MO; d. Aft. 1910, Monroe Co., MO?; m. EDWARD W. MARSHALL, Mar 10, 1885, Ralls Co., MO.
iv. ELONZO PENDLETON, b. Abt. 1866, Ralls Co., MO.
680. v. ROBERT L. PENDLETON, b. May 1868, MO.
vi. A. B. PENDLETON, b. Abt. 1871, MO.
vii. E. D. PENDLETON, b. Abt. 1877, MO.
viii. DAUGHTER PENDLETON, b. 1880, MO.

383. PRESLEY A.[10] PENDLETON (*PRESLEY*[9], *RICE*[8], *HENRY*[7], *JOHN*[6], *PHILIP*[5], *HENRY*[4], *HENRY*[3], *GEORGE*[2], *GEORGE*[1]) was born Abt. 1836 in Ralls Co., MO, and died Aft. 1880 in Monroe Co., MO? He married SARAH A. MILLON, daughter of JOHN MILLON. She was born Abt. 1842 in MO.

Presley Pendleton (32) and family are listed in the 1870 Ralls Co., MO census, Saline Township, pg. 67A. Sarah is deaf. Presley Pendleton was a witness for the will of John G. Dawson, probated Feb 18, 1870, Ralls Co., MO (Ref. 251).

Children of PRESLEY PENDLETON and SARAH MILLON are:
i. LAURA[11] PENDLETON, b. Abt. 1863, Ralls Co., MO.
ii. EDWARD PENDLETON, b. Abt. 1866, Ralls Co., MO.
iii. LULA PENDLETON, b. Abt. 1870, Ralls Co., MO.
iv. EFFA PENDLETON, b. Abt. 1875.
v. KELLIE PENDLETON, b. 1880.

384. DAVID J.[10] PENDLETON (*PRESLEY*[9], *RICE*[8], *HENRY*[7], *JOHN*[6], *PHILIP*[5], *HENRY*[4], *HENRY*[3], *GEORGE*[2], *GEORGE*[1]) was born Oct 29, 1837 in Ralls Co., MO, and died Dec 7, 1888 in Butteville, OR? He married SARAH WHITNEY Mar 9, 1862, daughter of WILLIAM WHITNEY and ELIZABETH TAYLOR. She was born Jul 7, 1842 in IN, and died Feb 4, 1922 in Donald, OR.

David J. Pendleton is listed in the 1870 and 1880 Marion Co., OR census records, Butteville.

Children of DAVID PENDLETON and SARAH WHITNEY are (Ref. 253):
i. WILLIAM E.[11] PENDLETON, b. Jan 30, 1863, OR; d. Aug 18, 1881, OR.
ii. ANDY P. PENDLETON, b. May 14, 1865, OR; d. Oct 16, 1888, OR.
iii. ENOS G. PENDLETON, b. Jun 19, 1867, OR; d. Aug 25, 1869, OR.
iv. DULCENA J. PENDLETON, b. Abt. 1869, OR; d. 1942.
v. ALICE R. PENDLETON, b. Abt. 1872, OR.
vi. MARTIN EUGENE PENDLETON, b. Apr 5, 1875, Hubbard, OR; d. Nov 3, 1946, Hubbard, Marion Co., OR.
    Eugene Pendleton registered for the WWI draft in Marion Co., OR listing his occupation as Farmer and his nearest relative as Sara Pendleton (mother). Martin Pendleton (farmer) is listed in the 1920 census, Marion Co., OR, pg. 3B near his brother, George A. Pendleton.

vii. MELVINA E. PENDLETON, b. Abt. 1878, OR; d. Jun 30, 1881, OR.
681. viii. DAVID ELMER PENDLETON, b. Feb 2, 1880, Butteville, OR; d. May 19, 1925, Marion Co., OR.
682. ix. GEORGE ALVIN PENDLETON, b. Aug 8, 1882, Butteville, OR; d. Feb 8, 1924, Broadacres, OR.

385. WILLIAM RICE[10] PENDLETON (*PRESLEY*[9], *RICE*[8], *HENRY*[7], *JOHN*[6], *PHILIP*[5], *HENRY*[4], *HENRY*[3], *GEORGE*[2], *GEORGE*[1]) was born May 20, 1840 in Ralls Co., MO, and died Nov 30, 1880 in Ralls Co., MO. He married NANCY ANN JAMES, daughter of MOSES JAMES and SARAH CUMMINS. She was born Nov 1, 1843 in KY, and died Mar 7, 1921 in Marion Co., MO.

Nancy A. Pendleton is listed in the 1910 and 1920 Marion Co., MO census records.

Children of WILLIAM PENDLETON and NANCY JAMES are:
i. SARAH[11] PENDLETON, b. Abt. 1862, MO.
ii. DULCENA PENDLETON, b. Abt. 1863, MO.
683. iii. CHARLES PORTER PENDLETON, b. Oct 5, 1865, Ralls Co., MO; d. Jul 17, 1936, Ralls Co., MO.

386. BERRYMAN H.[10] PENDLETON (*PRESTON*[9], *RICE*[8], *HENRY*[7], *JOHN*[6], *PHILIP*[5], *HENRY*[4], *HENRY*[3], *GEORGE*[2], *GEORGE*[1]) was born Dec 20, 1830 in Logan Co, IL, and died Apr 13, 1881 in IL. He married RHODA HADENS. She was born Abt. 1838 in OH, and died Aft. 1880.

B.H. Pendleton (farmer) and family are listed in the 1860 Logan Co., IL census, pg. 68. Barryman H. Pendleton of Lincoln, Illinois enlisted on 19 August 1861 in the Union Army as a private in Company H, 38th Infantry Regiment, Illinois.

Children of BERRYMAN PENDLETON and RHODA HADENS are:
684. i. FRANCES A.[11] PENDLETON, b. Abt. 1857, IL; d. Aft. 1882.
ii. MATTIE PENDLETON, b. Abt. 1861, IL.
iii. ARTHUR PENDLETON, b. Abt. 1862, IL.
iv. SUSIE PENDLETON, b. Abt. 1870, IL.
v. WILLIE PENDLETON, b. Abt. 1873, IL.

387. EDMUND[10] PENDLETON (*PRESTON*[9], *RICE*[8], *HENRY*[7], *JOHN*[6], *PHILIP*[5], *HENRY*[4], *HENRY*[3], *GEORGE*[2], *GEORGE*[1]) was born Jan 18, 1837 in Lincoln, Logan

Co., IL, and died Aft. 1880 in Logan Co., IL or CA? He married RACHEL ELLA HURT. She was born Abt. 1845 in OH, and died Aft. 1880.

Edmund Pendleton and family are listed in the 1880 Atlanta, Logan Co., IL census, pg. 44A. He is said to have moved to California.

Children of EDMUND PENDLETON and RACHEL HURT are:
i. ROSIE A.[11] PENDLETON, b. Abt. 1868, IL.
ii. CHARLES PENDLETON, b. Abt. 1870, IL.

685.   iii. JOHN M. PENDLETON, b. Abt. 1872, IL; d. Aft. 1920, Jackson Co., MO.
         iv. MERRETTIE PENDLETON, b. Abt. 1874, IL.
          v. CLARENCE PENDLETON, b. Abt. 1876, IL.

388. SAMUEL EVANS[10] PENDLETON *(PRESTON[9], RICE[8], HENRY[7], JOHN[6], PHILIP[5], HENRY[4], HENRY[3], GEORGE[2], GEORGE[1])* was born Aug 20, 1839 in Logan Co., IL, and died Aft. 1900 in Dickinson Co., KS? He married SARAH J. Abt. 1863. She was born Abt. 1844 in IL.

    Samuel E. Pendleton enlisted in the Union Army as a private twice. He claimed Residence in Springfield and served for the state of Illinois. He enlisted in E Co. 7th Infantry Regiment , IL on 03 June 1861 and mustered Out on 25 July 1861. He then enlisted on 30 May, 1862 in B Co. 70th Infantry Regiment, IL and mustered out at Camp Butler, Springfield, IL on 23 October 1862 as a Q.M. sergeant (Ref. 159). "He received his education at the Chaddock College of Illinois, and has attained prominence as one of the foremost clergymen in the United States. He has preached in all the principal cities of the union; for fifteen years has been presiding elder in the Kansas conference; and has been a delegate to the general conference four times" (Ref. 41). Samuel E. Pendleton (minister) and youngest two daughters are listed in the 1900 Dickinson Co., KS census, pg. 202.

Children of SAMUEL PENDLETON and SARAH J. are:
           i. SUELLA[11] PENDLETON, b. Abt. 1865, IL.
          ii. IDA R. PENDLETON, b. Abt. 1868, IL.
         iii. ALICE G. PENDLETON, b. 1870, IL.
          iv. SARAH G. PENDLETON, b. Aug 1880, KS.
           v. EDITH M. PENDLETON, b. Nov 1884, KS.

389. CYNTHIA A.[10] PENDLETON *(PRESTON[9], RICE[8], HENRY[7], JOHN[6], PHILIP[5], HENRY[4], HENRY[3], GEORGE[2], GEORGE[1])* was born Oct 29, 1843 in Lincoln, Logan Co., IL, and died Aft. 1880 in DeWitt Co, IL? She married JOHN F. ATCHISON. He was born Abt. 1837 in IL, and died Aft. 1880 in DeWitt Co., IL?

Children of CYNTHIA PENDLETON and JOHN ATCHISON are:
           i. ANNA BELL[11] ATCHISON, b. Abt. 1863.
          ii. MINNIE D. ATCHISON, b. Abt. 1865.
         iii. ULYSSES S. ATCHISON, b. Abt. 1868.
          iv. PRESTON S. ATCHISON, b. Abt. 1870.
           v. MARY R. ATCHISON, b. Abt. 1872.
          vi. EDITH G. ATCHISON, b. Abt. 1874.
         vii. SAMUEL A. ATCHISON, b. 1879.

390. JOHN S.[10] PENDLETON *(PRESTON[9], RICE[8], HENRY[7], JOHN[6], PHILIP[5], HENRY[4], HENRY[3], GEORGE[2], GEORGE[1])* was born Nov 18, 1849 in Lincoln, Logan Co., IL, and died Mar 3, 1918 in Clintonia Township, IL. He married JOESINA ELIZA MOUNTS Jun 3, 1876 in Beason, Logan Co., IL, daughter of JOSEPH MOUNTS and

VIRGINIA ROACH. She was born Apr 30, 1858 in OH, and died Jan 24, 1947 in Macon Co., IL.

      John Pendleton and family are listed in the 1900 Logan Co., IL census, pg. 70.

Children of JOHN PENDLETON and JOESINA MOUNTS are:
686.   i.   OSCAR GERMAIN[11] PENDLETON, b. Jul 10, 1881, Lincoln, Logan Co., IL; d. Aug 15, 1963, Morgan Co., IL.
687.   ii.   FLORENCE BELLE PENDLETON, b. Aug 24, 1885, Lincoln, Logan Co., IL; d. Jan 9, 1944, Lincoln, Logan Co., IL.

391. MICHAEL[10] PENDLETON (*CHAMPNEY*[9], *RICE*[8], *HENRY*[7], *JOHN*[6], *PHILIP*[5], *HENRY*[4], *HENRY*[3], *GEORGE*[2], *GEORGE*[1]) was born Jan 6, 1835 in IL, and died May 21, 1923 in Molalla, Clackamas Co., OR. He married (1) ELIZABETH JANE ABBOTT Sep 7, 1865 in Clackamas Co., OR, daughter of ISAIAH ABBOTT and ELIZABETH JANE MIDDLETON. She was born Jul 1850, and died Abt. 1868 in Clackamas Co., OR. He married (2) JULIA JOSEPHINE "ANN" BALL Feb 19, 1871 in Clackamas Co., OR, daughter of DAVID BALL and SUSAN SCHMIR. She was born Abt. 1850 in OR, and died Feb 12, 1937 in Clackamas Co., OR.

      Michael Penelton (sic) and family are listed in the 1880 Beaver Creek, Clackamas Co., OR census. He is listed in the 1890 Clackamas County, OR, Upper Molalla, Veterans Schedule. Michael Pendleton (farmer) and children are listed in the 1900 Clackamas Co., OR census, pg. 111a. The death of Julia Pendleton is recorded in the Oregon Death Index, 1903-98.

Child of MICHAEL PENDLETON and ELIZABETH ABBOTT is:
     i.   NANCY[11] PENDLETON, b. 1867, Clackamas Co., OR.

Children of MICHAEL PENDLETON and JULIA BALL are:
    ii.   LOUIS[11] PENDLETON, b. Jan 1872, OR.
   iii.   FRED CHAMPION PENDLETON, b. Oct 12, 1874, Portland, OR; d. Mar 13, 1910, Grant's Pass, OR.
        The death of Fred Champion Pendleton is recorded in the Oregon Death Index, 1903-98.

688.   iv.   DAVID EDWARD PENDLETON, b. Feb 14, 1878, OR; d. May 19, 1925, Marion Co., OR.

392. HANNAH[10] PENDLETON (*CHAMPNEY*[9], *RICE*[8], *HENRY*[7], *JOHN*[6], *PHILIP*[5], *HENRY*[4], *HENRY*[3], *GEORGE*[2], *GEORGE*[1]) was born Aug 1837 in IL, and died Aft. 1920 in Marion Co., OR? She married (1) ALAY C. DANIELS Mar 31, 1855 in OR. She married (2) ROBERT WHITNEY Feb 12, 1866. He was born Dec 1834 in IN, and died Aft. 1900 in Marion Co., OR?

      Hannnah Pendleton's first marriage is recorded in Reference 254. Hannah Whitney (82) is listed in the 1920 Oregon census, Marion Co. with Clara and Golsby Whitney and near George A. and Eugene Pendleton.

Child of HANNAH PENDLETON and ALAY DANIELS is:
    i.   SAMUEL T.[11] DANIELS, b. Abt. 1857, OR.

Children of HANNAH PENDLETON and ROBERT WHITNEY are:
    ii.   GEORGE[11] WHITNEY, b. 1867, OR.
    iii.   CLARA B. WHITNEY, b. Oct 1868, OR; d. Aft. 1920, Marion Co., OR?
    iv.   OLIVER C. WHITNEY, b. Abt. 1871, OR.
    v.   ARDULA WHITNEY, b. Abt. 1873, OR.
    vi.   CLARENCE A. WHITNEY, b. Jan 1875, OR.
    vii.   ANDREW L. WHITNEY, b. Aug 1876, OR; d. Aft. 1920, Marion Co., OR?; m. ALICE M.; b. Abt. 1889, MI.
    viii.   GOLSBY WHITNEY, b. Dec 1878, OR; d. Aft. 1920, Marion Co., OR?
    ix.   HONESTY WHITNEY, b. Feb 1881, OR.
    x.   LINCOLN WHITNEY, b. Oct 1884, OR.

393. FRANCIS M.[10] PENDLETON *(CHAMPNEY[9], RICE[8], HENRY[7], JOHN[6], PHILIP[5], HENRY[4], HENRY[3], GEORGE[2], GEORGE[1])* was born 1841 in IL, and died Aft. 1880. He married MARY FLETCHER. She was born Abt. 1856 in Washington Territory.

    Francis M. Pendleton served in the Union Army, 1st Regiment, Oregon Infantry. Francis M. Pendleton is listed in the 1880 Clark Co., WA, 23rd district census along with Ida E., Mary E., Nellie M. and Ira M. Pendleton.

Child of FRANCIS PENDLETON and MARY FLETCHER is:
    i.   IDA[11] PENDLETON, b. Abt. 1873; m. JOHN D. WILEY; b. Abt. 1856, WA; d. Aft. 1920, Portland, OR?
       John D. Wiley (64, laborer, widower) is listed in the 1920 Oregon Census, Portland, pg. 12A, born in Washington.

394. ELIZABETH[10] PENDLETON *(CHAMPNEY[9], RICE[8], HENRY[7], JOHN[6], PHILIP[5], HENRY[4], HENRY[3], GEORGE[2], GEORGE[1])* was born 1843 in IL. She married JAMES WHITNEY.

Children of ELIZABETH PENDLETON and JAMES WHITNEY are:
    i.   JOSEPH[11] WHITNEY, b. 1863, OR.
    ii.   ROSA WHITNEY, b. 1868, OR.

395. LUCY JANE[10] PENDLETON *(CHAMPNEY[9], RICE[8], HENRY[7], JOHN[6], PHILIP[5], HENRY[4], HENRY[3], GEORGE[2], GEORGE[1])* was born 1847 in OR, and died 1890 in Clackamas Co., OR. She married THOMAS L. FLETCHER Dec 24, 1871 in Clackamas Co., OR.

    The following is the inscription on the grave of Lucy Jane Fletcher, Pendleton Cemetery, Clackamas Co., OR: "Wife of T.L. Fletcher. Dau. of Champion Pendleton."

Children of LUCY PENDLETON and THOMAS FLETCHER are:
    i.   ANDREW[11] FLETCHER, b. 1872, OR; d. 1879, Canby, OR.
    ii.   SON FLETCHER, d. 1900, Clackamas Co., OR.

396. TILFORD[10] PENDLETON *(THRASHLEY[9], RICE[8], HENRY[7], JOHN[6], PHILIP[5], HENRY[4], HENRY[3], GEORGE[2], GEORGE[1])* was born May 1855 in Bath Co., KY, and died Aug 1, 1924 in Salt Lick, KY. He married LOU ELLEN GROSS Sep 3, 1884 in Bath Co., KY, daughter of F. GROSS and SARAH A. She was born 1867 in KY, and died 1953 in Salt Lick, KY.

Tilford inherited his portion of the family farm in 1896 upon the death of his father, Thrashley Pendleton (Ref. 163). In the 1900 Bath County Census the Tilford Pendleton family is listed adjacent to the household of his mother, Artemecia Pendleton, and his siblings. Tilford Pendleton sold his portion of the farm to his siblings in September, 1922 (Ref. 255). On his death certificate, Doctor C.T. Jones wrote "Was called but got another message that he was dead so didn't see him but from the symptoms that was told me I think he had a cerebral hemorrhage." He is buried in the Upper Salt Lick Cemetery adjacent to the Pendleton property.

Lou Ellen Gross Pendleton married J. E. Wilhoit after Tilford Pendleton died. J.E. Wilhoit, minister, and Lou Ellen, wife, are listed in the 1930 Census, Owingsville, Bath Co., KY. 'Grandma' Wilhoit smoked a pipe that she stored in her apron pocket. She lived with her son, Charles, in her final years (Ref. 164). Lou Ellen is buried in Upper Salt Lick Cemetery, Bath Co., KY next to her first husband, Tilford Pendleton.

Children of TILFORD PENDLETON and LOU GROSS are:

689.   i.   JOHN WESLEY[11] PENDLETON, b. Oct 28, 1885, Bath Co., KY; d. Jan 21, 1956, Middletown, OH.

690.   ii.   JESSE PENDLETON, b. Jul 1, 1887, Salt Lick, KY; d. Sep 18, 1967, Mt Sterling, KY.

        iii. BRACKEN PENDLETON, b. Abt. 1890, Bath Co., KY; d. bef. 1900.

            Bracken Pendleton does not appear in the 1900 census; his mother Lula Ellen Gross is listed as having 5 children, 4 living thus giving evidence that Bracken died young.

691.   iv. CHARLES A. PENDLETON, b. Jun 17, 1893, Bath Co., KY; d. Sep 3, 1977, Mt Sterling, KY.

        v.   LOU PEARL PENDLETON, b. Jan 1896, Bath Co., KY; d. Jun 23, 1916, Salt Lick, KY.

            Pearl Pendleton could sing beautifully and owned lots of elaborate hats. She would spend much of her time at the Upper Salt Lick Church near her home. She died of TB and is buried in Upper Salt Lick Cemetery (Ref. 164).

        vi. EFFIE LEE PENDLETON, b. Aug 26, 1900, Bath Co., KY; d. Jul 6, 1991, Dayton, OH; m. LOUTRELL PIERSALL Abt. 1920, Bath Co., KY; b. Apr 7, 1895, Bath Co., KY; d. Aug 1971, Covington, KY.

            Two infants of Effie Lee Loutrell are buried in the Upper Salt Lick Cemetery, Bath Co., KY.

397. SARAH E.[10] PENDLETON *(THRASHLEY[9], RICE[8], HENRY[7], JOHN[6], PHILIP[5], HENRY[4], HENRY[3], GEORGE[2], GEORGE[1])* was born May 26, 1860 in Bath Co., KY, and died 1925 in Bath Co., KY. She married JAMES WESLEY BLEVINS Sep 4, 1878 in

Bath Co., KY, son of JAMES BLEVINS and NANCY WILHOIT. He was born May 1855 in Bath Co., KY, and died Feb 7, 1925 in Bath Co., KY.

James Blevins is buried in Upper Salt Lick Cemetery, Bath Co., KY.

Children of SARAH PENDLETON and JAMES BLEVINS are (Ref. 256):

  i.   ELIZABETH[11] BLEVINS, b. 1879, Bath Co., KY; d. Mar 14, 1918, Bath Co., KY; m. LEONARD MCNABB, Jan 9, 1896, Bath Co., KY; b. 1870, Bath Co., KY; d. Jun 27, 1957, Bath Co., KY.

  ii.   GEORGE BLEVINS, b. Mar 1880, Bath Co., KY; d. Apr 7, 1967, Bath Co., KY.

  iii. EMMA BLEVINS, b. Dec 1882; m. CHARLES MOORE.

  iv.   BETTIE BLEVINS, b. Jan 31, 1883, Bath County, KY; d. Oct 1902, Bath County, KY.

        Bettie Blevins is buried in the Upper Salt Lick Cemetery, Bath Co., KY.

  v.   ISABELL BLEVINS, b. Jan 1885.

  vi.   WILLIAM BLEVINS, b. Sep 1887.

  vii. FRANKLIN BLEVINS, b. Jun 1889, Bath Co., KY; d. Dec 1, 1966, Bath Co., KY; m. (1) KATTIE PEARL BLEVINS; b. Feb 1895, Bath Co., KY; d. Nov 28, 1921, Bath Co., KY; m. (2) JESSE INGRAM; b. Feb 15, 1895; d. Jul 18, 1981.

  viii. SIMPSON BLEVINS, b. Apr 9, 1891, Bath Co., KY; d. May 21, 1953, Bath Co., KY; m. MAUDIE CASSITY; b. Jun 13, 1894, KY; d. May 12, 1980, KY.

  ix.   MENNIE BLEVINS, b. Apr 1894, Bath Co., KY; d. Mar 1, 1923, Bath Co., KY; m. JAMES T. HART; b. 1887; d. Aug 24, 1959, Bath Co., KY.

  x.   STELLA BLEVINS, b. Aug 1895, Bath Co., KY; d. Nov 8, 1981, Bath Co., KY; m. ELIZA INGRAM, Mar 31, 1915, Bath Co., KY; b. Nov 22, 1890, Owingsville, Bath Co., KY; d. Feb 8, 1967, Owingsville, Bath Co., KY.

  xi.   JOHN WESLEY BLEVINS, b. Aug 1897; d. Feb 3, 1969, Bath Co., KY; m. WILLIA CLARK; b. 1908; d. Jul 3, 1989, Rowan Co., KY.

  xii. LILLIE BLEVINS, b. May 1899.

398. ROBERT LEWIS[10] PENDLETON (*EDMUND B.*[9], *ROBERT*[8], *HENRY*[7], *JOHN*[6], *PHILIP*[5], *HENRY*[4], *HENRY*[3], *GEORGE*[2], *GEORGE*[1]) was born Aug 1843 in Spotsylvania Co., VA, and died 1906 in Spotsylvania Co., VA? He married (1) LAURA E. TINDER Aug 31, 1865 in VA, daughter of JOHN TINDER and MARY A. She was born Abt. 1845 in VA, and died Nov 1869 in Livingston, Spotsylvania Co., VA. He married (2) SAMUELLA TINDER Oct 29, 1873 in VA, daughter of JOHN TINDER and MARY A. She was born Abt. 1842 in VA, and died Jul 20, 1887 in Spotsylvania Co., VA. He married (3) ANNIE E. GAY Aug 27, 1890. She was born Jul 1855 in VA.

R.L. Pendleton (farmer) and family are listed in the 1900 Spotsylvania Co., VA census, pg. 243a. He was described as a farmer, six feet in height, with dark hair and blue eyes. The U.S. Federal Census Mortality Schedule of 1870 lists Laura Pendleton, cause of death, Consumption.

Children of ROBERT PENDLETON and LAURA TINDER are:
    i.   JOHN EDMUND[11] PENDLETON, b. 1867, VA; d. Aft. 1920, Spotsylvania
        Co., VA?; m. MRS. EMMA K. HALL, Abt. 1893; b. Apr 1862, VA; d. Aft.
        1920, Spotsylvania Co., VA?
           Edmund J. (farmer) and Emma Pendleton are listed in the 1920
        Spotsylvania Co., VA census, pg. 5B.

    ii. FRANCES ELLEN PENDLETON, b. 1869, Spotsylvania Co., VA.

Children of ROBERT PENDLETON and SAMUELLA TINDER are:
    iii. ROBERT S.[11] PENDLETON, b. Abt. 1877, VA; d. Jul 6, 1887, Spotsylvania
        Co., VA.
    iv. LOTTIE PENDLETON, b. Apr 1878, VA.

399. GEORGE ALLEN[10] PENDLETON (*ROBERT[9], ROBERT[8], HENRY[7], JOHN[6], PHILIP[5], HENRY[4], HENRY[3], GEORGE[2], GEORGE[1]*) was born Oct 18, 1848 in VA, and died Feb 6, 1912 in Spotsylvania Co., VA. He married NINA E. MASSEY Nov 12, 1879. She was born Oct 21, 1859 in VA, and died Jan 9, 1911 in Spotsylvania Co., VA.
      George A. Pendleton (farmer) and family are listed in the 1910 Spotsylvania Co., VA census. He is buried at Mine Road Baptist Church, Spotsylvania Co., VA.

Child of GEORGE PENDLETON and NINA MASSEY is:
    i.   KELSO WOODFOLK[11] PENDLETON, b. Sep 6, 1880, VA; d. Aft. 1920,
        Spotsylvania Co., VA?; m. (1) GRACE K. EMBREY, Nov 22, 1910, VA; b.
        Sep 5, 1885, VA; d. May 17, 1922, Spotsylvania Co., VA; m. (2) ETHEL K.
        FAULCONER, Jan 1, 1924, VA.
           Kelso Pendleton is listed 28 Dec. 1896 in a Spotsylvania Co. local
        newspaper as an Honor Roll Student. Kelso Woodfolk Pendleton registered
        in Spotsylvania for the WW I Draft (Ref. 210). He is listed as a farmer in the
        1920 census, Spotsylvania Co., pg. 1B.

400. ROBERT JAMES[10] PENDLETON (*ROBERT[9], ROBERT[8], HENRY[7], JOHN[6], PHILIP[5], HENRY[4], HENRY[3], GEORGE[2], GEORGE[1]*) was born Jul 30, 1851 in VA, and died Feb 18, 1927 in Spotsylvania Co., VA. He married (1) ANNIE ROOF Nov 18, 1882 in VA. He married (2) ELIZABETH CARTER Sep 19, 1893. She was born Jun 8, 1873 in VA, and died May 4, 1966 in Spotsylvania Co., VA.

      Robert J. Pendleton (farmer) and family are listed in the 1900 Spotsylvania Co., VA census, pg. 269a; in the 1910 census, pg 108B; and in the 1920 Spotsylvania Co., VA census, pg. 17A. The historical Pendleton House Site and Cemetery is a located 0.25 mile south of the intersection of Rts. 606 and 650. It consists of the home of Robert James Pendleton, a family cemetery as well as a slave cemetery nearby enclosed by a rock wall (Ref. 52). This may be the site of the Pendleton meeting house and adjacent cemetery established by his great uncle, Henry Pendleton, Jr. in 1790. Lizzie C. Pendleton is buried at the Mine Road Baptist Church cemetery in Spotsylvania Co.

Child of ROBERT PENDLETON and ELIZABETH CARTER is:
692.   i.   ROBERT JAMES[11] PENDLETON, JR., b. Apr 21, 1895, VA; d. Feb 1966, Bumpass, VA.

401. JOSEPH HOLMES[10] PENDLETON *(BENJAMIN[9], PHILIP[8], BENJAMIN[7], PHILIP[6], PHILIP[5], HENRY[4], HENRY[3], GEORGE[2], GEORGE[1])* was born Dec 19, 1809 in Of King and Queen Co., VA, and died 1848 in VA. He married SARAH M. HUNDLEY Apr 29, 1834 in Essex Co., VA, daughter of AMBROSE HUNDLEY and ELIZABETH HAILE. She was born 1814 in VA, and died 1901 in Tallapoosa, GA.

The marriage of Joseph Pendleton and Sarah Hundley is listed in Reference 25. Joseph Pendleton is listed in the 1840 King and Queen Co., VA census. Sarah Pendleton (36) along with Fanny (15), Elizabeth (13), Henry Clay (8), and Susan (4) are listed in the 1850 Essex Co., VA census. Sarah M. Pendleton and family are again listed in the 1860 King and Queen Co., VA census.

Children of JOSEPH PENDLETON and SARAH HUNDLEY are (Ref. 4):
         i.   FANNY[11] PENDLETON, b. Abt. 1835, VA.
         ii. ELIZABETH CATHERINE PENDLETON, b. Sep 11, 1837, VA; d. Aft. 1880, Calhoun Co., AL?
693.   iii. HENRY CLAY PENDLETON, b. Mar 29, 1842, VA; d. Feb 06, 1931, DeKalb Co., GA.
         iv. SUSAN ALICE PENDLETON, b. Abt. 1844; d. 1920, Tallapoosa, GA; m. THOMAS HIGDON.
694.   v.   LOUIS BAYLOR PENDLETON.
695.   vi. RICHARD PENDLETON.

402. PRISCILLA[10] PENDLETON *(BENJAMIN[9], PHILIP[8], BENJAMIN[7], PHILIP[6], PHILIP[5], HENRY[4], HENRY[3], GEORGE[2], GEORGE[1])* was born Jan 13, 1813 in VA. She married RICHARD LUMPKIN Nov 04, 1828 in King & Queen Co., VA. He was born Mar 21, 1797.

Child of PRISCILLA PENDLETON and RICHARD LUMPKIN is:
         i.   JOSEPHINE[11] LUMPKIN.

403. JAMES[10] PENDLETON *(PHILIP BAYLOR[9], PHILIP[8], BENJAMIN[7], PHILIP[6], PHILIP[5], HENRY[4], HENRY[3], GEORGE[2], GEORGE[1])* was born Abt. 1821 in King and Queen Co., VA, and died in Richmond, Henrico Co., VA? He married VIRGINIA CAMPBELL Dec 22, 1842 in Chesterfield Co., VA, daughter of HUGH CAMPBELL and MARY FLEET. She was born Aug 23, 1824 in VA.

James Pendleton is listed as a farmer, age 29, in 1850 King and Queen Co., VA census; value of farm $6500. James Pendleton (merchant) and family are listed in the 1860 Richmond, Henrico Co., VA census. "James Pendleton was an unkind husband, and his brothers-in-law, Hugh Campbell, William Mann, William Harrison, and perhaps Captain Thomas Dew, went to his house at night and gave him a severe whipping, which act involved them in serious trouble" (Ref. 257).

Children of JAMES PENDLETON and VIRGINIA CAMPBELL are:

   i. MARY HUGH[11] PENDLETON, b. 1844, VA.

   ii. VIRGINIUS PENDLETON, b. 1847, VA; d. Aft. 1890, Richmond, VA?

       Virginius Pendleton served as a private in the VA Cavalry, 40th Battalion, Company B, CSA. He is listed in the Richmond, Virginia City Directories, 1889-90, as a policeman, with an address of 2015 Broad E. Richmond, VA.

   iii. JAMES WILLIAM PENDLETON, b. 1849, VA.

   iv. WALTER PENDLETON, b. Abt. 1852, VA.

   v. TALLULAH PENDLETON, b. Abt. 1854, VA.

   vi. SALLY CAMPBELL PENDLETON, b. Abt. 1856, VA.

   vii. SUSAN ELLEN PENDLETON, b. Abt. 1858, VA; m. CHARLES WILLIAMS.

   viii. THOMAS PENDLETON, b. Abt. 1859, VA.

   ix. JULIAN PENDLETON, b. Abt. 1862, VA.

       Julian Pendleton (18) is listed in the 1880 Tuckahoe, Henrico Co., VA census in the household of Walter C. Andrews. It was likely this Julian Pendleton (born Abt. 1857 and died in Scotland Neck, NC) who married Alice May Lawrence about 1885 in Scotland Neck, NC. Their children included William Thomas Pendleton, b. Jan 21, 1886; d. Jan 31, 1944, George Edmund Pendleton, b. Sep 20, 1887, and Virginia Pendleton, b. Sep 28, 1893; d. Apr 9, 1935 (Ref. 258).

404. ROBINETTE[10] PENDLETON (*PHILIP BAYLOR*[9], *PHILIP*[8], *BENJAMIN*[7], *PHILIP*[6], *PHILIP*[5], *HENRY*[4], *HENRY*[3], *GEORGE*[2], *GEORGE*[1]) was born Jun 21, 1822 in VA, and died Dec 09, 1905 in King and Queen Co., VA? She married DR. SAMUEL STRAUGHAN HENLEY Oct 22, 1840 in King and Queen Co., VA, son of THOMAS HENLEY and ELIZABETH TEMPLE. He was born Jun 14, 1819 in VA, and died Jan 04, 1884 in King and Queen Co., VA?

       Samuel S. Henley and family are listed in the 1880 census, King and Queen Co., VA, pg. 469A.

Children of ROBINETTE PENDLETON and SAMUEL HENLEY are (Ref. 259):

   i. MARIAH ELIZABETH[11] HENLEY, b. Nov 11, 1841; d. Jan 22, 1842.

   ii. THOMAS BAYLOR HENLEY, b. Jan 27, 1843.

   iii. MARY STRAUGHAN HENLEY, b. Jul 29, 1845.

   iv. COLUMBIA B. HENLEY, b. Abt. 1857, VA.

   v. WILMA T. HENLEY, b. Abt. 1860, VA.

405. JR. PHILIP BAYLOR[10] PENDLETON (*PHILIP BAYLOR*[9], *PHILIP*[8], *BENJAMIN*[7], *PHILIP*[6], *PHILIP*[5], *HENRY*[4], *HENRY*[3], *GEORGE*[2], *GEORGE*[1]) was born Abt. 1826 in King and Queen Co., VA, and died Abt. 1860 in King and Queen Co., VA. He married CATHERINE ANNE PENDLETON Nov 10, 1846 in King & Queen Co., VA, daughter of GEORGE PENDLETON and KATHERINE LIPSCOMB. She was born Dec 1827 in VA, and died Aft. 1900 in King & Queen Co., VA?

Philip Pendleton is listed as a farmer in the 1850 King and Queen Co., VA census; value of farm $7,000. Catherine Pendleton and family are listed in the 1870 Stevensville, King & Queen Co., VA census. Catherine Pendleton (farmer) and 2 grandchildren are listed in the 1900 King & Queen Co., VA census, pg. 240.

Children of PHILIP PENDLETON and CATHERINE PENDLETON are:

    i.   ISABELLA[11] PENDLETON, b. Oct 23, 1847, King & Queen Co., VA; m. JOHN F. HARRIS, Dec 18, 1872, King & Queen Co., VA; b. Abt. 1822, Hanover Co., VA.
    ii. MARY CATHERINE PENDLETON, b. Jun 27, 1849; m. ALEXANDER GRAY HARROWER, 1876.
    iii. HYACINTH PENDLETON, b. May 12, 1851; d. Sep 06, 1851.
    iv. LILLIAN GERTRUDE PENDLETON, b. Jan 06, 1852; d. Jun 1919; m. BRUMBY MARTIN.
696. v. GEORGE BAYLOR PENDLETON, b. Sep 19, 1853, VA; d. Sep 16, 1904, King & Queen Co., VA?
697. vi. III PHILIP BAYLOR PENDLETON, b. Apr 20, 1858, King & Queen Co., VA; d. Nov 26, 1926, Richmond, VA.

406. ADELINE[10] PENDLETON (*GEORGE MACON[9], PHILIP[8], BENJAMIN[7], PHILIP[6], PHILIP[5], HENRY[4], HENRY[3], GEORGE[2], GEORGE[1]*) was born Oct 26, 1817 in King & Queen Co., VA, and died Aug 27, 1908 in Mount Lebanon, LA. She married FRANKLIN COURTNEY, DR. Nov 05, 1835 in VA. He was born Jun 04, 1812 in King & Queen Co., VA, and died May 28, 1896 in Grand Cane, LA.

Franklin Courtney (M.D.) and family are listed in the 1850 census, El Dorado, Union Co., AR.

Children of ADELINE PENDLETON and FRANKLIN COURTNEY are:

    i.   EUGENE[11] COURTNEY, b. Sep 18, 1836, Sumter Co., AL; d. Feb 22, 1920, Mount Lebanon, LA; m. MARY ELIZABETH HARDY, Sep 14, 1865, Mount Lebanon, LA; b. Nov 08, 1845, Mount Lebanon, LA; d. May 25, 1929, Mount Lebanon, LA.
    ii. JUNIUS COURTNEY, b. 1840, AL; d. 1878; m. CORNELIA F. MILLER, Dec 15, 1864; b. 1847; d. 1881, Marion, AL.
    iii. FRANKLIN COURTNEY, JR., b. Oct 27, 1841, Sumter Co., AL; d. Jan 27, 1927, Mount Lebanon, LA; m. (1) ANN HAELTINE HARDY; m. (2) MARY JOHNSON; m. (3) MARY ELIZABETH GREER; b. 1841; d. May 25, 1929; m. (4) EMMA JONES, Nov 04, 1906; b. Abt. 1873, Panola Co., TX.
    iv. ADA PENDLETON COURTNEY, b. Sep 07, 1845, Sumter Co., AL; d. May 04, 1900, Grand Cane, LA; m. GEORGE W. PEYTON; d. Apr 20, 1898, Grand Cane, LA.
    v.   MARY LOU COURTNEY, b. Aug 08, 1848, El Dorado, Union Co., AR; d. Dec 24, 1935, Gibsland, LA; m. JAMES DRAYTON HOLSTUN, SR., Dec 30, 1870; b. Jul 31, 1846, Chambers Co., AL; d. May 20, 1930, Gibsland, LA.

vi. ANNIE LEE COURTNEY, b. Aug 04, 1855, Mount Lebanon, LA; d. Jul 24, 1928, Keatchie, LA; m. THOMAS HARDY GATLIN; b. Dec 20, 1852, Keatchie, LA; d. Mar 12, 1910, Keatchie, LA.

407. WILLIAM HENRY[10] PENDLETON *(GEORGE MACON[9], PHILIP[8], BENJAMIN[7], PHILIP[6], PHILIP[5], HENRY[4], HENRY[3], GEORGE[2], GEORGE[1])* was born Oct 15, 1819 in King William Co., VA, and died Oct 25, 1895 in Downey, CA. He married HARRIETTE RAINEY May 27, 1840 in Clinton, Greene Co., GA. She was born Dec 16, 1821 in GA, and died Sep 14, 1894 in Downey, CA.

The Champagnolle, AR land office survey, dated November 01, 1848, lists William H. Pendleton with 39.96 total acres. William H. Pendleton and family are found in the 1850 census in Jackson Township, Union Co., AR. In the 1860 Union Co. census he is listed in Cornie township. William H. Pendleton is listed in the 1870 Los Nietos, Los Angeles Co., CA census, pg. 573. He is buried in the Downey Cemetery District; 9073 Gardendale Street, Downey, Los Angeles Co., California.

Children of WILLIAM PENDLETON and HARRIETTE RAINEY are:

      i. MARY CATHERINE[11] PENDLETON, b. 1843, Union, Arkansas; d. 1859, Union, Arkansas.

698. ii. CORA ALBINA PENDLETON, b. 1845, Union Co., AR; d. Dec 11, 1903, Bakersfield, CA.

699. iii. WILLIAM HENRY PENDLETON, b. Aug 31, 1846, Union Co., Arkansas; d. Jan 03, 1917, Downey, CA.

      iv. HARRIET ELLA PENDLETON, b. 1848, Union Co., AR; d. 1930, Downey, CA.

700. v. ADA COURTNEY PENDLETON, b. Sep 08, 1849, Union Co. Arkansas; d. Mar 14, 1930, Downey, CA.

701. vi. ALEXIS THEODORE PENDLETON, b. Mar 24, 1851, AR; d. Mar 24, 1928, Placentia, Orange Co., CA.

702. vii. GEORGE WALTER PENDLETON, b. Jan 1853, AR; d. Oct 25, 1934, Buena Park, CA.

     viii. EUGENE PENDLETON, b. Abt. 1855.

703. ix. EDWIN PENDLETON, b. Feb 1855, AR; d. Mar 25, 1933, Los Angeles, CA.

      x. JESSIE PENDLETON, b. Jan 21, 1859, AR; d. Feb 10, 1949, Downey, CA; m. MILTON SHIRLEY, Jan 30, 1894, Downey, CA.

      xi. ROBBINETTE PENDLETON, b. Abt. 1864, AR; d. 1939; m. LEROY CASEY FREDERICK, Aug 29, 1864.

704. xii. MATTHEW RAINEY PENDLETON, b. Jul 1866, Union, AR; d. Apr 18, 1934, Long Beach, CA.

408. GEORGE MACON[10] PENDLETON *(GEORGE MACON[9], PHILIP[8], BENJAMIN[7], PHILIP[6], PHILIP[5], HENRY[4], HENRY[3], GEORGE[2], GEORGE[1])* was born Dec 27, 1825 in VA, and died Mar 27, 1907 in Union Co., AR. He married MARY ANNE BROWN Oct 31, 1850 in Union Co., AR, daughter of JOHN BROWN and NANCY BATES. She was born Jun 02, 1832 in NC, and died Jun 22, 1916 in El Dorado, AR.

George Pendleton (24), druggist, is listed in the Union Co., Ark., El Dorado Township 1850 Census of Oct 2.; born in VA. The Champagnolle, AR land office survey, dated Apr 1, 1850, lists George M. Pendleton with 40 acres. George M Pendleton is also included in the 1860 and 1870 census records, Union Co., AR, respectively.

Children of GEORGE PENDLETON and MARY BROWN are (Ref. 260):
705. i.   MARY EMMA[11] PENDLETON, b. Jan 31, 1854, Union Co., AR; d. Jun 05, 1945, El Dorado, AR.
706. ii. MARIA LOUISA PENDLETON, b. Jun 02, 1856, AR; d. Feb 16, 1899, Union Co., AR.
707. iii. GEORGE ROBERT PENDLETON, b. May 27, 1858, AR; d. Jan 31, 1941, Junction City, AR.
708. iv. DELLA PENDLETON, b. Nov 26, 1860, AR; d. Nov 06, 1935, El Dorado, AR.
709. v.   JULIA PENDLETON, b. Feb 18, 1863, AR; d. Apr 26, 1945, Junction City, AR.
710. vi. LULA ELIZABETH PENDLETON, b. Feb 03, 1866, AR; d. Nov 14, 1916, El Dorado, AR.
711. vii. JOHN MACON PENDLETON, b. Aug 02, 1869, AR; d. Aft. 1930, El Dorado, Union Co., AR?
712. viii. KATHERINE LIPSCOMB PENDLETON, b. Nov 10, 1871, AR.

409. CATHERINE ANNE[10] PENDLETON *(GEORGE MACON[9], PHILIP[8], BENJAMIN[7], PHILIP[6], PHILIP[5], HENRY[4], HENRY[3], GEORGE[2], GEORGE[1])* was born Dec 1827 in VA, and died Aft. 1900 in King & Queen Co., VA? She married JR. PHILIP BAYLOR PENDLETON Nov 10, 1846 in King & Queen Co., VA, son of PHILIP PENDLETON and MARY WOOD. He was born Abt. 1826 in King and Queen Co., VA, and died Abt. 1860 in King and Queen Co., VA.

Children of Catherine Anne are listed above under (**405**) Philip Baylor Pendleton.

410. MARIA LOUISA[10] PENDLETON *(GEORGE MACON[9], PHILIP[8], BENJAMIN[7], PHILIP[6], PHILIP[5], HENRY[4], HENRY[3], GEORGE[2], GEORGE[1])* was born Abt. 1829 in VA, and died Aft. 1860 in King & Queen Co., VA? She married WILLIAM DAVID TURNER. He was born Abt. 1821 in VA, and died Aft. 1860 in King & Queen Co., VA?

Children of MARIA PENDLETON and WILLIAM TURNER are:
    i.   MARTHA[11] TURNER, b. Abt. 1850.
    ii. JENNY V. TURNER, b. Abt. 1852.
    iii. ADALINE TURNER, b. Abt. 1854.
    iv. WILLIAM L. TURNER, b. Abt. 1856.
    v.   BLANCH TURNER, b. Abt. 1859.

411. JOHN BAYLOR[10] PENDLETON *(GEORGE MACON[9], PHILIP[8], BENJAMIN[7], PHILIP[6], PHILIP[5], HENRY[4], HENRY[3], GEORGE[2], GEORGE[1])* was born Sep 1831 in

VA, and died Abt. 1901 in Dinwiddie Co., VA? He married FLORENCE C. JOHNSON Abt. 1884. She was born Feb 1862 in VA, and died Aft. 1920 in Richmond, VA?

The Richmond, Virginia City Directories, 1889-90 lists John B Pendleton, carpenter, address 732 5th St., N. Richmond, VA. J.B. Pendleton (carpenter) and family are listed in the 1900 Dinwiddie Co., VA census, pg. 223. Florence Cook Pendleton, Richmond, received a widow's pension in 1902 from the VA Confederate Pension Rolls. Florence C. Pendleton (keeper, boarding home) and daughters are listed in the 1920 Richmond, VA census, pg. 6A.

Children of JOHN PENDLETON and FLORENCE JOHNSON are:
  i. WINTERTON ASHBY[11] PENDLETON, b. Jul 08, 1884, VA.
      Winterton Ashby Pendleton registered in Richmond, VA for the WWI draft (Ref. 210).

  ii. JOHN PENDLETON, b. Feb 1888, VA.
  iii. DUDLEY FLEET PENDLETON, b. Feb 19, 1889, VA.
      Dudley Fleet Pendleton registered in Richmond, VA for the WWI draft (Ref. 210).

  iv. JACQUELINE PENDLETON, b. May 1892, VA.
   v. FLORENCE C. PENDLETON, b. Aug 1896, VA.
  vi. GRACE L. PENDLETON, b. Mar 1898, VA.

412. BENJAMIN FLEET[10] PENDLETON (*GEORGE MACON[9], PHILIP[8], BENJAMIN[7], PHILIP[6], PHILIP[5], HENRY[4], HENRY[3], GEORGE[2], GEORGE[1]*) was born 1835 in King and Queen Co., VA, and died 1862 in the Civil War. He married ELLA WEST SALE Jan 28, 1859. She was born Abt. 1838 in VA, and died Aft. 1902 in Richmond, VA?

Benjamin F. Pendleton was a member of St. Stephen's Church, King & Queen Co. He worked as a farmer before the war. Benjamin served in the VA 26th Infantry Companies I and C as a Sgt., CSA. He enlisted 24 June 1861, Gloucester Point. He transferred on 1 Sep 1862 from Company I to Company C (at Chaffin's Farm, VA). Benjamin was killed at Webb's Farm, VA on 17 Jun 1864.

The marriage of Benjamin F. Pendleton and Ella West, King and Queen County, was announced in the Daily Express, Petersburg, VA, January 28, 1859, page 2, column 4. Ella W. Pendleton and Chantina are listed in the 1870 Newton Township, King and Queen Co., VA census, pg. 442. Ella Pendleton is listed in the 1880 Newton, King and Queen Co., VA census in the household of her brother, Benjamin P. Sale. Ella W. Pendleton, widow of Benjamin F., is listed in the Richmond, Virginia City Directories, 1889-90, address 2112 Broad, E. Richmond, VA. Ella W. Pendleton, Richmond, is listed in the VA Confederate pension rolls (1902).

Child of BENJAMIN PENDLETON and ELLA SALE is:
  i. CHANTINA[11] PENDLETON, b. Abt. 1860.

413. ELLA[10] PENDLETON (*GEORGE MACON[9], PHILIP[8], BENJAMIN[7], PHILIP[6], PHILIP[5], HENRY[4], HENRY[3], GEORGE[2], GEORGE[1]*) was born Abt. 1841 in King and

Queen Co., VA, and died 1933 in Newton, King and Queen Co., VA? She married JOHN CRAWFORD CRUMP. He was born 1827 in VA, and died 1889 in King and Queen Co., VA?

John C. Crump and family are listed in the 1880 census, King and Queen Co., VA, pg. 449D.

Children of ELLA PENDLETON and JOHN CRUMP are:
    i.   JOHN[11] CRUMP, b. Abt. 1862, VA.
    ii. GEORGE R. CRUMP, b. Abt. 1868, VA.
    iii. MARGARET LOUISE CRUMP, b. 1872, VA; m. ROBERT LEE GATHRIGHT.
    iv. SALLIE CRUMP, b. Abt. 1876, VA.
    v.   ELLA CRUMP, b. Abt. 1878, VA.
    vi. CATHERINE A. CRUMP, b. Abt. 1888, VA.

414. JAMES B.[10] PENDLETON (*BENJAMIN[9], BENJAMIN[8], PHILIP[7], PHILIP[6], PHILIP[5], HENRY[4], HENRY[3], GEORGE[2], GEORGE[1]*) was born Abt. 1829 in KY. He married MARY C. She was born Abt. 1831 in TN.

James B. Pendleton (farmer) and family are listed in the 1860 Wayne Co., IL census adjacent to his father Benjamin's household. James B. Pendleton, 2nd Lt, served in the 111th Illinois infantry, K Company, Union Army. Company K was from Wayne and Marion Cos., IL.

Children of JAMES PENDLETON and MARY C. are:
    i.   MARY E.[11] PENDLETON, b. Abt. 1844, IL.
    ii. PHOEBE PENDLETON, b. Abt. 1847, IL.
    iii. WILLIAM B. PENDLETON, b. Abt. 1849, IL.
         William B. Pendleton is buried in the Cave Hill National Cemetery, Plot 1198 Louisville, Jefferson County, Kentucky. He died Nov 16, 1863 while a private in Company D, 84th Illinois Infantry, Union Army. Company D was from Marion Co., IL.

    iv. IDA MAY PENDLETON, b. 1860, IL.

415. ELIZABETH JENKINS[10] PENDLETON (*JOHN[9], JAMES[8], PHILIP[7], PHILIP[6], PHILIP[5], HENRY[4], HENRY[3], GEORGE[2], GEORGE[1]*) was born May 28, 1816 in Buckingham Co., VA, and died Feb 12, 1903 in Mt. Vernon, Lawrence, MO. She married PORTER JONES Nov 14, 1831 in Caldwell Co., KY. He was born Dec 11, 1808 in Hopkins Co., KY, and died Mar 22, 1884 in Mt. Vernon, Lawrence, MO.

Children of ELIZABETH PENDLETON and PORTER JONES are:
    i.   ELIZABETH[11] JONES, b. 1842; d. 1910.
    ii. ALICE J. JONES, b. 1858, Mt. Vernon, MO; m. ROBERT MILLSAP.
    iii. NATHAN B. JONES, b. Abt. 1852, MO.
    iv. NEELE W. JONES, b. Abt. 1854, MO.

416. WILLIAM MONROE[10] PENDLETON *(JOHN[9], JAMES[8], PHILIP[7], PHILIP[6], PHILIP[5], HENRY[4], HENRY[3], GEORGE[2], GEORGE[1])* was born 1821 in VA, and died 1909 in MO? He married (1) NANCY DUNNING Apr 21, 1840 in Caldwell Co., KY. She was born 1820 in KY, and died 1892 in Lawrence Co., MO. He married (2) NANCY U. SWEARINGEN Nov 21, 1893 in MO. She was born 1836.

The following account was written by Lula Pendleton, a descendant of William Pendleton and Nancy Dunning (Ref. 261).

William Pendleton was a young lad of about five or six years of age when his parents left Virginia and headed west. Evidently, several families of the Pendletons left Virginia on or about the same time. Quite a number of them appear in Tennessee about the same time. John, William's father, spent some time in Tennessee before heading on to Kentucky where they arrived in Caldwell County by 1831. The remainder of William's youth was spent in Caldwell and Christian County where a cousin lived. William was married in Caldwell County in 1840 and continued living there until 1846, when he, along with several other family members, moved to Lawrence County, Missouri. William obtained fifty-five acres of land from the General Land Office (Certificate No. 25063) in 1860, just down the road from the Dover Baptist Church. By 1879, he had eighty acres of land in Township 27, Range 25 West, Section 3. This is where he raised all nine of his children.

William was a farmer. When he first moved to Missouri, he lived in the Mount Vernon Township, later moving to the Turnback Township, where he farmed and lived until his death. He was a strong Republican and a staunch supporter of Abraham Lincoln when he was running for the Presidency. William was in the Civil War "Home Guard" enlisting May 18, 1861 at Elm Branch, and mustered in the same day by Captain Burrow, Company B. He was enrolled June 16, 1861 by John M. Filler, and discharged at Mount Vernon, August 10, 1861. He applied for a pension of disability, having paralysis and epileptic fits, in 1891, 1895, and 1901 and 1905, but he never received a pension. His four oldest sons also served in the Civil War.

On August 28, 1891, William paid $75 to A.L. Crane of Garland County, Arkansas, for his invention of a Washing Compound, Patent No. 413035. The Patent Deed agreement was good for a term of seventeen years. It is not known whether William ever made any money from this invention"

Nancy Dunning was married first in Caldwell County, Kentucky, on March 26, 1837 to James Pettit. He must have died soon after their marriage. She and William Pendleton were married by J. A. Cartwright and her name is given as Anney Pettit. This could have been misspelled or perhaps her middle name was Ann. Nancy was a midwife and delivered many of her grandchildren, nieces and nephews. The latest record found, so far, showing her as a midwife was in 1888, just four years prior to her death at the age of 72 years. One of the annual events that the family looked forward to every year was the Chesapeake Camp Ground religious camp meeting. It was during the one held in 1892 that Nancy Pendleton died. A record of some of the meeting was kept in the diary of Mr. Dobbin Hillhouse, and her death is mentioned in his diary. Her grave has a marker but there is not one on William's. He is presumed to be buried in the unmarked grave next to her.

Children of WILLIAM PENDLETON and NANCY DUNNING are:
713.   i.   JAMES MONROE[11] PENDLETON, b. Jan 1841, Caldwell Co., KY; d. Aft. 1900, Lawrence Co., MO?
714.   ii.   JOHN WILLIS PENDLETON, b. Oct 1842, Caldwell Co., KY; d. Aft. 1920, Lawrence Co., MO?
715.   iii.   GEORGE WASHINGTON PENDLETON, b. Jan 1845, Caldwell Co., KY; d. Oct 03, 1914, Mt. Vernon, MO.
716.   iv.   NATHANIEL CORDA PENDLETON, b. Jan 07, 1847, Lawrence Co., MO; d. 1923, Jasper, MO?
717.   v.   MARY CATHERINE PENDLETON, b. Mar 16, 1849, Lawrence Co., MO; d. Apr 1916, AR.
718.   vi.   ELIZABETH J. PENDLETON, b. Abt. 1851, Lawrence Co., MO.
719.   vii.   WILLIAM PORTER PENDLETON, b. 1853, Lawrence Co., MO.
      viii.   SIRENA JANE PENDLETON, b. 1855, Lawrence Co., MO; m. JOHN F. CULTON, Aug 14, 1879, Lawrence Co., MO; b. Abt. 1853, MO.
720.   ix.   ALFRED SIEGEL PENDLETON, b. Sep 02, 1861, Lawrence Co., MO; d. Aft. 1920, Erie Co., MO?

417. JOHN[10] PENDLETON (*JOHN[9], JAMES[8], PHILIP[7], PHILIP[6], PHILIP[5], HENRY[4], HENRY[3], GEORGE[2], GEORGE[1]*) was born 1824 in Buckingham Co., VA, and died Nov 11, 1897 in Lawrence Co., MO. He married (1) ELIZABETH J. COLLEY Oct 07, 1846 in Caldwell Co., KY. She was born Abt. 1830 in Caldwell Co., KY, and died Abt. 1855 in Caldwell Co., KY? He married (2) CLARISA F. COLLEY Nov 29, 1857 in Lawrence Co., MO. She was born Abt. 1836 in KY, and died Aft. 1880 in Lawrence Co., MO?

John Pendleton (farmer) and family are listed in the 1850 Caldwell Co., KY census. John and Clarissa Pendleton and family are listed in the 1860 Sebastian Co, AR census.

Children of JOHN PENDLETON and ELIZABETH COLLEY are:
      i.   WILLIAM DAVID[11] PENDLETON, b. Abt. 1847, Caldwell Co., KY.
      ii.   JAMES G. PENDLETON, b. Abt. 1849.
      iii.   ELLEN E. PENDLETON, b. Abt. 1854, KY.

Children of JOHN PENDLETON and CLARISA COLLEY are:
      iv.   MARTHA J.[11] PENDLETON, b. Abt. 1859, MO.
      v.   THOMAS J.T. PENDLETON, b. Abt. 1861, MO.
      vi.   GEORGE W. PENDLETON, b. Abt. 1865, MO.
      vii.   HENRY S. PENDLETON, b. Abt. 1868, MO.
      viii.   CLARISSA S. PENDLETON, b. Abt. 1874, MO.
      ix.   DORA A. PENDLETON, b. Abt. 1877, MO.
      x.   NANCY L. PENDLETON, b. Jan 1880, MO.

418. SARAH JANE[10] PENDLETON (*JOHN[9], JAMES[8], PHILIP[7], PHILIP[6], PHILIP[5], HENRY[4], HENRY[3], GEORGE[2], GEORGE[1]*) was born 1835 in Caldwell Co., KY, and died Aft. 1880 in Aurora, Lawrence Co., MO. She married ZACHARIAH DUNNING Nov 16, 1848 in Lawrence Co., MO.

Children of SARAH PENDLETON and ZACHARIAH DUNNING are:
- i. JESSE B.[11] DUNNING, b. Abt. 1849.
- ii. MARY F. DUNNING, b. Abt. 1851.
- iii. JONAH C. DUNNING, b. Abt. 1853.
- iv. JOHN W. DUNNING, b. Abt. 1855.
- v. JANY DUNNING, b. Abt. 1857.

419. LUCINDA[10] PENDLETON (*JOSEPH*[9], *MICAJAH*[8], *PHILIP*[7], *PHILIP*[6], *PHILIP*[5], *HENRY*[4], *HENRY*[3], *GEORGE*[2], *GEORGE*[1]) was born 1803. She married (1) WILLIAM MORGAN Nov 1821 in VA. He was born 1774 in VA, and died 1826 in Fort Niagara, NY. She married (2) GEORGE WASHINGTON HARRIS Nov 23, 1830 in Genessee Co., NY. He was born Apr 01, 1780. She married (3) JOSEPH SMITH 1838 in MO. He was born Dec 23, 1805 in Windsor Co., VT.

Children of LUCINDA PENDLETON and WILLIAM MORGAN are:
- i. LUCINDA WESLEY[11] MORGAN.
- ii. THOMAS JEFFERSON MORGAN.

420. PHILIP HARPER[10] PENDLETON (*JOSEPH*[9], *MICAJAH*[8], *PHILIP*[7], *PHILIP*[6], *PHILIP*[5], *HENRY*[4], *HENRY*[3], *GEORGE*[2], *GEORGE*[1]) was born Abt. 1810, and died Bef. 1850 in Niagara Falls, NY. He married ELIZABETH VAUGHN. She was born Abt. 1811 in VA, and died Aft. 1850.

An Elizabeth Pendleton (grandmother; 65) is listed in the household of James R. Ross in the 1880 Black Lick, Wythe Co., VA census.

Children of PHILIP PENDLETON and ELIZABETH VAUGHN are:
- 721. i. JOSEPH H.[11] PENDLETON, b. 1831, Wythe Co., VA; d. Civil War.
- ii. ELIZABETH PENDLETON, b. 1832, Wythe Co., VA; d. Aft. 1880.
- iii. SARAH "SALLY" PENDLETON, b. 1834, VA.
- 722. iv. MORGAN MITCHELL PENDLETON, b. Mar 15, 1836, Wythe Co., VA; d. Jul 09, 1894, Black Lick, Wythe Co., VA?
- v. HIRAM PENDLETON, b. Abt. 1838, Wythe Co., VA; d. Civil War.

421. JAMES VANCE[10] PENDLETON (*JOSEPH*[9], *MICAJAH*[8], *PHILIP*[7], *PHILIP*[6], *PHILIP*[5], *HENRY*[4], *HENRY*[3], *GEORGE*[2], *GEORGE*[1]) was born Feb 28, 1816 in Chilhowie, VA, and died Apr 1870 in Giles Co., VA? He married ANN MARIA MURPHY May 20, 1842 in Tazewell Co., VA. She was born Feb 1822 in VA, and died Aft. 1900 in Hamblen Co., TN?

James Pendleton is listed as a carpenter in the 1850 Pulaski Co., VA census (age 34) and in Pearisburg, Giles Co., VA in the 1860 census. In speaking of his father [James Vance Pendleton], Mr. Wirt W. Pendleton says: "My father was a fine architect. Many of the fine Old Colonial homes of southwest Virginia stand now to his credit, some few public buildings. He was far ahead of his time - always seeking knowledge" (Ref. 262).

Children of JAMES PENDLETON and ANN MURPHY are:

723.   i.   ANNE ELIZABETH[11] PENDLETON, b. Feb 11, 1845, VA; d. 1928, Bristol, TN.

724.   ii.   ALBERT GALLATIN PENDLETON, b. Feb 02, 1845, VA; d. Jul 24, 1891, San Marcos, TX.

      iii.   BENTLEY GAINES PENDLETON, b. Jul 02, 1847; d. Dec 26, 1847.

725.   iv.   LETITIA VIRGINIA PENDLETON, b. Mar 23, 1849, VA.

726.   v.   WILLIAM H. JORDAN PENDLETON, b. Jan 23, 1851, VA; d. Aft. 1900, Hamblen Co., TN?

      vi.   TAZEWELL MURPHY PENDLETON, b. Jul 1855; d. Nella, AR?

727.   vii.   BASCOM WOOD PENDLETON, b. Jul 23, 1857, VA; d. Mar 08, 1931, Sullivan Co., TN.

728.   viii.   WIRT WINTWORTH PENDLETON, b. May 07, 1860, VA; d. Aft. 1906, Baltimore, MD.

729.   ix.   FRANK LESLIE PENDLETON, b. Nov 10, 1867, VA; d. 1917.

Generation No. 11 – Reconstruction

The eleventh generation consists of the great (4) grandchildren of the immigrant Philip Pendleton and Isabella Hurt. The time period is from about 1840, when Elizabeth Pendleton, the first born of this generation, married in Kentucky, to at least 1975 when perhaps the last of this generation, Charles A. Pendleton, died at age 84 in Mt. Sterling, KY. Significant members of the eleventh generation who had no known children and are thus listed as children of tenth generation Pendletons include Louis Beauregard Pendleton (1802-1868), James Albert Pendleton (1844-1862), Robert Carter Pendleton (1870-1891), Alexander Robinson Pendleton (1848-aft. 1900), George Allen Pendleton (1823-1871), Rose Page Pendleton (1835-1910), John Overton Pendleton (1851-1916), Henry H. Pendleton (1853-), Lilbourn H. Pendleton (1838-1864), Baldwin Alexander Pendleton (1856-aft. 1920), William Wood Pendleton (1845-1870), Daniel Micajah Pendleton (1887-aft. 1920), Charles Edward Pendleton (1855-), John Malcolm Pendleton (1841-1862), and William B. Pendleton (1849-).

At least 32 men of this generation born before 1850 served in the Civil War; the majority, however, were born after that time and were spared that experience. In fact, at least 5 were born late enough to register for the World War I draft. Most spent their lives in the latter half of the 19th century during the period of reconstruction. The loss of property and lives throughout the south during the Civil War created great hardships; none greater than that in Virginia where much of the war took place.

The eleventh generation set up over 300 households in at least 27 different states from coast to coast. The portion that remained in Virginia continued to decline to about 25% of the total as families continued moving west. Just over 16% remained in Kentucky, about 14% in Missouri, while Texas residents increased to about 10%. Other predominant states included Tennessee, Georgia, Arkansas, and West Virginia. Still very few ventured north into Yankee territory or into the deep South.

Generation No. 11

422. JAMES[11] PENDLETON *(THOMAS CATLETT[10], HENRY[9], HENRY[8], JAMES[7], HENRY[6], PHILIP[5], HENRY[4], HENRY[3], GEORGE[2], GEORGE[1])* was born Abt. 1840 in KY. He married MARCELLA. She was born Abt. 1848 in KY.

James Pendleton and family are listed in the 1870 Allison's Precinct, Hardin Co., KY census.

Children of JAMES PENDLETON and MARCELLA are:
    i.   MARTHA[12] PENDLETON, b. Abt. 1867, KY.
   ii.   ELIZABETH PENDLETON, b. Abt. 1868, KY.
  iii.   ELIZA PENDLETON, b. 1869, KY.

423. WILLIAM E.[11] PENDLETON *(THOMAS CATLETT[10], HENRY[9], HENRY[8], JAMES[7], HENRY[6], PHILIP[5], HENRY[4], HENRY[3], GEORGE[2], GEORGE[1])* was born Abt. 1846 in KY, and died Aft. 1880 in Hardin Co., KY? He married MARY E. She was born Apr 20, 1844 in KY, and died Apr 04, 1895 in Hardin Co., KY.

William E. Pendleton (blacksmith) and family are listed in the 1870, Allison's Precinct, Hardin Co., KY census. Mary E. Pendleton is buried in St. Patrick's Cemetery, Fort Knox, Hardin Co., KY.

Children of WILLIAM PENDLETON and MARY E. are:

    i.   JAMES T.[12] PENDLETON, b. Nov 08, 1866, KY; d. Dec 12, 1915, Hardin Co., KY.

        J. T. Pendleton is buried in St. Patrick's Cemetery, Fort Knox, Hardin Co., KY.

730.   ii. JOHN H. PENDLETON, b. 1868, KY; d. Aft. 1910, Hardin Co., KY?

    iii. WILLIAM PENDLETON, b. Abt. 1869, KY.

    iv. R. E. PENDLETON, b. Abt. 1871, KY.

731.   v. RICHARD A. PENDLETON, b. Dec 1873, KY.

    vi. E. C. PENDLETON, b. Abt. 1877, KY.

    vii. V. D. PENDLETON, b. Abt. 1879, KY.

    viii. LORADA PENDLETON, b. Aug 1885, KY.

424. JOHN THOMAS[11] PENDLETON *(THOMAS CATLETT[10], HENRY[9], HENRY[8], JAMES[7], HENRY[6], PHILIP[5], HENRY[4], HENRY[3], GEORGE[2], GEORGE[1])* was born Jul 19, 1848 in KY, and died Apr 08, 1922 in Hardin Co., KY. He married THERESA CATHERINE REDMAN Abt. 1874. She was born Nov 29, 1857 in KY, and died Apr 1939 in Tippecanoe Co., IN?

John T. Pendleton (farmer) and family are listed in the 1880 and 1900 Hardin Co., KY census.

Children of JOHN PENDLETON and THERESA REDMAN are:

    i.   HENRY A.[12] PENDLETON, b. Dec 27, 1875.

    ii. PRINCE E. PENDLETON, b. Dec 02, 1877.

    iii. MARGARET PENDLETON, b. Jun 22, 1879.

    iv. MARY C. PENDLETON, b. May 11, 1881.

732.   v. PAUL COLUMBUS PENDLETON, b. Jun 27, 1883, Meade Co., KY?; d. Aft. 1930, Randolph, IN?

    vi. NETTIE A. PENDLETON, b. Jul 27, 1885.

733.   vii. GEORGE T. PENDLETON, b. Oct 18, 1887, KY; d. Aft. 1930, Tippecanoe Co., IN?

    viii. LOUIS ANDREW PENDLETON, b. Jun 12, 1891; d. Oct 1967, Gardnerville, NV; m. GRACE M.; b. Oct 19, 1898; d. Jan 1979, Gardnerville, NV.

    ix. NEZZIE M. PENDLETON, b. Feb 07, 1893.

    x. ZELMA E. PENDLETON, b. Sep 17, 1895.

xi. AGNES H. PENDLETON, b. Jul 02, 1898; d. Aft. 1960, Rineyville, KY?; m. JESSE L. BERRY; b. Jul 28, 1896; d. Dec 24, 1951, Meade Co., KY.

425. HELEN N.[11] PENDLETON (*THORNTON PRESLEY COCKE*[10], *EDMUND*[9], *HENRY*[8], *JAMES*[7], *HENRY*[6], *PHILIP*[5], *HENRY*[4], *HENRY*[3], *GEORGE*[2], *GEORGE*[1]) was born 1841 in VA, and died 1912 in MD? She married HAMMOND DORSEY 1869 in MD. He was born 1841 in MD, and died 1898 in Howard Co., MD?

Children of HELEN PENDLETON and HAMMOND DORSEY are:
    i. EMILY[12] DORSEY, b. Abt. 1874, MD; d. Aft. 1920, Washington DC?
       Emily Pendleton is listed in the 1920 Washington DC census in the household of her Aunt Charlotte Pendleton Plummer.

    ii. BAKER DORSEY, b. Abt. 1876, MD.

426. SOPHIA ELIZABETH[11] PENDLETON (*ROBERT WARD*[10], *EDMUND*[9], *HENRY*[8], *JAMES*[7], *HENRY*[6], *PHILIP*[5], *HENRY*[4], *HENRY*[3], *GEORGE*[2], *GEORGE*[1]) was born Apr 09, 1850 in Baltimore, MD, and died 1906 in Philadelphia, PA? She married J. LINDLEY GARBER 1872, son of S. GARBER and EMMA. He was born Abt. 1850 in PA, and died Aft. 1880 in Philadelphia, PA?
    J. Lindsey (keeps coal yard) and Sophia Garber are listed in the 1880 census, Philadelphia, PA in the household of his father.

Child of SOPHIA PENDLETON and J. GARBER is:
    i. PENDLETON[12] GARBER, b. Abt. 1875, PA.

427. DAVID ELLIS[11] PENDLETON (*PHILIP PETER*[10], *EDMUND*[9], *HENRY*[8], *JAMES*[7], *HENRY*[6], *PHILIP*[5], *HENRY*[4], *HENRY*[3], *GEORGE*[2], *GEORGE*[1]) was born 1844 in MD, and died Apr 07, 1900. He married LAURA CLAY SLATER 1864. She was born Abt. 1846 in VA.
    David E. Pendleton served three years in the Confederate Army; VA 7th Cavalry, Company A.

Child of DAVID PENDLETON and LAURA SLATER is:
    i. PHILIP PETER[12] PENDLETON, b. 1865; d. 1875.

428. NATHAN SMITH[11] PENDLETON (*PHILIP PETER*[10], *EDMUND*[9], *HENRY*[8], *JAMES*[7], *HENRY*[6], *PHILIP*[5], *HENRY*[4], *HENRY*[3], *GEORGE*[2], *GEORGE*[1]) was born 1856 in MD, and died Aft. 1920 in Baltimore, MD? He married JANE HEPBURN PATTERSON 1884. She was born Abt. 1870 in MD, and died Aft. 1920 in Baltimore, MD?
    Nathan Pendleton (pay master, B&O RR) and family are listed in the 1920 Baltimore, MD census.

Children of NATHAN PENDLETON and JANE PATTERSON are:
    i.   NATHAN SMITH[12] PENDLETON, JR., b. Dec 22, 1888, MD; d. Jan 1972, Baltimore, MD.

         N. S. Pendleton Jr. registered for the World War I draft in Baltimore, MD (Ref. 210).

    ii. ALFRED PATTERSON PENDLETON, b. May 23, 1890, MD; d. Sep 1965, Baltimore, MD.

         Alfred Patterson Pendleton registered for the World War I draft in Baltimore, MD (Ref. 210).

    iii. MARY LECHE PENDLETON, b. Dec 24, 1893, MD; d. Apr 1977, Baltimore, MD; m. HERBERT DAVIS STITH.

429. ALTHEA EARLY[11] PENDLETON (*GEORGE WASHINGTON[10], EDMUND[9], HENRY[8], JAMES[7], HENRY[6], PHILIP[5], HENRY[4], HENRY[3], GEORGE[2], GEORGE[1]*) was born 1850 in AR, and died Aft. 1930 in Hot Springs, AR? She married GEORGE LELAND LEATHERMAN, JUDGE 1876 in Star City, AR. He was born Abt. 1848 in of Hot Springs, AR, and died 1903 in Hot Springs, AR?
    A.E. Leatherman and family are listed in the 1910 Hot Springs, AR census.

Children of ALTHEA PENDLETON and GEORGE LEATHERMAN are:
    i.   GEORGE PENDLETON[12] LEATHERMAN, b. Abt. 1878, TN; d. Aft. 1930, AR.
    ii. MABEL LEATHERMAN, b. Abt. 1880, AR.

430. JOHN MORRIS[11] PENDLETON (*JOHN TAYLOR[10], JOHN[9], JAMES[8], JAMES[7], HENRY[6], PHILIP[5], HENRY[4], HENRY[3], GEORGE[2], GEORGE[1]*) was born Mar 08, 1823 in KY, and died Aft. 1900 in Montgomery Co., TN? He married ELIZA HUSTON 1855. She was born May 08, 1829 in KY, and died Jan 09, 1861 in Frankfort, KY?
    John Morris Pendleton is in the household of John Morris in 1850 Census, Franklin Co., KY, District 1, pg 6. John M Pendleton (47; Clerk in Post Office) and John T. Pendleton, his son (11; attending school) are listed in the 1870 Franklin, Frankfort Co., KY census. This may be the J.M Pendleton mentioned in the biography of N.B. Smith of Franklin Co. who went to Frankfort to clerk for J. M. Pendleton and remained two years; then clerked in other stores in Frankfort until June 1883 (Ref. 123).

Children of JOHN PENDLETON and ELIZA HUSTON are:
    i.   JOHN TAYLOR[12] PENDLETON, b. Dec 14, 1858.
    ii. SALLIE HUSTON PENDLETON, b. Jan 01, 1861; d. Apr 04, 1861.

431. ELIZABETH W.[11] PENDLETON (*JOHN TAYLOR[10], JOHN[9], JAMES[8], JAMES[7], HENRY[6], PHILIP[5], HENRY[4], HENRY[3], GEORGE[2], GEORGE[1]*) was born Feb 22, 1828 in KY, and died Aft. 1880 in Frankfort, KY? She married JAMES MONROE Jan 22, 1850 in Frankfort, KY. He was born Jun 15, 1823, and died Apr 20, 1860 in Frankfort, KY?

The family of Elizabeth Monroe is listed in the 1880 Frankfort, KY census, pg 175D.

Children of ELIZABETH PENDLETON and JAMES MONROE are:
   i.   ELIZABETH W.[12] MONROE, b. Abt. 1853.
   ii. JOHN P. MONROE, b. Abt. 1856.
   iii. ANNIE M. MONROE, b. Abt. 1859.

432. CATHERINE E.T.[11] PENDLETON *(JOHN TAYLOR[10], JOHN[9], JAMES[8], JAMES[7], HENRY[6], PHILIP[5], HENRY[4], HENRY[3], GEORGE[2], GEORGE[1])* was born Feb 04, 1830 in KY, and died Oct 27, 1882 in Paducah, KY? She married JOHN J. THOMAS Aug 13, 1852. He was born Abt. 1815 in VA, and died Aft. 1880 in Paducah, KY?
   Catherine Morris is included in the household of John Morris in 1850 Census, Franklin Co., KY, District 1, pg 6. The family of John J. Thomas is listed in the 1880 census, Paducah, KY, pg. 122B.

Children of CATHERINE PENDLETON and JOHN THOMAS are:
   i.   PENDLETON[12] THOMAS, b. Abt. 1855, KY.
   ii. ANNIE M. THOMAS, b. Abt. 1861, KY.
   iii. KATE THOMAS, b. Abt. 1874, TN.

433. ELIZABETH[11] PENDLETON *(THOMAS CLAYTON[10], JOHN[9], JAMES[8], JAMES[7], HENRY[6], PHILIP[5], HENRY[4], HENRY[3], GEORGE[2], GEORGE[1])* was born Abt. 1818 in KY, and died Aft. 1860 in Jefferson Co., KY? She married HENRY W. ALLISON. He was born 1804 in MD, and died Aft. 1860 in Jefferson Co., KY?

Children of ELIZABETH PENDLETON and HENRY ALLISON are:
   i.   LAURA[12] ALLISON, b. Abt. 1844, KY.
   ii. HENRY ALLISON, b. Abt. 1846, KY.
   iii. OLIVIA ALLISON, b. Abt. 1856, KY.

434. GEORGE TAYLOR[11] PENDLETON *(THOMAS CLAYTON[10], JOHN[9], JAMES[8], JAMES[7], HENRY[6], PHILIP[5], HENRY[4], HENRY[3], GEORGE[2], GEORGE[1])* was born Dec 18, 1823 in KY, and died Jan 25, 1883 in Cooper Co., MO. He married CATHERINE ANNE MAGRUDER May 01, 1851, daughter of OWEN MAGRUDER. She was born Oct 23, 1830 in KY, and died Oct 02, 1909 in Cooper Co., MO.
   George Pendleton, 27, is in the household of R.C.N. Barbour, farmer, in the 1850 Oldham Co., KY census, Dist. 1, pg. 152 (near John and Nannie Pendleton). G. T. Pendleton (farmer) and family are listed in the 1860 Cooper Co., MO census.

Children of GEORGE PENDLETON and CATHERINE MAGRUDER are:
734.   i.   THOMAS OWEN[12] PENDLETON, b. Jan 26, 1852, KY; d. Jan 1926, Cooper Co., MO.

ii. WILLIAM GIBSON PENDLETON, b. Jan 06, 1854, KY; d. Aft. 1930, Cooper Co., MO?; m. (1) HARRIET F. MCKENZIE, Dec 27, 1888; b. Oct 31, 1864, NY; d. Mar 11, 1926, Moniteau Co., MO; m. (2) MRS. DORA JONES HOWELL.

William Pendleton (lawyer) and Hattie are listed in the 1900 Cooper Co., MO census, pg. 61a. William G. Pendleton, lawyer, is listed in the Missouri State Gazetteer and Business Directory for 1881-82, Section B. The death of Mrs. Harriett F. McKenzie Pendleton is recorded in Reference 263.

iii. ELIZABETH ALLISON PENDLETON, b. Dec 27, 1856, KY; m. CHARLES R. FORSTER, Dec 27, 1887; b. 1857; d. 1924.
735. iv. CATHERINE HARRISON PENDLETON, b. Jan 16, 1860, MO; d. Dec 19, 1945, Cooper Co., MO.
736. v. STAPLETON CRUTCHFIELD PENDLETON, b. Jul 14, 1862, MO.
vi. SUSAN REBECCA PENDLETON, b. Mar 29, 1865, near Louisville, KY; d. 1958, Cooper Co., MO.
vii. GEORGE TAYLOR PENDLETON, b. Aug 12, 1867, MO; d. Mar 05, 1924, Moniteau Co., MO.
737. viii. ELEANOR CHINN PENDLETON, b. Sep 03, 1872, Cooper Co., MO; d. Aft. 1910.

435. MARY ELEANOR[11] PENDLETON (*THOMAS CLAYTON[10], JOHN[9], JAMES[8], JAMES[7], HENRY[6], PHILIP[5], HENRY[4], HENRY[3], GEORGE[2], GEORGE[1]*) was born Abt. 1824 in KY, and died Aug 20, 1853 in Mercer Co., KY? She married JOHN CHRISTOPHER CHINN Apr 22, 1845, son of CHRISTOPHER CHINN and SARAH HARDIN. He was born Nov 10, 1823 in KY, and died Oct 29, 1870 in Mercer Co., KY?

Children of MARY PENDLETON and JOHN CHINN are (Ref. 264):
i. CHRISTOPHER "KIT"[12] CHINN, b. Jun 29, 1846, KY; d. Abt. 1862, the battle of Salt Works, VA.
ii. JOHN PENDLETON CHINN, b. Feb 11, 1849, Harrodsburg, Mercer Co., KY; d. Jan 13, 1920; m. RUTH MORGAN, Feb 18, 1868; b. Feb 16, 1849, Mercer Co., KY.
iii. SARAH HARDIN CHINN, b. Mar 08, 1851, KY; d. Feb 13, 1853, KY.

436. REBECCA[11] PENDLETON (*THOMAS CLAYTON[10], JOHN[9], JAMES[8], JAMES[7], HENRY[6], PHILIP[5], HENRY[4], HENRY[3], GEORGE[2], GEORGE[1]*) was born Feb 25, 1830 in KY, and died Aft. 1880 in Oldham Co., KY? She married JAMES F. ALLISON. He was born Abt. 1803 in KY, and died Jan 19, 1877 in Oldham Co., KY?

Rebecca Allison and family are listed in the 1880 Oldham Co., KY census, pg 22D.

Children of REBECCA PENDLETON and JAMES ALLISON are:
i. JOHN P.[12] ALLISON, b. Abt. 1857.
ii. ELLA ALLISON, b. Abt. 1861.
iii. FLORENCE ALLISON, b. Abt. 1864.

iv. REBECCA ALLISON, b. Abt. 1866.
v. JAMES E. ALLISON, b. Abt. 1870.

437. JAMES FRENCH[11] PENDLETON (*JAMES[10], THOMAS[9], JAMES[8], JAMES[7], HENRY[6], PHILIP[5], HENRY[4], HENRY[3], GEORGE[2], GEORGE[1]*) was born Jul 09, 1834 in Culpeper Co., VA, and died Jun 15, 1918 in Ryan, OK. He married (1) MARY ANNE HART Sep 06, 1857 in Buchanan Co., MO. She was born 1837 in KY, and died 1860 in Buchanan Co., MO. He married (2) KITTY SMITH Aft. 1860.

James F. Pendleton served with the MO 1st Cavalry, Company E as a Sgt. French S. Pendleton (36; clerk in dry goods store) is listed in the 1870 Catalpa, Culpeper Co., VA census.

Children of JAMES PENDLETON and MARY HART are:
738. i. JAMES STROTHER[12] PENDLETON, b. Nov 15, 1858, DeKalb, MO; d. May 27, 1930, St. Joseph, MO.
ii. MARION A. PENDLETON, b. 1860, Buchanan Co., MO; d. Buchanan Co., MO.

Child of JAMES PENDLETON and KITTY SMITH is:
iii. JOHN SANFORD[12] PENDLETON.
John Sanford Pendleton registered for the WWI draft in Cincinnati, OH (Ref. 210).

438. HENRY CLAY[11] PENDLETON (*JAMES[10], THOMAS[9], JAMES[8], JAMES[7], HENRY[6], PHILIP[5], HENRY[4], HENRY[3], GEORGE[2], GEORGE[1]*) was born Oct 22, 1842 in VA, and died May 19, 1913 in Culpeper Co., VA. He married FLETA ANNE COONS Dec 27, 1877 in Culpeper Co., VA? She was born Mar 1856 in VA, and died Aft. 1910 in Culpeper Co., VA.

Henry Clay Pendleton enlisted in the Confederate Army at Culpeper Court House on 17 April 1861 as a Private in B Company, 13th Infantry Regiment, VA. He transferred by 1862 and served on Jackson's Brigade, Johnston's Division; trans. Gunner in Sturdevant's Battalion. He was wounded Nov 12, 1863, at Petersburg (Ref. 220). Henry C. Pendleton (farmer) and family are listed in the 1900 Culpeper Co., VA census, pg. 6a. and in the 1910 Culpeper Co. census.

Children of HENRY PENDLETON and FLETA COONS are:
i. EDWARD WALTER[12] PENDLETON, b. Apr 29, 1879, VA.
Edward Walter Pendleton registered for the World War I draft in Washington, DC (Ref. 210).

ii. CLARENCE EVERETT PENDLETON, b. Feb 25, 1882, VA.
Clarence Everett Pendleton registered for the World War I draft in Washington, DC (Ref. 210).

iii. VIOLA GERTRUDE PENDLETON, b. Jun 19, 1883; d. Jun 19, 1884.

iv. CONNER SPILLMAN PENDLETON, b. Feb 22, 1885, VA; d. Sep 08, 1902.
v. JESSIE STROTHER PENDLETON, b. Jan 30, 1886, VA.

439. ANNE ELIZABETH[11] PENDLETON *(GEORGE WASHINGTON[10], THOMAS[9], JAMES[8], JAMES[7], HENRY[6], PHILIP[5], HENRY[4], HENRY[3], GEORGE[2], GEORGE[1])* was born Jul 06, 1837 in VA, and died 1877 in Clinton Co., MO? She married CHAMPION JEFFERSON WILKERSON Mar 20, 1861. He was born Abt. 1838 in MO, and died Aft. 1870 in Clinton Co., MO?

Children of ANNE PENDLETON and CHAMPION WILKERSON are:
i. CARRIE[12] WILKERSON, b. Abt. 1862, MO.
ii. FANNIE WILKERSON, b. Abt. 1865, MO.
iii. EMMA COLEMAN WILKERSON, b. Jan 29, 1867, Clinton Co., MO; m. JOHN A. OLIPHANT.
iv. JOHN WILKERSON, b. 1869, MO.

440. WASHINGTON WINTER[11] PENDLETON *(GEORGE WASHINGTON[10], THOMAS[9], JAMES[8], JAMES[7], HENRY[6], PHILIP[5], HENRY[4], HENRY[3], GEORGE[2], GEORGE[1])* was born Apr 05, 1858 in VA, and died Aft. 1920 in Richmond, VA? He married MARY L. SYNAN Jun 15, 1884. She was born Abt. 1869 in VA, and died Aft. 1920 in Richmond, VA?

Winter W. (merchant) and Mary L. Pendleton are listed in the 1920 Richmond, VA census, pg. 15A.

Child of WASHINGTON PENDLETON and MARY SYNAN is:
i. WILLIAM EDWIN[12] PENDLETON, b. Apr 03, 1885, VA.
William Edwin Pendleton registered for the World War I draft in Dinwiddie Co., VA .

441. ALBERT FRENCH[11] PENDLETON *(JOHN BOWIE[10], THOMAS[9], JAMES[8], JAMES[7], HENRY[6], PHILIP[5], HENRY[4], HENRY[3], GEORGE[2], GEORGE[1])* was born Apr 22, 1835 in MO, and died 1912 in Monroe Co., MO. He married (1) LUCRETIA MALLORY in Caldwell Co., MO. She was born Abt. 1842 in MO, and died Bef. 1880 in Monroe Co., MO? He married (2) MATILDA J. She was born Jun 1861 in MO.

Albert Pendleton (day laborer) and family are listed in the 1900 Lawrence Co., MO census, pg. 110a.

Children of ALBERT PENDLETON and LUCRETIA MALLORY are:
i. ODELL[12] PENDLETON, b. Dec 28, 1869, MO.
ii. ANNA PENDLETON, b. Abt. 1876, MO.
739. iii. LUCY KATHERINE PENDLETON, b. Abt. 1878, MO; d. Aft. 1910, Monroe Co., MO?

Children of ALBERT PENDLETON and MATILDA J. are:
740.   iv.   CLARENCE M.[12] PENDLETON, b. Oct 13, 1886, MO; d. Jul 16, 1931,
               Randolph Co., MO.
        v.   ARTHUR PENDLETON, b. Oct 1896, MO.

442. ARTHUR MENEFEE[11] PENDLETON *(JOHN BOWIE[10], THOMAS[9], JAMES[8], JAMES[7], HENRY[6], PHILIP[5], HENRY[4], HENRY[3], GEORGE[2], GEORGE[1])* was born Dec 28, 1840 in Monroe Co., MO, and died Feb 03, 1915 in Chandlerville, IL? He married HESTER ROGERS HEWITT Aug 10, 1869 in IL, daughter of IMLA HEWITT and SARAH WITTAKER. She was born Nov 09, 1843 in IL, and died 1918.

The following account is derived from a history of colonial families and an early history of Illinois (Refs. 179 and 265).

   Arthur Menefee Pendleton, dealer in grain and agricultural implements,
   Chandlerville, was educated in Paris Academy of Monroe Co. MO and studied medicine.
   His father, John Pendleton was born in Culpepper County, Va., Aug. 1, 1805; emigrated
   to Missouri in 1830, where he is now residing, engaged in farming. His wife, Elizabeth
   Odell Pendleton, the mother of our subject, was born in Rappahannock, Va., Aug. 22,
   1812, and died in 1871. She was the mother of ten children, of whom Arthur M. was the
   third; of the ten children but four are now living. At about the age of twenty-one years, he
   entered as clerk in a drug store in Paris, Mo., where he continued until about the time of
   the war. In 1861, he enlisted in the Third Missouri Reg. State Troops, and served for
   about fifteen months. He was wounded at Battle of Wilson Creek After his return from
   the army, he again engaged as clerk in a dry goods store at St. Louis, and various other
   places. In 1867, he removed to Illinois, and engaged in teaching school in Menard and
   Cass Counties, and in Chandlerville High School, of which he was Principal for three
   years and a half. In 1869, he married Miss Hester Hewitt, a native of New Jersey; born
   Nov. 9, 1843; she is the mother of three children, two of whom are living: Stella, aged ten
   years, and Arthur M., jr. aged eight. In 1879, he engaged in the grain and agricultural
   implement business. Mr. Pendleton is a member of the A.F. and A.M.; is Secretary of the
   Lodge. He has held the office of Village Clerk for two years [in 1882]. He became
   Superintendent of Chandlerville Schools and an officer of People's State Bank since its
   organization. A life long democrat, he was elected county clerk of Cass County, IL 1898-
   1906.

   Arthur M. Pendleton (county clerk) and family are listed in the 1900 Cass Co.,
IL census, pg. 147.

Children of ARTHUR PENDLETON and HESTER HEWITT are:
        i.   MAUDE MENEFEE[12] PENDLETON, b. Jul 24, 1870, IL; d. Feb 06, 1874.
741.   ii.   STELLA LEE PENDLETON, b. 1871, Menard Co., IL; d. May 11, 1930,
               Springfield, IL.
742.   iii.   ARTHUR MENEFEE PENDLETON, b. Oct 22, 1873, IL; d. Aft. 1920,
               McLean Co., IL?
        iv.   MUSA MAY PENDLETON, b. Aug 18, 1882, IL.
        v.   JOHN IMLA PENDLETON, b. Dec 27, 1884, IL; d. Aft. 1920,
               Chandlerville, IL?; m. VIOLA M. COLEMAN, 1917; b. Abt. 1883, IL; d.
               Aft. 1920, Chandlerville, IL?

John I. (merchant; retail grocery) and Viola Pendleton are listed in the 1920 Chandlerville, IL census.

743. vi. MYRTLE HEWITT PENDLETON, b. Jan 17, 1887, IL; d. Aft. 1930, Chandlerville, Cass Co., IL?

443. RICHARD J.[11] PENDLETON (*JOHN BOWIE*[10], *THOMAS*[9], *JAMES*[8], *JAMES*[7], *HENRY*[6], *PHILIP*[5], *HENRY*[4], *HENRY*[3], *GEORGE*[2], *GEORGE*[1]) was born Mar 06, 1845 in MO, and died Aft. 1900 in Monroe Co., MO? He married CATHERINE WIGGINGTON Dec 28, 1869. She was born 1845 in MO, and died 1889 in Monroe Co., MO?

Richard Pendleton (farm laborer) and family are listed in the 1900 Monroe Co., MO census, pg. 101.

Children of RICHARD PENDLETON and CATHERINE WIGGINGTON are:
   i. IDA MAY[12] PENDLETON, b. Jan 31, 1871; MO.
   ii. DAISY DEANE PENDLETON, b. Jun 22, 1872, MO; d. Aug 05, 1904.
   iii. EDNA EARL PENDLETON, b. Sep 12, 1874; d. Jul 06, 1875.
744. iv. CLAUD ERNEST PENDLETON, b. Jun 23, 1876, MO; d. May 23, 1944, AR.
   v. CLYDE ELMER PENDLETON, b. Aug 13, 1878; d. Jan 28, 1899.
   vi. INEZ MAUD PENDLETON, b. Jan 28, 1881, MO; d. Jan 31, 1904.
   vii. ESSIE LEE PENDLETON, b. Apr 15, 1883, MO; d. Aft. 1920, Roswell, NM?; m. JOSEPH H. DEKKER, Oct 18, 1912; b. Abt. 1885, Holland; d. Aft. 1920, Roswell, NM?
      Joseph and Essie Lee Dekker are listed in the 1920 Roswell, NM census along with Mae Pendleton (48; sister-in-law).

   viii. ARTHUR PITTS PENDLETON, b. Jan 08, 1886; d. Jun 23, 1887.

444. ALBERT GALLATIN[11] PENDLETON (*JAMES FRENCH*[10], *WILLIAM*[9], *JAMES*[8], *JAMES*[7], *HENRY*[6], *PHILIP*[5], *HENRY*[4], *HENRY*[3], *GEORGE*[2], *GEORGE*[1]) was born Feb 20, 1836 in Smyth Co., VA, and died Mar 02, 1901 in Roanoke, VA. He married (1) CATHERINE BLANK 1862. She died 1862. He married (2) OLIVIA P. TINSLEY Dec 20, 1865 in Amherst Co., VA, daughter of ZACHARIAH D. TINSLEY and MARY DAWSON. She died Apr 03, 1869 in Amherst Co, VA. He married (3) ELIZABETH MADISON SHEFFEY Oct 28, 1872 in Marion, VA. She was born Jan 05, 1842, and died May 10, 1878. He married (4) MISSOURI FREELOVE THOMAS Feb 26, 1879 in Smyth Co., VA. She was born Feb 28, 1846 in VA, and died Mar 03, 1929.

A.G. Pendleton, attorney, is listed in the 1860 Smyth Co., VA census residing in a Marion hotel or rooming house. He enlisted Apr 18, 1861 as a Captain CSA and served in Company A, 4th Va. Infantry, Stonewall Brigade. His military experiences are recounted in The Virginia Regimental Histories Series (Ref. 266).

When the Blues left Marion Albert Gallatin Pendleton was their commanding officer. "The 4th Virginia established camp 4½ miles north of Winchester. Shortly after its arrival, Capt. Albert Pendleton of the Smyth Blues received a large bottle of whiskey from home. Pendleton dared not display the spirits when Jackson was nearby, for the general viewed alcohol as Satan in liquid form. However, at lunch one day Pendleton secretly passed the bottle among his compatriots; and according to one source, the officers left for afternoon drill in a haze of joyous anticipation. On January 20th [1862], Col. Preston died at his Montgomery County home....Captain Pendleton of the Smyth Blues was promoted to major, and for a time it appeared that he might be named to lead the 4th Virginia. Yet he had made a number of enemies in the regiment. Speculation ended when Capt. Charles A. Roland of the Montgomery Highlanders received promotion to lieutenant colonel and assignment to command the 4th Virginia." Albert G. Pendleton commanded the regiment at the battle of Kernstown on March 23, 1862. Because of physical disabilities, he applied in January 1863 for a position in the Quartermaster's Department. Later he served on the staff of Gen. James A. Walker, who commanded the Stonewall Brigade.

Albert and Wm. C. Pendleton (younger brother) are listed in the 1870 Lynchburg, VA census. Both are lawyers. A. G. Pendleton became County Superintendent of schools in 1875. In 1880 A. G. Pendleton, a 44 year old lawyer suffering from "sciatica," was living with his family in Marion. Albert G. Pendleton (lawyer) is listed in the 1900 Smyth Co., VA census, pg. 69. He is buried in Round Hill Cemetery, Marion.

Civil War Pension records include Missouri Freelove Pendleton, widow of Albert Gallatin Pendleton, Knox Co., TN.

Child of ALBERT PENDLETON and OLIVIA TINSLEY is:
745.   i.   KATE OLIVIA[12] PENDLETON, b. Oct 08, 1868, VA; d. Aft. 1920, Roanoke, VA?

Child of ALBERT PENDLETON and ELIZABETH SHEFFEY is:
       ii.   JAMES SHEFFEY[12] PENDLETON, b. Jan 01, 1874, VA; m. NANCY MARGARET FUDGE, Jun 15, 1898; b. Oct 1877, VA.
              J. Sheffey Pendleton (farmer) and family are listed in the 1900 Smyth Co., VA census, pg. 46a.

Children of ALBERT PENDLETON and MISSOURI THOMAS are:
      iii.   NARCISSA CAVINETT[12] PENDLETON, b. Nov 29, 1879; d. May 29, 1881.
       iv.   ALBERTA THOMAS PENDLETON, b. Jul 28, 1881, VA; d. Oct 10, 1908.
        v.   MARY VIRGINIA PENDLETON, b. Jan 15, 1884, VA; d. Jan 1977, Savannah, GA; m. FRANK BAKER MITCHELL; b. Mar 15, 1878; d. Oct 1975, Savannah, GA.

445. JOHN STROTHER[11] PENDLETON (*JAMES FRENCH*[10], *WILLIAM*[9], *JAMES*[8], *JAMES*[7], *HENRY*[6], *PHILIP*[5], *HENRY*[4], *HENRY*[3], *GEORGE*[2], *GEORGE*[1]) was born Oct 14, 1838 in VA, and died Aug 14, 1917 in Albemarle Co., VA? He married OLIVIA RUSSELL VENABLE Feb 07, 1857. She was born Aug 26, 1843 in VA, and died Jan 12, 1919.
       John S. Pendleton served as a surgeon and physician during the civil war, 63rd VA Infantry, 45th Battalion, CSA. After the war he became a prominent surgeon and

physician in Virginia, Tennessee and Arkansas. John S. (physician) and Olivia Pendleton are listed in the 1870 Marion, Smyth Co., VA census. John S. Pendleton (Doctor of Medicine) and family are listed in the 1900 Albemarle Co., VA census, pg. 204. Olivia Venable Pendleton applied for a widows pension, Richmond, VA, in 1902.

Children of JOHN PENDLETON and OLIVIA VENABLE are:

    i. WILLIAM CECIL[12] PENDLETON, b. Nov 05, 1873, VA; d. Aft. 1918, Jefferson Co., AL?

       William Cecil Pendleton registered for the World War I draft in Birmingham, Jefferson Co., AL (Ref. 210).

    ii. MARY ALICE PENDLETON, b. Feb 13, 1877, VA; m. WILLIAM T. SHEPHERD.

746.   iii. CARRIE STROTHER PENDLETON, b. Aug 06, 1879, VA; d. Aft. 1920, Knoxville, TN?

446. WILLIAM CECIL[11] PENDLETON (*JAMES FRENCH*[10], *WILLIAM*[9], *JAMES*[8], *JAMES*[7], *HENRY*[6], *PHILIP*[5], *HENRY*[4], *HENRY*[3], *GEORGE*[2], *GEORGE*[1]) was born Jan 16, 1847 in Smyth Co., VA, and died May 05, 1941 in Bluefield, Tazewell Co., VA. He married JULIA FRANCKE BITTLE Jun 17, 1875 in Salem, VA. She was born Apr 16, 1849 in MD, and died Feb 29, 1916.

    William C. Pendleton enlisted in VA as a private and served in A Company, 45th Infantry Regiment, CSA, VA. The marriage of William Pendleton, formerly of Lynchburg, and Julia F. Bittle was announced in the Petersburg Daily Newspaper on June 24, 1875, page 2, column 3. William C. Pendleton (editor) and family are listed in the 1900 Tazewell Co., VA census, pg. 162. He wrote "History of Tazewell County and Southwest Virginia 1748 - 1920," published by W.C. Hill Printing Co. in 1920. The book was "dedicated to the memory of my beloved son, James French Pendleton." He is included in the Veteran's Pension Lists of Smyth Co., VA.

Children of WILLIAM PENDLETON and JULIA BITTLE are:

    i. NARCISSA BITTLE[12] PENDLETON, b. Nov 03, 1876, VA; m. CONRAD F. TYNES, Apr 11, 1900.

    ii. FREDERICK WILLIAM PENDLETON, b. Jan 05, 1878, VA; m. MARY KELLY, Dec 20, 1907; b. Abt. 1888, VA.

       Frederick William Pendleton registered for the World War I draft in Mingo, WV (Ref. 210).

    iii. LOUISA CECIL PENDLETON, b. Sep 12, 1879, VA; m. WALTER LEE HODGES, Feb 14, 1907; b. Nov 02, 1865; d. Jun 28, 1930.

    iv. JULIA LEONARD PENDLETON, b. May 02, 1882, VA; d. Jul 30, 1938; m. GLENN MOORE ST. CLAIR, Feb 14, 1907.

    v. JAMES FRENCH PENDLETON, b. Jul 31, 1883, VA; d. Jun 18, 1918.

    vi. RUTH HOLLAND PENDLETON, b. Jul 25, 1885, VA.

vii. SALLIE STROTHER PENDLETON, b. Mar 07, 1889, VA; d. Sep 15, 1966, Bedford Co., VA; m. EDWIN CARTER TURPIN, Apr 27, 1916; b. Apr 11, 1877; d. Apr 15, 1967, Bedford Co., VA.

viii. JOHN STROTHER PENDLETON, b. Dec 04, 1890, VA; d. Apr 03, 1917.

447. EDMUND PIPER[11] PENDLETON *(JAMES FRENCH[10], WILLIAM[9], JAMES[8], JAMES[7], HENRY[6], PHILIP[5], HENRY[4], HENRY[3], GEORGE[2], GEORGE[1])* was born Mar 11, 1855 in Smyth Co., VA?, and died Aft. 1900 in Fort Worth, TX? He married HARRIET LEONA JOBE Sep 06, 1882 in Washington Co., TN, daughter of JOSEPH JOBE and EMMELINE R. She was born Oct 28, 1861 in Washington Co., TN, and died Aft. 1900 in Fort Worth, TX?

Edmund P. Pendleton (R. R. agent) and family are listed in the 1900 Unicoi Co., TN census, pg. 95.

Children of EDMUND PENDLETON and HARRIET JOBE are:
i. JAMES FRENCH[12] PENDLETON, b. May 27, 1883, VA.
ii. ALBERT GALLATIN PENDLETON, b. Jul 05, 1885, VA; d. Sep 05, 1915.

448. NANCY STROTHER[11] PENDLETON *(ALBERT GALLATIN[10], WILLIAM[9], JAMES[8], JAMES[7], HENRY[6], PHILIP[5], HENRY[4], HENRY[3], GEORGE[2], GEORGE[1])* was born Nov 11, 1847 in VA, and died Aug 25, 1925. She married PHILIP WILLIAMS STROTHER Jan 03, 1867 in VA. He was born 1839 in VA, and died 1922.

The family of Philip Strother, lawyer, is listed in the 1880 Giles Co., VA census, pg. 36D.

Children of NANCY PENDLETON and PHILIP STROTHER are:
i. JAMES[12] STROTHER, b. Abt. 1869, VA.
ii. ELAINA STROTHER, b. Abt. 1870, VA.
iii. ELIZABETH STROTHER, b. Abt. 1871, VA.
iv. PENDLETON STROTHER, b. Abt. 1872, VA.
v. SADIE STROTHER, b. Abt. 1874, VA.
vi. NANCY STROTHER, b. Abt. 1879, VA.

449. SARAH ELIZABETH STROTHER[11] PENDLETON *(ALBERT GALLATIN[10], WILLIAM[9], JAMES[8], JAMES[7], HENRY[6], PHILIP[5], HENRY[4], HENRY[3], GEORGE[2], GEORGE[1])* was born Jul 08, 1850 in VA. She married VAN TALIAFERRO Oct 20, 1869 in Giles Co., VA. He was born Abt. 1837 in VA.

Van Taliaferro and family are listed in the 1880 census, Lynchburg, Campbell Co., VA, pg. 356B.

Children of SARAH PENDLETON and VAN TALIAFERRO are:
i. MAMIE[12] TALIAFERRO, b. Abt. 1871, VA.
ii. A. P. TALIAFERRO, b. Abt. 1872, VA.
iii. EMILY F. TALIAFERRO, b. Abt. 1874, VA.
iv. MARY A. TALIAFERRO, b. Abt. 1876, VA.

v.   SALLIE P. TALIAFERRO, b. Abt. 1877, VA.
vi.   VAN TALIAFERRO, b. Abt. 1879, VA.

450. ALBERTA FRANKLIN[11] PENDLETON *(ALBERT GALLATIN[10], WILLIAM[9], JAMES[8], JAMES[7], HENRY[6], PHILIP[5], HENRY[4], HENRY[3], GEORGE[2], GEORGE[1])* was born Jan 31, 1856 in VA, and died Jul 28, 1902 in Wythe Co., VA. She married SAMUEL RUSH CROCKETT Oct 02, 1872, son of SAMUEL CROCKETT and MARY MCGAVOCK. He was born Jan 04, 1853 in VA, and died Jan 22, 1922 in Wythe Co., VA.

Samuel Crockett and family are listed in the 1880 Wythe Co., VA census, pg. 390B. Samuel and Alberta Franklin Crockett are buried in the Cove Presbyterian Church Cemetery, Wythe County.

Children of ALBERTA PENDLETON and SAMUEL CROCKETT are:
i.   THOMPSON S.[12] CROCKETT, b. Abt. 1874, VA.
ii.   NANCY S. CROCKETT, b. May 20, 1875, VA; d. Aug 10, 1932, Wythe Co., VA; m. ROBERT RAPER.
iii.   ALBERTA PENDLETON CROCKETT, b. Oct 06, 1876, VA; d. Jan 07, 1921, Wythe Co., VA.
      Alberta P. Crockett is buried in the Cove Presbyterian Church Cemetery, Wythe County.

iv.   CECIL LOUISA CROCKETT, b. Abt. 1879, VA.

451. MARY JANE[11] PENDLETON *(JAMES COLEMAN[10], JAMES[9], PHILIP[8], JAMES[7], HENRY[6], PHILIP[5], HENRY[4], HENRY[3], GEORGE[2], GEORGE[1])* was born Abt. 1827 in KY. She married WALTER B. M. BROOKS. He was born Abt. 1824 in KY.

Children of MARY PENDLETON and WALTER BROOKS are:
i.   COLEMAN C.[12] BROOKS, b. Abt. 1848, KY.
ii.   MARY BROOKS, b. May 1850, Bullitt Co. KY.

452. DAVID H.[11] PENDLETON *(JAMES COLEMAN[10], JAMES[9], PHILIP[8], JAMES[7], HENRY[6], PHILIP[5], HENRY[4], HENRY[3], GEORGE[2], GEORGE[1])* was born Dec 24, 1828 in KY, and died Aug 10, 1905 in Bullitt Co., KY. He married ABIGAIL MILLER. She was born 1841 in KY, and died Jan 24, 1911 in Bullitt Co., KY.

David H. Pendleton is listed in the 1860 Bullitt Co. census, Bitterwater, District 1 along with his mother, Susan Pendleton. David H. (farmer) and family are listed in the 1870 Shepherdsville, Bullitt Co., KY census. David H. Pendleton and his son Arthur L. Pendleton are buried in Pendleton Hill Cemetery, Bullitt Co, KY.

Children of DAVID PENDLETON and ABIGAIL MILLER are:
i.   GEORGE H.[12] PENDLETON, b. Jan 1870, KY.
ii.   JOHN PENDLETON, b. Oct 15, 1872, KY.
      John Pendleton registered for the WWI draft in Bullitt Co., KY. His nearest relative was listed as Linda Alma Pendleton.

iii. ARTHUR LEE PENDLETON, b. Nov 28, 1875, KY; d. May 2, 1981 Bullitt Co., KY.

747. iv. SUSAN VIRGINIA PENDLETON, b. 1878, Bullitt Co., KY; d. 1941.

v. LEWELLEN PENDLETON, b. 1879, Bullitt Co., KY.

453. WILLIAM D.[11] PENDLETON *(JAMES COLEMAN[10], JAMES[9], PHILIP[8], JAMES[7], HENRY[6], PHILIP[5], HENRY[4], HENRY[3], GEORGE[2], GEORGE[1])* was born Oct 30, 1830 in KY, and died Feb 14, 1920 in Bullitt Co., KY. He married EMALINE GARRETT Feb 03, 1853 in Bullitt Co., KY. She was born Abt. 1832 in Spencer Co., KY, and died Aft. 1880 in Clark Co., IN?

William Pendleton and family are listed in the 1860 Bullitt Co. census, Bitterwater, District 1. W. D. Pendleton (farmer) and family are listed in the 1870 Bullitt Co. census, pg. 57, Shepherdsville. William D. Pendleton and his son Walter B. Pendleton are buried in the Pendleton Hill Cemetery, Bullitt Co, KY.

Children of WILLIAM PENDLETON and EMALINE GARRETT are:

i. SARAH A.[12] PENDLETON, b. Abt. 1857, Bullitt Co., KY.

ii. COLEMAN PENDLETON, b. Abt. 1861, KY.

iii. WALTER B. PENDLETON, b. Oct 22, 1862, KY; d. Feb 15, 1909, Bullitt Co., KY.

iv. SUSAN E. PENDLETON, b. Abt. 1867, KY.

454. EMILY JANE[11] PENDLETON *(WILLIAM ROBERT[10], COLEMAN[9], PHILIP[8], JAMES[7], HENRY[6], PHILIP[5], HENRY[4], HENRY[3], GEORGE[2], GEORGE[1])* was born Apr 27, 1836 in GA, and died Jul 05, 1887 in Gainesville, GA. She married JEFFERSON JONES GAINES Dec 08, 1854. He was born Jun 06, 1835 in GA, and died Apr 18, 1914 in Gainesville, GA.

Jonas J. Gaines (blacksmith) and family are listed in the 1880 Gainesville, GA census, pg. 20D.

Children of EMILY PENDLETON and JEFFERSON GAINES are (Ref. 267):

i. JOHN EDMOND[12] GAINES, b. Abt. 1863, GA.

ii. INDIA O. GAINES, b. Abt. 1865, GA.

iii. PHILIP B. GAINES, b. Abt. 1870, GA.

iv. WILLIE J. GAINES, b. Abt. 1872, GA.

v. HENRY LEON GAINES, b. Dec 18, 1873, GA; m. GERTRUDE GILBERT.

vi. SARAH GAINES, b. Abt. 1876, GA.

vii. DANNIE GAINES, b. 1879, GA.

455. MARTHA ANNA PRISCILLA[11] PENDLETON *(WILLIAM ROBERT[10], COLEMAN[9], PHILIP[8], JAMES[7], HENRY[6], PHILIP[5], HENRY[4], HENRY[3], GEORGE[2], GEORGE[1])* was born Aug 13, 1837 in GA, and died Aug 18, 1880 in Hart Co., GA. She married ROLAND BROWN. He was born Abt. 1802 in GA, and died 1877 in Hart Co., GA.

Ann Brown, farmer, and family are listed in the 1880 census, Hart Co., GA, pg. 652D.

Children of MARTHA PENDLETON and ROLAND BROWN are (Ref. 268):

    i.   SALLIE A.[12] BROWN, b. 1857, GA.

    ii. WILLIAM EDMOND BROWN, b. Mar 09, 1862, Hart Co., GA; d. Apr 15, 1949, Long Beach, CA; m. LOLA FAIRRIE BRYSON, Oct 06, 1881, GA; b. Dec 26, 1865, GA; d. Feb 20, 1953, Long Beach, CA.

    iii. MARY E. BROWN, b. 1864, GA.

    iv. AEOLEAN LOLA BROWN, b. Feb 14, 1866, Hart Co., GA; m. WILLIAM DUQUESNE BURCH, May 17, 1885, Towns Co., GA; b. Oct 09, 1861, Towns Co., GA; d. 1926.

    v. AMICUS BROWN, b. Jun 01, 1869, Hart Co., GA; d. Jan 21, 1943.

456. WILLIAM FREDERICK[11] PENDLETON (*PHILIP COLEMAN[10], COLEMAN[9], PHILIP[8], JAMES[7], HENRY[6], PHILIP[5], HENRY[4], HENRY[3], GEORGE[2], GEORGE[1]*) was born Mar 25, 1845 in Savannah, GA, and died Nov 05, 1927 in Bryn Athyn, PA. He married MARY LAWSON YOUNG May 27, 1872, daughter of REMER YOUNG and MARY WYCHE. She was born 1851 in GA, and died 1938 in Bryn Athyn, PA?

An account of William Pendleton's life was written by his wife, Mary Young Pendleton (Ref. 269).

In 1862 William Frederic Pendleton joined the GA 50th Infantry, Company B of Ware Co. of which his father was major. He went with his unit as second sergeant to join the Confederate army of northern VA. At the close of the war he was a captain. His regiment was a part of Longstreet's Corps and participated in the battles of Salem Church, Gettysburg, Fort Loudon at Knoxville, the Wilderness, Spotsylvania, Cold Harbor, Cedar Creek (where he was wounded), Petersburg and Berryville, in all, about fifty skirmishes and battles. After the war he began the study of medicine at Sparta, GA under his uncle, Dr. Edmund Pendleton. He graduated from Savannah Medical College in 1869 and was ordained as minister in 1873 in Philadelphia having attended the New Church Theological School, Waltham, MA. He became a Professor of Theology with the Academy of the New Church and was consecrated Bishop in 1888. He became President of the academy in 1897 and served to 1914. He was the author of many religious books"

William Pendleton (minister) and family are listed in the 1920 Bryn Athyn, PA census, pg. 3A.

Children of WILLIAM PENDLETON and MARY YOUNG are:

748.   i.   AUGUSTA[12] PENDLETON, b. Mar 11, 1873, Delaware; d. Aft. 1920, Montgomery Co., MD?

749.   ii. LUELLE PENDLETON, b. Jan 04, 1875, PA.

        iii. VENITA PENDLETON, b. May 10, 1878, IL; m. PAUL CARPENTER, 1930; b. Abt. 1876.

        iv. AMENA PENDLETON, b. Jul 12, 1881, IL; d. Jan 1976, Bryn Athyn, PA; m. OLIVER SLOAN HAINES, DR., 1930; b. Feb 20, 1880; d. Jul 1966, Philadelphia, PA.

        v. FREDA PENDLETON, b. Mar 28, 1883, IL.

750.   vi. KORENE PENDLETON, b. Apr 08, 1885, PA; d. Aft. 1930, Bryn Athyn, PA?

        vii. CONSTANCE PENDLETON, b. Mar 05, 1887, PA.

   viii. ELOISE PENDLETON, b. Jun 10, 1889.

    ix. WERTHA PENDLETON, b. Jan 18, 1891, PA; d. Aft. 1930, Bryn Athyn, PA?; m. ROBERT MCFARLAND COLE, 1918; b. Abt. 1892, IL; d. Aft. 1930, Bryn Athyn, PA?

    x. ALAN PENDLETON, b. Jul 01, 1896, PA; d. 1936; m. MARION CHILDS PENDLETON May 30, 1921, dau. NATHANIEL PENDLETON and BEATRICE CHILDS; b. Jul 24, 1901, IL; d. 1963.

        Alan Pendleton served as a Major in the Infantry U.S. Army, A.E.F. in World War I.

457. CHARLES RITTENHOUSE[11] PENDLETON *(PHILIP COLEMAN[10], COLEMAN[9], PHILIP[8], JAMES[7], HENRY[6], PHILIP[5], HENRY[4], HENRY[3], GEORGE[2], GEORGE[1])* was born Jun 26, 1850 in Effingham Co., GA, and died Jan 16, 1914 in Bibb Co., GA. He married SARAH PEEPLES Nov 26, 1878 in Effingham Co., GA, daughter of RICHARD PEEPLES and SARAH CAMP. She was born Jun 1859 in GA, and died Aft. 1910 in Bibb Co., GA?

        Charles Pendleton was a member of the Georgia state legislature, 1882-1883; in 1896 he was a delegate to the Democratic National Convention. In 1904 he was delegate-at-large from Georgia to the Democratic National Convention. He was the distinguished editor of the Macon "Telegraph" for many years. He was a life member of the Bibb Co., GA Board of Education. Charles R. Pendleton and family are listed in the 1900 Bibb Co., GA census, pg. 76.

Children of CHARLES PENDLETON and SARAH PEEPLES are:

     i. CATHERINE PEEPLES[12] PENDLETON, b. Sep 12, 1880, GA; d. Jun 25, 1881.

    ii. MARY PENDLETON, b. May 29, 1882, GA; d. May 29, 1882.

751.   iii. CHARLES RITTENHOUSE PENDLETON, b. May 15, 1883, GA; d. Feb 1969, Bryn Athen, PA.

    iv. LUELLE PENDLETON, b. Sep 26, 1885, GA; d. Aft. 1930; m. CURTIS KEJLAR HICKS, 1913; b. Abt. 1883, GA.

    v. PHILOLA PENDLETON, b. Nov 15, 1887, GA; m. LEONARD GYLLENDAAL, 1914.

752.   vi. WILLIAM EDMUND PENDLETON, b. Dec 27, 1889, GA; d. Oct 09, 1959, Bibb Co., GA.

    vii. CARITA PENDLETON, b. Jan 13, 1892, GA; m. RICHARD DE CHARNES, 1917.

   viii. VIDA PENDLETON, b. Jan 01, 1894, GA; m. JOHN B. GYLLENDAAL, 1915.

    ix. LOUIS ALEXANDER PENDLETON, b. Aug 09, 1896, GA.

    x. ZERA FRANCES PENDLETON, b. May 08, 1898, GA; d. Feb 02, 1991, GA; m. GEORGE MARSTELLER NOTTINGHAM, Oct 18, 1921; b. May 25, 1892, Savannah, GA.

458. ALEXANDER SHAW[11] PENDLETON *(PHILIP COLEMAN[10], COLEMAN[9], PHILIP[8], JAMES[7], HENRY[6], PHILIP[5], HENRY[4], HENRY[3], GEORGE[2], GEORGE[1])* was born Mar 17, 1855 in Sandersville, VA, and died Apr 13, 1925 in Valdosta, GA. He married SUSAN PARRAMORE Nov 10, 1881 in Valdosta, GA, daughter of NOAH PARRAMORE and SUSAN DASHER. She was born May 1862 in GA, and died Feb 26, 1938 in Lowndes Co., GA.

A. S. Pendleton (wholesale discounter?) and family are listed in the 1900 Lowndes Co., GA census, pg. 120a. He was a prominent citizen of Valdosta, GA for many years.

Children of ALEXANDER PENDLETON and SUSAN PARRAMORE are:
753.   i.   PHILIP COLEMAN[12] PENDLETON, b. Dec 21, 1882, GA.
       ii.   ELIZABETH PARRAMORE PENDLETON, b. Oct 18, 1884, Valdosta, GA; d. Aft. 1930, Columbus, GA?; m. ALBERT JOHNSON LITTLE, JUDGE, Aug 23, 1920, Valdosta, GA?; b. Abt. 1887, GA.
          Mrs. Elizabeth Pendleton Little was a member of The National Society of the Daughters of the American Revolution (Volume 68, page 340).

       iii.   GERTRUDE ADALA PENDLETON, b. Mar 11, 1887, Valdosta, GA; d. Dec 02, 1925; m. CHARLES I. HARRELL, Nov 01, 1911; b. Abt. 1877, GA; d. Dec 03, 1930.
          Mrs. Gertrude A. Pendleton Harrell was a member of The National Society of the Daughters of the American Revolution (Volume 68, page 340).

       iv.   ALBERT SIDNEY PENDLETON, b. Aug 07, 1888, Valdosta, GA; d. Dec 16, 1965, Lowndes Co., GA; m. HELEN BROWN THOMAS Nov 17, 1923, GA; b. Oct 26, 1896, GA; d. Nov 28, 1972, Valdosta, GA.
          Albert Sidney Pendleton registered for the World War I draft in Lowndes Co., GA.

       v.   WILLIAM FREDERICK PENDLETON, b. Dec 03, 1889, GA; m. CLYDE FRANCIS THOMAS, Apr 09, 1913; b. Abt. 1892; d. Mar 18, 1989, DeKalb Co., GA.
          William Frederick Pendleton registered for the World War I draft in Lowndes Co., GA (Ref. 210).

       vi.   FRANCIS KEY PENDLETON, b. May 30, 1891, GA; d. Jul 05, 1911.
       vii.   ALEXIS RUNETTE PENDLETON, b. Oct 01, 1894, GA; d. Mar 25, 1967, Lowndes Co., GA.
          Alexis Runette Pendleton registered for the World War I draft in Lowndes Co., GA (Ref. 210).

459. NATHANIEL DANDRIDGE[11] PENDLETON *(PHILIP COLEMAN[10], COLEMAN[9], PHILIP[8], JAMES[7], HENRY[6], PHILIP[5], HENRY[4], HENRY[3], GEORGE[2], GEORGE[1])* was born Feb 19, 1865 in Valdosta, GA, and died 1937 in Bryn Athyn, PA. He married (1) CORNELIA VOSBURG Apr 08, 1889. She was born Dec 17, 1869, and died Jan 24, 1891. He married (2) BEATRICE WALTON CHILDS Aug 30, 1899, daughter of WALTER CHILDS and EDITH SMITH. She was born Abt. 1875 in PA, and died Aft. 1920.

Nathaniel Pendleton was Bishop of General Church of New Jerusalem with congregations in the U.S., Canada, England, France, The Netherlands, and Belgium. He was President of the Academy of the New Church, Bryn Athyn, Pennsylvania.

Child of NATHANIEL PENDLETON and CORNELIA VOSBURG is:

    i.   ORA CORNELIA[12] PENDLETON, b. Jan 07, 1891, IL.

Children of NATHANIEL PENDLETON and BEATRICE CHILDS are:

    ii.   PHILIP CHILDS[12] PENDLETON, b. Jul 03, 1900, IL; d. Apr 1977, Bryn Athyn, PA; m. DORIS GLENN Jun 18, 1925; b. Mar 11, 1902; d. Oct 1983, Bryn Athyn, PA.

754.   iii.   MARION CHILDS PENDLETON, b. Jul 24, 1901, IL; d. 1963; m. ALAN PENDLETON May 30, 1921, son of WILLIAM PENDLETON and MARY YOUNG; b. Jul 01, 1896, PA; d. 1936.

    iv.   JEAN LOWRIE PENDLETON, b. Apr 03, 1904, PA; d. May 1994, Bryn Athyn, PA; m. SAMUEL CROFT, Jun 28, 1925; b. Nov 07, 1899; d. Nov 1981, Bryn Athyn, PA.

    v.   WILLIAM DANDRIDGE PENDLETON.

    vi.   NANCY TEBEAU PENDLETON.

460. PHILIP THOMAS[11] PENDLETON (*EDMUND MONROE[10], COLEMAN[9], PHILIP[8], JAMES[7], HENRY[6], PHILIP[5], HENRY[4], HENRY[3], GEORGE[2], GEORGE[1]*) was born Dec 13, 1847 in GA, and died Feb 20, 1892 in Richmond Co., GA? He married MARTHA ANNE NELSON Apr 20, 1870 in Charleston, SC, daughter of SAMUEL NELSON and ANN MALLERY. She was born Dec 12, 1849 in Charleston, SC, and died Aft. 1880 in Richmond Co., GA?

The following marriage notice was published on April 29, 1870 (Ref. 270): "On April 20, in Trinity Church, Charleston, by Rev. W. P. Mouzon, Dr. P. T. Pendleton, of Sparta, Ga., and Miss Mattie A. Nelson, daughter of Samuel A. Nelson, of that city."

Children of PHILIP PENDLETON and MARTHA NELSON are:

    i.   PHILIP NELSON[12] PENDLETON, b. Jul 26, 1871, GA; m. ELLA BONNELL, Jul 14, 1894.

    ii.   MARIA GERTRUDE PENDLETON, b. Nov 24, 1873, GA; d. Feb 25, 1874, Sparta, GA.

The following death notice was published February 25, 1874 (Ref. 271): "In Sparta, Ga., Feb. 25th 1874, Maria Gertrude, daughter of Dr. P. T. and Mrs. M. A. Pendleton, aged 2 months and 3 weeks."

755.   iii.   SARAH JANE THOMAS PENDLETON, b. Apr 16, 1875, GA; d. Aft. 1920, Atlanta, GA?

461. WILLIAM MICAJAH[11] PENDLETON *(EDMUND MONROE[10], COLEMAN[9], PHILIP[8], JAMES[7], HENRY[6], PHILIP[5], HENRY[4], HENRY[3], GEORGE[2], GEORGE[1])* was born Aug 29, 1849 in GA, and died Feb 24, 1915 in Atlanta, GA. He married ELIZABETH D. TALMADGE Nov 09, 1870 in Forsyth, GA, daughter of MRS. ANN P. TALMADGE. She was born Apr 1854 in GA, and died Aft. 1900.

The following marriage notice was published on November 18, 1870 (Ref. 270): "By the Rev. Dr. Hillyer, on Wednesday Nov. 9, at the Baptist Church, Forsyth, Ga., Mr. Wm. M. Pendleton, of Macon, to Miss Lizzie D. Talmage, of Forsyth." William M. Pendleton (agent jus?) and family are listed in the household of his mother-in-law, Ann P. Talmadge, in the 1900 Atlanta, Fulton Co., GA census, pg. 290. He is buried in Oakland Cemetery, Atlanta, GA along with his infant children (Ref. 183).

Children of WILLIAM PENDLETON and ELIZABETH TALMADGE are:
  i. WILLIAM TALMADGE[12] PENDLETON, b. Oct 12, 1871.
  ii. EDMUND MONROE PENDLETON, b. 1873; d. May 20, 1878.
  iii. CORNELIA CHISHOLM PENDLETON, b. 1875; d. May 4, 1876.
  iv. JR. WILLIAM MICAJAH PENDLETON, b. 1877; d. Apr 8, 1878
  v. CHARLES MICAJAH PENDLETON, b. Jan 07, 1879, GA; d. Mar 25, 1948.
      Charles M. Pendleton (2nd Lt., U.S. Army, 29th Infantry) of Atlanta, GA, is listed in the1900 Census, Military and Naval Population, the Philippines, pg. 139. He served there during the Spanish-American War. He is buried in a National Cemetery (unnamed location), Capt. US Infantry.

  vi. ELIZABETH TALMADGE PENDLETON, b. Sep 30, 1884; d. infancy.
  vii. HELEN NEWSOME PENDLETON, b. Aug 13, 1885, GA.

462. SUSAN FRANCINA[11] PENDLETON *(EDMUND MONROE[10], COLEMAN[9], PHILIP[8], JAMES[7], HENRY[6], PHILIP[5], HENRY[4], HENRY[3], GEORGE[2], GEORGE[1])* was born Jul 24, 1851 in GA, and died Aft. 1900 in Atlanta, GA? She married LLEWELLYN HUDSON MUSE Jul 22, 1885 in Atlanta, GA? He was born Abt. 1849 in Atlanta, GA.

Children of SUSAN PENDLETON and LLEWELLYN MUSE are:
  i. ANNA P.[12] MUSE, b. May 1886.
  ii. LLEWELLYN H. MUSE, b. Jul 1891.

463. JAMES COLEMAN[11] PENDLETON *(EDMUND MONROE[10], COLEMAN[9], PHILIP[8], JAMES[7], HENRY[6], PHILIP[5], HENRY[4], HENRY[3], GEORGE[2], GEORGE[1])* was born May 28, 1853 in GA, and died Aug 20, 1929 in Fulton Co., GA. He married BERTHA EUGENIA SWIFT Dec 20, 1877 in Atlanta, GA, daughter of RICHARD SWIFT and ANNA TRISKETT. She was born Abt. 1861 in NY, and died Jun 09, 1941 in DeKalb Co., GA.

The following marriage notice was published on January 8, 1878 (Ref. 270): "By Rev. Dr. Spalding, in Atlanta, Ga., Dr. J. C. Pendleton to Miss Bertha Swift." J. C. and Bertha Pendleton are listed in the 1880 Augusta, GA census, pg. 373C. James C. Pendleton is listed in the household of his sister, Susie P. Muse, in the 1900 Atlanta,

Fulton Co., GA census. His infant daughter Bertha is buried in the Oakland Cemetery, Atlanta (Ref. 183).

Children of JAMES PENDLETON and BERTHA SWIFT are:
      i.   BERTHA ERNESTINE[12] PENDLETON, b. Sep 14, 1878, GA; d. Dec 28, 1878, Atlanta, GA.
     ii.   JAMES COLEMAN PENDLETON, b. Oct 24, 1880, GA; d. Feb 26, 1920.
         James Coleman Pendleton registered for the World War I draft in El Paso, TX (Ref. 210).

756.   iii.   SUSAN EUGENIA PENDLETON, b. Aug 29, 1883, GA; d. Aft. 1930, Atlanta, GA.

464. DIADAMIA HANNAH[11] PENDLETON (*JAMES C.*[10], *NATHANIEL*[9], *WILLIAM*[8], *NATHANIEL*[7], *HENRY*[6], *PHILIP*[5], *HENRY*[4], *HENRY*[3], *GEORGE*[2], *GEORGE*[1]) was born Abt. 1836 in MO, and died Nov 22, 1928 in Hopkins Co., TX. She married JAMES HENRY SMITH Jan 31, 1856 in Hopkins Co., TX, son of HENRY SMITH and LEMIRA ROGERS. He was born Apr 19, 1833 in KY, and died Jan 04, 1899 in Hopkins Co., TX.
     James H. Smith and family, including Evaline Pendleton (Rogers) are listed in the 1880 census, Hopkins Co., TX, pg. 191C.

Children of DIADAMIA PENDLETON and JAMES SMITH are:
      i.   CHARLES T.[12] SMITH, b. Abt. 1860, TX.
     ii.   HENRY J. SMITH, b. Abt. 1867, TX.
    iii.   JOHN W. SMITH, b. Abt. 1869, TX.
    iv.   ANN E. SMITH, b. Abt. 1872, TX.
     v.   GILBERT P. SMITH, b. Abt. 1875, TX.
    vi.   SAMUEL S. SMITH, b. Abt. 1877, TX.

465. NATHANIEL C.[11] PENDLETON (*JAMES C.*[10], *NATHANIEL*[9], *WILLIAM*[8], *NATHANIEL*[7], *HENRY*[6], *PHILIP*[5], *HENRY*[4], *HENRY*[3], *GEORGE*[2], *GEORGE*[1]) was born Nov 1837 in MO, and died Nov 21, 1906 in Hopkins Co., TX. He married AMANDA MCFALL Dec 26, 1859 in Hopkins Co., TX. She was born Feb 01, 1839 in IN, and died Apr 28, 1902 in Hopkins Co., TX.
     N.C. and Amanda Pendleton are listed in the 1860 Hopkins Co., TX census. Nate Pendleton (farmer) and family are listed in the 1900 Hopkins Co., TX census, pg. 202a.

Children of NATHANIEL PENDLETON and AMANDA MCFALL are:
      i.   AUGUSTUS[12] PENDLETON, b. Mar 12, 1862, TX.
     ii.   JAMES MCFALL PENDLETON, b. Nov 05, 1863, TX.
    iii.   ELIZABETH PENDLETON, b. Feb 27, 1866, TX.
757.   iv.   BENJAMIN PENDLETON, b. Mar 18, 1867, Hopkins Co., TX; d. 1915, Bennington, OK?
758.   v.   JOSHUA PENDLETON, b. Sep 1869, TX; d. Jun 09, 1945, Hopkins Co., TX?

vi. JOHN FLOYD PENDLETON, b. Dec 25, 1874, TX; d. Nov 04, 1929, Cumby, TX; m. ETHEL EVANS, Aft. 1900; b. of Cumby, TX.

vii. EMMA L. PENDLETON, b. Abt. 1875, TX; d. Aft. 1920, San Antonio, TX; m. ANDREW W. "DREW" BRASHER; b. Abt. 1874, of Aldrice, MO; d. Aft. 1920, San Antonio, TX.

   Andrew W. and Emma L. Brasher are listed in the 1920 Sulphur Springs, Hopkins Co., TX census.

viii. JOHN T. PENDLETON, b. Abt. 1879, TX.

ix. RALPH C. PENDLETON, b. Mar 1880, TX; d. Oct 03, 1928, Hopkins Co., TX?; m. LELLA DRAKE, Aft. 1900; b. Abt. 1883, TX; d. Feb 25, 1929, Hopkins Co., TX?

   Ralph C. Pendleton and wife are listed in the 1920 Hopkins Co., TX census.

759. x. RICHARD "DICK" PENDLETON, b. Abt. 1880, TX.

466. BENJAMIN STROTHER[11] PENDLETON *(JAMES WILLIAM[10], BENJAMIN[9], WILLIAM[8], NATHANIEL[7], HENRY[6], PHILIP[5], HENRY[4], HENRY[3], GEORGE[2], GEORGE[1])* was born Mar 28, 1842 in Little Rock, AR, and died Jan 19, 1931 in Jefferson Co., WV. He married (1) MARY HART Oct 31, 1877, daughter of JACOB HART and PRISCILLA MOORE. She was born Abt. 1856, and died Abt. 1880. He married (2) JULIA ELIZABETH RICKARD Oct 24, 1884. She was born Aug 1853 in WV, and died Aft. 1930 in Jefferson Co., WV?

Benjamin Pendleton is listed in the 1850 Ozark Co., AR, Census (8 years old) with his brother Albert (6) in the household of H.F. (30) and Margaret (29) White. An account of his life from that point is included in Confederate Veteran (Ref. 272).

His widowed mother moved to Shepherdstown, VA, in 1851. He joined the Confederate army at 18 and served throughout the war in Company B, 2nd VA Regiment in the Stonewall Brigade under Gen. Stewart Walker, receiving a wound in the battle of Chancellorsville. He was in every battle of the command except for Sharpsburg, MD, when he was home on furlough.., He was aide-de-camp to General Walker, Commander of the famous Stonewall Brigade. He returned to Potomac, Jefferson Co., WV for the 1880 census with his son. Benjamin S. Pendleton (gen'l merchant?) and family are listed in the 1900 Jefferson Co., WV census, pg. 161. Benjamin died in Shepherdstown, WV, on 19 Jan 1931, after an illness of several weeks. His funeral services were held in the Lutheran Church of Shepherdstown, of which he was an active member from early childhood. He is buried in old Elmwood Cemetery, at the edge of town. He was survived by his wife, who was Miss Julia Richards, and a son and daughter.

Child of BENJAMIN PENDLETON and MARY HART is:
   i. HARVEY HART[12] PENDLETON, b. Jun 04, 1879, WV; d. 1918.

Children of BENJAMIN PENDLETON and JULIA RICKARD are:
760. ii. MARY RICKARD[12] PENDLETON, b. Apr 24, 1886, WV; d. Dec 1976, Indianapolis, IN.

iii. BENJAMIN STROTHER PENDLETON, b. Feb 23, 1888, WV; d. Oct 1981, Washington, PA; m. ELIZABETH LORETTA MEYERS Aug 22, 1918; b. Apr 28, 1894; d. Nov 1980, Washington, PA.

Benjamin Strauther Pendleton registered for the World War I draft in Allegheny Co., PA.

467. ELLEN SHEPHERD[11] PENDLETON *(WILLIAM HENRY[10], WILLIAM[9], WILLIAM[8], NATHANIEL[7], HENRY[6], PHILIP[5], HENRY[4], HENRY[3], GEORGE[2], GEORGE[1])* was born Mar 21, 1862 in VA, and died May 19, 1894. She married LIONEL BLIGH PERRY-AYSCOUGH Sep 13, 1892. He was born Abt. 1858, and died Aft. 1910.

Child of ELLEN PENDLETON and LIONEL PERRY-AYSCOUGH is:
i. HENRIETTA RANDOLPH[12] PERRY-AYSCOUGH, b. Abt. 1894.

468. GARNETT PEYTON[11] PENDLETON *(WILLIAM HENRY[10], WILLIAM[9], WILLIAM[8], NATHANIEL[7], HENRY[6], PHILIP[5], HENRY[4], HENRY[3], GEORGE[2], GEORGE[1])* was born Oct 08, 1864 in VA, and died May 15, 1939. She married WILLIAM DABNEY WIRT Oct 02, 1894, son of WILLIAM WIRT and ELIZABETH PAYNE. He was born Jul 24, 1857, and died Mar 16, 1930.

Child of GARNETT PENDLETON and WILLIAM WIRT is:
i. HENRIETTA MARY RANDOLPH PEYTON[12] WIRT.

469. WILLIAM HENRY KINKLE[11] PENDLETON *(WILLIAM HENRY[10], WILLIAM[9], WILLIAM[8], NATHANIEL[7], HENRY[6], PHILIP[5], HENRY[4], HENRY[3], GEORGE[2], GEORGE[1])* was born Jan 17, 1867 in Bedford Co., VA, and died Aft. 1920 in Spartanburg, SC? He married ELIZABETH FORRER CHAPMAN Jul 28, 1897, daughter of WILLIAM CHAPMAN and JOSEPHINE JEFFRIES. She was born Jun 12, 1869 in VA, and died Jan 1969 in Asheville, NC.

William HK Pendleton is included in the Protestant Episcopal Church Clerical Directory, 1898: Residence, Fairfax Co. VA; Birth Place, Bedford Co. VA; Year became Deacon; 1896. William K. Pendleton (clergyman) and family are listed in the 1900 Prince William Co., VA census, pg. 190a. Mrs. Elizabeth Chapman Pendleton was a member of The National Society of the Daughters of the American Revolution (Volume 155, page 51).

Children of WILLIAM PENDLETON and ELIZABETH CHAPMAN are:
i. ELIZABETH RANDOLPH[12] PENDLETON, b. Dec 08, 1898, Prince William Co., VA.
ii. WILLIAM HENRY CHAPMAN PENDLETON, b. Jul 27, 1900, Prince William Co., VA; d. Dec 06, 1909.
iii. ROBERT RANDOLPH PENDLETON, b. Jun 15, 1902, VA; d. Mar 12, 1931.
iv. CARY VERDIER PENDLETON.
v. JOSEPHINE CHAPMAN PENDLETON.

470. WILLIAM HENRY[11] PENDLETON (*ROBERT SHEPHERD*[10], *WILLIAM*[9], *WILLIAM*[8], *NATHANIEL*[7], *HENRY*[6], *PHILIP*[5], *HENRY*[4], *HENRY*[3], *GEORGE*[2], *GEORGE*[1]) was born Jan 1850 in VA, and died Aft. 1880 in New Brunswick, NJ? He married ELLEN G. WRIGHT. She was born Abt. 1851 in NJ.

William H. (picture agent) and Ellen G. Pendleton are listed in the 1880 New Brunswick, Middlesex, NJ census, pg. 1B.

Children of WILLIAM PENDLETON and ELLEN WRIGHT are:
    i.   WILLIAM H.[12] PENDLETON, b. Abt. 1874, NJ.
    ii. JOHN P. PENDLETON, b. Abt. 1878, NJ.

471. JAMES PHILIP BOSMAN[11] PENDLETON (*ROBERT SHEPHERD*[10], *WILLIAM*[9], *WILLIAM*[8], *NATHANIEL*[7], *HENRY*[6], *PHILIP*[5], *HENRY*[4], *HENRY*[3], *GEORGE*[2], *GEORGE*[1]) was born Aft. 1850, and died in Schenectady, NY? He married EDITH HOWER.

James P.B. Pendleton was a Rector of St. Georges Church, Schenectady, N. Y.

Children of JAMES PENDLETON and EDITH HOWER are:
    i.   EDITH MAY ST. GEORGE[12] PENDLETON.
    ii. EDMUND RANDOLPH PENDLETON.
    iii. PHILIP CLAYTON PENDLETON.

472. WILLIAM HENRY[11] PENDLETON (*STEPHEN JAMES*[10], *WILLIAM*[9], *WILLIAM*[8], *NATHANIEL*[7], *HENRY*[6], *PHILIP*[5], *HENRY*[4], *HENRY*[3], *GEORGE*[2], *GEORGE*[1]) was born 1858 in Williamsburg, VA, and died 1915 in Lawrence, Douglas Co., KS? He married MATILDA MARY POEHLER 1882. She was born Abt. 1860 in Iowa, and died Aft. 1910 in Lawrence, Douglas Co., KS?

Children of WILLIAM PENDLETON and MATILDA POEHLER are:
    i.   CLAUDIA CLARA[12] PENDLETON, b. Abt. 1884.
    ii. WILLIAM HENLEY PENDLETON, b. Abt. 1887, KS; m. MARIE B. BIKLIN, 1914.
    iii. LAURA SOPHIE PENDLETON, b. Abt. 1890, KS.
    iv. EMMA HELEN PENDLETON, b. Abt. 1891, KS.
    v.   THEODORE POEHLER PENDLETON, b. Abt. 1898, KS.
    vi. VIRGINIA MAUD PENDLETON.

473. PHILIP CLAYTON[11] PENDLETON (*PHILIP CLAYTON*[10], *PHILIP CLAYTON*[9], *PHILIP*[8], *NATHANIEL*[7], *HENRY*[6], *PHILIP*[5], *HENRY*[4], *HENRY*[3], *GEORGE*[2], *GEORGE*[1]) was born Apr 16, 1839 in VA, and died in MD. He married MARY RUTH OGDEN Nov 23, 1864 in Adams Co., Miss., daughter of ELIAS OGDEN and ANNE ROUTH. She was born Mar 02, 1840 in VA, and died in MD.

Children of PHILIP PENDLETON and MARY OGDEN are:
    i.   MADELINE RUTH[12] PENDLETON, b. Oct 08, 1865; d. Oct 04, 1870.

761.   ii.   VIRGINIA OGDEN PENDLETON, b. Dec 06, 1866, MS; d. Aft. 1910, Camden NJ?
        iii. ANNIE OGDEN PENDLETON, b. Jun 17, 1868; d. Jun 18, 1868.
        iv.   JOHN KENNEDY PENDLETON, b. Dec 26, 1871.

474. EDMUND[11] PENDLETON *(PHILIP CLAYTON[10], PHILIP CLAYTON[9], PHILIP[8], NATHANIEL[7], HENRY[6], PHILIP[5], HENRY[4], HENRY[3], GEORGE[2], GEORGE[1])* was born Nov 27, 1840 in VA, and died Aft. 1900 in Morgan Co., WV? He married EMILY YOUNG Jan 13, 1864 in St. Louis, MO. She was born Abt. 1845 in NY, and died Aft. 1880.

Edmund Pendleton is listed in the 1900 Morgan Co., WV census, pg. 154.

Children of EDMUND PENDLETON and EMILY YOUNG are:
        i.   EDMUND[12] PENDLETON, b. Abt. 1865, WV.
        ii.   PHILIP C. PENDLETON, b. Abt. 1866, WV.
        iii. EDITH PENDLETON, b. Abt. 1873, WV.

475. CHARLES HENRY[11] PENDLETON *(ELISHA BOYD[10], PHILIP CLAYTON[9], PHILIP[8], NATHANIEL[7], HENRY[6], PHILIP[5], HENRY[4], HENRY[3], GEORGE[2], GEORGE[1])* was born Jan 21, 1845 in VA, and died Jul 13, 1914 in Morgan Co., WV? He married MATILDA SMITH BACKUS Dec 08, 1870. She was born Jan 05, 1847, and died Jan 25, 1877.

Charles H. Pendleton is listed in the 1900 Morgan Co., WV census, pg. 152. He was a Lieutenant Commander, U.S. Navy.

Children of CHARLES PENDLETON and MATILDA BACKUS are:
        i.   JOHN CHESTER BACKUS[12] PENDLETON, b. Sep 26, 1871, MD; d. Aft. 1920, Baltimore, MD?; m. MILDRED MORRIS; b. Jan 21, 1876, MD; d. Nov 1967, Baltimore, MD.

            John B. and Mildred Pendleton are listed in the 1920 Baltimore, MD census.

        ii.   MARIE LUCINDA PENDLETON, b. Jun 30, 1875.

476. NATHANIEL SPOTSWOOD DANDRIDGE[11] PENDLETON *(ELISHA BOYD[10], PHILIP CLAYTON[9], PHILIP[8], NATHANIEL[7], HENRY[6], PHILIP[5], HENRY[4], HENRY[3], GEORGE[2], GEORGE[1])* was born Nov 09, 1851 in VA, and died Jan 11, 1931 in Morgan Co., WV? He married AGNES KIRKLAND TAYLOR Jun 19, 1888. She was born Sep 08, 1862 in MD, and died Nov 21, 1907 in Morgan Co., WV?

N. S. D. Pendleton (editor) and family are listed in the 1900 Morgan Co., WV census, pg. 154a. He was a newspaper owner in Berkeley Springs, WV.

Children of NATHANIEL PENDLETON and AGNES TAYLOR are:
        i.   ELISHA BOYD[12] PENDLETON, b. Mar 09, 1889, WV; d. Aug 04, 1901.
        ii.   TALBOT TAYLOR PENDLETON, b. Feb 14, 1891, WV; d. Jun 1973, Tucson, AZ; m. FRANCES STEELE Nov 04, 1926; b. Abt. 1906 in TX.

Talbot Taylor Pendleton registered for the World War I draft in Houston, Harris Co., TX.

    iii. ELEANOR AGNES PENDLETON, b. Jan 29, 1899, WV; d. Sep 1983, Kennet Square, PA; m. HUGH CAMPBELL, Sep 14, 1927.

    iv. JAMES BLACKSTONE TAYLOR PENDLETON, b. Oct 22, 1900; d. Dec 1985, Huntington Beach, CA.

477. FRANCIS KEY[11] PENDLETON *(GEORGE HUNT[10], NATHANIEL GREENE[9], NATHANIEL[8], NATHANIEL[7], HENRY[6], PHILIP[5], HENRY[4], HENRY[3], GEORGE[2], GEORGE[1])* was born Jan 03, 1850 in Cincinnati, OH, and died Jul 26, 1930 in New York, NY. He married (1) SARAH MARIE' Jun 01, 1885. She died Mar 14, 1886. He married (2) ELIZABETH MARIANITS LA MONTAGNE Dec 10, 1889. She was born Abt. 1872 in NY, and died Aft. 1930 in New York, NY.

Francis Pendleton was a Justice of the Supreme Court of NY. He was president of the Society of the Cincinnati, NY.

Child of FRANCIS PENDLETON and ELIZABETH LA MONTAGNE is:
    i. GEORGE HUNT[12] PENDLETON, b. Aug 09, 1896, NY; d. Aft. 1930, NY?; m. CATHERINE PORTER, Jun 05, 1924; b. Abt. 1896, NY; d. Aft. 1930, NY?

       George Hunt Pendleton served with American Expeditionary Forces in France as a lieutenant in the 42nd Division, U.S. Army, and was twice wounded in action.

478. JANE FRANCES[11] PENDLETON *(GEORGE HUNT[10], NATHANIEL GREENE[9], NATHANIEL[8], NATHANIEL[7], HENRY[6], PHILIP[5], HENRY[4], HENRY[3], GEORGE[2], GEORGE[1])* was born Apr 22, 1860 in Washington DC, and died Aft. 1920 in Washington DC? She married ARTHUR TILGHMAN BRICE Dec 03, 1891. He was born Abt. 1855 in GA, and died Aft. 1920 in Washington DC?

Arthur T. Brice and family are listed in the 1920 Washington DC census, pg. 4A.

Children of JANE PENDLETON and ARTHUR BRICE are:
    i. JR. ARTHUR TILGHMAN[12] BRICE, b. Sep 11, 1892; d. Jun 1973, Santa Rosa, CA; m. ALICE LLOYD WINDER, Aug 29, 1929; b. Jul 08, 1886; d. Oct 1978, Santa Rosa, CA.

    ii. ALICE KEY PENDLETON BRICE, b. Dec 20, 1893, Washington DC; d. Mar 1983, Wayne, PA; m. JR. JOHN FORSYTHE JOLINE Sep 16, 1921; b. Abt. 1887, NJ; d. Aft. 1930, Delaware Co., PA?

    iii. JULIA FRANCES BRICE, b. Aug 22, 1896, NY; m. HERMAN BLANEY CHUBB, PROF., Jan 23, 1925.

479. LUCY GAYLORD[11] PENDLETON *(ELIOTT HUNT[10], NATHANIEL GREENE[9], NATHANIEL[8], NATHANIEL[7], HENRY[6], PHILIP[5], HENRY[4], HENRY[3], GEORGE[2], GEORGE[1])* was born Dec 1850 in OH, and died Aft. 1910 in Ambrose Co., OH? She married AMBROSE WHITE. He was born Abt. 1846 in OH, and died Aft. 1900 in Ambrose Co., OH?

Ambrose White and family are listed in the 1880 census, Hamilton Co., OH, pg. 337A.

Children of LUCY PENDLETON and AMBROSE WHITE are:
  i.   P. ELLIOT[12] WHITE, b. Abt. 1877, OH.
  ii.   AMBROSE WHITE, JR., b. Jul 1879, OH.
  iii. LUCY P. WHITE, b. Dec 1882, OH.
  iv.   JOHN WHITE, b. Sep 1885, OH.
  v.   NATHANIEL P. WHITE, b. Jul 1890, OH.
  vi.   ALICE WHITE, b. Feb 1895, OH.

480. JR. ELIOTT HUNT[11] PENDLETON *(ELIOTT HUNT[10], NATHANIEL GREENE[9], NATHANIEL[8], NATHANIEL[7], HENRY[6], PHILIP[5], HENRY[4], HENRY[3], GEORGE[2], GEORGE[1])* was born Dec 08, 1859 in OH, and died Jul 10, 1926 in Cincinnati, OH? He married ISABELLA ECKSTEIN Jun 14, 1885. She was born Abt. 1861 in OH, and died Aft. 1920 in Cincinnati, OH?

Children of ELIOTT PENDLETON and ISABELLA ECKSTEIN are:
  i.   HARRIET[12] PENDLETON, b. Abt. 1891, OH.
  ii.   ELIOTT HUNT PENDLETON, b. Feb 12, 1893, Cincinnati, OH.
        Elliott Hunt Pendleton Jr. registered for the World War I draft in
        Cincinnati, OH: Address, 1736 Madison Reserve Division, Cincinnati, Ohio.

  iii. ISABELLA E. PENDLETON, b. Abt. 1894, OH.

481. NATHANIEL GREENE[11] PENDLETON *(ELIOTT HUNT[10], NATHANIEL GREENE[9], NATHANIEL[8], NATHANIEL[7], HENRY[6], PHILIP[5], HENRY[4], HENRY[3], GEORGE[2], GEORGE[1])* was born Abt. 1862 in OH, and died Aft. 1910 in NJ? He married (1) BESSY JOHNSTON. He married (2) ADELAIDE E. Abt. 1895. She was born Abt. 1874 in NY, and died Aft. 1910.

Nathaniel G. Pendleton (Manager - Chemical Co.) and family are listed in the 1910 Bergen Co., NJ census.

Children of NATHANIEL PENDLETON and ADELAIDE E. are:
  i.   NATHANIEL G.[12] PENDLETON, b. Abt. 1896, Iowa.
  ii.   EDMUND J. PENDLETON, b. Mar 01, 1899, OH; d. Jan 1987, Paris,
        France.
        Edmund Pendleton was U.S. Consulate, Paris, France.

  iii. GEORGE PENDLETON, b. Abt. 1909, NY.

482. WILLIAM LARNED MARCY[11] PENDLETON *(EDMUND HENRY[10], NATHANIEL GREENE[9], NATHANIEL[8], NATHANIEL[7], HENRY[6], PHILIP[5], HENRY[4], HENRY[3], GEORGE[2], GEORGE[1])* was born Feb 19, 1865 in NY. He married (1) ALIDA

MARIA LUNDQUIST. She was born in Sweden. He married (2) EVELYN R. MOSEMAN Oct 02, 1913.

Children of WILLIAM PENDLETON and ALIDA LUNDQUIST are:
  i. ARVID H.[12] PENDLETON, b. Jan 23, 1890, Sweden; d. Oct 1964, CA; m. MARGARET, Abt. 1928; b. Abt. 1902, NY.
    Arvid H. Pendleton, Captain, is listed in the 1920 census, Naval Forces, Philippines, Fort Mills. He is buried in Arlington National Cemetery, VA.

  ii. CORNELIA PENDLETON, m. CLAUD MAYO, CDR.
  iii. ANNE PENDLETON, m. MANUEL D. JACKSON.

Child of WILLIAM PENDLETON and EVELYN MOSEMAN is:
  iv. MARY E.[12] PENDLETON, b. Aug 16, 1914.

483. WILLIAM ARMISTEAD[11] PENDLETON *(JOHN LEWIS[10], JOHN[9], EDMUND[8], JOHN[7], HENRY[6], PHILIP[5], HENRY[4], HENRY[3], GEORGE[2], GEORGE[1])* was born 1825 in VA, and died 1870 in St. Louis, MO? He married MARY ANNE BERRY COXE Feb 08, 1853 in St. Louis, MO. She was born Abt. 1823 in MO.
    W. A. Pendleton (lawyer) and family are listed in the 1860 Washington DC census.

Children of WILLIAM PENDLETON and MARY COXE are:
  i. MARY[12] PENDLETON, b. Abt. 1855, MO.
762. ii. JR. WILLIAM ARMISTEAD PENDLETON, b. Abt. 1856, St. Louis, MO; d. 1890.
  iii. IDA PENDLETON, b. Abt. 1858, Washington DC.

484. EUGENE BEAUHARNAIS[11] PENDLETON *(JOHN LEWIS[10], JOHN[9], EDMUND[8], JOHN[7], HENRY[6], PHILIP[5], HENRY[4], HENRY[3], GEORGE[2], GEORGE[1])* was born 1828 in Caroline Co., VA, and died 1901 in Rapides Parish, LA? He married ELIZABETH ANNE BAILEY 1867, daughter of WILLIAM BAILEY and HENRIETTA SCOTT. She was born Abt. 1838 in VA, and died Aft. 1880 in Rapides Co., LA?
    Eugene Pendleton's biography is included in an early history of Louisiana (Ref. 273).

    Major E. B. Pendleton of Alexandria, La., is one of the most extensive cotton planters of Rapides Parish, and is now residing on the old Bailey plantation four miles from Alexandria, on Bayou Robert's Road. The Bailey plantation was the home of the lamented Gen. Bailey, the father-in-law of our subject. It is one of the most picturesque places on Red River, and the stately old mansion is one of the landmarks that escaped destruction during the late Civil War. The spacious yards are filled with trees and shrubbery, the rarest that cultivated taste could desire or money purchase, and the massive pillars still bear witness as to the grandeur of its former days. Maj. Pendleton was born in Caroline County, Va., in 1828, and when about twenty years of age traveled to the Pacific slope by way of Cape Horn, going as sutler of Company A, United States Light Artillery, commanded by Col. Magruder. He located at San Diego, and there remained until 1857, engaged in general business. He was also treasurer of the county in

which he located for a term. In the last mentioned year he returned on a visit, was
induced to stay and entered business in St. Louis, Mo., remaining there until the breaking
out of the war. From there he went to New York City, thence to Baltimore, Md., and
later, on the underground railroad to Richmond, Va. He put up at Mrs. Surratt's Tavern,
which was kept by the lamented Mrs. Surratt who was hanged for being implicated in the
killing of President Lincoln. He was well acquainted with Mrs. Surratt and her daughter
and son. John Surratt drove our subject a considerable distance on the underground
railway. At Richmond, Va., Maj. Pendleton met his uncle Gen. Magruder and joined his
staff as chief commissary, serving in the Lone Star State. He fought in the battle of
Galveston, and when Gen. Magruder was ordered to Arkansas in 1864, the Major was
ordered to Richmond, Va., as bearer of dispatches. He was captured en route, taken to
New Orleans, thence to Fort La Fayette, and then to Fort Delaware, where he was
subsequently released by order of Gen. Grant. John Mitchell, the Irish patriot, who had
two sons in the Confederate Army, crossed the ocean to America, and was with Maj.
Pendleton on the underground railway, to Richmond. After the war Maj. Pendleton spent
some time in Canada and New York, and resumed business in St. Louis during 1866 and
1867. In 1867 he married Mrs. Elizabeth Pickett, daughter of Gen. William Bailey, and
withdrew from the firm in St. Louis taking charge of his father-in-law's plantation, where
he resides at the present time [1890].

Children of EUGENE PENDLETON and ELIZABETH BAILEY are:
  i.   EUGENE[12] PENDLETON, b. Abt. 1868, LA.
  ii. ALLEN B. PENDLETON, b. Abt. 1870, LA.
        Allen Pendleton was associated with Laclede National Bank, St. Louis,
        MO.

  iii. LAWRENCE PENDLETON, b. Abt. 1872; d. Bef. 1890.
  iv. HATTIE PENDLETON, b. Abt. 1874; d. Bef. 1890.
  v.   ALICE PENDLETON, b. Abt. 1876, Alexandria Co., LA; m. D. FRANK
        CLARKE.
        Mrs. Alice Pendleton Clarke was a member of The National Society of the
        Daughters of the American Revolution (Volume 50, page 119).

485. WILLIAM[11] PENDLETON *(EDMUND ALLEN[10], JOHN[9], EDMUND[8], JOHN[7],
HENRY[6], PHILIP[5], HENRY[4], HENRY[3], GEORGE[2], GEORGE[1])* was born Jun 21, 1828 in
VA, and died Aft. 1900 in Augusta, GA? He married ZEMULA C. WALKER Sep 24,
1862. She was born Jun 1841 in AL, and died Aft. 1900 in Augusta, GA?
        William Pendleton is listed in the 1870 Richmond Co., GA census, Augusta.
William Pendleton (machinist) and wife are listed in the 1900 Richmond Co., GA census,
pg. 117.

Children of WILLIAM PENDLETON and ZEMULA WALKER are:
        i.   BEVERLY WALKER[12] PENDLETON, b. Abt. 1869.
  763. ii. EDMUND ALLEN PENDLETON, b. Dec 20, 1872, GA; d. Aft. 1910,
              Richmond Co., GA?
        iii. WILLIAM KING PENDLETON, b. Jan 17, 1873; d. Aft. 1918, Jefferson
              Co., AL?

William King Pendleton registered for the World War I draft in Jefferson Co., AL.

486. HUGH[11] PENDLETON *(EDMUND ALLEN[10], JOHN[9], EDMUND[8], JOHN[7], HENRY[6], PHILIP[5], HENRY[4], HENRY[3], GEORGE[2], GEORGE[1])* was born Mar 15, 1834 in Caroline Co., VA, and died May 04, 1902 in Hamilton Co., TN? He married REBECCA JONES Dec 06, 1867. She was born Jan 1842 in VA, and died Aft. 1900.

Hugh and John Pendleton (machinists) are listed in the 1860 Mobile, AL census. Hugh Pendleton is listed in the 1870 Richmond Co., GA, Augusta census. Hugh Pendleton and family are listed in the 1900 Hamilton Co., TN census, pg. 324.

Children of HUGH PENDLETON and REBECCA JONES are:
- i. EDWARD CRAWLEY[12] PENDLETON, b. Sep 1867, VA.
- ii. JULIA PENDLETON, b. Abt. 1869, VA; m. LOUIS BERCKMANS HATCHER; b. 1867; d. 1932, Chattanooga, TN?.
- iii. HUGH WARD PENDLETON, b. Apr 1872, GA; d. Aft. 1920; m. MARIE L. OLIVER, Abt. 1899; b. Sep 1874, GA.
  Hugh W. Pendleton is listed in the Manhattan, NY 1920 census.

- iv. NANNIE ELSIE PENDLETON, m. LOUIS ANDERSON.
- v. JOHN PENDLETON, d. infancy.
- vi. ZEMULA WALKER PENDLETON, b. Sep 1879, GA.

487. ARMISTEAD FRANKLIN[11] PENDLETON *(EDMUND ALLEN[10], JOHN[9], EDMUND[8], JOHN[7], HENRY[6], PHILIP[5], HENRY[4], HENRY[3], GEORGE[2], GEORGE[1])* was born Sep 25, 1838 in VA, and died Aft. 1900 in Richmond Co., GA? He married (1) ISABELLA GARVIN 1868, daughter of ELEANOR P. She was born Abt. 1856 in GA.

Armistead Pendleton served as a private in the VA 1st Artillery, Company K, CSA. Armistead Pendleton (printer) and family are listed in the 1870 Augusta, Richmond Co., GA census.

Children of ARMISTEAD PENDLETON and ISABELLA GARVIN are:
- i. SARAH A.[12] PENDLETON, b. Abt. 1868, GA.
- ii. HOWARD PENDLETON, b. Abt. 1869, GA.
- 764. iii. EDMUND ALLEN PENDLETON, b. Abt. 1873, GA; d. Aft. 1910, Richmond Co., GA?
- iv. ANNA BELLA PENDLETON, b. Abt. 1879.

488. JR. WILLIAM ARMISTEAD[11] PENDLETON *(WILLIAM ARMISTEAD[10], JOHN[9], EDMUND[8], JOHN[7], HENRY[6], PHILIP[5], HENRY[4], HENRY[3], GEORGE[2], GEORGE[1])* was born May 11, 1844 in KY, and died Jan 06, 1882 in Campbell Co., KY? He married MEDDIE. She was born Abt. 1853 in TN.

William Pendleton (25; pilot) and his mother M.F. Pendleton (50) are listed in the 1870 Newport, Campbell Co., KY census. He is listed as a River Pilot in the 1880 Newport, Campbell Co., KY census, pg. 115D.

Children of WILLIAM PENDLETON and MEDDIE are:

765.   i.   III WILLIAM ARMISTEAD[12] PENDLETON, b. Apr 12, 1876, KY; d. Aft. 1930, Cincinnati, OH?
       ii. HARRY W. PENDLETON, b. Aug 23, 1877, KY.
       iii. ROBERT A. PENDLETON, b. Jun 26, 1879, Campbell Co., KY.
            Robert Pendleton registered for the World War I draft in Cincinnati, OH.

766.   iv. STEWART PENDLETON, b. Sep 26, 1881, Campbell Co., KY; d. Jun 1971, Louisville, OH.

489. ROBERT LEWIS[11] PENDLETON (*ROBERT TAYLOR[10], JOHN[9], EDMUND[8], JOHN[7], HENRY[6], PHILIP[5], HENRY[4], HENRY[3], GEORGE[2], GEORGE[1]*) was born Jan 24, 1830 in Caroline Co., VA, and died Dec 12, 1880 in Baltimore, MD. He married CHRISTIAN GORDON MICOU Jul 15, 1858 in Locust Grove, Essex Co., VA. She was born Oct 21, 1835 in Essex Co., VA, and died Aug 08, 1904 in Essex Co., VA.

Robert Pendleton (21) is listed in the 1850 Essex Co. census as a "Clerk in Store" in the household of Joseph Gouldman. The marriage of Robert L. Pendleton and Christian G. Micou is listed in Reference 25.

Children of ROBERT PENDLETON and CHRISTIAN MICOU are:
       i.   CONLEY[12] PENDLETON, b. 1861.
767.   ii. AGNES ROY PENDLETON, b. 1862, VA; d. Aft. 1930, Newport News, VA?
768.   iii. ROBERT L. PENDLETON, b. 1863, VA; d. Aft. 1920, Essex Co., VA?
       iv. C. C. PENDLETON, b. 1865.
       v.   R. PENDLETON, b. 1868.
769.   vi. REGINALD NOEL PENDLETON, b. Dec 09, 1873, Baltimore, MD; d. Apr 10, 1935, Baltimore, MD.

490. HENRIETTA[11] PENDLETON (*NATHANIEL PHILIP HENRY[10], JOHN[9], EDMUND[8], JOHN[7], HENRY[6], PHILIP[5], HENRY[4], HENRY[3], GEORGE[2], GEORGE[1]*) was born Dec 23, 1840 in VA, and died Oct 11, 1919. She married GEORGE TAYLOR Mar 03, 1868 in Caroline Co., VA. He died Bef. 1880 in Caroline Co., VA?

The marriage of George Taylor and Henrietta was announced Mar 9, 1868 in the Virginia Herald, Fredericksburg.

Child of HENRIETTA PENDLETON and GEORGE TAYLOR is:
       i.   SALLIE P.[12] TAYLOR, b. 1871, VA.

491. SARAH ANNE[11] PENDLETON (*NATHANIEL PHILIP HENRY[10], JOHN[9], EDMUND[8], JOHN[7], HENRY[6], PHILIP[5], HENRY[4], HENRY[3], GEORGE[2], GEORGE[1]*) was born Feb 22, 1842 in VA, and died Nov 27, 1930 in Elizabeth City, NJ? She married SAMUEL HEISLER PENDLETON 1864, son of JAMES PENDLETON and ANNALETHIA CARTER. He was born Jan 27, 1841 in VA, and died Sep 27, 1918 in Elizabeth City, NJ?

Samuel H. Pendleton enlisted in the Confederate Army as private on 26 Apr 1861, Appomattox Court House, VA, in A Company, 44th Infantry Regiment, VA. Samuel Pendleton (grain merchant) and family are listed in the 1880 Elizabeth, NJ census, pg. 249C.

Child of SARAH PENDLETON and SAMUEL PENDLETON is:
770.   i.   ARTHUR THOMAS[12] PENDLETON, b. Nov 20, 1865, VA; d. Aft. 1920, Elizabeth City, NJ?

492. JULIA NELSON[11] PENDLETON *(HUGH NELSON[10], EDMUND[9], EDMUND[8], JOHN[7], HENRY[6], PHILIP[5], HENRY[4], HENRY[3], GEORGE[2], GEORGE[1])* was born Jan 21, 1830 in VA, and died Jul 23, 1865. She married JAMES W. ALLEN, COL. 1856. He was born in of Bedford Co., VA, and died 1862 killed at Cold Harbor.

Child of JULIA PENDLETON and JAMES ALLEN is:
     i.   HUGH[12] ALLEN, b. Abt. 1857.

493. DUDLEY DIGGES[11] PENDLETON *(HUGH NELSON[10], EDMUND[9], EDMUND[8], JOHN[7], HENRY[6], PHILIP[5], HENRY[4], HENRY[3], GEORGE[2], GEORGE[1])* was born Mar 02, 1840 in Jefferson Co., VA, and died Aug 25, 1886 in Shepherdstown, WV? He married HELEN MCCOMB BOTELER Apr 25, 1866, daughter of ALEXANDER BOTELER and HELEN STOCKTON. She was born 1840 in VA.

Dudley D. Pendleton served as Private in the 1st Rockbridge Artillery, the VA 6th Cavalry Company D and the VA Light Artillery, Graham's Company. Dudley D. Pendleton and family are listed in the 1870 Battletown, Clarke Co., VA census. He was accidentally caught in machinery while threshing wheat, 25th Aug 1886, and so crushed that he died a few hours afterward, leaving his widow and several children (Ref. 274).

Children of DUDLEY PENDLETON and HELEN BOTELER are:
     i.   HELEN BOTELER[12] PENDLETON, b. Apr 02, 1867, WV; d. Aft. 1943, Shepherdstown, WV?

         Helen Boteler Pendleton is the author of "The Bedinger Family" (Ref. 275).

    ii.   ALICE PAGE PENDLETON, b. Oct 1868, Jefferson Co., WV; d. Jun 26, 1898.
   iii.   ELIZABETH STOCKTON PENDLETON, b. Abt. 1870, WV; d. Feb 28, 1916.
771. iv.   JR. DUDLEY DIGGES PENDLETON, b. Mar 24, 1873, WV; d. Aft. 1930, Pittsburgh, PA?
772.   v.   HUGH NELSON PENDLETON, b. Jan 11, 1875, WV; d. Bef. 1954.
   vi.   CHARLOTTE PENDLETON, b. Oct 27, 1876, WV; m. EDMOND LEE GOLDSBOROUGH, Dec 04, 1915; b. Abt. 1869, VA.
773. vii.   ROSALIE PENDLETON, b. May 14, 1880, WV; d. Aft. 1920, Pittsburgh, PA?

494. ROBERT NELSON[11] PENDLETON *(HUGH NELSON[10], EDMUND[9], EDMUND[8], JOHN[7], HENRY[6], PHILIP[5], HENRY[4], HENRY[3], GEORGE[2], GEORGE[1])* was born Feb 04, 1843 in Jefferson Co., VA, and died Jun 22, 1905. He married FRANCES HITE GIBSON Jun 16, 1869. She was born 1848 in MD, and died Aft. 1920 in Roanoke, VA?

A Robert N. Pendleton served in the VA 6th Cavalry, Company D, CSA. Robert N. Pendleton is listed in the 1870 WV census, Jefferson Co., Grant township. Robert N. Pendleton and family are listed in the 1880 Wythe Co., VA census. A biographical sketch of Robert Nelson Pendleton (Ref. 276) is listed in the Virginia Historical Society

Children of ROBERT PENDLETON and FRANCES GIBSON are:

     i. ALEXANDER WALKER[12] PENDLETON, b. Mar 31, 1870, VA; d. Jan 02, 1881.

    ii. LUCY NELSON PENDLETON, b. Feb 03, 1872, Wytheville, VA; m. (1) WILLIAM THOMAS LEAVELL Apr 14, 1898; b. 1854; d. 1900; m. (2) JAMES R. K. BELL Sep 28, 1904.

774. iii. SUE GIBSON PENDLETON, b. Oct 30, 1873, Wytheville, VA; d. Aft. 1920, Wytheville, VA?

775. iv. KATE BERKELEY PENDLETON, b. Jul 29, 1875, Wytheville, VA; d. Aft. 1920.

    v. ELLEN PENDLETON, b. 1878; d. Nov 28, 1880.

    vi. D.D. WILLIAM GIBSON PENDLETON, b. Feb 11, 1880, VA; d. 1964, Lynchburg, VA?; m. (1) MARIA MASON DAWSON Oct 08, 1908; b. Abt. 1885, VA; d. 1921, Fauquier Co., VA; m. (2) ELEANOR FLETCHER HOTCHKISS Dec 12, 1922.

       William (minister) and Maria Pendleton are listed in the 1920 Central Township, Faquier Co., VA census. William Pendleton was a Rector of Grace Church, Lynchburg, VA. He wrote "The character of Robert Edward Lee" (Ref. 277).

495. MILDRED EDMONIA[11] PENDLETON *(FRANCIS WALKER[10], EDMUND[9], EDMUND[8], JOHN[7], HENRY[6], PHILIP[5], HENRY[4], HENRY[3], GEORGE[2], GEORGE[1])* was born 1843 in Richmond Co., VA. She married TASKER CRABBE 1861. He was born Abt. 1844 in VA.

Child of MILDRED PENDLETON and TASKER CRABBE is:

     i. FANNIE[12] CRABBE, b. Abt. 1869.

496. SUSAN[11] PENDLETON *(WILLIAM NELSON[10], EDMUND[9], EDMUND[8], JOHN[7], HENRY[6], PHILIP[5], HENRY[4], HENRY[3], GEORGE[2], GEORGE[1])* was born Dec 10, 1831 in VA, and died Dec 10, 1911 in Lexington, VA. She married EDWIN GRAY LEE, GEN. Nov 16, 1859 in Rockbridge Co., VA, son of EDMUND LEE and HENRIETTA BEDINGER. He was born 1836 in WV, and died Aug 24, 1870 in Montgomery Co., VA.

Susan Pendleton wrote "Memoirs of William Nelson Pendleton" (Ref. 278).

Child of SUSAN PENDLETON and EDWIN LEE is:
    i. SUSAN P.[12] LEE.

497. ALEXANDER SWIFT "SANDY"[11] PENDLETON (*WILLIAM NELSON*[10], *EDMUND*[9], *EDMUND*[8], *JOHN*[7], *HENRY*[6], *PHILIP*[5], *HENRY*[4], *HENRY*[3], *GEORGE*[2], *GEORGE*[1]) was born Sep 28, 1840 in Fairfax Co., VA, and died Sep 22, 1864 in Battle of Fisher's Hill. He married CATHERINE CORBIN Dec 1863 in Moss Neck, VA, daughter of JAMES PARKE CORBIN. She was born 1839, and died 1918.

The short life of Alexander Pendleton, a Confederate hero, is included in the Encyclopedia of Virginia Biography (Ref. 200).

Alexander Pendleton was born at what is now the Episcopal High School, of which his father, the Rev. Dr. William N. Pendleton, was then the rector. Alexander S. Pendleton received his early education under his father's tuition. At thirteen years of age he entered Washington College, Lexington, Virginia, and in his senior year, before he was sixteen years old, was tutor in mathematics. In 1857, before he was seventeen, he was graduated at the head of his class, receiving the first honor of the college, and being appointed to deliver the "Cincinnati Oration." He entered the University of Virginia, in 1859, and in one year was graduated in half of the academic classes, intending to apply for the master's degree the following year. This was prevented by his entering the Confederate army, in which he was offered a second lieutenantcy. He was on the staff of Col. Thomas J. Jackson, and his successors. He was promoted for conspicuous gallantry at Falling Waters and at Manassas, and was again and again recommended for promotion. After the seven days' fight around Richmond, he was made a captain and was also promoted major in the same year. He was with Gen. Jackson at Chancellorsville when the latter was shot. When Gen. Ewell succeeded Gen. Jackson, he was promoted lieutenant-colonel and occupied the same position upon the staff. He was offered a brigade, but declined it to hold the position which he preferred. He was Gen. Early's chief-of-staff in the famous march that he made from the Chickahominy to the gates of Washington, and was known by all acquainted with the history of that movement as among the most efficient officers in that command. After the battle of Winchester, in trying to stay the retreat at Fisher's Hill, he was truck by a piece of shell, which proved to be his death wound. Thus he died September 23, 1864, before he was twenty-four years old. Of him Col. Allen said "In the long catalogue of useful sons who sprang to arms at her bidding and fell in her defense, Virginia mourns no one more worthy of her grand renown and whose open life gave promise of a more useful and distinguished future." His wife, Kate (Corbin) Pendleton, of Moss Neck, survived him.

He well merited an inscription at Versailles - student at 19; soldier at 20; captain at 21; major at 22; lieutenant-colonel and adjutant of the Second Corps at 23; dead at 24.

Child of ALEXANDER PENDLETON and CATHERINE CORBIN is:
    i. ALEXANDER "LITTLE SANDY"[12] PENDLETON, b. Nov 04, 1864; d. Sep 01, 1865.

498. SAMUEL HEISLER[11] PENDLETON *(JAMES LAWRENCE[10], EDMUND[9], EDMUND[8], JOHN[7], HENRY[6], PHILIP[5], HENRY[4], HENRY[3], GEORGE[2], GEORGE[1])* was born Jan 27, 1841 in VA, and died Sep 27, 1918 in Elizabeth City, NJ? He married SARAH ANNE PENDLETON 1864, daughter of NATHANIEL PENDLETON and ANNE TURNER. She was born Feb 22, 1842 in VA, and died Nov 27, 1930 in Elizabeth City, NJ?

Child of Samuel is listed above under (**491**) Sarah Anne Pendleton.

499. WILLIAM J.[11] PENDLETON *(JAMES LAWRENCE[10], EDMUND[9], EDMUND[8], JOHN[7], HENRY[6], PHILIP[5], HENRY[4], HENRY[3], GEORGE[2], GEORGE[1])* was born Abt. 1850 in VA. He married MARY J. ROYALL Oct 1870 in Richmond, VA, daughter of JOHN M. ROYALL.

The marriage of William J. Pendleton and Mary J. Royall, both of Richmond, was announced in the Daily Courier (Petersburg, Va.), October 10, 1870, page 2, column 3.

Children of WILLIAM PENDLETON and MARY ROYALL are:
    i. JAMES L.[12] PENDLETON, b. Mar 1880, VA.
        James L. Pendleton (clerk) is listed in the 1900 Henrico Co., VA in the household of his uncle, Samuel Royall.

    ii. ISABEL R. PENDLETON, b. Nov 1881, VA.

500. EDMUND[11] PENDLETON *(GUERDON HUNTINGDON[10], EDMUND[9], EDMUND[8], JOHN[7], HENRY[6], PHILIP[5], HENRY[4], HENRY[3], GEORGE[2], GEORGE[1])* was born May 22, 1856 in of Wytheville, VA, and died 1935. He married ELEANOR LOVE WILLIS Oct 02, 1895, daughter of NATHANIEL WILLIS and JEAN CHARLOTTE WASHINGTON. She was born Jul 17, 1871 in WV, and died Aug 17, 1908.

Children of EDMUND PENDLETON and ELEANOR WILLIS are:
    i. JANE BYRD[12] PENDLETON, b. Aug 13, 1896, Wytheville, VA; d. 1953.
        Miss Jane Byrd Pendleton was a member of The National Society of the Daughters of the American Revolution (Volume 155, page 52).

    ii. NATHANIEL WILLIS PENDLETON, b. Jun 04, 1898, Wytheville, VA; d. 1968; m. MARGARET ELLA TINDER; b. Oct 23, 1907, of Fredericksburg, VA; d. Dec 17, 1995, Wytheville, VA.
        A biographical sketch of Nathaniel Willis Pendleton (Ref. 279) is listed in the Virginia Historical Society Catalog.

    iii. ELEANOR LOVE PENDLETON, b. Nov 10, 1900, Wytheville, VA; d. 1974; m. GEORGE STUART HASTINGS.
    iv. EDMUND PENDLETON, b. Sep 17, 1902, VA; d. Feb 1976, Wytheville, VA; m. AMELIA CATHERINE DEEKENS; b. Jun 26, 1908; d. Mar 30, 2001, Wytheville, VA.
    v. JEAN WASHINGTON PENDLETON, b. May 26, 1905, VA; d. 1964.

vi. MILDRED LEE PENDLETON, b. Sep 01, 1907, VA; d. Nov 18, 1907.
vii. THOMAS WILLIS PENDLETON.

501. MANN RANDOLPH PAGE[11] PENDLETON *(GUERDON HUNTINGDON[10], EDMUND[9], EDMUND[8], JOHN[7], HENRY[6], PHILIP[5], HENRY[4], HENRY[3], GEORGE[2], GEORGE[1])* was born Mar 01, 1858 in VA, and died Jul 06, 1922 in Wytheville, Wythe Co., VA? He married LEONORA CLAGGETT Jul 22, 1903. She was born Mar 22, 1875 in Of Fairfax Co., VA, and died May 24, 1955 in Wythe Co., VA?

Mann P. Pendleton (farmer) and family are listed in the 1920 Wytheville, Wythe Co., VA census, pg. 1B. The log and frame residence of Mann and Nora C. Pendleton, built in 1820, is a historical site. It is located on 22nd St., Wytheville, VA (Ref. 280).

Children of MANN PENDLETON and LEONORA CLAGGETT are:
i. HAMMETT CLAGGETT[12] PENDLETON, b. Jan 09, 1906, VA; d. Jul 1937; m. RUTH EVELYN GUY, Jul 05, 1930.
ii. BYRD PAGE PENDLETON, b. Mar 28, 1908, Wytheville, VA; d. Nov 1982, Wytheville, VA; m. JACOB MCGAVOCK; b. Jul 08, 1893; d. Jan 1989, Wytheville, VA.

502. JULIA NELSON[11] PENDLETON *(GUERDON HUNTINGDON[10], EDMUND[9], EDMUND[8], JOHN[7], HENRY[6], PHILIP[5], HENRY[4], HENRY[3], GEORGE[2], GEORGE[1])* was born Apr 20, 1865 in WV, and died Aft. 1920 in Wytheville, VA? She married AMADEUS FOSTER POTTS Feb 03, 1903. He was born May 07, 1850 in MS, and died Dec 08, 1925 in Wytheville, VA?

Amadeus Potts and family are listed in the 1920 census, Wytheville, VA.

Children of JULIA PENDLETON and AMADEUS POTTS are:
i. MILDRED ROBINSON[12] POTTS, b. Oct 23, 1903; d. Aug 25, 1904.
ii. JANE BYRD POTTS.

503. MILDRED LOUISE[11] PENDLETON *(GUERDON HUNTINGDON[10], EDMUND[9], EDMUND[8], JOHN[7], HENRY[6], PHILIP[5], HENRY[4], HENRY[3], GEORGE[2], GEORGE[1])* was born May 22, 1867 in Wytheville, VA, and died Mar 25, 1944 in Charlotte, NC. She married EDMUND MYERS ROBINSON Oct 03, 1888 in Wytheville, VA, son of THOMAS ROBINSON and SARAH HUSKE. He was born Oct 27, 1860 in Georgetown, DC, and died Jul 26, 1944 in Charlotte, NC.

Children of MILDRED PENDLETON and EDMUND ROBINSON are:
i. EDMUND DANA[12] ROBINSON, b. Jul 11, 1889; m. ELIZABETH LA FORTUNE, Jan 30, 1923.
ii. PAGE PENDLETON ROBINSON, b. Dec 15, 1890; d. Jan 1972, FL; m. BELLA PRIVETTE Jun 14, 1923.
iii. ANNE HUSKE ROBINSON, b. Mar 06, 1897.
iv. JULIA NELSON ROBINSON, b. Nov 19, 1900; d. Oct 18, 1901.

504. JANE BYRD[11] PENDLETON *(GUERDON HUNTINGDON[10], EDMUND[9], EDMUND[8], JOHN[7], HENRY[6], PHILIP[5], HENRY[4], HENRY[3], GEORGE[2], GEORGE[1])* was born Jun 26, 1869 in Jefferson Co., WV, and died Aft. 1910 in Wythe Co., VA? She married JOHN WILLIAMSON MCGAVOCK Jun 17, 1891. He was born Oct 25, 1846 in VA, and died Aft. 1910 in Wythe Co., VA?

Children of JANE PENDLETON and JOHN MCGAVOCK are:
    i. EMILY GRAHAM[12] MCGAVOCK, b. Jun 16, 1892; d. May 07, 1919; m. ALCOTT NEARY, Jul 13, 1918.
    ii. BYRD PAGE MCGAVOCK, b. Jul 09, 1894; d. Feb 14, 1995, Pulaski, VA.
    iii. SARAH JACKSON MCGAVOCK, b. Jun 06, 1896; d. Dec 26, 1988, Draper, VA; m. JOHN CRAIG ALLISON, Dec 30, 1919.
    iv. GUERDON PENDLETON MCGAVOCK, b. Nov 15, 1898.
    v. STEPHEN MCGAVOCK, b. Nov 25, 1901; d. Jan 1983, Max Meadows, VA.
    vi. FRANCIS NELSON MCGAVOCK.

505. FRANCES LAWRENCE[11] PENDLETON *(GUERDON HUNTINGDON[10], EDMUND[9], EDMUND[8], JOHN[7], HENRY[6], PHILIP[5], HENRY[4], HENRY[3], GEORGE[2], GEORGE[1])* was born Apr 15, 1873 in Wytheville, VA, and died Aft. 1920 in Wytheville, VA? She married CHARLES BARNITZ Feb 09, 1898. He was born Abt. 1870 in VA, and died Aft. 1920 in Wytheville, VA?
    Mrs. Frances Pendleton Barnitz was a member of The National Society of the Daughters of the American Revolution (Volume 72, page 238).

Children of FRANCES PENDLETON and CHARLES BARNITZ are:
    i. MARY CHRISTIAN[12] BARNITZ, b. Jul 09, 1899; d. May 14, 1916.
    ii. FRANCES PAGE BARNITZ, b. Jan 11, 1901; d. Aug 1975, Wytheville, VA; m. RICHARD FRANCIS KELLUM TOTHILL, Feb 18, 1924; b. Feb 01, 1887; d. Dec 1971, Wytheville, VA.
    iii. CHARLES BARNITZ, b. Sep 04, 1906; d. Feb 04, 1997, Elizabeth City, NC.

506. JOHN BARRETT[11] PENDLETON *(MADISON[10], EDMUND[9], HENRY[8], JOHN[7], HENRY[6], PHILIP[5], HENRY[4], HENRY[3], GEORGE[2], GEORGE[1])* was born Oct 21, 1830 in Louisa Co., VA, and died Jul 10, 1861 in killed while in C.S.A. He married SALLIE ANNE MEREDITH Dec 16, 1858. She was born Nov 15, 1839, and died Dec 25, 1889.
    John Barrett Pendleton is listed as a student in the 1850 Louisa Co., VA census. The Civil War letters of John Barrett Pendleton (Ref. 281) are listed in the Virginia Historical Society Catalog. He is buried at "The Hermitage," Louisa Co., VA. Sallie A. Pendleton is in the household of Madison and Elizabeth K. Pendleton in the 1870 census, Louisa Co., Northern District.

Child of JOHN PENDLETON and SALLIE MEREDITH is:
776.   i. ELIZABETH "BETTIE" BARRETT[12] PENDLETON, b. Apr 28, 1860, VA; d. Aft. 1920, Cuckoo, Louisa Co., VA?

507. EDMUND STRACHAN[11] PENDLETON (*MADISON*[10], *EDMUND*[9], *HENRY*[8], *JOHN*[7], *HENRY*[6], *PHILIP*[5], *HENRY*[4], *HENRY*[3], *GEORGE*[2], *GEORGE*[1]) was born May 09, 1833 in Louisa Co., VA, and died Dec 27, 1909 in Iron Gate, Louisa Co., VA. He married (1) SUSAN MANSFIELD TRICE Dec 07, 1856, daughter of JAMES TRICE and CATHERINE G. She was born Sep 18, 1835 in VA, and died Apr 18, 1879 in VA. He married (2) SALLIE WOOLFOLK FLIPPO Dec 19, 1883, daughter of LITTLETON FLIPPO and SARAH COLEMAN. She was born Mar 03, 1855.

  Edmund S. Pendleton was an assistant surgeon in the C.S.A (Ref. 69). Edmund S. Pendleton (physician) and family are listed in the 1870 Byrd, Goochland Co., VA census. A biographical sketch of Edmund Strachan Pendleton (Ref. 272) is listed in the Virginia Historical Society Catalog.

Children of EDMUND PENDLETON and SUSAN TRICE are:

   i. MARY UNITY[12] PENDLETON, b. Jan 28, 1858, VA.
   ii. JAMES MADISON PENDLETON, b. Feb 13, 1861, VA; d. Jan 14, 1898.
777. iii. JOHN HENRY PENDLETON, b. Jun 26, 1867, VA; d. Mar 05, 1899.
   iv. CATHERINE KIMBROUGH PENDLETON, b. Sep 05, 1872, VA; m. JOSEPH MORRISON SMITH, Sep 11, 1895; d. Elkton, NC?
778. v. SUSAN STRACHAN PENDLETON, b. Feb 18, 1877, VA; d. Apr 28, 1957, Botetourt Co., VA?

Children of EDMUND PENDLETON and SALLIE FLIPPO are:

   vi. EDMUND LITTLETON[12] PENDLETON, b. Sep 29, 1884; d. Aug 06, 1888.
   vii. EDMUND STRACHAN PENDLETON, b. Dec 19, 1886, VA; d. Jun 06, 1917.
     Edmund Strachan Pendleton registered for the World War I Draft in Alleghany Co., VA (Ref. 210).

   viii. LITTLETON FLIPPO PENDLETON, b. Sep 16, 1888, VA; m. RUTH EDGAR Jan 17, 1925; dau. WARREN EDGAR and VIRGINIA M.; b. Abt. 1893, PA.
     Littleton Flippo Pendleton registered for the World War I draft in Alleghany Co. (Ref. 210).

508. CHARLES KIMBROUGH[11] PENDLETON (*MADISON*[10], *EDMUND*[9], *HENRY*[8], *JOHN*[7], *HENRY*[6], *PHILIP*[5], *HENRY*[4], *HENRY*[3], *GEORGE*[2], *GEORGE*[1]) was born Nov 30, 1835 in Louisa Co., VA, and died Feb 10, 1918 in Ashland, VA. He married LUCY TURNER CHANDLER Mar 15, 1875 in Louisa Co., VA? She was born Mar 15, 1851 in VA, and died Aft. 1920 in Ashland, VA?

  Charles K. Pendleton was with his three brothers in the C.S.A. and took with him to his grave a minnie ball. He served in the VA 4th Cavalry, Company F, Sgt. CSA. He was captured 8 May 1864, Spotsylvania Court House and paroled at Fort Delaware, 20 June 1865. Charles K. Pendleton (farmer) and family are listed in the 1900 Louisa Co., VA census, pg. 217. C.K. Pendleton and Lucy (widow) are listed in the Confederate Pension Rolls, Hanover Co., VA.

Children of CHARLES PENDLETON and LUCY CHANDLER are:
  i.   MADISON STRACHAN[12] PENDLETON, b. Mar 27, 1876, VA; d. Oct 14, 1927.
  ii. THOMAS CHANDLER PENDLETON, b. Apr 05, 1878, VA; d. Oct 19, 1903.
779. iii. ELIZABETH KIMBROUGH PENDLETON, b. Dec 28, 1879, Louisa Co., VA; d. Aft. 1920, Ashland, VA?
780. iv. MARY WASHINGTON PENDLETON, b. Dec 20, 1881, Louisa Co., VA; d. Aft. 1920, Ashland, VA?
  v.   CHARLES KIMBROUGH PENDLETON, b. Sep 18, 1885, VA; d. Jun 03, 1911.
  vi. HARRY LEIGH PENDLETON, b. Jun 30, 1888, VA; d. Dec 06, 1915.
  vii. BRODIE HERNDON PENDLETON, b. Oct 08, 1891, VA; d. Jun 08, 1892.

509. WILLIAM BARRETT[11] PENDLETON *(MADISON[10], EDMUND[9], HENRY[8], JOHN[7], HENRY[6], PHILIP[5], HENRY[4], HENRY[3], GEORGE[2], GEORGE[1])* was born Feb 12, 1838 in Louisa Co., VA, and died Jan 17, 1914 in Louisa Co., VA. He married JULIANA PENDLETON May 03, 1870 in Louisa Co., VA, daughter of WILLIAM PENDLETON and CATHERINE HARRIS. She was born May 13, 1839 in Louisa Co., VA, and died May 12, 1926 in Cuckoo, Louisa Co., VA?

William B. Pendleton served in the 23rd Infantry Regiment, Company G, C.S.A. where he was promoted to Captain. He was wounded at Cedar Mountain, losing a leg. He was Adjutant in Taliaferro's brigade. Wm B. Pendleton (farmer) and family are listed in the 1900 Louisa Co., VA census, pg. 24. He died at "Cuckoo" about 1914.

Children of William Barrett are listed above under **(261)** Juliana Pendleton.

510. WILLIAM CAMPBELL[11] PENDLETON *(WILLIAM KIMBROUGH[10], EDMUND[9], HENRY[8], JOHN[7], HENRY[6], PHILIP[5], HENRY[4], HENRY[3], GEORGE[2], GEORGE[1])* was born May 03, 1849 in Bethany, Brooke Co., VA, and died Oct 07, 1922 in Trumbull Co., OH? He married HELEN KING AUSTIN Jan 15, 1880, daughter of HARMON AUSTIN and MINERVA SACKETT. She was born Dec 15, 1853 in Trumbull Co., OH, and died Oct 22, 1922 in Trumbull Co., OH?

Child of WILLIAM PENDLETON and HELEN AUSTIN is:
781. i.   AUSTIN CAMPBELL[12] PENDLETON, b. Aug 03, 1881, Trumbull Co., OH; d. Apr 27, 1921, Trumbull Co., OH.

511. CLARINDA HUNTINGTON[11] PENDLETON *(WILLIAM KIMBROUGH[10], EDMUND[9], HENRY[8], JOHN[7], HENRY[6], PHILIP[5], HENRY[4], HENRY[3], GEORGE[2], GEORGE[1])* was born Aug 26, 1856 in WV, and died Apr 27, 1943 in Atlanta, GA. She married JOSEPH RUCKER LAMAR Jan 30, 1879 in Bethany, WV, son of JAMES S. LAMAR and MARY RUCKER. He was born Oct 14, 1857 in GA, and died Jan 02, 1916.

Joseph Rucker Lamar was appointed to the United States Supreme Court by the affable William H. Taft. His choice was excellent for Justice Lamar served the nation with unwavering faith, ability and fidelity. Lamar's father was Reverend James S. Lamar who married Mary Rucker; his grandfather, Phillip Lamar Jr. Married Margaret Anthony; his great grandfather Phillip Sr., married Ruth Davis, and his great-great grandfather, Robert, married Sarah Wilson. Mrs. Joseph Rucker Lamar, prominent in Georgia society and club work, was Clarinda Huntington Pendleton, daughter of Dr. William K. Pendleton once President of Bethany College.

Children of CLARINDA PENDLETON and JOSEPH LAMAR are:
    i. PHILIP RUCKER[12] LAMAR, b. Jun 16, 1880.
    ii. WILLIAM PENDLETON LAMAR, b. Oct 05, 1882.
    iii. MARY LAMAR, b. Apr 15, 1885; d. Jul 11, 1885.

512. HUNTINGTON KING[11] PENDLETON *(WILLIAM KIMBROUGH*[10]*, EDMUND*[9]*, HENRY*[8]*, JOHN*[7]*, HENRY*[6]*, PHILIP*[5]*, HENRY*[4]*, HENRY*[3]*, GEORGE*[2]*, GEORGE*[1]*)* was born Sep 07, 1861 in WV. He married MARTHA WELLMAN PAXTON Jun 05, 1884. She was born 1862 in WV.

Children of HUNTINGTON PENDLETON and MARTHA PAXTON are:
    i. KATHERINE KING[12] PENDLETON, b. Apr 16, 1885, New Albany, IN; d. Jun 16, 1925; m. JR. ROBERT H. HADDOW, Jun 02, 1910.
        Mrs. Katharine Pendleton Haddow was a member of The National Society of the Daughters of the American Revolution (Volume 46, page 85).

    ii. MARY WHITEHEAD PENDLETON, b. Sep 11, 1886; m. (1) JASPER NEWTON, Oct 09, 1907; m. (2) OZRA DODGE THOMAS.
    iii. GEORGE PAXTON PENDLETON, b. Feb 18, 1888; d. May 09, 1893.
    iv. JEAN FRANCES PENDLETON, b. Oct 27, 1889; m. HARRY AVERY FERRAN, Sep 24, 1909.

513. PHILIP YANCEY[11] PENDLETON *(WILLIAM KIMBROUGH*[10]*, EDMUND*[9]*, HENRY*[8]*, JOHN*[7]*, HENRY*[6]*, PHILIP*[5]*, HENRY*[4]*, HENRY*[3]*, GEORGE*[2]*, GEORGE*[1]*)* was born Sep 25, 1863 in WV, and died Feb 01, 1930. He married (1) ADA (HARVUOT) LLOYD Jun 13, 1893. She was born 1863 in OH, and died 1925. He married (2) PEARL MARIE BUTLER Apr 29, 1928.

Children of PHILIP PENDLETON and ADA LLOYD are:
    i. WILLIAM LAMAR[12] PENDLETON, b. May 28, 1895; m. RUTH THOMAS.
    ii. ELEANOR FORD PENDLETON, b. Mar 02, 1899; d. Mar 24, 1921.
    iii. JR. PHILIP YANCEY PENDLETON, b. Feb 02, 1905; d. Jan 1956, CA?; m. MRS. HELEN (FRANES) ELDER, Jun 09, 1930.
        Philip Y. Pendleton was Assistant County Attorney, Maricopa Co., AZ, 1928.

514. WINSTON KENT[11] PENDLETON *(WILLIAM KIMBROUGH*[10]*, EDMUND*[9]*, HENRY*[8]*, JOHN*[7]*, HENRY*[6]*, PHILIP*[5]*, HENRY*[4]*, HENRY*[3]*, GEORGE*[2]*, GEORGE*[1]*)* was born Oct 24, 1869 in Bethany, WV, and died in Eustis, FL? He married DAISY BELLE WATT Dec 27, 1897. She was born Aug 1876 in VA.

Children of WINSTON PENDLETON and DAISY WATT are:
- i.   STEWART WATT[12] PENDLETON, b. Jun 08, 1899, Eustis, FL; d. Jun 1969, Miami, FL; m. (1) ELVA ROBERTS Jun 27, 1919; b. Jan 21, 1901, FL; d. Aug 08, 1996, Alachua, FL; m. (2) BETTY RAWLS.
- ii. CATHERINE HUNTINGTON PENDLETON.
- iii. ALEXANDER CASSIL PENDLETON.
- iv. JANE ANN PENDLETON, b. Jan 16, 1905; d. May 09, 1990; m. JOHN W. WHITEMAN 1925.
- v.   WINSTON KENT PENDLETON, b. Nov 27, 1910; d. Feb 18, 2000, Orange Co., FL.
- vi. JOE LAMAR PENDLETON, b. Oct 04, 1914; d. Nov 27, 1987, Fort Myers, FL.

515. DWIGHT LYMAN[11] PENDLETON *(WILLIAM KIMBROUGH[10], EDMUND[9], HENRY[8], JOHN[7], HENRY[6], PHILIP[5], HENRY[4], HENRY[3], GEORGE[2], GEORGE[1])* was born Oct 14, 1871 in WV, and died Feb 12, 1955 in Clark Co, KY- Winchester Cemetery. He married SARA TEBBS PREWITT Nov 29, 1899. She was born Mar 16, 1870 in KY, and died Jan 14, 1941 in Clark Co, KY- Winchester Cemetery.

Dwight L. Pendleton was a graduate of Bethany College, WV and was a admitted to the Bar at Pittsburg, PA. Mr. Pendleton was a prominent lawyer in Winchester, KY and was listed as such in the 1900 Clark Co., KY census.

Children of DWIGHT PENDLETON and SARA PREWITT are:
- i.   ELIZABETH TEBBS[12] PENDLETON, b. Jul 26, 1901, Winchester, Clark Co., KY; d. Apr 1986, Winchester, Clark Co., KY; m. ROBERT DUDLEY TAYLOR, Nov 27, 1929; b. Abt. 1897, KY.
- ii. KATE HUNTINGTON PENDLETON.
- iii. STANLEY DUDLEY PENDLETON, b. Aug 30, 1906; d. Oct 1979, Winchester, KY.
- iv. DWIGHT LYMAN PENDLETON, b. May 10, 1910, KY; d. May 1978, Lexington, KY.

    The following notice appeared May 8, 1978 in Lexington newspapers (Ref. 282): "Development Council director D.L. Pendleton, age 67, dies; Dwight Lyman Pendleton, 67, Court Street [Stanton], owner of Pen-Dal Farms and director of the Blue Grass Area Development Council, died Sunday."

- v.   WILLIAM KIMBROUGH PENDLETON.

516. EUGENE B.[11] PENDLETON, DR. *(PHILIP BARBOUR[10], EDMUND[9], HENRY[8], JOHN[7], HENRY[6], PHILIP[5], HENRY[4], HENRY[3], GEORGE[2], GEORGE[1])* was born Jun 22, 1851 in VA, and died Sep 09, 1927 in Cuckoo, Louisa Co., VA? He married ELIZABETH "BETTIE" BARRETT PENDLETON Sep 09, 1880, daughter of JOHN

PENDLETON and SALLIE MEREDITH. She was born Apr 28, 1860 in VA, and died Aft. 1920 in Cuckoo, Louisa Co., VA?

Eugene Pendleton (Dr. of Medicine) and family are listed in the 1900 Louisa Co., VA census, pg. 30 and the 1920 census, Cuckoo, Louisa Co., pg. 10A.

Children of EUGENE PENDLETON and ELIZABETH PENDLETON are:

      i.   JOHN BARRETT[12] PENDLETON, b. Aug 28, 1881; d. Jun 26, 1888.

782.   ii.   EUGENE BARBOUR PENDLETON, b. Jun 01, 1885, VA; d. Aft. 1920, Cuckoo, Louisa Co., VA?

     iii.   LEWIS SMITH PENDLETON, b. May 01, 1889, VA; m. (1) MADELINE BURRIS Oct 07, 1920; b. Oct 24, 1896; d. Jan 19, 1923; m.(2) CHRISTINE FURNIVAL Feb 08, 1930.

        Lewis S. Pendleton (lawyer) is listed in the household of his father in the 1920 Louisa Co., VA census.

     iv.   ANNE MEREDITH PENDLETON, b. Aug 05, 1895, VA; d. Aug 1974, Mineral, VA; m. WILLIAM MENTZEL FORREST, Jun 21, 1932, Louisa Co., VA.

        Anne M. Pendleton is listed in the household of her father in the 1920 Louisa Co., VA census. She contributed the Civil War letters of John Barrett Pendleton to the Virginia Historical Society Library.

517. SALLY LOUISE[11] PENDLETON *(PHILIP BARBOUR[10], EDMUND[9], HENRY[8], JOHN[7], HENRY[6], PHILIP[5], HENRY[4], HENRY[3], GEORGE[2], GEORGE[1])* was born Feb 04, 1853 in VA, and died Jul 15, 1932. She married ISAAC J. SPENCER Sep 19, 1878. He was born Nov 10, 1851 in Belmont Co., OH, and died Mar 01, 1922 in Peoria, IL.

Children of SALLY PENDLETON and ISAAC SPENCER are:

      i.   JESSIE PENDLETON[12] SPENCER, b. Jan 25, 1880.

     ii.   HOWARD GALE SPENCER, b. Aug 24, 1881; m. MARY CURTIS, Dec 23, 1915.

     iii.   EVELYN HOLLADAY SPENCER, b. Sep 03, 1883.

     iv.   JULIA HOGE SPENCER, b. Sep 16, 1889; d. Mar 1977, Bourbon Co., KY; m. WILLIAM BRECKENBRIDGE ARDERY Mar 14, 1910; b. Aug 11, 1887; d. Jul 1967 in Bourbon Co., KY.

518. JOSEPH KIMBROUGH[11] PENDLETON *(PHILIP BARBOUR[10], EDMUND[9], HENRY[8], JOHN[7], HENRY[6], PHILIP[5], HENRY[4], HENRY[3], GEORGE[2], GEORGE[1])* was born Feb 11, 1855 in VA. He married IDA E. KAUFMAN Jan 02, 1896. She was born Aug 1871 in WI.

Joseph K. Pendleton (hardware merchant) and family are listed in the 1900 Alleghany Co., VA census, pg. 125a.

Child of JOSEPH PENDLETON and IDA KAUFMAN is:

      i.   JANE KIMBROUGH[12] PENDLETON, b. Apr 07, 1900; d. Mar 1979, Los Angeles, CA; m. ERNEST CHRISTIAN MADSEN, Jun 01, 1922.

519. WILLIAM "WILLIE" WALLER[11] PENDLETON (*PHILIP BARBOUR*[10], *EDMUND*[9], *HENRY*[8], *JOHN*[7], *HENRY*[6], *PHILIP*[5], *HENRY*[4], *HENRY*[3], *GEORGE*[2], *GEORGE*[1]) was born Sep 26, 1856 in Louisa Co., VA, and died Aft. 1920 in Clifton Forge, VA? He married MARY BLANCHE CARGILL Nov 06, 1884. She was born Aug 1866 in WV, and died Aft. 1920 in Clifton Forge, VA?

William W Pendleton, clerk, is listed in the Richmond, Virginia City Directories, 1889-90 with an address of 1535 Main St., E. Richmond, VA. William W. Pendleton (school superintendent) and family are listed in the 1900 Alleghany Co., VA census, pg. 116 and as garage owner in the 1920 Clifton Forge, VA census, pg. 18A.

Child of WILLIAM PENDLETON and MARY CARGILL is:

    i.   PHILIP CARGILL[12] PENDLETON, b. Feb 07, 1886, VA; d. Jul 1963, Clifton Forge, VA?; m. MARY MERCER DUERSON Oct 19, 1911, dau. of EMMA; b. Abt. 1887, VA; d. Aft. 1930, Clifton Forge, VA?

        Philip Cargill Pendleton registered for the World War I draft in Alleghany Co., VA. Philip C. Pendleton (automobile supply) and family are listed in the 1920 Clifton Forge, VA census.

520. ELIZABETH YANCEY[11] PENDLETON (*PHILIP BARBOUR*[10], *EDMUND*[9], *HENRY*[8], *JOHN*[7], *HENRY*[6], *PHILIP*[5], *HENRY*[4], *HENRY*[3], *GEORGE*[2], *GEORGE*[1]) was born Jan 12, 1862 in VA, and died Bef. 1920. She married WILLIAM PERCY THORNTON May 04, 1886. He was born Jun 09, 1863 in VA, and died Jul 12, 1925 in Accomack Co., VA?

William P. Thornton (Laborer) is listed in the 1920 Accomack Co., VA census.

Child of ELIZABETH PENDLETON and WILLIAM THORNTON is:

    i.   ANDREW W.[12] THORNTON.

521. PHILIP BARBOUR[11] PENDLETON (*PHILIP BARBOUR*[10], *EDMUND*[9], *HENRY*[8], *JOHN*[7], *HENRY*[6], *PHILIP*[5], *HENRY*[4], *HENRY*[3], *GEORGE*[2], *GEORGE*[1]) was born Jun 23, 1868 in VA, and died Jun 05, 1908. He married ALMA FLORENCE STAFFORD Jul 03, 1906, daughter of CHARLES STAFFORD and JULIA KUHN. She was born May 23, 1887 in Kanawha Valley, WV.

Philip B Pendleton, medical student, is listed in the Richmond, Virginia City Directories, 1889-90, boards at 521 8th St., N. Richmond, VA. Mrs. Alma (Stafford) Pendleton was a member of The National Society of the Daughters of the American Revolution (Volume 157, page 155).

Children of PHILIP PENDLETON and ALMA STAFFORD are:

    i.   JANE STAFFORD[12] PENDLETON, b. Jul 08, 1907; d. Dec 26, 1995, Greensboro, NC; m. JR. CHARLES WESLEY CAUSEY, May 22, 1931; b. May 27, 1909; d. Jun 13, 1992, Greensboro, NC.

    ii.   JULIA LOUISA PENDLETON.

522. ERNEST COPELAND[11] PENDLETON (*HENRY*[10], *JOHN BICKERTON*[9], *HENRY*[8], *JOHN*[7], *HENRY*[6], *PHILIP*[5], *HENRY*[4], *HENRY*[3], *GEORGE*[2], *GEORGE*[1]) was born Feb 24, 1877 in Pickens Co., AL, and died Feb 05, 1941. He married WILLIE ALLEN Feb 20, 1902. She was born Jan 30, 1881 in AL, and died Feb 22, 1950 in Marshall Co., AL.

Children of ERNEST PENDLETON and WILLIE ALLEN are:
- i. PAUL[12] PENDLETON, b. Nov 23, 1902, AL; d. Apr 03, 1923, Marshall Co., AL.
- ii. AUBREY PENDLETON, b. Jul 01, 1904, AL; d. Apr 10, 1990; m. (1) VIRGIE B. STARNES; b. Apr 14, 1904; d. Jan 16, 1953, Marshall Co., AL.; m. (2) ROSALIE CLEVELAND KENNAMER; b. Sep 23, 1910, AL; d. Dec 26, 2000, Marshall Co., AL.
- iii. THELMA PENDLETON, b. Jul 20, 1907, AL; d. Jan 14, 2005, De Kalb Co., AL; m. FRANKLIN NORWOOD CONNER; b. Jan 09, 1905.
- iv. HERBERT BEESON PENDLETON, b. Apr 12, 1910, AL; d. May 09, 1950, Marshall Co., AL.

523. IDA EWING[11] PENDLETON *(JOSEPH HENRY[10], JOSEPH WINSTON[9], HENRY[8], JOHN[7], HENRY[6], PHILIP[5], HENRY[4], HENRY[3], GEORGE[2], GEORGE[1])* was born 1858 in VA. She married FRANK P. JEPSON 1876, son of FRANK JEPSON. He was born Abt. 1854 in WV.

Frank Jepson and family are listed in the 1880 census, Wheeling, WV, pg. 447A.

Child of IDA PENDLETON and FRANK JEPSON is:
- i. EVALINE[12] JEPSON, b. Abt. 1879, WV.

524. VIRGINIA CAMPBELL[11] PENDLETON *(JOSEPH HENRY[10], JOSEPH WINSTON[9], HENRY[8], JOHN[7], HENRY[6], PHILIP[5], HENRY[4], HENRY[3], GEORGE[2], GEORGE[1])* was born 1861 in VA. She married ANDREW U. WILSON 1888.

Child of VIRGINIA PENDLETON and ANDREW WILSON is:
- i. JOHN PENDLETON[12] WILSON.

525. JOHN O. H.[11] PENDLETON *(JOHN OVERTON[10], JOSEPH WINSTON[9], HENRY[8], JOHN[7], HENRY[6], PHILIP[5], HENRY[4], HENRY[3], GEORGE[2], GEORGE[1])* was born Feb 1861 in VA, and died Aft. 1910 in Albemarle Co., VA? He married CORINNE M. DIGGES Jul 05, 1883 in Albemarle Co., VA, daughter of DAVID DIGGES and MARTHA PRICE. She was born Sep 1863 in VA, and died Aft. 1910 in Albemarle Co., VA?

John O.H. Pendleton (book keeper) and family are listed in the 1900 Albemarle Co., VA census, pg. 251.

Children of JOHN PENDLETON and CORINNE DIGGES are:
- i. EDMUND COLE[12] PENDLETON, b. Jan 15, 1885, VA.

    Edmond Cole Pendleton registered for the World War I draft in Albemarle Co., VA.

ii. ANNIE LEWIS PENDLETON, b. Aug 1886, VA.

iii. IDA DAVIS PENDLETON, b. Jul 29, 1888, Albemarle Co., VA.

iv. HENRY A. PENDLETON, b. Apr 08, 1890, Albemarle Co., VA; d. Aug 1962.

v. DAVID M. PENDLETON, b. Nov 20, 1892, Albemarle Co., VA.

vi. JOHN SHIRLEY PENDLETON, b. Sep 08, 1893, Albemarle Co., VA.

John Shirley Pendleton registered for the World War I draft in Prince George Co., VA.

vii. PHILIP DAVIS PENDLETON, b. Dec 1897, Albemarle Co., VA.

526. ELIZABETH B.[11] PENDLETON *(ELISHA HENRY[10], THOMAS MADISON[9], HENRY[8], JOHN[7], HENRY[6], PHILIP[5], HENRY[4], HENRY[3], GEORGE[2], GEORGE[1])* was born Jul 28, 1872 in VA, and died 1957 in WV. She married (1) CLARENCE RADER Oct 26, 1898 in Charleston, WV. She married (2) WILLIAM WOOD Mar 19, 1918.

Elizabeth Pendleton is in the household of her aunt Eliza M. Jackson (64) in the 1880 Cumberland Co., VA census.

Child of ELIZABETH PENDLETON and CLARENCE RADER is:

i. LYNN P.[12] RADER, b. 1899; d. 1963.

527. CHARLES WILLIAM[11] PENDLETON *(ELISHA HENRY[10], THOMAS MADISON[9], HENRY[8], JOHN[7], HENRY[6], PHILIP[5], HENRY[4], HENRY[3], GEORGE[2], GEORGE[1])* was born May 26, 1878 in VA, and died Jul 20, 1970 in WV? He married MARGARET KERNS Jun 14, 1899. She was born Abt. 1879 in VA, and died Aft. 1920 in Spring Hill, WV?

Charley William Pendleton registered for the World War I draft in Charleston, Kanawha Co., WV. Charles W. Pendleton (Carpenter) and family are listed in the 1920 Spring Hill, Kanawha Co., WV census.

Child of CHARLES PENDLETON and MARGARET KERNS is:

i. GUY BRIGGS[12] PENDLETON, b. Jun 27, 1900, WV; d. Mar 22, 1949, Washington Co., MD?; m. AVA IRENE SUMMERS, Sep 18, 1928; b. Abt. 1907, MD.

Guy Briggs Pendleton registered for the World War I draft in Charleston, Kanawha Co., WV.

528. JOHN HUNTER[11] PENDLETON *(DAVID HARRIS[10], WILLIAM JAMES[9], HENRY[8], JOHN[7], HENRY[6], PHILIP[5], HENRY[4], HENRY[3], GEORGE[2], GEORGE[1])* was born Jan 22, 1858 in VA, and died Aug 01, 1940 in Rockbridge, VA? He married LOUISA WHITE Jun 23, 1891. She was born Sep 1869 in VA, and died Aft. 1920 in Rockbridge, VA?

Hunter Pendleton (Professor at VMI) and family are listed in the 1900 Rockbridge, Lexington Co., VA census, pg. 100a. J. Hunter Pendleton and family are listed in the 1920 Rockbridge census. Col. Hunter Pendleton was a Professor of Chemistry at VMI from 1890 to 1935.

Children of JOHN PENDLETON and LOUISA WHITE are:
- i. NANCY LEWIS[12] PENDLETON, b. Oct 13, 1895, VA; d. Feb 1972, Atlanta, GA; m. WALTER B. ELCOCK, Aug 14, 1917; b. Dec 06, 1888; d. Jun 1964, GA?.
- ii. HILAH WHITE PENDLETON, b. Dec 25, 1898, VA; m. STUART MOORE Nov 09, 1927; b. Abt. 1894, VA.
- iii. HUNTER PENDLETON, b. Oct 23, 1900, VA; d. Sep 16, 1992, Fort Worth, TX; m. MARGUERITE SCALING Oct 16, 1926, dau. LAURA W; b. Abt. 1900, MO.
- iv. JOHN WHITE PENDLETON, b. Feb 07, 1908; d. Mar 1971.

529. PHILIP HENRY[11] PENDLETON *(WILLIAM BARRETT[10], MADISON[9], EDMUND[8], HENRY[7], JOHN[6], HENRY[5], PHILIP[4], HENRY[3], HENRY[2], GEORGE[1])* was born May 05, 1871 in VA, and died Nov 26, 1916 in Fayette Co., PA? He married CHARLOTTE STAUFFER REID Dec 13, 1895. She was born Abt. 1875 in PA.

Children of PHILIP PENDLETON and CHARLOTTE REID are:
- i. JULIA JOSEPHINE[12] PENDLETON, b. Jul 26, 1896, PA.
- ii. ELIZABETH MOORE PENDLETON, b. Nov 03, 1897, PA; m. HENRY EASTMAN HACKNEY, Uniontown, PA.
- iii. REID PENDLETON, b. Sep 15, 1902; d. Sep 20, 2002, Turlock, CA; m. MARGARET DRAPER.
- iv. CONSTANCE PENDLETON.

530. ALICE OVERTON[11] PENDLETON *(WILLIAM BARRETT[10], MADISON[9], EDMUND[8], HENRY[7], JOHN[6], HENRY[5], PHILIP[4], HENRY[3], HENRY[2], GEORGE[1])* was born Mar 06, 1873. She married SCHUYLER BARCLAY MOON, DR. Sep 26, 1896, son of JOHN MOON and ELIZABETH TOMPKINS.

Child of ALICE PENDLETON and SCHUYLER MOON is:
- i. ELIZABETH BARCLAY[12] MOON.

531. WILLIAM BARRETT[11] PENDLETON *(WILLIAM BARRETT[10], MADISON[9], EDMUND[8], HENRY[7], JOHN[6], HENRY[5], PHILIP[4], HENRY[3], HENRY[2], GEORGE[1])* was born Feb 12, 1880 in VA, and died Nov 1969 in VA. He married NORVELLE WINSTON Oct 31, 1914. She was born Abt. 1883 in VA.

William B. Pendleton (farmer), family and mother, Juliana Pendleton, are listed in the 1920 Cuckoo, Louisa Co., VA census.

Child of WILLIAM PENDLETON and NORVELLE WINSTON is:
- i. WILLIAM WINSTON[12] PENDLETON.

532. JAMES TRIGG[11] PENDLETON *(IRA NASH[10], REUBEN[9], BENJAMIN[8], WILLIAM[7], JOHN[6], PHILIP[5], HENRY[4], HENRY[3], GEORGE[2], GEORGE[1])* was born Nov 15, 1827 in Lee Co., VA, and died Dec 18, 1880 in Johnson Co., KY. He married SARAH HILTON KILGORE. She was born Sep 28, 1828 in Lee Co., VA, and died Mar 25, 1912 in Morgan Co., KY.

James T. Pendleton is listed in the 1850 Scott Co., VA census, age 21, with his wife, Sarah T. (21), younger brother Samuel G. (10), younger sisters, Josephine (6), and Rosamon, (4), and his son, William (1). He served in the VA 25th Cavalry, Company A, CSA, with his brother Samuel G. Pendleton. He enlisted as a private on 27 May, 1861, in Abingdon, VA James Pendleton is listed in the 1880 Morgan Co., KY census, as a farm and dry goods merchant, age 52, along with Sarah J. (51, Robert (21), Ardena (18), Virginia (16), Samuel G. (14), and George H. (12).

Children of JAMES PENDLETON and SARAH KILGORE are (Ref. 283):

      i. WILLIAM[12] PENDLETON, b. Aug 1850, Scott Co., VA; d. Dec 31, 1928, Johnson Co., KY; m. MARY LEMASTER, Nov 18, 1870, Johnson Co., KY; b. Nov 1853, KY; d. Apr 26, 1915, Johnson Co., KY.

          William Pendleton (farmer?) and Mary are listed in the 1900 Johnson Co., KY census. Mary is listed as having 1 child, none living.

783.   ii. IRA NEWTON PENDLETON, b. Jun 05, 1851, Scott Co., VA; d. Mar 25, 1907, KY.

784.   iii. JOHN PENDLETON, b. May 10, 1853, VA; d. Nov 24, 1911, Morgan Co., KY.

785.   iv. JAMES M. PENDLETON, b. Abt. 1854, VA.

      v. ROBERT PENDLETON, b. 1860, KY; m. CYNTHIA SAGRAVES, Jan 20, 1882, Johnson Co., KY; b. Jan 07, 1861, Johnson Co., KY.

786.   vi. ARDENA PENDLETON, b. Abt. 1862, KY; d. Aft. 1900.

787. vii. VIRGINIA PENDLETON, b. May 05, 1865, KY; d. Mar 29, 1931, Morgan Co., KY.

   viii. SAMUEL G. PENDLETON, b. Abt. 1866.

788.   ix. GEORGE H. PENDLETON, b. Oct 19, 1868, KY; d. Oct 19, 1911, Johnson Co., KY.

533. DULCENA[11] PENDLETON *(IRA NASH[10], REUBEN[9], BENJAMIN[8], WILLIAM[7], JOHN[6], PHILIP[5], HENRY[4], HENRY[3], GEORGE[2], GEORGE[1])* was born Abt. 1830 in VA, and died Abt. 1915 in Scott Co., VA? She married HENRY MAHAN. He was born Abt. 1820 in VA, and died Aft. 1880.

Henry Mahan, farmer, and family are listed in the 1880 Scott Co., VA census, pg. 301D.

Children of DULCENA PENDLETON and HENRY MAHAN are:

      i. PETER[12] MAHAN, b. Abt. 1857, VA.

     ii. ELIZABETH MAHAN, b. Abt. 1865, VA.

   iii. FRANCES A. MAHAN, b. Abt. 1867, VA.

   iv. JOSEPHINE MAHAN, b. Abt. 1870, VA.

v.   HENRY W. MAHAN, b. Abt. 1872, VA.
vi. ROSA MAHAN, b. Abt. 1875, VA.

534. SAMUEL G.[11] PENDLETON *(IRA NASH[10], REUBEN[9], BENJAMIN[8], WILLIAM[7], JOHN[6], PHILIP[5], HENRY[4], HENRY[3], GEORGE[2], GEORGE[1])* was born Apr 29, 1840 in Scott Co., VA, and died 1907 in Johnson Co., KY? He married (1) MARTHA CARTER Jan 08, 1866 in Scott Co., VA, daughter of JAMES CARTER. She was born Abt. 1846 in Scott Co., VA. He married (2) MARGARET NEELY. She was born May 29, 1847 in VA, and died Jul 17, 1929.

Samuel G. Pendleton served in the VA 25th Cavalry, Company A, CSA as a Sgt. with his brother James T. Pendleton. He enlisted 27 May, 1862 (age 22) as a private in Abingdon, VA, with height 5' 11", fair complexion and hair, and blue eyes. He enlisted in D Company, 37th Regiment, VA. Samuel Pendleton (farmer) and second family are listed in the 1900 Johnson Co., KY census, pg. 208a.

Children of SAMUEL PENDLETON and MARTHA CARTER are:
789. i.   CHARLES[12] PENDLETON, b. Abt. 1868, VA; d. Aft. 1910, Chelan Co., WA?
      ii. TIMOTHY PENDLETON, b. Abt. 1870, KY.
      iii. ROSA K. PENDLETON, b. Abt. 1873, KY; m. G. W. BOND, Feb 26, 1891, Johnson Co., KY; b. Abt. 1863.
      iv. LEE ROY PENDLETON, b. Abt. 1875, KY.
      v.   EASTER PENDLETON, b. Abt. 1879, KY.

Children of SAMUEL PENDLETON and MARGARET NEELY are:
      vi. ADA RULE[12] PENDLETON, b. Jun 18, 1883, KY; d. Jan 30, 1926; m. HOWARD SEBASTIAN WILLIAMS, Jan 03, 1903, Johnson Co., KY; b. Oct 09, 1880; d. Dec 17, 1968.
      vii. JESSE EMRY PENDLETON, b. Sep 05, 1887, KY.
           Jesse Emry Pendleton registered for the World War I draft in Chelan Co., WA .

535. SARAH T.[11] PENDLETON *(IRA NASH[10], REUBEN[9], BENJAMIN[8], WILLIAM[7], JOHN[6], PHILIP[5], HENRY[4], HENRY[3], GEORGE[2], GEORGE[1])* was born Abt. 1841 in VA, and died Aft. 1880 in Scott Co., VA? She married MARTIN G. STONE, son of JOHN STONE and REBECCA SARGENT. He was born Abt. 1833 in Scott Co., VA, and died Aft. 1880 in Scott Co., VA?

Martin Stone and family are listed in the 1880 census, Scott Co., VA, pg. 254C.

Children of SARAH PENDLETON and MARTIN STONE are:
      i.   IRA TRIGG[12] STONE, b. Apr 26, 1856, VA.
      ii. HELEN R. STONE, b. Abt. 1858, VA.
      iii. SAMUEL STEPHEN STONE, b. Apr 06, 1861, VA.
      iv. JAMES B. STONE, b. Abt. 1865, VA.
      v.   MARTIN G. STONE, b. Abt. 1868, VA.
      vi. NANCY M. STONE, b. Abt. 1872, VA.

vii. LYDIA V. STONE, b. Abt. 1875, VA.

viii. ESTHER STONE, b. Abt. 1878, VA.

536. ROSAMOND[11] PENDLETON *(IRA NASH[10], REUBEN[9], BENJAMIN[8], WILLIAM[7], JOHN[6], PHILIP[5], HENRY[4], HENRY[3], GEORGE[2], GEORGE[1])* was born Dec 28, 1846 in VA, and died Mar 12, 1924 in Lee Co., VA. She married GEORGE WASHINGTON PRIDEMORE Jan 11, 1866 in Hancock Co., TN, son of SAMUEL PRIDEMORE and NANCY MADDEN. He was born Sep 16, 1842 in Kyles Ford, KY, and died Jun 13, 1923 in Lee Co., VA.

G. W. Pridemore (farmer) and family are listed in the 1880 Hancock Co., TN census, pg. 290A.

Children of ROSAMOND PENDLETON and GEORGE PRIDEMORE are:

i. SHERMAN[12] PRIDEMORE, b. Abt. 1867, TN.

ii. SARAH E. PRIDEMORE, b. Abt. 1869, TN.

iii. JAMES ANDERSON PRIDEMORE, b. Abt. 1871, TN.

iv. NANCY JOSEPHINE PRIDEMORE, b. Jun 04, 1873, TN; m. LEONARD WALLEN, Jul 29, 1894, TN.

v. MARY E. PRIDEMORE, b. Abt. 1875, TN.

vi. LAURA E. PRIDEMORE, b. Abt. 1879, TN.

vii. LOYD SAMUEL PRIDEMORE, b. Jan 24, 1882.

537. MARTHA JANE[11] PENDLETON *(SAMUEL GUTHRIE[10], REUBEN[9], BENJAMIN[8], WILLIAM[7], JOHN[6], PHILIP[5], HENRY[4], HENRY[3], GEORGE[2], GEORGE[1])* was born 1827 in Scott Co., VA, and died 1906 in Scott Co., VA. She married JAMES N. TAYLOR Jun 04, 1844 in Scott Co., VA. He was born Abt. 1820 in VA, and died 1892.

Children of MARTHA PENDLETON and JAMES TAYLOR are:

i. IRA[12] TAYLOR, b. Abt. 1845.

ii. SAMUEL TAYLOR, b. Abt. 1848.

iii. SALLY TAYLOR, b. Abt. 1868.

538. IRA NASH[11] PENDLETON *(SAMUEL GUTHRIE[10], REUBEN[9], BENJAMIN[8], WILLIAM[7], JOHN[6], PHILIP[5], HENRY[4], HENRY[3], GEORGE[2], GEORGE[1])* was born Jun 16, 1828 in VA, and died Feb 26, 1918 in Washington Co., VA? He married NANCY F. YOUNG Aug 08, 1854 in Lee Co., VA. She was born Oct 13, 1835 in VA, and died Jul 02, 1928 in Bristol, VA.

This is apparently the Ira Pendleton listed as Merchant in 1850 Scott Co., VA census, (age 21); property value ($400). an "Ina" N. Pendleton, private, served in the 25th Virginia Cavalry, Company A. Ira N. Pendleton (stock broker) and family are listed in the 1900 Washington Co., VA census, pg. 164. Nancy F. Pendleton (83) is listed in the 1920 Bristol, VA census, pg. 7B in the household of William B. Kilgore, her son-in-law. Iran N. Pendleton and wife Nancy are buried in Bristol Cemetery, VA.

Children of IRA PENDLETON and NANCY YOUNG are:

790.   i.   EDWIN DUDLEY[12] PENDLETON, b. Dec 01, 1855, VA; d. Dec 28, 1928, Bristol, VA.

791.   ii.   LAURA REBECCA PENDLETON, b. Oct 05, 1857, VA; d. Aft. 1920, Bristol, VA?

792.   iii. JAMES PRESLEY PENDLETON, b. Nov 19, 1860, VA.

        iv.   WILLIAM SILAS PENDLETON, b. May 06, 1863, VA; m. HATTIE HAUGHTON, Jan 30, 1908.

793.   v.   RUFUS BOYD PENDLETON, b. Nov 08, 1866, VA; d. May 31, 1900, Richmond, Henrico Co., VA.

        vi.   MARY "MOLLIE" DUNCAN PENDLETON, b. Mar 24, 1871, VA; m. DUKE SCOTT, Jan 28, 1901.

794.   vii. BEVERLY NEAL PENDLETON, b. May 19, 1874, VA; d. Aft. 1920, Bristol, VA?

795.   viii. KATHERINE B. PENDLETON, b. Oct 14, 1879, VA; d. Jan 1977, Bristol, TN.

539. WILLIAM SAMUEL[11] PENDLETON *(SAMUEL GUTHRIE[10], REUBEN[9], BENJAMIN[8], WILLIAM[7], JOHN[6], PHILIP[5], HENRY[4], HENRY[3], GEORGE[2], GEORGE[1])* was born Apr 1834 in Scott Co., VA, and died 1905 in Hancock Co., TN. He married JULIA ANN QUILLEN Sep 17, 1850 in Scott Co., VA, daughter of THOMAS QUILLEN and POLLY STRONG. She was born Mar 1836 in Scott Co., VA, and died 1909 in Hancock Co., TN.

William S. Pendleton, Farmer, is listed in the 1850 Scott Co., VA census, age 17, in the household of James Taylor, his brother-in-law. William Pendleton (farmer) and family are listed in the 1900 Hancock Co., TN census, pg. 215 adjacent to his son Christopher.

Children of WILLIAM PENDLETON and JULIA QUILLEN are:

        i.   LYDIA[12] PENDLETON, b. 1851, VA; d. 1923; m. SKEETS.

796.   ii.   JAMES M. PENDLETON, b. Sep 17, 1852, VA; d. Aft. 1920, Jonesville, VA?

        iii. IRA JOSEPH PENDLETON, b. 1856, VA.

        iv.   MARA REBECCA PENDLETON, b. 1858, VA.

797.   v.   CHRISTOPHER PENDLETON, b. Aug 1861, TN; d. Aft. 1920, Hancock Co., TN?

798.   vi.   WILLIAM BENTON PENDLETON, b. Aug 04, 1861, TN; d. Feb 11, 1944, Sullivan Co., TN.

        vii. SARAH PENDLETON, b. 1863.

        viii. THOMAS L. PENDLETON, b. 1866; m. MARTHA STRONG, Jul 29, 1882.

        ix.   MARTHA "MOLLY" PENDLETON, b. 1869.

        x.   LAURA PENDLETON, b. 1872.

        xi.   EMILE PENDLETON, b. 1874.

        xii. LODESSA PENDLETON, b. 1877.

        xiii. ULYSSES PENDLETON, b. Feb 1881, Hancock Co., TN; m. MATTIS RAINEY, Jan 04, 1906, Scott Co., VA.

540. MALINDA[11] PENDLETON *(JOHN L.*[10]*, JAMES A.*[9]*, BENJAMIN*[8]*, WILLIAM*[7]*, JOHN*[6]*, PHILIP*[5]*, HENRY*[4]*, HENRY*[3]*, GEORGE*[2]*, GEORGE*[1]*)* was born Jan 09, 1832 in Scott Co., VA, and died Jan 24, 1889 in Scott Co., VA. She married (1) RIAL HENRY JENNINGS Aug 18, 1853 in Scott Co., VA, son of BASIL JENNINGS. He was born Oct 08, 1835, and died Apr 02, 1863 in Confederate Prison during Civil War. She married (2) SAMUEL LANE Mar 05, 1874 in Scott Co., VA. He was born Nov 1827 in Scott Co., VA, and died Aft. 1880.

Children of MALINDA PENDLETON and RIAL JENNINGS are:
    i.   CHILD[12] JENNINGS, b. Aug 20, 1855, young.
    ii. MARY E. JENNINGS, b. Sep 1856; m. WILLIAM H. LANE.
    iii. BOSWELL FLOYD JENNINGS, b. May 03, 1859; m. BELLE LANE.
    iv. JOHN ROYAL JENNINGS, b. 1862; m. ELIZA M. LANE; b. Abt. 1864.

Child of MALINDA PENDLETON and SAMUEL LANE is:
    v.   JOSEPH S.[12] LANE, b. Abt. 1876.

541. JOSEPH DOUGLAS[11] PENDLETON *(JOHN L.*[10]*, JAMES A.*[9]*, BENJAMIN*[8]*, WILLIAM*[7]*, JOHN*[6]*, PHILIP*[5]*, HENRY*[4]*, HENRY*[3]*, GEORGE*[2]*, GEORGE*[1]*)* was born 1835 in VA, and died May 17, 1871 in Scott Co., VA? He married ELIZA LAWSON Jun 10, 1856 in Scott Co., VA. She was born 1839 in VA, and died Jun 06, 1909.
    Joseph D. Pendleton served as a Union Soldier in Civil War in Company D, KY, 7th Infantry. He served from April 17, 1862 to Apr 17, 1865 and was discharged at Baton Rouge, LA.

Children of JOSEPH PENDLETON and ELIZA LAWSON are:
    i.   ISABEL VIRGINIA[12] PENDLETON, b. Feb 17, 1859, Scott Co., VA; d. Jan 18, 1929, Scott Co., VA; m. WILLAM M. LANE, Mar 19, 1873; b. Nov 16, 1851, VA; d. Nov 27, 1929, Scott Co., VA.
    ii. MARTHA VICTORIA PENDLETON, b. Nov 24, 1862, VA; m. WILLIAM HIRAM STRONG.
    iii. HAMPTON FLANARY PENDLETON, b. Jun 10, 1866, VA; d. 1890; m. SARAH ELLEN ALLEY; b. Nov 11, 1876, Scott Co., VA; d. Aug 07, 1938, Scott Co., VA.
799.   iv. POLLY ANN PENDLETON, b. Mar 31, 1870, VA; d. 1944, Scott Co., VA.

542. JOHN EMERSON[11] PENDLETON *(JOHN L.*[10]*, JAMES A.*[9]*, BENJAMIN*[8]*, WILLIAM*[7]*, JOHN*[6]*, PHILIP*[5]*, HENRY*[4]*, HENRY*[3]*, GEORGE*[2]*, GEORGE*[1]*)* was born Sep 09, 1836 in VA, and died Jan 10, 1903 in Scott Co., VA? He married MARY A. QUILLEN Jan 26, 1866. She was born Mar 19, 1846 in Hill Station, VA, and died Aft. 1920 in Scott Co., VA?
    John E. Pendleton served as a Union Soldier in the Civil War along with his brother Joseph D. The term of service was from April 17, 1862 to Apr 17, 1865; discharged at Baton Rouge, LA. John E. was know as "Uncle Jack" to most of the people in his community (Ref. 124). John E. Pendleton is listed in the 1880 Taylor, Scott Co.,

VA census. John E. Pendleton (farmer) and family are listed in the 1900 Scott Co., VA census, pg. 101.

Children of JOHN PENDLETON and MARY QUILLEN are:
      i. IRA QUILLEN[12] PENDLETON, b. Jan 01, 1867, VA; d. Nov 17, 1947, Scott Co., VA?
800. ii. JOHN LILBOURNE PENDLETON, b. Jul 29, 1868, VA; d. Jan 18, 1947.
801. iii. ELIZABETH JANE PENDLETON, b. Jun 01, 1870, VA.
      iv. HUSTON C. PENDLETON, b. Aug 20, 1872, VA.
      v. SALLY PENDLETON, b. Jul 25, 1875, VA.
      vi. DANIEL C. PENDLETON, b. May 27, 1878, VA.
802. vii. CHARLES SUMNER PENDLETON, b. Mar 28, 1880, VA; d. 1952, Scott Co., VA?

543. JAMES F.[11] PENDLETON (*JOHN L.*[10], *JAMES A.*[9], *BENJAMIN*[8], *WILLIAM*[7], *JOHN*[6], *PHILIP*[5], *HENRY*[4], *HENRY*[3], *GEORGE*[2], *GEORGE*[1]) was born May 07, 1841 in Scott Co., VA, and died Aug 16, 1916 in Letcher Co., KY. He married HARRIET STRONG Nov 04, 1867 in Scott Co., VA, daughter of THOMAS STRONG and MARY DRAPER. She was born Oct 26, 1839 in Scott Co., VA, and died Dec 12, 1892 in Letcher Co., KY.
    James F. Pendleton is buried near Whitesburg, Letcher Co., KY.

Children of JAMES PENDLETON and HARRIET STRONG are:
803. i. JOSEPH DELAWARE[12] PENDLETON, b. Sep 01, 1868, Scott Co., VA; d. Nov 02, 1934, Letcher Co., KY.
804. ii. WILLIAM E. PENDLETON, b. May 05, 1870, Scott Co., VA; d. Mar 29, 1950, Letcher Co., KY.
805. iii. JAMES SAMUEL PENDLETON, b. Dec 31, 1871, Scott Co., VA; d. Oct 25, 1956, VA.
      iv. EMILY E. PENDLETON, b. Mar 05, 1873, Scott Co., VA; d. 1954; m. ZION G. WELLS, Apr 24, 1890, Letcher Co., KY.
806. v. JOHN ALLY PENDLETON, b. Jun 04, 1874, Scott Co., VA; d. Oct 27, 1936, Letcher Co., KY.
      vi. LLOYD KIDD PENDLETON, b. Jul 12, 1876, Scott Co., VA; d. Jun 16, 1955, Scott Co., VA; m. IDA CATHERINE ARWOOD, Nov 01, 1908, Scott Co., VA; b. Oct 29, 1885, Scott Co., VA; d. Oct 16, 1945, Scott Co., VA.
      vii. CHARLES ELIHU PENDLETON, b. Sep 26, 1879, Letcher Co., KY.
      viii. ALICE PENDLETON, b. Apr 26, 1890, Letcher Co., KY; d. Oct 28, 1963, Warren Co., OH; m. JAMES MONROE ENGLAND; b. Sep 07, 1885, Scott Co., VA; d. Feb 20, 1962, Warren Co., OH.
          Alice was a niece who was adopted (Ref. 124).

544. SAMUEL DAVID[11] PENDLETON (*JOHN L.*[10], *JAMES A.*[9], *BENJAMIN*[8], *WILLIAM*[7], *JOHN*[6], *PHILIP*[5], *HENRY*[4], *HENRY*[3], *GEORGE*[2], *GEORGE*[1]) was born Jul 29, 1844 in VA, and died Nov 17, 1911 in Scott Co., VA? He married (1) ANNA E. BISHOP Nov 17, 1874 in Scott Co., VA, daughter of JESSE BISHOP and MARY JANE.

She was born 1857 in VA, and died Abt. 1885 in Scott Co., VA. He married (2) MARY CATHERINE DEZARN Nov 24, 1893 in Scott Co., VA. She was born Sep 08, 1864 in VA, and died 1943.

Samuel D. Pendleton (farmer) and family are listed in the 1900 Scott Co., VA census, pg. 240a. S. D. Pendleton, veteran of Scott Co., is listed in the 1902 VA Pension Rolls (Confederate). He died of pneumonia.

Children of SAMUEL PENDLETON and ANNA BISHOP are:

807.   i.   ROBERT PATTON[12] PENDLETON, b. Oct 09, 1875, VA; d. Apr 07, 1936, Scott Co., VA?

    ii.   ASIA AURORA PENDLETON, b. May 02, 1877, VA.

    iii.   JESSE HAYDEN PENDLETON, b. Apr 04, 1879, VA; d. Aug 15, 1964.

    iv.   JOSEPH DOUGLAS PENDLETON, b. Mar 20, 1882, VA; d. Nov 12, 1897.

Children of SAMUEL PENDLETON and MARY DEZARN are:

    v.   CORA B.[12] PENDLETON, b. Mar 22, 1895; d. Apr 09, 1895.

    vi.   EDWARD M. PENDLETON, b. Oct 27, 1896, VA; d. Mar 1978, Jonesville, Lee Co., VA.

    vii.   MYRTLE B. PENDLETON, b. May 25, 1899, VA; d. 1972.

    viii.   DAVID F. PENDLETON, b. Oct 11, 1902, VA; d. Mar 1963.

    ix.   IDA VICTORIA PENDLETON, b. Sep 05, 1907; d. May 29, 1993.

545. ROBERT KENNUS[11] PENDLETON (*JOHN L.*[10], *JAMES A.*[9], *BENJAMIN*[8], *WILLIAM*[7], *JOHN*[6], *PHILIP*[5], *HENRY*[4], *HENRY*[3], *GEORGE*[2], *GEORGE*[1]) was born Jun 1846 in VA, and died Jan 15, 1913 in Scott Co., VA? He married MARGARET E. TEMPLETON Apr 29, 1871 in Hawkins Co., TN, daughter of THOMAS TEMPLETON and MARY WILLIAMS. She was born Jul 1856 in VA, and died 1915 in Scott Co., VA?

Robert K. Pendleton, farmer, and family are listed in the 1900 Scott Co., VA census, pg. 102.

Children of ROBERT PENDLETON and MARGARET TEMPLETON are:

    i.   POLLY[12] PENDLETON, b. Jun 1873, VA; m. ABRAHAM LANE, Aug 20, 1887, Scott Co., VA; b. Jul 19, 1867, Scott Co., VA; d. Apr 23, 1956, Scott Co., VA.

    ii.   SALLIE PENDLETON, b. Sep 24, 1874; m. GILLIAM.

    iii.   MARTHA ELIZABETH PENDLETON, b. Oct 22, 1879; d. Mar 23, 1953; m. JAMES MARTIN TIPTON; b. 1883; d. Feb 24, 1960.

808.   iv.   AMOS DANIEL PENDLETON, b. Jun 10, 1882, VA; d. Jul 29, 1968, Scott Co., VA.

    v.   ISAAC H. "IKE" PENDLETON, b. Sep 1884, VA.

    vi.   LINDA ISABELL PENDLETON, b. May 03, 1888, VA; d. 1947, Scott Co., VA?; m. JOSEPH CHRISTIAN; b. Abt. 1870, VA; d. Aft. 1930, Scott Co., VA?

809.   vii.   JAMES MONROE PENDLETON, b. Dec 01, 1890, VA; d. Feb 06, 1978.

    viii.   CLARA ETTA PENDLETON, b. May 1893, VA; m. BILL CHRISTIAN.

ix.   NANCY M. PENDLETON, b. Mar 1898, VA; m. HARVEY TIPTON.
x.   CORA PENDLETON, b. Jan 09, 1901, VA; d. Nov 27, 1968; m. WILLIAMS.

546. WILLIAM DANIEL E.[11] PENDLETON (*JOHN L.[10], JAMES A.[9], BENJAMIN[8], WILLIAM[7], JOHN[6], PHILIP[5], HENRY[4], HENRY[3], GEORGE[2], GEORGE[1]*) was born Apr 28, 1850 in VA, and died Dec 24, 1912 in Scott Co., VA? He married (1) NANCY MARY L. TEMPLETON Sep 30, 1869 in Hawkins Co., TN. She was born Mar 1852 in VA, and died Aug 08, 1908. He married (2) LOUISA F. 'PETERS' GILLIAM Feb 19, 1910 in Scott Co., VA.

Daniel Pendleton (farmer) and family are listed in the 1900 Scott Co., VA census, pg. 105.

Children of WILLIAM PENDLETON and NANCY TEMPLETON are:
i.   POLLY[12] PENDLETON, b. Sep 17, 1870; d. Dec 11, 1956.
ii.   MALINDA V. PENDLETON, b. Apr 04, 1872; d. Nov 03, 1881.
iii.   SARAH PENDLETON, b. Sep 01, 1873; d. Aug 01, 1964.
iv.   LILBOURN H. PENDLETON, b. Apr 19, 1875; d. Jun 30, 1899.
v.   AMOS T. PENDLETON, b. Nov 12, 1876; d. Aug 17, 1888.
vi.   HANNAH F. PENDLETON, b. Dec 11, 1879; d. Nov 15, 1974.
vii.   CORA E. PENDLETON, b. Apr 05, 1882; d. Feb 03, 1899.
viii.   CALLEY DONA PENDLETON, b. May 10, 1884, VA; d. Mar 23, 1956.
ix.   CONLEY F. PENDLETON, b. Jun 21, 1885, VA; d. Jul 23, 1931.
Conley F. Pendleton registered for the World War I draft in Scott Co., VA.

x.   ELIZA CAROLINE PENDLETON, b. Dec 23, 1886, VA; d. Nov 02, 1973.
810.   xi.   JOHN D. PENDLETON, b. Sep 08, 1889, Scott Co., VA; d. Mar 02, 1984.
xii.   CLARENCE N. PENDLETON, b. Oct 29, 1892, VA; d. Jan 15, 1984.
xiii.   ABRAHAM W. PENDLETON, b. Sep 05, 1896, VA.

547. JEMIMA[11] PENDLETON (*JAMES A.[10], JAMES A.[9], BENJAMIN[8], WILLIAM[7], JOHN[6], PHILIP[5], HENRY[4], HENRY[3], GEORGE[2], GEORGE[1]*) was born Abt. 1840 in VA. She married WILLIAM REEVES DAVIDSON Abt. 1859, son of WILLIAM DAVIDSON and SARAH STURGILL. He was born Abt. 1840 in Scott Co., VA, and died Jun 11, 1892 in Wise Co., VA.

Children of JEMIMA PENDLETON and WILLIAM DAVIDSON are:
i.   ROBERT FRANK[12] DAVIDSON, b. 1860.
ii.   WILLIAM REEVES DAVIDSON, b. 1862.
iii.   JOHN M. DAVIDSON, b. 1864.
iv.   MARY L. DAVIDSON, b. 1866.
v.   ANNA B. DAVIDSON, b. 1869.
vi.   LEE EVALINE DAVIDSON, b. 1871.
vii.   JANE DAVIDSON, b. 1873.
viii.   ELLA DAVIDSON, b. 1875.

ix. CINIA M. DAVIDSON, b. 1878.

x. SARAH DAVIDSON.

548. ROBERT[11] PENDLETON *(JAMES A.[10], JAMES A.[9], BENJAMIN[8], WILLIAM[7], JOHN[6], PHILIP[5], HENRY[4], HENRY[3], GEORGE[2], GEORGE[1])* was born Feb 1845 in VA, and died Aft. 1900 in Scott Co., VA? He married (1) MARTHA E. FRAZIER Abt. 1868. She was born Abt. 1851 in VA. He married (2) MELISSA HELEN GILLENWATER Abt. 1894, daughter of WILLIAM GILLENWATER and SUSANNAH COUNTS. She was born Sep 26, 1861 in VA, and died Mar 1942.

Robert Pendleton (farmer) and family are listed in the 1900 Scott Co., VA census, pg. 220.

Children of ROBERT PENDLETON and MARTHA FRAZIER are:
811.   i. CHRISTOPHER C.[12] PENDLETON, b. Abt. 1869, VA; d. Aft. 1920, Scott Co., VA?

ii. MARY DAVIS PENDLETON, b. Abt. 1871, VA.

iii. HAROLD WORTH PENDLETON, b. Sep 1874, VA.

iv. RICHARD PENDLETON, b. Aft. 1880.

549. IRA M.[11] PENDLETON *(JAMES A.[10], JAMES A.[9], BENJAMIN[8], WILLIAM[7], JOHN[6], PHILIP[5], HENRY[4], HENRY[3], GEORGE[2], GEORGE[1])* was born Feb 10, 1848 in VA, and died Jun 19, 1894 in Scott Co., VA. He married (1) ELIZABETH FRAZIER. She was born Abt. 1846 in VA. He married (2) MARTHA ELIZABETH STRONG. She was born May 27, 1845, and died Jul 16, 1884 in Scott Co., VA.

Ira Pendleton (32), Elizabeth (34) and Sarah E. (13) are listed in the 1880 De Kalb, Scott Co., VA census, pg 167b.

Child of IRA PENDLETON and ELIZABETH FRAZIER is:
i. SARAH ELIZABETH[12] PENDLETON, b. Abt. 1867, VA; m. STONEY J. CARTER; b. Abt. 1864.

Children of IRA PENDLETON and MARTHA STRONG are:
ii. WILLIAM[12] PENDLETON.

iii. OSCAR PENDLETON.
812.   iv. RUFUS PENDLETON, d. 1916.

v. ODESA M. PENDLETON.

550. SARAH S.[11] PENDLETON *(JAMES A.[10], JAMES A.[9], BENJAMIN[8], WILLIAM[7], JOHN[6], PHILIP[5], HENRY[4], HENRY[3], GEORGE[2], GEORGE[1])* was born Abt. 1856 in VA. She married HENRY STEWART. He was born Abt. 1850 in VA.

Child of SARAH PENDLETON and HENRY STEWART is:
i. ELLEN[12] STEWART, b. Abt. 1878.

551. ELBERT M.[11] PENDLETON *(JAMES A.[10], JAMES A.[9], BENJAMIN[8], WILLIAM[7], JOHN[6], PHILIP[5], HENRY[4], HENRY[3], GEORGE[2], GEORGE[1])* was born Feb 1859 in VA, and died Aft. 1920 in Scott Co., VA? He married (1) MALINDA. She was born Abt. 1860 in VA. He married (2) ROSIE BELL Abt. 1890. She was born Mar 1877 in VA, and died Aft. 1920 in Scott Co., VA?

Elbert M. Pendleton (farmer) and family are listed in the 1900 Scott Co., VA census, pg. 220 and the 1920 Scott Co. census, pg.

Child of ELBERT PENDLETON and MALINDA is:
     i. ROBERT C.[12] PENDLETON, b. Jan 1880.

Children of ELBERT PENDLETON and ROSIE BELL are:
     ii. CALLIE R.[12] PENDLETON, b. Feb 1891, VA.
     iii. WILLIAM R. PENDLETON, b. Mar 1893, VA.
     iv. ELLA F. PENDLETON, b. Nov 1895, VA.
     v. NORA PENDLETON, b. Mar 1897, VA.
     vi. AFIMA A. PENDLETON, b. Feb 1899, VA.
     vii. MAY PENDLETON.
     viii. LUCIE PENDLETON.
     ix. RUBIE PENDLETON.
     x. RUTHIE PENDLETON.

552. ELDRIDGE HOWARD[11] PENDLETON *(WILLIAM GAINES[10], JOHN[9], BENJAMIN[8], WILLIAM[7], JOHN[6], PHILIP[5], HENRY[4], HENRY[3], GEORGE[2], GEORGE[1])* was born Aug 02, 1843 in TN, and died 1906 in Collin Co., TX? He married SARAH CASSANDRA ROBINSON Jan 16, 1869, daughter of CHARLES ROBINSON and ELIZABETH PRYOR. She was born Jul 12, 1853 in VA, and died Dec 06, 1903 in Collin Co., TX?

E.H. Pendleton came to Texas with his grandparents in 1858. In 1861 he enlisted in the Confederate Army. He was wounded in the battles of Cotton Plant and of Milliken's Bend. At the close of the war his rank was first lieutenant, Company "E," 16th Texas Dismounted Cavalry (Fitzhugh's). Eldridge Pendleton is listed in the 1870 Collins Co., TX census index, Farmersville. El H. Pendleton (farmer) and family are listed in the 1900 Collins Co., TX census, pg. 236a.

Children of ELDRIDGE PENDLETON and SARAH ROBINSON are:
     i. CHARLES DOUGLASS[12] PENDLETON, b. 1873, TX; d. 1896; m. ETTA HONAKER, Dec 19, 1894; b. Jun 1876, TX.
813.   ii. WILLIAM FREDERICK PENDLETON, b. Apr 01, 1875, TX; d. Nov 30, 1945.
814.   iii. THOMAS EDWARD PENDLETON, b. May 1876, TX; d. 1906, Collin Co., TX?
     iv. GRACE LABELLE PENDLETON, b. 1877, TX; d. 1878.
815.   v. JAMES ELDRIDGE PENDLETON, b. Jul 1880, TX; d. 1933, Farmersville, TX?
     vi. CLAUDE HOWARD PENDLETON, b. 1882, TX; d. Aft. 1910, Tom Green, TX?; m. LAURA KELLER; b. 1883, TX; d. Aft. 1910, Tom Green, TX?

816.   vii.   HOMER ALEXANDER PENDLETON, b. May 06, 1888, TX; d. Aug 1967, TX.

817.   viii. CHARLOTTE ELIZABETH PENDLETON, b. Dec 24, 1890, TX; d. Nov 1979.

       ix.   GEORGE CLARK PENDLETON, b. May 08, 1893, TX; d. Sep 1986, Durant, OK; m. RUTH GOODMAN, Mar 22, 1923; b. Oct 20, 1896; d. Jan 1985, Durant, OK.

             George Clark Pendleton registered for the World War I draft in Bryan Co., OK

       x.   CLARE CASSANDRA PENDLETON, b. Jan 1895, TX; d. Jul 17, 1990, Farmersville, TX; m. OSCAR EDWIN CARLISLE, Dec 05, 1923; b. Jun 29, 1894; d. Jul 07, 1989, TX.

553. HENRY[11] PENDLETON *(WILLIAM GAINES[10], JOHN[9], BENJAMIN[8], WILLIAM[7], JOHN[6], PHILIP[5], HENRY[4], HENRY[3], GEORGE[2], GEORGE[1])* was born 1866, and died 1894. He married MOLLIE HARRISON 1889. She died 1890 in TX.

Child of HENRY PENDLETON and MOLLIE HARRISON is:
       i.   ROY[12] PENDLETON, b. Abt. 1890, TX.

554. PARALEE[11] PENDLETON *(WILLIAM GAINES[10], JOHN[9], BENJAMIN[8], WILLIAM[7], JOHN[6], PHILIP[5], HENRY[4], HENRY[3], GEORGE[2], GEORGE[1])* was born 1870, and died Dec 29, 1919 in Cherokee Co., AL. She married ABLE THOMAS OXFORD Nov 17, 1886, son of WILLIAM OXFORD and NANCY SOWELL. He was born Aug 22, 1867 in Erath Co., TX, and died May 03, 1936 in Erath Co., TX.

Children of PARALEE PENDLETON and ABLE OXFORD are (Ref. 284):
       i.   RHODA[12] OXFORD, b. Jul 24, 1887, Erath Co., TX; d. Jan 15, 1972, Jefferson Co., TX.
       ii.   OTTIE RANDOLPH OXFORD, b. Dec 12, 1891, Johnson Co., TX; d. Dec 01, 1949, Kimble Co., TX.
       iii. FLOYD W. OXFORD, b. May 18, 1895; d. May 12, 1974, Bell Co., TX.
       iv.   LUTHER OXFORD, b. Dec 14, 1897, Erath Co., TX; d. Oct 31, 1900.
       v.   CLAYTON OXFORD, b. Bef. 1900; d. Bef. 1900.
       vi.   SALLIE NAN OXFORD, b. Apr 22, 1904, Erath Co., TX; d. Mar 15, 1990, Rockville, MD.

555. JOSEPH DAY[11] PENDLETON *(WILLIAM GAINES[10], JOHN[9], BENJAMIN[8], WILLIAM[7], JOHN[6], PHILIP[5], HENRY[4], HENRY[3], GEORGE[2], GEORGE[1])* was born Aug 1869 in TX, and died Aft. 1920 in Van Zandt Co., TX? He married MAGGIE ELLA WARD Oct 05, 1893 in Hunt Co., TX. She was born Sep 1875 in TX, and died Aft. 1920 in Van Zandt Co., TX?

       Joseph D. Pendleton (farmer) and family are listed in the 1900 Hunt Co. and 1920 Van Zandt Co TX census records.

Children of JOSEPH PENDLETON and MAGGIE WARD are:
> i.   GRACIE[12] PENDLETON, b. Mar 1895, TX.
> ii. HOWARD JACKSON PENDLETON, b. Jan 04, 1897, Farmersville, TX; d. Apr 1979, Dallas, TX; m. IRENE E. BASS; b. Jul 01, 1903, TX; d. May 1987, Kaufman Co., TX.
>   Howard Jackson Pendleton registered for the World War I draft in Van Zandt Co., TX.
>
> iii. JOSEPH BAILEY PENDLETON, b. Jul 25, 1899, TX; m. CLEAVE BASS.
>   Joseph Bailey Pendleton registered for the World War I draft in Van Zandt Co., TX.
>
> iv. GRADYS PENDLETON.
> v.   WILLIAM G. PENDLETON.
> vi. PERALLE L. PENDLETON.
> vii. JAMES W. PENDLETON.

556. CORDELIA[11] PENDLETON *(WILLIAM GAINES[10], JOHN[9], BENJAMIN[8], WILLIAM[7], JOHN[6], PHILIP[5], HENRY[4], HENRY[3], GEORGE[2], GEORGE[1])* was born 1873 in TX, and died Aft. 1920 in Waco, TX? She married FRANK A. CURTIS, son of W. CURTIS and SARAH CHAIM. He was born 1865 in IL, and died Aft. 1920 in Waco, TX?

Child of CORDELIA PENDLETON and FRANK CURTIS is:
> i.   MABLE[12] CURTIS.

557. WILLIAM MARION[11] PENDLETON *(HIRAM KILGORE[10], JOHN[9], BENJAMIN[8], WILLIAM[7], JOHN[6], PHILIP[5], HENRY[4], HENRY[3], GEORGE[2], GEORGE[1])* was born Jul 1844 in VA, and died 1921 in Scott Co., VA. He married (1) MINNIE RAMEY Apr 14, 1875. He married (2) ALICE "NANCY" COX Nov 07, 1879. She was born Nov 1861 in VA, and died Aft. 1920 in Scott Co., VA?

W.M. Pendleton was Treasurer of Scott County and fought in the Civil War. He spent his youth in Texas and Oklahoma, coming east to Virginia later and settling on the Clinch River near Dungannon, Virginia. His former home on Rt. 71 in Dungannon is now a historical site (Ref. 285). William Pendleton (farmer) and family are listed in the 1900 Scott Co., VA census, pg. 284A and the 1920 Floyd, Scott Co census, pg. 3A.

Children of WILLIAM PENDLETON and ALICE COX are:
>   i.   WORLEY BASCUM[12] PENDLETON, b. Aug 08, 1880, VA; d. Oct 1964, VA; m. MOLLIE SERGENT.
> 818.   ii. SAMUEL WALTER PENDLETON, b. May 1883, VA; d. 1935, Scott Co., VA?
> 819.   iii. MAXIE ELIZABETH PENDLETON, b. Mar 1886, VA.
> 820.   iv. HARRISON BURTON PENDLETON, b. Jul 28, 1889, VA; d. Aft. 1930, Scott Co., VA?

821.   v.   EDITH ALICE PNDLETON, b. Jan 01, 1893, Rye Cove, Scott Co., VA; d.
             Jul 07, 1947, Scott Co., VA.
        vi. CHARLES CLINTON PENDLETON, b. Apr 12, 1895, VA; d. May 1977,
             Scott Co., VA; m. TROY COLEMAN, Aug 31, 1927; b. Apr 02, 1906; d. Jun
             1984, Scott Co., VA.
        vii. ELDRIDGE MCKINLEY PENDLETON, b. Jun 04, 1899, VA; d. Apr 1984,
             Vicksburg, MS; m. VIOLA HARMON; b. Oct 26, 1919; d. Feb 15, 1998,
             Copiah Co., MS.
                  Eldridge McKinley Pendleton registered for the World War I draft in
             Logan Co., WV (Ref. 210).

       viii. CECIL RICHMOND PENDLETON, DR., b. May 22, 1902; d. May 1987,
             Maryville, Blount Co., TN; m. RUTH BOATRIGHT, Feb 20, 1927; b. Apr
             08, 1906; d. Sep 1993, Blount Co., TN.

558. JOHN W.[11] PENDLETON (*HIRAM KILGORE*[10], *JOHN*[9], *BENJAMIN*[8],
WILLIAM[7], *JOHN*[6], *PHILIP*[5], *HENRY*[4], *HENRY*[3], *GEORGE*[2], *GEORGE*[1]) was born 1847
in VA. He married MARY ANN ADDINGTON Oct 05, 1870, daughter of JAMES
ADDINGTON and HARRIET QUILLEN. She was born Abt. 1852 in Scott Co., VA.
      John Pendleton is reported to have moved to CA or OR.

Children of JOHN PENDLETON and MARY ADDINGTON are:
        i.   PATRICK HENRY[12] PENDLETON, b. Abt. 1872, VA.
822.   ii. JAMES E. PENDLETON, b. Abt. 1874, VA; d. Aft. 1930, Siskiyou Co., CA?
823.   iii. SALLIE PENDLETON, b. Abt. 1876, VA.
        iv. WILLARD PENDLETON, b. Abt. 1878, VA.

559. SARAH HELEN[11] PENDLETON (*HIRAM KILGORE*[10], *JOHN*[9], *BENJAMIN*[8],
WILLIAM[7], *JOHN*[6], *PHILIP*[5], *HENRY*[4], *HENRY*[3], *GEORGE*[2], *GEORGE*[1]) was born 1849
in VA, and died 1872. She married JAMES PIPER ALLEY Abt. 1865. He was born
Abt. 1841 in VA, and died Aft. 1880.

Children of SARAH PENDLETON and JAMES ALLEY are:
        i.   MINERVA C.[12] ALLEY, b. 1868, VA.
        ii. IDA MARIE ALLEY, b. 1870, VA; d. 1955; m. CHARLES A.
             MCMULLEN; b. 1873.

560. THOMAS CLINTON[11] PENDLETON (*HIRAM KILGORE*[10], *JOHN*[9], *BENJAMIN*[8],
WILLIAM[7], *JOHN*[6], *PHILIP*[5], *HENRY*[4], *HENRY*[3], *GEORGE*[2], *GEORGE*[1]) was born Abt.
1852 in VA. He married ELLEN RICHMOND, daughter of WILLIAM RICHMOND
and SARAH COX. She was born 1865.
      Thomas Pendleton may have had a twin who died in 1864.

Child of THOMAS PENDLETON and ELLEN RICHMOND is:
        i.   LILLIAN[12] PENDLETON.

561. BENJAMIN FRANKLIN[11] PENDLETON *(HIRAM KILGORE[10], JOHN[9], BENJAMIN[8], WILLIAM[7], JOHN[6], PHILIP[5], HENRY[4], HENRY[3], GEORGE[2], GEORGE[1])* was born Mar 1854 in VA, and died Aft. 1920 in Sullivan Co., TN? He married SUSANNA COX Abt. 1879. She was born Feb 1866 in VA, and died Aft. 1920 in Sullivan Co., TN?

Benjamin Pendleton (farmer) and family are listed in the 1900 Sullivan Co., TN census, pg. 61a.

Children of BENJAMIN PENDLETON and SUSANNA COX are:
  i. EMMA B.[12] PENDLETON, b. Sep 1880, VA.
  ii. CALLIE R. PENDLETON, b. Dec 1883, VA.
  iii. NANCY J. PENDLETON, b. Sep 1886, VA.
  iv. OLLIE M. PENDLETON, b. Oct 1888, VA.
  v. BESSIE K. PENDLETON, b. Jul 1892, VA.
  vi. HENRY K. PENDLETON, b. Apr 09, 1895, VA; d. Mar 1969, Kingsport, Sullivan Co., TN.

   Henry K. Pendleton registered for the World War I draft in Sullivan Co., TN.

  vii. GLADYS L. PENDLETON, b. Sep 1897, TN.
  viii. FANNIE L. PENDLETON, b. Oct 1899, TN.
  ix. WILLIAM C. PENDLETON.

562. JEMIMA JANE[11] PENDLETON *(HIRAM KILGORE[10], JOHN[9], BENJAMIN[8], WILLIAM[7], JOHN[6], PHILIP[5], HENRY[4], HENRY[3], GEORGE[2], GEORGE[1])* was born 1856 in VA, and died Aft. 1920 in Russell Co., VA? She married JAMES BUCHANAN FRALEY Nov 03, 1881, son of MARTIN FRALEY and POLLY HORNE. He was born 1861 in VA, and died 1940.

James B. Fraley (farmer) and family are listed in the Castlewood, Russell Co., VA 1920 census.

Children of JEMIMA PENDLETON and JAMES FRALEY are:
  i. ETHEL[12] FRALEY.
  ii. DELLE FRALEY, b. Abt. 1890, VA.
  iii. LILLIAN FRALEY, b. Abt. 1899, VA.
  iv. ELLA FRALEY.
  v. EDGAR FRALEY.

563. ROBERT MELVIN[11] PENDLETON *(HIRAM KILGORE[10], JOHN[9], BENJAMIN[8], WILLIAM[7], JOHN[6], PHILIP[5], HENRY[4], HENRY[3], GEORGE[2], GEORGE[1])* was born Apr 1861 in VA, and died Aft. 1930 in Sullivan Co., TN? He married LAURA MEADE Abt. 1892, daughter of GEORGE MEADE and LUCY HARRIS. She was born Jul 27, 1871 in Scott Co., VA, and died Aft. 1930 in Sullivan Co., TN?

Robert M. Pendleton (farmer) and family are listed in the 1900 Sullivan Co., VA census, pg. 61a.

Children of ROBERT PENDLETON and LAURA MEADE are:
    i.   BARNEY C.[12] PENDLETON, b. Mar 28, 1893, TN.
          Barney C. Pendleton registered for the World War I draft in Sullivan Co., TN.

    ii.   LILLIE FAY PENDLETON, b. Jun 1897, TN.
   iii. JANE L. PENDLETON, b. Oct 1898, TN.
    iv. BEN K. PENDLETON.
    v.   VICTOR E. PENDLETON, b. Apr 20, 1903, TN; d. Dec 1969, Kingsport, TN.
    vi. SADIE P. PENDLETON.
   vii. PARIS L. PENDLETON, b. Aug 12, 1906, TN; d. Jul 1982, Blountville, TN.
  viii. ODIS PENDLETON.
    ix. ROBERT M. PENDLETON.
    x.   FRED H. PENDLETON.

564. REBECCA JANE[11] PENDLETON *(IVY TAYLOR[10], JOHN[9], BENJAMIN[8], WILLIAM[7], JOHN[6], PHILIP[5], HENRY[4], HENRY[3], GEORGE[2], GEORGE[1])* was born 1845 in VA, and died Aft. 1900 in Owsley Co., KY? She married STEPHEN MCPHERSON. He was born Abt. 1826 in VA, and died Aft. 1880 in Owsley Co., KY?
    Stephen McPhearson (farmer) and family are listed in the 1880 Owsley Co., KY census, pg. 298A.

Children of REBECCA PENDLETON and STEPHEN MCPHERSON are:
    i.   SOPHIA B.[12] MCPHERSON, b. Abt. 1865, KY.
    ii.   MANERVY MCPHERSON, b. Abt. 1867, KY.
   iii. JOSEPHINE MCPHERSON, b. Abt. 1869, KY.
    iv. ELIZABETH D. MCPHERSON, b. Abt. 1871, KY.
    v.   SARAH C. MCPHERSON, b. Abt. 1873, KY.
    vi. JOHN S. MCPHERSON, b. Abt. 1875, KY.
   vii. WILSON A. MCPHERSON, b. Abt. 1877, KY.
  viii. NANCY MCPHERSON, b. 1880, KY.
    ix. VIRGINIA MCPHERSON, b. Abt. 1882.
    x.   WILLIE MCPHERSON, b. Abt. 1885.

565. ELIZABETH E.[11] PENDLETON *(IVY TAYLOR[10], JOHN[9], BENJAMIN[8], WILLIAM[7], JOHN[6], PHILIP[5], HENRY[4], HENRY[3], GEORGE[2], GEORGE[1])* was born Abt. 1848 in VA. She married REUBEN MANUS. He was born Abt. 1848 in VA.
    Reuben Maness and family are listed in the 1880 census, Scott Co., VA, pg. 301C.

Children of ELIZABETH PENDLETON and REUBEN MANUS are:
    i.   JACOB[12] MANUS, b. Abt. 1870, VA.
    ii.   MARY J. MANUS, b. Abt. 1872, VA.

566. EMILY[11] PENDLETON *(IVY TAYLOR[10], JOHN[9], BENJAMIN[8], WILLIAM[7], JOHN[6], PHILIP[5], HENRY[4], HENRY[3], GEORGE[2], GEORGE[1])* was born Abt. 1849 in VA. She married THOMAS MAUPIN. He was born Abt. 1834 in KY, and died Aft. 1880 in Owsley Co., KY?

Children of EMILY PENDLETON and THOMAS MAUPIN are:
- i. CHARLIE[12] MAUPIN, b. Abt. 1878, KY.
- ii. DORA B. MAUPIN, b. Abt. 1879, KY.

567. CATHERINE[11] PENDLETON *(IVY TAYLOR[10], JOHN[9], BENJAMIN[8], WILLIAM[7], JOHN[6], PHILIP[5], HENRY[4], HENRY[3], GEORGE[2], GEORGE[1])* was born Dec 04, 1851 in VA, and died Sep 16, 1887 in Owsley Co., KY. She married ALEX J. HAMILTON, son of LINDA. He was born Jan 14, 1852 in VA, and died Dec 20, 1887 in Owsley Co., KY.

A. J. Hamilton and family are listed in the 1880 census, Rocky Station, Lee Co., VA, pg. 226C.

Children of CATHERINE PENDLETON and ALEX HAMILTON are:
- i. JOSEPHINE[12] HAMILTON, b. Abt. 1874, VA.
- ii. WILLIAM STEVENS HAMILTON, b. Abt. 1876, VA; d. Nov 1965; m. MARTHA J. ISAACS; b. Aug 17, 1879; d. Oct 22, 1935, Owsley Co., KY.
- iii. CORA HAMILTON, b. Abt. 1878, VA.

568. GEORGE W.[11] PENDLETON *(IVY TAYLOR[10], JOHN[9], BENJAMIN[8], WILLIAM[7], JOHN[6], PHILIP[5], HENRY[4], HENRY[3], GEORGE[2], GEORGE[1])* was born Apr 30, 1859 in KY, and died Sep 17, 1931 in Owsley Co., KY. He married MARY JANE FLANNERY Abt. 1880 in Owsley Co., KY. She was born Mar 27, 1864 in Owsley Co., KY, and died Sep 25, 1944 in Perry Co., KY.

Children of GEORGE PENDLETON and MARY FLANNERY are:
- i. WILLIAM[12] PENDLETON, b. Aug 19, 1881, Owsley Co., KY; d. Jul 18, 1948, Owsley Co., KY; m. VIVIAN INEZ HERNDON, Feb 24, 1910, Owsley Co., KY; b. Apr 15, 1881, Owsley Co., KY; d. Jul 18, 1948, Perry Co., KY.
- 824.   ii. HAMPTON W. PENDLETON, b. Jan 18, 1884, Owsley Co., KY; d. May 31, 1951, Perry Co., KY.
- iii. ROBERT S. PENDLETON, b. Feb 02, 1886, Owsley Co., KY; d. 1906.
- iv. EDNA PENDLETON, b. Mar 13, 1888, Owsley Co., KY; d. Jan 28, 1935, Owsley Co., KY; m. LUCIAN R. PORTER, May 1910; b. Mar 1888.
- v. ARCH GLASS PENDLETON, b. Mar 19, 1892, Owsley Co., KY; d. Sep 21, 1970, Lexington, KY; m. CARRIE HERNDON, Jun 04, 1915; b. 1894; d. Sep 04, 1944, Perry Co., KY.
- vi. NANCY PENDLETON, b. 1895; m. M. H. ALC?, Aug 1915.
- vii. CHARLES W. PENDLETON, b. Apr 29, 1897, Lee Co., KY; d. Oct 10, 1918, France; m. MAVIS, Jan 1918.

   A Charles W. Pendleton (22, house painter) born in KY and wife, Loralee (19), are listed in the 1920 Elizabeth City, VA census, pg. 24A.

viii. MATTIE PENDLETON.
ix. BERTHA PENDLETON, b. 1907, Owsley Co., KY; d. Abt. 1980, Fayette Co., KY.

569. MARY JANE[11] PENDLETON (*JOHN CRAIG*[10], *JOHN*[9], *BENJAMIN*[8], *WILLIAM*[7], *JOHN*[6], *PHILIP*[5], *HENRY*[4], *HENRY*[3], *GEORGE*[2], *GEORGE*[1]) was born Aug 1861 in Fannin Co., TX, and died Jun 17, 1939. She married JOHN ALBERT ANDERSON Jan 13, 1881, son of WILLIAM ANDERSON and ELIZABETH JACKSON.

Children of MARY PENDLETON and JOHN ANDERSON are:
   i. CLEOPATRA[12] ANDERSON, b. Nov 14, 1881, TX.
   ii. JESSE ASBERRY ANDERSON, b. Jan 08, 1888, Bryan Co., OK.
   iii. CRAIG ANDERSON.

570. JEMIMA ELIZABETH[11] PENDLETON (*JOHN CRAIG*[10], *JOHN*[9], *BENJAMIN*[8], *WILLIAM*[7], *JOHN*[6], *PHILIP*[5], *HENRY*[4], *HENRY*[3], *GEORGE*[2], *GEORGE*[1]) was born Feb 1862 in TX, and died 1905 in Choctaw Nation, OK? She married ROBERT FRANKLIN SEIGLER Nov 13, 1880 in Collins Co., TX, son of ROBERT SEIGLER and MARIAH GILLESPIE. He was born Nov 1858 in MS, and died Aft. 1900 in Choctaw Nation, OK?

Children of JEMIMA PENDLETON and ROBERT SEIGLER are:
   i. MAMIE E.[12] SEIGLER, b. Oct 1881, TX.
   ii. NANNIE B. SEIGLER, b. Jul 1884, TX.
   iii. ROSA E. SEIGLER, b. May 1886, TX.
   iv. HOMER N. SEIGLER, b. Jan 1889, TX.
   v. CRAWFORD C. SEIGLER, b. May 1890, TX.
   vi. MINOLA SEIGLER, b. Jul 1893, TX.
   vii. MYRTLE R. SEIGLER, b. Jan 1895, TX.
   viii. ALICE SEIGLER.

571. MARTHA ADELINE[11] PENDLETON (*JOHN CRAIG*[10], *JOHN*[9], *BENJAMIN*[8], *WILLIAM*[7], *JOHN*[6], *PHILIP*[5], *HENRY*[4], *HENRY*[3], *GEORGE*[2], *GEORGE*[1]) was born 1865 in TX, and died Aft. 1920 in Hunt Co., TX? She married GEORGE WALTER COFFEY Jan 05, 1881 in Hunt Co., TX, son of WILLIAM COFFEY and MARY WHEAT. He was born 1856 in KY, and died 1927 in Hunt Co., TX?
   George W. Coffey (merchant) and family are listed in the 1920 Hunt Co., TX census.

Children of MARTHA PENDLETON and GEORGE COFFEY are:
   i. OTHA A.[12] COFFEY, b. 1883.
   ii. EFFIE M. COFFEY, b. 1885.
   iii. ARCH C. COFFEY, b. 1886.
   iv. JIMMIE A. COFFEY, b. 1888.
   v. MATTIE G. COFFEY, b. 1889.

572. ANGINETTA VIRGINIA[11] PENDLETON *(JOHN CRAIG*[10]*, JOHN*[9]*, BENJAMIN*[8]*, WILLIAM*[7]*, JOHN*[6]*, PHILIP*[5]*, HENRY*[4]*, HENRY*[3]*, GEORGE*[2]*, GEORGE*[1]*)* was born 1867 in TX, and died Aft. 1910 in Custer Co., OK? She married STONEWALL JACKSON TIPPENS Nov 03, 1889 in Hunt Co., TX. He was born Abt. 1863 in TX, and died Aft. 1910 in Custer Co., OK?

Children of ANGINETTA PENDLETON and STONEWALL TIPPENS are:
- i. EDDIE[12] TIPPENS, b. 1890; d. Infancy.
- ii. MABLE CLARA TIPPENS, b. 1892; d. 1934.
- iii. RUTH TIPPENS, b. 1894.
- iv. ESTHER TIPPENS, b. 1896.
- v. WILLIE TIPPENS, b. 1898; d. Infancy.
- vi. THOMAS EDISON TIPPENS.
- vii. BENJAMIN TIPPENS, d. Infancy.
- viii. WHITCOMB RILEY TIPPENS.
- ix. JOSEPH TIPPENS, b. 1905; d. 1907.

573. JOHN ASBURY[11] PENDLETON *(JOHN CRAIG*[10]*, JOHN*[9]*, BENJAMIN*[8]*, WILLIAM*[7]*, JOHN*[6]*, PHILIP*[5]*, HENRY*[4]*, HENRY*[3]*, GEORGE*[2]*, GEORGE*[1]*)* was born Mar 1868 in TX, and died Aft. 1920 in Collin Co., TX? He married MARY EVELYN HOLSONBAKE Oct 30, 1895, daughter of WADE HOLSONBAKE and ELIZABETH HOWELL. She was born Jul 1876 in TX, and died Aft. 1920 in Collin Co., TX?

John A. Pendleton (salesman) and family are listed in the 1900 Collin Co., TX census, pg. 234.

Children of JOHN PENDLETON and MARY HOLSONBAKE are:
- 825. i. BESSIE NOMA[12] PENDLETON, b. 1897, TX.
- ii. ROY HOLSONBAKE PENDLETON, b. Jul 11, 1899, TX; d. Jan 1977, Duncan, OK; m. MELVIA POTEET, Apr 18, 1920; b. Apr 06, 1902, TX; d. Jul 06, 1990, Amarillo, TX.
- iii. WILLIE WADE PENDLETON, b. Mar 26, 1901, TX; d. Dec 28, 1997, Dallas, TX; m. NETA CARLTON, Nov 17, 1923.
- iv. BROOKSIE ELIZABETH PENDLETON, b. Feb 19, 1903, TX; d. Feb 17, 1997, Garland, TX; m. WALLACE A. MASON, Dec 25, 1919.
- v. IRMA LOUISE PENDLETON.
- vi. FRANCES CATHERINE PENDLETON, b. May 13, 1907, TX; d. Dec 26, 2001, Galveston, TX; m. LONNIE FRANK ALLMOND, Jul 04, 1927; b. Jun 11, 1907; d. May 1984, Conroe, TX.
- vii. RUTH LORINE PENDLETON.
- viii. JOHN ASBURY PENDLETON, JR.

574. ALICE NORA[11] PENDLETON *(JOHN CRAIG*[10]*, JOHN*[9]*, BENJAMIN*[8]*, WILLIAM*[7]*, JOHN*[6]*, PHILIP*[5]*, HENRY*[4]*, HENRY*[3]*, GEORGE*[2]*, GEORGE*[1]*)* was born Feb 1871 in TX, and died in Fannin Co., TX? She married JOHN THOMAS RICHARDSON Feb 01, 1891, son of PETER RICHARDSON and ELIZABETH TAYLOR. He was born Jun 1863 in TN.

Children of ALICE PENDLETON and JOHN RICHARDSON are:
  i.   MYRTLE B.[12] RICHARDSON, b. Apr 1892.
  ii. THOMAS H. RICHARDSON, b. Oct 1893.
  iii. CLARA L. RICHARDSON, b. Jun 1895.
  iv. GRACE M. RICHARDSON, b. Aug 1898.

575. WILLIAM CRAIG[11] PENDLETON (*JOHN CRAIG[10], JOHN[9], BENJAMIN[8], WILLIAM[7], JOHN[6], PHILIP[5], HENRY[4], HENRY[3], GEORGE[2], GEORGE[1]*) was born 1879 in TX, and died Sep 20, 1965 in Collin Co., TX. He married JESSIE BERRY ROBINSON Dec 27, 1905, daughter of GREEN ROBINSON and HENRIETTA ROSS. She was born Abt. 1888 in TX, and died Aft. 1930 in Collin Co., TX?

Children of WILLIAM PENDLETON and JESSIE ROBINSON are:
  i.   WILLIAM ROSS[12] PENDLETON, b. Jun 19, 1911, Collin Co., TX; d. Sep 21, 1999, Sunray, TX.
  ii. CLARK ASBURY PENDLETON, b. Feb 20, 1916, TX; d. Oct 1981, Sunray, TX.
  iii. JESSIE WRIGHT PENDLETON.

576. LUTHER DOUGLAS[11] PENDLETON (*JOHN CRAIG[10], JOHN[9], BENJAMIN[8], WILLIAM[7], JOHN[6], PHILIP[5], HENRY[4], HENRY[3], GEORGE[2], GEORGE[1]*) was born Dec 05, 1881 in TX, and died Feb 15, 1975 in Lubbock, TX. He married MAUDE A. CARR, daughter of DAVID CARR and MARY HAMMONDS. She was born 1889 in TX.

Children of LUTHER PENDLETON and MAUDE CARR are:
  i.   MARTHA[12] PENDLETON.
  ii. DOROTHY PENDLETON.
  iii. JIMMY PENDLETON.

577. ELMER WENDELL[11] PENDLETON (*JOHN CRAIG[10], JOHN[9], BENJAMIN[8], WILLIAM[7], JOHN[6], PHILIP[5], HENRY[4], HENRY[3], GEORGE[2], GEORGE[1]*) was born Dec 12, 1884 in TX. He married LULA KELLER Oct 11, 1905, daughter of HENRY KELLER and MAGGIE MCBRIDE. She was born 1885.

Elmer Wendell Pendleton registered for the World War I draft in Fort Worth, Tarrant Co., TX,

Children of ELMER PENDLETON and LULA KELLER are:
  i.   WINDELL[12] PENDLETON.
  ii. MARGARET PENDLETON.
  iii. JOSEPHINE PENDLETON, b. Feb 26, 1916; d. Aug 09, 1994, Walnut Creek, CA; m. MCCLENDON M. STALLINGS, Jan 28, 1938; b. Nov 06, 1915, TX; d. May 1978.
  iv. THOMAS PENDLETON.

578. JAMES MARION[11] PENDLETON (*ANDREW JACKSON[10], JOHN[9], BENJAMIN[8], WILLIAM[7], JOHN[6], PHILIP[5], HENRY[4], HENRY[3], GEORGE[2], GEORGE[1]*) was born Oct

04, 1870 in VA. He married HATTIE E. HILTON, daughter of JOHN HILTON and NANCY J. She was born Jun 1878 in VA.

James M. Pendleton (farm laborer) and family are listed in the 1900 Hawkins Co., TN census, pg. 231a.

Children of JAMES PENDLETON and HATTIE HILTON are:
   i. GARLAND E.[12] PENDLETON, b. Jul 05, 1894, TN.
      Garland and Clyde Pendleton registered for the World War I draft in Cooke Co., TX.

   ii. FRANCIS PENDLETON, b. Sep 1895, TN.
   iii. JOHN PENDLETON, b. May 05, 1897, TN.

579. BONNIE LAURA[11] PENDLETON *(ANDREW JACKSON[10], JOHN[9], BENJAMIN[8], WILLIAM[7], JOHN[6], PHILIP[5], HENRY[4], HENRY[3], GEORGE[2], GEORGE[1])* was born Jul 11, 1878 in VA, and died Feb 26, 1948. She married WILLIAM HUGH KIRKLAND. Resided in the Thackerville, OK area in 1915.

Children of BONNIE PENDLETON and WILLIAM KIRKLAND are:
   i. AVA[12] KIRKLAND.
   ii. JACK KIRKLAND.
   iii. BONNIE KIRKLAND.
   iv. HORTENSE KIRKLAND.

580. HIRAM KILGORE[11] PENDLETON *(ALLISON OSBORN[10], JOHN[9], BENJAMIN[8], WILLIAM[7], JOHN[6], PHILIP[5], HENRY[4], HENRY[3], GEORGE[2], GEORGE[1])* was born Mar 10, 1859 in Collin Co., TX, and died Oct 06, 1938 in Erath Co., TX. He married BARBARA ELLEN SOUTH Dec 20, 1893 in Pottawatomie Co., OK. She was born Apr 07, 1877 in Montague Co., TX, and died Mar 05, 1959 in Erath Co., TX.

Children of HIRAM PENDLETON and BARBARA SOUTH are:
   i. WILLIAM OTIS[12] PENDLETON, b. Jan 09, 1895, Pottawtomie Co., OK; d. Aug 01, 1954, Erath Co., TX; m. OMA VIOLA CURRIER; b. Jul 11, 1898, Cherokee Co., TX; d. Feb 15, 1985, Houston, TX.
   ii. JAMES FREDERICK ARTHUR PENDLETON, b. Nov 25, 1897, Collin Co., TX; d. Nov 04, 1971, Stephenville, TX; m. BERTHA MAE SHEFFIELD; b. Abt. 1908, TX; d. Aug 03, 1991, Tarrant Co., TX.
   iii. JOHNNY PENDLETON, b. 1899, Montague Co., TX; d. 1899, Montague Co., TX.
   iv. WILSON LEE PENDLETON, b. Aug 13, 1900, Coryell Co., TX; d. Jun 08, 1985, Stephenville, TX; m. (1) ENA WHITE, May 29, 1925; b. 1907; m. (2) ALMA PAULINE ALLMOND, May 14, 1930; b. Sep 17, 1906; d. Oct 07, 1983, Erath Co., TX.
   v. MAY PEARL PENDLETON, b. Jan 06, 1907, Erath Co., TX; d. Mar 16, 1999, Corpus Christi, TX; m. PERRY M. CAREY, Jul 19, 1924, Erath Co., TX; b. Sep 17, 1903; d. Nov 1974, Erath Co., TX.

vi. MAMIE B. PENDLETON, b. Nov 08, 1908, Erath Co., TX; d. Nov 03, 1990, Amarillo, TX; m. ALLIE SNEED, Nov 10, 1939, Comanche Co., TX.

vii. GLADYS PENDLETON, b. Dec 04, 1910, Erath Co., TX; d. Apr 22, 1986, Stephenville, TX; m. EARL THURMAN, Dec 22, 1930, Erath Co., TX.

viii. HOMER B. PENDLETON, b. Jun 07, 1914, Erath Co., TX; d. Mar 26, 1992; m. DIXIE CULWELL, Sep 11, 1935.

ix. JESSE CLARK PENDLETON, b. Abt. 1918, TX; d. Jan 04, 1994, Erath Co., TX; m. DELMA J. CURRIER; b. Dec 23, 1908, TX; d. Mar 23, 2001, Orange Park, FL.

581. PATTON MONROE[11] PENDLETON *(ALLISON OSBORN[10], JOHN[9], BENJAMIN[8], WILLIAM[7], JOHN[6], PHILIP[5], HENRY[4], HENRY[3], GEORGE[2], GEORGE[1])* was born Jul 19, 1864 in Collin Co., TX, and died Jan 15, 1957 in Erath Co., TX. He married NORA ELLEN WALLACE Abt. 1890. She was born Dec 22, 1874 in TX, and died Oct 09, 1946 in Erath Co., TX.

P. M. Pendleton (farmer) and family are listed in the 1900 Hunt Co., TX census, pg. 90a.

Children of PATTON PENDLETON and NORA WALLACE are:

826. i. SAMUEL ELDRIDGE[12] PENDLETON, b. Nov 06, 1891, TX; d. Dec 03, 1953, Coryell Co., TX.

ii. LILLIE PENDLETON, b. Nov 14, 1894, TX; d. Oct 17, 1918, Coryell Co., TX; m. ARTHUR FAUBION; b. Apr 23, 1890; d. Mar 1963, TX.

iii. ERNEST M. PENDLETON, b. Apr 16, 1896, TX; d. Jun 1978, Coryell Co., TX; m. GLADYS LOVEJOY; b. Jun 26, 1900; d. May 1981, Coryell Co., TX.

Ernest M. Pendleton registered for the World War I Draft in Coryell Co., TX.

iv. ROSELLA PENDLETON, b. Jul 24, 1897, Coryell Co., TX; d. Oct 21, 1956, Waco, TX; m. OMER HARRELL, Apr 17, 1913, Coryell Co., TX.

v. JOHNNY PENDLETON, b. Nov 29, 1900; d. Jan 26, 1901, Coryell Co., TX.

vi. HORACE PENDLETON, b. May 19, 1903, TX; d. Oct 1984, Hays Co., TX; m. LUCY E. MARION; b. Jan 10, 1906; d. Apr 30, 1997, Hunt Co., TX.

vii. VERN ODELL PENDLETON, b. Mar 11, 1912, Coryell Co., TX; d. Jul 18, 2000, Stephenville, TX; m. CHRISTINE JONES Nov 29, 1934, Hamilton, TX.

582. HARVEY ELDRIDGE[11] PENDLETON *(ALLISON OSBORN[10], JOHN[9], BENJAMIN[8], WILLIAM[7], JOHN[6], PHILIP[5], HENRY[4], HENRY[3], GEORGE[2], GEORGE[1])* was born Jan 29, 1870 in Gainesville, TX, and died Apr 29, 1942 in Breckinridge, TX. He married JUNE ETTA RUSSELL Jan 14, 1893, daughter of WILLIAM RUSSELL and DELLA JONES. She was born Jun 06, 1875 in Coryell Co., TX, and died Feb 16, 1955 in Breckinridge, TX.

Harvey Pendleton (farmer) and family are listed in the 1900 Erath Co., TX census, pg. 150.

Children of HARVEY PENDLETON and JUNE RUSSELL are:

    i.   VIOLA^{12} PENDLETON, b. Oct 04, 1893, TX; d. Bef. 1900.

   ii. RAYMOND PENDLETON, b. Aug 30, 1896, TX; d. May 1970, Gatesville, TX; m. (1) ANN BELL COCKERELL, Apr 07, 1920; b. Feb 28, 1902; d. Oct 10, 1948, Graham, TX.; m. (2) HATTIE MAE BLAKELY WEBB, Nov 08, 1950; b. Oct 03, 1891.

  iii. JOHN EARL PENDLETON, b. Mar 02, 1899, TX; d. Mar 30, 1962; m. LUCY ELLEN COX, Jun 22, 1944; b. Jan 10, 1906, TX; d. Apr 30, 1997, Commerce, TX.

  iv. HUBERT MONROE PENDLETON, b. Jul 27, 1901; d. Jan 02, 1979, Breckinridge, TX; m. SUSIE PEARL STEWART, Jul 01, 1933; b. Jun 10, 1902; d. Dec 11, 1971, Breckinridge, TX.

   v. SUSIE REBECCA PENDLETON.

  vi. BUSTER WILLIE PENDLETON, b. Apr 19, 1907, Stephens Co., TX; d. Nov 29, 1970, Erath Co., TX; m. ANNIE JUANITA WALLACE, Mar 30, 1931, Walton, OK; b. Mar 30, 1914, Erath Co., TX; d. Jan 10, 1991, Erath Co., TX.

  vii. DOLLY ODESSA PENDLETON.

 viii. ILLA CORENE PENDLETON.

  ix. VELVA VIOLENE PENDLETON.

   x. HARVEY RUSSELL PENDLETON, b. Aug 24, 1918, Breckinridge, TX; d. Sep 02, 2003, Breckinridge, TX; m. PAULINE LOUDDER, Jun 11, 1957; b. Jun 11, 1924, Breckinridge, TX.

583. SARAH BELLE^{11} PENDLETON *(MELVIN C.^{10}, JOHN^9, BENJAMIN^8, WILLIAM^7, JOHN^6, PHILIP^5, HENRY^4, HENRY^3, GEORGE^2, GEORGE^1)* She married RICHARD MILLER FORRESTER Sep 03, 1890 in Hunt Co., TX, son of JAMES FORRESTER and JANE SUTTON. He was born 1856, and died 1939.

Children of SARAH PENDLETON and RICHARD FORRESTER are:

    i.   ED^{12} FORRESTER.

   ii. DOCIA ELLEN FORRESTER.

  iii. JAMES FORRESTER.

  iv. ORA FORRESTER.

   v. GERTRUDE FORRESTER.

584. ANDREW J. "JACK"^{11} PENDLETON *(MELVIN C.^{10}, JOHN^9, BENJAMIN^8, WILLIAM^7, JOHN^6, PHILIP^5, HENRY^4, HENRY^3, GEORGE^2, GEORGE^1)* was born Sep 1868 in MO. He married MATTIE GRIFFIN Dec 24, 1899 in Hunt Co., TX, daughter of ROBERT GRIFFIN and SALLEY DRISKELL. She was born Oct 1879 in TX.

     A. J. Pendleton (engineer - cotton gin) and Mattie are listed in the 1900 Hunt Co., KY census, pg. 172a.

Children of ANDREW PENDLETON and MATTIE GRIFFIN are:

    i.   BONNIE^{12} PENDLETON.

   ii. WELDON PENDLETON.

iii. TROY JAMES PENDLETON, b. Jul 08, 1908, TX; d. Jan 24, 1978, Hunt
Co., TX; m. MABEL E. THOMASON; b. Apr 27, 1914, TX; d. Sep 30,
1983, Hunt Co., TX.

585. SAMUEL D.[11] PENDLETON (*JAMES LUCAS*[10], *JOHN*[9], *EDMUND*[8], *WILLIAM*[7],
JOHN[6], *PHILIP*[5], *HENRY*[4], *HENRY*[3], *GEORGE*[2], *GEORGE*[1]) was born Jun 10, 1836 in
TN, and died Bef. 1900 in Izard Co., AR? He married MARTHA JANE WARRICK Jan
09, 1861 in Coffee Co., TN, daughter of JESSE WARRRICK and MARTHA. She was
born Abt. 1839 in TN, and died Aft. 1900 in Izard Co., AR?

Samuel D. Pendleton served in the Confederate Army, 4th Regiment, Tennessee
Cavalry (McLemore's).   Samuel D. Pendleton and family homesteaded near Sage,
Arkansas at about the site of what is now known as "Bone Town" (Ref. 286). Martha J.
Pendleton (farmer), Nora, her youngest daughter, and Mary J. Pendleton, her sister-in-
law, are listed in the 1900 Izard Co., AR census, pg. 370a.

Children of SAMUEL PENDLETON and MARTHA WARRICK are:
827. i. DERINDA ELIZABETH[12] PENDLETON, b. Nov 08, 1861, Bell Buckle,
TN; d. Jan 10, 1956, Hanford, Fresno Co., CA.
ii. ISABEL A. PENDLETON, b. Abt. 1865.
iii. J. L. PENDLETON, b. Abt. 1866; d. young?
828. iv. DOVEY JANE PENDLETON, b. Sep 1869, TN; d. Aft. 1920, Piney Fork,
AR?
v. JAMES A. PENDLETON, b. Abt. 1871, AR.
vi. SARAH PENDLETON, b. Abt. 1873.
vii. JOHN F. PENDLETON, b. Jun 1877, AR.
viii. WILLIAM A. PENDLETON, b. Abt. 1878.
ix. NORA B. PENDLETON, b. Aug 1880, AR.

586. JOHN L.[11] PENDLETON (*SAMUEL L.*[10], *JOHN*[9], *EDMUND*[8], *WILLIAM*[7], *JOHN*[6],
PHILIP[5], *HENRY*[4], *HENRY*[3], *GEORGE*[2], *GEORGE*[1]) was born Feb 01, 1848 in Cannon
Co., TN, and died Mar 24, 1930 in Cannon Co., TN. He married MARY ELIZABETH
LYNN Sep 26, 1867 in Cannon Co., TN, daughter of DAVID LYNN and MARTHA
FREEZE. She was born Sep 23, 1850 in TN, and died Nov 25, 1920 in Cannon Co., TN.

John L. Pendleton (black smithing) and family are listed in the 1900 Cannon Co.,
TN census, pg. 46. John L. Pendleton and his wife Mary are buried in Cherry Cemetery,
Cannon Co., TN (Ref. 287).

Children of JOHN PENDLETON and MARY LYNN are:
i. RACHEL E.[12] PENDLETON, b. Feb 05, 1869, Cannon Co., TN; d. Nov 04,
1884.
ii. MARY ELIZABETH PENDLETON, b. Aug 24, 1871, Cannon Co., TN.
iii. MARTHA L. PENDLETON, b. Mar 29, 1873, Cannon Co., TN.
iv. SALLIE A. PENDLETON, b. Jun 24, 1875, Cannon Co., TN; d. Nov 01,
1971.
v. MAGGIE B. PENDLETON, b. Oct 22, 1877, Cannon Co., TN; d. Oct 22,
1878.

    vi.   FANNIE CAROLINE PENDLETON, b. Oct 20, 1879, Cannon Co., TN; d. Mar 22, 1955, Cannon Co., TN; m. JAMES CALVIN TAYLOR, Aug 14, 1899, Cannon Co., TN; b. Feb 22, 1880, Cannon Co., TN; d. Aug 10, 1970, Cannon Co., TN.

   vii.   JOHN WILLIAM PENDLETON, b. Mar 23, 1882, Cannon Co., TN; d. Mar 21, 1932.

        John William Pendleton registered for the World War I draft in Hill Co., TX.

  viii.   JOSIE N. PENDLETON, b. Oct 09, 1885.

    ix.   JULIE A. PENDLETON, b. Sep 29, 1887, Cannon Co., TN; d. Aug 31, 1888.

     x.   DAVID W. PENDLETON, b. Aug 07, 1890, Cannon Co., TN; d. Jul 30, 1926.

        David Pendleton registered for the World War I draft in Cannon Co., TN.

587. WILLIAM GREEN[11] PENDLETON *(SAMUEL L.[10], JOHN[9], EDMUND[8], WILLIAM[7], JOHN[6], PHILIP[5], HENRY[4], HENRY[3], GEORGE[2], GEORGE[1])* was born Oct 16, 1853 in Woodbury, Cannon Co., TN, and died Nov 11, 1927 in Hill Co., TX. He married ELIZA GILMORE DUNCAN Oct 19, 1870, daughter of JOHN DUNCAN and MARY BUTLER. She was born Apr 19, 1848 in Cannon Co., TN, and died Jan 1943 in Hill Co., TX.

Children of WILLIAM PENDLETON and ELIZA DUNCAN are (Ref. 288):

829.   i.   SAMUEL ZACHARY[12] PENDLETON, b. Nov 21, 1872, Woodbury, Cannon Co., TN; d. Mar 04, 1959, Hillsboro, TX.

830.   ii.   HARRIS PENDLETON, b. Oct 01, 1874, TN; d. Bef. 1964, South Corbin, KY?

831. iii.   RACHEL ELIZABETH PENDLETON, b. Apr 01, 1876, Woodbury, Cannon Co., TN; d. Dec 18, 1960, Hill Co., TX.

832. iv.   EMMA JAQULINE PENDLETON, b. Jul 27, 1878, Woodbury, Cannon Co., TN; d. Apr 27, 1964, Hillsboro, Hill Co., TX.

     v.   WILLIAM STEPHEN PENDLETON, b. Aug 22, 1886, Woodbury, Cannon Co., TN; d. Sep 15, 1964, Hillsboro, TX.

        William Stephen Pendleton registered for the World War I draft in Hill Co., TX (Ref. 210).

    vi.   JUNIS PENDLETON, b. Mar 15, 1888, Woodbury, Cannon Co., TN; d. Jun 13, 1888, Woodbury, Cannon Co., TN.

   vii.   WILLIAM G. PENDLETON, b. Oct 16, 1889, Woodbury, Cannon Co., TN; d. Bef. 1964, Woodbury, Cannon Co., TN.

588. EDMOND HARRIS[11] PENDLETON *(WILLIAM G.[10], JOHN[9], EDMUND[8], WILLIAM[7], JOHN[6], PHILIP[5], HENRY[4], HENRY[3], GEORGE[2], GEORGE[1])* was born Sep 23, 1858 in Cannon Co., TN, and died Aug 22, 1952 in Birmingham, AL. He married MARY "MOLLY" EVALINE CROSSLIN Oct 13, 1881 in Coffee Co., TN. She was born Dec 28, 1866 in Cannon Co., TN, and died Jun 29, 1937 in Cannon Co., TN.

Edmond Pendleton (farmer) and family are listed in the 1900 and 1910 Coffee Co., TN census records.

Children of EDMOND PENDLETON and MARY CROSSLIN are:
    i.   FLORA[12] PENDLETON, b. Jul 1882, TN.
    ii. CORA HARRIS PENDLETON, b. Jan 1886, TN.
    iii. STONEWALL JACKSON PENDLETON, b. Apr 25, 1889, TN; d. Apr 1972, Akron, OH.
         Stonewall Jackson Pendleton registered for the World War I draft in Franklin Co., TN.

    iv. WHIT FRANCIS PENDLETON, b. May 06, 1893, TN.
         Wit Francis Pendleton registered for the World War I draft in Escambia Co., FL.

    v.   TULLY PENDLETON, b. Feb 1898, TN.
    vi. EVA PENDLETON.
    vii. BRADY PENDLETON, b. Jul 10, 1908, TN; d. May 1974, Bessemer, AL.

589. WILLIAM SEAMOR[11] PENDLETON *(WILLIAM G.[10], JOHN[9], EDMUND[8], WILLIAM[7], JOHN[6], PHILIP[5], HENRY[4], HENRY[3], GEORGE[2], GEORGE[1])* was born May 1867 in TN, and died Aft. 1930 in Warren Co., TN? He married LAURA Abt. 1888. She was born Jun 1869 in TN, and died Aft. 1930 in Warren Co., TN?
    Seymore Pendleton (farmer) and family are listed in the 1900 Coffee Co., TN census, pg. 219.

Children of WILLIAM PENDLETON and LAURA are:
833.   i.   ETHEL[12] PENDLETON, b. Mar 1889, TN.
834.   ii. R. D. PENDLETON, b. Mar 1890, TN.
        iii. DORA L. PENDLETON, b. Mar 1892, TN.
        iv. EWING E. PENDLETON, b. Jan 1895, TN.
        v.   DEWEY ELWOOD PENDLETON, b. May 04, 1900, TN; d. Aug 1985, Madison, Davidson Co., TN.
             Dewey Ellwood Pendleton registered for the World War I draft in Coffee Co., TN.

590. GEORGE CASSETY[11] PENDLETON *(EDMUND[10], BENJAMIN[9], EDMUND[8], WILLIAM[7], JOHN[6], PHILIP[5], HENRY[4], HENRY[3], GEORGE[2], GEORGE[1])* was born Apr 23, 1845 in Coffee Co., TN, and died Jan 19, 1913 in Temple, Bell Co., TX. He married HELEN EMBREE May 16, 1870. She was born May 23, 1848 in KY, and died Sep 03, 1924 in Bell Co., TX?
    The biography of George Pendleton is included in the Biographical Directory of the American Congress (Ref. 111).

    George Cassety Pendleton moved with his parents from TN to Ellis County, TX., in 1857 and settled in Belton, TX where he engaged in mercantile and agricultural pursuits. During the Civil War he entered the Confederate service as a private in Captain Forrest's

Company, Watson's Regiment, Parson's Brigade, Texas Cavalry. At the close of the war, he attended Waxahachie Academy in Ellis County, TX. He was employed as a commercial traveler for twelve years and continued to be engaged in mercantile and agricultural pursuits. George Pendleton is listed in the 1880 Bell Co., TX census, E.D. 5, along with Katie A. and David Pendleton. He was a delegate to every Democratic State convention from 1876 to 1910 and a member of the State house of representatives 1882-1888 where he served as speaker in 1886. He was Lieutenant Governor of Texas 1890-1892 and a delegate to the Democratic National Convention at Chicago in 1896. He was elected as a Democrat to the Fifty-third and Fifty-fourth Congresses (March 4, 1893-March 3, 1897). He declined to be a candidate for renomination in 1896 and instead engaged in banking in Temple, Bell County, TX. He studied law, was admitted to the bar in 1900, and practiced in Temple until his death. He is buried in the Temple City Cemetery.

The following notice of his death appeared Jun 25, 1913 in local newspapers (Ref. 289): "Former Lieut., Governor Dies, Temple, Texas. George C. Pendleton, lieutenant governor of Texas under James S. Hogg and formerly congressman from the old Ninth district, died at his home in this city Sunday morning. He was 68 years old. Mr. Pendleton suffered a stroke of paralysis Saturday morning, from which he never rallied and was unconscious much of Saturday. The funeral was held in Temple Monday."

Children of GEORGE PENDLETON and HELEN EMBREE are:

    i.   MABLE[12] PENDLETON, b. Dec 17, 1872, TX; m. ANDREW NOBLE SAYRE, Dec 22, 1897; d. Feb 03, 1924.

        Mrs. Mabel Pendleton Sayre was a member of The National Society of the Daughters of the American Revolution (Volume 46, page 75).

    ii. MYRTLE PENDLETON, b. Mar 31, 1877, TX; m. LEE F. COWAN, Sep 05, 1902.

        Mrs. Myrtle Pendleton Cowan was a member of The National Society of the Daughters of the American Revolution (Volume 48, page 190.

   iii. ARIA PENDLETON, b. Sep 02, 1881, Temple, TX; m. MORTON J. LYSTER, May 15, 1904.

        Mrs. Aria Pendleton Lyster was a member of The National Society of the Daughters of the American Revolution (Volume 46, page 75).

    iv. LUCILLE PENDLETON, b. May 19, 1886, TX; d. Sep 03, 1924, Houston, TX?; m. HARRY TAYLOR KENDALL; b. Abt. 1883, KS; d. Aft. 1920.

835.   v. EDMUND EMBREE PENDLETON, b. Aug 31, 1888, TX; d. Aft. 1930, San Antonio, TX?

591. WILLIAM SMARTT[11] PENDLETON *(EDMUND[10], BENJAMIN[9], EDMUND[8], WILLIAM[7], JOHN[6], PHILIP[5], HENRY[4], HENRY[3], GEORGE[2], GEORGE[1])* was born Feb 06, 1848 in TN, and died Aft. 1900 in Fort Worth, TX? He married ANNE SHELTON 1875. She was born Abt. 1856 in KY.

Children of WILLIAM PENDLETON and ANNE SHELTON are:
     i.   ANNA BELLE[12] PENDLETON, b. 1876.
    ii.   ROBERT EDMUND (HERBERT E.) PENDLETON, b. Oct 03, 1878, TX; d. Jan 1971, Seward, KS; m. CLARRIE L.; b. Abt. 1886, MS.
         Herbert E. Pendleton (stock man) is listed in the 1900 Wheeler Co., TX census, pg. 183. Robert Edmund Pendleton registered for the World War I draft in Wheeler Co., TX.

    iii. WALTER SHELTON PENDLETON, b. Aug 26, 1880, Fort Worth, TX; d. Jun 15, 1952; m. MARY NONA EVANS, Apr 11, 1911, Greenville, Hunt Co., TX; b. Jul 07, 1889, Morris Co., TX; d. Dec 18, 1971.
         Walter S. Pendleton (ranch hand) is listed in the 1900 Wheeler Co., TX census, pg. 182. Walter Shelton Pendleton registered for the World War I draft in Wheeler Co., TX.

    iv. ANNALU PENDLETON, b. Feb 1883, TX.
     v. EDNA PENDLETON, b. Jan 1886, TX.

592. EDMUND GAINES[11] PENDLETON *(EDMUND[10], BENJAMIN[9], EDMUND[8], WILLIAM[7], JOHN[6], PHILIP[5], HENRY[4], HENRY[3], GEORGE[2], GEORGE[1])* was born Sep 28, 1852 in TN, and died Nov 19, 1931 in Sherman Co., TX? He married KETURAH ELLIOTT Oct 07, 1879. She was born Jun 1861 in KY, and died Aft. 1920 in Sherman Co., TX?

    E. G. Pendleton is listed as grantee of 37.5 acres of land in Bell Co., TX, Milam District, on Jan 15, 1889 (Ref. 290). E. G. Pendleton (farmer) and family are listed in the 1900 Randall Co., TX census, pg. 203.

Children of EDMUND PENDLETON and KETURAH ELLIOTT are:
     i.   DAVID ELLIOTT[12] PENDLETON, b. Jul 28, 1880, TX; d. Oct 24, 1926.
    ii.   BESSIE D. PENDLETON, b. Apr 23, 1882, TX.
    iii. ROYAL PENDLETON, b. Jun 16, 1884, TX; d. Dec 1973, TX.
         Royal Pendleton registered for the World War I draft in Sherman Co., TX.

    iv. GEORGE C. PENDLETON, b. Sep 29, 1886, TX; d. May 1963.
         George C. Pendleton registered for the World War I draft in Union Co., NM.

     v. MARY J. PENDLETON, b. Nov 24, 1888, TX.
    vi. JOHN ROBERT PENDLETON, b. Mar 01, 1892, TX; d. Oct 30, 1996, Stratford, TX.
         John Robert Pendleton registered for the World War I draft in Sherman Co., TX.

    vii. FAY PENDLETON, b. Aug 27, 1895, TX.
   viii. FERN PENDLETON, b. Aug 27, 1895.

ix. OLIVE H. PENDLETON, b. Jul 13, 1898, TX.
x. VELMA B. PENDLETON.

593. OCTAVIA[11] PENDLETON *(EDMUND[10], BENJAMIN[9], EDMUND[8], WILLIAM[7], JOHN[6], PHILIP[5], HENRY[4], HENRY[3], GEORGE[2], GEORGE[1])* was born Jan 1858 in TX, and died Jul 03, 1947 in Fort Worth, TX. She married KLEBER MILLER VAN ZANDT Oct 1885 in Fort Worth, TX, son of ISAAC VAN ZANDT and FANNY LIPSCOMB. He was born Nov 07, 1836 in Franklin Co., TX, and died Mar 19, 1930 in Fort Worth, TX.

Children of OCTAVIA PENDLETON and KLEBER VAN ZANDT are (Ref. 291):
i. EDMUND PENDLETON[12] VAN ZANDT, b. 1886.
ii. FRANCES COOKE VAN ZANDT, b. Oct 03, 1890, Fort Worth, TX; d. Apr 08, 1967, Fort Worth, TX; m. CLARENCE DAVIS SLOAN; b. Jul 21, 1888, Cherryville, KS.
iii. ALICE VAN ZANDT.
iv. MARGARET VAN ZANDT.
v. A. S. J. VAN ZANDT.

594. DAVID RAMSEY[11] PENDLETON *(EDMUND[10], BENJAMIN[9], EDMUND[8], WILLIAM[7], JOHN[6], PHILIP[5], HENRY[4], HENRY[3], GEORGE[2], GEORGE[1])* was born Feb 06, 1861 in TX, and died Aft. 1910 in Bell Co., TX? He married (1) ETTA MAY EASTON Sep 17, 1891, daughter of LUCY EASTON. He married (2) JULIA PROCTOR May 05, 1901, daughter of SARAH P. She was born Abt. 1871 in TX, and died Aft. 1910 in Bell Co., TX?

David Pendleton is listed in the 1880 Bell Co., TX census index, E.D. 5, with his older brother George C. Pendleton. His sons, George C. and Harry E. Pendleton, are in the household of Lucy Easton, their grandmother, in the 1900 Travis Co., TX census, pg. 53a.

Children of DAVID PENDLETON and ETTA EASTON are:
i. HARRY EASTON[12] PENDLETON, b. Sep 13, 1892, TX; d. Feb 1977, Tyler, TX.

Harry E. Pendleton registered for the World War I draft in Dallas, TX. He was a Captain, Combined Arms Command, U.S. Army.

ii. GEORGE C. PENDLETON, b. Oct 24, 1894, TX.

Children of DAVID PENDLETON and JULIA PROCTOR are:
iii. HALL P.[12] PENDLETON, b. Sep 08, 1902, TX; d. May 04, 1997, Amarillo, TX; m. VELMA DENSON; b. Aug 12, 1907; d. Apr 1976, Amarillo, TX.
iv. ENOCH LEE PENDLETON.
v. SARAH PENDLETON.
vi. JULIA PENDLETON.
vii. ELIZABETH PENDLETON.

595. ANDREW A.[11] PENDLETON *(THOMAS DILLARD[10], BENJAMIN[9], EDMUND[8], WILLIAM[7], JOHN[6], PHILIP[5], HENRY[4], HENRY[3], GEORGE[2], GEORGE[1])* was born 1844 in Cannon Co., TN, and died in Hill Co., TX? He married MARTHA WALKER Dec 28, 1865 in Christian Co., MO. She was born Abt. 1849 in MS, and died Aft. 1880 in Hill Co., TX?

Andrew A. Pendleton is named in Missouri Land Patents on Jun 1,1859, and Jun 1, 1860 in Christian Co. MO, and Jan 10, 1874 in Douglas Co., MO. Andrew A. Pendleton served in the 11th Missouri Cavalry, Union Army.

Child of ANDREW PENDLETON and MARTHA WALKER is:
  i.   NANCY[12] PENDLETON, b. Abt. 1869.

596. JOHN BENJAMIN[11] PENDLETON *(DILLARD[10], BENJAMIN[9], EDMUND[8], WILLIAM[7], JOHN[6], PHILIP[5], HENRY[4], HENRY[3], GEORGE[2], GEORGE[1])* was born Jul 1858 in Christian Co., MO, and died Aug 11, 1928 in Caldwell Co., TX. He married (1) EMMA C. ZUMWALT Dec 02, 1887 in Gonzales Co., TX. He married (2) MARTHA LANE NORTON Sep 19, 1893 in Caldwell Co., TX. She was born Aug 31, 1876 in Travis Co., TX, and died Oct 06, 1958 in Gonzales Co., TX.

John B. Pendleton (farmer) and family are listed in the 1900 Caldwell Co., TX census, pg. 223a.

Children of JOHN PENDLETON and MARTHA NORTON are:
  i.   TYRE STOKES[12] PENDLETON, b. Sep 17, 1894, Caldwell Co., TX; d. Feb 08, 1964, San Antonio, TX; m. MYRTLE ADELL POPPS, Apr 19, 1922, Gonzales Co., TX; b. Dec 08, 1904, Caldwell Co., TX; d. Nov 01, 1973, Caldwell Co., TX.
       Tyre Stokes Pendleton registered for the World War I draft in Caldwell Co., TX.

  ii. WILLIAM EARL PENDLETON, b. Mar 17, 1896, Caldwell Co., TX; d. Feb 11, 1985, Caldwell Co., TX.
       Willie Earl Pendleton registered for the World War I draft in Caldwell Co., TX.

597. STACY A.[11] PENDLETON *(DILLARD[10], BENJAMIN[9], EDMUND[8], WILLIAM[7], JOHN[6], PHILIP[5], HENRY[4], HENRY[3], GEORGE[2], GEORGE[1])* was born 1866 in Christian Co., MO, and died Nov 01, 1888 in Gonzales Co., TX. She married E.S. CARLOS Dec 04, 1878 in Gonzales Co., TX. He was born Abt. 1854 in MO, and died Aft. 1880.

E. S. Carlos and family are listed in the 1880 Gonzales Co., TX census.

Child of STACY PENDLETON and E.S. CARLOS is:
  i.   ADA[12] CARLOS, b. 1879, TX.

598. SELINA DICKSON[11] PENDLETON *(ALEXANDER GARLAND[10], WILLIAM GARLAND[9], REUBEN[8], WILLIAM[7], JOHN[6], PHILIP[5], HENRY[4], HENRY[3], GEORGE[2], GEORGE[1])* was born Abt. 1844 in VA, and died Aft. 1910 in Montgomery Co., MD?

She married JOHN C. WILSON Aug 11, 1863 in Montgomery Co., MD. He was born Abt. 1834 in MD, and died Aft. 1880 in Montgomery Co., MD?

John C. Wilson and family are listed in the 1880 census, Montgomery Co., MD, pg. 381C.

Children of SELINA PENDLETON and JOHN WILSON are:
  i. SALLIE P.[12] WILSON, b. Abt. 1866, MD.
  ii. ROSA WILSON, b. Abt. 1870, MD.
  iii. JOHN C. WILSON, b. Abt. 1872, MD.
  iv. WILLIAM P. WILSON, b. Abt. 1874, MD.
  v. EMMA WILSON, b. Abt. 1876, MD.
  vi. ELLEN WILSON, b. Abt. 1879, MD.

599. ROSE B.[11] PENDLETON *(ALEXANDER GARLAND[10], WILLIAM GARLAND[9], REUBEN[8], WILLIAM[7], JOHN[6], PHILIP[5], HENRY[4], HENRY[3], GEORGE[2], GEORGE[1])* was born Abt. 1846 in VA. She married JOHN H. DARRELL. He was born Abt. 1837 in VA.

John H. Darrell (dentist) and family are listed in the 1870 Washington DC census. Rose B. Darrall and family are listed in the 1880 census, Washington DC.

Children of ROSE PENDLETON and JOHN DARRELL are:
  i. OLIVER B.[12] DARRELL, b. Abt. 1863, DC.
  ii. LOUIS P. DARRELL, b. Abt. 1875, DC.
  iii. EFFIE DARRELL, b. Abt. 1879, DC.

600. EDWIN CONWAY[11] PENDLETON *(ALEXANDER GARLAND[10], WILLIAM GARLAND[9], REUBEN[8], WILLIAM[7], JOHN[6], PHILIP[5], HENRY[4], HENRY[3], GEORGE[2], GEORGE[1])* was born May 27, 1847 in Richmond, VA, and died Sep 28, 1919 in Philadelphia, PA -U.S. Naval Hosp. He married MARY RIDDLE SAXTON Apr 02, 1872, daughter of JOSEPH SAXTON and MARY ABERCROMBIE. She was born Jun 23, 1858 in Washington DC, and died Apr 22, 1926.

Edwin Conway Pendleton graduated from the U.S. Naval Academy in 1867. He served on the "Marion" in pursuit of the Confederate steamers "Florida" and "Tallahassee." He was Superintendent of the Naval Gun Factory in Washington 1897-1899 and 1902-1905. He was Commandant of the Navy Yard, Washington in 1905. Edwin Pendleton was promoted to rear Admiral and served as Commandant of the League Island Navy Yard, PA, 1907-1909 where he retired 27 May 1909. He is buried in Arlington National Cemetery.

Child of EDWIN PENDLETON and MARY SAXTON is:
836.   i. JOSEPH SAXTON[12] PENDLETON, b. Oct 28, 1871.

601. ALEXANDER GREENHEW[11] PENDLETON *(ALEXANDER GARLAND[10], WILLIAM GARLAND[9], REUBEN[8], WILLIAM[7], JOHN[6], PHILIP[5], HENRY[4], HENRY[3], GEORGE[2], GEORGE[1])* was born Abt. 1852 in Wash DC, and died Aft. 1900 in Gila Co.,

AZ? He married ROSA B. BARCLAY. She was born Abt. 1851 in VA, and died Aft. 1900 in Gila Co., AZ?

Alexander, civil engineer, and Rosa Pendleton are listed in the 1880 AZ census, Pinal Co., pg. 400D. Alex G. Pendleton and family are listed in the 1900 Gila Co., AZ census.

Children of ALEXANDER PENDLETON and ROSA BARCLAY are:

837.   i.   ALEXANDER G.^{12} PENDLETON, b. Abt. 1882, AZ; d. Aft. 1930, Pittsburgh, PA?
         ii.   ROSA PENDLETON, b. Abt. 1884, AZ.
         iii.   ANNA PENDLETON, b. Abt. 1885, AZ.
         iv.   EDWIN CONWAY PENDLETON, b. Mar 11, 1892, AZ.
             Edwin Conway Pendleton, Civil Engineer, Interstate Commerce Commission, registered for the WWI draft in Berkeley, Alameda County.

         v.   JOHN WALTON PENDLETON, b. Abt. 1898, AZ.

602. WILLIAM ADDISON^{11} PENDLETON *(ROBERT ALDRIDGE^{10}, JAMES SHEPHERD^9, REUBEN^8, WILLIAM^7, JOHN^6, PHILIP^5, HENRY^4, HENRY^3, GEORGE^2, GEORGE^1)* was born Aug 1840 in VA, and died Aft. 1920 in Amherst Co., VA? He married DORA Abt. 1893. She was born Jan 1875 in VA, and died Aft. 1920 in Amherst Co., VA?

William Addison Pendleton (occupation: farmer) enlisted 15 Apr 1865 as private, age 20, Amherst Court House, Confederacy. W. A. Pendleton of Amherst is listed in the 1888 VA Pension Roles (Confederate). William Pendleton (farmer) and family are listed in the 1900 Amherst Co., VA census and the 1920 Temperance, Amherst Co. census, pg. 17A.

Children of WILLIAM PENDLETON and DORA are:

         i.   LENA^{12} PENDLETON, b. Mar 1894, VA.
         ii.   ALICE PENDLETON, b. Jul 1895, VA.
         iii.   ALMA PENDLETON, b. May 1898, VA.
         iv.   ELIZABETH PENDLETON, b. Jun 1899, VA.
         v.   CARSON PENDLETON.
         vi.   HENRIETTA PENDLETON.
         vii.   VIRGINIA PENDLETON.
         viii.   DOROTHY PENDLETON.

603. RICHARD S.^{11} PENDLETON *(ROBERT ALDRIDGE^{10}, JAMES SHEPHERD^9, REUBEN^8, WILLIAM^7, JOHN^6, PHILIP^5, HENRY^4, HENRY^3, GEORGE^2, GEORGE^1)* was born Apr 1867 in VA, and died Aft. 1920 in Lynchburg, VA? He married EMMA H. WINGFIELD Abt. 1890. She was born Mar 1872 in VA, and died Aft. 1920 in Lynchburg, VA?

Richard Pendleton (City Deputy Constable) and family are listed in the 1920 Lynchburg, VA census, pg. 19A.

Children of RICHARD PENDLETON and EMMA WINGFIELD are:
- i. GLADYS[12] PENDLETON, b. Oct 1891, VA.
- ii. RICHARD PENDLETON, b. May 1893, VA.

  Richard Pendleton is listed as a sergeant who served in WWI, from Lynchburg, VA (Ref. 292).

- iii. JAMES PENDLETON, b. Dec 1894, VA.
- iv. JESSE JOHNSON PENDLETON, b. Nov 1898, VA.

  Jesse Johnson Pendleton registered for the World War I draft in Lynchburg, Campbell Co., VA.

- v. CLARENCE CLARK PENDLETON, b. Oct 26, 1900, VA; d. Mar 1969, Lynchburg, VA.

  Clarence Clark Pendleton registered for the World War I draft in Lynchburg, Campbell Co., VA.

- vi. CATHERINE PENDLETON.
- vii. MARY PENDLETON.

604. ANNA CATREN[11] PENDLETON (*WILLIAM GARLAND*[10], *JAMES SHEPHERD*[9], *REUBEN*[8], *WILLIAM*[7], *JOHN*[6], *PHILIP*[5], *HENRY*[4], *HENRY*[3], *GEORGE*[2], *GEORGE*[1]) was born Jun 22, 1856 in AR, and died Sep 10, 1910 in Union Co., AR? She married CHARLES WILLIAM HEARIN Oct 16, 1868, son of JOHN HEARIN and RHODA BUSSEY. He was born Oct 16, 1847 in Union Co., AR, and died Aft. 1910 in Union Co., AR?

Children of ANNA PENDLETON and CHARLES HEARIN are:
- i. FLORENCE[12] HEARIN, b. 1872, AR.
- ii. HARRY SMITH HEARIN, b. Feb 22, 1877, AR; d. Sep 06, 1879.
- iii. EMMETTE HOLCOMBE HEARIN, b. Apr 12, 1880, AR.

605. HERBERT GEORGE[11] PENDLETON (*WILLIAM GARLAND*[10], *JAMES SHEPHERD*[9], *REUBEN*[8], *WILLIAM*[7], *JOHN*[6], *PHILIP*[5], *HENRY*[4], *HENRY*[3], *GEORGE*[2], *GEORGE*[1]) was born Dec 31, 1863 in AR, and died Jan 27, 1950 in Union Co., AR. He married JULIA E. MORRISON Abt. 1889 in Union Co., Arkansas. She was born Nov 1872 in AR, and died Feb 09, 1948 in Union Co., AR.

H. G. Pendleton (stock broker) and family are listed in the 1900 Union Co., AR census, pg. 52a, El Dorado Township.

Children of HERBERT PENDLETON and JULIA MORRISON are:
- 838. i. JOHN S.[12] PENDLETON, b. Nov 1889, AR.
- 839. ii. JACK H. PENDLETON, b. Jan 12, 1891, AR; d. May 1973, Union Co., AR.
- iii. MAY ANNA PENDLETON, b. Nov 23, 1895, AR; d. Jul 1983, Pulaski Co., AR; m. WALTER SIMPSON; b. Abt. 1893, AR.
- 840. iv. AUGUSTUS GARLAND PENDLETON, b. Oct 26, 1897, AR; d. Dec 20, 1965, Union Co., AR.

        v.   FANNIE L. PENDLETON.
       vi.   WILLIE PENDLETON, b. Aft. 1900; d. infancy.
      vii.   ROBERT HENRY PENDLETON.
     viii.   ADELINE PENDLETON.
       ix.   LELA GRACE PENDLETON.
        x.   JOSEPH MORRIS PENDLETON.
       xi.   BOYAKIN PENDLETON.

606. LELIA A.[11] PENDLETON *(JAMES SHEPHERD[10], JAMES SHEPHERD[9], REUBEN[8], WILLIAM[7], JOHN[6], PHILIP[5], HENRY[4], HENRY[3], GEORGE[2], GEORGE[1])* was born Abt. 1854 in VA. She married GREENWOOD HOPKINS NOWLIN, son of PEYTON NOWLIN and SUSAN ATKINS. He was born Abt. 1845 in MO, and died Aft. 1910 in Lynchburg, VA?
        Green H. Nowlin and family are listed in the 1880 census, Lynchburg, VA, pg. 320D. Also listed are his mother-in-law, Lucy Pendleton and Lelia's siblings, Lucy S. and Charles D. Pendleton.

Children of LELIA PENDLETON and GREENWOOD NOWLIN are:
        i.   GREENWOOD H.[12] NOWLIN, JR., b. Abt. 1879, VA.
       ii.   RICHARD PEYTON NOWLIN, b. Abt. 1886, VA.
      iii.   ROBERT A. NOWLIN, b. Abt. 1889, VA.
       iv.   JAMES PENDLETON NOWLIN, b. Abt. 1895, VA.

607. LUCIE SHEPHERD[11] PENDLETON *(JAMES SHEPHERD[10], JAMES SHEPHERD[9], REUBEN[8], WILLIAM[7], JOHN[6], PHILIP[5], HENRY[4], HENRY[3], GEORGE[2], GEORGE[1])* was born Abt. 1864 in VA, and died Aft. 1920 in Lynchburg, VA? She married GREENWOOD HOPKINS NOWLIN, son of PEYTON NOWLIN and SUSAN ATKINS. He was born Abt. 1845 in MO, and died Aft. 1910 in Lynchburg, VA?
        Green H. Nowlin was first married to Lelia Pendleton, Lucie's older sister.

Child of LUCIE PENDLETON and GREENWOOD NOWLIN is:
        i.   CHARLES SHEPHERD[12] NOWLIN, b. Abt. 1908, VA.

608. ELIZABETH CHILES[11] PENDLETON *(EDMUND[10], MICAJAH[9], REUBEN[8], WILLIAM[7], JOHN[6], PHILIP[5], HENRY[4], HENRY[3], GEORGE[2], GEORGE[1])* was born Mar 08, 1849 in VA, and died Oct 16, 1929 in Rockbridge, VA? She married WALTER COLES, DR. Jun 19, 1872. He was born Feb 25, 1839, and died Jul 10, 1892.
        Elizabeth P. Coles and Elizabeth C. Marshall (daughter) are listed in the 1920 Rockbridge, VA census.

Child of ELIZABETH PENDLETON and WALTER COLES is:
        i.   ELIZABETH CARTER[12] COLES, b. Abt. 1879, MO; m. MARSHALL.

609. EPHRAIM MORGAN[11] PENDLETON *(EDMUND[10], MICAJAH[9], REUBEN[8], WILLIAM[7], JOHN[6], PHILIP[5], HENRY[4], HENRY[3], GEORGE[2], GEORGE[1])* was born Aug 25, 1857 in VA, and died Feb 16, 1919. He married LAURA RANDOLPH TUCKER

Nov 08, 1888, daughter of JOHN RANDOLPH TUCKER and LAURA POWELL. She was born 1860 in VA, and died Aft. 1920 in Washington DC?

A biographical sketch (Ref. 293) of E. Morgan Pendleton of Lexington, Rockbridge Co., VA is listed in the Virginia Historical Society Catalog.

Children of EPHRAIM PENDLETON and LAURA TUCKER are:
  i.   RANDOLPH TUCKER[12] PENDLETON, b. Aug 23, 1889, VA; d. Jan 1973, FL; m. CORNELIA MONTGOMERY CURTIS, b. Jul 08, 1897; d. Apr 1973, FL.
  ii. EDMUND RANDOLPH PENDLETON, b. Jan 01, 1892; d. Apr 21, 1893.
  iii. LAURA TUCKER PENDLETON, b. Mar 19, 1894; m. (1) FREDERICK WARD ROEGE, Oct 28, 1920; d. 1929; m. (2) RICHARD SETON MCCARTNEY, Oct 08, 1929.
  iv. EDWIN MORGAN PENDLETON, b. Mar 19, 1897, MD?; d. Jun 1975, Baltimore, MD.
  v.   GERTRUDE POWELL PENDLETON, b. Jun 02, 1899, VA; m. GEORGE EDGAR BRANDT, Jan 17, 1925; b. Abt. 1896, PA.

610. EDMUND[11] PENDLETON (*JAMES DUDLEY*[10], *MICAJAH*[9], *REUBEN*[8], *WILLIAM*[7], *JOHN*[6], *PHILIP*[5], *HENRY*[4], *HENRY*[3], *GEORGE*[2], *GEORGE*[1]) was born Nov 30, 1862 in VA, and died Jun 08, 1927 in Powhatan Co., VA? He married MARY BROOKES STEVENSON Jun 01, 1886. She was born Abt. 1869 in VA, and died Aft. 1920 in Powhatan Co., VA?

Children of EDMUND PENDLETON and MARY STEVENSON are:
  i.   JR. EDMUND[12] PENDLETON, b. Apr 02, 1887, VA; m. ANNA MAUPIN OWEN, Apr 26, 1930.
  ii. JAMES DUDLEY PENDLETON, b. Feb 19, 1890, VA; m. LOTTIE ALEXANDER, Jun 15, 1916.
  iii. BROOKES STEVENSON PENDLETON, b. Oct 15, 1891, VA; d. Jul 1974, Powhatan, VA.

       Brooks S. Pendleton (farmer) is listed in the Huguenot Dist., Powhatan Co., 1920 VA census, pg. 4A.

  iv. ROBERT STEVENSON PENDLETON, b. Jan 01, 1896, VA; d. Feb 03, 1960; m. MARGUERITE MARTIN, Dec 31, 1920; b. Sep 19, 1890; d. Jul 26, 1967.

       Robert Stevenson and Marquerite Pendleton are buried in Arlington National Cemetery.

  v.   EVELYN BYRD PENDLETON, b. Sep 01, 1898, VA; m. WILLIAM PALMER FERVEY, Oct 07, 1919.

611. MARY PEARL[11] PENDLETON (*WILLIAM F.*[10], *MICAJAH*[9], *REUBEN*[8], *WILLIAM*[7], *JOHN*[6], *PHILIP*[5], *HENRY*[4], *HENRY*[3], *GEORGE*[2], *GEORGE*[1]) was born Nov 1879 in VA, and died Aft. 1910 in Roanoke Co., VA? She married FRANCIS WILLIA

MICHAEL 1901. He was born Abt. 1875 in MD, and died Aft. 1910 in Roanoke Co., VA?

Child of MARY PENDLETON and FRANCIS MICHAEL is:
    i. FRANCIS P.[12] MICHAEL.

612. WILLIAM HARMON[11] PENDLETON *(WILLIAM F.[10], MICAJAH[9], REUBEN[8], WILLIAM[7], JOHN[6], PHILIP[5], HENRY[4], HENRY[3], GEORGE[2], GEORGE[1])* was born Oct 08, 1881 in VA, and died 1928 in Washington DC? He married CARRIE C. STANLEY 1905. She was born Abt. 1888 in VA, and died Aft. 1930 in Washington DC?
    William Harman Pendleton registered for the World War I draft in Roanoke, VA. William H. Pendleton (contract electrician) and family are listed in the 1920 Washington DC census.

Children of WILLIAM PENDLETON and CARRIE STANLEY are:
    i. MARY KENT[12] PENDLETON, b. 1906, VA; d. 1931; m. GANID POWER STANTON, 1928; b. Abt. 1905, DC.
    ii. MARGARET ELIZABETH PENDLETON.
    iii. CAROLINE PENDLETON.

613. EDMUND MICAJAH[11] PENDLETON *(WILLIAM F.[10], MICAJAH[9], REUBEN[8], WILLIAM[7], JOHN[6], PHILIP[5], HENRY[4], HENRY[3], GEORGE[2], GEORGE[1])* was born May 1883 in VA. He married ANNE CRAVEN. She was born Abt. 1891 in MA.
    Edmund (farmer) and Annie Pendleton are listed in the 1920 Little River, Floyd Co., VA census.

Child of EDMUND PENDLETON and ANNE CRAVEN is:
    i. ANNE[12] PENDLETON.

614. WILCHER LEWIS[11] PENDLETON *(ROBERT H.[10], JAMES[9], RICHARD[8], WILLIAM[7], JOHN[6], PHILIP[5], HENRY[4], HENRY[3], GEORGE[2], GEORGE[1])* was born Sep 09, 1847 in Wright City, MO, and died Nov 24, 1923 in Whittier, CA. He married (1) UNKNOWN Abt. 1875 in Warren Co., MO.   He married (2) ALICE HARVIL Oct 22, 1882 in Colorado City, TX. She was born Feb 19, 1860 in Arkansas, and died Sep 27, 1927 in Whittier, CA.

Child of WILCHER PENDLETON and UNKNOWN is:
    i. HERSCHEL[12] PENDLETON, b. Jul 17, 1876, Wright City, MO; d. Aft. 1920, Oklahoma City, OK?; m. OLA; b. Abt. 1897, TX.
        Herschel Pendleton registered for the World War I draft in Oklahoma City, OK. Herschel (retail merchant) and Ola Pendleton are listed in the 1920 Oklahoma City census.

Children of WILCHER PENDLETON and ALICE HARVIL are:
    ii. ROBERT MILTON[12] PENDLETON, b. Sep 17, 1883, Colorado City, TX; d. Oct 1978, Whittier, CA; m. ETTA M., Bef. 1918.

Robert M. Pendleton registered for the World War I draft in Oklahoma City, OK.

iii. GROVER CLEVELAND PENDLETON, b. Oct 30, 1885, Georgetown, TX; d. Nov 1965, Oklahoma City, OK; m. MARTHA, Bef. 1918.
Grover Cleveland Pendleton registered for the World War I draft in Oklahoma City, OK.

iv. ENOCH MARVIN PENDLETON, b. Jan 27, 1888, Hickory Hill, TX.
v. GEORGIE ALICE PENDLETON, b. Apr 17, 1890, Oklahoma City, OK.
vi. MARTHA JANE PENDLETON, b. Jul 11, 1892.
vii. JOHN ROLAND PENDLETON, b. Sep 19, 1894, Oklahoma City, OK.
viii. JAMES H. PENDLETON, b. Apr 15, 1897, Oklahoma City, OK; d. Nov 18, 1971.
James Pendleton registered for the World War I draft in Oklahoma City, OK.

ix. RUTH P. PENDLETON, b. Apr 11, 1899, Oklahoma City, OK.
x. NELLIE ETHEL PENDLETON.

615. CORNELIA[11] PENDLETON *(ROBERT H.[10], JAMES[9], RICHARD[8], WILLIAM[7], JOHN[6], PHILIP[5], HENRY[4], HENRY[3], GEORGE[2], GEORGE[1])* was born Dec 18, 1850 in MO. She married DUDLEY.
Cornelia Dudley (28) is listed in the 1880 census, Warren Co., MO along with her sons, H. T. Pendleton (3), and J. E. Harris (2).

Children of CORNELIA PENDLETON and DUDLEY are:
i. H. T. PENDLETON[12] DUDLEY, b. Abt. 1877.
ii. J. E. HARRIS DUDLEY, b. Abt. 1878.

616. LAFAYETTE[11] PENDLETON *(ROBERT H.[10], JAMES[9], RICHARD[8], WILLIAM[7], JOHN[6], PHILIP[5], HENRY[4], HENRY[3], GEORGE[2], GEORGE[1])* was born Apr 09, 1861 in MO, and died Aft. 1920 in Lincoln Co., MO? He married MARY ANN STORY May 02, 1883 in Lincoln Co., MO. She was born May 1866 in MO, and died Aft. 1920 in Lincoln Co., MO?
Lafayette Pendleton (physician) and family are listed in the 1900 Lincoln Co., MO census, pg. 202. Lafayette (doctor) and Mary A. Pendleton are listed in the 1920 Bedford, Lincoln Co., MO census.

Children of LAFAYETTE PENDLETON and MARY STORY are:
i. SON[12] PENDLETON, b. Dec 1885, MO; d. Nov 05, 1886, Lincoln Co., MO.
ii. NEVA PENDLETON, b. Aug 1887, MO.
iii. FAYETTE D. PENDLETON, b. Dec 18, 1895, MO; d. Aug 1976, Taney, MO.

617. JENNIE[11] PENDLETON *(JAMES LEWIS[10], JAMES[9], RICHARD[8], WILLIAM[7], JOHN[6], PHILIP[5], HENRY[4], HENRY[3], GEORGE[2], GEORGE[1])* was born Jul 1867 in IL. She married STEELE.

Children of JENNIE PENDLETON and STEELE are:
- i. JOHN J.[12] STEELE, b. May 1892, MO.
- ii. MAMIE M. STEELE, b. Nov 1895, MO.
- iii. GEORGIA E. STEELE, b. Apr 1898, MO.

618. ANDREW DAVIS[11] PENDLETON *(WILLIAM[10], WILLIAM[9], RICHARD[8], WILLIAM[7], JOHN[6], PHILIP[5], HENRY[4], HENRY[3], GEORGE[2], GEORGE[1])* was born Jan 1847 in MO, and died Aft. 1910 in Miller Co., MO? He married MARY ELLEN BILYEU Dec 08, 1867 in Miller Co., MO. She was born Abt. 1849, and died Bef. 1900 in Miller Co., MO?

Andrew Pendleton (farmer) and family are listed in the 1900 Miller Co., MO census, pg. 101a.

Children of ANDREW PENDLETON and MARY BILYEU are (Ref. 294):
- i. SARAH E.[12] PENDLETON, b. Abt. 1869, MO.
- ii. M. JACKSON PENDLETON, b. Abt. 1870, MO.
- iii. MARTHA J. PENDLETON, b. Abt. 1874, MO.
- iv. OWEN E. PENDLETON, b. Mar 1877, MO.

    Owen Pendleton (boarder; watchman) is listed in the Miller Co., MO census.

- v. HENRY A. PENDLETON, b. Jan 1880, Miller Co., MO.
- 841. vi. EVERETT S. PENDLETON, b. Nov 1882, MO; d. Aug 1966, St. Louis, MO.
- vii. IVA PENDLETON, b. Feb 1885, MO.
- viii. IDA PENDLETON, b. Feb 1885, MO.
- ix. ADOLPHUS PENDLETON, b. Apr 24, 1891, MO; d. Jul 06, 1953, St. Louis, MO.

    Adolph Pendleton (machinist; 28 and single) is listed in the 1920 St. Louis, MO census. Adolphus Pendleton is buried in Jefferson Barracks National Cemetery, St. Louis, MO.

- x. PERRY PENDLETON, b. Jun 1896, MO; d. Dec 03, 1930, Jefferson Co, AR.

619. OWEN R.[11] PENDLETON *(WILLIAM[10], WILLIAM[9], RICHARD[8], WILLIAM[7], JOHN[6], PHILIP[5], HENRY[4], HENRY[3], GEORGE[2], GEORGE[1])* was born Sep 1855 in MO. He married (1) JENNIE ATKINSON Dec 06, 1885 in Miller Co., MO. He married (2) MARY B. THOMPSON Dec 11, 1892 in Miller Co., MO. She was born Feb 1872 in MO.

Owen R. Pendleton, clerk, is listed in the Missouri State Gazetteer and Business Directory for 1881-82, Part S, St. Elizabeth. Owen (Elwen?) Pendleton (farmer) and family are listed in the 1900 Miller Co., MO census, pg. 101a.

Child of OWEN PENDLETON and JENNIE ATKINSON is:
  i. WILLIAM H.[12] PENDLETON, b. Sep 1885.

Children of OWEN PENDLETON and MARY THOMPSON are:
  ii. OLSY[12] PENDLETON, b. Sep 1895.
  iii. HOLMES PENDLETON, b. Nov 1898.

620. CHARLES WESLEY[11] PENDLETON *(WILLIAM[10], WILLIAM[9], RICHARD[8], WILLIAM[7], JOHN[6], PHILIP[5], HENRY[4], HENRY[3], GEORGE[2], GEORGE[1])* was born Feb 08, 1859 in Cole Co., MO, and died Mar 16, 1935 in Jefferson City, MO. He married SARAH EMALINE STRATTON Sep 01, 1880 in Miller Co., MO. She was born Oct 1862 in MO, and died Aug 15, 1939 in Miller Co., MO.
     Charles Pendleton (farmer) and family are listed in the 1900 Miller Co., MO census, pg. 101a.

Children of CHARLES PENDLETON and SARAH STRATTON are:
  i. STELLA MAE[12] PENDLETON, b. Sep 17, 1882, Miller Co., MO; d. Sep 22, 1969, Maries Co., MO; m. JOHN R. HICKS, 1898, MO; b. 1877; d. 1958.
  ii. MINNIE A. PENDLETON, b. Jul 1889, MO.
  iii. OLLIE M. PENDLETON, b. Jul 20, 1891, MO; d. Jan 04, 1972.
  iv. JOHN W. PENDLETON, b. Nov 1893, MO.
  v. RAY W. PENDLETON, b. Mar 1897, MO.
  vi. LUTHER E. PENDLETON, b. Apr 23, 1899, MO; d. Oct 1972, Abilene, TX.
  vii. OTIS LESLIE PENDLETON, b. Jan 20, 1902, Miller Co., MO; d. Mar 1968, Jefferson City, MO.

621. JOSEPH M.[11] PENDLETON *(WILLIAM[10], WILLIAM[9], RICHARD[8], WILLIAM[7], JOHN[6], PHILIP[5], HENRY[4], HENRY[3], GEORGE[2], GEORGE[1])* was born Nov 20, 1861 in Miller Co., MO. He married SARAH C. Abt. 1885. She was born Oct 1863 in MO.
     Joseph Pendleton (farmer) and family are listed in the 1900 Miller Co., MO census, pg. 101a.

Children of JOSEPH PENDLETON and SARAH C. are:
  i. EMMA H.[12] PENDLETON, b. Dec 1889.
  ii. WILLIAM E. PENDLETON, b. Sep 1892.
842. iii. CHARLES ARTHUR PENDLETON, b. Jan 27, 1896, MO.

622. JOHN E.[11] PENDLETON *(WILLIAM[10], WILLIAM[9], RICHARD[8], WILLIAM[7], JOHN[6], PHILIP[5], HENRY[4], HENRY[3], GEORGE[2], GEORGE[1])* was born Sep 1863 in MO, and died Aft. 1910 in Miller Co., MO? He married SALLIE T. Abt. 1892. She was born Mar 1868 in MO, and died Aft. 1910 in Miller Co., MO?

Child of JOHN PENDLETON and SALLIE T. is:
  i. ERNEST T.[12] PENDLETON, b. Dec 1897, MO.

623. THOMAS E.[11] PENDLETON *(WILLIAM[10], WILLIAM[9], RICHARD[8], WILLIAM[7], JOHN[6], PHILIP[5], HENRY[4], HENRY[3], GEORGE[2], GEORGE[1])* was born Jul 02, 1869 in MO, and died Aft. 1920 in Cole Co., MO? He married KATIE. She was born Abt. 1887 in MO.

Children of THOMAS PENDLETON and KATIE are:
- i.   MARTHA[12] PENDLETON.
- ii. MARY PENDLETON.
- iii. THOMAS PENDLETON.

624. WILLIAM HOOVER[11] PENDLETON *(ZACHARIAH[10], WILLIAM[9], RICHARD[8], WILLIAM[7], JOHN[6], PHILIP[5], HENRY[4], HENRY[3], GEORGE[2], GEORGE[1])* was born Oct 03, 1850 in MO, and died Jun 15, 1917 in Maries Co., MO? He married MARTHA "ANNA" MOSS Dec 26, 1875 in Maries Co., MO. She was born Feb 1859 in MO, and died Aft. 1910 in Maries Co., MO?

William Pendleton (farmer) and family are listed in the 1900 Maries Co., MO census, pg. 13.

Children of WILLIAM PENDLETON and MARTHA MOSS are:
- i.   JAMES I.[12] PENDLETON, b. Jan 1877, Maries Co., MO.
- ii. CHARLES A. PENDLETON, b. Aug 1879, Maries Co., MO.
- iii. SARAH JANE PENDLETON, b. Oct 1883, Maries Co., MO; m. OLIVER HELTON, Oct 20, 1901, Maries Co., MO.
- iv. LUCY A. PENDLETON, b. Apr 1886, Maries Co., MO; m. JAMES EVANS.
- v.   ULYSSES PENDLETON, b. Jan 21, 1894, Maries Co., MO; d. Aug 24, 1960, Maries Co., MO; m. NELLIE WEST, b. Abt. 1906, MO.

625. JAMES RICHARD[11] PENDLETON *(ZACHARIAH[10], WILLIAM[9], RICHARD[8], WILLIAM[7], JOHN[6], PHILIP[5], HENRY[4], HENRY[3], GEORGE[2], GEORGE[1])* was born Dec 24, 1854 in Osage Co., MO, and died Sep 14, 1903 in Cooper Co., MO. He married DICA M. BUCHANAN Apr 09, 1884 in Miller Co., MO.

James R. Pendleton is buried in Clayton Cemetery, Cooper County, MO (Ref. 295).

Children of JAMES PENDLETON and DICA BUCHANAN are:
- i.   OTIS J.[12] PENDLETON, b. Jul 04, 1885.
- ii. WILLIAM R. PENDLETON, b. Jul 12, 1888.
- iii. EFFIE PENDLETON, b. Mar 18, 1890.
- iv. BESSIE JANE PENDLETON, b. Apr 12, 1893.
- v.   BROOKSIE MAY PENDLETON, b. May 1895.
- vi. CORA EVELYN PENDLETON, b. Feb 20, 1897.
- vii. EXCE OPAL PENDLETON.

626. GEORGE PINCKNEY[11] PENDLETON *(ZACHARIAH[10], WILLIAM[9], RICHARD[8], WILLIAM[7], JOHN[6], PHILIP[5], HENRY[4], HENRY[3], GEORGE[2], GEORGE[1])* was born Aug 21, 1861 in Maries Co., MO, and died Bef. 1920 in Maries Co., MO? He married

RACHEL BARNHART Jan 03, 1880 in Maries Co., MO, daughter of JACKSON
BARNHART and MARTHA BABB. She was born Oct 03, 1858 in MO, and died Jul
22, 1934 in Maries Co., MO.

Children of GEORGE PENDLETON and RACHEL BARNHART are:
    i. ZACHARIAH W.[12] PENDLETON, b. Aug 1882, MO.
        Zachariah Pendleton is listed in the 1920 census, Callaway Co., MO,
        inmate - State Hospital.

    ii. JEFFERSON D. PENDLETON, b. Dec 01, 1886, MO; d. Nov 02, 1972,
        Maries Co., MO; m. (1) ANNA J. MACHON Abt. 1912, MO; b. Abt. 1893;
        d. 1920, Miller Co., MO; m. (2) PATSY Jul 05, 1926, Miller Co., MO; b. Jan
        1900, MO; d. Oct 22, 1982, Miller Co., MO.
        Anna J. Pendleton and her infant son are buried in Lawson Cemetery,
        Miller Co., MO (Ref. 296).

    iii. ANDY J. PENDLETON, b. Jan 1888, MO; m. MAGGIE GREEN, Abt.
        1904; b. Abt. 1887.
    iv. EDWARD PENDLETON, b. Oct 1890, MO.
    v. OSCAR PENDLETON, b. Aug 1892, MO.
    vi. ANTONE PENDLETON, b. Feb 15, 1895, MO; d. Apr 21, 1976.
    vii. AUSBY W. PENDLETON, b. Mar 1897, MO.

627. MARTHA ELIZABETH[11] PENDLETON (*ZACHARIAH[10], WILLIAM[9],
RICHARD[8], WILLIAM[7], JOHN[6], PHILIP[5], HENRY[4], HENRY[3], GEORGE[2], GEORGE[1]*)
was born Feb 07, 1863 in Maries Co., MO, and died Nov 27, 1939 in Jefferson City, MO.
She married WILLIAM HENDERSON WILLIAMS Jan 06, 1879 in MO. He was born
Abt. 1853 in MO, and died Aft. 1910 in Maries Co., MO?

Children of MARTHA PENDLETON and WILLIAM WILLIAMS are:
    i. JOSEPH[12] WILLIAMS, b. Abt. 1890, MO.
    ii. EDNA WILLIAMS, b. Abt. 1895, MO.
    iii. WILLARD WILLIAMS, b. Abt. 1897, MO.
    iv. MINNIE WILLIAMS.
    v. DOVE WILLIAMS.
    vi. DELLA WILLIAMS.

628. AZARIAH B.[11] PENDLETON (*GEORGE WASHINGTON[10], WILLIAM[9],
RICHARD[8], WILLIAM[7], JOHN[6], PHILIP[5], HENRY[4], HENRY[3], GEORGE[2], GEORGE[1]*)
was born May 07, 1850 in Meta, MO, and died Sep 14, 1888 in Maries Co., MO. He
married TENNESSEE M. BARNHART May 16, 1871 in Maries Co., MO, daughter of
HENRY BARNHART and JANE WILSON. She was born Aug 29, 1851 in TN, and
died May 11, 1941 in Maries Co., MO.
    Tennessee Pendleton and family are listed in the 1900 Miller Co., MO census, pg.
99.

Children of AZARIAH PENDLETON and TENNESSEE BARNHART are:

843.   i.   GEORGE H.[12] PENDLETON, b. Oct 26, 1872, Miller Co., MO; d. Feb 22, 1965, Jay, OK.

844.   ii.   CHARLES E. PENDLETON, b. Oct 25, 1874, MO; d. Jan 01, 1963, Iberia, MO.

845.   iii.   ROSETTA PENDLETON, b. Jan 01, 1876, MO; d. Aug 30, 1961, Maries Co., MO.

846.   iv.   WILLIAM D. PENDLETON, b. Dec 16, 1878, MO; d. Feb 01, 1949, Owensville, MO.

       v.   ROBERTA PENDLETON, b. Dec 26, 1880, MO; d. Apr 24, 1924, Maries Co., MO; m. PERRY HEALEY.

       vi.   VINASEY PENDLETON, b. Feb 15, 1881, MO; d. Oct 30, 1884, MO.

847.   vii.   CLEVELAND PENDLETON, b. Mar 09, 1885, MO; d. May 08, 1979, Iberia, MO.

       viii.   OLIVER W. PENDLETON, b. Mar 20, 1887, MO; d. Jan 19, 1950, Maries Co., MO; m. MAMIE CLAYTON; b. Abt. 1893, MO; d. Sep 02, 1939, Maries Co., MO.

629. WILLIAM E.[11] PENDLETON (*GEORGE WASHINGTON*[10], *WILLIAM*[9], *RICHARD*[8], *WILLIAM*[7], *JOHN*[6], *PHILIP*[5], *HENRY*[4], *HENRY*[3], *GEORGE*[2], *GEORGE*[1]) was born Feb 09, 1854 in Maries Co., MO, and died Dec 10, 1905 in Meta, MO. He married MARY C. STOKES May 05, 1881. She was born Aug 11, 1861 in Osage Co., MO, and died Jul 10, 1900 in Meta, MO.

    William Pendleton (farmer) and family are listed in the 1900 Maries Co., MO census, pg. 8a. The following eulogy for Mary C. Pendleton was penned by William Robands (re-written, 1964).

    It becomes my sad duty to once more chronicle the death of one of our dearly beloved, Mrs. Mary C. Pendleton, whose spirit having winged its flight to that Mansion above on the morning of July 10th, 1900, at her home in Maries County. Deceased, who was the daughter of Mr. and Mrs. W. P. Stokes, was born August 11, 1861 in Osage County, Missouri, and with her parents moved to Maries County where she resided until our heavenly Master called her to that goodly land. On May 5, 1881, she was united in marriage to William E. Pendleton, of which three children blessed their union, the first, Jessie F., a son, the second, Lilly C., having preceded her mother's spirit to that better land over the rolling Jordon of death. The third, Elsie Belle, a most beautiful and intelligent little girl 4 years of age...

Children of WILLIAM PENDLETON and MARY STOKES are:

       i.   JESSE FRANK[12] PENDLETON, b. Oct 15, 1882, Maries Co., MO; d. Dec 09, 1959, Jefferson City, MO; m. IVY CAROLINE HAWK, Oct 05, 1904, Miller Co., MO; b. Jun 05, 1886, Maries Co., MO; d. Dec 26, 1949, Jefferson City, MO.

       ii.   LILY C. PENDLETON, b. Dec 01, 1888, Meta, MO; d. Feb 28, 1889, Meta, MO.

       iii.   ELSIE BELLE PENDLETON, b. Mar 27, 1896, Maries Co., MO; d. Apr 21, 1998, Kansas City, MO; m. (1) EDWARD WILLIAMS; b. Abt. 1882, MO; d. Aft. 1930, Kansas City, MO?; m. (2) EVERETT HAWK Sep 01, 1912, Van

Cleve, MO; b. born May 07, 1889, Maries Co., MO; d. Jul 03, 1921, Van Cleve, MO.

630. ZACHARIAH[11] PENDLETON (*GEORGE WASHINGTON[10], WILLIAM[9], RICHARD[8], WILLIAM[7], JOHN[6], PHILIP[5], HENRY[4], HENRY[3], GEORGE[2], GEORGE[1]*) was born Jan 18, 1856 in Meta, MO, and died Sep 01, 1934 in Clinton, MO. He married (1) CATHERINE BURD Aug 26, 1877 in Osage Co., MO, daughter of DANIEL BURD and MARGARET LAWSON. She was born May 1855 in MO, and died Feb 01, 1908 in Maries Co., MO. He married (2) VIRGINIA FLORENCE MEREDITH Sep 07, 1909 in Clinton, MO. She was born Sep 16, 1876 in Henry Co., MO, and died May 28, 1961 in Chula Vista, CA.

Zach Pendleton (farmer) and family are listed in the 1900 Maries Co., MO census, pg. 8a.

Children of ZACHARIAH PENDLETON and CATHERINE BURD are:
848.   i.   MARY ARIZONA[12] PENDLETON, b. Jul 14, 1878, Van Cleve, MO; d. Nov 26, 1949, Osage Co., MO.
       ii. FIDELLA PENDLETON, b. Feb 20, 1881, Van Cleve, MO; d. Apr 17, 1927, Maries Co., MO; m. WILLIAM THEODORE GRAY, Oct 22, 1897; b. Aug 11, 1876, Miller Co., MO; d. Feb 07, 1959, Maries Co., MO.
     iii. HESTELLA PENDLETON, b. Feb 20, 1881, Van Cleve, MO; d. Sep 25, 1959, Van Cleve, MO; m. ADAM HARMON BARNHART, Nov 06, 1898, Miller Co., MO; b. Oct 01, 1877, Miller Co., MO; d. Sep 12, 1955, Van Cleve, MO.
     iv. OLLIE M. PENDLETON, b. May 1886.

Child of ZACHARIAH PENDLETON and VIRGINIA MEREDITH is:
      v. EMMA[12] PENDLETON.

631. JAMES HENRY[11] PENDLETON (*GEORGE WASHINGTON[10], WILLIAM[9], RICHARD[8], WILLIAM[7], JOHN[6], PHILIP[5], HENRY[4], HENRY[3], GEORGE[2], GEORGE[1]*) was born Oct 12, 1859 in Meta, MO, and died Dec 13, 1931 in Maries Co., MO. He married MARTHA ELIZABETH ROBERDS Jun 04, 1880 in Maries Co., MO. She was born Mar 22, 1862 in MO, and died Sep 09, 1948 in Maries Co., MO.

Henry Pendleton (farmer) and family are listed in the 1900 Maries Co., MO census, pg. 8a.

Children of JAMES PENDLETON and MARTHA ROBERDS are:
849.   i.   ANDREW J.[12] PENDLETON, b. Aug 1883, MO; d. Aft. 1920, Maries Co., MO?
      ii. BERTIE E. PENDLETON, b. Mar 1889, MO.
     iii. CLARABELLA PENDLETON, b. Apr 1892, MO; d. 1983, Maries Co., MO; m. CHARLES M. GREEN; b. 1887; d. 1942, Maries Co., MO.
     iv. CHARLES PENDLETON, b. Apr 1894, MO.
     v. NELLIE PENDLETON.

632. JOHN RILEY[11] PENDLETON *(GEORGE WASHINGTON[10], WILLIAM[9], RICHARD[8], WILLIAM[7], JOHN[6], PHILIP[5], HENRY[4], HENRY[3], GEORGE[2], GEORGE[1])* was born Jul 14, 1860 in Meta, MO, and died Aft. 1920 in Maries Co., MO? He married FANNIE WOODY Mar 09, 1882, daughter of JOHN WOODY and IRENA BURD. She was born Aug 11, 1862 in Osage Co., MO, and died Dec 30, 1937 in Maries Co., MO?

John R. Pendleton (farmer) and family are listed in the 1900 and 1920 Maries Co., MO census records.

Children of JOHN PENDLETON and FANNIE WOODY are:
- i. IDA BELL[12] PENDLETON, b. May 25, 1884, MO; d. Aug 30, 1949, Maries Co., MO; m. LEROY STOKES; b. Mar 18, 1882, Maries Co., MO; d. Jun 01, 1959, Maries Co., MO.
- ii. IRENE R. PENDLETON, b. Mar 25, 1888, MO; d. Sep 14, 1971, Pulaski Co., MO; m. (1) LAMON J. ADKINS, Apr 26, 1906, Maries Co., MO; b. Feb 23, 1884, Maries Co., MO; d. Sep 14, 1971, MO; m. (2) WILLIAM RAY COPELAND, Jun 1932.

633. SARAH E.[11] PENDLETON *(GEORGE WASHINGTON[10], WILLIAM[9], RICHARD[8], WILLIAM[7], JOHN[6], PHILIP[5], HENRY[4], HENRY[3], GEORGE[2], GEORGE[1])* was born May 23, 1862 in Meta, MO, and died Apr 01, 1929 in Meta, MO. She married ROBERT WITTEN BARNHART Dec 23, 1877, son of HENRY BARNHART and JANE WILSON. He was born Aug 14, 1857 in MO, and died May 26, 1933 in Maries Co., MO.

Children of SARAH PENDLETON and ROBERT BARNHART are:
- i. ROBERT P.[12] BARNHART, b. Aug 30, 1883, MO; d. Apr 1963, MO.
- ii. COSHI BARNHART, b. May 1885, MO.
- iii. MARY S. BARNHART, b. Mar 1887, MO.
- iv. BERTIE L. BARNHART, b. Apr 1889, MO.
- v. GEORGE H. BARNHART, b. Mar 29, 1894, MO; d. Dec 23, 1990.
- vi. PERCY BARNHART, b. May 1896, MO.
- vii. CLAUDE BARNHART, b. May 1898, MO.
- viii. MILLARD BARNHART, b. Abt. 1899, MO.

634. GEORGE W.[11] PENDLETON *(GEORGE WASHINGTON[10], WILLIAM[9], RICHARD[8], WILLIAM[7], JOHN[6], PHILIP[5], HENRY[4], HENRY[3], GEORGE[2], GEORGE[1])* was born Mar 25, 1864 in Meta, MO, and died Abt. 1937 in Meta, MO. He married NANCY LEONA BARNHART Oct 09, 1888 in Maries Co., MO, daughter of THOMAS BARNHART and JANE WEST. She was born Jul 28, 1867 in MO, and died Feb 23, 1939 in Meta, MO.

George W. Pendleton (farmer) and family are listed in the 1900 Maries Co., MO census, pg. 9a.

Children of GEORGE PENDLETON and NANCY BARNHART are:

i. MINA B.[12] PENDLETON, b. Feb 02, 1886, Meta, Maries Co., MO; d. Jul 1966, Long Beach, CA; m. HARMON BARNHART, Aft. 1900; b. Feb 1874, Osage Co., MO; d. 1952, Maries Co., MO.

ii. WILLIAM L. PENDLETON, b. Mar 1892, MO.

iii. RANEY PENDLETON, b. Jun 18, 1895, MO; d. May 1971, Jefferson City, MO.

635. CORDELIA[11] PENDLETON (*GEORGE WASHINGTON[10]*, *WILLIAM[9]*, *RICHARD[8]*, *WILLIAM[7]*, *JOHN[6]*, *PHILIP[5]*, *HENRY[4]*, *HENRY[3]*, *GEORGE[2]*, *GEORGE[1]*) was born Apr 03, 1868 in Meta, MO, and died Jun 15, 1944 in Maries Co., MO. She married GEORGE DAVIDSON BARNHART Jul 26, 1885 in Maries Co., MO, son of JACKSON BARNHART and MARTHA BABB. He was born Jul 24, 1864 in MO, and died Mar 24, 1939 in Maries Co., MO.

Children of CORDELIA PENDLETON and GEORGE BARNHART are:

i. EVA[12] BARNHART, b. Aug 06, 1885, MO.

ii. RILEY BARNHART, b. May 1888, MO.

iii. INFANT BARNHART, b. Feb 13, 1893, MO.

iv. ELLA L. BARNHART, b. Apr 1896, MO.

v. ARLA BARNHART, b. Mar 1898, MO.

vi. OLLIE BARNHART, b. Mar 1898, MO.

vii. ELIZA BARNHART.

viii. MARTHA BARNHART.

ix. WILLIAM BARNHART.

x. MARY BARNHART.

xi. CORDELIA BARNHART.

636. JAMES H.[11] PENDLETON (*JAMES RICHARD[10]*, *WILLIAM[9]*, *RICHARD[8]*, *WILLIAM[7]*, *JOHN[6]*, *PHILIP[5]*, *HENRY[4]*, *HENRY[3]*, *GEORGE[2]*, *GEORGE[1]*) was born Aug 15, 1855 in Osage Co., MO, and died Dec 15, 1944 in Boone Township, Meta Co., MO. He married MARGARET JANE WOODY Jan 16, 1879 in Maries Co., MO, daughter of JOHN HARGER WOODY and IRENA BURD. She was born Mar 09, 1860 in Boone Township, Meta Co., MO, and died Jan 23, 1905 in Van Cleve, Maries Co., MO.

The marriage of James H. Pendleton and Margaret J. Woody is recorded in Reference 177. James Pendleton (farmer) and family are listed in the 1900 Maries Co., MO census, pg. 12a.

Children of JAMES PENDLETON and MARGARET WOODY are:

i. JOHN FRANKLIN[12] PENDLETON, b. Dec 29, 1879, Osage Co., MO; d. Apr 16, 1913, Van Cleve, Maries Co., MO; m. (1) LILLIE LAWSON, 1900; b. Feb 23, 1880, MO; d. Apr 05, 1901, Maries Co., MO; m. (2) ORA ETTA SKELTON, Oct 29, 1903, Maries Co., MO; b. Jan 18, 1882, Warrick Co., IN.

Frank Pendleton (farmer) and first wife Lillie are listed in the 1900 Maries Co., MO census, pg. 12a.

    ii.   JAMES RICHARD PENDLETON, b. Aug 19, 1881, Boone Township, Meta Co., MO; d. Aug 03, 1907, Boone Township, Meta Co., MO.

   iii.   THOMAS J. PENDLETON, b. Oct 21, 1883, Boone Township, Meta Co., MO; d. Apr 02, 1908, Boone Township, Meta Co., MO.

850.   iv.   WARREN BURD PENDLETON, b. May 25, 1887, Van Cleve, Maries Co., MO; d. Mar 1972, Canon City, CO.

    v.   CLARA MAE PENDLETON, b. Mar 28, 1890, Van Cleve, Maries Co., MO; d. May 1974, Pueblo, CO; m. LOUIS EMORY, May 02, 1908, Pueblo, CO; b. Jan 1886; d. 1953.

   vi.   IDA FRANCES PENDLETON, b. Jun 09, 1892, Van Cleve, Maries Co., MO; d. Feb 1981, De Soto, MO; m. LEONARD WALGREN; b. Jul 1889, Osage Co., MO; d. Jun 1958, Grubville, MO.

   vii.   ARTHUR FREDERICK PENDLETON, b. Sep 10, 1894, Van Cleve, Maries Co., MO; d. May 1984, Rushville, IL; m. VIOLA MELVA FLAUGHER; b. May 01, 1899; d. Feb 23, 1993, Rushville, IL.

   viii.   AMELIA PENDLETON.

637. LAURA[11] PENDLETON *(JOHN EDWARD[10], RICHARD[9], JOHN[8], WILLIAM[7], JOHN[6], PHILIP[5], HENRY[4], HENRY[3], GEORGE[2], GEORGE[1])* was born Abt. 1856 in KY. She married HOWARD GRAY Oct 28, 1874 in Hartford, KY, son of CIMBSY GRAY. He was born Abt. 1851 in KY.

Children of LAURA PENDLETON and HOWARD GRAY are:
    i.   PENDLETON O.[12] GRAY, b. Abt. 1876, KY.
   ii.   MARY GRAY, b. Abt. 1878, KY.

638. MARY[11] PENDLETON *(JOHN EDWARD[10], RICHARD[9], JOHN[8], WILLIAM[7], JOHN[6], PHILIP[5], HENRY[4], HENRY[3], GEORGE[2], GEORGE[1])* was born Feb 13, 1858 in KY, and died Dec 19, 1919 in Ohio Co., KY. She married HARRISON PIRTLE TAYLOR 1884. He was born Jul 1857 in KY, and died Aft. 1900 in Ohio Co., KY?

Children of MARY PENDLETON and HARRISON TAYLOR are:
    i.   SARAH FIELD DAVIS[12] TAYLOR, b. Nov 24, 1885, Hartford, KY.
   ii.   JOHN P. TAYLOR, b. Oct 1887, KY.

639. EUGENE BANKS[11] PENDLETON *(JOHN EDWARD[10], RICHARD[9], JOHN[8], WILLIAM[7], JOHN[6], PHILIP[5], HENRY[4], HENRY[3], GEORGE[2], GEORGE[1])* was born Feb 1866 in KY, and died Apr 09, 1930 in Daviess Co., KY. He married LULA 1891. She was born Nov 1869 in KY, and died Bef. 1920.

    Eugene B. Pendleton (physician) and family are listed in the 1900 and 1920 Ohio Co., KY census records.

Children of EUGENE PENDLETON and LULA are:
    i.   WILLIAM TRIMBLE[12] PENDLETON, b. Jun 16, 1892, KY; d. May 15, 1975, Daviess Co., KY.

William Trimble Pendleton, farmer, registered for the WWI draft in Kuttawa, Lyon Co., KY. His dependents included a wife and child.

 ii. CATHERINE M. PENDLETON, b. Oct 1894, KY.
 iii. MARY LAURA PENDLETON, b. Jul 1897, KY.
 iv. JOHN E. PENDLETON, b. Sep 1899, KY.
 v. EMILY H. PENDLETON.
 vi. EUGENE BANKS PENDLETON, JR., b. Mar 15, 1917; d. Jun 14, 1999.
   Eugene Banks Pendleton, Jr. is buried in Arlington National Cemetery.

640. THOMAS R.[11] PENDLETON (*ALFRED*[10], *JAMES*[9], *JOHN*[8], *WILLIAM*[7], *JOHN*[6], *PHILIP*[5], *HENRY*[4], *HENRY*[3], *GEORGE*[2], *GEORGE*[1]) was born Jul 1865 in MO, and died 1932 in Kansas City, MO. He married DEBORAH ELIZABETH MCCORMICK, daughter of ORRIS MCCORMICK and ELIZABETH FURNISH. She was born Jul 12, 1863 in KY, and died Dec 11, 1945 in Jackson Co., MO.

Child of THOMAS PENDLETON and DEBORAH MCCORMICK is:
 i. ANNA L.[12] PENDLETON, b. Jul 1888.

641. CLAUDE L.[11] PENDLETON (*EBERLE*[10], *JAMES*[9], *JOHN*[8], *WILLIAM*[7], *JOHN*[6], *PHILIP*[5], *HENRY*[4], *HENRY*[3], *GEORGE*[2], *GEORGE*[1]) was born Aug 1869 in MO, and died Aft. 1920 in Jackson Co., MO? He married EVALINE MCCLAY 1899. She was born Jul 1880 in MO, and died Aft. 1920 in Jackson Co., MO?
 Claude Pendleton (Grocery Merchant) and family are listed in the 1920 Blue, Jackson Co., MO census.

Children of CLAUDE PENDLETON and EVALINE MCCLAY are:
 i. THOMAS[12] PENDLETON.
 ii. EVERETT PENDLETON.
 iii. ANNA PENDLETON.
 iv. RALPH PENDLETON, b. Jul 28, 1907, MO; d. Jul 1975, Cooper Co., MO.
 v. MARGARETTE PENDLETON.

642. WILLIAM M.[11] PENDLETON (*JOHN T.*[10], *BENJAMIN*[9], *HENRY*[8], *HENRY*[7], *JOHN*[6], *PHILIP*[5], *HENRY*[4], *HENRY*[3], *GEORGE*[2], *GEORGE*[1]) was born 1833 in VA, and died Aft. 1870 in Spotsylvania Co., VA? He married (1) ANNE ARNOLD. She was born Abt. 1837 in VA. He married (2) SARAH A. JONES. She was born 1827 in VA.
 William M. Pendleton, private, served with the Co. E 9th. Mercer Cavalry from Spotsylvania Co. He enlisted April 25, 1861 under Capt. Corbin Crutchfield and Capt. Robert Smith. William M. Pendleton (works on farm) and family are listed adjacent to the household of his father John T. Pendleton in the 1870 Cortland, Spotsylvania Co., VA census.

Children of WILLIAM PENDLETON and ANNE ARNOLD are:
 i. MARY C.[12] PENDLETON, b. Abt. 1859, Spotsylvania Co., VA.
 ii. ROSA L. PENDLETON, b. 1861.

643. JOHN HAMILTON[11] PENDLETON *(JOHN T.[10], BENJAMIN[9], HENRY[8], HENRY[7], JOHN[6], PHILIP[5], HENRY[4], HENRY[3], GEORGE[2], GEORGE[1])* was born 1838 in VA, and died Aft. 1920 in Spotsylvania Co., VA? He married FANNIE G. HAWKINS. She was born 1845 in VA, and died Aft. 1885.

John H. Pendleton (works on farm) and family are listed in the household of his father John T. Pendleton is in the 1870 Cortland, Spotsylvania Co., VA census. John H. Pendleton (71; farmer), Nannie B. (38; daughter), and Allie T. (25; son), are listed in the 1910 Spotsylvania Co., VA census.

Children of JOHN PENDLETON and FANNIE HAWKINS are:

    i.   JAMES T.[12] PENDLETON, b. Abt. 1868, VA.
    ii. EUSTACE B. PENDLETON, b. 1871.
    iii. NANNIE BELL PENDLETON, b. 1872, VA; d. Aft. 1920, Spotsylvania Co., VA?
    iv. ALEX T. PENDLETON, b. Abt. 1885, VA; d. Aft. 1920, Spotsylvania Co., VA?

644. LAWRENCE BATAILLE[11] PENDLETON *(JOHN T.[10], BENJAMIN[9], HENRY[8], HENRY[7], JOHN[6], PHILIP[5], HENRY[4], HENRY[3], GEORGE[2], GEORGE[1])* was born Aug 11, 1840 in Westmoreland, VA, and died Dec 1903 in Spotsylvania Co., VA. He married MAGGIE H. ALSOP Oct 24, 1867. She was born Dec 1845 in VA, and died Aug 27, 1918 in Spotsylvania Co., VA?

Lawrence Bataille Pendleton served in the VA 30th Infantry Company D as a Sgt., CSA. L.B. Pendleton (farmer) and family are listed in the 1870 Chancellor, Spotsylvania Co., VA census. Lawrence B. Pendleton is included in the index of Confederate Disability Applications and Receipts (Artificial Limbs): 1884, Fredericksburg, VA. He is included in the Confederate VA Pension Rolls, 1888, Spotsylvania Co., VA. L. B. Pendleton (farmer) and family are listed in the 1900 Spotsylvania Co., VA census, pg. 238a. A biographical sketch of L. B. Pendleton (Ref. 272) is listed in the Virginia Historical Society Catalog. Maggie L. Pendleton is listed in the VA Confederate Pension Rolls, 1902, Spotsylvania Co., VA.

Children of LAWRENCE PENDLETON and MAGGIE ALSOP are:

    i.   LUCY H.[12] PENDLETON, b. Abt. 1870, Spotsylvania Co., VA.
    ii. BEN PENDLETON, b. Abt. 1872, Spotsylvania Co., VA.
         A Benjamin F. Pendleton (gen'l merchandise) is listed in the 1910 Montgomery Co., MD census.

    iii. JOHN PENDLETON, b. Abt. 1873, Spotsylvania Co., VA.
851. iv. LAWRENCE BATAILLE PENDLETON, b. Jan 13, 1875, Spotsylvania Co., VA; d. Oct 20, 1959, Wash. DC?
    v. ARTHUR O. PENDLETON, b. Jan 25, 1877, Spotsylvania Co., VA; d. Aft. 1917, Wash. D.C.?
         Othniel Alsop Pendleton registered for the World War I draft in Washington, DC.

vi. MARTHA PENDLETON, b. Sep 1879, Spotsylvania Co., VA.

vii. GUY CHETWOOD PENDLETON, b. Aug 1881, VA.

852. viii. MARY ALSOP PENDLETON, b. Jul 1884, VA; d. Oct 1967, Fredericksburg, VA.

645. JOSEPH ALBERT[11] PENDLETON (*HUGH CLAIBORNE[10], HENRY[9], HENRY[8], HENRY[7], JOHN[6], PHILIP[5], HENRY[4], HENRY[3], GEORGE[2], GEORGE[1]*) was born May 30, 1851 in VA, and died Feb 15, 1933 in Spotsylvania Co., VA. He married MARTHA DAWSON CARNER Jan 17, 1876 in Spotsylvania Co., VA, daughter of ALLAN CARNER and ELIZABETH SPINDLE? She was born Feb 26, 1853 in Green Co., VA, and died Apr 15, 1930 in Spotsylvania Co., VA.

The marriage of Joseph A. Pendleton and Mattie D. Carner, both of Spotsylvania Co. was announced in the Petersburg, VA Daily on January 31, 1876. Mattie Pendleton (head; farmer) and family are listed in the 1900 Spotsylvania Co., VA census. Maxie and Edith are listed as teachers; Joseph Albert is absent.

Children of JOSEPH PENDLETON and MARTHA CARNER are:

i. MAXIE MARVIN[12] PENDLETON, b. Nov 1, 1876, VA; d. Jan 1943; m. JAMES AUSTIN, May 25, 1922.

Maxie M. Pendleton, Spotsylvania school teacher, is mentioned in a Fredericksburg newspaper, 18 Sep 1897.

853. ii. EDITH MAY PENDLETON, b. Abt. 1879, VA; d. Aft. 1910, Wichita, KS?

iii. CARRIE CRISMOND PENDLETON, b. Nov 14, 1883, VA; d. Mar 3, 1963; m. THOMAS SHADRACK GREER, Feb 22, 1911.

854. iv. FANNIE ELIZABETH PENDLETON, b. May 18, 1885, Alleghany Co., VA; d. 1974.

646. SALLIE A.[11] PENDLETON (*HUGH CLAIBORNE[10], HENRY[9], HENRY[8], HENRY[7], JOHN[6], PHILIP[5], HENRY[4], HENRY[3], GEORGE[2], GEORGE[1]*) was born Sep 20, 1853 in VA. She married WILLIAM E. WHITLOCK in Spotsylvania Co., VA? He was born Abt. 1850 in VA.

Children of SALLIE PENDLETON and WILLIAM WHITLOCK are:

i. A. M.[12] WHITLOCK, b. Abt. 1876.

ii. EDDIE WHITLOCK, b. Abt. 1879.

647. JAMES MONROE[11] PENDLETON (*HUGH CLAIBORNE[10], HENRY[9], HENRY[8], HENRY[7], JOHN[6], PHILIP[5], HENRY[4], HENRY[3], GEORGE[2], GEORGE[1]*) was born Dec 1861 in VA, and died Aft. 1900. He married ISABELLA PARK HOLLADAY Dec 29, 1881 in Spotsylvania Co., VA, daughter of TAVERNER HOLLADAY and SARAH B. WAITE. She was born Mar 11, 1858 in VA, and died Jul 12, 1913 in Spotsylvania Co., VA.

J.M. Pendleton (carpenter) and family are listed in the 1900 Orange Co., VA census, pg. 109a.

Children of JAMES PENDLETON and ISABELLA HOLLADAY are:

855.   i.   HARRY HOLLADAY[12] PENDLETON, b. Oct 8, 1883, VA; d. Feb 20, 1965.

     ii.   MAGGIE PENDLETON, b. Dec 17, 1884, VA; d. Jun 1885.

    iii.   MAGGIE PENDLETON, b. Jun 1886, VA; d. Oct 1886.

856.   iv.   NELLIE M. PENDLETON, b. Jul 1890, VA.

648. OSCAR L.[11] PENDLETON *(HUGH CLAIBORNE[10], HENRY[9], HENRY[8], HENRY[7], JOHN[6], PHILIP[5], HENRY[4], HENRY[3], GEORGE[2], GEORGE[1])* was born 1865 in VA. He married LILLIAN M. HOLLADAY Apr 26, 1888 in Spotsylvania Co., VA, daughter of TAVERNER HOLLADAY and HELEN YOUNG. She was born Abt. 1871 in VA, and died Aft. 1910 in Spotsylvania Co., VA?

Child of OSCAR PENDLETON and LILLIAN HOLLADAY is:

     i.   HUGH C.[12] PENDLETON, b. Aug 1889, VA.

         Hugh C. Pendleton (19, laborer, stepson) is listed in the household of his stepfather, James R. Evans and his mother, Lillie Evans, Helen B. Holladay, his grandmother, Ida J. Kenningham, his aunt, and his step brothers and sisters, in the 1910 Spotsylvania Co., VA census. He registered for the World War I draft in McDowell Co., WV.

649. FRANCES "FANNY"[11] PENDLETON *(JAMES MADISON[10], JOHN[9], HENRY[8], HENRY[7], JOHN[6], PHILIP[5], HENRY[4], HENRY[3], GEORGE[2], GEORGE[1])* was born 1843 in Warren Co., KY, and died 1925. She married LESLIE WAGGONER Jun 27, 1867. He was born Sep 11, 1841 in Todd Co., KY, and died Aug 19, 1896 in CO.

    Leslie Waggoner (Pres. College) and family are listed in the 1880 Logan Co., KY census, pg. 451B.

Children of FRANCES PENDLETON and LESLIE WAGGONER are:

     i.   KATIE[12] WAGGONER, b. Abt. 1868.

    ii.   LIZZIE WAGGONER, b. Abt. 1870.

   iii.   LILA BELLE WAGGONER, b. Abt. 1872.

   iv.   LESLIE WAGGONER, b. Abt. 1877.

    v.   FANNIE WAGGONER, b. Abt. 1879.

650. GARNETT[11] PENDLETON *(JAMES MADISON[10], JOHN[9], HENRY[8], HENRY[7], JOHN[6], PHILIP[5], HENRY[4], HENRY[3], GEORGE[2], GEORGE[1])* was born 1855 in KY, and died 1921 in Upland, PA? He married (1) HELENA WARD. He married (2) ANNA BLACK.

    Garnett Pendleton is listed in the 1910 Upland, PA census.

Child of GARNETT PENDLETON and HELENA WARD is:

     i.   EMMA[12] PENDLETON, b. Abt. 1890, PA.

651. JOHN THOMAS[11] PENDLETON *(WILLIAM HENRY[10], JOHN[9], HENRY[8], HENRY[7], JOHN[6], PHILIP[5], HENRY[4], HENRY[3], GEORGE[2], GEORGE[1])* was born Abt.

1845 in Christian Co., KY, and died Oct 5, 1922 in Atlanta, GA. He married ELLA JANE BOWIE. She was born Abt. 1844 in VA, and died Sep 17, 1922 in Fulton Co., GA.

John Thomas Pendleton entered the Southern Army at 16. He mustered into service on October 8, 1862, at Hopkinsville, Kentucky, by General Clarke and ordered to report to Colonel B.H. Helm at Bowling Green, Kentucky, November 1, 1862, and there put into First Kentucky Cavalry, C.S.A., Company H. He remained in the service until the war's end. After the war, he graduated from Washington and Lee College. J.T. Pendleton (lawyer) and family are listed in the 1880 Atlanta, GA census. John T. (lawyer) and Ella J. Pendleton are listed in the 1920 Atlanta, GA census. At some point in his career he was appointed Judge.

Children of JOHN PENDLETON and ELLA BOWIE are:
857.   i. MARY BELLE[12] PENDLETON, b. Abt. 1871, Atlanta, GA; d. Aft. 1920, DeKalb Co., GA?
       ii. KATE PENDLETON, b. Abt. 1874; m. CHARLES T. NUNNALLY.
          Mrs. Kate Pendleton Nunnally was a member of The National Society of the Daughters of the American Revolution (Volume 39, page 353).

652. PHILANDER BARCLAY[11] PENDLETON (*EDMUND WALLER*[10], *JOHN*[9], *HENRY*[8], *HENRY*[7], *JOHN*[6], *PHILIP*[5], *HENRY*[4], *HENRY*[3], *GEORGE*[2], *GEORGE*[1]) was born Jul 4, 1852 in Logan Co., KY, and died Aft. 1904 in Christian Co., KY? He married ELIZABETH C. LEAVELL May 31, 1881 in Christian Co., KY, daughter of HENRY LEAVELL and SALLIE CLARDY. She was born 1858 in Christian Co., KY, and died 1952 in Pembroke, Christian Co., KY.

An account of Philander Pendleton's life is included in an early history of Christian and Trigg Counties (Ref. 245).

Philander B. Pendleton was born July 4, 1852, in Logan County, Ky., and was reared in Christian County, Ky., his present residence. He is the son of Edward Waller Pendleton, who was born in Christian County, Ky., in 1822, and who died here in 1870. Subject's mother, Mrs. Anna E. (Barclay) Jameson, was born in 1829, and is still living, Subject attended the select schools of the country until his eighteenth year, and then attended college at Georgetown, Ky. In 1881 he was married to Miss Lizzie C,, daughter of Col. Henry C, and Mrs. Sallie A. (Clardy) Leavelle, of Christian County, Ky. They are both members of the Salem Baptist Church. Subject was reared a farmer (which is his present vocation), and he now owns 27'_' acres of valuable and very productive land; in a high state of cultivation. He is a member of the Grange, also of the Masonic fraternity, and in politics is connected with the Democratic party"

P. B. Pendleton was included in a list of sixty-five wheat growers of Christian County in 1904.

Children of PHILANDER PENDLETON and ELIZABETH LEAVELL are:
       i. HENRY LEAVELL[12] PENDLETON, b. Apr 9, 1885, Christian Co., KY.
       ii. WALLER GRAHAM PENDLETON, b. Sep 19, 1888, Christian Co., KY; d. Aug 28, 1955, Christian Co., KY; m. ELIZABETH MARTIN COVINGTON; b. Mar 13, 1903, KY; d. Dec 22, 1989, Christian Co., KY.

Walter G. Pendleton served in World War I enlisting in Christian Co., KY (Ref. 297).

   iii. FRANCES PENDLETON, b. Nov 1891, Richland, KY; m. J. J. RUCKER BRISTOW.

       Mrs. Frances Pendleton Bristow was a member of The National Society of the Daughters of the American Revolution (Volume 157, page 293).

   iv. JAMES MALCOLM PENDLETON, b. Feb 14, 1894, Christian Co., KY.

       James Malcolm Pendleton, farmer employed by P. B. Pendleton, registered for the WWI draft in Pembroke, Christian Co., KY.

   v. ELIZABETH PENDLETON, b. Oct 1895, Christian Co., KY.

653. LOOLYE B.[11] PENDLETON (*EDMUND WALLER*[10], *JOHN*[9], *HENRY*[8], *HENRY*[7], *JOHN*[6], *PHILIP*[5], *HENRY*[4], *HENRY*[3], *GEORGE*[2], *GEORGE*[1]) was born Abt. 1867 in Christian Co., KY, and died 1964 in Clarksville, TN. She married FRANK SUMMERFIELD BEAUMONT, son of FRANK BEAUMONT and LAURA CONRAD. He was born Mar 28, 1861 in KY, and died Nov 13, 1908 in Montgomery Co, TN.

     Mrs. Loolye Pendleton Beaumont was a member of The National Society of the Daughters of the American Revolution (Volume 55, page 312). Loolye Beaumont and family are listed in the 1910 Clarksville City, Montgomery Co., TN census. Information on the children of Frank and Loolye Beaumont is, in part, from.

Children of LOOLYE PENDLETON and FRANK BEAUMONT are (Ref. 298):
   i. ANNA[12] BEAUMONT, b. Abt. 1888, KY.
   ii. FRANK BEAUMONT, b. Abt. 1891, TN.
   iii. MARTHA BEAUMONT, b. Abt. 1894, TN.
   iv. PHIL PENDLETON BEAUMONT, b. Aug 24, 1895, TN.
       Phil Pendleton Beaumont registered for the World War I Draft in Montgomery Co., TN.

   v. CORSTIAN BEAUMONT.
   vi. SARAH BEAUMONT.

654. MARY FRANCES[11] PENDLETON (*CYRUS NEVILLE*[10], *JOHN*[9], *HENRY*[8], *HENRY*[7], *JOHN*[6], *PHILIP*[5], *HENRY*[4], *HENRY*[3], *GEORGE*[2], *GEORGE*[1]) was born May 26, 1863 in KY. She married WILLIAM CHADWICK OLMSTEAD. He was born in from Lockport, NY.

Children of MARY PENDLETON and WILLIAM OLMSTEAD are:
   i. KINGSLEY[12] OLMSTEAD.
   ii. FLORENCE OLMSTEAD.

655. NEVILLE[11] PENDLETON (*CYRUS NEVILLE*[10], *JOHN*[9], *HENRY*[8], *HENRY*[7], *JOHN*[6], *PHILIP*[5], *HENRY*[4], *HENRY*[3], *GEORGE*[2], *GEORGE*[1]) was born Jan 3, 1869 in

Christian Co., KY, and died 1949 in Albuquerque, NM. She married STEPHEN POWERS Feb 25, 1892 in Rockport, IN, son of JOSHUA POWERS and CLARA HAWES. He was born Sep 2, 1866 in Hancock Co., KY, and died Feb 25, 1944 in Coronado, CA.

Children of NEVILLE PENDLETON and STEPHEN POWERS are:
   i.   JOSHUA DEVERS[12] POWERS III, b. Feb 27, 1893, Nogul, NM; d. Nov 1966, Coronado, CA; m. LOIS ELIZABETH HIDDEN.
   ii. ROSALIE PIERCE POWERS, b. Oct 13, 1894, Las Vegas, NM; d. May 1969, Portales, NM; m. ROBERT EDWARD WHITE, Jun 6, 1923, Santa Rosa, NM.
   iii. MARY STEPHANIE POWERS, b. Jul 20, 1896, Las Vegas, NM; d. Oct 13, 1989, Albuquerque, NM.
   iv. ROBERT BOYD POWERS, b. Oct 3, 1900, Las Vegas, NM; d. Nov 19, 1976, Bethany, OK; m. MILDRED ADELANE IRWIN, Dec 5, 1928, Bakersfield, CA.
   v.   RUTH POWERS, b. Apr 1, 1903, Las Vegas, NM; d. Aug 30, 1993, Albuquerque, NM; m. JOSEPH FRANK TONDRE, Oct 10, 1921, Las Vegas, NM.
   vi. KATHERINE JULIET POWERS, b. Jun 7, 1906, Las Vegas, NM; d. Jan 1992, Valencia Co., NM; m. ELIGIO GALLEGOS, Mar 3, 1929, Isleta, NM.
   vii. MARTHA GARNET POWERS, b. Dec 18, 1909, NM; d. Oct 10, 1989, San Diego, CA; m. WILLIAMS.

656. JAMES MONTAGUE[11] PENDLETON (*CYRUS NEVILLE[10], JOHN[9], HENRY[8], HENRY[7], JOHN[6], PHILIP[5], HENRY[4], HENRY[3], GEORGE[2], GEORGE[1]*) was born Aug 24, 1880 in KY, and died Mar 10, 1942 in Daviess Co., KY. He married JANET L. REID. She was born Abt. 1890 in KY, and died Feb 25, 1980 in Daviess Co., KY.

James M. Pendleton is listed as editor of daily paper in the 1920 Owensboro census.

Children of JAMES PENDLETON and JANET REID are:
   i. ALLENE[12] PENDLETON.
   ii. JANET R. PENDLETON.

657. JOHN A.[11] PENDLETON (*CHESLEY THACKER[10], JOHN[9], JOHN[8], HENRY[7], JOHN[6], PHILIP[5], HENRY[4], HENRY[3], GEORGE[2], GEORGE[1]*) was born Oct 23, 1843 in Adair Co., KY, and died May 17, 1892 in Metcalfe Co., KY. He married SUSANNA CALEDONIA WOODWARD Oct 23, 1866 in Metcalfe Co., KY. She was born Oct 28, 1847 in Bridgeport, KY, and died Aft. 1880 in Metcalfe Co., KY?

John Pendleton's life was recounted in an early history of Kentucky (Ref. 123).

John A. Pendleton was born in Adair (now Metcalfe) County, October 23, 1843. His father, Chesley T., who is also a native of Kentucky, was born in Adair County, March 6, 1824, and is living at the age of nearly sixty-two years; he is hale and stout, and superintends his farming interests with vigor. He married Eliza J. Pulliam in 1842. She was a Virginian by birth, and died on the 6th of October, 1858, leaving six children, four of whom are yet living, John A. being the eldest, followed by James H., Elizabeth J. and Martha J. John Pendleton, the father of Chesley T., was a native of the Old Dominion, born in 1795; came to Kentucky in 1819; married Polly M. Estes in 1821. He was engaged in agricultural pursuits, and at his death in 1834 left a fine property which is inherited by his children. Polly (Estes) Pendleton was of English descent, and a daughter of Peter Estes, of Adair (now Metcalfe) County, Ky. John A. Pendleton received a good education in early life, and is possessed of fine business abilities. He remained on the home farm until his marriage with Susanna C. Woodward, on the 23rd of October, 1866, being the twenty-third anniversary of his birth. Since that time he has been engaged in agricultural pursuits in connection with the milling business, which he carries on to some extent. His farm of 420 acres is well improved and well kept, and yields good profits. Mr. Pendleton served four years, from 1878 to 1882, as tax assessor of Metcalfe County, in which office he gave general satisfaction, and was very popular with his constituents. In politics he is a Democrat, and takes an interest in the political issues of the day. He and wife are members of the Baptist Church. They are the parents of two daughters: Mary V. and Evalina, the latter deceased. Mr. Pendleton is a member of the Masonic fraternity, and is a Master Mason in Beech Grove Lodge, No. 399. His influence is extended to the temperance cause, and as a public-spirited citizen and man of strict business principles he does much for the improvement of the morals of the neighborhood in which he resides.

Children of JOHN PENDLETON and SUSANNA WOODWARD are:

858.   i.   MARY VALONIA^{12} PENDLETON, b. Sep 28, 1867, Metcalfe Co., KY.
      ii.   EVALINA PENDLETON, b. Aft. 1870, Metcalfe Co., KY; d. Bef. 1880, Metcalfe Co., KY.

658. MARY ANN^{11} PENDLETON *(CHESLEY THACKER^{10}, JOHN^9, JOHN^8, HENRY^7, JOHN^6, PHILIP^5, HENRY^4, HENRY^3, GEORGE^2, GEORGE^1)* was born 1845 in Adair Co., KY, and died 1877 in Metcalfe Co., KY. She married PLEASANT THOMAS ESTES 1865 in Metcalfe Co., KY, son of THOMAS ESTES and MARTHA EASTERS. He was born 1837 in KY, and died 1919 in Hart Co., KY.

Children of MARY PENDLETON and PLEASANT ESTES are:
      i.   ELIZIA^{12} ESTES, b. 1866, Metcalfe Co., KY.
      ii.   WILY MARTIAL ESTES, b. 1867, Metcalfe Co., KY.
      iii.   ALLEN HOSKINS ESTES, b. 1869, Metcalfe Co., KY; d. 1931.

659. JAMES H.^{11} PENDLETON *(CHESLEY THACKER^{10}, JOHN^9, JOHN^8, HENRY^7, JOHN^6, PHILIP^5, HENRY^4, HENRY^3, GEORGE^2, GEORGE^1)* was born Mar 1848 in Adair Co., KY, and died Apr 15, 1928 in Adair Co., KY. He married (1) ANNE E. BUCKNER Abt. 1872, daughter of WILLIAM BUCKNER and MARY EDWARDS. She was born Abt. 1853 in Green Co., KY, and died Aft. 1890 in Adair Co., KY? He married (2) LIZZIE E. Abt. 1892. She was born Apr 1862 in KY.

      James H. Pendleton, farmer, is listed in the 1900 Metcalfe Co., KY census, pg. 34, with his second wife and his father (Chesley T.).

Children of JAMES PENDLETON and ANNE BUCKNER are:
859.   i.   CHESLEY BUCKNER^{12} PENDLETON, b. Feb 1, 1873, KY; d. May 9, 1937, Hart Co., KY.

    ii.   MARY M. PENDLETON, b. Aug 23, 1875, Green Co., KY.

    iii.   ANNA B. PENDLETON, b. Abt. 1879, KY.

    iv.   CHARLES H. PENDLETON, b. Feb 1881, KY.

    v.   HETTIE E. PENDLETON, b. Nov 1882, KY.

    vi.   MYSTIE M. PENDLETON, b. Sep 1884, KY.

    vii.   ROSA L. PENDLETON, b. Dec 1887, KY.

    viii.   JOHN MILLER PENDLETON, b. May 10, 1891, KY.

           John Miller Pendleton registered for the WWI draft in Adair Co., KY.

660. MARY JANE[11] PENDLETON *(ABNER J.[10], JOHN[9], JOHN[8], HENRY[7], JOHN[6], PHILIP[5], HENRY[4], HENRY[3], GEORGE[2], GEORGE[1])* was born Nov 16, 1845 in Adair Co., KY, and died May 6, 1935 in Metcalfe Co., KY. She married JOHN W. NORRIS Jan 1, 1871 in Metcalfe Co., KY, son of JOSEPH NORRIS and MARY RANDLES. He was born 1849 in Barren Co., KY, and died Sep 9, 1916 in Metcalfe Co., KY.

Children of MARY PENDLETON and JOHN NORRIS are (Ref. 299):

    i.   SAMUEL T.[12] NORRIS, b. Oct 12, 1871, Metcalfe Co., KY.

    ii.   CALADONIA NORRIS, b. May 16, 1874, Metcalfe Co., KY.

    iii.   MARTHA A. NORRIS, b. May 26, 1876, Metcalfe Co., KY.

    iv.   LEE MURRELL NORRIS, b. 1878, Metcalfe Co., KY.

    v.   ABIGAIL M. NORRIS, b. 1880, Metcalfe Co., KY.

    vi.   SARAH NORRIS, b. 1882, Metcalfe Co., KY.

    vii.   GROVER NORRIS, b. 1884, Metcalfe Co., KY.

    viii.   ELIZABETH NORRIS, b. 1886, Metcalfe Co., KY.

    ix.   CHESLEY NORRIS, b. May 11, 1888, Metcalfe Co., KY; d. Feb 18, 1969, Green Co., KY.

    x.   HENRY WATERSON NORRIS, b. Nov 26, 1890, Metcalfe Co., KY.

661. ELIZABETH ELLEN[11] PENDLETON *(ABNER J.[10], JOHN[9], JOHN[8], HENRY[7], JOHN[6], PHILIP[5], HENRY[4], HENRY[3], GEORGE[2], GEORGE[1])* was born Jul 1, 1848 in Metcalfe Co., KY. She married ROBERT J. WILLIAMS Apr 15, 1868 in Metcalfe Co., KY. He was born Abt. 1835 in KY.

Children of ELIZABETH PENDLETON and ROBERT WILLIAMS are:

    i.   WILLIAM[12] WILLIAMS, b. Abt. 1865, KY.

    ii.   JAMES M. WILLIAMS, b. Abt. 1870, KY.

    iii.   ROSA B. WILLIAMS, b. Abt. 1873, KY.

    iv.   THOMAS K. WILLIAMS, b. Abt. 1877, KY.

662. ABNER J.[11] PENDLETON, JR. *(ABNER J.[10], JOHN[9], JOHN[8], HENRY[7], JOHN[6], PHILIP[5], HENRY[4], HENRY[3], GEORGE[2], GEORGE[1])* was born Jan 1, 1853 in Metcalfe Co., KY, and died Sep 27, 1904 in Metcalfe Co., KY. He married HENRIETTA CASSADY 1873 in Metcalfe Co., KY. She was born Abt. 1853 in KY, and died Jan 27, 1922 in Garrard Co., KY.

Children of ABNER PENDLETON and HENRIETTA CASSADY are:
860.   i.   CLARENCE[12] PENDLETON, b. 1873, Metcalfe Co., KY; d. Aft. 1920,
             Garrard Co., KY?
       ii.   VIRGIL PENDLETON, b. 1875, Metcalfe Co., KY.
      iii.   LENI PENDLETON, b. 1879, Metcalfe Co., KY.
       iv.   CALLIE PENDLETON, b. 1880, Metcalfe Co., KY.
        v.   IVY JANE PENDLETON, b. 1882.

663. KIZZIAH[11] PENDLETON *(ABNER J.[10], JOHN[9], JOHN[8], HENRY[7], JOHN[6],*
PHILIP[5], HENRY[4], HENRY[3], GEORGE[2], GEORGE[1]) was born Feb 10, 1855 in Metcalfe
Co., KY, and died Jan 8, 1934 in Metcalfe Co., KY. She married GEORGE W.
BLAYDES Apr 29, 1875 in Adair Co., KY. He was born Abt. 1844 in KY, and died Oct
14, 1887 in Metcalfe Co., KY.

Children of KIZZIAH PENDLETON and GEORGE BLAYDES are (Ref. 300):
        i.   WOOD ROWLET[12] BLAYDES, b. Oct 28, 1878, Metcalfe Co., KY.
       ii.   DOVER TITUS BLAYDES, b. Feb 28, 1881.
      iii.   ARTHUR THOMAS BLAYDES, b. Jan 18, 1884.

664. JOHN A.[11] PENDLETON *(ABNER J.[10], JOHN[9], JOHN[8], HENRY[7], JOHN[6],*
PHILIP[5], HENRY[4], HENRY[3], GEORGE[2], GEORGE[1]) was born Jun 1, 1857 in Metcalfe
Co., KY, and died Oct 30, 1944 in Garrard Co., KY. He married LOUISA ELIZABETH
BURRIS 1879 in Metcalfe Co., KY. She was born 1859 in KY, and died Nov 18, 1940
in Garrard Co., KY.

Child of JOHN PENDLETON and LOUISA BURRIS is:
861.   i.   JEFFERSON[12] PENDLETON, b. Feb 4, 1892, Adair Co., KY.

665. HIRAM[11] PENDLETON *(ABNER J.[10], JOHN[9], JOHN[8], HENRY[7], JOHN[6],*
PHILIP[5], HENRY[4], HENRY[3], GEORGE[2], GEORGE[1]) was born Nov 30, 1858 in Metcalfe
Co., KY, and died Dec 21, 1951 in Cincinnati, OH. He married LAURA SAVANNAH
"MOLLIE" YATES. She was born Apr 9, 1865, and died May 22, 1909 in Garrard Co.,
KY?

Children of HIRAM PENDLETON and LAURA YATES are (Ref. 74):
        i.   EDGAR[12] PENDLETON, b. Jan 27, 1882, Metcalfe Co., KY.
       ii.   LULUA PENDLETON, b. Oct 5, 1883, Metcalfe Co., KY; m. MOSE
             MILLER.
862.   iii.   ALLEN LEE PENDLETON, b. Oct 15, 1886, Metcalfe Co., KY; d. Sep 24,
             1972.
863.   iv.   GROVER CLEVELAND PENDLETON, b. Apr 23, 1889, Metcalfe Co., KY.
864.   v.   ELIZABETH "BESSIE" PENDLETON, b. Nov 30, 1890, Metcalfe Co., KY;
             d. Jul 31, 1972.
865.   vi.   RUFUS PENDLETON, b. Sep 30, 1892, Metcalfe Co., KY; d. Jun 2, 1972,
             LeRoy, IL.

866. vii. HENRIETTA "HATTIE MAE" PENDLETON, b. Sep 17, 1894, Metcalfe Co., KY; d. Oct 9, 1917, Deland, IL.

867. viii. CARL LESTER PENDLETON, b. Jul 10, 1896, IN; d. Dec 18, 1982, Lancaster, Garrard Co., KY.

   ix. GEORGE BECKHAM PENDLETON, b. May 28, 1898, Lancaster, Garrard Co., KY; d. Mar 27, 1974, Heyworth, IL; m. VIOLA MARIE BUCKLEY Dec 22, 1922; b. Feb 25, 1903, IL; d. Sep 19, 1999, Clinton, IL.

      George Pendleton (laborer: Texas pipe line) and family are listed in the 1930 McLean Co., Heyworth, IL census, pg. 9A.

   x. WILLIAM GOEBEL PENDLETON, b. Apr 20, 1900, Lancaster, Garrard Co., KY; d. May 27, 1985, Garrard Co., KY; m. JENNIE MAE HAMMACK; b. Feb 10, 1903; d. Jan 1984, Lancaster, Garrard Co., KY.

   xi. JAMES PENDLETON, b. Jan 20, 1903, Lancaster, Garrard Co., KY; d. Oct 1971, Cincinnati, OH; m. ETHEL ANDERSON; b. Feb 4, 1902; d. Jul 1987, Cincinnati, OH.

666. SARAH PORTER[11] PENDLETON *(ABNER J.[10], JOHN[9], JOHN[8], HENRY[7], JOHN[6], PHILIP[5], HENRY[4], HENRY[3], GEORGE[2], GEORGE[1])* was born Feb 10, 1862 in Metcalfe Co., KY, and died Dec 6, 1947 in Metcalfe Co., KY. She married DUARD BELMONT DOWELL Mar 29, 1885 in Metcalfe Co., KY, son of THOMAS DOWELL and SARAH ROSE. He was born Jul 10, 1859 in Green Co., KY, and died May 16, 1911 in Metcalfe Co., KY.

      D.B. Dowell (farmer) and family are listed in the 1910 Metcalfe Co., KY census.

Children of SARAH PENDLETON and DUARD DOWELL are:
   i. LINDSEY DUARD[12] DOWELL, b. Jan 10, 1886, Green Co., KY.
   ii. FRANK HENRY DOWELL, b. 1888, Green Co., KY.

667. THOMAS CHESLEY[11] PENDLETON *(ABNER J.[10], JOHN[9], JOHN[8], HENRY[7], JOHN[6], PHILIP[5], HENRY[4], HENRY[3], GEORGE[2], GEORGE[1])* was born Jun 9, 1865 in Metcalfe Co., KY, and died Oct 7, 1908 in Metcalfe Co., KY? He married HENNY ELENA BUCKNER Jul 9, 1888 in Metcalfe Co., KY, daughter of CHARLES BUCKNER and NARCISSA BLACKMAN. She was born Jan 1870 in KY, and died Dec 27, 1927 in Metcalfe Co., KY.

      Thomas C. Pendleton (farmer) and family are listed in the 1900 Metcalfe Co., KY census, pg. 33a.

Children of THOMAS PENDLETON and HENNY BUCKNER are:
868. i. LEE ALLEN[12] PENDLETON, b. Nov 24, 1889, Metcalfe Co., KY; d. Jun 17, 1981, Edmonson, KY.

869. ii. WILLIAM STEWART PENDLETON, b. Sep 3, 1891, Metcalfe Co., KY; d. Apr 1977, Edmonton, KY.

   iii. BERTHA PENDLETON, b. Sep 27, 1894, Metcalfe Co., KY; d. Oct 11, 1918; m. WALTER COFFEY, 1913, Metcalfe Co., KY.

iv. MARGARET PENDLETON, b. Aug 31, 1897, Metcalfe Co., KY; m. THURMAN RUSSELL, 1916, Taylor, KY.
v. NANCY PENDLETON.
vi. ANN MARY PENDLETON.

668. THEOPHILIS[11] PENDLETON *(JOHN HIRAM*[10]*, JOHN*[9]*, JOHN*[8]*, HENRY*[7]*, JOHN*[6]*, PHILIP*[5]*, HENRY*[4]*, HENRY*[3]*, GEORGE*[2]*, GEORGE*[1]) was born Abt. 1851 in Adair Co., KY, and died Apr 8, 1922 in Metcalfe Co., KY. He married SARAH V. PACE. She was born Abt. 1854 in KY, and died Feb 23, 1917 in Metcalfe Co., KY.

Thomas Pendleton (farmer) and family are listed in the 1880 and 1910 Metcalfe Co., KY census. Theophilis Pendleton (farmer) is listed in the 1920 Sulphur Well, Metcalfe Co. census, pg. 3A along with his daughter's family.

Children of THEOPHILIS PENDLETON and SARAH PACE are:
      i. JOHN F.[12] PENDLETON, b. Jun 18, 1874, Metcalfe Co., KY.
870.   ii. ANNE S. "PEARL" PENDLETON, b. Abt. 1882, KY; d. Aft. 1930, Metcalfe Co., KY?
      iii. LENORA PENDLETON, b. Abt. 1887.

669. SARAH FRANCES BECK[11] PENDLETON *(JOHN HIRAM*[10]*, JOHN*[9]*, JOHN*[8]*, HENRY*[7]*, JOHN*[6]*, PHILIP*[5]*, HENRY*[4]*, HENRY*[3]*, GEORGE*[2]*, GEORGE*[1]) was born Nov 1, 1859 in Adair Co., KY, and died Oct 18, 1946 in Adair Co., KY. She married CHRISTOPHER C. STEPHENS Sep 24, 1877 in Hickman Co., TN. He was born Abt. 1853 in KY.

Christopher Stephens and family are listed in the 1880 census, Metcalfe Co., KY, pg. 210A.

Children of SARAH PENDLETON and CHRISTOPHER STEPHENS are:
      i. MAUDAUNT T.[12] STEPHENS, b. Abt. 1879, KY.
      ii. CORA A. STEPHENS, b. 1880, KY.

670. MARY ELLEN[11] PENDLETON *(JOHN HAMILTON*[10]*, ROBERT YATES*[9]*, PHILIP*[8]*, HENRY*[7]*, JOHN*[6]*, PHILIP*[5]*, HENRY*[4]*, HENRY*[3]*, GEORGE*[2]*, GEORGE*[1]) was born Abt. 1848, and died 1875 in Christian Co., KY. She married HORACE PLUMMER RIVES Nov 1, 1867, son of HENRY RIVES and ELEANOR TILLETSON. He was born Jan 20, 1845 in Montgomery Co., TN, and died Aft. 1900 in Christian Co., KY?
A biography of Horace Rives is included in an early history of Christian and Trigg Counties (Ref. 245).

Horace P. Rives was born in Montgomery County, Tenn., on January 20, 1845, and is a son of Henry A. and Eleanor P. (Tillotson) Rives. The grandfather was Stephen Rives, and was born in Virginia; he moved to Tennessee in 1829, where he subsequently died. The father was born in Virginia in 1816, and came to Tennessee with his father; he is now living in Montgomery County, that State. The mother was born in Virginia; died in Montgomery County, Tenn., in 1882. To her were born the following children : Mildred E., W. M., Stephen E. and Horace P. (subject). Horace P. attended school in Kentucky, where to graduated and afterward followed surveying ; he is now quite an extensive farmer and tobacco-grower, and owns about 350 acres; he was married to Miss Mary E.

Pendleton. Two children blessed this union Willie and May. Mrs. Rives died in 1875, and Mr. Rives was next married to Miss Nannie A. Garrott, a daughter of Robert W. Garrott. To this union were born two children-Harry A. and Maggie. Mr. Rives is a Democrat.

Children of MARY PENDLETON and HORACE RIVES are:
     i.   WILLIE[12] RIVES.
    ii.   MAY RIVES.

671. ANNIE[11] PENDLETON *(JOHN HAMILTON[10], ROBERT YATES[9], PHILIP[8], HENRY[7], JOHN[6], PHILIP[5], HENRY[4], HENRY[3], GEORGE[2], GEORGE[1])* was born Abt. 1851 in KY. She married STEPHEN EDWARD RIVES in Christian Co., KY?, son of HENRY RIVES and ELEANOR TILLETSON. He was born 1843 in TN, and died 1926.

Children of ANNIE PENDLETON and STEPHEN RIVES are:
     i.   MAGGIE[12] RIVES, b. Abt. 1873, TN.
    ii.   EUNICE RIVES, b. Abt. 1875.
   iii.   HENRY RIVES, b. Abt. 1878.

672. ROBERT YATES[11] PENDLETON III *(ROBERT YATES[10], ROBERT YATES[9], PHILIP[8], HENRY[7], JOHN[6], PHILIP[5], HENRY[4], HENRY[3], GEORGE[2], GEORGE[1])* was born Mar 1866 in Christian Co., KY, and died Apr 8, 1952 in Christian Co., KY. He married ELIZABETH M. Abt. 1890. She was born Sep 1867 in KY, and died Oct 8, 1932 in Christian Co., KY.

   R.Y. Pendleton (farmer) and family are listed in the 1900 Christian Co., KY census, pg. 162a. R. Y. Pendleton was a deacon of the Pembroke Church, Christian Co., KY, as of 1930 (Ref. 146).

Child of ROBERT PENDLETON and ELIZABETH M. is:
     i.   HELEN S.[12] PENDLETON, b. Jul 1895, KY; m. THOMAS EASTMAN; b. Abt. 1893, KY.

673. JAMES R.[11] PENDLETON *(HARVEY B.[10], JOHN[9], CURTIS[8], HENRY[7], JOHN[6], PHILIP[5], HENRY[4], HENRY[3], GEORGE[2], GEORGE[1])* was born Nov 20, 1850 in Todd Co., KY, and died Oct 15, 1925 in Todd Co., KY. He married SARAH VIRGINIA WEBB Nov 10, 1874 in Todd Co., KY, daughter of NOFLETT WEBB and SALLIE MARSHALL. She was born Apr 1855 in KY, and died Apr 6, 1936 in Todd Co., KY.

   A biography of James Pendleton is included in an early history of Todd Co. (Ref. 139).

   James R. Pendleton has always retained his residence in Trenton, Todd County, Ky. His father, Harvey B. Pendleton, was born in 1811 and died about 1854; he was the son of John Pendleton. Subject's mother, Louisa M., daughter of George and Betsey Carnall, of Todd County, was born in 1831. To her and her husband, Harvey B., were born: Martha A. (deceased), James R. and Cenara (deceased). James R. in youth procured a good English education, and is a reader of good books and papers. He was married, November 10, 1874, to Miss Sarah V., daughter of Noflet and Sallie A. (Marshall) Webb, of Todd County, Ky., and to them were born: Marcellus E., August 5, 1875; Louisa E., October 7, 1876; Sallie A., June 8, 1878; Nancy C., November 10, 1879, and James E.,

January 18, 1882. Mr. Pendleton is a farmer owning 245 acres of first-class land in a fine state of cultivation and in good condition. He is a member of the I.O.O.F. also of the Christian Church, and is a Democrat.

James R. Pendleton (farmer) and family are listed in the 1900 Todd Co., KY census.

Children of JAMES PENDLETON and SARAH WEBB are:
-    i. MARCELLUS E.[12] PENDLETON, b. Aug 5, 1875, KY.
- 871. ii. LOUISA ELIZABETH PENDLETON, b. Oct 7, 1876, KY; d. Aft. 1930, Nashville, TN?
-   iii. SALLIE A. PENDLETON, b. Jun 8, 1878, KY.
-   iv. NANCY C. PENDLETON, b. Nov 10, 1879, KY.
-    v. JAMES E. PENDLETON, b. Jan 18, 1882, KY.

674. ISAAC THOMAS[11] PENDLETON *(RICE[10], THACKER[9], RICE[8], HENRY[7], JOHN[6], PHILIP[5], HENRY[4], HENRY[3], GEORGE[2], GEORGE[1])* was born 1849 in Clark Co., KY, and died Jun 12, 1923 in Fayette Co., KY. He married LUCY OLEATHA HOVERMALE Nov 13, 1870 in Bath Co., KY. She was born Feb 1855 in Bath County, KY, and died Dec 22, 1935 in Fayette Co., KY.

Children of ISAAC PENDLETON and LUCY HOVERMALE are (Ref. 301):
- 872.   i. MATTIE LEE[12] PENDLETON, b. Jan 2, 1872, KY; d. Mar 12, 1905.
- 873.   ii. JAMES RICE PENDLETON, b. Apr 19, 1875, Bath County, KY; d. Jan 27, 1947, Clark County, KY.
-   iii. DAISY PENDLETON, b. Apr 3, 1876, KY; d. Jul 30, 1950.
-   iv. THOMAS JEFFERSON PENDLETON, b. May 4, 1878, KY; d. Feb 18, 1947, Montgomery Co., KY; m. NANCY BELLE; b. Abt. 1878, KY.
  Thomas Jefferson Pendleton, residence Mt. Sterling and occupation Carpenter, registered for the WWI draft in Montgomery Co., KY. His Nearest Relative was listed as Nancy Belle Pendleton

-    v. HALLIE WOODFORD PENDLETON.
-   vi. PETE PENDLETON.
- vii. VIRGINIA PENDLETON.
- 874. viii. EDWARD SPEARS PENDLETON, b. Jun 6, 1891, Bourbon Co., KY; d. Dec 23, 1965, Paris, KY.
-   ix. ELIZABETH PENDLETON, b. Jan 4, 1894; d. Jun 16, 1949; m. GUYER.
-    x. LUCY MAY PENDLETON, b. Dec 18, 1899, KY; d. Dec 29, 1952, Cincinnati, OH.

675. THACKER V.[11] PENDLETON *(RICE[10], THACKER[9], RICE[8], HENRY[7], JOHN[6], PHILIP[5], HENRY[4], HENRY[3], GEORGE[2], GEORGE[1])* was born Dec 1, 1854 in Bath Co., KY, and died Oct 1, 1936 in Clark Co., KY. He married CLARISSA C. DONALON. She was born Nov 1857 in KY, and died Mar 12, 1935 in Clark Co., KY.

Thacker Pendleton is listed in the 1880 Clark Co. census, Blue Ball, Dist 3. Thacker (blacksmith) and family are listed in the 1910 Clark Co., KY census. Thacker (farmer), Clara, and Nancy G. Pendleton are listed in the 1920 Clark Co. census, pg. 4A, Wader Mill Township. Thacker V. Pendleton and his wife, Clarissa are buried in Winchester Cemetery, Winchester, KY.

Children of THACKER PENDLETON and CLARISSA DONALON are:
875.   i.   EDWARD LESLIE[12] PENDLETON, b. Nov 1878, Clark Co., KY; d. Apr 18, 1944, Fayette Co., KY.
        ii. FRANK PENDLETON, b. Mar 1885, Clark Co., KY.
       iii. GUS? PENDLETON, b. May 1888, Clark Co., KY.
       iv. STANLEY PENDLETON, b. Aug 1890, Clark Co., KY.
       v. MARGERIE PENDLETON, b. Aug 1894, Clark Co., KY.
      vi. NANCY G. PENDLETON, b. Feb 1897, Clark Co., KY.

676. JOHN RICE[11] PENDLETON *(RICE[10], THACKER[9], RICE[8], HENRY[7], JOHN[6], PHILIP[5], HENRY[4], HENRY[3], GEORGE[2], GEORGE[1])* was born Dec 1858 in Clark Co., KY, and died Jun 10, 1923 in Montgomery Co., KY. He married ELIZA. She was born Mar 1860 in OH, and died Feb 12, 1934 in Montgomery Co., KY.

John and Eliza are listed in the 1880 Clark Co. census, Blue Ball, Dist 3. The following news appeared in the Sentinel Democrat (Montgomery Co., KY) on 21 May 1880: "Camargo. John Pendleton bought, last Monday, of Mr. B. S. J. Tipton, 6 acres of land adjoining his lott for $200." John Pendleton and family are listed in the 1900 and 1910 census records, Clark Co., KY. He is buried at Wade Cemetery, Mt. Sterling, KY.

Children of JOHN PENDLETON and ELIZA are:
        i. GIRTA?[12] PENDLETON, b. 1880, Clark Co., KY.
876.   ii. JOHN RICE PENDLETON, b. Jan 1886, Clark Co., KY; d. Dec 11, 1915, Montgomery Co, KY.
       iii. ROY PENDLETON, b. Jul 1889, Clark Co., KY.
          A Roy Pendleton (32) born in KY is listed in the 1920 census, Fort Niagara, Youngstown, NY as a soldier (private).

877.   iv. ASAH PENDLETON, b. Mar 1893, Clark Co., KY; d. Sep 11, 1960, Montgomery Co., KY.
       v. RAY PENDLETON, b. Jan 1895, Clark Co., KY.
          A Ray Pendleton (age 24, waiter in restaurant) is listed in the 1920 Cincinnati, OH census with his family, Birdie (23), Robert (5), and Margarete (2 7/12), all born in KY.

677. THOMAS JEFFERSON[11] PENDLETON *(RICE[10], THACKER[9], RICE[8], HENRY[7], JOHN[6], PHILIP[5], HENRY[4], HENRY[3], GEORGE[2], GEORGE[1])* was born Dec 12, 1860 in Clark Co., KY, and died May 30, 1948 in Fayette Co., KY. He married MARY E. She was born Nov 13, 1860 in KY, and died Dec 3, 1895 in Clark Co., KY?

Thomas Pendleton is included in the 1880 Clark Co., KY census, Blue Ball, Dist 3. Thomas J. Pendleton (farmer) and family are listed in the 1900 Clark Co., KY census, pg. 206. Thomas J. Pendleton and wife, Mary E., are buried at the Wade Cemetery, Mt. Sterling, KY. The following is inscribed on the gravestone of Mary E. Pendleton: "Wife of T J Pendleton; Mother, thou art now at home, many angels fair above. But yet below thy child must roam, till summon'd by his love."

Children of THOMAS PENDLETON and MARY E. are:
    i.   MOLLIE[12] PENDLETON, b. Aug 1879.
    ii. ANNIE PENDLETON, b. Sep 1880.
    iii. JOHANNA PENDLETON, b. May 1886.
    iv. HENA PENDLETON, b. Apr 1888.
    v.   BESSIE PENDLETON, b. May 1890.
    vi. JOSIE PENDLETON, b. Mar 1892.

678. FRANKLIN P.[11] PENDLETON *(DAVID J.[10], RICE[9], RICE[8], HENRY[7], JOHN[6], PHILIP[5], HENRY[4], HENRY[3], GEORGE[2], GEORGE[1])* was born Nov 1852 in Clark Co., KY, and died 1946 in Clark Co., KY. He married HANNAH "ANNIE" BALDWIN. She was born May 1860 in KY, and died 1940 in KY.

Frank Pendleton is listed in the 1880 Clark Co. census, Winchester, Dist 6. Frank Pendleton (Hotel Proprietor) and family are listed in the 1900 Clark Co. census, KY, Winchester, City. Franklin P. Pendleton and his wife Hannah are buried in the Winchester Cemetery. His gravestone is inscribed with "God's finger touched him and he slept."

Children of FRANKLIN PENDLETON and HANNAH BALDWIN are:
    i.   EMMA S.[12] PENDLETON, b. 1880, KY.
    ii. MARY PENDLETON, b. Apr 1883, KY.
    iii. CHARLIE PENDLETON, b. Sep 1885, KY.
    iv. ELLA PENDLETON, b. Aug 1888, KY.
    v.   FRANCES PENDLETON, b. Nov 1894, KY.

679. JAMES WILLIAM[11] PENDLETON *(MARTIN J.[10], PRESLEY[9], RICE[8], HENRY[7], JOHN[6], PHILIP[5], HENRY[4], HENRY[3], GEORGE[2], GEORGE[1])* was born Aug 8, 1855 in Ralls Co., MO, and died Sep 7, 1897 in Shannon Co., MO. He married MARY ELLEN GOWINS Abt. 1883, daughter of JOHN GOWINS and MARTHA STONE. She was born Aug 18, 1858 in Green Co., IL, and died Dec 26, 1940 in Hereford, MO.

Children of JAMES PENDLETON and MARY GOWINS are:
878.   i.   WILLIAM ARTIE[12] PENDLETON, b. Aug 28, 1890, Centralia, MO; d. May 19, 1962, Neodesha, KS.
        ii. ANNIE MAY PENDLETON, b. Abt. 1895, MO; m. JACK WHEELER; b. Abt. 1897, MO.

680. ROBERT L.[11] PENDLETON *(MARTIN J.[10], PRESLEY[9], RICE[8], HENRY[7], JOHN[6], PHILIP[5], HENRY[4], HENRY[3], GEORGE[2], GEORGE[1])* was born May 1868 in MO. He married ALMIRA F. She was born Apr 1865 in MO.

Robert L. Pendleton (farmer) and family are listed in the 1900 Monroe Co., MO census, pg. 90.

Child of ROBERT PENDLETON and ALMIRA F. is:
    i.   CANDIS? L.[12] PENDLETON, b. Apr 1893.

681. DAVID ELMER[11] PENDLETON *(DAVID J.[10], PRESLEY[9], RICE[8], HENRY[7], JOHN[6], PHILIP[5], HENRY[4], HENRY[3], GEORGE[2], GEORGE[1])* was born Feb 2, 1880 in Butteville, OR, and died May 19, 1925 in Marion Co., OR. He married (1) IDA S. She was born Abt. 1884 in OR. He married (2) MARGARET Aft. 1920. She was born Abt. 1898 in WA.

    David E. Pendleton (farmer) and family are listed in the 1910 Marion Co., OR census adjacent to his brother Martin E. David Elmer Pendleton, occupation butcher, registered for the WWI draft in Marion Co., OR. His nearest relative is listed as Ida S. Pendleton. His disabilities were listed as "Infected with Rheumatism."

Children of DAVID PENDLETON and IDA S. are:
    i.   ALICE L.[12] PENDLETON.
    ii.   ELDON DAVID PENDLETON, b. Jan 15, 1909, OR; d. Jun 30, 1969, Umatilla Co., OR.
          Eldon Pendleton is buried in Willamette National Cemetery, OR.

682. GEORGE ALVIN[11] PENDLETON *(DAVID J.[10], PRESLEY[9], RICE[8], HENRY[7], JOHN[6], PHILIP[5], HENRY[4], HENRY[3], GEORGE[2], GEORGE[1])* was born Aug 8, 1882 in Butteville, OR, and died Feb 8, 1924 in Broadacres, OR. He married MAUDE LENA ALLEN Jan 22, 1906 in Marion Co., OR, daughter of GEORGE ALLEN and KATIE HESS. She was born Apr 14, 1887 in Grey Eagle, MN, and died Aug 1, 1972 in Woodburn, OR.

    George Alvin Pendleton, farmer, registered for the WWI draft in Marion Co., OR. George A. Pendleton (farmer) and family are listed in the 1920 census, Marion Co., OR, pg. 3B.

Children of GEORGE PENDLETON and MAUDE ALLEN are:
    i.   FAY ELENOR[12] PENDLETON.
    ii.   ALVIN EDWIN PENDLETON, b. Dec 19, 1910, Hubbard, OR; d. Sep 14, 1939, Newberg, OR.
    iii. EDNA MARGARET PENDLETON, b. Nov 3, 1912, Hubbard, OR; d. Mar 1982, Woodburn, Marion Co., OR; m. JOHN PAUL CAMERON JONES; b. Jan 30, 1909, Clintonville, WI; d. Mar 1981, Woodburn, Marion Co., OR.

683. CHARLES PORTER[11] PENDLETON *(WILLIAM RICE[10], PRESLEY[9], RICE[8], HENRY[7], JOHN[6], PHILIP[5], HENRY[4], HENRY[3], GEORGE[2], GEORGE[1])* was born Oct 5, 1865 in Ralls Co., MO, and died Jul 17, 1936 in Ralls Co., MO. He married HANNAH LOUISA GREEVES Mar 30, 1891 in Ralls Co., MO. She was born Sep 22, 1865 in Ralls Co., MO, and died Sep 14, 1930 in Ralls Co., MO.

    Charles P. Pendleton (farmer) and family are listed in the 1900 Ralls Co., MO census, pg. 240a.

Children of CHARLES PENDLETON and HANNAH GREEVES are:

879.   i.   CORNELIA ANN[12] PENDLETON, b. Jan 9, 1892, Ralls Co., MO; d. Aft. 1930, Ralls Co., MO.
        ii.   HARRY CURTIS PENDLETON, b. Dec 7, 1893, MO; d. Oct 2, 1897, MO.
        iii. WILLIAM RUSSELL PENDLETON, b. Aug 30, 1898, MO; d. Jul 4, 1957, Green Mountain Falls, CO; m. (1) LOUELLA INEZ VARNER; b. 1900; m. (2) VIRGINIA JANE GILTNER.
        iv.   MARY L. PENDLETON, b. Jul 18, 1900, MO; d. May 5, 1989, Enid, OK; m. RONALD EDWARD WILLCOXON; b. Jul 14, 1901, MO; d. Jan 13, 1969, New Bloomfield, MO.
        v.   ALICE C. PENDLETON.

684. FRANCES A.[11] PENDLETON *(BERRYMAN H.[10], PRESTON[9], RICE[8], HENRY[7], JOHN[6], PHILIP[5], HENRY[4], HENRY[3], GEORGE[2], GEORGE[1])* was born Abt. 1857 in IL, and died Aft. 1882. She married CHARLES M. CONNER. He was born Abt. 1855 in IN.

        Charles M. Conner (farmer) and family are listed in the 1880 De Witt Co., IL census.

Child of FRANCES PENDLETON and CHARLES CONNER is:
        i.   ADA[12] CONNER, b. Abt. 1879, IL.

685. JOHN M.[11] PENDLETON *(EDMUND[10], PRESTON[9], RICE[8], HENRY[7], JOHN[6], PHILIP[5], HENRY[4], HENRY[3], GEORGE[2], GEORGE[1])* was born Abt. 1872 in IL, and died Aft. 1920 in Jackson Co., MO. He married CLARA S. Abt. 1907. She was born Abt. 1876 in KS, and died Aft. 1920 in Jackson Co., MO.

Children of JOHN PENDLETON and CLARA S. are:
        i.   MARELLA ELIZABETH[12] PENDLETON.
        ii.   RICHARD PENDLETON.
        iii. MARGARETTE PENDLETON.

686. OSCAR GERMAIN[11] PENDLETON *(JOHN S.[10], PRESTON[9], RICE[8], HENRY[7], JOHN[6], PHILIP[5], HENRY[4], HENRY[3], GEORGE[2], GEORGE[1])* was born Jul 10, 1881 in Lincoln, Logan Co., IL, and died Aug 15, 1963 in Morgan Co., IL. He married ALICE MAY WHITE Sep 28, 1905. She was born Apr 30, 1887 in Macon Co., IL, and died Mar 11, 1970 in Dewitt Co., IL.

        Oscar Jermane (sic) Pendleton (worked as a brakeman on the railroad) registered for the World War I draft in Decatur, Macon Co., IL.

Children of OSCAR PENDLETON and ALICE WHITE are:
        i.   FLORENCE[12] PENDLETON, b. Aug 27, 1906, Dewitt Co., IL; d. Apr 9, 2003, St. Peters, MO; m. FRED TILINSKI, May 23, 1931; b. Dec 5, 1908; d. Aug 1968.

ii. MILDRED PENDLETON, b. Aug 25, 1908, IL; d. Oct 6, 1999, Mcallen, TX; m. KEITH RHEA, DR., Dec 23, 1931, Springfield, IL; b. Aug 14, 1910; d. Dec 11, 1997, Mcallen, TX.

iii. MERCEDES LAMAR PENDLETON, b. Oct 9, 1910, Macon Co., IL; d. Jul 23, 1996, Decatur Co., IL; m. GERHARD KEYL, Apr 3, 1932, Moultrie Co., IL.

687. FLORENCE BELLE[11] PENDLETON *(JOHN S.[10], PRESTON[9], RICE[8], HENRY[7], JOHN[6], PHILIP[5], HENRY[4], HENRY[3], GEORGE[2], GEORGE[1])* was born Aug 24, 1885 in Lincoln, Logan Co., IL, and died Jan 9, 1944 in Lincoln, Logan Co., IL. She married GEORGE CLARENCE JOHNSTON Aug 30, 1910 in Lincoln, Logan Co., IL, son of JOHN JOHNSTON and ALICE HOFFMAN. He was born Feb 1, 1889 in Lincoln, Logan Co., IL, and died Jul 9, 1964 in Tazwell Co., IL.

Child of FLORENCE PENDLETON and GEORGE JOHNSTON is:
   i. HAROLD STANLEY[12] JOHNSTON.

688. DAVID EDWARD[11] PENDLETON *(MICHAEL[10], CHAMPNEY[9], RICE[8], HENRY[7], JOHN[6], PHILIP[5], HENRY[4], HENRY[3], GEORGE[2], GEORGE[1])* was born Feb 14, 1878 in OR, and died May 19, 1925 in Marion Co., OR. He married ANNA K. Abt. 1898. She was born Jun 1880 in MI, and died Apr 9, 1929 in Clackamas Co., OR.

David Edward Pendleton (owns farm) registered for the WWI draft in Clackamas Co., OR. His nearest relative is listed as Anna Pendleton.

Children of DAVID PENDLETON and ANNA K. are:
   i. HERBERT ELMER[12] PENDLETON, b. Jan 6, 1900, Canby, OR; d. Apr 24, 1964, OR; m. ELIZABETH FRANCES JONES, Oct 12, 1946, Salem, OR; b. Jul 15, 1911.
      Herbert Pendleton is buried in Willamette National Cemetery, OR.

   ii. CLYDE D. PENDLETON.
   iii. EDITH D. PENDLETON.
   iv. DORSEY E. PENDLETON.

689. JOHN WESLEY[11] PENDLETON *(TILFORD[10], THRASHLEY[9], RICE[8], HENRY[7], JOHN[6], PHILIP[5], HENRY[4], HENRY[3], GEORGE[2], GEORGE[1])* was born Oct 28, 1885 in Bath Co., KY, and died Jan 21, 1956 in Middletown, OH. He married WILLA DELL CARR Feb 22, 1906 in Bath Co., KY, daughter of CHARLES CARR and LOU GOAD. She was born Jan 24, 1890 in Morgan Co., KY, and died Feb 5, 1984 in Middletown, OH.

John W. Pendleton is listed as a farmer in the 1906 marriage bond of Feb 16, 1906, Bath Co., KY: "to be married at bride's home on the 21st Feb. 1906." C.L. Carr and Tilford Pendleton signed the bond. The John Pendleton family removed to Ohio from Bath Co., KY about 1913. John Wesley Pendleton, fireman, registered for the draft on Sep 12, 1918 in Middletown, Butler Co., OH. His employer was Wrenn Paper Co., 4th St., Middletown. His nearest relative is listed as Willa D. Pendleton (wife). The following description of John Pendleton was included: height, medium; build, medium; color of eyes, brown; color of hair, brown; physical [disabilities], none. In the 1920 Bath Co., KY census, pg. 4B, Lena, Milford and Wilbur Pendleton (John Wesley's children) are listed in the Tilford Pendleton (farmer) household. John Pendleton worked at Wrens Paper Mill, Middletown, OH until the day he retired; the same day he died.

Children of JOHN PENDLETON and WILLA CARR are:
    i. HELENA BERNICE[12] PENDLETON, b. Feb 18, 1907, Breathitt Co., KY; d. Mar 3, 1999, Middletown, OH; m. JOHN WILLIAM MILLER Abt. 1930, b. Jun 25, 1904, PA, d. Sep 3, 1985, Middletown, OH.
    ii. DOLORES "DO" MARENE PENDLETON, b. Apr 1, 1909, KY; d. Sep 7, 1999, Orlando, FL; m. GLENN M. MEARS Apr 8, 1929, Newport, KY; b. Nov 30, 1910; d. Jan 27, 1993, Elkhart, IN.
    iii. MILDRED RUTH PENDLETON, b. Jul 10, 1910, KY; d. Jul 15, 1984, Middletown, OH; m. ROBERT HARRY MARKERT Jul 10, 1934, IN, son of HARRY MARKERT and BLANCH NIXON; b. Aug 14, 1913, Middletown, OH; d. Oct 7, 1997 in Middletown, OH.
    iv. MILFORD LYMAN PENDLETON.
    v. JOHN WILBUR PENDLETON, b. Apr 3, 1915, Middletown, OH; d. Apr 29, 2005, Corona, CA.

690. JESSE[11] PENDLETON *(TILFORD[10], THRASHLEY[9], RICE[8], HENRY[7], JOHN[6], PHILIP[5], HENRY[4], HENRY[3], GEORGE[2], GEORGE[1])* was born Jul 1, 1887 in Salt Lick, KY, and died Sep 18, 1967 in Mt Sterling, KY. He married (1) ADA B. ADAMS Dec 26, 1907 in KY, daughter of H.D. "JOHN" ADAMS. She was born Abt. 1893 in KY, and died Apr 2, 1946 in Bath Co., KY. He married (2) FLORENCE WELLS Aft. 1946. She was born Abt. 1902 in KY, and died Jun 15, 1981 in Montgomery Co., KY.

    Jesse Pendleton (self employed, farm) registered for the WWI draft on June 5, 1917 in Sharpsburg, Bath Co., KY. He is described as tall, medium build, brown eyes, and black hair. He spent much of his life as a tenant farmer near or along Flat Creek, Bath Co., KY. Jesse Pendleton and his wife Ada are buried in Crown Hill Cemetery, Bath Co., KY.

Children of JESSE PENDLETON and ADA ADAMS are:
    i. FESTUS RAY[12] PENDLETON, b. Jan 25, 1909, Bath Co., KY; d. Dec 2, 1973, Mt. Sterling, KY; m. INA FARRIS MAZE Feb 23, 1929; b. May 28, 1912; d. Jul 4, 1995, Sharpsburg, KY.
    ii. HENRY CLAY PENDLETON, b. May 10, 1911, Bath Co., KY; d. May 23, 1980, Mt Sterling, KY; m. FRANCES FOLEY Apr 20, 1934; b. Abt. 1915; d. Nov 12, 1999, Montgomery Co., KY.
    iii. WARREN CECIL PENDLETON, b. May 31, 1913, Bath Co., KY; d. Nov 10, 1972, Louisville, KY.
    iv. ROWENNA MAE PENDLETON, b. Mar 1, 1916, Bath Co., KY; d. Dec 15, 1978, Montgomery Co., KY; m. HAROLD N. SORRELL; b. May 30, 1913 in KY; d. Oct 1966, Paris, KY.

691. CHARLES A.[11] PENDLETON *(TILFORD[10], THRASHLEY[9], RICE[8], HENRY[7], JOHN[6], PHILIP[5], HENRY[4], HENRY[3], GEORGE[2], GEORGE[1])* was born Jun 17, 1893 in Bath Co., KY, and died Sep 3, 1977 in Mt Sterling, KY. He married WINNIE MAE SPENCER Jul 9, 1916 in Menifee Co., KY, daughter of J. EDMOND SPENCER and OLLIE BENSON. She was born Jul 22, 1899 in KY, and died Nov 26, 1981 in Montgomery Co., KY.

Charles Pendleton (self employed, farm) registered for the WWI draft in Sharpsburg, Bath Co., KY. He is described as tall, medium build, blue eyes, and brown hair.

Child of CHARLES PENDLETON and WINNIE SPENCER is:
     i.   ALMA IRENE[12] PENDLETON.

692. ROBERT JAMES[11] PENDLETON, JR. *(ROBERT JAMES[10], ROBERT[9], ROBERT[8], HENRY[7], JOHN[6], PHILIP[5], HENRY[4], HENRY[3], GEORGE[2], GEORGE[1])* was born Apr 21, 1895 in VA, and died Feb 1966 in Bumpass, VA. He married ANNIE RUTH PAYNE. She was born Abt. 1892 in VA, and died Aft. 1930 in Spotsylvania Co., VA?

Robert James Pendleton registered for the World War I draft in Spotsylvania Co., VA.

Child of ROBERT PENDLETON and ANNIE PAYNE are:
     i.   ROBERT JAMES[12] PENDLETON III.

692. ELIZABETH CATHERINE[11] PENDLETON *(JOSEPH HOLMES[10], BENJAMIN[9], PHILIP[8], BENJAMIN[7], PHILIP[6], PHILIP[5], HENRY[4], HENRY[3], GEORGE[2], GEORGE[1])* was born Sep 11, 1837 in VA, and died Aft. 1880 in Calhoun Co., AL? She married CHARLES TALLIAFERRO HILTON in Oxford, Calhoun Co., AL. He was born Abt. 1834 in TN, and died Aft. 1900 in Calhoun Co., AL?

Charles Hilton and family, including Sarah Pendleton his mother-in-law and Susan H. Pendleton his sister-in-law, are listed in the 1880 census, Calhoun Co., AL, pg. 702A.

Children of ELIZABETH PENDLETON and CHARLES HILTON are:
     i.   ROLAND[12] HILTON, b. Abt. 1871, AL.
     ii.   CHARLES HILTON, b. Abt. 1874, AL.
     iii.   MARY PENDLETON HILTON, b. Abt. 1878, AL.

693. HENRY CLAY[11] PENDLETON *(JOSEPH HOLMES[10], BENJAMIN[9], PHILIP[8], BENJAMIN[7], PHILIP[6], PHILIP[5], HENRY[4], HENRY[3], GEORGE[2], GEORGE[1])* was born Mar 29, 1842 in VA, and died Feb 06, 1931 in DeKalb Co., GA. He married NANCY ELIZABETH ROBINSON Apr 08, 1869, daughter of JOHN ROBINSON and POLLIE LAVENDAR. She was born Aug 13, 1845 in GA, and died Mar 10, 1927 in DeKalb Co., GA.

Henry C. Pendleton is the author of "The Death of Colonel Dahlgren" (Ref. 302).

Children of HENRY PENDLETON and NANCY ROBINSON are:

    i. WALTER HOLMES[12] PENDLETON, b. Jun 04, 1870, GA; d. Aug 28, 1870, Rome, GA.

    ii. EUGENE ROBINSON PENDLETON, b. Nov 14, 1871, GA.

        Eugene Pendleton (single; clergyman) is listed in the 1900 Fayette Co., GA census, pg. 236. Eugene R. Pendleton is the author of Reference 4.

    iii. HENRY CLAY PENDLETON, b. Dec 06, 1873, GA; d. Marin Co., CA?

        This may be the Henry Pendleton (mgr. publishing company) in the 1900 Marin Co., CA census, pg. 207.

880.   iv. LOUIS BAYLOR PENDLETON, b. Nov 19, 1875, GA; d. May 1964, MO.

    v. RICHARD HUNDLEY PENDLETON, b. Oct 26, 1877, GA; d. Jan 1963, NY.

        Richard Hunley Pendleton registered for the World War I draft in Augusta, Richmond Co., GA.

    vi. NELLIE ISABELLE PENDLETON, b. Aug 12, 1879, Atlanta, GA; d. Aft. 1920, DeKalb Co., GA?; m. JAMES BLEDSOE ARMSTRONG; b. Abt. 1874, GA; d. Aft. 1920, DeKalb Co., GA?

        Mrs. Nellie Pendleton Armstrong was a member of The National Society of the Daughters of the American Revolution (Volume 107, page 238). James B. and Nellie Armstrong are listed in the 1920 DeKalb Co., GA census.

    vii. WILLIAM ALBERT PENDLETON, b. Oct 03, 1881; d. Oct 25, 1959, DeKalb Co., GA; m. ETHEL L.; b. Oct 12, 1886; d. Apr 27, 1984, Forsyth Co., GA.

        The following is inscribed on the tombstone of William Pendleton in the Clarkston Town Cemetery Dekalb Co. Georgia: "Albert's Life Has Been Like A Good Watch; Open Face, Busy Hands, Pure Gold, Well Regulated, And Full Of Good Works."

    viii. VIRGINIA FAY PENDLETON, b. Dec 22, 1883.

    ix. ETHEL LENOIR PENDLETON, b. Oct 12, 1886.

    x. ROY LAVENDER PENDLETON, b. Mar 10, 1890; d. Mar 31, 1961, DeKalb Co., GA.

694. LOUIS BAYLOR[11] PENDLETON (*JOSEPH HOLMES[10]*, *BENJAMIN[9]*, *PHILIP[8]*, *BENJAMIN[7]*, *PHILIP[6]*, *PHILIP[5]*, *HENRY[4]*, *HENRY[3]*, *GEORGE[2]*, *GEORGE[1]*) He married UNKNOWN.

Children of LOUIS PENDLETON and UNKNOWN are:

    i. NANCY AMELIA[12] PENDLETON.

    ii. ELEANOR PENDLETON.

695. RICHARD[11] PENDLETON *(JOSEPH HOLMES[10], BENJAMIN[9], PHILIP[8], BENJAMIN[7], PHILIP[6], PHILIP[5], HENRY[4], HENRY[3], GEORGE[2], GEORGE[1])* He married UNKNOWN.

Children of RICHARD PENDLETON and UNKNOWN are:
- i. RICHARD[12] PENDLETON.
- ii. JOHN PENDLETON.
- iii. HENRY PENDLETON.
- iv. THOMAS PENDLETON.

696. GEORGE BAYLOR[11] PENDLETON *(PHILIP BAYLOR[10], PHILIP BAYLOR[9], PHILIP[8], BENJAMIN[7], PHILIP[6], PHILIP[5], HENRY[4], HENRY[3], GEORGE[2], GEORGE[1])* was born Sep 19, 1853 in VA, and died Sep 16, 1904 in King & Queen Co., VA? He married (1) MISS WOODY. He married (2) RUTH L. COURTNEY Abt. 1886. She was born Apr 1860 in VA, and died Aft. 1920 in King & Queen Co., VA?

George Pendleton (farmer) and family are listed in the 1900 King and Queen Co., VA census, pg. 256a. Ruth Pendleton is listed in the 1920 Stevensville, King and Queen Co., VA census.

Children of GEORGE PENDLETON and RUTH COURTNEY are:
- i. PHILIP CAMPBELL[12] PENDLETON, b. Mar 1887, VA.
- ii. JULIA A. PENDLETON, b. Oct 1888, VA.
- iii. ELIZABETH PENDLETON, b. Apr 1892, VA.
- iv. MATTIE E. PENDLETON, b. Jun 1898, VA.
- v. GEORGE PENDLETON.

697. III PHILIP BAYLOR[11] PENDLETON *(PHILIP BAYLOR[10], PHILIP BAYLOR[9], PHILIP[8], BENJAMIN[7], PHILIP[6], PHILIP[5], HENRY[4], HENRY[3], GEORGE[2], GEORGE[1])* was born Apr 20, 1858 in King & Queen Co., VA, and died Nov 26, 1926 in Richmond, VA. He married NEENAH BUTLER May 06, 1880. She was born Abt. 1858 in VA, and died Aft. 1920 in Richmond, VA?

Philip B Pendleton, mattress maker, is included in the Richmond, Virginia City Directories, 1889-90. Philip Pendleton (laborer, lumber) and family are listed in the 1920 Richmond, VA census, pg. 24B.

Children of PHILIP PENDLETON and NEENAH BUTLER are:
- i. ANN LAMB[12] PENDLETON, b. Dec 02, 1880, VA; d. Aft. 1920, Richmond, VA?; m. ELI AUGUST MINER, Oct 06, 1914; b. 1878, VA; d. Aft. 1920, Richmond, VA?
- ii. VIRGINIA BUTLER PENDLETON, b. Nov 13, 1888, VA; d. Nov 16, 1888.
- 881. iii. IV PHILIP BAYLOR PENDLETON, b. Jul 22, 1891, VA; d. Richmond, VA?
- iv. OSCAR RAY PENDLETON, b. Oct 03, 1895, VA; d. Mar 11, 1898.
- v. HUNTER ASHBY PENDLETON, b. Oct 17, 1897, VA; d. Jan 1978, Richmond, VA; m. SARAH IRVING SHINO Dec 09, 1922; b. Aug 22, 1897; d. Dec 1969, Richmond, VA.

Hunter A Pendleton was a Captain in the Virginia National Guard (Ref. 303).

    vi.   ELSIE LOUISE PENDLETON.

698. CORA ALBINA[11] PENDLETON *(WILLIAM HENRY[10], GEORGE MACON[9], PHILIP[8], BENJAMIN[7], PHILIP[6], PHILIP[5], HENRY[4], HENRY[3], GEORGE[2], GEORGE[1])* was born 1845 in Union Co., AR, and died Dec 11, 1903 in Bakersfield, CA. She married HARRIS ANDERSON SLEDGE Abt. 1866 in AR. He was born 1840 in AR, and died Dec 07, 1903 in Bakersfield, CA.

Children of CORA PENDLETON and HARRIS SLEDGE are (Ref. 304):
    i.   NETTIE[12] SLEDGE, b. Abt. 1869, Downey, CA.
    ii.   ADA SLEDGE, b. Abt. 1873; d. Sep 1903; m. J. E. MEYERS.
    iii.   HENRY SLEDGE, b. Abt. 1874; m. KATE MCNEIL, Abt. 1902, San Diego, CA.

699. WILLIAM HENRY[11] PENDLETON *(WILLIAM HENRY[10], GEORGE MACON[9], PHILIP[8], BENJAMIN[7], PHILIP[6], PHILIP[5], HENRY[4], HENRY[3], GEORGE[2], GEORGE[1])* was born Aug 31, 1846 in Union Co., Arkansas, and died Jan 03, 1917 in Downey, CA. He married SARAH CORNELIA REYNOLDS Nov 09, 1865 in Union Co., Arkansas. She was born Aug 1848 in Perry Co., AL, and died Feb 01, 1912 in Downey, CA.

    William Pendleton (preacher) and family are listed in the 1900 Los Angeles Co., CA census, pg. 22.

Children of WILLIAM PENDLETON and SARAH REYNOLDS are:
    i.   EUGENE REYNOLDS[12] PENDLETON, b. Sep 02, 1866, Union Co., AR; d. Mar 22, 1870, Downey, CA.
    ii.   MARY SULA PENDLETON, b. Sep 22, 1868, Union Co., AR; d. May 04, 1870, Downey, CA.
    iii.   WILLIAM FRANKLIN PENDLETON, b. Jul 01, 1870, Downey, CA; d. Jul 09, 1936, Downey, CA; m. LULA L., Abt. 1898; b. Oct 1866, IL; d. Aft. 1920.
        William F. Pendleton (milker) and wife are listed in the 1900 Downey, Los Angeles Co., Ca census, pg. 109a.

882.   iv.   JENNIE ALVINA PENDLETON, b. Aug 14, 1871, Downey, CA; d. Jun 02, 1929, Long Beach, CA.
883.   v.   GEORGE RANEY PENDLETON, b. May 14, 1873, Downey, CA; d. Jan 03, 1917, Tulare Co., CA.
       vi.   HENRY LEE PENDLETON, b. Dec 13, 1874.
884.   vii.   JESSE CASWELL PENDLETON, b. Apr 05, 1876, Downey, CA; d. Dec 29, 1940, Venice, CA.
      viii.   THEODORE LOUIE PENDLETON, b. Jan 13, 1878, CA; d. Mar 29, 1932, Downey, CA; m. ESTELLA M.; b. Abt. 1883.

      ix. SUDIE ELLA PENDLETON, b. Nov 17, 1879, Downey, CA; d. Apr 13, 1881, Downey, CA.

      x. MINNIE MAY PENDLETON, b. Jul 29, 1881, Downey, CA; d. Nov 10, 1956, Burbank, CA.

      xi. ERNEST PENDLETON, b. Nov 17, 1883, Downey, CA; d. Mar 02, 1945, Van Nuys, CA.

885. xii. EARL PENDLETON, b. Sep 01, 1885, Downey, CA; d. Aft. 1930, Glendale, CA?

      xiii. HOMER HERMAN PENDLETON, b. Nov 25, 1888, Downey, CA; d. Sep 25, 1908, Downey, CA.

700. ADA COURTNEY[11] PENDLETON *(WILLIAM HENRY[10], GEORGE MACON[9], PHILIP[8], BENJAMIN[7], PHILIP[6], PHILIP[5], HENRY[4], HENRY[3], GEORGE[2], GEORGE[1])* was born Sep 08, 1849 in Union Co. Arkansas, and died Mar 14, 1930 in Downey, CA. She married (1) COCHRAN Abt. 1871 in CA. He was born Abt. 1845. She married (2) SMITH.

    T.P. Cochran (farmer) and Ada Smith (mother) are listed in the 1920 Downey, CA census.

Children of ADA PENDLETON and COCHRAN are:

      i. EMMET[12] COCHRAN, b. Abt. 1872.

      ii. THOMAS P. COCHRAN, b. Abt. 1874, CA; d. Aft. 1920, Downey, CA?

Child of ADA PENDLETON and SMITH is:

      iii. THOMAS[12] SMITH, b. Abt. 1875, CA.

701. ALEXIS THEODORE[11] PENDLETON *(WILLIAM HENRY[10], GEORGE MACON[9], PHILIP[8], BENJAMIN[7], PHILIP[6], PHILIP[5], HENRY[4], HENRY[3], GEORGE[2], GEORGE[1])* was born Mar 24, 1851 in AR, and died Mar 24, 1928 in Placentia, Orange Co., CA. He married SARA J. Abt. 1885. She was born Mar 1857 in PA, and died Aft. 1910 in Placentia, Orange Co., CA?

    Alexis Pendleton (farmer) and family are listed in the 1900 Orange Co., CA census, pg. 48a.

Children of ALEXIS PENDLETON and SARA J. are:

      i. BESSIE[12] PENDLETON, b. May 1887, CA.

      ii. JOSIE J. PENDLETON, b. Aug 1888, CA.

      iii. LLOYD A. PENDLETON, b. Oct 1891, CA.

702. GEORGE WALTER[11] PENDLETON *(WILLIAM HENRY[10], GEORGE MACON[9], PHILIP[8], BENJAMIN[7], PHILIP[6], PHILIP[5], HENRY[4], HENRY[3], GEORGE[2], GEORGE[1])* was born Jan 1853 in AR, and died Oct 25, 1934 in Buena Park, CA. He married ELMA H. DAWSON 1880 in Downey, CA, daughter of DAWSON and MARY. She was born Mar 1860 in AR, and died Aft. 1920 in CA.

    George W. Pendleton (farmer) and family are listed in the 1900 Los Angeles Co., CA census, pg. 57.

Children of GEORGE PENDLETON and ELMA DAWSON are:
  i. ELLA E.[12] PENDLETON, b. Dec 1881, CA.
  ii. THOMAS M. PENDLETON, b. Jul 30, 1883, CA; d. Jul 1962.
  iii. JOSEPH R. PENDLETON, b. Mar 22, 1885, CA; d. Feb 1965, CA.
  iv. CLARENCE E. PENDLETON, b. Apr 1891, CA.
  v. DAWSON R. PENDLETON, b. Oct 27, 1893, CA; d. Dec 1973, Westminster, CA.
  vi. ELMA MAY PENDLETON, b. May 1899, CA.

703. EDWIN[11] PENDLETON *(WILLIAM HENRY[10], GEORGE MACON[9], PHILIP[8], BENJAMIN[7], PHILIP[6], PHILIP[5], HENRY[4], HENRY[3], GEORGE[2], GEORGE[1])* was born Feb 1855 in AR, and died Mar 25, 1933 in Los Angeles, CA. He married EMMA O. BELL Dec 28, 1879 in Downey, CA. She was born Oct 1861 in TX.
  Edwin Pendleton (expressman) and family are listed in the 1900 Los Angeles Co., CA census, pg. 190a.

Children of EDWIN PENDLETON and EMMA BELL are:
  i. ARTHUR W.[12] PENDLETON, b. Apr 1882, CA.
    An Arthur H. Pendleton (37; butcher) is listed in the 1920 Barstow, CA census.

  ii. IVAN V. PENDLETON, b. Jun 12, 1889, CA.
    Ivor Edwin (sic) Pendleton registered for the World War I draft in Los Angeles, CA.

  iii. ORA B. PENDLETON, b. Feb 1899, CA.

704. MATTHEW RAINEY[11] PENDLETON *(WILLIAM HENRY[10], GEORGE MACON[9], PHILIP[8], BENJAMIN[7], PHILIP[6], PHILIP[5], HENRY[4], HENRY[3], GEORGE[2], GEORGE[1])* was born Jul 1866 in Union, AR, and died Apr 18, 1934 in Long Beach, CA. He married CLARA M. Abt. 1893. She was born Feb 1867 in CA, and died Aft. 1920 in Long Beach, CA?
  Matthew R. Pendleton and wife are listed in the 1900 Los Angeles Co., CA census, pg. 95. Matthew Pendleton (grammar school principal) and family are listed in the 1920 Long Beach, CA census.

Children of MATTHEW PENDLETON and CLARA M. are:
  i. WALTER BROYLES[12] PENDLETON, b. Jul 23, 1900, AR; d. Apr 1972, Santa Paula, CA.
    Walter Broyles Pendleton registered for the World War I draft in Sebastian Co., AR.

  ii. ALFRED PENDLETON, b. Oct 24, 1901; d. Dec 1985, Whittier, CA.
  iii. HERBERT PENDLETON, b. Sep 03, 1906; d. Jul 1980, Long Beach, CA.

705. MARY EMMA[11] PENDLETON (*GEORGE MACON*[10], *GEORGE MACON*[9], *PHILIP*[8], *BENJAMIN*[7], *PHILIP*[6], *PHILIP*[5], *HENRY*[4], *HENRY*[3], *GEORGE*[2], *GEORGE*[1]) was born Jan 31, 1854 in Union Co., AR, and died Jun 05, 1945 in El Dorado, AR. She married ANTHONY REYNOLDS Dec 13, 1872, son of JAMES REYNOLDS and ELIZABETH SLAYTER. He was born Mar 13, 1849 in Union Co., AR, and died Oct 09, 1928 in El Dorado, AR.

Children of MARY PENDLETON and ANTHONY REYNOLDS are:
 i. LUCY O.[12] REYNOLDS, b. Nov 09, 1872, Union Co., AR.
 ii. JAMES MARK REYNOLDS, b. Sep 27, 1875, Union Co., AR.
 iii. ARTHUR PIERCE REYNOLDS, b. Sep 27, 1877, Union Co., AR.
 iv. MACON LEE REYNOLDS, b. Feb 22, 1880, Union Co., AR.
 v. HENRY ENOCH REYNOLDS, b. Jun 24, 1882, Union Co., AR.
 vi. MILLIE IDELL REYNOLDS, b. Feb 11, 1885, Union Co., AR.
 vii. MARY EMMA REYNOLDS, b. Aug 03, 1887, Union Co., AR.
 viii. GEORGE GORDON REYNOLDS, b. Mar 08, 1889, Union Co., AR.
 ix. JOSEPH WATSON REYNOLDS, b. Aug 08, 1891, Union Co., AR.
 x. DAVID CRAIG REYNOLDS, b. Aug 01, 1897, Union Co., AR.
 xi. RALPH ANTHONY REYNOLDS.

706. MARIA LOUISA[11] PENDLETON (*GEORGE MACON*[10], *GEORGE MACON*[9], *PHILIP*[8], *BENJAMIN*[7], *PHILIP*[6], *PHILIP*[5], *HENRY*[4], *HENRY*[3], *GEORGE*[2], *GEORGE*[1]) was born Jun 02, 1856 in AR, and died Feb 16, 1899 in Union Co., AR. She married JOHN H. CATE Dec 12, 1878 in AR, son of HENRY CATE and MARY. He was born 1856 in AR, and died in El Dorado, AR?

Children of MARIA PENDLETON and JOHN CATE are:
 i. GEORGE LUTHER[12] CATE, b. Aug 12, 1880, AR.
 ii. ANNIE CATE, b. 1883, AR.
 iii. JEWEL CATE, b. 1886, AR.
 iv. LUCY CATE, b. 1888, AR.
 v. J. HENRY CATE, b. 1891, AR.

707. GEORGE ROBERT[11] PENDLETON (*GEORGE MACON*[10], *GEORGE MACON*[9], *PHILIP*[8], *BENJAMIN*[7], *PHILIP*[6], *PHILIP*[5], *HENRY*[4], *HENRY*[3], *GEORGE*[2], *GEORGE*[1]) was born May 27, 1858 in AR, and died Jan 31, 1941 in Junction City, AR. He married MARY ELIZABETH REASONS Aug 26, 1885 in Nevada Co., AR, daughter of W. REASONS and MAHALY. She was born 1865 in AR, and died 1939 in Junction City, AR.

Children of GEORGE PENDLETON and MARY REASONS are:
 i. G. LUTHER[12] PENDLETON, b. Dec 08, 1887, AR; d. Dec 05, 1899, Union Co., AR.
 ii. CARL MACON PENDLETON, b. Sep 19, 1889, AR; d. Jan 1978, Idabel, OK.

Carl Macon Pendleton registered for the World War I draft in McCurtain Co., OK.

   iii. GRADY REASONS PENDLETON, b. 1891, AR.
   iv. MYRTLE LOUISE PENDLETON, b. 1894, AR; d. Nov 02, 1986, Union Co., AR; m. ROBERT RAYMOND POOLE, Feb 15, 1925, AR; b. Jan 11, 1889, Columbia Co., AR; d. Mar 23, 1964, Union Co., AR.
   v. HYATT FLEET PENDLETON, b. Dec 07, 1894, AR.
      Hyatt Fleet Pendleton registered for the World War I draft in Union Co., AR.

708. DELLA[11] PENDLETON (*GEORGE MACON[10], GEORGE MACON[9], PHILIP[8], BENJAMIN[7], PHILIP[6], PHILIP[5], HENRY[4], HENRY[3], GEORGE[2], GEORGE[1]*) was born Nov 26, 1860 in AR, and died Nov 06, 1935 in El Dorado, AR. She married WILLIAM M. SWILLEY Dec 12, 1878 in Union Co., AR, son of LAWSON SWILLEY and MARGARET STILES. He was born Jul 22, 1854 in El Dorado, AR, and died Feb 17, 1916 in El Dorado, AR.

Children of DELLA PENDLETON and WILLIAM SWILLEY are:
   i. M. F.[12] SWILLEY, b. Nov 1880, AR.
   ii. A. A. C. SWILLEY, b. Feb 1883, AR.
   iii. Z. E. SWILLEY, b. May 1885, AR.
   iv. WALTER LEE SWILLEY, b. Oct 26, 1887, AR.
   v. MAUDE ESTELLE SWILLEY, b. Aug 26, 1890, AR.
   vi. GEORGE WILLIAM SWILLEY, b. Dec 09, 1893, AR.
   vii. EDWARD S. SWILLEY, b. Aug 1899, AR.
   viii. C. D. SWILLEY.

709. JULIA[11] PENDLETON (*GEORGE MACON[10], GEORGE MACON[9], PHILIP[8], BENJAMIN[7], PHILIP[6], PHILIP[5], HENRY[4], HENRY[3], GEORGE[2], GEORGE[1]*) was born Feb 18, 1863 in AR, and died Apr 26, 1945 in Junction City, AR. She married AMOS JAMES REYNOLDS Jul 14, 1883 in Union Co., AR, son of JAMES REYNOLDS and ELIZABETH SLAYTER. He was born Dec 24, 1858 in Union Co., AR, and died Sep 03, 1937 in Junction City, AR.

Children of JULIA PENDLETON and AMOS REYNOLDS are:
   i. PETER PAUL[12] REYNOLDS, b. Jul 11, 1884, AR.
   ii. PEARL R. REYNOLDS, b. Jan 1886, AR.
   iii. STELLA MAY REYNOLDS, b. Sep 1888, AR.
   iv. HUGH DECIMUS REYNOLDS, b. Jun 21, 1891, AR.
   v. BIRDIE ANN REYNOLDS, b. Jul 01, 1893, AR.
   vi. ELIZABETH REYNOLDS, b. Dec 1895, AR.
   vii. GEORGE DWIGHT REYNOLDS, b. May 1897, AR.
   viii. GRACE REYNOLDS.
   ix. JAMES HALE REYNOLDS.

710. LULA ELIZABETH[11] PENDLETON *(GEORGE MACON[10], GEORGE MACON[9], PHILIP[8], BENJAMIN[7], PHILIP[6], PHILIP[5], HENRY[4], HENRY[3], GEORGE[2], GEORGE[1])* was born Feb 03, 1866 in AR, and died Nov 14, 1916 in El Dorado, AR. She married JOHN F. REASONS Jun 09, 1889 in Union Co., AR, son of W. REASONS and MAHALY. He was born Oct 09, 1857 in AR, and died Jul 03, 1939 in El Dorado, AR.

Children of LULA PENDLETON and JOHN REASONS are:
- i.   WILLIAM PENDLETON[12] REASONS, b. Dec 02, 1889.
- ii. EDNA F. REASONS, b. 1893, AR.
- iii. RUTH LOIS REASONS.

711. JOHN MACON[11] PENDLETON *(GEORGE MACON[10], GEORGE MACON[9], PHILIP[8], BENJAMIN[7], PHILIP[6], PHILIP[5], HENRY[4], HENRY[3], GEORGE[2], GEORGE[1])* was born Aug 02, 1869 in AR, and died Aft. 1930 in El Dorado, Union Co., AR? He married MARTHA ANN SWILLEY Nov 09, 1893 in Union Co., Arkansas, daughter of LAWSON SWILLEY and MARGARET STILES. She was born Jul 1872 in AR, and died Aft. 1930 in El Dorado, Union Co., AR?

John Pendleton (farmer) and family are listed in the 1900 Union Co., AR census, pg. 83.

Children of JOHN PENDLETON and MARTHA SWILLEY are:
- i.   G. L.[12] PENDLETON, b. Sep 1894, AR; d. Bef. 1910.
- ii.   FLOYD L. Q. PENDLETON, b. Feb 02, 1896, AR; d. Mar 20, 1913, Union Co., AR.
- iii. ROBERT LAVELLE PENDLETON, b. Jul 25, 1899, AR; d. Apr 02, 1991, El Dorado, AR; m. (1) DAISY MORGAN; b. Jul 16, 1899; d. Dec 1978, El Dorado, AR.; m. (2) ANNIE MAG POOLE.
       Robert Lovelle Pendleton registered for the World War I draft in Union Co., AR.

- iv.   ETHEL MAE PENDLETON, b. Feb 04, 1903, AR; d. Dec 21, 1999, El Dorado, AR; m. SAM EARL BAKER; b. Jan 03, 1896, AR; d. Aug 1968, El Dorado, AR.
- v.   RUTH L. PENDLETON.
- vi.   JESSIE N. PENDLETON.
- vii. W. MADISON PENDLETON.
- viii. MATTIE LOU PENDLETON.
- ix.   GERTRUDE PENDLETON.
- x.   JOHN MACON PENDLETON.

712. KATHERINE LIPSCOMB[11] PENDLETON *(GEORGE MACON[10], GEORGE MACON[9], PHILIP[8], BENJAMIN[7], PHILIP[6], PHILIP[5], HENRY[4], HENRY[3], GEORGE[2], GEORGE[1])* was born Nov 10, 1871 in AR. She married GEORGE WASHINGTON MASON Jun 06, 1894 in Oaklawn, LA. He was born Oct 1865 in LA, and died in Union Co., AR.

Children of KATHERINE PENDLETON and GEORGE MASON are:
    i.   IDELLE LUCY[12] MASON, b. Mar 24, 1895, Spearsville, LA.
    ii. MARY ETTA MASON, b. Oct 1898, AR.
   iii. GEORGE WASHINGTON MASON.

713. JAMES MONROE[11] PENDLETON *(WILLIAM MONROE[10], JOHN[9], JAMES[8], PHILIP[7], PHILIP[6], PHILIP[5], HENRY[4], HENRY[3], GEORGE[2], GEORGE[1])* was born Jan 1841 in Caldwell Co., KY, and died Aft. 1900 in Lawrence Co., MO? He married (1) MARY JANE REYNOLDS. She was born Abt. 1838 in IL, and died Apr 17, 1893 in Christian Co., MO? He married (2) MALISSA P. JOHNSON Abt. 1894. She was born Jul 1839 in TN, and died Aft. 1900.

       A James M. Pendleton was the Atchison Co., MO County and Circuit Clerk in 1865. James M. Pendleton (farmer) and family are listed in the 1880 Christian Co. census, Polk township. James M. Pendleton, harness maker, is listed in the Missouri State Gazetteer and Business Directory for 1881-82, Section B. James Pendleton (zinc miner) and family are listed in the 1900 Lawrence Co., MO census, pg. 73a. Mary Jane Reynolds Pendleton left for KY to help settle the estate of her grandparents in 1893 but she died on the way to KY (Ref. 305).

Children of JAMES PENDLETON and MARY REYNOLDS are:
      i.   MARY A.[12] PENDLETON, b. Abt. 1862, MO.
      ii. NANCY PENDLETON, b. Abt. 1864, MO.
886.   iii. ROBERT HENRY PENDLETON, b. Sep 20, 1865, MO; d. Aug 13, 1946, Pope Co., AR.
887.   iv. WILLIAM M. PENDLETON, b. Dec 1867, MO; d. Aft. 1920, Pope Co., AR?
      v. ROSETTA PENDLETON, b. Abt. 1871, MO.
     vi. BENJAMIN L. PENDLETON, b. May 1878, MO; d. Aft. 1920, Barry Co., MO?; m. MAUDE P. NEWMAN; b. Abt. 1877, TN; d. Aft. 1920, Barry Co., MO?

        Benjamin L. Pendleton (farmer) is listed in the 1920 Barry Co., MO census, Crane Creek Township.

    vii. ALFORD PENDLETON, b. Jul 1880, MO.

714. JOHN WILLIS[11] PENDLETON *(WILLIAM MONROE[10], JOHN[9], JAMES[8], PHILIP[7], PHILIP[6], PHILIP[5], HENRY[4], HENRY[3], GEORGE[2], GEORGE[1])* was born Oct 1842 in Caldwell Co., KY, and died Aft. 1920 in Lawrence Co., MO? He married (1) MATILDA K. BURROW. She was born Abt. 1844 in TN, and died Aft. 1881. He married (2) MARY CONANT Abt. 1884. She was born Nov 1861 in KS.

       A John W. Pendleton, private, served in Capt. Burrows' Company B, Home Guard Regiment, Missouri, Union Army. John Willis Pendleton (day laborer) and second family are listed in the 1900 Lawrence Co., MO census, pg. 60a. John Pendleton is in the household of his son-in-law, John Mosher, in the 1920 census.

Children of JOHN PENDLETON and MATILDA BURROW are:

888. i. MARY C.[12] PENDLETON, b. Abt. 1865, MO; d. Aft. 1920, Lawrence Co., MO?
889. ii. WILEY G. PENDLETON, b. Aug 1866, MO; d. Aft. 1920, Ottawa Co., OK?
890. iii. DOCKY H. PENDLETON, b. Sep 1868, MO; d. Aft. 1910, Lawrence Co., MO?
891. iv. JOHN W. PENDLETON, b. Jun 1871, MO; d. Aft. 1920, Lawrence Co., MO?
      v. ALEX C. PENDLETON, b. Abt. 1874.
      vi. FANNY CISIRE PENDLETON, b. Feb 1876, MO; d. Nov 20, 1957, Joplin, MO; m. JOSEPH LARKIN CAVENER, Jul 23, 1899, Joplin, MO; b. Sep 05, 1876, MO; d. Jun 15, 1915, Joplin, MO.
      vii. NATHAN J. PENDLETON, b. Oct 1877, MO.
      viii. JAMES G. PENDLETON, b. Jun 1881, MO.

Children of JOHN PENDLETON and MARY CONANT are:

      ix. GEORGE T.[12] PENDLETON, b. Jan 1885, MO.
      x. CHARLES A. PENDLETON, b. Jul 1888, MO.
      xi. ANNIE PENDLETON, b. Aug 1891, MO.
      xii. JERRY PENDLETON, b. Jun 1895, MO.
      xiii. LIDDIE PENDLETON, b. Oct 1897, MO.

715. GEORGE WASHINGTON[11] PENDLETON (*WILLIAM MONROE[10], JOHN[9], JAMES[8], PHILIP[7], PHILIP[6], PHILIP[5], HENRY[4], HENRY[3], GEORGE[2], GEORGE[1]*) was born Jan 1845 in Caldwell Co., KY, and died Oct 03, 1914 in Mt. Vernon, MO. He married MIRIAM GEMETTA COWAN May 16, 1869 in Lawrence Co., MO. She was born 1852 in AR, and died Abt. 1888 in Mt. Vernon, MO.

George Washington Pendleton was a soldier in the Civil War, Company B, 15th Missouri Cavalry. G.W. Pendleton (farm laborer) and his daughter, Annie, are listed in the 1900 Lawrence Co., MO census, pg. 294a. The Marionville, MO Free Press stated in Oct 1914 that George Pendleton died, age 69, when a wagon overturned, throwing him out. He had been a widower for 26 years and had two surviving children at that time.

Children of GEORGE PENDLETON and MIRIAM COWAN are:

      i. AZZORA[12] PENDLETON, b. 1871, MO.
      ii. CALDONIA PENDLETON, b. 1872, MO.
      iii. DORA E. PENDLETON, b. 1875, MO.
892. iv. ELMER E. PENDLETON, b. May 1877, MO; d. Aft. 1920, Lawrence Co., MO?
      v. ANNIE PENDLETON, b. Jun 18, 1884.

716. NATHANIEL CORDA[11] PENDLETON (*WILLIAM MONROE[10], JOHN[9], JAMES[8], PHILIP[7], PHILIP[6], PHILIP[5], HENRY[4], HENRY[3], GEORGE[2], GEORGE[1]*) was born Jan 07, 1847 in Lawrence Co., MO, and died 1923 in Jasper, MO? He married NANCY MARIVA BURROW Abt. 1865, daughter of JOSHUA BURROW and MARTHA NEUSUM. She was born Nov 1846 in TN, and died 1920 in Jasper, MO?

N. C. Pendleton (engineer-sawmill) and family are listed in the 1900 Lawrence Co., MO census, pg. 292.

Children of NATHANIEL PENDLETON and NANCY BURROW are:
    i. MARTHA A.[12] PENDLETON, b. Abt. 1867.
    ii. LUCY J. PENDLETON, b. Abt. 1873.
    iii. ALFORD PORTER PENDLETON, b. Nov 1878, MO; d. Aft. 1920, Jasper, MO?
    iv. LULA CALDONIA PENDLETON, b. Apr 1885, Lawrence Co., MO; m. FRED SMITH.
    v. CARR M. PENDLETON, b. Oct 1887.

717. MARY CATHERINE[11] PENDLETON *(WILLIAM MONROE[10], JOHN[9], JAMES[8], PHILIP[7], PHILIP[6], PHILIP[5], HENRY[4], HENRY[3], GEORGE[2], GEORGE[1])* was born Mar 16, 1849 in Lawrence Co., MO, and died Apr 1916 in AR. She married WILLIAM RILEY CASTOE Aug 14, 1873 in Lawrence Co., MO, son of JOHN CASTOE and JUSTINE COOTS. He was born Nov 1851 in Barry Co., MO, and died Apr 24, 1933 in Benton, AR.
    William Castoe and family are listed in the 1880 census, Lawrence Co., MO, pg. 455D.

Children of MARY PENDLETON and WILLIAM CASTOE are:
    i. SELINA[12] CASTOE, b. Abt. 1875; d. 1929; m. SAMUEL NELSON GRAHAM, 1893.
    ii. SERENA B. J. CASTOE, b. Abt. 1877.

718. ELIZABETH J.[11] PENDLETON *(WILLIAM MONROE[10], JOHN[9], JAMES[8], PHILIP[7], PHILIP[6], PHILIP[5], HENRY[4], HENRY[3], GEORGE[2], GEORGE[1])* was born Abt. 1851 in Lawrence Co., MO. She married JESSE W. ARNHART. He was born Abt. 1852 in MO.
    J. W. Arnhart (farmer) and family are listed in the 1880 Lawrence Co., MO census, pg. 453C.

Children of ELIZABETH PENDLETON and JESSE ARNHART are:
    i. WILLIAM M.[12] ARNHART, b. Abt. 1870, MO.
    ii. CORDY M. ARNHART, b. Abt. 1873, MO.
    iii. DORA A. ARNHART, b. Abt. 1877, MO.
    iv. SARAH C. ARNHART, b. Abt. 1879, MO.

719. WILLIAM PORTER[11] PENDLETON *(WILLIAM MONROE[10], JOHN[9], JAMES[8], PHILIP[7], PHILIP[6], PHILIP[5], HENRY[4], HENRY[3], GEORGE[2], GEORGE[1])* was born 1853 in Lawrence Co., MO. He married KISSIAH ELIZABETH ARNHART Jan 03, 1871. She was born Abt. 1854 in MO.

Children of WILLIAM PENDLETON and KISSIAH ARNHART are:
    i. MARY[12] PENDLETON, b. 1873, MO.

ii. NATHAN PENDLETON, b. 1876, MO.
iii. JOHN PENDLETON, b. Sep 1878, MO.
iv. GENERAL PENDLETON, b. Sep 1880.
v. ANNA B. ETHEL PENDLETON, b. Feb 01, 1884.
vi. DEAMY PENDLETON, d. Mar 11, 1890, Mt. Vernon, MO.

720. ALFRED SIEGEL[11] PENDLETON *(WILLIAM MONROE[10], JOHN[9], JAMES[8], PHILIP[7], PHILIP[6], PHILIP[5], HENRY[4], HENRY[3], GEORGE[2], GEORGE[1])* was born Sep 02, 1861 in Lawrence Co., MO, and died Aft. 1920 in Erie Co., MO? He married RACHEL CONDARA EPPERSON Dec 03, 1882. She was born Sep 1864 in MO, and died Aft. 1920 in Erie Co., MO?

A. S. Pendleton (farmer) and family are listed in the 1900 Lawrence Co., MO census, pg. 293.

Children of ALFRED PENDLETON and RACHEL EPPERSON are:
893.   i. DANIEL N.[12] PENDLETON, b. Jun 1886, MO.
  ii. BESSIE C. PENDLETON, b. Aug 1894, MO.
  iii. EVERETT M. PENDLETON, b. Jun 1898, MO.

721. JOSEPH H.[11] PENDLETON *(PHILIP HARPER[10], JOSEPH[9], MICAJAH[8], PHILIP[7], PHILIP[6], PHILIP[5], HENRY[4], HENRY[3], GEORGE[2], GEORGE[1])* was born 1831 in Wythe Co., VA, and died in the Civil War. He married MARY JANE KEISLING Apr 11, 1852. She was born Abt. 1832 in VA, and died Aft. 1870 in Wythe Co., VA?

Joseph Pendleton (miller) and family are listed in the 1860 Wythe Co., VA census. Joseph H. Pendleton, private, served in the 63rd VA infantry, Company H. Mary J. Pendleton and Lorenza are listed as domestic servants in the 1870 Wythe Co., VA census.

Children of JOSEPH PENDLETON and MARY KEISLING are:
  i. SARAH[12] PENDLETON, b. Abt. 1852, VA.
  ii. LORENZA HARRIET PENDLETON, b. Abt. 1854, VA.
  iii. JAMES PENDLETON, b. Abt. 1856, VA.
894.   iv. GEORGE HIRAM PENDLETON, b. Jan 26, 1862, VA; d. Feb 21, 1935, Letcher Co., KY.

722. MORGAN MITCHELL[11] PENDLETON *(PHILIP HARPER[10], JOSEPH[9], MICAJAH[8], PHILIP[7], PHILIP[6], PHILIP[5], HENRY[4], HENRY[3], GEORGE[2], GEORGE[1])* was born Mar 15, 1836 in Wythe Co., VA, and died Jul 09, 1894 in Black Lick, Wythe Co., VA? He married MARGARET SHERFEY 1857. She was born Abt. 1837 in TN.

Morgan Pendleton served as Sgt. in the VA 1st Cavalry, 2nd Company D, CSA. Morgan Pendleton (farm laborer) and family are listed in the 1870 Elk Creek, Grayson Co., VA census.

Children of MORGAN PENDLETON and MARGARET SHERFEY are (Ref. 306):
895.   i. JOSHUA BORAN[12] PENDLETON, b. May 19, 1858, Washington Co., TN; d. Jun 21, 1929, Clark Co., IL.

    ii. ELIZABETH PENDLETON, b. Oct 05, 1861, Washington Co., TN; d. 1928.

   iii. CATHERINE PENDLETON, b. Aug 25, 1866, Wythe Co., VA; d. Aft. 1880.
Catherine Pendleton is listed in the 1880 Black Lick, Wythe Co., VA census in the household of James W. Stuart.

896.   iv. SARAH ANGELINE PENDLETON, b. Sep 11, 1868, Wythe Co., VA; d. Jul 15, 1953.

897.   v. JOHN HARVEY PENDLETON, b. Sep 13, 1870, Wythe Co., VA; d. Feb 09, 1937, Dunklin Co., MO.

898.   vi. JAMES E. WILSON PENDLETON, b. Apr 28, 1872, Wythe Co., VA; d. Mar 22, 1957, Rhea Co., TN?

   vii. PETER HENRY V. PENDLETON, b. Aug 05, 1874, Wythe Co., VA; d. 1955, Clay Co., AR?
Peter Henry Pendleton registered for the World War I draft in Clay Co., AR.

  viii. WILLIAM B. PENDLETON, b. Mar 07, 1877, Wythe Co., VA; d. Jun 27, 1904.

   ix. CLARA FRANCES PENDLETON, b. Mar 08, 1879, Wythe Co., VA; m. JARRED KEITH, Jul 30, 1897.

   x. MINNIE PENDLETON, b. Apr 13, 1881; d. May 20, 1968; m. FRANK PHILLIPI, Sep 28, 1902.

   xi. LAURA ESTHER PENDLETON, b. Apr 12, 1883; d. Aug 04, 1965; m. NATHAN KEITH, 1939.

723. ANNE ELIZABETH[11] PENDLETON (*JAMES VANCE*[10], *JOSEPH*[9], *MICAJAH*[8], *PHILIP*[7], *PHILIP*[6], *PHILIP*[5], *HENRY*[4], *HENRY*[3], *GEORGE*[2], *GEORGE*[1]) was born Feb 11, 1845 in VA, and died 1928 in Bristol, TN. She married ANDREW JACKSON GIBSON Aug 13, 1866 in Tazewell Co., VA, son of SAMUEL GIBSON and MARGARET WARD. He was born Aug 04, 1845 in Tazewell Co., VA, and died Feb 11, 1902.

Children of ANNE PENDLETON and ANDREW GIBSON are:

   i. ROSA BELLE[12] GIBSON.

   ii. ALBERT GAINES GIBSON, b. Feb 11, 1871, Tazewell Co, VA; d. Jun 02, 1923, Shubert, Nebraska; m. CAROLINE VIRGINIA BROCE, Nov 25, 1891, Bristol, TN; b. Feb 25, 1863, TN.

   iii. BLAIR THOMPSON GIBSON, b. 1874.

   iv. WILLIAM G. GIBSON, b. 1876.

   v. GEORGE GOSE GIBSON, b. Sep 20, 1879.

   vi. WIRT W. GIBSON, b. May 04, 1886; d. Dec 1973, Cleveland, TN.

724. ALBERT GALLATIN[11] PENDLETON (*JAMES VANCE*[10], *JOSEPH*[9], *MICAJAH*[8], *PHILIP*[7], *PHILIP*[6], *PHILIP*[5], *HENRY*[4], *HENRY*[3], *GEORGE*[2], *GEORGE*[1]) was born Feb 02, 1845 in VA, and died Jul 24, 1891 in San Marcos, TX. He married KATE D. MILLER Jan 29, 1873 in Jackson, TN, daughter of JOHN MILLER and SARAH

PHIPPS. She was born Feb 04, 1854 in Jackson, TN, and died Oct 18, 1901 in Hays Co., TX.

"At 15 years of age, he volunteered in the Confederate Army, where he served with honors until the end of the Civil War. In 1868 he was a captain of a Klu Klux Klan. He studied medicine, was a surgeon of extended reputation, having passed satisfactory examinations at the highest institutions of Scotland and England. He was a Fellow of the Royal Academy of Surgeons of London, England" (Ref. 307). Albert G. Pendleton (physician) and family are listed in the 1880 Hays Co., TX census.

Children of ALBERT PENDLETON and KATE MILLER are:
899.   i. ALBERTA[12] PENDLETON, b. Jun 1874, TN.
       ii. MILLER VANCE PENDLETON, b. Jul 11, 1878, TX.
           Miller Vance Pendleton registered for the World War I draft in San Antonio, Bexar Co., TX.

      iii. ANNA BYRD PENDLETON, b. Nov 11, 1881, Hays Co., TX; d. Mar 27, 1971, San Antonio, TX; m. WILLIAM HOWELL CLARK, Sep 14, 1904; b. May 02, 1875, Aransas Co., TX; d. Sep 03, 1949, Tarrant Co., TX.
      iv. LOUALLIE PENDLETON, b. Dec 1884, TX; m. H. H. BURCHARD.
      v. ALBERT G. PENDLETON, JR., b. Apr 1891, TX.

725. LETITIA VIRGINIA[11] PENDLETON *(JAMES VANCE[10], JOSEPH[9], MICAJAH[8], PHILIP[7], PHILIP[6], PHILIP[5], HENRY[4], HENRY[3], GEORGE[2], GEORGE[1])* was born Mar 23, 1849 in VA. She married JOHN HENRY NELMS Jan 04, 1870 in Kingsport, TN, son of WILLIAM NELMS and ELIZABETH CHILDRESS. He was born Abt. 1841 in TN.

John Nelms and family are listed in the 1880 census, Hamblen Co., TN, pg. 353C.

Children of LETITIA PENDLETON and JOHN NELMS are:
      i. MYRTLE ANNA ELIZABETH[12] NELMS, b. Abt. 1872, TN; m. FLETCHER CAMPBELL, Jun 22, 1892, Morristown, TN.
      ii. KATHLEEN PENDLETON NELMS, b. Abt. 1873, TN.
      iii. JOSEPH MONROE NELMS, b. Abt. 1876, TN; m. HELEN HOFFMAN, TN.
      iv. NELLIE B. NELMS, b. Abt. 1879, TN.
      v. VIRGINIA GAINES NELMS.
      vi. HELEN VANCE NELMS, m. EDWARD E. TARR.

726. WILLIAM H. JORDAN[11] PENDLETON *(JAMES VANCE[10], JOSEPH[9], MICAJAH[8], PHILIP[7], PHILIP[6], PHILIP[5], HENRY[4], HENRY[3], GEORGE[2], GEORGE[1])* was born Jan 23, 1851 in VA, and died Aft. 1900 in Hamblen Co., TN? He married LOU Abt. 1875. She was born Aug 1840 in TN.

William H. Pendleton (carpenter) and family are listed in the 1900 Hamblen Co., TN census, pg. 88.

Children of WILLIAM PENDLETON and LOU are:

     i.   ANNA P.[12] PENDLETON, b. Oct 1877, TN.

     ii. LINN L. PENDLETON, b. Oct 1879, TN.

     iii. CHARLES V. PENDLETON, b. Sep 1882, TN.

     iv. WIRT FRANK PENDLETON, b. Dec 23, 1885, TN.

          Wirt Frank Pendleton registered for the World War I draft in Hamblen Co., TN.

727. BASCOM WOOD[11] PENDLETON (*JAMES VANCE[10], JOSEPH[9], MICAJAH[8], PHILIP[7], PHILIP[6], PHILIP[5], HENRY[4], HENRY[3], GEORGE[2], GEORGE[1]*) was born Jul 23, 1857 in VA, and died Mar 08, 1931 in Sullivan Co., TN. He married MARY T. WAXTON HORNE Nov 30, 1898 in San Marcos, TX. She was born Jan 01, 1868 in San Marcos, TX, and died Oct 11, 1919 in Baltimore, MD.

    Bascom W. Pendleton and family are listed in the 1900 Sullivan Co., TN census, pg. 205.

Children of BASCOM PENDLETON and MARY HORNE are:

     i.   BESSIE GOULD[12] PENDLETON.

     ii. BASCOM WOOD PENDLETON, JR., b. Mar 02, 1904, TN; d. Dec 20, 1983, MD?

     iii. MARY LOUISE PENDLETON.

     iv. KATHLEEN BEE PENDLETON.

     v. MARGARET VANCE PENDLETON.

728. WIRT WINTWORTH[11] PENDLETON (*JAMES VANCE[10], JOSEPH[9], MICAJAH[8], PHILIP[7], PHILIP[6], PHILIP[5], HENRY[4], HENRY[3], GEORGE[2], GEORGE[1]*) was born May 07, 1860 in VA, and died Aft. 1906 in Baltimore, MD. He married ADA W. WINSTON. She was born Abt. 1864 in Richmond, VA, and died Aft. 1920 in Wytheville, Wythe Co., VA?

    Wirt Wintworth is the author of "Christian church, its foundation. And history and reminiscences of the Christian church at Clifton Forge, Va," published in 1935. Ada W. Pendleton (56; manager) is listed in the 1920 Wytheville, Wythe Co., VA census, pg. 9B.

Child of WIRT PENDLETON and ADA WINSTON is:

     i.   MARGUERITE[12] PENDLETON.

729. FRANK LESLIE[11] PENDLETON (*JAMES VANCE[10], JOSEPH[9], MICAJAH[8], PHILIP[7], PHILIP[6], PHILIP[5], HENRY[4], HENRY[3], GEORGE[2], GEORGE[1]*) was born Nov 10, 1867 in VA, and died 1917. He married VERINA DAVIS MATTOX 1886. She was born in GA.

Children of FRANK PENDLETON and VERINA MATTOX are:

     i.   MYRTLE VERINA[12] PENDLETON, b. 1887.

     ii. LESLIE WIRT PENDLETON, b. Jan 25, 1889, GA.

          Leslie Wirt Pendleton registered for the World War I draft in Polk Co., FL.

iii. ALBERT GAINES PENDLETON, b. May 26, 1891, Bristol, VA; d. Nov 26, 1950; m. MARY MAGDALENE ALLEN; b. Mar 25, 1890, Steinhatchee, FL; d. Aug 16, 1969.

Albert Gaines Pendleton registered for the World War I draft in Lafayette Co., FL.

iv. HERBERT ELLSWORTH PENDLETON, b. Mar 22, 1894, Bristol, VA; d. Dec 1984, Lancaster Co., PA; m. GRACE VIRGINIA GATES; b. Dec 08, 1899, Of Baltimore, MD; d. Oct 1982, Lancaster Co., PA.

Herbert Ellsworth Pendleton registered for the World War I draft in Baltimore, MD.

v. JAMES LUCIUS PENDLETON, b. 1898.

Generation No. 12 – Twentieth Century

The twelfth generation consists of the great (5) grandchildren of the immigrant Philip Pendleton and Isabella Hurt. The time period is from about 1873, when Ira Newton Pendleton, Laura Rebecca Pendleton, and James M. Pendleton were each married in Virginia or Kentucky, to at least 2006, the date of this publication. Many later born members of this generation are still living and thus are not included in this history to protect their privacy. In addition, a greater number of this twelfth generation, having only living children (not included), are listed only as children of the eleventh generation.

A few of the early born of this generation were old enough to have remembered the Civil War. Most, however, were born toward the end of the 19th century. Virtually all of this generation still living were born after 1900; the last about 1930.

The full story of the twelfth generation is yet to be told. But for those included in this history, households were found in 21 different states. The portion of households found in Virginia continued to decline to about 21% of the total as families continued moving west. About 19% remained in Kentucky, about 14% in Missouri, and about 8% were Texas residents. Other predominant states included Tennessee, Georgia, Arkansas, and Illinois.

Generation No. 12

730. JOHN H.[12] PENDLETON *(WILLIAM E.*[11]*, THOMAS CATLETT*[10]*, HENRY*[9]*, HENRY*[8]*, JAMES*[7]*, HENRY*[6]*, PHILIP*[5]*, HENRY*[4]*, HENRY*[3]*, GEORGE*[2]*, GEORGE*[1]*)* was born 1868 in KY, and died Aft. 1910 in Hardin Co., KY? He married LORDA? She was born Abt. 1871 in KY.

Children of JOHN PENDLETON and LORDA? are:
  i.   WILLIAM H.[13] PENDLETON, b. Jul 24, 1897, KY.
       William H Pendleton registered for the WWI draft in Hardin Co., KY.

  ii. MARY H. PENDLETON.
  iii. NELLIE C. PENDLETON.
  iv. ADA ANN PENDLETON.
  v.   LORANA? PENDLETON.

731. RICHARD A.[12] PENDLETON *(WILLIAM E.*[11]*, THOMAS CATLETT*[10]*, HENRY*[9]*, HENRY*[8]*, JAMES*[7]*, HENRY*[6]*, PHILIP*[5]*, HENRY*[4]*, HENRY*[3]*, GEORGE*[2]*, GEORGE*[1]*)* was born Dec 1873 in KY. He married CLARA. She was born Jan 1879 in KY.

Child of RICHARD PENDLETON and CLARA is:
  i.   VICTOR G.[13] PENDLETON, b. Oct 1896, KY.

732. PAUL COLUMBUS[12] PENDLETON *(JOHN THOMAS[11], THOMAS CATLETT[10], HENRY[9], HENRY[8], JAMES[7], HENRY[6], PHILIP[5], HENRY[4], HENRY[3], GEORGE[2], GEORGE[1])* was born Jun 27, 1883 in Meade Co., KY?, and died Aft. 1930 in Randolph, IN? He married KATHRYN ISABELLE VOWELS Nov 23, 1909 in KY, daughter of WILLIAM VOWELS and MARTHA RAY. She was born 1884 in KY, and died Aft. 1930 in Randolph, IN?

Children of PAUL PENDLETON and KATHRYN VOWELS are:
  i.   HENRY[13] PENDLETON.
  ii. RAYMOND THOMAS PENDLETON.
  iii. PAYTON A. PENDLETON.
  iv. WALTER M. PENDLETON.

733. GEORGE T.[12] PENDLETON *(JOHN THOMAS[11], THOMAS CATLETT[10], HENRY[9], HENRY[8], JAMES[7], HENRY[6], PHILIP[5], HENRY[4], HENRY[3], GEORGE[2], GEORGE[1])* was born Oct 18, 1887 in KY, and died Aft. 1930 in Tippecanoe Co., IN? He married ALVA E. RITCHIE, daughter of JAMES RITCHIE and MARY SHACKLETT. She was born Oct 1895 in KY, and died Aft. 1930 in Tippecanoe Co., IN?
     George Pendleton registered for the World War I draft in Tippecanoe, IN.

Children of GEORGE PENDLETON and ALVA RITCHIE are:
  i. PAULINE[13] PENDLETON.
  ii. LEONA M. PENDLETON.

734. THOMAS OWEN[12] PENDLETON *(GEORGE TAYLOR[11], THOMAS CLAYTON[10], JOHN[9], JAMES[8], JAMES[7], HENRY[6], PHILIP[5], HENRY[4], HENRY[3], GEORGE[2], GEORGE[1])* was born Jan 26, 1852 in KY, and died Jan 1926 in Cooper Co., MO. He married ELIZABETH CATHERINE CUNNINGHAM Jul 31, 1877. She was born Jul 30, 1857 in Of St. Charles, MO, and died Jul 20, 1933.
     T.O. Pendleton, physician, is listed in the Missouri State Gazetteer and Business Directory for 1881-82, Part P. T. Pendleton (doctor) and family are listed in the 1900 Cooper Co., MO census, pg. 199. His wife is not listed. Mrs. Eliza Cunningham Pendleton was a member of The National Society of the Daughters of the American Revolution (Volume 93, page 40).

Child of THOMAS PENDLETON and ELIZABETH CUNNINGHAM is:
  i. GERTRUDE OWEN[13] PENDLETON, b. Aug 06, 1878, Pilot Grove, MO.
      Miss Gertrude O. Pendleton was a member of The National Society of the Daughters of the American Revolution (Volume 85, page 325).

735. CATHERINE HARRISON[12] PENDLETON *(GEORGE TAYLOR[11], THOMAS CLAYTON[10], JOHN[9], JAMES[8], JAMES[7], HENRY[6], PHILIP[5], HENRY[4], HENRY[3], GEORGE[2], GEORGE[1])* was born Jan 16, 1860 in MO, and died Dec 19, 1945 in Cooper Co., MO. She married STEPHEN LOUIS STITES Dec 26, 1888. He was born Mar 02, 1865 in TX, and died Feb 07, 1942 in Cooper Co., MO.

Children of CATHERINE PENDLETON and STEPHEN STITES are:
> i. KATHERINE[13] STITES, b. Mar 30, 1892, Cooper Co., MO; d. May 26, 1939, Cooper Co., MO; m. HAYS.
> ii. MADELINE A. STITES, b. Jan 24, 1894; d. May 16, 1894, Cooper Co., MO.
> iii. EDITH STITES.

736. STAPLETON CRUTCHFIELD[12] PENDLETON *(GEORGE TAYLOR[11], THOMAS CLAYTON[10], JOHN[9], JAMES[8], JAMES[7], HENRY[6], PHILIP[5], HENRY[4], HENRY[3], GEORGE[2], GEORGE[1])* was born Jul 14, 1862 in MO. He married (1) KATHERINE SALMON. He married (2) ALICE LICKLIDER Jan 24, 1888.
> Stapleton C Pendleton was a railway official in Denver, CO (Ref. 308).

Children of STAPLETON PENDLETON and KATHERINE SALMON are:
> i. GEORGE EDWIN[13] PENDLETON.
> ii. FRANCES CRUTCHFIELD PENDLETON.
> iii. ELIZABETH FORSTER PENDLETON.

737. ELEANOR CHINN[12] PENDLETON *(GEORGE TAYLOR[11], THOMAS CLAYTON[10], JOHN[9], JAMES[8], JAMES[7], HENRY[6], PHILIP[5], HENRY[4], HENRY[3], GEORGE[2], GEORGE[1])* was born Sep 03, 1872 in Cooper Co., MO, and died Aft. 1910. She married RICHARD W. EMBRY Oct 31, 1894, son of LEONIDES EMBRY. He was born 1869 in MO, and died Aft. 1910 in Moniteau Co., MO?
> Mrs. Nellie Pendleton Embry was a member of The National Society of the Daughters of the American Revolution (Volume 103, page 308).

Children of ELEANOR PENDLETON and RICHARD EMBRY are:
> i. LEONIDES[13] EMBRY, b. Abt. 1896.
> ii. ELEANOR HOOD EMBRY, b. Abt. 1898, California, MO.

738. JAMES STROTHER[12] PENDLETON *(JAMES FRENCH[11], JAMES[10], THOMAS[9], JAMES[8], JAMES[7], HENRY[6], PHILIP[5], HENRY[4], HENRY[3], GEORGE[2], GEORGE[1])* was born Nov 15, 1858 in DeKalb, MO, and died May 27, 1930 in St. Joseph, MO. He married (1) FANNIE R. CHITWOOD Mar 01, 1886 in Buchanan Co., Missouri. She was born Feb 16, 1858, and died May 29, 1888 in St. Joseph, Missouri. He married (2) ADELINE S. GOODWIN Abt. 1892, daughter of IRA GOODWIN and LOUISE BORCHERS. She was born Aug 30, 1868 in St. Joseph, MO, and died Apr 06, 1963 in St. Joseph, MO.
> James S. Pendleton (home carpenter) and family are listed in the 1900 Buchanan Co., MO census, pg. 87a.

Child of JAMES PENDLETON and FANNIE CHITWOOD is:
> i. FRANCIS R.[13] PENDLETON, b. May 29, 1888, St. Joseph, Missouri; d. Jun 29, 1888, St. Joseph, Missouri.

Children of JAMES PENDLETON and ADELINE GOODWIN are:

900.　ii.　LILLIAN[13] PENDLETON, b. Sep 06, 1893, MO; d. Oct 1980, Richmond, MO.

901.　iii.　LOUISE PENDLETON, b. May 11, 1895, MO; d. May 20, 1987, St. Joseph, MO.

　　　iv.　MARY FRANCES PENDLETON, b. May 11, 1895, MO.

902.　v.　MARGARET ETHEL PENDLETON, b. Jan 19, 1897, St. Joseph, MO; d. Dec 1971, Dallas, TX.

　　　vi.　JAMES IRA PENDLETON, b. Apr 12, 1899, St. Joseph, Missouri; d. Jul 21, 1961, St. Joseph, Missouri; m. RUBY LUCRETIA SMITH Aug 23, 1922; b. Mar 13, 1897, Atlanta, KS; d. Oct 16, 1980, Ventura, CA.

739. LUCY KATHERINE[12] PENDLETON *(ALBERT FRENCH[11], JOHN BOWIE[10], THOMAS[9], JAMES[8], JAMES[7], HENRY[6], PHILIP[5], HENRY[4], HENRY[3], GEORGE[2], GEORGE[1])* was born Abt. 1878 in MO, and died Aft. 1910 in Monroe Co., MO? She married ARTHUR P. WOODSON in Madison, MO. He was born Abt. 1876 in MO, and died Aft. 1910 in Monroe Co., MO?

Children of LUCY PENDLETON and ARTHUR WOODSON are:
　　　i.　EVA LU[13] WOODSON.
　　　ii.　JO ETTA WOODSON.
　　　iii.　WILLIAM V. WOODSON.

740. CLARENCE M.[12] PENDLETON *(ALBERT FRENCH[11], JOHN BOWIE[10], THOMAS[9], JAMES[8], JAMES[7], HENRY[6], PHILIP[5], HENRY[4], HENRY[3], GEORGE[2], GEORGE[1])* was born Oct 13, 1886 in MO, and died Jul 16, 1931 in Randolph Co., MO. He married NINA M. DOWDY. She was born Nov 19, 1888 in MO, and died Mar 29, 1964 in Randolph Co., MO.

Children of CLARENCE PENDLETON and NINA DOWDY are:
　　　i.　JOHN R.[13] PENDLETON.
　　　ii.　LUCY K. PENDLETON.
　　　iii.　EDNA FRANCES PENDLETON.

741. STELLA LEE[12] PENDLETON *(ARTHUR MENEFEE[11], JOHN BOWIE[10], THOMAS[9], JAMES[8], JAMES[7], HENRY[6], PHILIP[5], HENRY[4], HENRY[3], GEORGE[2], GEORGE[1])* was born 1871 in Menard Co., IL, and died May 11, 1930 in Springfield, IL. She married ALBERT RUFUS LYLES, DR. Jun 22, 1898 in Chandlerville, IL, son of MOSES LYLES and SARAH WALKER. He was born Jul 10, 1860 in Allen Co., KY, and died Dec 18, 1945 in Springfield, IL.

　　Mrs. Stella Pendleton Lyles was a member of The National Society of the Daughters of the American Revolution (Volume 100, page 32).

Children of STELLA PENDLETON and ALBERT LYLES are:
　　　i.　MIRIAM EUNICE PENDLETON[13] LYLES.
　　　ii.　PAULINE LAVINIA PENDLETON LYLES.

742. ARTHUR MENEFEE[12] PENDLETON *(ARTHUR MENEFEE[11], JOHN BOWIE[10], THOMAS[9], JAMES[8], JAMES[7], HENRY[6], PHILIP[5], HENRY[4], HENRY[3], GEORGE[2], GEORGE[1])* was born Oct 22, 1873 in IL, and died Aft. 1920 in McLean Co., IL? He married OLIVE R. TURNER Mar 07, 1901. She was born Jun 06, 1873 in IL, and died May 05, 1922 in McLean Co., IL?

Arthur M. Pendleton and family are listed in the 1920 Bloomington, McLean Co., IL census.

Children of ARTHUR PENDLETON and OLIVE TURNER are:
     i.   LYLE TURNER[13] PENDLETON, b. Feb 19, 1902, IL; d. May 1973, Louisville, KY.
    ii. GAIL ALBERT PENDLETON.
   iii. PAUL GORDON PENDLETON.

743. MYRTLE HEWITT[12] PENDLETON *(ARTHUR MENEFEE[11], JOHN BOWIE[10], THOMAS[9], JAMES[8], JAMES[7], HENRY[6], PHILIP[5], HENRY[4], HENRY[3], GEORGE[2], GEORGE[1])* was born Jan 17, 1887 in IL, and died Aft. 1930 in Chandlerville, Cass Co., IL? She married WILLIAM DUDLEY LEEPER. He was born Abt. 1877 in IL, and died Aft. 1920 in Chandlerville, Cass Co., IL?

W. D. Leeper (retail merchant) and family are listed in the 1920 Cass Co., IL census. Myrtle Leeper (43, Manager Hat Shop) and daughter are listed in the 1930 Chandlerville, Cass Co., IL census.

Child of MYRTLE PENDLETON and WILLIAM LEEPER is:
     i.   EMILY ANN[13] LEEPER.

744. CLAUD ERNEST[12] PENDLETON *(RICHARD J.[11], JOHN BOWIE[10], THOMAS[9], JAMES[8], JAMES[7], HENRY[6], PHILIP[5], HENRY[4], HENRY[3], GEORGE[2], GEORGE[1])* was born Jun 23, 1876 in MO, and died May 23, 1944 in AR. He married MARGARET THORNBURGH May 31, 1907.

Claude Ernest Pendleton registered for the World War I draft in Little Rock, Pulaski Co., AR.

Children of CLAUD PENDLETON and MARGARET THORNBURGH are:
     i.   MARY KATHERINE[13] PENDLETON.
    ii. JOHN RICHARD PENDLETON, b. Apr 08, 1911; d. Nov 02, 1950, Pulaski Co., AR.
   iii. MARGARET ELIZABETH PENDLETON.

745. KATE OLIVIA[12] PENDLETON *(ALBERT GALLATIN[11], JAMES FRENCH[10], WILLIAM[9], JAMES[8], JAMES[7], HENRY[6], PHILIP[5], HENRY[4], HENRY[3], GEORGE[2], GEORGE[1])* was born Oct 08, 1868 in VA, and died Aft. 1920 in Roanoke, VA? She married FRANK W. CRAIG Oct 25, 1887. He was born Apr 1858 in TN, and died Aft. 1920 in Roanoke, VA?

Frank W. Craig (real estate agent) and family are listed in the 1920 Roanoke, VA census.

Children of KATE PENDLETON and FRANK CRAIG are:
    i.   ALBERT P.[13] CRAIG, b. Jul 10, 1888, VA; d. Jan 1963, TX.
    ii. JACK T. CRAIG, b. Jul 1890, VA.
    iii. KATHLEEN CRAIG, b. Dec 1891, VA.
    iv. FRANKLIN W. CRAIG, JR., b. Oct 1898, VA.

746. CARRIE STROTHER[12] PENDLETON (*JOHN STROTHER*[11], *JAMES FRENCH*[10], *WILLIAM*[9], *JAMES*[8], *JAMES*[7], *HENRY*[6], *PHILIP*[5], *HENRY*[4], *HENRY*[3], *GEORGE*[2], *GEORGE*[1]) was born Aug 06, 1879 in VA, and died Aft. 1920 in Knoxville, TN? She married JAMES CLYDE LOVE Jul 31, 1901. He was born Abt. 1880 in TN, and died Aft. 1920 in Knoxville, TN?

Children of CARRIE PENDLETON and JAMES LOVE are:
    i.   VIRGINIA T.[13] LOVE, b. Sep 26, 1903, TN; d. Nov 1982, Hampton, VA; m. BENJAMIN W. CHURCHILL Jul 17, 1923; b. Oct 25, 1903, d. Jan 1977, Houston, TX.
    ii. JOHN WILLIAM PENDLETON LOVE.
    iii. JR. JAMES CLYDE LOVE.

747. SUSAN VIRGINIA[12] PENDLETON (*DAVID H.*[11], *JAMES COLEMAN*[10], *JAMES*[9], *PHILIP*[8], *JAMES*[7], *HENRY*[6], *PHILIP*[5], *HENRY*[4], *HENRY*[3], *GEORGE*[2], *GEORGE*[1]) was born 1878 in Bullitt Co., KY, and died 1941. She married ERNEST DEMOVILLE JONES Jul 06, 1904, son of ROBERT JONES and MARY CHURCH. He was born Sep 11, 1871, and died Jan 27, 1936.

Child of SUSAN PENDLETON and ERNEST JONES is:
    i.   DEMOVILLE PENDLETON[13] JONES.

748. AUGUSTA[12] PENDLETON (*WILLIAM FREDERIC*[11], *PHILIP COLEMAN*[10], *COLEMAN*[9], *PHILIP*[8], *JAMES*[7], *HENRY*[6], *PHILIP*[5], *HENRY*[4], *HENRY*[3], *GEORGE*[2], *GEORGE*[1]) was born Mar 11, 1873 in Delaware, and died Aft. 1920 in Montgomery Co., MD? She married (1) MADISON COOPER, DR. 1899. He was born 1873, and died 1910. She married (2) REGINALD WILLIAM BROWN, REV. 1912. He was born Abt. 1878 in Canada, and died Aft. 1920 in Montgomery Co., MD?

Children of AUGUSTA PENDLETON and MADISON COOPER are:
    i.   DOROTHY[13] COOPER.
    ii. MARGARET COOPER.
    iii. LAWSON COOPER.
    iv. PHILIP COOPER.

749. LUELLE[12] PENDLETON (*WILLIAM FREDERIC*[11], *PHILIP COLEMAN*[10], *COLEMAN*[9], *PHILIP*[8], *JAMES*[7], *HENRY*[6], *PHILIP*[5], *HENRY*[4], *HENRY*[3], *GEORGE*[2], *GEORGE*[1]) was born Jan 04, 1875 in PA. She married ROBERT BEEBE CALDWELL 1903. He was born Abt. 1875 in PA.

Child of LUELLE PENDLETON and ROBERT CALDWELL is:
  i. JOHN P.[13] CALDWELL.

750. KORENE[12] PENDLETON *(WILLIAM FREDERIC[11], PHILIP COLEMAN[10], COLEMAN[9], PHILIP[8], JAMES[7], HENRY[6], PHILIP[5], HENRY[4], HENRY[3], GEORGE[2], GEORGE[1])* was born Apr 08, 1885 in PA, and died Aft. 1930 in Bryn Athyn, PA? She married WILLIAM BEEBE CALDWELL. He was born Abt. 1884 in PA, and died Aft. 1930 in Bryn Athyn, PA?

Children of KORENE PENDLETON and WILLIAM CALDWELL are:
  i. BERYL B.[13] CALDWELL.
  ii. JEANETTE CALDWELL.

751. CHARLES RITTENHOUSE[12] PENDLETON *(CHARLES RITTENHOUSE[11], PHILIP COLEMAN[10], COLEMAN[9], PHILIP[8], JAMES[7], HENRY[6], PHILIP[5], HENRY[4], HENRY[3], GEORGE[2], GEORGE[1])* was born May 15, 1883 in GA, and died Feb 1969 in Bryn Athen, PA. He married RUTH HICKS 1912. She was born Mar 05, 1884 in PA, and died May 1974 in Bryn Athen, PA.
  C. R. Pendleton was a delegate to the Democratic National Convention from Georgia in 1912. Charles R. Pendleton (Teacher of Science-Academy of New Church) and family are listed in the 1920 Montgomery Co., MD census.

Child of CHARLES PENDLETON and RUTH HICKS is:
  i. SHAWN[13] PENDLETON.

752. WILLIAM EDMUND[12] PENDLETON *(CHARLES RITTENHOUSE[11], PHILIP COLEMAN[10], COLEMAN[9], PHILIP[8], JAMES[7], HENRY[6], PHILIP[5], HENRY[4], HENRY[3], GEORGE[2], GEORGE[1])* was born Dec 27, 1889 in GA, and died Oct 09, 1959 in Bibb Co., GA. He married STELLA ROBERTS Oct 01, 1914 in Valdosta, Ga., daughter of J. T. ROBERTS. She was born Abt. 1894, and died May 06, 1968 in Bibb Co., GA.
  William Edward Pendleton registered for the World War I draft in Macon, Bibb Co., GA.

Child of WILLIAM PENDLETON and STELLA ROBERTS is:
  i. WILLIAM EDMUND[13] PENDLETON, b. Jul 30, 1915, GA; d. Apr 13, 1995, Macon, GA.

753. PHILIP COLEMAN[12] PENDLETON *(ALEXANDER SHAW[11], PHILIP COLEMAN[10], COLEMAN[9], PHILIP[8], JAMES[7], HENRY[6], PHILIP[5], HENRY[4], HENRY[3], GEORGE[2], GEORGE[1])* was born Dec 21, 1882 in GA. He married SUE HOPE CORNER Apr 25, 1906 in Valdosta, GA. She was born Abt. 1885 in TN, and died Nov 12, 1981 in Lowndes Co., GA.
  Philip Coleman Pendleton registered for the World War I draft in Lowndes Co., GA.

Children of PHILIP PENDLETON and SUE CORNER are:
   i. CATHERINE SARAH[13] PENDLETON, b. Apr 24, 1907; d. Dec 1974, Valdosta, GA; m. THOMAS GORDON CRANFORD, LT., Sep 16, 1930.
   ii. ELIZABETH HOPE PENDLETON.
   iii. SUE CORNER PENDLETON.

754. MARION CHILDS[12] PENDLETON *(NATHANIEL DANDRIDGE[11], PHILIP COLEMAN[10], COLEMAN[9], PHILIP[8], JAMES[7], HENRY[6], PHILIP[5], HENRY[4], HENRY[3], GEORGE[2], GEORGE[1])* was born Jul 24, 1901 in IL, and died 1963. She married ALAN PENDLETON May 30, 1921, son of WILLIAM PENDLETON and MARY YOUNG. He was born Jul 01, 1896 in PA, and died 1936.

755. SARAH JANE THOMAS[12] PENDLETON *(PHILIP THOMAS[11], EDMUND MONROE[10], COLEMAN[9], PHILIP[8], JAMES[7], HENRY[6], PHILIP[5], HENRY[4], HENRY[3], GEORGE[2], GEORGE[1])* was born Apr 16, 1875 in GA, and died Aft. 1920 in Atlanta, GA? She married RICHARD M. EUBANKS Nov 18, 1896 in GA. He was born Abt. 1872 in SC, and died Aft. 1920 in Atlanta, GA?

Children of SARAH PENDLETON and RICHARD EUBANKS are (Ref. 309):
   i. JANE[13] EUBANKS.
   ii. ELIZABETH EUBANKS.
   iii. MARTHA EUBANKS.

756. SUSAN EUGENIA[12] PENDLETON *(JAMES COLEMAN[11], EDMUND MONROE[10], COLEMAN[9], PHILIP[8], JAMES[7], HENRY[6], PHILIP[5], HENRY[4], HENRY[3], GEORGE[2], GEORGE[1])* was born Aug 29, 1883 in GA, and died Aft. 1930 in Atlanta, GA. She married GEORGE HERBERT PHILLIPS Apr 02, 1903 in GA. He was born Oct 04, 1874 in GA, and died Mar 1963 in GA.

Children of SUSAN PENDLETON and GEORGE PHILLIPS are:
   i. JR. GEORGE HERBERT[13] PHILLIPS.
   ii. SUSIE LOUISE PHILLIPS, b. Mar 16, 1908; d. Jan 12, 1914.
   iii. EDMUND PENDLETON PHILLIPS.

757. BENJAMIN[12] PENDLETON *(NATHANIEL C.[11], JAMES C.[10], NATHANIEL[9], WILLIAM[8], NATHANIEL[7], HENRY[6], PHILIP[5], HENRY[4], HENRY[3], GEORGE[2], GEORGE[1])* was born Mar 18, 1867 in Hopkins Co., TX, and died 1915 in Bennington, OK? He married (1) MARY MARTIN Abt. 1894. She was born Mar 1874 in TX, and died Sep 04, 1902 in Franklin Co., TX? He married (2) WILLIE BELLE BINGHAM Jun 21, 1905 in Dokeville, Indian Territory, OK, daughter of ELISHA BINGHAM. She was born Mar 19, 1887 in Bryan Co., OK, and died Apr 05, 1944.

   Ben Pendleton (dentist) and family are listed in the 1900 Franklin Co., TX census, pg. 19a. After the death of his first wife, Benjamin migrated to Bennington, OK, Indian Territory, where he practiced dentistry for many years.

Children of BENJAMIN PENDLETON and MARY MARTIN are:
  i.   ZONA[13] PENDLETON, b. May 15, 1895, TX; m. JOHN HULSEY; of Honey Grove, TX.
  ii. CUNNINGHAM PENDLETON, b. Sep 1898, TX.
  iii. BEN PENDLETON.

Children of BENJAMIN PENDLETON and WILLIE BINGHAM are:
  iv. RICHARD MCFALL[13] PENDLETON, b. Aug 06, 1906; d. Mar 28, 1909.
  v.   DREW BRASHER PENDLETON, b. Dec 01, 1909; d. May 01, 1910.
  vi. EMMA ELIZABETH PENDLETON, b. Oct 12, 1912, Bennington, OK; d. Mar 04, 1966, Covina, CA; m. JAMES C. TRUAX; b. of San Antonio, TX.
  vii. JOHN EDGAR PENDLETON, b. Apr 01, 1915, Bennington, OK; d. Aug 16, 1999; m. DULCIE NORMA DISHER, Apr 27, 1943, Claremont, Western Australia; b. of Cottesloe, Western Australia.

758. JOSHUA[12] PENDLETON *(NATHANIEL C.[11], JAMES C.[10], NATHANIEL[9], WILLIAM[8], NATHANIEL[7], HENRY[6], PHILIP[5], HENRY[4], HENRY[3], GEORGE[2], GEORGE[1])* was born Sep 1869 in TX, and died Jun 09, 1945 in Hopkins Co., TX? He married MARY ELMIRA BARTLETT Abt. 1899, daughter of HENRY BARTLETT and CELIA PICKLE. She was born Jun 1870 in TX, and died Aft. 1920 in Hopkins Co., TX?
      Josh Pendleton, farmer, and family are listed in the 1920 Hopkins Co., TX census.

Children of JOSHUA PENDLETON and MARY BARTLETT are:
  i.   VERA M.[13] PENDLETON.
  ii. BOYD PENDLETON.
  iii. GLADYS PENDLETON.

759. RICHARD "DICK"[12] PENDLETON *(NATHANIEL C.[11], JAMES C.[10], NATHANIEL[9], WILLIAM[8], NATHANIEL[7], HENRY[6], PHILIP[5], HENRY[4], HENRY[3], GEORGE[2], GEORGE[1])* was born Abt. 1880 in TX. He married ELIZABETH CHURCH. She was born Abt. 1884 in TX.
      Dick Pendleton owned and operated a drug store in Mineola, TX for many years and also served as a Justice of the Peace.

Children of RICHARD PENDLETON and ELIZABETH CHURCH are:
  i.   NANA LEE[13] PENDLETON.
  ii. JAMES CHURCH PENDLETON.
  iii. ELIZABETH PENDLETON.
  iv. RICHARD PENDLETON, JR.

760. MARY RICKARD[12] PENDLETON *(BENJAMIN STROTHER[11], JAMES WILLIAM[10], BENJAMIN[9], WILLIAM[8], NATHANIEL[7], HENRY[6], PHILIP[5], HENRY[4], HENRY[3], GEORGE[2], GEORGE[1])* was born Apr 24, 1886 in WV, and died Dec 1976 in Indianapolis, IN. She married CHARLES ALMOND PEARSON Oct 07, 1913. He was born Jun 10, 1878, and died Aug 1967 in Indianapolis, IN.

Children of MARY PENDLETON and CHARLES PEARSON are:
  i. CHARLES ALMOND[13] PEARSON, JR.
  ii. JOHN STROTHER PEARSON.
  iii. THOMAS RICKARD PEARSON.

761. VIRGINIA OGDEN[12] PENDLETON *(PHILIP CLAYTON[11], PHILIP CLAYTON[10], PHILIP CLAYTON[9], PHILIP[8], NATHANIEL[7], HENRY[6], PHILIP[5], HENRY[4], HENRY[3], GEORGE[2], GEORGE[1])* was born Dec 06, 1866 in MS, and died Aft. 1910 in Camden NJ? She married PAGE.

Children of VIRGINIA PENDLETON and PAGE are:
  i. ISABELLE W.[13] PAGE, b. Abt. 1895, NJ.
  ii. WILLIAM B. PAGE.

762. JR. WILLIAM ARMISTEAD[12] PENDLETON *(WILLIAM ARMISTEAD[11], JOHN LEWIS[10], JOHN[9], EDMUND[8], JOHN[7], HENRY[6], PHILIP[5], HENRY[4], HENRY[3], GEORGE[2], GEORGE[1])* was born Abt. 1856 in St. Louis, MO, and died 1890. He married MARY ALEXANDER BRUCE Sep 02, 1885 in Lexington, Rockbridge Co., VA, daughter of ALEXANDER BRUCE and MARY ANDERSON. She was born Abt. 1860 in Halifax Co. VA?

Children of WILLIAM PENDLETON and MARY BRUCE are:
  i. III WILLIAM ARMISTEAD[13] PENDLETON, b. Jun 24, 1886, VA; m. ELSIE G. HUNT Jun 09, 1923; b. 1897, NY.
    William A. Pendleton graduated from the U.S. Military Academy at West Point in 1910. He served with the A.E.F. as a Major, Field Artillery, U.S. Army.

903. ii. ALEXANDER BRUCE PENDLETON, b. Mar 14, 1888, VA; d. May 04, 1919, Halifax Co., VA.
  iii. ALLAN BRUCE PENDLETON, b. Abt. 1890, VA; d. Jul 09, 1900, St. Louis, MO.

763. EDMUND ALLEN[12] PENDLETON *(WILLIAM[11], EDMUND ALLEN[10], JOHN[9], EDMUND[8], JOHN[7], HENRY[6], PHILIP[5], HENRY[4], HENRY[3], GEORGE[2], GEORGE[1])* was born Dec 20, 1872 in GA, and died Aft. 1910 in Richmond Co., GA? He married ALBERTA M. MEYERS Abt. 1897 in Richmond Co., GA?, daughter of BERTHA J. She was born Oct 1877 in GA, and died Aft. 1910 in Richmond Co., GA?

  E. A. Pendleton (bank teller) and wife are listed in the 1900 Richmond Co., GA census, pg. 197a. Edmund Allen Pendleton registered for the World War I draft in Augusta, Richmond Co., GA. This Edmund, however, may be the son of Armistead Franklin Pendleton (see next page).

Child of EDMUND PENDLETON and ALBERTA MEYERS is:
  i. BERTHA[13] PENDLETON, b. Abt. 1899.

764. EDMUND ALLEN[12] PENDLETON *(ARMISTEAD FRANKLIN[11], EDMUND ALLEN[10], JOHN[9], EDMUND[8], JOHN[7], HENRY[6], PHILIP[5], HENRY[4], HENRY[3], GEORGE[2], GEORGE[1])* was born Abt. 1873 in GA, and died Aft. 1910 in Richmond Co., GA? He married AGNES WALKER Abt. 1886. She died Sep 30, 1944 in De Kalb Co., GA.

Child of EDMUND PENDLETON and AGNES WALKER is:
     v. WALKER PAGE[12] PENDLETON, b. Dec 13, 1888, GA; d. Dec 1962.

765. III WILLIAM ARMISTEAD[12] PENDLETON *(WILLIAM ARMISTEAD[11], WILLIAM ARMISTEAD[10], JOHN[9], EDMUND[8], JOHN[7], HENRY[6], PHILIP[5], HENRY[4], HENRY[3], GEORGE[2], GEORGE[1])* was born Apr 12, 1876 in KY, and died Aft. 1930 in Cincinnati, OH? He married (1) LILLIE MAY RASPAM Abt. 1900. She was born 1882 in OH, and died Aft. 1920 in Cincinnati, OH? He married (2) EDNA. She was born 1894 in PA, and died Aft. 1930.
     William Armstead Pendleton (occupation engineer) registered for the World War I draft in Cincinnati, Hamilton Co., OH.

Children of WILLIAM PENDLETON and LILLIE RASPAM are:
     i. FRANCIS L.[13] PENDLETON.
     ii. VIOLET O. PENDLETON.
     iii. WILLIAM PENDLETON.

766. STEWART[12] PENDLETON *(WILLIAM ARMISTEAD[11], WILLIAM ARMISTEAD[10], JOHN[9], EDMUND[8], JOHN[7], HENRY[6], PHILIP[5], HENRY[4], HENRY[3], GEORGE[2], GEORGE[1])* was born Sep 26, 1881 in Campbell Co., KY, and died Jun 1971 in Louisville, OH. He married ALICE B. She was born Abt. 1892 in NY, and died Aft. 1930 in Wayne Co., OH?
     Stewart Pendleton (bead trimmer; rubber works) and family are listed in the 1920 Canton, Stark Co., OH census.

Children of STEWART PENDLETON and ALICE B. are:
     i. STEWART DARRELL[13] PENDLETON, b. Apr 23, 1911, OH; d. Jul 21, 1991.
     ii. ARNOLD HENRY PENDLETON.

767. AGNES ROY[12] PENDLETON *(ROBERT LEWIS[11], ROBERT TAYLOR[10], JOHN[9], EDMUND[8], JOHN[7], HENRY[6], PHILIP[5], HENRY[4], HENRY[3], GEORGE[2], GEORGE[1])* was born 1862 in VA, and died Aft. 1930 in Newport News, VA? She married EDWARD W. CHRISTIAN Nov 03, 1885 in Essex Co., VA. He was born Abt. 1861 in VA, and died Aft. 1930 in Newport News, VA?
     The marriage of Agnes Pendleton and Edward Christian is recorded in Reference 25.

Child of AGNES PENDLETON and EDWARD CHRISTIAN is:
     i. CATHERINE S.[13] CHRISTIAN.

768. ROBERT L.[12] PENDLETON *(ROBERT LEWIS[11], ROBERT TAYLOR[10], JOHN[9], EDMUND[8], JOHN[7], HENRY[6], PHILIP[5], HENRY[4], HENRY[3], GEORGE[2], GEORGE[1])* was born 1863 in VA, and died Aft. 1920 in Essex Co., VA? He married MABEL M. She was born Abt. 1869 in VA, and died Aft. 1920 in Essex Co., VA?

R. L. Pendleton (farmer, 56) and family are listed in the 1920 Central Township, Essex Co., VA census, pg. 6B.

Child of ROBERT PENDLETON and MABEL M. is:
    i. CATHERINE M.[13] PENDLETON.

769. REGINALD NOEL[12] PENDLETON *(ROBERT LEWIS[11], ROBERT TAYLOR[10], JOHN[9], EDMUND[8], JOHN[7], HENRY[6], PHILIP[5], HENRY[4], HENRY[3], GEORGE[2], GEORGE[1])* was born Dec 09, 1873 in Baltimore, MD, and died Apr 10, 1935 in Baltimore, MD. He married MARY CORDELIA GARTHRIGHT Dec 09, 1901 in Newport News, Warwick, VA. She was born Jun 20, 1882 in Richmond, VA, and died Apr 02, 1967 in Baltimore, MD.

Reginald Noel Pendleton registered for the World War I draft in Baltimore, MD. Reginald N. Pendleton (shipfitter; steel maker) and family are listed in the 1920 Baltimore, MD census.

Children of REGINALD PENDLETON and MARY GARTHRIGHT are:
    i. EDELLA G.[13] PENDLETON.
    ii. DORIS M. PENDLETON.

770. ARTHUR THOMAS[12] PENDLETON *(SAMUEL HEISLER[11], JAMES LAWRENCE[10], EDMUND[9], EDMUND[8], JOHN[7], HENRY[6], PHILIP[5], HENRY[4], HENRY[3], GEORGE[2], GEORGE[1])* was born Nov 20, 1865 in VA, and died Aft. 1920 in Elizabeth City, NJ? He married IDA L. TALIAFERRO Abt. 1903. She was born Abt. 1876 in VA, and died Aft. 1920 in Elizabeth City, NJ?

Arthur T. Pendleton (Estate Manager) and family are listed in the 1920 Elizabeth City, NJ census.

Children of ARTHUR PENDLETON and IDA TALIAFERRO are:
    i. SAMUEL TALIAFERRO[13] PENDLETON, b. Jul 28, 1906, NJ; d. Feb 1971, Charlottesville, VA.
    ii. ANNE LOUISE PENDLETON.
    iii. ELIZABETH TAYLOR PENDLETON.

771. JR. DUDLEY DIGGES[12] PENDLETON *(DUDLEY DIGGES[11], HUGH NELSON[10], EDMUND[9], EDMUND[8], JOHN[7], HENRY[6], PHILIP[5], HENRY[4], HENRY[3], GEORGE[2], GEORGE[1])* was born Mar 24, 1873 in WV, and died Aft. 1930 in Pittsburgh, PA? He married MARGUERITE BRUNELLE LAKE Oct 11, 1913. She was born Abt. 1883 in MD, and died Aft. 1930 in Pittsburgh, PA?

Children of DUDLEY PENDLETON and MARGUERITE LAKE are:
  i.   III DUDLEY DIGGES[13] PENDLETON, b. Jan 12, 1915, NJ; d. Aug 1974, Long Beach, CA.
  ii. JAMES LAKE PENDLETON, b. Mar 26, 1917, PA; d. Mar 1980, Galveston, TX.

772. HUGH NELSON[12] PENDLETON *(DUDLEY DIGGES[11], HUGH NELSON[10], EDMUND[9], EDMUND[8], JOHN[7], HENRY[6], PHILIP[5], HENRY[4], HENRY[3], GEORGE[2], GEORGE[1])* was born Jan 11, 1875 in WV, and died Bef. 1954. He married SERENA PENDLETON DANDRIDGE Sep 11, 1901. She was born Abt. 1878 in VA, and died Aft. 1920 in Jefferson Co., WV.
  Hugh N. Pendleton and family are listed in the McKeesport, Alleghany Co., PA 1920 census.

Children of HUGH PENDLETON and SERENA DANDRIDGE are:
  i.   SERENA DANDRIDGE[13] PENDLETON.
  ii. HUGH NELSON PENDLETON, b. Aug 30, 1906, PA; d. Jul 30, 1996, CO.
  iii. HELEN BOTELER PENDLETON.
  iv. ISABELLA LAWRENCE PENDLETON.

773. ROSALIE[12] PENDLETON *(DUDLEY DIGGES[11], HUGH NELSON[10], EDMUND[9], EDMUND[8], JOHN[7], HENRY[6], PHILIP[5], HENRY[4], HENRY[3], GEORGE[2], GEORGE[1])* was born May 14, 1880 in WV, and died Aft. 1920 in Pittsburgh, PA? She married CORNELIUS DECATUR SCULLY. He was born Abt. 1874 in PA, and died Aft. 1920 in Pittsburgh, PA?

Children of ROSALIE PENDLETON and CORNELIUS SCULLY are:
  i.   ALICE PENDLETON[13] SCULLY.
  ii. ELIZABETH NEGLEY SCULLY.
  iii. JR. CORNELIUS DECATUR SCULLY.
  iv. JOHN PENDLETON SCULLY.

774. SUE GIBSON[12] PENDLETON *(ROBERT NELSON[11], HUGH NELSON[10], EDMUND[9], EDMUND[8], JOHN[7], HENRY[6], PHILIP[5], HENRY[4], HENRY[3], GEORGE[2], GEORGE[1])* was born Oct 30, 1873 in Wytheville, VA, and died Aft. 1920 in Wytheville, VA? She married FRANK PAINTER CHAFFIN, DR. Feb 14, 1898. He was born Abt. 1872 in VA, and died Aft. 1920 in Wytheville, VA?
  Frank P. Chaffin and family are listed in the 1920 Wytheville, VA census.

Child of SUE PENDLETON and FRANK CHAFFIN is:
  i.   ALEXANDER NATHAN[13] CHAFFIN, b. Sep 07, 1899, VA; d. Apr 1958.

775. KATE BERKELEY[12] PENDLETON *(ROBERT NELSON[11], HUGH NELSON[10], EDMUND[9], EDMUND[8], JOHN[7], HENRY[6], PHILIP[5], HENRY[4], HENRY[3], GEORGE[2], GEORGE[1])* was born Jul 29, 1875 in Wytheville, VA, and died Aft. 1920. She married

GEORGE GILMORE MOORE, DR. He was born 1875 in VA, and died 1925 in Lexington, VA?

Mrs. Kate Burkley Pendleton Moore was a member of The National Society of the Daughters of the American Revolution (Volume 77, page 63).

Children of KATE PENDLETON and GEORGE MOORE are:
    i. ROBERT PENDLETON[13] MOORE, b. Oct 24, 1908, VA; d. Apr 26, 1911.
    ii. GEORGE GILMORE MOORE.

776. ELIZABETH "BETTIE" BARRETT[12] PENDLETON *(JOHN BARRETT[11], MADISON[10], EDMUND[9], HENRY[8], JOHN[7], HENRY[6], PHILIP[5], HENRY[4], HENRY[3], GEORGE[2], GEORGE[1])* was born Apr 28, 1860 in VA, and died Aft. 1920 in Cuckoo, Louisa Co., VA? She married EUGENE B. PENDLETON, DR. Sep 09, 1880, son of PHILIP PENDLETON and JANE HOLLIDAY. He was born Jun 22, 1851 in VA, and died Sep 09, 1927 in Cuckoo, Louisa Co., VA?

Children are listed above under **(516)** Eugene B. Pendleton, Dr.

777. JOHN HENRY[12] PENDLETON *(EDMUND STRACHAN[11], MADISON[10], EDMUND[9], HENRY[8], JOHN[7], HENRY[6], PHILIP[5], HENRY[4], HENRY[3], GEORGE[2], GEORGE[1])* was born Jun 26, 1867 in VA, and died Mar 05, 1899. He married MAMIE G. PORTER.

Child of JOHN PENDLETON and MAMIE PORTER is:
    i. EDMUND PORTER[13] PENDLETON, b. Mar 21, 1893.

778. SUSAN STRACHAN[12] PENDLETON *(EDMUND STRACHAN[11], MADISON[10], EDMUND[9], HENRY[8], JOHN[7], HENRY[6], PHILIP[5], HENRY[4], HENRY[3], GEORGE[2], GEORGE[1])* was born Feb 18, 1877 in VA, and died Apr 28, 1957 in Botetourt Co., VA? She married EDWARD DILLON Oct 06, 1897, son of EDWARD DILLON and FRANCES POLK. He was born Oct 19, 1871 in VA, and died Mar 24, 1922 in Buchanan, Botetourt Co., VA?

Edward Dillon (manufacturing) and family are listed in the 1920 Buchanan, Botetourt Co., VA census.

Children of SUSAN PENDLETON and EDWARD DILLON are:
    i. EDMUND P.[13] DILLON.
    ii. MARY W. DILLON.
    iii. WILLIAM P. DILLON.

779. ELIZABETH KIMBROUGH[12] PENDLETON *(CHARLES KIMBROUGH[11], MADISON[10], EDMUND[9], HENRY[8], JOHN[7], HENRY[6], PHILIP[5], HENRY[4], HENRY[3], GEORGE[2], GEORGE[1])* was born Dec 28, 1879 in Louisa Co., VA, and died Aft. 1920 in Ashland, VA? She married JAMES MARCELLUS COX Jan 16, 1906. He was born Abt. 1875 in VA, and died Aft. 1920 in Ashland, VA?

James Cox (Retail Merchant, Dry Goods) and family are listed in the 1920 Ashland, Hanover Co., VA census. Mrs. Elizabeth Pendleton Cox was a member of The National Society of the Daughters of the American Revolution (Volume 115, page 174).

Children of ELIZABETH PENDLETON and JAMES COX are:
    i. ELIZABETH PENDLETON[13] COX.
    ii. JAMES KIMBROUGH COX, b. Nov 24, 1908, VA; d. Apr 1962.

780. MARY WASHINGTON[12] PENDLETON (*CHARLES KIMBROUGH[11], MADISON[10], EDMUND[9], HENRY[8], JOHN[7], HENRY[6], PHILIP[5], HENRY[4], HENRY[3], GEORGE[2], GEORGE[1]*) was born Dec 20, 1881 in Louisa Co., VA, and died Aft. 1920 in Ashland, VA? She married HENRY ROSE CARTER, DR. Oct 18, 1905. He was born Abt. 1875 in VA, and died Aft. 1920.
    Mrs. Mary Pendleton Carter was a member of The National Society of the Daughters of the American Revolution (Volume 127, page 2).

Child of MARY PENDLETON and HENRY CARTER is:
    i. HILL[13] CARTER.

781. AUSTIN CAMPBELL[12] PENDLETON (*WILLIAM CAMPBELL[11], WILLIAM KIMBROUGH[10], EDMUND[9], HENRY[8], JOHN[7], HENRY[6], PHILIP[5], HENRY[4], HENRY[3], GEORGE[2], GEORGE[1]*) was born Aug 03, 1881 in Trumbull Co., OH, and died Apr 27, 1921 in Trumbull Co., OH. He married WINIFRED THORN Oct 01, 1903. She was born Nov 04, 1880 in Mahoning Co., OH, and died Aft. 1920 in Trumbull Co., OH?

Children of AUSTIN PENDLETON and WINIFRED THORN are:
    i. VIRGINIA THORN[13] PENDLETON.
    ii. EMLEN THORN PENDLETON, b. Jun 24, 1907, OH; d. Jun 1985, Trumbull Co., OH.

782. EUGENE BARBOUR[12] PENDLETON (*EUGENE B.[11], PHILIP BARBOUR[10], EDMUND[9], HENRY[8], JOHN[7], HENRY[6], PHILIP[5], HENRY[4], HENRY[3], GEORGE[2], GEORGE[1]*) was born Jun 01, 1885 in VA, and died Aft. 1920 in Cuckoo, Louisa Co., VA? He married VIRGINIA HUNTER GOODMAN Oct 23, 1909. She was born Abt. 1883 in VA, and died Aft. 1920 in Cuckoo, Louisa Co., VA?
    Eugene Barbour Pendleton (doctor) and family are listed in the 1920 census, Cuckoo, Louisa Co., VA, pg. 7B.

Children of EUGENE PENDLETON and VIRGINIA GOODMAN are:
    i. ELIZABETH EUGENIA[13] PENDLETON.
    ii. EUGENE BARBOUR PENDLETON, b. Apr 02, 1913, VA; d. Jan 23, 2004, Louisa Co., VA.

783. IRA NEWTON[12] PENDLETON (*JAMES TRIGG[11], IRA NASH[10], REUBEN[9], BENJAMIN[8], WILLIAM[7], JOHN[6], PHILIP[5], HENRY[4], HENRY[3], GEORGE[2], GEORGE[1]*) was born Jun 05, 1851 in Scott Co., VA, and died Mar 25, 1907 in KY. He married

ARMINTA BRANHAM Sep 17, 1873 in Johnson Co., KY, daughter of TURNER BRANHAM and CATHERINE MEAD. She was born Jan 23, 1859 in Johnson Co., KY, and died Apr 06, 1903 in KY.

Children of IRA PENDLETON and ARMINTA BRANHAM are:
904.   i.   JAMES TRIGG[13] PENDLETON, b. Oct 10, 1874, Johnson Co., KY; d. 1940.
        ii.   TURNER PENDLETON, b. May 05, 1877, Morgan Co., KY; d. Nov 22, 1944, Scioto Co., OH; m. MYRTLE BELL WILLIAM, Sep 19, 1903, Johnson Co., KY; b. Dec 26, 1877, Red Bush, KY; d. Feb 28, 1935, Scioto Co., OH.
           Turner Pendleton registered for the WWI draft in Johnson Co., KY. His residence was Portsmouth, Scioto Co., OH

       iii.   FLORA PENDLETON, b. Abt. 1879, KY; m. JAMES M. COMPTON, Jan 10, 1900, Johnson Co., KY; b. 1876, KY.
905.   iv.   LOU PENDLETON, b. Mar 1883, KY; d. Aft. 1920, Johnson Co., KY?
       v.   GROVER PENDLETON, b. Apr 23, 1885, KY; d. Jun 1968, Scioto Co., OH; m. AMANDA BROWN, Jun 29, 1904, Johnson Co., KY; b. Abt. 1884.
       vi.   JOHN PENDLETON, b. Abt. 1890, KY.
       vii.   WILLIAM PENDLETON, b. Nov 22, 1892, KY; d. Dec 27, 1916, Hamilton Co., OH; m. TENNIE HILL; b. Apr 14, 1890; d. Jan 19, 1947, Morgan Co., KY.
       viii.   MOLLIE PENDLETON, b. Nov 1893, KY.

784. JOHN[12] PENDLETON (*JAMES TRIGG*[11], *IRA NASH*[10], *REUBEN*[9], *BENJAMIN*[8], *WILLIAM*[7], *JOHN*[6], *PHILIP*[5], *HENRY*[4], *HENRY*[3], *GEORGE*[2], *GEORGE*[1]) was born May 10, 1853 in VA, and died Nov 24, 1911 in Morgan Co., KY. He married (1) EMILY WIREMAN Aug 07, 1874 in Johnson Co., KY. She was born Abt. 1857 in VA, and died in Johnson Co., KY. He married (2) LUCINA MEAD Dec 20, 1881 in Johnson Co., KY. She was born 1861.
      John Pendleton (farmer) and family are listed in the 1900 Johnson Co., KY census, pg. 206.

Children of JOHN PENDLETON and EMILY WIREMAN are:
       i.   WILLIAM JAMES[13] PENDLETON, b. Jul 05, 1876, Johnson Co., KY; m. JENNY; b. Abt. 1890, KY.
           William James Pendleton registered for the WWI draft in Johnson Co., KY. His nearest relative is listed as Mrs. Vada Pendleton and residence as Paintsville, KY.

       ii.   ROBERT TRIGG PENDLETON, b. Oct 17, 1878, Johnson Co., KY; d. Jul 28, 1943, Johnson Co., KY; m. MARY L.; b. Jan 21, 1889; d. Feb 1964, Morgan Co., KY.
           Robert Trigg Pendleton (occupation farming) registered for the WWI draft in Morgan Co., KY. His nearest relative was Mary Pendleton and residence was Ophir, Morgan Co., KY.

Children of JOHN PENDLETON and LUCINA MEAD are:
  iii. MOLLIE[13] PENDLETON, b. Oct 1882, KY; m. L. E. WILLIAMS, Sep 15, 1900, Johnson Co., KY; b. Abt. 1879.
  iv. SARAH PENDLETON, b. Feb 1885, KY.

785. JAMES M.[12] PENDLETON *(JAMES TRIGG[11], IRA NASH[10], REUBEN[9], BENJAMIN[8], WILLIAM[7], JOHN[6], PHILIP[5], HENRY[4], HENRY[3], GEORGE[2], GEORGE[1])* was born Abt. 1854 in VA. He married RHODA ELLEN BRANHAM Apr 25, 1878 in Morgan Co., KY. She was born Abt. 1864 in KY.

Child of JAMES PENDLETON and RHODA BRANHAM is:
  i. POLK[13] PENDLETON, b. Jun 04, 1880, Morgan Co., KY?; d. Jun 20, 1957, Floyd Co., IN; m. IDA WILLIAMS, Oct 25, 1907; b. Feb 16, 1884; d. Jun 15, 1974, Floyd Co., IN.
      Polk Pendleton (occupation farming) registered for the WWI draft in Morgan Co., KY.

786. ARDENA[12] PENDLETON *(JAMES TRIGG[11], IRA NASH[10], REUBEN[9], BENJAMIN[8], WILLIAM[7], JOHN[6], PHILIP[5], HENRY[4], HENRY[3], GEORGE[2], GEORGE[1])* was born Abt. 1862 in KY, and died Aft. 1900. She married CHRISTOPHER COLUMBUS ISON Aug 14, 1884 in Morgan Co., KY, son of MARTIN ISON and ELIZABETH SMITH. He was born Jul 29, 1865 in Elliot Co., KY, and died Jul 01, 1946.

Children of ARDENA PENDLETON and CHRISTOPHER ISON are:
  i.   CALONA[13] ISON, b. May 1885.
  ii.   GEORGE W. ISON, b. Feb 1887.
  iii. SHERMAN ISON, b. Nov 1888.
  iv.   AMANDA ISON, b. Nov 1889.
  v.   CORA ISON, b. Nov 1892.
  vi.   TRIGG ISON, b. Mar 1895.
  vii. DAUGHTER ISON, b. May 1897.

787. VIRGINIA[12] PENDLETON *(JAMES TRIGG[11], IRA NASH[10], REUBEN[9], BENJAMIN[8], WILLIAM[7], JOHN[6], PHILIP[5], HENRY[4], HENRY[3], GEORGE[2], GEORGE[1])* was born May 05, 1865 in KY, and died Mar 29, 1931 in Morgan Co., KY. She married JOSEPH COLE Abt. 1883, son of JESSE COLE and PENELOPE HOWINGTON. He was born Feb 12, 1848 in Yadkin Co., NC, and died Aug 30, 1934 in Morgan Co., KY.

Children of VIRGINIA PENDLETON and JOSEPH COLE are:
  i.   GENOE H.[13] COLE, b. 1880, Morgan Co., KY; d. 1881, Morgan Co., KY.
  ii. SARAH CALOMA COLE, b. Jun 12, 1884, Morgan Co., KY; d. Dec 09, 1940, Morgan Co., KY; m. SAM HELTON; b. Mar 01, 1889, Morgan Co., KY; d. Nov 24, 1970, Morgan Co., KY.

iii. JESSE TRUMAN COLE, b. Feb 12, 1886, Morgan Co., KY; d. Sep 28, 1961, Jackson Co., OH; m. LOU VESTA MCCURRY, Dec 25, 1907, Johnson Co., KY; b. Oct 25, 1888, Johnson Co., KY; d. Oct 17, 1972, Pike Co., KY.

iv. JOHN ANDREW COLE, b. Jun 09, 1891, Morgan Co., KY; d. May 1967, Montgomery Co., OH; m. MARTHA GULLETT; b. Oct 11, 1891, Magoffin Co., KY; d. 1966, Magoffin Co., KY.

v. WILLIAM D. COLE, b. 1893; d. Aug 20, 1916, Morgan Co., KY.

vi. ARMINTA ELIZABETH COLE, b. Dec 18, 1896, Morgan Co., KY; d. Oct 14, 1969, Morgan Co., KY; m. JIM HELTON, Dec 25, 1912, Morgan Co., KY; b. Nov 18, 1894; d. Jan 12, 1969, Morgan Co., KY.

vii. ARDENA CATHERINE COLE, b. Sep 24, 1900; d. Dec 1986, OH; m. (1) SAM COCHRAN; m. (2) GEORGE HELTON, Morgan Co., KY; d. 1949.

viii. TRIGG COLE, b. Feb 12, 1903, Morgan Co., KY; d. Apr 03, 1929, Morgan Co., KY; m. GRACIE COX, Jan 19, 1921; d. Apr 27, 1990, Rowan Co., KY.

788. GEORGE H.[12] PENDLETON (*JAMES TRIGG*[11], *IRA NASH*[10], *REUBEN*[9], *BENJAMIN*[8], *WILLIAM*[7], *JOHN*[6], *PHILIP*[5], *HENRY*[4], *HENRY*[3], *GEORGE*[2], *GEORGE*[1]) was born Oct 19, 1868 in KY, and died Oct 19, 1911 in Johnson Co., KY. He married MAHALA DELPHIE LEMASTER Mar 15, 1894. She was born Mar 20, 1874 in KY, and died Oct 30, 1911 in Johnson Co., KY.

Children of GEORGE PENDLETON and MAHALA LEMASTER are:

i. SAMUEL[13] PENDLETON, b. Sep 23, 1895, Morgan Co., KY; d. Feb 14, 1958, Chillicothe, OH; m. JOSEPHINE HALL Aug 12, 1919, Wheelersburg, KY, dau. JAMES HALL and ELIZABETH CONLEY; b. Oct 09, 1903, McGuffin, KY; d. Oct 17, 1985, Pike Co., OH.

ii. ARDENA PENDLETON, b. 1899, Johnson Co., KY; d. Dec 14, 1978, Portsmouth, OH; m. ANDREW JAYNE; b. 1892, Magoffin Co., KY; d. Jan 15, 1977, Portsmouth, OH.

906. iii. WILLIAM PENDLETON, b. Mar 28, 1899; d. Jan 04, 1966, KY.

iv. MAGGIE P. PENDLETON.

v. JOHN ALFRED PENDLETON.

vi. CHARLES PENDLETON.

vii. SARAH L. PENDLETON, b. 1909; d. Dec 16, 1984, Cincinnati, OH; m. JAMES CLIFFORD CROSS; b. 1909; d. 1987.

viii. GAIL PENDLETON.

789. CHARLES[12] PENDLETON (*SAMUEL G.*[11], *IRA NASH*[10], *REUBEN*[9], *BENJAMIN*[8], *WILLIAM*[7], *JOHN*[6], *PHILIP*[5], *HENRY*[4], *HENRY*[3], *GEORGE*[2], *GEORGE*[1]) was born Abt. 1868 in VA, and died Aft. 1910 in Chelan Co., WA? He married JULIA HAMILTON Feb 16, 1889 in Johnson Co., KY. She was born Abt. 1870 in KY, and died Aft. 1910 in Chelan Co., WA?

Children of CHARLES PENDLETON and JULIA HAMILTON are:

i. JULIA A.[13] PENDLETON, b. Abt. 1890, KY.

ii. NORA PENDLETON, b. Abt. 1892, KY.

iii. ESTA PENDLETON, b. Abt. 1895, KY; m. L. A. HAFFERTY; b. Abt. 1887, Iowa.
iv. BESSIE PENDLETON, b. Abt. 1897, KY.
v. CHARLES PENDLETON.
vi. ROSA PENDLETON.
vii. WILLIE PENDLETON.
viii. DOROTHY PENDLETON.

790. EDWIN DUDLEY[12] PENDLETON (*IRA NASH*[11], *SAMUEL GUTHRIE*[10], *REUBEN*[9], *BENJAMIN*[8], *WILLIAM*[7], *JOHN*[6], *PHILIP*[5], *HENRY*[4], *HENRY*[3], *GEORGE*[2], *GEORGE*[1]) was born Dec 01, 1855 in VA, and died Dec 28, 1928 in Bristol, VA. He married MARY ELIZABETH HORTON Jan 31, 1877. She was born Jun 30, 1862 in VA, and died Jan 31, 1928 in Bristol, VA.

Edwin D. and family are listed in the 1920 St. Clair Co., IL census, East St. Louis, pg. 1B.

Children of EDWIN PENDLETON and MARY HORTON are:
i. DORA BLANCHE[13] PENDLETON, b. Jul 11, 1879, VA; d. 1959; m. HOLLY MORGAN HALE, REV., Nov 25, 1903; b. Oct 01, 1878, MO; d. Apr 10, 1954.

907. ii. ALBERT HORTON PENDLETON, b. Jul 31, 1881, VA; d. Aft. 1930, Chicago, IL?

iii. ERASMUS MCCLEARY PENDLETON, b. Oct 19, 1883, VA; d. Aft. 1930, St. Louis, MO.?; m. LOLITA COMPAS, Dec 06, 1926; b. Jan 26, 1893, CA; d. Feb 1973, San Diego, CA.

iv. IRA LYNN PENDLETON, b. Sep 26, 1886, VA; d. Mar 1965, MT; m. ANNA LEE (ANDREWS) HINSON, May 15, 1929; b. Abt. 1893, IL.
Ira Lynn Pendleton registered for the World War I draft in East St Louis, St Clair, IL. I. L. (Clerk, Booking Co.) and Anna Lee Pendleton are listed in the 1930 E. St. Louis, IL census.

v. NANNIE BERTHA PENDLETON, b. Nov 29, 1888, VA; m. J. FRED MEYER, Jun 06, 1914.

vi. RUFUS EDWIN PENDLETON, b. Oct 16, 1892, VA; m. MAUD (DANIELS) LATHAM, Feb 12, 1916.

vii. CLYDE FUGATE PENDLETON, b. Oct 10, 1894, VA; d. Sep 27, 1918, in action WWI, Bristol, France.
Clyde F. Pendleton registered for the World War I draft in East St Louis, St Clair Co., IL. Clyde F. Pendleton, Corporal, East St. Louis, was a soldier of the Great War (Ref. 292).

791. LAURA REBECCA[12] PENDLETON (*IRA NASH*[11], *SAMUEL GUTHRIE*[10], *REUBEN*[9], *BENJAMIN*[8], *WILLIAM*[7], *JOHN*[6], *PHILIP*[5], *HENRY*[4], *HENRY*[3], *GEORGE*[2], *GEORGE*[1]) was born Oct 05, 1857 in VA, and died Aft. 1920 in Bristol, VA? She married WILLIAM B. KILGORE Feb 04, 1873, son of GRANVILLE KILGORE and

ESTHER FUGATE. He was born Apr 18, 1854 in VA, and died Abt. 1929 in Bristol, VA?

William B. Kilgore and family are listed in the 1880 census, Scott Co., VA, pg. 246C.

Children of LAURA PENDLETON and WILLIAM KILGORE are:
  i.   HIRAM R.[13] KILGORE, b. Abt. 1875.
  ii. JAMES D. KILGORE, b. Abt. 1878.
  iii. WILLIAM E. KILGORE, b. 1879.
  iv. FRANK A. KILGORE, b. Abt. 1890.
  v.   MYRTLE KILGORE, b. Abt. 1894.

792. JAMES PRESLEY[12] PENDLETON *(IRA NASH[11], SAMUEL GUTHRIE[10], REUBEN[9], BENJAMIN[8], WILLIAM[7], JOHN[6], PHILIP[5], HENRY[4], HENRY[3], GEORGE[2], GEORGE[1])* was born Nov 19, 1860 in VA. He married ELIZABETH FERGESON Jun 28, 1893. She was born Jun 1869 in VA.

Child of JAMES PENDLETON and ELIZABETH FERGESON is:
908.   i.   ARTHUR CLIFTON[13] PENDLETON, b. Jun 20, 1894, VA; d. Jul 21, 1926, Washington Co., VA?

793. RUFUS BOYD[12] PENDLETON *(IRA NASH[11], SAMUEL GUTHRIE[10], REUBEN[9], BENJAMIN[8], WILLIAM[7], JOHN[6], PHILIP[5], HENRY[4], HENRY[3], GEORGE[2], GEORGE[1])* was born Nov 08, 1866 in VA, and died May 31, 1900 in Richmond, Henrico Co., VA. He married MARGARET DUKE Oct 03, 1893. She was born Nov 1872 in VA, and died Aft. 1920 in Norfolk, VA?

Margaret Pendleton and family are listed in the 1920 census in the household of her brother, William H. Duke.

Children of RUFUS PENDLETON and MARGARET DUKE are:
  i.   YOUNG DUKE[13] PENDLETON, b. Jul 25, 1894, VA.
  ii. CATHERINE MAY PENDLETON, b. May 11, 1897, VA; d. Feb 03, 1989, Portsmouth, VA; m. WILLIAM VANN SAVAGE, Oct 25, 1921.
  iii. NANCY MARGARET PENDLETON, b. Dec 06, 1898, VA; d. Dec 06, 1991; m. ROBERT DREWRY GODSEY, Oct 10, 1923, Norfolk Co., VA; b. Jul 17, 1896, VA.
  iv. RUFUS BOYD PENDLETON, b. May 07, 1900, VA; d. Dec 25, 1927.

794. BEVERLY NEAL[12] PENDLETON *(IRA NASH[11], SAMUEL GUTHRIE[10], REUBEN[9], BENJAMIN[8], WILLIAM[7], JOHN[6], PHILIP[5], HENRY[4], HENRY[3], GEORGE[2], GEORGE[1])* was born May 19, 1874 in VA, and died Aft. 1920 in Bristol, VA? He married MAMIE COLLMAN Nov 06, 1901. She was born Abt. 1876 in VT, and died Aft. 1920 in Bristol, VA?

Beverly Neal Pendleton registered for the World War I draft in Washington Co., VA. Beverly Pendleton (jewelry store salesman) and family are listed in the 1920 Bristol, VA census.

Child of BEVERLY PENDLETON and MAMIE COLLMAN is:
    i. N. COLLMAN[13] PENDLETON.

795. KATHERINE B.[12] PENDLETON *(IRA NASH[11], SAMUEL GUTHRIE[10], REUBEN[9], BENJAMIN[8], WILLIAM[7], JOHN[6], PHILIP[5], HENRY[4], HENRY[3], GEORGE[2], GEORGE[1])* was born Oct 14, 1879 in VA, and died Jan 1977 in Bristol, TN. She married JAMES T. CECIL Nov 06, 1901. He was born Abt. 1878 in VA, and died Aft. 1920 in Bristol, TN?

James T. Cecil (hardware salesman) and family are listed in the 1920 Bristol, VA census.

Child of KATHERINE PENDLETON and JAMES CECIL is:
    i. DOROTHY K.[13] CECIL.

796. JAMES M.[12] PENDLETON *(WILLIAM SAMUEL[11], SAMUEL GUTHRIE[10], REUBEN[9], BENJAMIN[8], WILLIAM[7], JOHN[6], PHILIP[5], HENRY[4], HENRY[3], GEORGE[2], GEORGE[1])* was born Sep 17, 1852 in VA, and died Aft. 1920 in Jonesville, VA? He married MARY JANE SUMPTER Abt. 1873, daughter of LAFAYETTE SUMPTER. She was born Jan 1857 in TN, and died Aft. 1920 in Jonesville, VA?

James Pendleton (farmer) and family are listed in the 1900 Hancock Co., TN census, pg. 217 and the 1920 Jonesville, Lee Co., VA census.

Children of JAMES PENDLETON and MARY SUMPTER are:
    i.   LOUISA[13] PENDLETON, b. Mar 1875, TN.
    ii. ARCHILOUS PENDLETON, b. Abt. 1876, TN.
            An Arch Pendleton (farmer; 52) and family are listed in the 1920 Claiborne Co., TN census.

909.   iii. WILLIAM B. PENDLETON, b. Abt. 1878, TN; d. Aft. 1920, Lee Co., VA?
        iv. ELIZABETH PENDLETON, b. Sep 1879, TN.
        v.   GROVER C. PENDLETON, b. Mar 1887, TN; d. Aft. 1920, Lee Co., VA?; m. BELLE M.; b. Abt. 1876, VA; d. Aft. 1920, Lee Co., VA?
            Grover C. Pendleton and family are listed in the 1920 Jonesville, Lee Co., VA census.

        vi. SARAH PENDLETON, b. Aug 1890, TN.
910.   vii. BEDFORD HORNER PENDLETON, b. Apr 1892, Hancock Co., TN; d. Aug 05, 1958, Lee Co., VA.
        viii. OLLIE PENDLETON, b. May 1894, TN.
        ix. ROY PENDLETON, b. May 1896, TN.
        x.   BESSIE E. PENDLETON, b. Jul 1898, TN.

797. CHRISTOPHER[12] PENDLETON *(WILLIAM SAMUEL[11], SAMUEL GUTHRIE[10], REUBEN[9], BENJAMIN[8], WILLIAM[7], JOHN[6], PHILIP[5], HENRY[4], HENRY[3], GEORGE[2], GEORGE[1])* was born Aug 1861 in TN, and died Aft. 1920 in Hancock Co., TN? He married JOSEPHINE SUMPTER, daughter of LAFAYETTE SUMPTER. She was born Oct 1868 in TN, and died Bef. 1910 in Hancock Co., TN?

Christopher Pendleton (farmer) and family are listed in the 1900 Hancock Co., TN census, pg. 215.

Children of CHRISTOPHER PENDLETON and JOSEPHINE SUMPTER are:

    i.   LAURA[13] PENDLETON, b. Jun 1886, TN.

    ii. PALESTINE PENDLETON, b. Apr 22, 1889, TN.

         Palestine Pendleton registered for the World War I draft in Hancock Co., TN.

    iii. HATTIE PENDLETON, b. Oct 1891, TN.

    iv. HAP F. PENDLETON, b. Dec 04, 1893, TN.

         Hop F. Pendleton registered for the World War I draft in Hancock Co., TN.

    v.   ARVILL PENDLETON, b. Feb 1895, TN.

         Arville Pendleton registered for the World War I draft in Hancock Co., TN.

    vi. COLE PENDLETON, b. Aug 07, 1898, TN; d. Apr 1979, Tazewell, TN.

         Colby Pendleton registered for the World War I draft in Hancock Co., TN.

    vii. LLOYD PENDLETON.

    viii. LINDY PENDLETON.

    ix. CHARLES PENDLETON.

    x.   JULIA PENDLETON.

798. WILLIAM BENTON[12] PENDLETON *(WILLIAM SAMUEL[11], SAMUEL GUTHRIE[10], REUBEN[9], BENJAMIN[8], WILLIAM[7], JOHN[6], PHILIP[5], HENRY[4], HENRY[3], GEORGE[2], GEORGE[1])* was born Aug 04, 1861 in TN, and died Feb 11, 1944 in Sullivan Co., TN. He married NANCY JANE ALLEY 1882 in Scott Co., VA, daughter of DAVID ALLEY and MARY WILLIAMS. She was born Nov 1861 in VA, and died 1937 in Sullivan Co., TN.

    William Pendleton (farmer) and family are listed in the 1900 Scott Co., VA census, pg. 100a.

Children of WILLIAM PENDLETON and NANCY ALLEY are:

    i.   DOCIA LEE[13] PENDLETON, b. Mar 1883, Scott Co., VA; d. 1938, Sullivan Co., TN; m. ANDREW NELSON WILLIAMS, Abt. 1923, Scott Co., VA; b. 1881; d. 1923.

    ii. MARTHA V. PENDLETON, b. Oct 1888, VA.

911. iii. HAMPTON LLOYD PENDLETON, b. May 26, 1890, Scott Co., VA; d. Bonita Springs, Lee Co., FL.

    iv. EMMA ALLEY PENDLETON, b. Oct 31, 1893, Magoffin Co., KY; d. Mar 03, 1938, Baltimore, MD; m. ORBAN FLEETWOOD TEMPLETON, 1923; b. Jul 07, 1883, Morgan Co., KY; d. May 21, 1963, Baltimore, MD.

v.   DAVID WRIGHTLY R. PENDLETON, b. Mar 17, 1895, Scott Co., VA; d. Sep 14, 1980, Sullivan Co., TN; m. ETHEL R. BLAIR, Abt. 1917, Wise Co., VA; b. Mar 18, 1900; d. Apr 29, 1996, Sullivan Co., TN.

vi.   MARGARET PENDLETON, b. 1900, Scott Co., VA; d. Oct 10, 1966, Sullivan Co., TN; m. WILLARD ROBINETTE, Scott Co., VA.

vii.   DONNELLY PENDLETON.

viii.   CURTIS RAY PENDLETON, b. 1906, Scott Co., VA; d. Oct 1973, Morgantown, NC; m. GRACE DICKENSON; b. Apr 30, 1911, NC?; d. Jan 1985, Morgantown, NC.

ix.   WILLIAM BENTON PENDLETON, JR., b. Jun 22, 1907, Scott Co., VA; d. Feb 18, 1972, Sullivan Co., TN; m. MARY FURR, Charleston, WV.

799. POLLY ANN[12] PENDLETON (*JOSEPH DOUGLAS*[11], *JOHN L.*[10], *JAMES A.*[9], *BENJAMIN*[8], *WILLIAM*[7], *JOHN*[6], *PHILIP*[5], *HENRY*[4], *HENRY*[3], *GEORGE*[2], *GEORGE*[1]) was born Mar 31, 1870 in VA, and died 1944 in Scott Co., VA. She married DAVID B. ALLEY. He was born Abt. 1867 in VA, and died Aft. 1920 in Scott Co., VA?

David B. Alley (farmer) and family are listed in the Taylor, Scott Co., VA 1920 census.

Children of POLLY PENDLETON and DAVID ALLEY are:
i.   POLLY B.[13] ALLEY, b. Abt. 1898, VA.
ii.   PEARL E. ALLEY.
iii.   CHARLES R. ALLEY.
iv.   JAMES D. ALLEY.

800. JOHN LILBOURNE[12] PENDLETON (*JOHN EMERSON*[11], *JOHN L.*[10], *JAMES A.*[9], *BENJAMIN*[8], *WILLIAM*[7], *JOHN*[6], *PHILIP*[5], *HENRY*[4], *HENRY*[3], *GEORGE*[2], *GEORGE*[1]) was born Jul 29, 1868 in VA, and died Jan 18, 1947. He married (1) ELEANOR BRILLA PENLEY Abt. 1888. She was born Nov 29, 1873 in VA, and died Jan 15, 1918. He married (2) MARTHA A. RICHERSON. She was born Sep 12, 1868, and died May 28, 1936.

John L. Pendleton (farmer) and family are listed in the 1900 Scott Co., VA census, pg. 101a.

Children of JOHN PENDLETON and ELEANOR PENLEY are (Ref. 310):
i.   MARY ESTELL[13] PENDLETON, m. KYLE.
ii.   MYRTLE PENDLETON, b. Nov 1890, VA; m. BATES.
iii.   ROY EDMON PENDLETON, b. Jan 18, 1893, VA; d. Mar 05, 1978, Gate City, VA; m. POLLY MYRTLE TEMPLETON, Aug 20, 1914, Scott Co., VA; b. Aug 09, 1892, Morgan Co., KY; d. Aug 27, 1976, Scott Co., VA.
iv.   ROBERT WALKER PENDLETON, b. Apr 07, 1895, VA; d. Apr 01, 1919, WWI.

Robert W. Pendleton registered for the World War I draft in Scott Co., VA.

v. ISAAC ARLO PENDLETON, b. Aug 24, 1897, VA; d. Jan 02, 1979, Gate City, VA.

vi. CHARLES CLAYTON PENDLETON, b. Apr 29, 1900, Scott Co., VA; d. Jan 27, 2000, Scott Co., VA; m. EMMA ALICE TEMPLETON, Dec 11, 1920, Scott Co., VA; b. Apr 19, 1899, Scott Co., VA; d. Dec 08, 1970, Scott Co., VA.

vii. JOHN EMERSON PENDLETON, b. 1903; d. Mar 1989.

viii. LLOYD WARREN PENDLETON, b. Apr 13, 1906; d. Oct 01, 1985.

ix. CLARENCE BASCOM PENDLETON, b. Jun 28, 1910, Scott Co., VA; d. Jun 12, 1993, Sullivan Co., TN.

801. ELIZABETH JANE[12] PENDLETON (*JOHN EMERSON[11], JOHN L.[10], JAMES A.[9], BENJAMIN[8], WILLIAM[7], JOHN[6], PHILIP[5], HENRY[4], HENRY[3], GEORGE[2], GEORGE[1]*) was born Jun 01, 1870 in VA. She married MONEYHAM? Abt. 1893.

Children of ELIZABETH PENDLETON and MONEYHAM? are:

i. RALPH C.[13] MONEYHAM?, b. Jan 1895.

ii. NATHANIEL F. MONEYHAM?, b. Sep 1896.

iii. ROSIE O. MONEYHAM?, b. Sep 1898.

802. CHARLES SUMNER[12] PENDLETON (*JOHN EMERSON[11], JOHN L.[10], JAMES A.[9], BENJAMIN[8], WILLIAM[7], JOHN[6], PHILIP[5], HENRY[4], HENRY[3], GEORGE[2], GEORGE[1]*) was born Mar 28, 1880 in VA, and died 1952 in Scott Co., VA? He married PEARL M. She was born Nov 13, 1884 in VA, and died Jun 1975 in Scott Co., VA.

A biographical sketch (Ref. 311) of Charles Sumner Pendleton is listed in the Virginia Historical Society Library. The C.S Pendleton home built of logs in 1825 is included in a survey of historical sites of Virginia. It is located 8 miles north of Gate City on Rt. 665, Scott Co., VA (Ref. 312).

Children of CHARLES PENDLETON and PEARL M. are:

i. FLORY[13] PENDLETON.

ii. IRA S. PENDLETON.

iii. ABRAHAM R. PENDLETON.

iv. RYLAND H. PENDLETON.

v. ROBERT PENDLETON.

vi. CHARLES S. PENDLETON, b. Apr 17, 1918; d. Feb 06, 2003, Kingsport, TN.

803. JOSEPH DELAWARE[12] PENDLETON (*JAMES F.[11], JOHN L.[10], JAMES A.[9], BENJAMIN[8], WILLIAM[7], JOHN[6], PHILIP[5], HENRY[4], HENRY[3], GEORGE[2], GEORGE[1]*) was born Sep 01, 1868 in Scott Co., VA, and died Nov 02, 1934 in Letcher Co., KY. He married CYNTHIA M. BLAIR Jul 15, 1891 in Letcher Co., KY, daughter of JOHN BLAIR and MALISSA WELLS. She was born Nov 26, 1872 in KY, and died Jun 07, 1952 in Letcher Co., KY.

Joseph Pendleton (farmer) and family are listed in the 1900 and 1920 Letcher Co., KY census records.

Children of JOSEPH PENDLETON and CYNTHIA BLAIR are:
- i.   FLETCHER[13] PENDLETON, b. Jan 1891, KY.
- ii. BERTHA PENDLETON, b. Aug 1894, KY.
- iii. MYRTLE PENDLETON, b. May 1897, KY.
- iv. JOHNNY PENDLETON.
- v.   ROSA PENDLETON.

804. WILLIAM E.[12] PENDLETON (*JAMES F.[11], JOHN L.[10], JAMES A.[9], BENJAMIN[8], WILLIAM[7], JOHN[6], PHILIP[5], HENRY[4], HENRY[3], GEORGE[2], GEORGE[1]*) was born May 05, 1870 in Scott Co., VA, and died Mar 29, 1950 in Letcher Co., KY. He married MARY DAY Oct 02, 1895 in Letcher Co., KY. She was born May 1874 in KY, and died Mar 31, 1950 in Letcher Co., KY.

William E. Pendleton (farmer) and family are listed in the 1920 Letcher Co., KY census.

Children of WILLIAM PENDLETON and MARY DAY are:
- i.   PERLIA[13] PENDLETON, b. Jun 1895.
- ii. CHARLES PENDLETON.

805. JAMES SAMUEL[12] PENDLETON (*JAMES F.[11], JOHN L.[10], JAMES A.[9], BENJAMIN[8], WILLIAM[7], JOHN[6], PHILIP[5], HENRY[4], HENRY[3], GEORGE[2], GEORGE[1]*) was born Dec 31, 1871 in Scott Co., VA, and died Oct 25, 1956 in VA. He married CRISSIE ADDINGTON Jan 19, 1893 in Letcher Co., KY. She was born Oct 15, 1870 in Letcher Co., KY, and died Jan 08, 1925 in Letcher Co., KY.

Children of JAMES PENDLETON and CRISSIE ADDINGTON are:
- i.   ETHEL A.[13] PENDLETON, b. Mar 05, 1898, Letcher Co., KY; d. Nov 05, 1999, Big Stone Gap, Wise Co., VA; m. CALEB HAYNES, May 13, 1916; b. Jul 06, 1894, Letcher Co., KY; d. May 21, 1950, Letcher Co., KY.
- ii. JOHN H. PENDLETON.
- iii. BALLARD PENDLETON.
- iv. CARLOS PENDLETON.

806. JOHN ALLY[12] PENDLETON (*JAMES F.[11], JOHN L.[10], JAMES A.[9], BENJAMIN[8], WILLIAM[7], JOHN[6], PHILIP[5], HENRY[4], HENRY[3], GEORGE[2], GEORGE[1]*) was born Jun 04, 1874 in Scott Co., VA, and died Oct 27, 1936 in Letcher Co., KY. He married NANCY MUSIC, daughter of THOMAS MUSIC. She was born Dec 26, 1880 in VA, and died Dec 1965 in Letcher Co., KY.

John Ally Pendleton registered for the WWI draft in Letcher Co., KY. His residence is listed as Pally, Letcher Co., KY and nearest relative Nancy Pendleton, his wife. John A. Pendleton (farmer) and family are listed in the Letcher Co., KY 1920 census.

Children of JOHN PENDLETON and NANCY MUSIC are:
- i.   JANUL?[13] PENDLETON.
- ii. GILES PENDLETON.

iii. EDNA PENDLETON.
iv. RUTH PENDLETON.

807. ROBERT PATTON[12] PENDLETON *(SAMUEL DAVID[11], JOHN L.[10], JAMES A.[9], BENJAMIN[8], WILLIAM[7], JOHN[6], PHILIP[5], HENRY[4], HENRY[3], GEORGE[2], GEORGE[1])* was born Oct 09, 1875 in VA, and died Apr 07, 1936 in Scott Co., VA? He married SARAH D. Abt. 1899. She was born Mar 1878 in VA, and died Aft. 1920 in Scott Co., VA?

Robert P. Pendleton and family are listed in the 1920 Scott Co., VA census.

Children of ROBERT PENDLETON and SARAH D. are:
   i. WILLIAM HIRAM[13] PENDLETON, b. Nov 01, 1899, VA; d. Feb 1978, Kingsport, TN.
      William Hiram Pendleton registered for the World War I draft in Scott Co., VA

   ii. THOMAS HAYDEN PENDLETON, b. 1901; d. 1999.
   iii. EDITH PENDLETON.
   iv. JAMES S. PENDLETON.
   v. MAGGIE PENDLETON.
   vi. ELIZA M. PENDLETON.
   vii. ANNIE PENDLETON.

808. AMOS DANIEL[12] PENDLETON *(ROBERT KENNUS[11], JOHN L.[10], JAMES A.[9], BENJAMIN[8], WILLIAM[7], JOHN[6], PHILIP[5], HENRY[4], HENRY[3], GEORGE[2], GEORGE[1])* was born Jun 10, 1882 in VA, and died Jul 29, 1968 in Scott Co., VA. He married ELIZA V. GILLIAM Abt. 1900. She was born Jul 1881 in VA, and died Aft. 1930 in Scott Co., VA?

Children of AMOS PENDLETON and ELIZA GILLIAM are:
   i. TURNEY M.[13] PENDLETON.
   ii. LOYD C. PENDLETON.
   iii. BILLIE J. PENDLETON.
   iv. HANNAH L. PENDLETON.
   v. EFFA L. PENDLETON.
   vi. EDNA C. PENDLETON.
   vii. ROBERT K. PENDLETON.
   viii. MAGGIE K. PENDLETON.

809. JAMES MONROE[12] PENDLETON *(ROBERT KENNUS[11], JOHN L.[10], JAMES A.[9], BENJAMIN[8], WILLIAM[7], JOHN[6], PHILIP[5], HENRY[4], HENRY[3], GEORGE[2], GEORGE[1])* was born Dec 01, 1890 in VA, and died Feb 06, 1978. He married CORA L. She was born Abt. 1888 in VA, and died Aft. 1920.

James Monroe Pendleton registered for the World War I draft in Scott Co., VA. James M. Pendleton and family are listed in the 1920 Estillville Dist., Scott Co., VA census.

Children of JAMES PENDLETON and CORA L. are:
    i.   EZEKIEL B.[13] PENDLETON.
    ii. BAISARD T. PENDLETON.
    iii. RIBA N. PENDLETON.
    iv. JAMES H. PENDLETON.

810. JOHN D.[12] PENDLETON *(WILLIAM DANIEL E.[11], JOHN L.[10], JAMES A.[9], BENJAMIN[8], WILLIAM[7], JOHN[6], PHILIP[5], HENRY[4], HENRY[3], GEORGE[2], GEORGE[1])* was born Sep 08, 1889 in Scott Co., VA, and died Mar 02, 1984. He married MARY ETTA BRAY Oct 09, 1918 in Scott Co., VA. She was born Feb 06, 1895 in Scott Co., VA, and died Dec 23, 1975 in Kingsport, Sullivan Co., TN.

Children of JOHN PENDLETON and MARY BRAY are:
    i.   ALPHA ANISE[13] PENDLETON, b. Jan 10, 1919; d. Jul 1985 in Los Angeles, CA 1920.
    ii. HOKE JAMES PENDLETON.

811. CHRISTOPHER C.[12] PENDLETON *(ROBERT[11], JAMES A.[10], JAMES A.[9], BENJAMIN[8], WILLIAM[7], JOHN[6], PHILIP[5], HENRY[4], HENRY[3], GEORGE[2], GEORGE[1])* was born Abt. 1869 in VA, and died Aft. 1920 in Scott Co., VA? He married MISS SAUNDERS, daughter of GEORGE SAUNDERS and MAHALA. She was born in VA, and died Bef. 1920 in Scott Co., VA?
    Christopher C. Pendleton (farm labor) is listed in the household of his father-in-law in the 1920, Scott Co., VA census.

Children of CHRISTOPHER PENDLETON and MISS SAUNDERS are:
    i.   ROBERT L.[13] PENDLETON.
    ii. MARTHA PENDLETON.

812. RUFUS[12] PENDLETON *(IRA M.[11], JAMES A.[10], JAMES A.[9], BENJAMIN[8], WILLIAM[7], JOHN[6], PHILIP[5], HENRY[4], HENRY[3], GEORGE[2], GEORGE[1])* died 1916. He married TEMPA ELIZABETH LAWSON. She was born Abt. 1892, and died 1986.

Children of RUFUS PENDLETON and TEMPA LAWSON are:
    i.   ETHEL[13] PENDLETON.
    ii. GRACE MAE PENDLETON.

813. WILLIAM FREDERICK[12] PENDLETON *(ELDRIDGE HOWARD[11], WILLIAM GAINES[10], JOHN[9], BENJAMIN[8], WILLIAM[7], JOHN[6], PHILIP[5], HENRY[4], HENRY[3], GEORGE[2], GEORGE[1])* was born Apr 01, 1875 in TX, and died Nov 30, 1945. He married MAMIE KELLER Sep 11, 1895, daughter of HENRY KELLER and MAGGIE MCBRIDE. She was born Jul 1875 in TX, and died Dec 25, 1969.
    Fred Pendleton (grocery man) and family are listed in the 1900 Collin Co., TX census, pg. 231a. William Frederick Pendleton registered for the World War I draft in Bryan Co., OK.

Children of WILLIAM PENDLETON and MAMIE KELLER are:
- i.   ETTA LOUISE[13] PENDLETON, b. Mar 1897, TX; m. JOHN A. MCDONALD, May 17, 1922; b. 1891.
- ii. CASSANDRA BERNICE PENDLETON, b. Aug 1899, TX; m. REQUA W. BELL, Oct 24, 1925; b. Oct 20, 1893; d. Mar 1968, Gainesville, FL.
- iii. MATTIE IRENE PENDLETON.
- iv. NORMA PENDLETON, b. Sep 20, 1904, TX; d. May 1986, San Marino, CA; m. WILLIAM FRANCIS LYTE, Jan 09, 1926; b. 1901.
- v.   HUGH HALSELL PENDLETON.
- vi. ALFRED MOORE PENDLETON, b. Jan 18, 1911, Collin Co., TX; d. Aug 21, 2005; m. LAURITA BELL YEAGER; b. Jan 03, 1915; d. May 1983, Dallas, TX.

814. THOMAS EDWARD[12] PENDLETON (*ELDRIDGE HOWARD[11]*, *WILLIAM GAINES[10]*, *JOHN[9]*, *BENJAMIN[8]*, *WILLIAM[7]*, *JOHN[6]*, *PHILIP[5]*, *HENRY[4]*, *HENRY[3]*, *GEORGE[2]*, *GEORGE[1]*) was born May 1876 in TX, and died 1906 in Collin Co., TX? He married LYDA ANNA ELIZA HONAKER Apr 12, 1899, daughter of HENRY HONAKER and MARY BAIN. She was born Jun 1878 in TX.

Tom Pendleton (grocer) and Eliza are listed in the 1900 Collin Co., TX census, pg. 235a.

Children of THOMAS PENDLETON and LYDA HONAKER are:
- i. ELDRIDGE HONAKER[13] PENDLETON, b. Oct 12, 1900; d. Oct 1967, Richardson, TX; m. KATHRYN MONTGOMERY; b. 1906.
- ii. MARY ELIZABETH PENDLETON.

815. JAMES ELDRIDGE[12] PENDLETON (*ELDRIDGE HOWARD[11]*, *WILLIAM GAINES[10]*, *JOHN[9]*, *BENJAMIN[8]*, *WILLIAM[7]*, *JOHN[6]*, *PHILIP[5]*, *HENRY[4]*, *HENRY[3]*, *GEORGE[2]*, *GEORGE[1]*) was born Jul 1880 in TX, and died 1933 in Farmersville, TX? He married BLANCHE I. BATTLE Aug 15, 1900, daughter of MILTON BATTLE and SUE NEWSOME. She was born 1881 in TX, and died Aft. 1920.

James Eldridge Pendleton registered for the World War I draft in Collin Co., TX. James E. Pendleton (cotton exchange) and family are listed in the 1920 Farmersville, TX census.

Children of JAMES PENDLETON and BLANCHE BATTLE are:
- i.   MILDRED KATHRYN[13] PENDLETON, b. Jun 19, 1902, TX; d. Dec 18, 1994, Collin Co., TX; m. W. BYRON HOPE, Nov 18, 1924; b. 1900, TX.
- ii. MADGE PENDLETON, b. Nov 13, 1906, TX; d. May 27, 2000, Austin, TX; m. HOWARD STEINLE, May 23, 1935; b. Nov 26, 1900; d. Nov 1982, Austin, TX.
- iii. JAMES ELDRIDGE PENDLETON, JR.

816. HOMER ALEXANDER[12] PENDLETON (*ELDRIDGE HOWARD[11]*, *WILLIAM GAINES[10]*, *JOHN[9]*, *BENJAMIN[8]*, *WILLIAM[7]*, *JOHN[6]*, *PHILIP[5]*, *HENRY[4]*, *HENRY[3]*, *GEORGE[2]*, *GEORGE[1]*) was born May 06, 1888 in TX, and died Aug 1967 in TX. He married MARGUERITE B. SHINE Oct 17, 1908. She was born Dec 10, 1888 in TX, and died Aug 1974 in TX.

Homer Alexander Pendleton registered for the World War I draft in Knox Co., TX .

Children of HOMER PENDLETON and MARGUERITE SHINE are:
- i. HOMER ALEXANDER[13] PENDLETON, JR., b. Feb 25, 1910, TX; d. Dec 1959; m. FRANCES MCCORD, Sep 08, 1933; b. Aug 11, 1914; d. Jan 12, 2002, Henrietta, TX.
- ii. MAXINE JEANETTE PENDLETON, b. Oct 08, 1912, TX; d. Sep 1995, Wichita Falls, TX; m. ROY SANDERS, Aug 05, 1933; b. Apr 11, 1910; d. Aug 1982, Wichita Falls, TX.
- iii. PAUL BERNARD PENDLETON, b. Mar 02, 1915, TX; d. Jan 08, 1994, Munday, TX; m. NINA KATHRYN SPENCER, Jun 05, 1938; b. Mar 04, 1911; d. Jul 20, 1996, TX.

817. CHARLOTTE ELIZABETH[12] PENDLETON *(ELDRIDGE HOWARD[11], WILLIAM GAINES[10], JOHN[9], BENJAMIN[8], WILLIAM[7], JOHN[6], PHILIP[5], HENRY[4], HENRY[3], GEORGE[2], GEORGE[1])* was born Dec 24, 1890 in TX, and died Nov 1979. She married ROY E. PHILLIPS Jun 08, 1910, son of TAYLOR PHILLIPS and CORA HENTIES. He was born Apr 08, 1885 in TX, and died Dec 1974 in TX.

Children of CHARLOTTE PENDLETON and ROY PHILLIPS are:
- i. JAMES WILBUR[13] PHILLIPS.
- ii. SARAH CLARE PHILLIPS.

818. SAMUEL WALTER[12] PENDLETON *(WILLIAM MARION[11], HIRAM KILGORE[10], JOHN[9], BENJAMIN[8], WILLIAM[7], JOHN[6], PHILIP[5], HENRY[4], HENRY[3], GEORGE[2], GEORGE[1])* was born May 1883 in VA, and died 1935 in Scott Co., VA? He married VIRGINIA CLICK Nov 22, 1911. She was born Abt. 1893 in VA.

Walter P. Pendleton (bank cashier) and family are listed in the 1920 Scott Co., VA census.

Child of SAMUEL PENDLETON and VIRGINIA CLICK is:
- i. LOUISA V.[13] PENDLETON.

819. MAXIE ELIZABETH[12] PENDLETON *(WILLIAM MARION[11], HIRAM KILGORE[10], JOHN[9], BENJAMIN[8], WILLIAM[7], JOHN[6], PHILIP[5], HENRY[4], HENRY[3], GEORGE[2], GEORGE[1])* was born Mar 1886 in VA. She married ORBAN W. WINEGAR, son of WILLIAM M. WINEGAR and IDA ELLIS. He was born Jan 07, 1882, and died Jan 1974 in VA.

Child of MAXIE PENDLETON and ORBAN WINEGAR is:
- i. CHARLIE WILLIAM[13] WINEGAR.

414

820. HARRISON BURTON[12] PENDLETON *(WILLIAM MARION[11], HIRAM KILGORE[10], JOHN[9], BENJAMIN[8], WILLIAM[7], JOHN[6], PHILIP[5], HENRY[4], HENRY[3], GEORGE[2], GEORGE[1])* was born Jul 28, 1889 in VA, and died Aft. 1930 in Scott Co., VA? He married VERDA D. STONE Feb 22, 1916, daughter of WILLIAM STONE and EMILY TYLER. She was born 1891 in VA, and died Aft. 1930 in Scott Co., VA?

Harry B. Pendleton and family are listed in the 1920 Floyd, Scott Co., VA census, pg. 3B.

Child of HARRISON PENDLETON and VERDA STONE is:
   i. EULA FAY[13] PENDLETON, b. Dec 31, 1919, VA; d. Jul 03, 1994, Houston, AL; m. OTTO JAMES TADLOCK.

821. EDITH ALICE[12] PENDLETON *(WILLIAM MARION[11], HIRAM KILGORE[10], JOHN[9], BENJAMIN[8], WILLIAM[7], JOHN[6], PHILIP[5], HENRY[4], HENRY[3], GEORGE[2], GEORGE[1])* was born Jan 01, 1893 in Rye Cove, Scott Co., VA, and died Jul 07, 1947 in Scott Co., VA. She married HAMPTON LLOYD PENDLETON Jun 13, 1914, son of WILLIAM PENDLETON and NANCY ALLEY. He was born May 26, 1890 in Scott Co., VA, and died in Bonita Springs, Lee Co., FL.

Haupton (sic) Loyd Pendleton registered for the World War I draft in Scott Co., VA.

Child of EDITH PENDLETON and HAMPTON PENDLETON is:
   i. HAMPTON LLOYD[13] PENDLETON, JR., b. Jan 28, 1918, Scott Co., VA; d. Sep 16, 1949, Kingsport, TN.

822. JAMES E.[12] PENDLETON *(JOHN W.[11], HIRAM KILGORE[10], JOHN[9], BENJAMIN[8], WILLIAM[7], JOHN[6], PHILIP[5], HENRY[4], HENRY[3], GEORGE[2], GEORGE[1])* was born Abt. 1874 in VA, and died Aft. 1930 in Siskiyou Co., CA? He married GRACE K. She was born Abt. 1885 in VA, and died Aft. 1930 in Siskiyou Co., CA?

James E. Pendleton (retail merchant) and family are listed in the 1920 Siskiyou Co., CA census.

Children of JAMES PENDLETON and GRACE K. are:
   i. DOROTHY V.[13] PENDLETON.
   ii. ORA M. PENDLETON.
   iii. JAMES E. PENDLETON.

823. SALLIE[12] PENDLETON *(JOHN W.[11], HIRAM KILGORE[10], JOHN[9], BENJAMIN[8], WILLIAM[7], JOHN[6], PHILIP[5], HENRY[4], HENRY[3], GEORGE[2], GEORGE[1])* was born Abt. 1876 in VA. She married AMOS M. TEMPLETON Dec 31, 1894 in Scott Co., VA. He was born Sep 27, 1853, and died Jul 22, 1928 in Scott Co., VA.

The marriage of Amos Templeton and Sallie Pendleton is recorded in Reference 3133.

Child of SALLIE PENDLETON and AMOS TEMPLETON is:
   i. ROBERT RAY[13] TEMPLETON, b. 1897.

824. HAMPTON W.[12] PENDLETON *(GEORGE W.[11], IVY TAYLOR[10], JOHN[9], BENJAMIN[8], WILLIAM[7], JOHN[6], PHILIP[5], HENRY[4], HENRY[3], GEORGE[2], GEORGE[1])* was born Jan 18, 1884 in Owsley Co., KY, and died May 31, 1951 in Perry Co., KY. He married CALLIE H. HOWELL Jan 18, 1905, daughter of NANCY JANE KELLY. She was born Oct 03, 1887 in KY, and died Apr 20, 1964 in Perry Co., KY.

Hampton Pendleton (farm laborer) and family are listed in the 1920 Fayette Co., KY census.

Children of HAMPTON PENDLETON and CALLIE HOWELL are:
- i. DAISY MAE[13] PENDLETON, b. Jan 08, 1906, KY; d. 1984, Perry Co., KY.
- ii. RUTH JANE PENDLETON, b. Aug 10, 1910, KY; d. Aug 30, 1973, Mercer Co., KY.
- iii. GEORGE HAMPTON PENDLETON, b. Oct 10, 1918, Mercer Co., KY; d. Jan 24, 1995, Perry Co., KY.

825. BESSIE NOMA[12] PENDLETON *(JOHN ASBURY[11], JOHN CRAIG[10], JOHN[9], BENJAMIN[8], WILLIAM[7], JOHN[6], PHILIP[5], HENRY[4], HENRY[3], GEORGE[2], GEORGE[1])* was born 1897 in TX. She married JOHN THEODORE MOORE Jun 04, 1916.

Children of BESSIE PENDLETON and JOHN MOORE are:
- i. JOHN THEODORE[13] MOORE, JR.
- ii. JAMES PENDLETON MOORE.

826. SAMUEL ELDRIDGE[12] PENDLETON *(PATTON MONROE[11], ALLISON OSBORN[10], JOHN[9], BENJAMIN[8], WILLIAM[7], JOHN[6], PHILIP[5], HENRY[4], HENRY[3], GEORGE[2], GEORGE[1])* was born Nov 06, 1891 in TX, and died Dec 03, 1953 in Coryell Co., TX. He married VINNIE ORA WOODARD. She was born Abt. 1894 in TX, and died Aft. 1930 in Coryell Co., TX?

Samuel E. Pendleton registered for the World War I draft in Coryell Co., TX.

Children of SAMUEL PENDLETON and VINNIE WOODARD are:
- i. JESSIE[13] PENDLETON.
- ii. AGNES PENDLETON.

827. DERINDA ELIZABETH[12] PENDLETON *(SAMUEL D.[11], JAMES LUCAS[10], JOHN[9], EDMUND[8], WILLIAM[7], JOHN[6], PHILIP[5], HENRY[4], HENRY[3], GEORGE[2], GEORGE[1])* was born Nov 08, 1861 in Bell Buckle, TN, and died Jan 10, 1956 in Hanford, Fresno Co., CA. She married RUSSELL CALVIN HALEY 1878 in Izard Co., AR. He was born Aug 23, 1858 in Bell Buckle, TN, and died 1929 in Ash Flat, AR.

Children of DERINDA PENDLETON and RUSSELL HALEY are:
- i. SAMUEL BARNEY[13] HALEY, b. Aug 03, 1879; m. (1) STELLA FRAZIER; m. (2) MARY PAYNE, Mar 21, 1900.
- ii. CLARENCE ALVIN HALEY, b. Sep 26, 1880; m. ETHEL TAYLOR.
- iii. WILLIAM VIRGEL HALEY, b. Dec 29, 1882; d. 1932; m. AGNES STEWART.

iv. MARTHA JANE HALEY, b. 1883.

v. SALLIE BELLE HALEY, b. Nov 19, 1884; d. 1932; m. JOHN H. QUALLS.

vi. DAVID THEODORE HALEY, b. Dec 21, 1886; m. SUE BLACK.

vii. OPHA ANN HALEY, b. Dec 15, 1888; m. JOHN BRAY.

viii. ROBERT RUSSELL HALEY, b. Dec 29, 1889; d. Jul 1971, Armona, CA; m. TOLA BERRY.

ix. MARY FRANCIS HALEY, b. Jan 1891.

x. OLLIE MAE HALEY, b. May 04, 1892; m. SIDNEY HINKLE WILLIAMS, Sep 11, 1911; b. Jan 04, 1891.

xi. JOHN FRANKLIN HALEY, b. Aug 26, 1893; m. IDA MEDLEY.

xii. ETHEL HALEY, b. Jan 27, 1895, AR; d. Feb 15, 1977, Reedley, CA; m. RONEY HALL TOLLESON; b. Aug 05, 1890, Independence Co., AR; d. Dec 07, 1976, Reedley, CA.

xiii. ALICE NORA HALEY, b. Jan 27, 1896; m. WILLIAM FUDGE, 1915.

xiv. JIMMIE HALEY, b. Jan 27, 1896; d. Infancy.

xv. SUSIE ELMER HALEY.

xvi. OSCAR LEE HALEY, b. May 16, 1902; d. Nov 16, 1992, Selma, CA; m. MIRIAM WILSON.

xvii. RUTH ELLEN HALEY.

xviii. EDGAR THURMAN HALEY, b. Aug 26, 1904; d. Mar 1986, Ash Flat, AR; m. FAYE HALL; b. Oct 28, 1904; d. Dec 21, 1991, Ash Flat, AR.

828. DOVEY JANE[12] PENDLETON *(SAMUEL D.[11], JAMES LUCAS[10], JOHN[9], EDMUND[8], WILLIAM[7], JOHN[6], PHILIP[5], HENRY[4], HENRY[3], GEORGE[2], GEORGE[1])* was born Sep 1869 in TN, and died Aft. 1920 in Piney Fork, AR? She married GEORGE FINLEY, son of WILLIAM FINLEY and BAILS. He was born in AR.

Dovey Finley (farmer), her children, and John F. Pendleton, her brother are listed in the 1900 Izard Co., AR census, pg. 321.

Children of DOVEY PENDLETON and GEORGE FINLEY are:

i. RAYMOND F.[13] FINLEY, b. Aug 1886, AR.

ii. ROXIE A. FINLEY, b. Feb 1890, AR.

iii. GEORGE R. FINLEY, b. Feb 1894, AR.

829. SAMUEL ZACHARY[12] PENDLETON *(WILLIAM GREEN[11], SAMUEL L.[10], JOHN[9], EDMUND[8], WILLIAM[7], JOHN[6], PHILIP[5], HENRY[4], HENRY[3], GEORGE[2], GEORGE[1])* was born Nov 21, 1872 in Woodbury, Cannon Co., TN, and died Mar 04, 1959 in Hillsboro, TX. He married LAURA MAE THOMAS Sep 13, 1896 in Emmitt, TX, daughter of PA THOMAS and MARY ADAMS. She was born Nov 30, 1879 in TX, and died Jun 25, 1967 in Hillsboro, TX.

Sam Z. Pendleton (farmer) and family are listed in the 1900 Hill Co., TX census, pg. 180a. Samuel Z. Pendleton registered for the World War I draft in Hill Co., TX.

Children of SAMUEL PENDLETON and LAURA THOMAS are:
    i.   EWELL WILLIAM[13] PENDLETON, b. Dec 1899, Mertens, TX; d. Feb 07,
         1935, Waco, TX; m. ONA BELLE HILL, Oct 25, 1919, Hillsboro, Hill Co.,
         TX; b. Oct 02, 1900, Hillsboro, Hill Co., TX; d. Jul 19, 1992, Dallas Co., TX.
    ii. ERNEST DEWEY PENDLETON, b. Nov 20, 1901, TX; d. Jan 10, 1993,
         Harris Co., TX.
    iii. SAMUEL FINIS PENDLETON, b. Mar 31, 1906, Malone, TX; d. Apr 11,
         1996, Mesa, AZ.
            Samuel Pendleton is buried in the National Memorial Cemetery of
         Arizona in Phoenix.

    iv. GLADYS PENDLETON, b. Jan 31, 1904, TX; d. Feb 1982, Hillsboro, TX;
         m. LAUDIE MYERS; b. Apr 15, 1896, AL; d. Apr 1974, Hillsboro, TX.
    v.   CARRIE MAE PENDLETON, b. Feb 11, 1910, TX; d. May 19, 1985,
         Hillsboro, TX; m. FLOYD CAMPBELL.
    vi. HAZEL VIVIAN PENDLETON, b. Aug 05, 1912, TX; d. Jul 03, 1996,
         Lubbock, TX; m. JOHN SHERROD.

830. HARRIS[12] PENDLETON (*WILLIAM GREEN[11], SAMUEL L.[10], JOHN[9],
EDMUND[8], WILLIAM[7], JOHN[6], PHILIP[5], HENRY[4], HENRY[3], GEORGE[2], GEORGE[1]*)
was born Oct 01, 1874 in TN, and died Bef. 1964 in South Corbin, KY? He married
EVERGREEN. She was born Abt. 1884 in TN, and died Aft. 1920.
        Harris Pendleton (steam shovel crewman) and family are listed in the Whitley
Co., South Corbin, KY 1920 census.

Children of HARRIS PENDLETON and EVERGREEN are:
    i.   FRED[13] PENDLETON.
    ii. LORINE PENDLETON.
    iii. ATA PENDLETON.
    iv. LOLA M. PENDLETON.
    v.   CHARLES PENDLETON.

831. RACHEL ELIZABETH[12] PENDLETON (*WILLIAM GREEN[11], SAMUEL L.[10],
JOHN[9], EDMUND[8], WILLIAM[7], JOHN[6], PHILIP[5], HENRY[4], HENRY[3], GEORGE[2],
GEORGE[1]*) was born Apr 01, 1876 in Woodbury, Cannon Co., TN, and died Dec 18,
1960 in Hill Co., TX. She married (1) ANDREW JACKSON MITCHELL Sep 16, 1894
in Hillsboro, Hill Co., TX. He was born Nov 05, 1866 in TX, and died Dec 05, 1915 in
Malone, Hill Co., TX. She married (2) EARLY ELLIS Aft. 1915.

Children of RACHEL PENDLETON and ANDREW MITCHELL are:
    i.   LURA ETHEL[13] MITCHELL, b. Feb 08, 1895; d. Jul 20, 1985, Hillsboro,
         Hill Co., TX.
    ii. LULA RACHEL MITCHELL, b. May 07, 1897.
    iii. MAE FRANCIS GILMORE MITCHELL, b. Sep 20, 1898, TX.
    iv. JOHN WILLIAM MITCHELL, b. Feb 05, 1900; d. 1999, Hillsboro, Hill Co.,
         TX.

v. TISHIA LEE MITCHELL, b. Aug 31, 1901; d. Oct 02, 1901, TX.
vi. GEORGE ERNEST MITCHELL.
vii. MACON ARETTA MITCHELL.
viii. PEARL IRENE MITCHELL.
ix. MARY EMMA MITCHELL.
x. JOSEPH CARLYLE MITCHELL.
xi. DOROTHY JUANITA MITCHELL.
xii. ERNEST WOODROW MITCHELL.

Child of RACHEL PENDLETON and EARLY ELLIS is:
xiii. INA FAYE[13] ELLIS.

832. EMMA JAQULINE[12] PENDLETON *(WILLIAM GREEN[11], SAMUEL L.[10], JOHN[9], EDMUND[8], WILLIAM[7], JOHN[6], PHILIP[5], HENRY[4], HENRY[3], GEORGE[2], GEORGE[1])* was born Jul 27, 1878 in Woodbury, Cannon Co., TN, and died Apr 27, 1964 in Hillsboro, Hill Co., TX. She married EARL WILDER ERWIN Oct 13, 1900, son of LEONDOUS ERWIN and ZIPPORAH BONDS. He was born May 20, 1877 in Pulaski, Giles Co., TN, and died May 09, 1951.

Children of EMMA PENDLETON and EARL ERWIN are:
i. HERBET BEE[13] ERWIN, b. Sep 05, 1903, Irene, Hill Co., TX; d. Nov 07, 1935, Waco, TX.
ii. MARGIE LEE ERWIN, b. Jun 04, 1902, Irene, Hill Co., TX; d. Jan 27, 1991, Sweetwater, TX.
iii. EDDIE WILDER ERWIN, b. Jul 31, 1905, Irene, Hill Co., TX; d. Dec 04, 1999, Arlington, TX.
iv. JOSEPH WELDON ERWIN, b. Jul 25, 1908, Irene, Hill Co., TX; d. Oct 16, 1997, Hillsboro, Hill Co., TX.
v. RUTH ELIZABETH ERWIN.
vi. ELIZA SYLVADO ERWIN, b. Feb 12, 1914, Mayfield, Switch Co., TX; d. Jun 03, 1991, Hillsboro, Hill Co., TX.

833. ETHEL[12] PENDLETON *(WILLIAM SEAMOR[11], WILLIAM G.[10], JOHN[9], EDMUND[8], WILLIAM[7], JOHN[6], PHILIP[5], HENRY[4], HENRY[3], GEORGE[2], GEORGE[1])* was born Mar 1889 in TN. He married ODEA. She was born Abt. 1893 in TN.

Child of ETHEL PENDLETON and ODEA is:
i. CHARLES[13] PENDLETON, b. Abt. 1917, TN.

834. R. D.[12] PENDLETON *(WILLIAM SEAMOR[11], WILLIAM G.[10], JOHN[9], EDMUND[8], WILLIAM[7], JOHN[6], PHILIP[5], HENRY[4], HENRY[3], GEORGE[2], GEORGE[1])* was born Mar 1890 in TN. He married CHARLINE WILLIE. She was born Abt. 1891 in TN.

Child of R. PENDLETON and WILLIE is:
i. FLOYD[13] PENDLETON.

835. EDMUND EMBREE[12] PENDLETON *(GEORGE CASSETY[11], EDMUND[10], BENJAMIN[9], EDMUND[8], WILLIAM[7], JOHN[6], PHILIP[5], HENRY[4], HENRY[3], GEORGE[2], GEORGE[1])* was born Aug 31, 1888 in TX, and died Aft. 1930 in San Antonio, TX? He married KATHERINE VAN BUREN Jun 03, 1918. She was born Abt. 1892 in TX, and died Aft. 1930 in San Antonio, TX?

Edmund Embree Pendleton registered for the World War I draft in Bell Co., TX.

Child of EDMUND PENDLETON and KATHERINE VAN BUREN is:

    i.   GEORGE C.[13] PENDLETON, b. Oct 15, 1919, MO; d. Apr 1985, Montgomery Co., MD.

836. JOSEPH SAXTON[12] PENDLETON *(EDWIN CONWAY[11], ALEXANDER GARLAND[10], WILLIAM GARLAND[9], REUBEN[8], WILLIAM[7], JOHN[6], PHILIP[5], HENRY[4], HENRY[3], GEORGE[2], GEORGE[1])* was born Oct 28, 1871. He married MARY YOCUM May 16, 1911.

Joseph Pendleton (48; b. PA; lodger; laborer) is listed in the 1920 Kansas City, MO census.

Children of JOSEPH PENDLETON and MARY YOCUM are:

    i.   II EDWIN CONWAY[13] PENDLETON, b. May 27, 1912; d. Jul 14, 1935, Princeton Light Artillery Unit, R.O.T.C.

    ii.   JOSEPH SAXTON PENDLETON, b. Sep 11, 1917; d. Apr 1983, Berks, PA.

837. ALEXANDER G.[12] PENDLETON *(ALEXANDER GREENHEW[11], ALEXANDER GARLAND[10], WILLIAM GARLAND[9], REUBEN[8], WILLIAM[7], JOHN[6], PHILIP[5], HENRY[4], HENRY[3], GEORGE[2], GEORGE[1])* was born Abt. 1882 in AZ, and died Aft. 1930 in Pittsburgh, PA? He married MARTHA F. She was born Abt. 1881 in PA, and died Aft. 1930 in Pittsburgh, PA?

Alexander G. Pendleton, Jr. (cadet) is listed in the 1900 census, West Point, Orange Co., NY. Alexander G. (army officer) and Martha R. Pendleton are listed in the 1910 Southold, Suffolk Co., NY census.

Children of ALEXANDER PENDLETON and MARTHA F. are:

    i.   HELEN M.[13] PENDLETON.

    ii.   JOSEPHINE B. PENDLETON.

838. JOHN S.[12] PENDLETON *(HERBERT GEORGE[11], WILLIAM GARLAND[10], JAMES SHEPHERD[9], REUBEN[8], WILLIAM[7], JOHN[6], PHILIP[5], HENRY[4], HENRY[3], GEORGE[2], GEORGE[1])* was born Nov 1889 in AR. He married CORAL KING 1910 in Union Co., Arkansas. She was born Abt. 1889, and died Apr 09, 1948 in Jefferson Co., AR.

Children of JOHN PENDLETON and CORAL KING are:

    i.   OLLIE KING[13] PENDLETON, d. Jul 29, 1937, Union Co., AR.

    ii.   JAMES CORAL PENDLETON.

839. JACK H.^{12} PENDLETON *(HERBERT GEORGE^{11}, WILLIAM GARLAND^{10}, JAMES SHEPHERD^9, REUBEN^8, WILLIAM^7, JOHN^6, PHILIP^5, HENRY^4, HENRY^3, GEORGE^2, GEORGE^1)* was born Jan 12, 1891 in AR, and died May 1973 in Union Co., AR. He married EVELINA MORGAN 1913 in Union Co., Arkansas.

Jack H. Pendleton registered for the World War I draft in Union Co., AR.

Children of JACK PENDLETON and EVELINA MORGAN are:
- i. WILLIAM HERBERT^{13} PENDLETON.
- ii. JACK PENDLETON.
- iii. FRANK PENDLETON.

840. AUGUSTUS GARLAND^{12} PENDLETON *(HERBERT GEORGE^{11}, WILLIAM GARLAND^{10}, JAMES SHEPHERD^9, REUBEN^8, WILLIAM^7, JOHN^6, PHILIP^5, HENRY^4, HENRY^3, GEORGE^2, GEORGE^1)* was born Oct 26, 1897 in AR, and died Dec 20, 1965 in Union Co., AR. He married HELEN ORLEAN ENIS Apr 01, 1917 in Union Co., AR, daughter of WILLIAM ENIS and ARTIE LINDER. She was born Oct 29, 1898 in Claiborne Parish, LA, and died Apr 28, 1977 in Union Co., AR.

Child of AUGUSTUS PENDLETON and HELEN ENIS is:
- i. JULIA VIRGINIA^{13} PENDLETON.

841. EVERETT S.^{12} PENDLETON *(ANDREW DAVIS^{11}, WILLIAM^{10}, WILLIAM^9, RICHARD^8, WILLIAM^7, JOHN^6, PHILIP^5, HENRY^4, HENRY^3, GEORGE^2, GEORGE^1)* was born Nov 1882 in MO, and died Aug 1966 in St. Louis, MO. He married ROSA. She was born Abt. 1890 in MO, and died Aft. 1930 in MO?

Everett Pendleton (laborer; railroad) and family are listed in the 1910 Lincoln Co., MO census.

Children of EVERETT PENDLETON and ROSA are:
- i. FAYE^{13} PENDLETON.
- ii. WILLARD PENDLETON.

    A Willard I. Pendleton (22) is listed as an inmate in the 1930 census, San Quentin Prison, Marin Co., CA. The middle initial 'I' could be a 'J.'

- iii. LOUISE PENDLETON.
- iv. RUTH PENDLETON.

842. CHARLES ARTHUR^{12} PENDLETON *(JOSEPH M.^{11}, WILLIAM^{10}, WILLIAM^9, RICHARD^8, WILLIAM^7, JOHN^6, PHILIP^5, HENRY^4, HENRY^3, GEORGE^2, GEORGE^1)* was born Jan 27, 1896 in MO. He married BESS. She was born Abt. 1894 in MO.

Charles Arthur Pendleton registered for the WWI draft in Cole Co., MO.

Child of CHARLES PENDLETON and BESS is:
- i. NELSON^{13} PENDLETON.

843. GEORGE H.[12] PENDLETON *(AZARIAH B.[11], GEORGE WASHINGTON[10], WILLIAM[9], RICHARD[8], WILLIAM[7], JOHN[6], PHILIP[5], HENRY[4], HENRY[3], GEORGE[2], GEORGE[1])* was born Oct 26, 1872 in Miller Co., MO, and died Feb 22, 1965 in Jay, OK. He married MARY ETTA RENFROW Sep 14, 1893 in Miller Co., MO. She was born Jul 27, 1875 in Miller Co., MO, and died Dec 04, 1957 in Jay, OK.

Children of GEORGE PENDLETON and MARY RENFROW are (Ref. 314):

    i. DELLA[13] PENDLETON, b. Dec 05, 1894, Sedalia, Pettis Co., MO; d. Jan 13, 1965, Ketchum, OK; m. BENJAMIN HARRISON LYNCH, Apr 05, 1914; b. Mar 20, 1891, OK; d. Jan 11, 1960, Ketchum, OK.

        Benjamin Harrison Lynch was a full-blooded Indian of the Delaware tribe.

    ii. IDA PEARL PENDLETON, b. Jul 14, 1897, Miller Co., MO; d. Oct 27, 1973, Broken Arrow, OK; m. THOMAS ALLEN BROWN, Dec 07, 1916, Joplin, MO; b. Sep 08, 1891, Howell Co., AR; d. Jun 15, 1964, Broken Arrow, OK.

    iii. STELLA PENDLETON, b. Jan 04, 1900, Miller Co., MO; d. Aug 1987, Stanislaus, CA; m. CLYDE MAYSHACK CARNES, Jan 17, 1920, Salina, OK; b. Feb 09, 1897, Horse Shoe, NC; d. Jun 26, 1972, Broken Arrow, OK.

    iv. DORSIE EDWARD PENDLETON, b. Jul 15, 1902, Miller Co., MO; d. Mar 16, 1988, Jay, OK; m. HATTIE SUSAN NEET, Feb 25, 1933, Talequah, OK; b. AR.

    v. BESSIE PENDLETON, b. Jul 30, 1904, Miller Co., MO; d. Mar 24, 1993, Collinsville, OK; m. (1) JAMES MONROE CUNNINGHAM, May 24, 1924, Pryor, OK; b. Spavinaw, OK; d. Dec 09, 1949, Spavinaw, OK; m. (2) JACK J. PARIS, Aft. 1949; b. Jan 04, 1882.

        James Cunningham was a full-blooded Cherokee Indian.

    vi. ALMA EASTER PENDLETON, b. Apr 20, 1908, Miami, OK; d. Dec 24, 2000, Broken Arrow, OK; m. SAM ALLEN WATTAM, Sep 25, 1933, Vinita, OK; b. Feb 12, 1911, Denton, TX; d. Feb 02, 1996, Salina, OK.

844. CHARLES E.[12] PENDLETON *(AZARIAH B.[11], GEORGE WASHINGTON[10], WILLIAM[9], RICHARD[8], WILLIAM[7], JOHN[6], PHILIP[5], HENRY[4], HENRY[3], GEORGE[2], GEORGE[1])* was born Oct 25, 1874 in MO, and died Jan 01, 1963 in Iberia, MO. He married MATTIE LAIR Abt. 1899 in Miller Co., MO? She was born Feb 1877 in MO, and died 1954.

Children of CHARLES PENDLETON and MATTIE LAIR are:

    i. HERMAN R.[13] PENDLETON, b. Jan 05, 1901, MO; d. Jan 28, 1954, Maries Co., MO; m. LILLIAN BARNHART; b. Abt. 1909, MO.

    ii. ELENA M. PENDLETON.

    iii. THOMAS D. PENDLETON.

    iv. CLYDE C. PENDLETON, b. Nov 24, 1907, MO; d. Nov 1971, Union, MO.

    v. EMMET R. PENDLETON, b. Mar 28, 1909, MO; d. Aug 20, 1998, Osage Co., MO.

vi.   DORA E. PENDLETON.
vii. ETHEL PENDLETON.
viii. LOUELLA PENDLETON.
ix.   LILLIE PENDLETON.

845. ROSETTA[12] PENDLETON (*AZARIAH B.*[11], *GEORGE WASHINGTON*[10], *WILLIAM*[9], *RICHARD*[8], *WILLIAM*[7], *JOHN*[6], *PHILIP*[5], *HENRY*[4], *HENRY*[3], *GEORGE*[2], *GEORGE*[1]) was born Jan 01, 1876 in MO, and died Aug 30, 1961 in Maries Co., MO. She married WILLIAM H. COPELAND Oct 17, 1895 in Maries Co., MO, son of WILLIAM COPELAND and SARAH HUGHES. He was born Jan 19, 1872 in MO, and died Sep 17, 1952 in MO.

Children of ROSETTA PENDLETON and WILLIAM COPELAND are:
    i.   GUTHRIE B.[13] COPELAND, b. Sep 27, 1896, Maries Co., MO.
    ii. EVA MAY COPELAND, b. Nov 1898, Maries Co., MO.
    iii. VIRGIL COPELAND, b. Mar 14, 1901, MO; d. Sep 03, 1988, Phelps Co., MO.
    iv. ORVILLE COPELAND, b. Aug 28, 1907, MO; d. Oct 1950.
    v.   IVAN COPELAND, b. Sep 05, 1909, MO; d. Mar 1974, Union, MO.
    vi. AGNES COPELAND.
    vii. LILLIAN L. COPELAND.

846. WILLIAM D.[12] PENDLETON (*AZARIAH B.*[11], *GEORGE WASHINGTON*[10], *WILLIAM*[9], *RICHARD*[8], *WILLIAM*[7], *JOHN*[6], *PHILIP*[5], *HENRY*[4], *HENRY*[3], *GEORGE*[2], *GEORGE*[1]) was born Dec 16, 1878 in MO, and died Feb 01, 1949 in Owensville, MO. He married EVA SLOAN Feb 02, 1905. She was born Aug 02, 1888 in MO, and died Aft. 1920 in Miller Co., MO?
    William D. Pendleton and family are listed in the 1910 Miller Co., MO census.

Children of WILLIAM PENDLETON and EVA SLOAN are:
    i.   GARRETT[13] PENDLETON.
    ii. CLARENCE PENDLETON.
    iii. EDITH PENDLETON.
    iv. GOLDEN PENDLETON, b. Apr 12, 1912, MO; d. Jan 28, 1994, Maries Co., MO.
    v.   MARY PENDLETON.

847. CLEVELAND[12] PENDLETON (*AZARIAH B.*[11], *GEORGE WASHINGTON*[10], *WILLIAM*[9], *RICHARD*[8], *WILLIAM*[7], *JOHN*[6], *PHILIP*[5], *HENRY*[4], *HENRY*[3], *GEORGE*[2], *GEORGE*[1]) was born Mar 09, 1885 in MO, and died May 08, 1979 in Iberia, MO. He married (1) LOUISE ROLLINS. She was born Abt. 1893 in MO, and died Aft. 1910 in Miller Co., MO? He married (2) STELLA HUMPHREY.

Child of CLEVELAND PENDLETON and LOUISE ROLLINS is:
    i.   MABEL[13] PENDLETON.

848. MARY ARIZONA[12] PENDLETON *(ZACHARIAH[11], GEORGE WASHINGTON[10], WILLIAM[9], RICHARD[8], WILLIAM[7], JOHN[6], PHILIP[5], HENRY[4], HENRY[3], GEORGE[2], GEORGE[1])* was born Jul 14, 1878 in Van Cleve, MO, and died Nov 26, 1949 in Osage Co., MO. She married CHARLES SAMUEL BURNHAM Sep 20, 1896 in Maries Co., MO. He was born Nov 22, 1877 in Osage Co., MO.

Children of MARY PENDLETON and CHARLES BURNHAM are:
     i.   TONY[13] BURNHAM, b. Dec 06, 1896, MO.
    ii.   DULCEY MAE BURNHAM.

849. ANDREW J.[12] PENDLETON *(JAMES HENRY[11], GEORGE WASHINGTON[10], WILLIAM[9], RICHARD[8], WILLIAM[7], JOHN[6], PHILIP[5], HENRY[4], HENRY[3], GEORGE[2], GEORGE[1])* was born Aug 1883 in MO, and died Aft. 1920 in Maries Co., MO? He married MARGARET GREENE, daughter of JOHN GREENE. She was born Abt. 1884 in MO, and died Aft. 1920 in Maries Co., MO?

    Andrew Pendleton and family are listed in the 1920 Maries Co., MO census, Miller township.

Children of ANDREW PENDLETON and MARGARET GREENE are:
     i.   MAUDIE[13] PENDLETON.
    ii.   BENNETT PENDLETON, b. Mar 03, 1906, MO; d. Sep 1968, Pulaski Co., MO.
   iii.   ALICE PENDLETON.
   iv.   OPEL PENDLETON.

850. WARREN BURD[12] PENDLETON *(JAMES H.[11], JAMES RICHARD[10], WILLIAM[9], RICHARD[8], WILLIAM[7], JOHN[6], PHILIP[5], HENRY[4], HENRY[3], GEORGE[2], GEORGE[1])* was born May 25, 1887 in Van Cleve, Maries Co., MO, and died Mar 1972 in Canon City, CO. He married LOUELLA SKELTON Abt. 1910. She was born 1891 in MO, and died Aft. 1930 in Pueblo, CO?

Children of WARREN PENDLETON and LOUELLA SKELTON are:
     i.   MONTE W.[13] PENDLETON, b. Aug 18, 1911; d. May 1986, Pueblo, CO.
    ii.   THURMAN C. PENDLETON, b. Apr 03, 1917, CO; d. Apr 08, 1998, Pueblo, CO.

851. LAWRENCE BATAILLE[12] PENDLETON *(LAWRENCE BATAILLE[11], JOHN T.[10], BENJAMIN[9], HENRY[8], HENRY[7], JOHN[6], PHILIP[5], HENRY[4], HENRY[3], GEORGE[2], GEORGE[1])* was born Jan 13, 1875 in Spotsylvania Co., VA, and died Oct 20, 1959 in Wash. DC? He married HARRIET E. She was born Abt. 1881 in VA, and died Jan 4, 1944 in Wash. DC?

    Lawrence B. Pendleton (salesman; grocery) and family are listed in the 1910 Washington DC census. Lawrence Battile (sic) Pendleton registered for the World War I draft in Washington, DC.

Children of LAWRENCE PENDLETON and HARRIET E. are:
   i.   GARETT A.[13] PENDLETON.
   ii. MARY E. PENDLETON.
   iii. LAWRENCE B. PENDLETON, b. Dec 16, 1909, Wash. DC; d. Aug 8, 1999, Silver Spring, MD.
   iv. GEORGE E. PENDLETON, b. Oct 23, 1912, MD; d. Aug 27, 1988, Garrett Park, MD.

852. MARY ALSOP[12] PENDLETON (*LAWRENCE BATAILLE*[11], *JOHN T.*[10], *BENJAMIN*[9], *HENRY*[8], *HENRY*[7], *JOHN*[6], *PHILIP*[5], *HENRY*[4], *HENRY*[3], *GEORGE*[2], *GEORGE*[1]) was born Jul 1884 in VA, and died Oct 1967 in Fredericksburg, VA. She married JAMES H. CANADAY Oct 18, 1906 in Spotsylvania Co., VA. He was born Abt. 1877 in VA, and died Aft. 1930 in Spotsylvania Co., VA?

James Canaday (general farmer) and family are listed in the 1930 Chancellor, Spotsylvania Co., VA census.

Children of MARY PENDLETON and JAMES CANADAY are:
   i.   EVERETT EARL[13] CANADAY, b. Aug 17, 1907, VA; d. Nov 1966.
   ii. JAMES H. CANADAY, b. Feb 3, 1914, VA; d. Jul 10, 1999, Fredericksburg, VA.

853. EDITH MAY[12] PENDLETON (*JOSEPH ALBERT*[11], *HUGH CLAIBORNE*[10], *HENRY*[9], *HENRY*[8], *HENRY*[7], *JOHN*[6], *PHILIP*[5], *HENRY*[4], *HENRY*[3], *GEORGE*[2], *GEORGE*[1]) was born Abt. 1879 in VA, and died Aft. 1910 in Wichita, KS? She married INNIS DURETTE HARRIS Sep 20, 1900 in VA. He was born Abt. 1876 in VA, and died Aft. 1910 in Wichita, KS?

Edith Pendleton is listed as a student in the Free Lance Newspaper, Fredericksburg, VA on 6 May, 1890 along with Carrie, Maxie and Fannie Pendleton. Edith Pendleton is a Chancellor teacher in a Virginia Star article of 20 Sep 1899. Innis D. Harris (minister) and family are listed in the 1910 Wichita, KS census. Edith Harris contributed her family history chart to the Fredericksburg, VA library.

Children of EDITH PENDLETON and INNIS HARRIS are:
   i.   ELISE E.[13] HARRIS.
   ii. MARION M. HARRIS.
   iii. INNIS G. HARRIS.

854. FANNIE ELIZABETH[12] PENDLETON (*JOSEPH ALBERT*[11], *HUGH CLAIBORNE*[10], *HENRY*[9], *HENRY*[8], *HENRY*[7], *JOHN*[6], *PHILIP*[5], *HENRY*[4], *HENRY*[3], *GEORGE*[2], *GEORGE*[1]) was born May 18, 1885 in Alleghany Co., VA, and died 1974. She married ROBERT WARNER HILDRUP Sep 1905, son of EDWARD HILDRUP and MARY SMITH. He was born 1873 in VA, and died 1955.

The birth of Fannie Pendleton is recorded in Reference 315. Robert Hildrup (farm laborer) and family are listed in the 1910 Spotsylvania Co., VA census.

Children of FANNIE PENDLETON and ROBERT HILDRUP are:
    i. LEROY[13] HILDRUP.
   ii. ALBERT HILDRUP.

855. HARRY HOLLADAY[12] PENDLETON *(JAMES MONROE[11], HUGH CLAIBORNE[10], HENRY[9], HENRY[8], HENRY[7], JOHN[6], PHILIP[5], HENRY[4], HENRY[3], GEORGE[2], GEORGE[1])* was born Oct 8, 1883 in VA, and died Feb 20, 1965. He married (1) SADIE ELVISTON HUGHES Feb 23, 1904, daughter of JOHN HUGHES and SARAH LEE. She was born 1886 in VA, and died Feb 1920 in Orange Co., VA. He married (2) BETTIE WHITLOCK Oct 26, 1921 in Orange Co., VA, daughter of ROBERT WHITLOCK and LUCY ATKINS. She was born 1891 in VA, and died Abt. 1925 in Orange Co., VA? He married (3) VICTORIA L. WHITLOCK Jul 24, 1930 in Orange Co., VA, daughter of JIM WHITLOCK and LELIA SIZEMORE. She was born Abt. 1913.

      Harry Pendleton (farm laborer) and family are listed in the 1920 Taylor, Orange Co., VA census, pg. 9A.

Children of HARRY PENDLETON and SADIE HUGHES are:
     i. LULA J.[13] PENDLETON, b. 1905, VA; d. Abt. 1998; m. ROY HICKS, Aug 22, 1931; b. Abt. 1912.
    ii. LEWIS WILLIAM PENDLETON.
   iii. BELLE CRITTENDON PENDLETON.
   iv. HARRY MONROE PENDLETON, b. Feb 6, 1915, Orange Co., VA; d. 1969; m. RAY SMITH, dau. ALFRED SMITH and ALICE LOWE.
    v. BARCLAY HOLLADAY PENDLETON, b. Jul 11, 1918, Orange Co., VA; d. Mar 7, 1982; m. (1) DOROTHY SMITH May 1940, dau. ALFRED SMITH and ALICE LOWE; b. Nov 19, 1919; d. Sep 10, 1963; m. (2) JOYCE BRAMLETT; d. Abt. 1986.

856. NELLIE M.[12] PENDLETON *(JAMES MONROE[11], HUGH CLAIBORNE[10], HENRY[9], HENRY[8], HENRY[7], JOHN[6], PHILIP[5], HENRY[4], HENRY[3], GEORGE[2], GEORGE[1])* was born Jul 1890 in VA. She married EARNEST HUGHES, son of JOHN HUGHES and SARAH LEE.

Children of NELLIE PENDLETON and EARNEST HUGHES are:
     i. RUTH L.[13] HUGHES.
    ii. EARNEST HUGHES.
   iii. ELIZABETH HUGHES.
   iv. WILLIAM HUGHES.
    v. EDWARD HUGHES.

857. MARY BELLE[12] PENDLETON *(JOHN THOMAS[11], WILLIAM HENRY[10], JOHN[9], HENRY[8], HENRY[7], JOHN[6], PHILIP[5], HENRY[4], HENRY[3], GEORGE[2], GEORGE[1])* was born Abt. 1871 in Atlanta, GA, and died Aft. 1920 in DeKalb Co., GA? She married EDWIN C. STEWART. He was born Abt. 1868 in GA, and died Aft. 1920 in DeKalb Co., GA?

Children of MARY PENDLETON and EDWIN STEWART are:
  i.   JOHN P.[13] STEWART, b. Abt. 1896, GA.
  ii. MARY LOUISE STEWART, b. Abt. 1897, GA.
  iii. KATHERINE STEWART.

858. MARY VALONIA[12] PENDLETON *(JOHN A.[11], CHESLEY THACKER[10], JOHN[9], JOHN[8], HENRY[7], JOHN[6], PHILIP[5], HENRY[4], HENRY[3], GEORGE[2], GEORGE[1])* was born Sep 28, 1867 in Metcalfe Co., KY. She married BENJAMIN FRANKLIN PILE. He was born Jan 8, 1861 in Adair Co., KY.

Child of MARY PENDLETON and BENJAMIN PILE is:
  i.   THOMAS PENDLETON[13] PILE.

859. CHESLEY BUCKNER[12] PENDLETON *(JAMES H.[11], CHESLEY THACKER[10], JOHN[9], JOHN[8], HENRY[7], JOHN[6], PHILIP[5], HENRY[4], HENRY[3], GEORGE[2], GEORGE[1])* was born Feb 1, 1873 in KY, and died May 9, 1937 in Hart Co., KY. He married FIDA M. She was born Abt. 1877 in KY.

Chesley Pendleton (farmer) and family are listed in the 1910 Metcalfe Co., KY census. Chesley Buckner Pendleton (carpenter) registered for the WWI draft in Louisville, Jefferson Co., KY. His nearest relative listed is his wife, Mrs. Fida M. Pendleton.

Child of CHESLEY PENDLETON and FIDA M. is:
  i.   BRAULT C.[13] PENDLETON, b. Sep 11, 1895, Edmonton, KY.
       Brault C. Pendleton (Machinist Helper) registered for the WWI draft in
       Metcalfe Co., KY.

860. CLARENCE[12] PENDLETON *(ABNER J.[11], ABNER J.[10], JOHN[9], JOHN[8], HENRY[7], JOHN[6], PHILIP[5], HENRY[4], HENRY[3], GEORGE[2], GEORGE[1])* was born 1873 in Metcalfe Co., KY, and died Aft. 1920 in Garrard Co., KY? He married IDA LOGAN. She was born Abt. 1890 in KY, and died Aft. 1920 in Garrard Co., KY?

Clarence Pendleton registered for the WWI draft in Lancaster, Garrard Co., KY. His nearest relative is listed as Ida Pendleton (wife). Clarence Pendleton (farmer) and family are listed in the 1920 Garrard Co. census, Buckeye.

Children of CLARENCE PENDLETON and IDA LOGAN are:
  i.   JESSE J.[13] PENDLETON, b. May 7, 1915, Boyle Co., KY; d. Feb 8, 1997,
       Lancaster, Garrard Co., KY.
  ii. IDA C. PENDLETON.

861. JEFFERSON[12] PENDLETON *(JOHN A.[11], ABNER J.[10], JOHN[9], JOHN[8], HENRY[7], JOHN[6], PHILIP[5], HENRY[4], HENRY[3], GEORGE[2], GEORGE[1])* was born Feb 4, 1892 in Adair Co., KY. He married LILLIE LONG. She was born Abt. 1895 in KY.

Jeff Pendleton (occupation, own farm) registered for the WWI draft in Lancaster, Garrard Co., KY.

Child of JEFFERSON PENDLETON and LILLIE LONG is:
    i. ONEIL[13] PENDLETON, b. Feb 3, 1913, KY; d. Feb 12, 1970, KY.
        Oneal Pendleton is buried in Lebanon National Cemetery, KY.

862. ALLEN LEE[12] PENDLETON *(HIRAM[11], ABNER J.[10], JOHN[9], JOHN[8], HENRY[7], JOHN[6], PHILIP[5], HENRY[4], HENRY[3], GEORGE[2], GEORGE[1])* was born Oct 15, 1886 in Metcalfe Co., KY, and died Sep 24, 1972. He married SALLIE B. LOCKER Abt. 1908. She was born 1886, and died Nov 1967.

Children of ALLEN PENDLETON and SALLIE LOCKER are:
    i.   ELIZABETH MARIE[13] PENDLETON.
    ii. LILLIAN PENDLETON.
    iii. STELLA MAE PENDLETON, b. Jun 21, 1911, Garrard Co., KY; d. Nov 26,
         2001, Garrard Co., KY; m. ALVA HUFFMAN.

863. GROVER CLEVELAND[12] PENDLETON *(HIRAM[11], ABNER J.[10], JOHN[9], JOHN[8], HENRY[7], JOHN[6], PHILIP[5], HENRY[4], HENRY[3], GEORGE[2], GEORGE[1])* was born Apr 23, 1889 in Metcalfe Co., KY. He married EDITH MORLING.

Children of GROVER PENDLETON and EDITH MORLING are:
    i.   BETTY[13] PENDLETON.
    ii. HELEN PENDLETON.
    iii. JOANN PENDLETON.
    iv. MARY PENDLETON.
    v.   MORRIS PENDLETON.
    vi. RAYMOND PENDLETON.
    vii. OLIVE RUTH PENDLETON.

864. ELIZABETH "BESSIE"[12] PENDLETON *(HIRAM[11], ABNER J.[10], JOHN[9], JOHN[8], HENRY[7], JOHN[6], PHILIP[5], HENRY[4], HENRY[3], GEORGE[2], GEORGE[1])* was born Nov 30, 1890 in Metcalfe Co., KY, and died Jul 31, 1972. She married WILL LANE Jul 28, 1906.

Children of ELIZABETH PENDLETON and WILL LANE are:
    i.   FLONNIE MAE[13] LANE, b. May 2, 1907; d. Aug 1975, Garrard Co., KY; m.
         MILLER.
    ii. MARGARET SAVANNAH LANE.
    iii. ELZIE LANE.

865. RUFUS[12] PENDLETON *(HIRAM[11], ABNER J.[10], JOHN[9], JOHN[8], HENRY[7], JOHN[6], PHILIP[5], HENRY[4], HENRY[3], GEORGE[2], GEORGE[1])* was born Sep 30, 1892 in Metcalfe Co., KY, and died Jun 2, 1972 in LeRoy, IL. He married IVA HALL 1904. She was born Oct 31, 1890 in Garrard Co., KY, and died Nov 1982 in Peoria, IL.

Children of RUFUS PENDLETON and IVA HALL are:
  i.   JOHN G.[13] PENDLETON, b. Mar 9, 1913, Madison Co., KY; d. May 12, 2004, Loveland, CO; m. MARGRADEL DOOLEY Jun 4, 1939, LeRoy, IL.; b. Dec 31, 1914, Bloomington, IL.
  ii. AGNES F. PENDLETON.
  iii. CLYDE PENDLETON.

866. HENRIETTA "HATTIE MAE"[12] PENDLETON *(HIRAM[11], ABNER J.[10], JOHN[9], JOHN[8], HENRY[7], JOHN[6], PHILIP[5], HENRY[4], HENRY[3], GEORGE[2], GEORGE[1])* was born Sep 17, 1894 in Metcalfe Co., KY, and died Oct 9, 1917 in Deland, IL. She married OSCAR FOLEY.

Children of HENRIETTA PENDLETON and OSCAR FOLEY are:
  i.   MARY EDITH[13] FOLEY.
  ii. HERBERT FOLEY.

867. CARL LESTER[12] PENDLETON *(HIRAM[11], ABNER J.[10], JOHN[9], JOHN[8], HENRY[7], JOHN[6], PHILIP[5], HENRY[4], HENRY[3], GEORGE[2], GEORGE[1])* was born Jul 10, 1896 in IN, and died Dec 18, 1982 in Lancaster, Garrard Co., KY. He married NELL.

Children of CARL PENDLETON and NELL are:
  i.   MARTHA[13] PENDLETON.
  ii. FLONNIE PENDLETON.
  iii. AMY PENDLETON.

868. LEE ALLEN[12] PENDLETON *(THOMAS CHESLEY[11], ABNER J.[10], JOHN[9], JOHN[8], HENRY[7], JOHN[6], PHILIP[5], HENRY[4], HENRY[3], GEORGE[2], GEORGE[1])* was born Nov 24, 1889 in Metcalfe Co., KY, and died Jun 17, 1981 in Edmonson, KY. He married ELIZABETH O. JONES 1910 in Barren Co., KY. She was born Abt. 1890 in KY, and died Sep 10, 1941 in Barren Co., KY.

Lee Allen Pendleton (Minister, Baptist Churches) registered for the WWI draft in Metcalfe Co., KY. Lee Pendleton (farmer) and family are listed in the 1930 Green Co., KY census.

Children of LEE PENDLETON and ELIZABETH JONES are:
  i.   PHILIP[13] PENDLETON.
  ii. BECKHAM PENDLETON, b. Jun 3, 1914, KY; d. Dec 6, 1995, Glasgow, Barren Co., KY.

869. WILLIAM STEWART[12] PENDLETON *(THOMAS CHESLEY[11], ABNER J.[10], JOHN[9], JOHN[8], HENRY[7], JOHN[6], PHILIP[5], HENRY[4], HENRY[3], GEORGE[2], GEORGE[1])* was born Sep 3, 1891 in Metcalfe Co., KY, and died Apr 1977 in Edmonton, KY. He married NANCY KELTNER 1911 in Metcalfe Co., KY. She was born Abt. 1892 in KY, and died Aft. 1930 in Edmonton, KY?

William S. Pendleton (farming) registered for the WWI draft in Metcalfe Co., KY. Stewart Pendleton (farmer) and family are listed in the 1920 Metcalfe Co., KY census.

Children of WILLIAM PENDLETON and NANCY KELTNER are:
    i.   LILLIAN[13] PENDLETON.
    ii. THOMAS PENDLETON.
    iii. LORRAINE PENDLETON.

870. ANNE S. "PEARL"[12] PENDLETON (*THEOPHILIS[11], JOHN HIRAM[10], JOHN[9], JOHN[8], HENRY[7], JOHN[6], PHILIP[5], HENRY[4], HENRY[3], GEORGE[2], GEORGE[1]*) was born Abt. 1882 in KY, and died Aft. 1930 in Metcalfe Co., KY? She married ROBERT HENRY BUTLER. He was born Abt. 1878 in KY, and died Oct 11, 1958 in Metcalfe Co., KY.

Children of ANNE PENDLETON and ROBERT BUTLER are:
    i.   HORACE P.[13] BUTLER.
    ii.   WINDELL C. BUTLER.
    iii. POLLY R. BUTLER.
    iv. WILLARD BUTLER.
    v.   EDWARD S. BUTLER.

871. LOUISA ELIZABETH[12] PENDLETON (*JAMES R.[11], HARVEY B.[10], JOHN[9], CURTIS[8], HENRY[7], JOHN[6], PHILIP[5], HENRY[4], HENRY[3], GEORGE[2], GEORGE[1]*) was born Oct 7, 1876 in KY, and died Aft. 1930 in Nashville, TN? She married BENJAMIN OTHELLO GARRETT Aft. 1900. He was born Abt. 1875 in KY, and died Aft. 1930 in Nashville, TN?
    Benjamin O. Garrett (farmer) and family are listed in the 1910 and 1920 Christian Co., KY census records. The family is listed in the 1930 Nashville, TN census.

Children of LOUISA PENDLETON and BENJAMIN GARRETT are:
    i.   JAMES PENDLETON[13] GARRETT.
    ii.   ERNEST WALTON GARRETT.
    iii.   BENJAMIN OTHELLO GARRETT.
    iv.   HARVEY CAMPBELL GARRETT.
    v.   CORD WEBB GARRETT.
    vi.   JENNIE B. GARRETT.
    vii. DOROTHY ELIZABETH GARRETT.
   viii. LELIA SALLEE GARRETT.
    ix.   RADFORD AGEE GARRETT.

872. MATTIE LEE[12] PENDLETON (*ISAAC THOMAS[11], RICE[10], THACKER[9], RICE[8], HENRY[7], JOHN[6], PHILIP[5], HENRY[4], HENRY[3], GEORGE[2], GEORGE[1]*) was born Jan 2, 1872 in KY, and died Mar 12, 1905. She married THOMAS HARDIN.
    A Mattie Hardin (29; b. KY) is listed in the Kentucky Asylum for Insane, Fayette Co., KY in the 1900 census.

Child of MATTIE PENDLETON and THOMAS HARDIN is:
    i.   LULU[13] HARDIN, b. 1899, KY; d. Aft. 1920, Montgomery Co., KY?
         Lula Hardin is in the household of Tom and Manny B. Pendleton in the
         1920 Montgomery Co., KY census.

873. JAMES RICE[12] PENDLETON (*ISAAC THOMAS*[11], *RICE*[10], *THACKER*[9], *RICE*[8], *HENRY*[7], *JOHN*[6], *PHILIP*[5], *HENRY*[4], *HENRY*[3], *GEORGE*[2], *GEORGE*[1]) was born Apr 19, 1875 in Bath County, KY, and died Jan 27, 1947 in Clark County, KY. He married HATTIE BEACHIE CROUCH Nov 2, 1905 in Ironton, OH. She was born Feb 22, 1885 in Salt Lick, KY, and died Feb 12, 1936 in Clark Co., KY.

The following account appeared in Bath County newspapers on Nov 2, 1905 (Ref. 316): "James Pendleton and Beachie Crouch eloped Sunday and were married at Ironton, Ohio. She is the daughter of Mrs. Betts Crouch and granddaughter of Mrs. Amanda Crouch. He is a railroad bridge carpenter for the L&N Railroad." Hattie Pendleton is buried in Winchester Cemetery, Clark Co., KY.

Children of JAMES PENDLETON and HATTIE CROUCH are:
    i.   HOWARD FERRIS[13] PENDLETON, b. Dec 20, 1907; d. Jan 1981,
         Louisville, KY.
    ii. CHARLES WILGUS PENDLETON, b. 1911, KY; d. May 21, 1911,
         Bourbon Co., KY.
    iii. FRANCES ELEANOR PENDLETON.
    iv. JAMES RUSSELL PENDLETON, b. Jan 27, 1919, Bourbon Co., KY; d.
         Nov 1, 1991.

874. EDWARD SPEARS[12] PENDLETON (*ISAAC THOMAS*[11], *RICE*[10], *THACKER*[9], *RICE*[8], *HENRY*[7], *JOHN*[6], *PHILIP*[5], *HENRY*[4], *HENRY*[3], *GEORGE*[2], *GEORGE*[1]) was born Jun 6, 1891 in Bourbon Co., KY, and died Dec 23, 1965 in Paris, KY. He married (1) MYRTLE CATES. He married (2) FLORA LOU ROBERTS MENG, He married (3) RUTH GLADYS BECKWITH daughter of ELLIOTT BECKWITH and CHARITY WHITING. She was born Apr 13, 1906, and died Feb 17, 1974.

Edward Spears Pendleton registered for the World War I draft in Hamilton Co., OH.

Children of EDWARD PENDLETON and MYRTLE CATES are:
    i.   PATRICIA L.[13] PENDLETON.
    ii. ALEETA PENDLETON.

875. EDWARD LESLIE[12] PENDLETON (*THACKER V.*[11], *RICE*[10], *THACKER*[9], *RICE*[8], *HENRY*[7], *JOHN*[6], *PHILIP*[5], *HENRY*[4], *HENRY*[3], *GEORGE*[2], *GEORGE*[1]) was born Nov 1878 in Clark Co., KY, and died Apr 18, 1944 in Fayette Co., KY. He married (1) DELIA ELDRIDGE. She was born Jul 14, 1878 in VA, and died Mar 13, 1921 in Fayette Co., KY. He married (2) EULIE K. She was born Abt. 1877 in KY, and died Jun 30, 1962 in Fayette Co., KY.

Edward Pendleton (fireman - wagon works) and family are listed in the 1920 Lexington, Fayette Co., KY census. Edward Leslie Pendleton and his wife, Delia Eldridge are buried in Winchester Cemetery, Clark Co., KY.

Children of EDWARD PENDLETON and DELIA ELDRIDGE are:
    i. MAE LOUISE[13] PENDLETON.
    ii. EDWARD FRANKLIN PENDLETON, b. Abt. 1905, KY; d. Jul 20, 1969, Fayette Co., KY; m. MARIE LAKE, b. Jan 11, 1911; d. Oct 4, 1987, Lexington, KY.
    iii. LESLIE DUDLEY PENDLETON.
    iv. VIRGIL THACKER PENDLETON, b. Abt. 1909, KY; d. Apr 20, 1926, Fayette Co., KY.
        Virgil Pendleton is buried in Lexington Cemetery, KY.

    v. CLARA L. PENDLETON.
    vi. DELIA ELIZABETH PENDLETON.
    vii. NANCY DONALON PENDLETON.
    viii. PHILLIP HENRY PENDLETON, b. Nov 24, 1918, Fayette Co., KY; d. Oct 17, 1940, Fayette Co., KY.

876. JOHN RICE[12] PENDLETON (*JOHN RICE[11], RICE[10], THACKER[9], RICE[8], HENRY[7], JOHN[6], PHILIP[5], HENRY[4], HENRY[3], GEORGE[2], GEORGE[1]*) was born Jan 1886 in Clark Co., KY, and died Dec 11, 1915 in Montgomery Co, KY. He married BESSIE ADELL THOMAS. She was born 1887, and died Sep 19, 1975 in Montgomery Co, KY.

Children of JOHN PENDLETON and BESSIE THOMAS are:
    i. WILLIAM R.[13] PENDLETON, b. Apr 9, 1913, Montgomery Co., KY; d. Sep 30, 1969, Bath Co., KY.
    ii. CHARLES DAVID PENDLETON, b. Jun 26, 1915, Montgomery Co., KY; d. Nov 6, 1974, Butler Co., OH.

877. ASAH[12] PENDLETON (*JOHN RICE[11], RICE[10], THACKER[9], RICE[8], HENRY[7], JOHN[6], PHILIP[5], HENRY[4], HENRY[3], GEORGE[2], GEORGE[1]*) was born Mar 1893 in Clark Co., KY, and died Sep 11, 1960 in Montgomery Co., KY. He married LILLIAN. She was born Abt. 1899 in KY.

Children of ASAH PENDLETON and LILLIAN are:
    i. MARY E.[13] PENDLETON.
    ii. LIDA M. PENDLETON.

878. WILLIAM ARTIE[12] PENDLETON (*JAMES WILLIAM[11], MARTIN J.[10], PRESLEY[9], RICE[8], HENRY[7], JOHN[6], PHILIP[5], HENRY[4], HENRY[3], GEORGE[2], GEORGE[1]*) was born Aug 28, 1890 in Centralia, MO, and died May 19, 1962 in Neodesha, KS. He married KATIE ROSCUM RIGGS Oct 4, 1915 in Miami Co., KS, daughter of FRED RIGGS and LUCY FOSTER. She was born Oct 12, 1900 in Centralia, MO, and died Jan 4, 1968 in Neodesha, KS.

Children of WILLIAM PENDLETON and KATIE RIGGS are:
     i. WILLIAM[13] PENDLETON.
    ii. MARY R. PENDLETON.

879. CORNELIA ANN[12] PENDLETON *(CHARLES PORTER[11], WILLIAM RICE[10], PRESLEY[9], RICE[8], HENRY[7], JOHN[6], PHILIP[5], HENRY[4], HENRY[3], GEORGE[2], GEORGE[1])* was born Jan 9, 1892 in Ralls Co., MO, and died Aft. 1930 in Ralls Co., MO. She married HARRY RUSSELL NORRIS Oct 16, 1912, son of JOHN NORRIS and ELIZABETH MARTIN. He was born Feb 26, 1880 in MO, and died Aft. 1930 in Ralls Co., MO.

Child of CORNELIA PENDLETON and HARRY NORRIS is:
     i. PAULINE[13] NORRIS.

880. LOUIS BAYLOR[12] PENDLETON *(HENRY CLAY[11], JOSEPH HOLMES[10], BENJAMIN[9], PHILIP[8], BENJAMIN[7], PHILIP[6], PHILIP[5], HENRY[4], HENRY[3], GEORGE[2], GEORGE[1])* was born Nov 19, 1875 in GA, and died May 1964 in MO. He married BERTHA E. She was born Abt. 1882 in MO, and died Aft. 1920.
      Louis B. Pendleton (architect) and family are listed in the 1920 St. Louis, MO census.

Children of LOUIS PENDLETON and BERTHA E. are:
     i. NANCY A.[13] PENDLETON.
    ii. ELEANOR PENDLETON.

881. IV PHILIP BAYLOR[12] PENDLETON *(PHILIP BAYLOR[11], PHILIP BAYLOR[10], PHILIP BAYLOR[9], PHILIP[8], BENJAMIN[7], PHILIP[6], PHILIP[5], HENRY[4], HENRY[3], GEORGE[2], GEORGE[1])* was born Jul 22, 1891 in VA, and died in Richmond, VA? He married MARJORIA WASHINGTON MARSHALL Apr 21, 1913. She was born Abt. 1891 in VA, and died in Richmond, VA?
      Philip B. Pendleton (post office clerk) and family are listed in the 1920 Richmond census, pg. 3B.

Child of PHILIP PENDLETON and MARJORIA MARSHALL are:
     i. ALVIN ELWOOD[13] PENDLETON.

882. JENNIE ALVINA[12] PENDLETON *(WILLIAM HENRY[11], WILLIAM HENRY[10], GEORGE MACON[9], PHILIP[8], BENJAMIN[7], PHILIP[6], PHILIP[5], HENRY[4], HENRY[3], GEORGE[2], GEORGE[1])* was born Aug 14, 1871 in Downey, CA, and died Jun 02, 1929 in Long Beach, CA. She married ELMER ENYART BALL Dec 05, 1891 in Downey, CA, son of ENYART BALL and FLORELLA SIMS. He was born Nov 23, 1869 in Chautaugua Co., KS, and died Nov 10, 1943 in Alhambra, CA.

Child of JENNIE PENDLETON and ELMER BALL is:
> i. ELMER HORACE[13] BALL, b. Mar 13, 1894, Carmenita, CA; d. Oct 17, 1965, Oceanside, CA.

883. GEORGE RANEY[12] PENDLETON (*WILLIAM HENRY[11], WILLIAM HENRY[10], GEORGE MACON[9], PHILIP[8], BENJAMIN[7], PHILIP[6], PHILIP[5], HENRY[4], HENRY[3], GEORGE[2], GEORGE[1]*) was born May 14, 1873 in Downey, CA, and died Jan 03, 1917 in Tulare Co., CA. He married LUELLA N. She was born Oct 1878 in WI.

George R. Pendleton (farmer) and family are listed in the 1900 Los Angeles Co., CA, pg. 77.

Child of GEORGE PENDLETON and LUELLA N. is:
> i. GEORGE A.[13] PENDLETON, b. Oct 1896, CA.

884. JESSE CASWELL[12] PENDLETON (*WILLIAM HENRY[11], WILLIAM HENRY[10], GEORGE MACON[9], PHILIP[8], BENJAMIN[7], PHILIP[6], PHILIP[5], HENRY[4], HENRY[3], GEORGE[2], GEORGE[1]*) was born Apr 05, 1876 in Downey, CA, and died Dec 29, 1940 in Venice, CA. He married ESTHER OCTAVIA MATNEY Nov 28, 1896 in CA. She was born Oct 18, 1881 in Topeka, KS, and died Jan 28, 1942 in Downey, CA.

Jessie Pendleton (teamster) and family are listed in the 1900 Los Angeles Co., CA census, pg. 283. Jesse Caswell Pendleton registered for the World War I draft in Los Angeles, CA.

Children of JESSE PENDLETON and ESTHER MATNEY are (Ref. 317):
> i. IRENE B.[13] PENDLETON, b. Feb 02, 1898, Los Angeles, CA; d. Sep 22, 1958, Glendale, CA.
> ii. GLADYS R. PENDLETON, b. Nov 18, 1899, Los Angeles, CA; d. Jan 08, 1939, Glendale, CA.
> iii. WILLIAM HENRY PENDLETON, b. Dec 02, 1904, Los Angeles, CA; d. Apr 04, 1945, Glendale, CA.
> iv. MATTHEW CLINTON PENDLETON, b. Jul 13, 1906, Los Angeles, CA; d. Sep 20, 1963, Glendale, CA.
> v. PAUL E. PENDLETON, b. Jun 20, 1910, Los Angeles, CA; d. Sep 1963, Glendale, CA.
> vi. EVA OCTAVIA PENDLETON, b. May 04, 1914, Los Angeles, CA; d. Apr 15, 1995, Phoenix, AZ; m. CARROL DEWITT SMITH.

885. EARL[12] PENDLETON (*WILLIAM HENRY[11], WILLIAM HENRY[10], GEORGE MACON[9], PHILIP[8], BENJAMIN[7], PHILIP[6], PHILIP[5], HENRY[4], HENRY[3], GEORGE[2], GEORGE[1]*) was born Sep 01, 1885 in Downey, CA, and died Aft. 1930 in Glendale, CA? He married RUTH L. FORSTER Jun 01, 1908 in CA. She was born 1889 in MN, and died Aft. 1930 in Glendale, CA?

Earl Pendleton registered for the World War I draft in Los Angeles, CA. Earl Pendleton and family are listed in the 1920 Los Angeles census.

Child of EARL PENDLETON and RUTH FORSTER is:
> i. DOROTHY[13] PENDLETON.

886. ROBERT HENRY[12] PENDLETON (*JAMES MONROE[11], WILLIAM MONROE[10], JOHN[9], JAMES[8], PHILIP[7], PHILIP[6], PHILIP[5], HENRY[4], HENRY[3], GEORGE[2], GEORGE[1]*) was born Sep 20, 1865 in MO, and died Aug 13, 1946 in Pope Co., AR. He married MARY JANE CASTOE Dec 14, 1887 in AR, daughter of DAVID CASTOE and SALINA BATSEL. She was born Feb 1872 in MO, and died Mar 20, 1946.

R. H. Pendleton (farm laborer) and family are listed in the 1900 Lawrence Co., MO census, pg. 285a.

Children of ROBERT PENDLETON and MARY CASTOE are (Ref. 318):

    i.   DAVID ELVA[13] PENDLETON, b. Jul 12, 1890, MO; d. Pope Co., AR?; m. NEVIE; b. Abt. 1892, AR.

        David Elva Pendleton registered for the World War I draft in Pope Co., AR.

    ii. SALINA ETHEL PENDLETON, b. Mar 17, 1894, MO.

    iii. EARL JAMES PENDLETON, b. Jul 24, 1896, MO; d. Oct 1975, Russellville, AR.

        Earl James Pendleton registered for the World War I draft in Pope Co., AR.

    iv. PEARLY JANE PENDLETON, b. Jul 24, 1896, MO.

    v.   NICIE FAY PENDLETON, b. Nov 09, 1899, MO.

    vi. DICIE FAY PENDLETON, b. Nov 09, 1899, MO.

    vii. CORDIE LEE PENDLETON.

    viii. ALFORD J. PENDLETON.

887. WILLIAM M.[12] PENDLETON (*JAMES MONROE[11], WILLIAM MONROE[10], JOHN[9], JAMES[8], PHILIP[7], PHILIP[6], PHILIP[5], HENRY[4], HENRY[3], GEORGE[2], GEORGE[1]*) was born Dec 1867 in MO, and died Aft. 1920 in Pope Co., AR? He married FLORA P. Abt. 1892. She was born May 1875 in IN, and died Aft. 1920 in Pope Co., AR?

Children of WILLIAM PENDLETON and FLORA P. are:

    i.   ESTER R.[13] PENDLETON.

    ii. WILLIAM H. PENDLETON.

    iii. MARY E. PENDLETON.

    iv. LELIA C. PENDLETON.

    v.   ROBERT H. PENDLETON.

888. MARY C.[12] PENDLETON (*JOHN WILLIS[11], WILLIAM MONROE[10], JOHN[9], JAMES[8], PHILIP[7], PHILIP[6], PHILIP[5], HENRY[4], HENRY[3], GEORGE[2], GEORGE[1]*) was born Abt. 1865 in MO, and died Aft. 1920 in Lawrence Co., MO? She married JOHN A. MOSHER. He was born Abt. 1857 in IL, and died Aft. 1920 in Lawrence Co., MO?

John Mosher (laborer) and family are listed in the 1920 Lawrence Co., MO census.

Children of MARY PENDLETON and JOHN MOSHER are:
    i.   ROY[13] MOSHER, b. Abt. 1887, MO.
   ii.   MARY MOSHER, b. Abt. 1893, MO.

889. WILEY G.[12] PENDLETON *(JOHN WILLIS[11], WILLIAM MONROE[10], JOHN[9], JAMES[8], PHILIP[7], PHILIP[6], PHILIP[5], HENRY[4], HENRY[3], GEORGE[2], GEORGE[1])* was born Aug 1866 in MO, and died Aft. 1920 in Ottawa Co., OK? He married MARY E. Abt. 1895. She was born Jul 1874 in MO, and died Aft. 1920 in Ottawa Co., OK?

       Wiley G. Pendleton (zinc farmer) and family are listed in the 1900 Lawrence Co., MO census, pg. 45a. Wiley G. Pendleton (mill; carpenter) and family are listed in the 1920 Ottawa Co., OK census.

Children of WILEY PENDLETON and MARY E. are:
     i.   BLANCHE[13] PENDLETON, b. Jun 1896, MO.
    ii.   BESSIE M. PENDLETON, b. Dec 1898, MO.
   iii.   DELIA PENDLETON.
   iv.   GOLDIE PENDLETON.
    v.   JEWEL PENDLETON.

890. DOCKY H.[12] PENDLETON *(JOHN WILLIS[11], WILLIAM MONROE[10], JOHN[9], JAMES[8], PHILIP[7], PHILIP[6], PHILIP[5], HENRY[4], HENRY[3], GEORGE[2], GEORGE[1])* was born Sep 1868 in MO, and died Aft. 1910 in Lawrence Co., MO? He married MARY CAROLINE TALLEY Abt. 1889. She was born Jun 1866 in KS, and died Aft. 1910 in Lawrence Co., MO?

Children of DOCKY PENDLETON and MARY TALLEY are:
     i.   ERNEST[13] PENDLETON, b. Jul 1892, MO.
    ii.   LUCRETIA M. PENDLETON, b. Aug 1899, Lawrence Co., MO.
   iii.   JUNUS W. PENDLETON.

891. JOHN W.[12] PENDLETON *(JOHN WILLIS[11], WILLIAM MONROE[10], JOHN[9], JAMES[8], PHILIP[7], PHILIP[6], PHILIP[5], HENRY[4], HENRY[3], GEORGE[2], GEORGE[1])* was born Jun 1871 in MO, and died Aft. 1920 in Lawrence Co., MO? He married (1) UNKNOWN.   He married (2) ROSA J. Abt. 1900 in Lawrence Co., MO. She was born Sep 1882 in MO.

       John W. Pendleton (zinc miner) and wife are listed in the 1900 Lawrence Co., MO census, pg. 45a.

Child of JOHN PENDLETON and UNKNOWN is:
     i.   LIVIE G.[13] PENDLETON, b. Feb 1892.

892. ELMER E.[12] PENDLETON *(GEORGE WASHINGTON[11], WILLIAM MONROE[10], JOHN[9], JAMES[8], PHILIP[7], PHILIP[6], PHILIP[5], HENRY[4], HENRY[3], GEORGE[2], GEORGE[1])* was born May 1877 in MO, and died Aft. 1920 in Lawrence Co., MO? He married NETTIE. She was born Sep 1877 in TX, and died Aft. 1920 in Lawrence Co., MO?

Elmer E. Pendleton (miller) and family are listed in the 1900 Lawrence Co., MO census, pg. 152.

Children of ELMER PENDLETON and NETTIE are:
    i.   LEONA M.[13] PENDLETON, b. Oct 1899, Lawrence Co., MO.
    ii.   GEORGE PENDLETON.
    iii. GINEVER PENDLETON.
    iv.   DORIS PENDLETON.
    v.   MAY PENDLETON.
    vi.   MILDRED PENDLETON.
    vii. GERTRUDE PENDLETON.

893. DANIEL N.[12] PENDLETON (*ALFRED SIEGEL[11], WILLIAM MONROE[10], JOHN[9], JAMES[8], PHILIP[7], PHILIP[6], PHILIP[5], HENRY[4], HENRY[3], GEORGE[2], GEORGE[1]*) was born Jun 1886 in MO. He married HELENA H. She was born Abt. 1888 in MO.

Child of DANIEL PENDLETON and HELENA H. is:
    i.   DOROTHY E.[13] PENDLETON.

894. GEORGE HIRAM[12] PENDLETON (*JOSEPH H.[11], PHILIP HARPER[10], JOSEPH[9], MICAJAH[8], PHILIP[7], PHILIP[6], PHILIP[5], HENRY[4], HENRY[3], GEORGE[2], GEORGE[1]*) was born Jan 26, 1862 in VA, and died Feb 21, 1935 in Letcher Co., KY. He married ALICE SERENA EADS Abt. 1888, daughter of ANDREW EADS and BARBARA WOLFE. She was born Mar 14, 1869 in Smyth Co., VA, and died Jan 13, 1965 in Ashland, Boyd Co., KY.
    George Pendleton (sawyer) and family are listed in the 1900 Smyth Co., VA census, pg. 6a.

Children of GEORGE PENDLETON and ALICE EADS are:
          i.   WILLIAM BASIL[13] PENDLETON, b. Jul 14, 1889, VA; d. Jan 26, 1919, VA; m. CATHERINE MUSIC, 1912.
    912. ii. MARY ELLA PENDLETON, b. Jun 01, 1891, Wythe Co., VA; d. Jan 20, 1986, Hocking Co., OH.
          iii. JOSEPH LINTON PENDLETON, b. Mar 11, 1893, VA; d. Nov 26, 1962, VA; m. MRS. PICKLEHEIMER, 1920.
          iv. KYLE MONTAGUE PENDLETON, b. Sep 22, 1895, VA; d. Aug 18, 1948, Letcher Co., KY?; m. VERA MENGUS, 1922; b. Abt. 1905, KY.
          v.   JULIAN LEE PENDLETON, b. Jul 30, 1898, VA; d. May 29, 1908, VA.

895. JOSHUA BORAN[12] PENDLETON (*MORGAN MITCHELL[11], PHILIP HARPER[10], JOSEPH[9], MICAJAH[8], PHILIP[7], PHILIP[6], PHILIP[5], HENRY[4], HENRY[3], GEORGE[2], GEORGE[1]*) was born May 19, 1858 in Washington Co., TN, and died Jun 21, 1929 in Clark Co., IL. He married PHEREBA CHRISTINE STRAKER Mar 08, 1888. She was born Abt. 1861 in IL, and died Aft. 1910 in Clark Co., IL?
    Josh Pendleton (22), born in TN, is found in the 1880 census, Clark Co., IL, pg. 153A in the household of George Glankenbeker.

Children of JOSHUA PENDLETON and PHEREBA STRAKER are:

    i.   MYRTLE[13] PENDLETON, b. Abt. 1891, IL.

   ii. HERMAN PENDLETON, b. Oct 22, 1892, IL; d. Dec 1975, Marshall, IL.

  iii. DENNIS PENDLETON, b. Abt. 1895, IL.

   iv. LUCY PENDLETON, b. Abt. 1898, IL.

    v. CLIFFORD PENDLETON, b. Jul 29, 1901, IL; d. Apr 1979, Peoria, IL.

   vi. PHILIP PENDLETON, b. Sep 16, 1903, IL; d. Oct 1973, Peoria, IL.

896. SARAH ANGELINE[12] PENDLETON (*MORGAN MITCHELL*[11], *PHILIP HARPER*[10], *JOSEPH*[9], *MICAJAH*[8], *PHILIP*[7], *PHILIP*[6], *PHILIP*[5], *HENRY*[4], *HENRY*[3], *GEORGE*[2], *GEORGE*[1]) was born Sep 11, 1868 in Wythe Co., VA, and died Jul 15, 1953. She married SAMUEL ANDERSON POWERS Jul 09, 1888, son of JAMES POWERS and NANCY HOPE. He was born Aug 01, 1867 in TN, and died Sep 26, 1937 in Morgan Co., TN.

Children of SARAH PENDLETON and SAMUEL POWERS are:

    i.   MINNIE[13] POWERS, b. Mar 26, 1892, TN.

   ii. MAGGIE POWERS, b. Sep 06, 1894, TN.

  iii. MAY POWERS, b. May 1896, TN.

897. JOHN HARVEY[12] PENDLETON (*MORGAN MITCHELL*[11], *PHILIP HARPER*[10], *JOSEPH*[9], *MICAJAH*[8], *PHILIP*[7], *PHILIP*[6], *PHILIP*[5], *HENRY*[4], *HENRY*[3], *GEORGE*[2], *GEORGE*[1]) was born Sep 13, 1870 in Wythe Co., VA, and died Feb 09, 1937 in Dunklin Co., MO. He married SARAH FRANCES BOLEN Jul 16, 1894 in Mississippi Co., MO. She was born Nov 1879 in KY, and died Aft. 1920 in Dunklin Co., MO?

    John Pendleton (farm laborer) and family are listed in the 1900 Mississippi Co., MO census, pg. 234. John Pendleton (timber man; insurance) and family are listed in the 1920 Independence, MO census.

Children of JOHN PENDLETON and SARAH BOLEN are:

    i.   SAMUEL VERN[13] PENDLETON, b. Sep 19, 1895, Mississippi Co., MO; d. Apr 12, 1947.

       Sam Pendleton (common laborer) registered for the WWI draft in Dunklin Co., MO. He had a disability of weak eyes.

   ii. PHEREBA DELANE PENDLETON, b. Jan 04, 1901, Mississippi Co., MO; d. Jan 23, 1982, St. Louis, MO; m. IRA BLANCHARD MINNER, Apr 05, 1917, Dunklin Co., MO; b. Abt. 1894, AR; d. Aft. 1930, Bollinger Co., MO?

  iii. JAMES RAY PENDLETON, b. May 29, 1903, New Madrid Co., MO; d. Jun 03, 1957.

   iv. HERMAN PETER PENDLETON, b. Nov 13, 1906, MO; d. Oct 1984, St. Louis, MO.

    v. MINNIE FRANCES PENDLETON.

   vi. MARC DAVIS PENDLETON, b. Jun 29, 1911; d. Jun 26, 1988, Dunklin Co., MO.

vii. ROMULAS DOYLE PENDLETON, b. Feb 08, 1914, Dunklin Co., MO; d. Oct 18, 1914.

viii. KATHALEEN IMOGENE PENDLETON.

898. JAMES E. WILSON[12] PENDLETON *(MORGAN MITCHELL[11], PHILIP HARPER[10], JOSEPH[9], MICAJAH[8], PHILIP[7], PHILIP[6], PHILIP[5], HENRY[4], HENRY[3], GEORGE[2], GEORGE[1])* was born Apr 28, 1872 in Wythe Co., VA, and died Mar 22, 1957 in Rhea Co., TN? He married JENNY "MARY JANE" KEYLON Abt. 1888, daughter of WILLIAM KEYLON and MARGARET HOPE. She was born Apr 18, 1875 in TN, and died Jan 27, 1953 in Rhea Co., TN?

James Pendleton (farm laborer) and family are listed in the 1900 Meigs Co., TN census, pg. 71.

Children of JAMES PENDLETON and JENNY KEYLON are:

i. MARGARET JANE[13] PENDLETON, b. Sep 25, 1889, TN; d. Jan 26, 1975.

ii. ALICE PENDLETON, b. Mar 1893, TN; d. 1914.

iii. WORLEY H. PENDLETON, b. Dec 1894, Warren Co., TN; d. Nov 11, 1948.

iv. LILLIE PENDLETON, b. Jul 1897, TN.

913. v. FRANK BURK PENDLETON, b. May 22, 1900, TN; d. Apr 13, 1982, Spring City, TN.

vi. HATTIE PENDLETON, b. Abt. 1903, TN; d. Jul 06, 1950.

vii. LEONARD PENDLETON.

viii. ADA PENDLETON, b. Abt. 1906, TN; d. Oct 15, 1931.

ix. JAMES E. PENDLETON, b. 1908, TN; d. Jul 21, 1934; m. RUTH D.; b. Abt. 1910, TN.

x. BONNIE PENDLETON, b. Dec 1911, TN; d. Mar 1927.

xi. ARCH PAUL PENDLETON, b. Mar 01, 1914, TN; d. May 03, 1998.

xii. CHARLES E. PENDLETON.

899. ALBERTA[12] PENDLETON *(ALBERT GALLATIN[11], JAMES VANCE[10], JOSEPH[9], MICAJAH[8], PHILIP[7], PHILIP[6], PHILIP[5], HENRY[4], HENRY[3], GEORGE[2], GEORGE[1])* was born Jun 1874 in TN. She married THOMAS A. HINSON. He was born May 1874 in England.

Child of ALBERTA PENDLETON and THOMAS HINSON is:

i. KATHERINE[13] HINSON, b. Dec 1899, TX.

Generation No. 13

The thirteenth generation consists of the great (6) grandchildren of the immigrant Philip Pendleton and Isabella Hurt. The time period is from about 1894, when James Trigg Pendleton married in Kentucky, to a date well beyond 2006, the date of this history. Most members of this generation are living yet and thus are not included in this history to protect their privacy. A few of the early born of this generation were old enough to have served as soldiers in World War I, others in World War II, and still others, no doubt, in later conflicts of the twentieth century. A full account of this generation will not be written for some time.

Generation No. 13

900. LILLIAN[13] PENDLETON *(JAMES STROTHER[12], JAMES FRENCH[11], JAMES[10], THOMAS[9], JAMES[8], JAMES[7], HENRY[6], PHILIP[5], HENRY[4], HENRY[3], GEORGE[2], GEORGE[1])* was born Sep 06, 1893 in MO, and died Oct 1980 in Richmond, MO. She married JOHN B. ABERCROMBIE. He was born Mar 03, 1894 in MO, and died Apr 1983 in Cape Girardeau, MO.

Children of LILLIAN PENDLETON and JOHN ABERCROMBIE are:
    i.   MARY MARGARET[14] ABERCROMBIE, b. Jul 01, 1915, St. Joseph, Mo; d. Mar 1981, Atlanta, GA; m. NORWOOD NEVILLE COBB; d. May 1968, Birmingham, Al.
    ii. JEAN GOODWIN ABERCROMBIE.

901. LOUISE[13] PENDLETON *(JAMES STROTHER[12], JAMES FRENCH[11], JAMES[10], THOMAS[9], JAMES[8], JAMES[7], HENRY[6], PHILIP[5], HENRY[4], HENRY[3], GEORGE[2], GEORGE[1])* was born May 11, 1895 in MO, and died May 20, 1987 in St. Joseph, MO. She married LOUIS SAYLES. He was born Feb 05, 1894, and died Oct 1983 in St. Joseph, MO.

Children of LOUISE PENDLETON and LOUIS SAYLES are:
    i.   NORMAN[14] SAYLES.
    ii. NICHOLAS SAYLES.
    iii. PATSY SAYLES.

902. MARGARET ETHEL[13] PENDLETON *(JAMES STROTHER[12], JAMES FRENCH[11], JAMES[10], THOMAS[9], JAMES[8], JAMES[7], HENRY[6], PHILIP[5], HENRY[4], HENRY[3], GEORGE[2], GEORGE[1])* was born Jan 19, 1897 in St. Joseph, MO, and died Dec 1971 in Dallas, TX. She married FRANK EMMERT POE Jun 14, 1917 in St. Joseph, MO, son of ELISHA POE and MARY RILEY. He was born Jun 23, 1887 in St. Joseph, MO, and died Nov 25, 1953 in Kansas City, MO.

Child of MARGARET PENDLETON and FRANK POE is:
    i. JERRY LOUISE[14] POE.

903. ALEXANDER BRUCE[13] PENDLETON *(WILLIAM ARMISTEAD[12], WILLIAM ARMISTEAD[11], JOHN LEWIS[10], JOHN[9], EDMUND[8], JOHN[7], HENRY[6], PHILIP[5], HENRY[4], HENRY[3], GEORGE[2], GEORGE[1])* was born Mar 14, 1888 in VA, and died May 04, 1919 in Halifax Co., VA. He married MARIE IRVING EASLEY Dec 17, 1913, daughter of JOHN EASLEY and JENNIE C. She was born Abt. 1891 in VA, and died Aft. 1920 in Halifax Co., VA?

    Alexander B. Pendleton (salesman) registered for the WWI draft in Atlanta, GA. Alexander Bruce Pendleton is buried in the Bruce Family Cemetery, Berry Hill Plantation, Halifax Co., VA.

Child of ALEXANDER PENDLETON and MARIE EASLEY is:
    i. ALEXANDER BRUCE[14] PENDLETON, JR.

904. JAMES TRIGG[13] PENDLETON *(IRA NEWTON[12], JAMES TRIGG[11], IRA NASH[10], REUBEN[9], BENJAMIN[8], WILLIAM[7], JOHN[6], PHILIP[5], HENRY[4], HENRY[3], GEORGE[2], GEORGE[1])* was born Oct 10, 1874 in Johnson Co., KY, and died 1940. He married CYNTHIA BROWN Abt. 1894. She was born Sep 1878 in KY.

    James Trigg Pendleton (farmer) and family are listed in the 1900 Johnson Co., KY census, pg. 240.

Children of JAMES PENDLETON and CYNTHIA BROWN are:
    i. CATHERINE[14] PENDLETON, b. Jan 10, 1897; d. Dec 27, 1999; m. BRUCE COCHRAN.
    ii. MENTIE PENDLETON, b. Mar 23, 1899; d. Aug 03, 1914, KY.
    iii. AMANDA PENDLETON.
    iv. TIA PENDLETON, b. Jul 10, 1903, KY; d. At birth.
    v. JAMES IRA PENDLETON, b. Sep 25, 1905, Johnson Co., KY; d. Nov 26, 1981, Wilmington, OH; m. LUCILLE THOMAS, Nov 15, 1929, Rush, KY.
    vi. BERTIE PENDLETON.
    vii. HURSHEL HASTIN PENDLETON, b. Apr 30, 1918; d. Jan 10, 2000, Mount Sterling, OH; m. DONNA.
    viii. GLADYS PENDLETON.
    ix. RUBY B. PENDLETON.

905. LOU[13] PENDLETON *(IRA NEWTON[12], JAMES TRIGG[11], IRA NASH[10], REUBEN[9], BENJAMIN[8], WILLIAM[7], JOHN[6], PHILIP[5], HENRY[4], HENRY[3], GEORGE[2], GEORGE[1])* was born Mar 1883 in KY, and died Aft. 1920 in Johnson Co., KY? She married MACE CANTRILL Jun 12, 1901 in Johnson Co., KY. He was born Abt. 1882 in KY, and died Aft. 1920 in Johnson Co., KY?

Children of LOU PENDLETON and MACE CANTRILL are:
    i. IRA[14] CANTRILL.
    ii. HENRY CANTRILL.

906. WILLIAM[13] PENDLETON *(GEORGE H.[12], JAMES TRIGG[11], IRA NASH[10], REUBEN[9], BENJAMIN[8], WILLIAM[7], JOHN[6], PHILIP[5], HENRY[4], HENRY[3], GEORGE[2], GEORGE[1])* was born Mar 28, 1899, and died Jan 04, 1966 in KY. He married NANCY SMITH. She was born Oct 15, 1908 in Morgan Co., KY, and died Jul 25, 2000, West Liberty, Morgan Co., KY.

Children of WILLIAM PENDLETON and NANCY SMITH are:
    i.   MARGARET[14] PENDLETON.
    ii. GEORGE H. PENDLETON.

907. ALBERT HORTON[13] PENDLETON *(EDWIN DUDLEY[12], IRA NASH[11], SAMUEL GUTHRIE[10], REUBEN[9], BENJAMIN[8], WILLIAM[7], JOHN[6], PHILIP[5], HENRY[4], HENRY[3], GEORGE[2], GEORGE[1])* was born Jul 31, 1881 in VA, and died Aft. 1930 in Chicago, IL? He married MARY CECILIA LAYTON Oct 01, 1906. She was born Abt. 1886 in PA, and died Nov 21, 1922 in E. St. Louis, IL?
    Albert H. Pendleton (horse dealer; stock works) and family are listed in the 1910 East St. Louis, IL census. Albert H. Pendleton (Manager, Horses Retail Co.) and daughter Jane are listed in the 1930 Chicago, IL census.

Child of ALBERT PENDLETON and MARY LAYTON is:
    i.   JANE MARIE[14] PENDLETON.

908. ARTHUR CLIFTON[13] PENDLETON *(JAMES PRESLEY[12], IRA NASH[11], SAMUEL GUTHRIE[10], REUBEN[9], BENJAMIN[8], WILLIAM[7], JOHN[6], PHILIP[5], HENRY[4], HENRY[3], GEORGE[2], GEORGE[1])* was born Jun 20, 1894 in VA, and died Jul 21, 1926 in Washington Co., VA? He married MARGARET HAYNES Jan 12, 1916.
    Arthur Clifton Pendleton World registered for the War I draft in Washington Co., VA.

Child of ARTHUR PENDLETON and MARGARET HAYNES is:
    i.   MARY[14] PENDLETON.

909. WILLIAM B.[13] PENDLETON *(JAMES M.[12], WILLIAM SAMUEL[11], SAMUEL GUTHRIE[10], REUBEN[9], BENJAMIN[8], WILLIAM[7], JOHN[6], PHILIP[5], HENRY[4], HENRY[3], GEORGE[2], GEORGE[1])* was born Abt. 1878 in TN, and died Aft. 1920 in Lee Co., VA? He married MATILDA J. She was born Abt. 1875 in TN, and died Aft. 1920 in Lee Co., VA?

Children of WILLIAM PENDLETON and MATILDA J. are:
    i.   JEFFRIE[14] PENDLETON.
    ii. MARY A. PENDLETON.
    iii. BONNIE? PENDLETON.

910. BEDFORD HORNER[13] PENDLETON *(JAMES M.[12], WILLIAM SAMUEL[11], SAMUEL GUTHRIE[10], REUBEN[9], BENJAMIN[8], WILLIAM[7], JOHN[6], PHILIP[5], HENRY[4], HENRY[3], GEORGE[2], GEORGE[1])* was born Apr 1892 in Hancock Co., TN, and died Aug

05, 1958 in Lee Co., VA. He married LUCY MAE WOLFENBARGER Mar 14, 1912. She was born Aug 05, 1894 in Hancock Co., TN, and died Nov 08, 1978 in Lee Co., VA.

Bedford Pendleton (farmer, 29) and family are listed in the 1920 White Shoals, Lee Co., VA census, pg. 5A.

Children of BEDFORD PENDLETON and LUCY WOLFENBARGER are:
- i. BONNIE H.[14] PENDLETON.
- ii. VIRGINIA B. PENDLETON.

911. HAMPTON LLOYD[13] PENDLETON *(WILLIAM BENTON[12], WILLIAM SAMUEL[11], SAMUEL GUTHRIE[10], REUBEN[9], BENJAMIN[8], WILLIAM[7], JOHN[6], PHILIP[5], HENRY[4], HENRY[3], GEORGE[2], GEORGE[1])* was born May 26, 1890 in Scott Co., VA, and died in Bonita Springs, Lee Co., FL. He married EDITH ALICE PENDLETON Jun 13, 1914, daughter of WILLIAM PENDLETON and ALICE COX. She was born Jan 01, 1893 in Rye Cove, Scott Co., VA, and died Jul 07, 1947 in Scott Co., VA.

Child of Hampton Lloyd is listed above under (**821**) Edith Alice Pendleton.

912. MARY ELLA[13] PENDLETON *(GEORGE HIRAM[12], JOSEPH H.[11], PHILIP HARPER[10], JOSEPH[9], MICAJAH[8], PHILIP[7], PHILIP[6], PHILIP[5], HENRY[4], HENRY[3], GEORGE[2], GEORGE[1])* was born Jun 01, 1891 in Wythe Co., VA, and died Jan 20, 1986 in Hocking Co., OH. She married (1) DAVID SULLEN SPENCER Aug 22, 1909 in McDowell Co., WV?, son of WILLIAM SPENCER and ELIZABETH HURST. He was born Dec 14, 1876 in KY, and died Oct 15, 1928 in Harlan Co., KY. She married (2) WILLIAM HENRY EVANS, son of BENJAMIN EVANS and ABIGAIL VAN METER. He was born Jan 01, 1881 in Lawrence Co., OH, and died Apr 17, 1961 in Hocking Co., OH.

Children of MARY PENDLETON and DAVID SPENCER are:
- i. BYRON OLIN[14] SPENCER, b. Jun 08, 1910, McDowell Co., WV; d. Sep 1986, Locking Co., OH.
- ii. BASIL THOMAS SPENCER.
- iii. JACK SPENCER, b. Sep 07, 1915, McDowell Co., WV; d. Dec 15, 1999, Dover, DE.
- iv. JAMES O'CONNOR SPENCER.
- v. DAVID SULLEN SPENCER, b. Dec 19, 1919, Floyd Co., KY; d. Jul 06, 1960, New Orleans, LA.

913. FRANK BURK[13] PENDLETON *(JAMES E. WILSON[12], MORGAN MITCHELL[11], PHILIP HARPER[10], JOSEPH[9], MICAJAH[8], PHILIP[7], PHILIP[6], PHILIP[5], HENRY[4], HENRY[3], GEORGE[2], GEORGE[1])* was born May 22, 1900 in TN, and died Apr 13, 1982 in Spring City, TN. He married BETTIE. She was born Dec 17, 1905 in TN, and died Abt. 1929 in TN.

Frank Burk Pendleton registered for the World War I draft in Rhea Co., TN.

Child of FRANK PENDLETON and BETTIE is:
    i. GENEVA[14] PENDLETON.

References

1. "Genealogical and Historical Notes on Culpeper County, Virginia. Embracing a Revised and Enlarged Edition of Dr. Philip Slaughter's History of St. Mark's Parish," Compiled by Raleigh Travers Green, 1900.

2. "Old Churches, Ministers & Families Of Virginia," by Bishop William Meade, 2 volumes, 490 + 495 Pgs. (1857, 1910) 1997. Genealogies of Virginia families, with emphasis on families of the Episcopalian church.

3. "The Pendleton Family" by Mrs. Katherine Cox Gottschalk and Major John Bailey Calvert Nicklin, published serially between 1933 and 1937 and reprinted In Genealogies of Virginia Families From the Virginia Magazine of History and Biography, Vol. IV, Genealogical Publishing Co., Inc. Baltimore, 1981.

4. "One Pendleton Family, Nine Generations of Unbroken Male Descent, 1674-1944 From Essex and King and Queen Counties Virginia" compiled by Eugene R. Pendleton In Genealogies of Virginia Families, From Tyler's Quarterly History and Genealogical Magazine, Vol. II, Genealogical Publishing Co., Inc. Baltimore, 1981.

5. "The Kay-Pendleton-Neel Families," by George and Margaret Rose, published by J. Grant Stevenson, Provo, Utah, 1969.

6. Lancashire Records Office, Preston England, provided by Graham Pendleton of Liverpool, England.

7. "Brian Pendleton and His Descendants, 1599-1910," by Everett H. Pendleton, privately printed by E.H. Pendleton, 1911.

8. Lancashire Court of Final Records in Lancashire and Chester Record Society, Vol. XXXIX, p. 105.

9. Internet site www.pendle.net.

10. "Edmund Pendleton, A Biography," by David John Mays, 1952, Virginia State Library, 1984 Reprint.

11. "The First Generation of the Pendleton Family in Virginia," In Genealogies of Virginia Families From the William and Mary College Quarterly Historical Magazine, Vol. IV, Genealogical Publishing Co., Inc. Baltimore, 1982.

12. "Virginia, The New Dominion, A History from 1607 to the Present," by Virginius Dabney, Doubleday Inc., NY, 1971.

13. "Old Albemarle and Its Absentee Landlords," by Worth J. Ray, Genealogical Publishing Co., 1960.

14. "The Records of the Virginia Company of London," Vol. III, Susan Myra Kingsbury, Ed., U.S. Government Printing Office, 1933.

15. "The Complete Book of Emigrants," by Peter Wilson Coldham, Genealogical Publishing Co., Inc., 1990.

16. "Gleanings of Virginia History, Newman Family of Virginia," Pg. 246.

17. "Genealogical Gleanings in England," Volume 70, Pg. 42.

18. Court records of King William Co., 20 Jun 1702, Book 1. 1702-1707. p. 10.

19. Virginia Patent Book 3, page 217 (transcribed by Robert M. Allen).

20. "The Colony of Virginia," by Dan Lacy, Franklin Watts, Inc. NY, 1973.

21. "The Shaping of Colonial Virginia," by Thomas J. Wertenbaker, Russell and Russell, New York, 1958.

22. Essex County Records, Deed Book #12, pgs. 437-439.

23. King and Queen Items in Essex Co. Deeds (1742 - 1757): Deed Bood No. 23 1742-1745. Page 1. Lease and Release; 11 and 12 Feb. 1742/3.

24. "Virginia, A History," by Luis D. Rubin, W.W. Norton & Co., Inc., NY, 1977.

25. "Index to Marriages of Old Rappahannock and Essex Counties, Virginia," Pg. 188.

26. Virginia Genealogical Society Quarterly, Vol. XXVIII No. 1, 1 Feb, 1990.

27. "Virginia, The English Heritage in America," by Parke Rouse, Jr., Hastings House Publishers, NY, 1966.

28. "History of Early Spotsylvania," by James R. Mansfield, Green Publishers, Inc., 1977.

29. "History of the Baptists in Virginia," by Robert Baylor Semple, 1810.

30. Spotsylvania Deed Book A, 1722-1729, pg. 100.

31. "Early Virginia Marriages, Lancaster County," page 50.

32. Spotsylvania Deed Book C, 1734-1742, pg. 160.

33. Culpeper Will Book A, pg. 305.

34. Essex Co, VA Deeds Book 30, p.188, 14 Jul 1768.

35. Virginia Vital Records #1, 1600s-1800s; Virginia Vital Records, Madison Family Bible Records, Pg. 696.

36. Virginia Tax Records, True and Exact Poll of the Election of Burgesses, Essex County, Va., November 20, 1741, Page 81.

37. Essex Co. Will Book 5, page 349, dated 16 January 1734 and probated 19 August 1735.

38. Deed Book No. 26, Essex Co., page 28, Deed. 21 April 1752.

39. Abstract of Graves of Revolutionary Patriots, Vol.3, p. Serial: 11912; Volume 4.

40. Memo Re. Estate of Joseph Anderson, 1743, Essex Co. Will Book 7, pg 23.

41. "Encyclopedia of American Biography," by Thomas William Herringshaw.

42. "The South in the Building of the Nation." Richmond, VA. v.12 (1909-1913), p. 267.

43. Post by Karen Yankosky In Gen Forum: Pendleton Family, Jan 27, 2004.

44. "Encyclopedia of Virginia Biography," by Lyon G. Tyler, 1915.

45. "Officers of the Senate of Virginia," by George Wesley Rogers, Richmond, VA, 1959.

46. Will Book 1, page 507 & 508 Dated 2 Jan. 1774, Amherst County, Virginia.

47. Post by Anita B. Baldock-Bryant In Gen Forum: Pendleton Family, June 23, 2000.

48. Marriage Records ('M' Surnames), 1796-1800 of Amherst County, Virginia.

49. Spotsylvania County, VA Marriages License - 1726-1744: W. G. Stanard, from 1735 to 1767, minister of St. George's Parish, Spotsylvania.

50. Spotsylvania County Deed Book F 1761-1766, pg. 229, May 9, 1763.

51. Spotsylvania Co. Deed Book E, 1751-1761 pg. 220.

52. "Handbook of Historic Sites in Spotsylvania County, VA," edited by Virginia W. Durrett and Sonya V. Harrison, Spotsylvania, VA, 1987.

53. Augusta Co. Court Records, Order Book No. 1.

54. Spotsylvania Co. Deed Book A 1722-1759, pg. 517.

55. "Virginia Land Records, A List of Early Land Patents and Grants," Pg. 782.

56. VA Land Grants: Spice Pendleton, Buckingham Co., 3 Apr 1790, grant no. 23, pg. 114.

57. Abstracts from 18th-Century Virginia Newspapers, Surnames W-X, Page 368.

58. Post by Bill Davidson In Gen Forum: Pendleton Family, January 03, 2005.

59. Culpeper Co., VA Will Book dated 24 March, 1768, P. 122 Pages 466-67.

60. [Virginia Historical Buildings] from a survey report March 8, 1936 - research made by Margaret Jeffries.

61. "Chronicles of The Scotch-Irish Settlement Of Virginia," by Lyman Chalkley.

62. "Papers of Thomas Jefferson," ed. by Julian P. Boyd, Princeton: Princeton University Press, 1950, 1:504.

63. "Genealogies of West Virginia Families," from the West Virginia Historical Magazine Quarterly, 1901 - 1905: West Virginians in the American Revolution.

64. Virginia Grants for service in the Revolutionary War.

65. "The Kentucky Land Grants," by Willard Rouse Jillson, Filson Club Publications, 1925.

66. "Historical Register of Officers of the Continental Army," by Francis B. Heitman, Pg. 435.

67. "Colonial Caroline, A History of Caroline Co., VA" by T.E. Campbell, 1984.

68. "Records of Ante-Bellum Southern Plantations From the Revolution Through the Civil War Series J: Selections from the Southern Historical Collection, Part 9: Virginia."

69. "A History of Louisa County, Virginia," by Malcolm H. Harris.

70. "Tennessee, The Volunteer State," Volume I, by John Trotwood Moore, 1923.

71. Virginia Land Grants 37, 1796-98, pg. 528, 11 Dec 1797; 64 acres on the south branch of Harris Creek, Amherst Co.

72. Post by Jack Templeton In Gen Forum: Pendleton Family, November 9, 2000.

73. Daughters of the American Revolution Patriot Index, Centennial Edition.

74. Personal Communication: Gary A. Wade, Galveston Island, TX.

75. VA Land Grants pat. 42- pg. 395, 19 June, 1799, Russell Co., 281 ac. on Clinch River and Cove Creek adjoining Thomas Carter Grants.

76. Marriage and Death Notices from "The Visitor," Vol. I, No. 23., pg. 182, Dec. 16, 1809.

77. "Amherst County, Virginia, in the Revolution," by Lenora Higginbottom Sweeny, 1951.

78. Deed Book "T" page 1, Amherst Co., 30 Sept. 1829.

79. LDS Family Group Record AF-101416 by Thomas Dale Ashby, Bradford, IL.

80. Biographical Sketches of Ohio Co., Dr. John E. Pendleton.

81. Virginia Marriage Index, 1740-1850.

82. Personal Communication: Vince Brandlein, Aug 21, 1999, "Kentucky Cousins."

83. Marriage Register Index, 1763 – 1852, Amherst Co., Virginia.

84. Spotsylvania County Deed Book J 1774-1782; page 332: Novr. 10, 1777.

85. Spotsylvania County Deed Book J 1774-1782, page 432: March 2, 1790.

86. Spotsylvania County 1721-1800 Revolutionary Records, 1774-1782, Deed Book A 1722-1729, Page 530.

87. "A Religious History of Spotsylvania County, 1767-1976."

88. Lewis Family Papers, 1804-1884, Spotsylvania County, Virginia.

89. Spotsylvania Co. Deed Book, Novr. 8, 1787.

90. Carl C. Thomas' Home Page "Thomas Family History."

91. Will Records of Clark County, Kentucky, Volume II, 28 August 1809-April 1826, Book C.

92. Personal Communication: Sandra Brockmeyer Button, Oct 13, 1999.

93. "Clark Co., KY Marriages," compiled by Dr. George Doyle in the 1920's.

94. "Some Delinquent Taxpayers 1787-1790," In The Virginia Genealogist, Vol. 21, No. 1, 1977.

95. The "A.C. Quisenberry Book."

96. "The Winchester Democrat," Clark County, Kentucky, 26 February, 1915.

97. "Kentucky Court of Appeals Deed Book 1811-1821," by M.L. Cook and B.A. Cook, 1985.

98. Bath Co. Court House Sales Book B, pg. 9, December 19, 1823.

99. Bath Co. Court House Settlements Book B, pg. 77.

100. Bath Co. Court House Dower Book A, pg. 444, February 15, 1825.

101. "Early Families of Montgomery County and Pioneer Kentucky," a series of syndicated columns by Harry W. Mills.

102. Spotsylvania County Deed Book O, 1794-1797, page 483, April 4, 1796.

103. King and Queen County Petitions, Nov 2, 1776.

104. "Old Houses of King and Queen County, Virginia," by V.D. Cox and W.T. Weathers, King and Queen Co. Historical Society, 1973.

105. Marriage and obituary citations compiled by Bernard J. Henley from Virginia newspapers on microfilm at the Library of Virginia.

106. "American Biographical Notes," by Franklin B. Hough, Pg. 318.

107. Residents Petition to VA House of Delegates, 1785 - Buckingham Co. VA.

108. VA Land Grants No. 29 pg. 70, 13 May 1793, Buckingham Co.

109. Deed Abstract, 1785-1815, Amherst Co. VA & Loudon Co. VA: p 386, 31 Aug, 1810.

110. "Abstracts from the First 131 Wills of Jefferson County, Kentucky," Volume 6, September, 1783 to June, 1813.

111. "Biographical Directory of the American Congress, 1774-1949," Biographies, Pg.1666.

112. Nelson Co., KY Will Book A, 1784-1807.

113. Bullitt Co., KY Will Book C, pg 193.

114. Kentucky Marriage Records, Jefferson County, Volume 13, 1800 to 1826.

115. "Lives of Christian Ministers, Richmond, VA," (1909), Pg. 54.

116. "Colonial Families of The Southern States of America; Orrick Family," page 402.

117. "History of the Early Settlers of Sangamon County, Illinois," by John Carroll Power.

118. "A History of the Pioneer Families of Missouri," by Wm S. Bryan and Robert Rose, published by Bryan, Brand & Co, St. Louis, MO, 1876.

119. Handbook of Texas Online, s.v. "Dawson Massacre."

120. "Philip C. Pendleton: Biographical Sketch, In Pulliam's: The Constitutional Conventions of Virginia. Richmond, Virginia," 1901, Pg. 80.

121. "The 20th Century Biographical Dictionary of Notable Americans," Vol. 2, p.364.

122. "Records of Ante-Bellum Southern Plantations From the Revolution Through the Civil War;" Series M: Selections from the Virginia Historical Society, Part 4: Central Piedmont Virginia.

123. "Kentucky: A History of the State," Battle, Perrin, & Kniffin, 7th ed., 1887, Campbell County.

124. Personal Communication: Jack Templeton.

125. Personal Communication: Ronald L. Pendleton, Kingsport, TN.

126. Personal Communication: Dianna Gilliam.

127. "The Pendleton Family: Being Concerned Chiefly with the Descendants of the Reverend John Pendleton," by James W. Phillips, 1939.

128. Personal Communication: Fred Pendleton, Sep. 20, 2000; Genealogy Update, Family of Rev. John Pendleton.

129. "Cannon County History of Tennessee," Chicago And Nashville, The Goodspeed Publishing Co., 1887.

130. Personal Communication: Becky Dixon-Messier.

131. Greene Co., MO Probate Records, Will Book A, pg. 68.

132. "Hughes and Phillips Families of Virginia," by Virginia Phillips-Smith.

133. Old Kentucky Entries and Deeds, Chapter VII, Court of Appeals, Deeds - Grantees, 1783 - 1909, Pg. 439.

134. Reynolds-Miller-Woods Bible Record from Virginia Genealogical Society Quarterly, Vol. XVIII, number 1, 1 Jan., 1980).

135. Personal Communication: Steve Gredell, Aug. 19, 1999 and Dec. 5, 2001.

136. "Yesterday's Roots, Today's Branches," by Pauline Pendleton Wall.

137. Personal Communication: Martha Myers, Austin, TX.

138. Henry County Kentucky Will Book 13, pp. 464-66, 24 July 1860.

139. "History of Todd County, Kentucky," ed. J. H. Battle, 1884, F. A. Battey Publishing Co., 1884, Pg. 282.

140. Personal Communication: Everette Tucker, descendant of Agnes Ann Pendleton Swan.

141. "A History of Kentucky Baptists," by J. H. Spencer, Cincinnati, 1885, Vol. 2, Pg. 388.

142. "A history of Bethel Church 1813-1838," by John Pendleton, p. 40.

143. Christian Co KY Will Book K, pgs 319-324.

144. Personal Communication: Nan Hankovich, Jan 7, 2002.

145. Personal Communication: Vicki Ringer, Oct 11, 1999

146. "History of Christian County Kentucky," by Charles M. Meacham, 1930.

147. Post by Mark Lause In Gen Forum: Pendleton Family on Jun 27, 1999.

148. Personal Communication: Sandi Gorin.

149. The Fayette County (KY) Genealogical Society Quarterly, Vol. 4, No. 3, Fall 1989.

150. "Will Records of Clark County, Kentucky," Volume II, 28 August, 1809 - April 1826, Book 5, Page 193.

151. Personal Communication: Jeanette Jahntz.

152. "The 20th Century Biographical Dictionary of Notable Americans," Vol. 4, Pg. 279.

153. Personal Communication: Robert Karrick, Aug 30, 1998.

154. Personal Communication: Anne Palmeter Threlkeld.

155. Personal Communication: Mary E. Price.

156. Will Book No.7, Winchester, Clark Co., KY, p.653.

157. Personal Communication: Janet de la Pena.

158. Personal Communication: Eugene R. Johnston, Port Angeles, WA.

159. Illinois Roster of Officers and Enlisted Men [Union Army, Civil War].

160. Bath County, KY Court Records.

161. Personal Communication: James B. Skilton, Dec. 16, 1998.

162. General Index to Mortgages, Bath Co., KY Court House.

163. Bath Co., KY Court record "Pendleton Heirs To Deed Sarah E. Blevins, April 23, 1896."

164. Personal Communication: Kathryn Pendleton Gilvin.

165. St. Louis Genealogical Society Quarterly, Spring 1999, Vol. XXXII, No. 1.

166. "History of St. Louis City and County," by J. Thomas Schaef, 1883. Pg. 1927.

167. Kentucky Marriages, 1797-1865, KY Historical Society (Lexington Newspapers).

168. Personal Communication: Kenneth Shelton.

169. KY Grants in County Court, Book 7, Pg. 316 [June 15, 1841] in Warren Co., KY.

170. The Robert Battle Home Page.

171. "Legocki Family History," by Thomas F. Legocki.

172. Personal Communication: Jeff Jernegan.

173. "The Long family Bible Record, 1753-1928," Library of Virginia.

174. "Old Kentucky Entries and Deeds," Chapter VII, Court of Appeals, Deeds - Grantees, 1783 - 1909, Page 439.

175. "Society of Montana Pioneers," Volume I., ed. by James U. Sanders, 1899.

176. "Tim Conner's Database."

177. Missouri Marriages, 1851-1900.

178. Montana Death Index (No. 87-286).

179. "Colonial Families of The United States of America," Volume 4, by George Norbury Mackenzie, Baltimore, Genealogical Publishing Co. Inc., 1907.

180. Personal Communication: Rees Chapman, August 2004.

181. Pamela Dyess Mann at Ancestry.com.

182. "Virtual American Biographies," Edited Appletons Encyclopedia, Copyright © 2001 VirtualologyTM.

183. "Historic Oakland Cemetery, Atlanta, Georgia," transcribed by Rachal Leigh Grizzle, 1998-1999.

184. "The Tale of Time," by Dick Hare, a story about the Sulphur Bluff, Texas Community.

185. "History of Franklin County," The Goodspeed Publishing Co., Chicago, IL, 1889.

186. "Reverend Christian Frederick Post and Peter Humrickhouse and Some of the Latter's Family," by Harry H. Humrickhouse, 1913.

187. Document No. 4 of the Governor's Message and Annual Reports of the Public Officers of the State, and Boards of Directors, Visitors, Superintendents, and other Agents of Public Institutions or Interests of Virginia Printed under resolutions March 18, 1847, Samuel Shepherd, Public Printer, Richmond, 1847.

188. [Virginia Historical Buildings] Survey Report, May 19, 1937, from research made by Francis B. Foster.

189. "Old Chapel, Clarke County, Virginia," by Charles Randolph Hughes, Berryville, VA, pg. 64, 1906.

190. "E. Boyd Pendleton. February 12, 1875...Mr. Sheldon, from the Committee on Ways and Means, submitted the following report: To accompany bill H.R. 3750," United States Congress. House Committee on Ways and Means, 43rd Congress.

191. Personal Communication: Ned Boyajian, Sep 12, 2000.

192. "Shenandoah Valley Pioneers and Their Descendants, A History of Frederick County, Virginia, From its Formation in 1738 to 1908 Compiled Mainly from Original Records of Old Frederick County, now Hampshire, Berkeley, Shenandoah, Jefferson, Hardy, Clarke, Warren, Morgan and Frederick," by T. K. Cartmell, Clerk of the Old County Court, pgs 186-205.

193. "Valleau and Variations with Other Surnamed Descendants," by Rich Turnblom.

194. "Ancestors and Cousins of Dane Coefer," by Dane Coefer.

195. Message by John Troyer, Ancestry Message Board.

196. "Justice In Old Town," by Donna K. Sefton, The Journal of San Diego History, October 1956, Volume 2, Number 4.

197. National Register of the Society Sons of the American Revolution.

198. St. Louis City Death Records, 1850-1908.

199. Virginia Vital Records, Inscriptions from Tombstones in King and Queen, Westmoreland, Hanover and Albemarle, Page 570.

200. "Encyclopedia of Virginia Biography," Volume III - The Confederacy, Military and Naval Offices.

201. William Nelson Pendleton Papers, #1466, 1798-1889.

202. "General David Hunter's sack of Lexington, Virginia, June 10-14, 1864: An Account by Rose Page Pendleton," In Virginia magazine of history and biography, Richmond, VA. v.83 (1975), p. 173-183.

203. "Life of William Kimbrough Pendleton, LL. D., President of Bethany College," by Frederick D. Power, Christian Publishing Company, St. Louis, 1902.

204. "Lana & Carlton Floyd Lines," by Lana Floyd.

205. Personal Communication: Eleanor Joyce Carman.

206. "Selected Scott County Marriage Records," by Mary Barnett.

207. "Highland Home Page Surnames List," by Dan Mohn.

208. "Descendants of Thomas Flannary," by John Wilson.

209. Personal Communication: James W. Phillips.

210. World War I Draft Registration Cards, 1917-1918 from Ancestry.com.

211. Personal Communication: Sue Seibert, Mineral Wells, TX.

212. Personal Communication: Doris Pendleton, Jan 18, 2002.

213. Personal Communication: Marion Nichols, May 20, 1999.

214. "The 24th Missouri Volunteer Infantry 'Lyon Legion,'" by J. Randall Houp.

215. "The Stone Descendants of Linden," by Kathleen Stone Short, In Christian Co., MO Historian Vols. 1 & 2, 1988-1989.

216. Personal Communication: Mike and Vera Marie Leisure, San Diego, CA.

217. Post by Candy Cox In Gen Forum, Pendleton Family on Nov 7, 2000.

218. "Persons Buried in the 'Winton' Graveyard," Virginia Genealogical Society Quarterly, Vol. XI, No. 2, Apr 1, 1973.

219. "The V.M.I. New Market Cadets," by William Couper, Charlottesville, VA, pgs. 153-154, 1933.

220. "Hardesty's Historical and Geographical Encyclopedia," H. H. Hardesty and Company Publishers, NY, Richmond, and Toledo, pg. 411,1884.

221. Personal Communication: Richard Bailey.

222. [Virginia Historical Buildings] Survey Report, May 19, 1937, from research made by Elizabeth A. Rust.

223. "The History of West Virginia, Old and New," Volume III, The American Historical Society, Inc., Chicago and New York, pg. 457, 1923.

224. Personal Communication: Bob Prater, Tulsa, OK.

225. Personal Communication: April Janvrin.

226. Kentucky Genealogy and Biography, Vol. V, edited by Westerfield, 1975.

227. Kansas City and Jackson County, Missouri Biographical Record, 1896.

228. Personal Communication: Dorothy Cook Burt.

229. Post by Virginia Anderson in Gen Forum, Pendleton Family on Feb 23, 2003.

230. Personal Communication: Wayne Irwin.

231. "Ancestors of John Walden and Mickey Schroth," by John Shelby Walden.

232. Cemetery Records of Daviess County, Missouri Volume II.

233. Alabama Marriages, 1800-1920.

234. "American Almanac," 1844, pg 314.

235. A genealogical chart by Edith May Pendleton, Fredericksburg, Virginia Library.

236. Personal Communication: Kristi Pendleton Brantley, Feb 28, 2000.

237. "Gunn and Burrus Families of Virginia," by Cheryl Maxwell.

238. "History of Trigg County, Historical and Biographical," edited by W.H. Perrin, F.A. Battey Pub. Co., Chicago, 1884. pp. 187-188.

239. "County of Christian, Kentucky Historical And Biographical," edited By William Henry Perrin.

240. "James Madison Pendleton: A Southern Crusader Against Slavery," a biographical article by Victor B. Howard, The Register; the KY Historical Society, July 1976.

241. "The South in History and Literature," by Mildred Lewis Rutherford, Athens, GA. (1906), p. 803.

242. "Reminiscences of a Long Life," by J. M. Pendleton, Louisville, Ky., Press Baptist Book Concern, 1891.

243. The Military Annals of Tennessee Confederate. First Series: Embracing a Review of Military Operations with Regimental Histories and Memorial Rolls. Ninth Tennessee Infantry.

244. Church Minutes, Bethel Baptist Church, Christian Co., KY.

245. "Counties of Christian and Trigg, Kentucky. Historical and Biographical," edited by William Henry Perrin, Chicago and Louisville, F. A. Battey Publishing, 1884.

246. Personal Communication: Robert Powers, Salt Lake City, Utah.

247. Land grants in KY County Court Records: Adair County Grant Book.

248. Land grants in KY County Court Records: Metcalfe County Grant Book.

249. Personal Communication: Roger K Powell, Lake Point, UT.

250. "A History of Todd Co, KY," by Rev. Silas Emmett Lucas, Jr, pub. from original ed. in Lib. of The Filson Club, Louisville, KY, 1979, pg. 333.

251. Will Records of Ralls County, Missouri, Volume I, 1824-1872, Will Records Book B.

252. Personal Communication: Martha Boyers.

253. "The Borofka Family Tree," by Robert Borofka.

254. Oregon Marriages From1853 to 1899.

255. Bath County Deed Book 84, p. 252, 26 September, 1922.

256. "Descendants of Sarah E. Pendleton," by Ray Copher, Oct. 2000.

257. "A History of King and Queen Co., Virginia."

258. "Dates in Historical Southern Families," Vol.1, by John Bennett Boddie, 1958 page 187.

259. The Henley family Bible record, 1778-1929, Library of Virginia.

260. "Warner Brown Family - Virginia to Arkansas," by Linda Medley.

261. "Pendleton Family Records, ca. 1500-1965," by Lula Caldonia Pendleton.

262. Personal Communication: Everett E. Hicks, Jun 29, 2002.

263. Moniteau County, Missouri Deaths, 1858-1931, from Ancestry.com.

264. The Chinn Bible transcribed by Emma Jane Walker and Virginia Wilson.

265. "Illinois: History of Cass County, Illinois," edited by William Henry Perrin, O. L. Baskin & Co. Historical Publishers, Chicago, 1882.

266. "The Virginia Regimental Histories Series, Robertson's 4th Virginia Infantry," 1987.

267. Personal Communication: John H. Gaines.

268. Personal Communication: Susan L. Clark.

269. "Confederate Memoirs, Early Life and Family History [of] William Frederic Pendleton [and] Mary Lawson Young Pendleton," edited by Constance Pendleton with a supplement by Amena Pendleton Haines, Bryn Athyn, Pa., 1958.

270. Marriage Notices from The Southern Christian Advocate 1867-1878.

271. Death And Obituary Notices from The Southern Christian Advocate 1867-1878.

272. "Confederate Veteran," by Katherine E. Entler, Nashville, TN, pg. 149, 1931.

273. "Biographical and Historical Memoirs of Northwest Louisiana," the Southern Publishing Company, Chicago & Nashville, 1890.

274. "Genealogy of the Page Family in Virginia."

275. "The Bedinger Family," by Helen Boteler Pendleton, In Jefferson County Historical Society. Its Magazine, Shepherdstown, WV. v.9 (1943), p. 41-48.

276. "Confederate Military History," by Clement Anselm Evans, Atlanta, GA. v.4 (1987), p. 1106-1107.

277. "The Character of Robert Edward Lee," by William G. Pendleton, Winchester-Frederick County Historical Society, 1962.

278. "Memoirs of William Nelson Pendleton," by Susan Pendleton, J.B. Lippincott Publ., 1893.

279. "The General Assembly of the Commonwealth of Virginia, 1940-1960," by Edward Griffith Dodson, Richmond, VA. (1961), p. 571.

280. [Virginia Historical Buildings] Survey Report, Aug 24, 1937, from research made by Regina M. Coughlan.

281. Louisa County Historical Magazine. Louisa, VA. v.6, no.1 (Summer 1974), p. 34-39.

282. Lexington Local History Index.

283. Personal Communication: Eleanor Joyce Carman, July 15, 2001.

284. "Oxford-Baker," by William D. Andrews.

285. [Virginia Historical Buildings] Survey report, Nov 22, 1937, from research made by Lelia P. Davidson.

286. Personal Communication: Ellen Tolleson Reesh.

287. Cannon Co. Cemetery Book.

288. Posts by Candy Kimberly In Gen Forum, Pendleton Family, July 2000.

289. The Irving Index (Dallas County, TX).

290. Texas Land Title Abstracts.

291. Personal Communication: Everett T Jorgenson.

292. "Soldiers of the Great War, Volumes I-III," compiled by W. M. Haulsee, F.G. Howe, and A.C. Doyle, Washington, D.C., 1920.

293. "Biographical Sketch: E. Morgan Pendleton," by Paul Brandon Barringer, University of Virginia, New York, NY. Vol. 2 (1904), p. 121-122.

294. Post by Bob Prater In Gen Forum, Pendleton Family, Nov 13, 2001.

295. Missouri Cemetery Records, Vol. 1-12.

296. Cemetery Records of Miller County, Missouri, Volume I.

297. Army and Navy Men from Christian County, Kentucky, Who Served in The World War, 1917 - 1919.

298. Personal Communication: Wayne R. and Fran West.

299. Ancestry Of Melvin W. Schwartz.

300. LDS Ancestral File # 1KV1-1X0.

301. Personal Communication: Robert Harold Pendleton, Sep 23, 2002.

302. "The death of Colonel Dahlgren," by Henry C. Pendleton, In College of William and Mary. Its Quarterly. Williamsburg, VA. Ser.2, v.12 (1932), p. [1]-3.

303. U.S. Military Records, 1925: Official National Guard Register.

304. Personal Communication: Annette Andersen.

305. Personal Communication: Beverly Self.

306. Personal Communication: Robert Anderson of Sikeston, MO.

307. "Barking Up My Family Tree," by Curtis Bright.

308. "History of Cooper County Missouri," by W. F. Johnson, Historical Publishing Co., Topeka and Cleveland, 1919, pg 494.

309. Handwritten information provided by Mrs. Jane Eubanks Johnson.

310. Personal Communication: Olin Pendleton, Dec 20, 2001.

311. "Official Virginia," by Duval Porter, Richmond, VA. (1920), p. 93-94.

312. [Virginia Historical Buildings] Survey Report, Dec 8, 1937, from research made by Hazel G. Bellamy.

313. Scott County Marriages 1858 to 1900, VA State Library.

314. "Family Research," by Donna Hall.

315. Alleghany County, VA Birth Records, 1853-96.

316. "Local Vital Records from Newspapers of Bath Co. Ky. 1884-1910" page 127: Owingsville Outlook, 11- 2-1905.

317. Personal Communication: Dianna Reed.

318. Personal Communication: Wanda Castoe.

Index of Names

Boatright, Louisa, 186
Boatright, Meadow, 186
Boatright, Sarah J., 186
Bococh, Sarah Louise, 137
Boggs, Robert P., 70
Bohannon, Lydia, 226
Bolen, Sarah Frances, 439
Boles, Edmund, 61
Bolton, Elizabeth, 183
Bond, Constance, 31
Bond, G. W., 305
Bond, William, 32
Bonds, Zipporah, 420
Bonnell, Ella, 277
Bonnycastle, Ann Mason, 52
Borchers, Louise, 388
Boteler, Helen McComb, 290
Boteler, Alexander, 290
Botts, Elizabeth, 32
Boulware, William, 74
Bowes, Matthew, 203
Bowie, Catherine, 47, 48, 79, 84
Bowie, Ella Jane, 354
Bowie, John, 47
Bowler, George Pendleton, 166
Bowler, Jane Hunter, 166
Bowler, Jesse Hunter, 166
Bowler, Louisa Foote, 166
Bowler, Nathaniel Pendleton, 166
Bowler, Robert Bonner, 165, 166
Bowles, Elizabeth, 181
Bowman, 145
Boyce, Moses, 75
Boyd, I. D., 228
Boyd, Sarah Ann, 92
Boyd, Sarah Goldsborough (Dandridge), 64
Bradburn, William, 19
Braddock, Gen., 30
Bragg, James Madison, 121
Bramlett, Joyce, 426
Branch, Maranda, 237
Brandt, George Edgar, 338
Branham, Arminta, 401
Branham, Rhoda Ellen, 402
Branham, Turner, 401
Brasher, Andrew W. "Drew," 280
Bratton, Dee, 238
Bray, John, 417
Bray, Mary Etta, 412
Brazelton, Mary "Polly," 111
Breckinridge, Miss, 76, 77
Brewer, Abraham V., 156
Brewer, Thomas, 11
Brice, Alice Key Pendleton, 283
Brice, Arthur Tilghman, 283
Brice, Julia Frances, 283

Brickey, 57
Brittendese, Catherine D., 172
Briscoe, G. H., 111
Bristow, J. J. Rucker, 354
Broadux, Lucy, 86, 87
Brohard, Elizabeth, 236, 237
Bronaugh, William, 63
Brooking, Alvan, 213
Brooking, Serena Matilda, 213
Brooks, Coleman C., 271
Brooks, Mary, 271
Brooks, Walter B. M., 271
Brown, Aeolean Lola, 273
Brown, Amanda, 401
Brown, Amicus, 273
Brown, Ann (Elkins), 103, 104
Brown, Cynthia, 441
Brown, Daniel, 31
Brown, Elizabeth, 153
Brown, John, 251
Brown, Lydia E., 195, 196
Brown, Mary, 147, 148
Brown, Mary Anne, 251
Brown, Mary E., 273
Brown, Prudence Ann, 61
Brown, Reginald William, Rev., 391
Brown, Roland, 272, 273
Brown, Sallie A., 273
Brown, Susan, 225
Brown, Thomas, 31
Brown, Thomas Allen, 422
Brown, William C., 46, 47
Brown, William Edmond, 273
Browning, John, 46
Browning, R. L, 228
Bruce, Alexander, 395
Bruce, Mary Alexander, 395
Brugh, Alice Dudley, 203
Brugh, Anne G., 107
Brugh, Cornelia Pendleton, 203
Brugh, Daniel, 202
Brugh, Lewis, 202, 203
Brugh, Louisa Jane Davis, 203
Brugh, Nancy Lewis
Brugh, Virginia Grove, 203
Brummett, Narcissus M., 192
Bryant, Rachel Melissa, 101
Bryson, Lola Fairrie, 273
Buchanan, A., 63
Buchanan, Dica M., 342
Buchanan, Floyd Peter, 192
Buchanan, Genetia, 191
Buchanan, Jane Allison, 199
Buchanan, Joseph Rice, 191
Buchanan, Lafayette Douglas, 192
Buchanan, Lenora G., 191

Clayton, William, 84
Clayton, Mamie, 344
Click, Virginia, 414
Clough, Eben, 86
Cobb, Neville, 210
Cobb, Norwood, 210
Cobb, Sally, 210
Cochran, Bruce, 441
Cock, 57
Cocke, 47
Cocke, David, 183
Cocke, Elisah, 183
Cocke, Elizah, 183
Cocke, Enoch, 183
Cocke, James, 183
Cocke, James B., 183
Cocke, Nancy, 183
Cocke, Robert, 183
Cocke, William, 183
Cockerell, Ann Bell, 325
Coffey, Arch C., 320
Coffey, Effie M., 320
Coffey, George Walter, 320
Coffey, Jimmie A., 320
Coffey, Mattie G., 320
Coffey, Otha A., 320
Coffey, Walter, 359
Coffey, William, 320
Coffman, Aaron, 147
Coffman, Abraham, 147
Coffman, Henry Pendleton, 147
Cogdell, Richard, 202
Coghill, Robert A., 106
Cole, Arminta Elizabeth, 403
Cole, Ardena Catherine, 403
Cole, Genoe H., 402
Cole, Jesse, 402
Cole, Jesse Truman, 403
Cole, John Andrew, 403
Cole, Joseph, 402
Cole, Robert McFarland, 274
Cole, Sarah Caloma, 402
Cole, Trigg, 403
Cole, William D., 403
Coleman, Ann, 24, 169
Coleman, Ann Mourning 74
Coleman, Ann W., 117
Coleman, Betsey, 74
Coleman, Francis, 65
Coleman, George, 74
Coleman, Jane, 74
Coleman, Liza, 74
Coleman, Robert, 75
Coleman, Robert Spilsbe, 18, 33
Coleman, Sally, 75
Coleman, Samuel, 75

Coleman, Sarah, 295
Coleman, Thomas, 62
Coleman, Troy, 316
Coleman, Viola M., 266
Coles, Elizabeth Carter, 336
Coles, Walter, Dr., 336
Colley, Clarisa F., 255
Colley, Elizabeth J., 255
Collier, Mary, 181
Collins, Bartley, 157
Collman, Mamie, 405, 406
Colquhoun, James, 40
Colston, 186
Colston, Raleigh, 50
Colville, Margaret, 194
Compas, Lolita, 404
Compton, James M., 401
Conant, Mary, 378
Conn, Andrew Jackson, 101
Conn, Catherine, 101
Conn, Cynthia, 101
Conn, Elizabeth, 101
Conn, James, 101
Conn, Jesse Wilson, 101
Conn, John, 101
Conn, Josiah, 101
Conn, Lucinda, 101
Conn, Margaret, 101
Conn, Polly, 100
Conn, Reuben Harrison, 101
Conn, Samuel, 101
Connely, Espy, 160
Conner, Ada, 366
Conner, Charles M., 366
Conner, Franklin Norwood, 301
Conner, Susan M., 152
Conner, Uriel, 152
Conrad, Laura, 354
Cooke, Edmund Pendleton, 92
Cooke, John Esten, 9, 92
Cooke, John Rogers, 92
Cooke, Mordecai, 73
Cooke, Philip Pendleton, 92
Cooke, Sallie Dandridge, 92
Coons, Fleta Anne, 264
Coons, Pamelia, 66
Cooper, Dorothy, 391
Cooper, Jane, 105
Cooper, Lawson, 391
Cooper, Madison, Dr., 391
Cooper, Margaret, 391
Cooper, Philip, 391
Coots, Justine, 380
Copeland, Agnes, 423
Copeland, Eva May, 423
Copeland, Guthrie B., 423

Cunningham, John, 50
Currier, Delma J., 324
Curry, W. R., 213
Curtis, Cornelia Montgomery, 337
Curtis, Elizabeth, 40
Curtis, Frank A., 186, 315
Curtis, Henry, 98
Curtis, Jane, 40
Curtis, Mable, 315
Curtis, Martha, 40, 41
Curtis, Mary, 299
Curtis, Rice, 40
Curtis, W., 315
Dabney, Sarah, 109
Dakin, Joseph, 203
Dandridge, Adam Stephen, 91, 164
Dandridge, Alexander S., 164
Dandridge, Alexander Spotswood, 91, 92, 165
Dandridge, Alice K., 165
Dandridge, Ann Spotswood, 91
Dandridge, Bolling, 180
Dandridge, Edmund P., 164
Dandridge, Jane P., 165
Dandridge, Lucy, 180
Dandridge, Martha, 165
Dandridge, Mary Evalina, 165
Dandridge, Mary R., 164
Dandridge, Nathaniel Pendleton, 165
Dandridge, Philip P., 164
Dandridge, Philip Pendleton, 92
Dandridge, Samuel P., 164
Dandridge, Sarah Kennedy, 165
Dandridge, Sarah P., 164
Dandridge, Sarah Stephena, 91
Dandridge, Serena C., 164
Dandridge, Serena Pendleton, 398
Dandridge, Spotswood, 58
Dandridge, Susan Bowler, 165
Daniel, J.B., 223
Daniel, Jane, 67
Daniel, John, 62
Daniels, Alay C., 242, 243
Daniels, Elizabeth, 50
Daniels, Pauline, 234
Daniels, Samuel T., 243
Darden, George M., 104
Darrell, Effie, 333
Darrell, John H., 333
Darrell, Louis P., 333
Darrell, Oliver B., 333
Dasher, Susan, 275
Davenport, Fannie Ophelia, 238
Davidson, Anna B., 311
Davidson, Cinia M., 312
Davidson, David, 44
Davidson, Ella, 311

Davidson, Giles, 43, 44
Davidson, Jane, 311
Davidson, John M., 311
Davidson, Joseph P., 44
Davidson, Lee Evaline, 311
Davidson, Mary L, 311
Davidson, Robert Frank, 311
Davidson, Sarah, 312
Davidson, William Reeves, 311
Davis, Catherine, 82, 144
Davis, E. Mildred, 177
Davis, Francis, 83
Davis, James, 106
Davis, Jefferson, 172
Davis, John Thomas, 115, 116
Davis, Katie, 144
Davis, Leona Tinsley, 191
Davis, Louisa Jane, 106, 202
Davis, Luther Hunt, 204
Davis, Mary E., 192
Davis, Mary Elizabeth, 116
Davis, Ruth, 297
Davis, Sally, 131
Davis, Sarah A., 115, 116
Davis, William, 65
Dawson, Berkley, 67
Dawson, Elma H., 373, 374
Dawson, John G., 239
Dawson, Maria Mason, 290
Dawson, Mary, 267
Day, Joseph, 186
Day, Mary, 410
de Charnes, Richard, 274
de-Pendleton, Agnes-, 3
de-Pendleton, Aviel-, 3
de-Pendleton, Ellis-, 3
de-Pendleton, Reginald-, 3
de-Pendleton, Sebastus-, 3
de-Pendleton, Siward-, 3, 4
de-Pendleton, Thomas-, 3
de Penelton, Matilda, 4
de Penelton, Richard, 4
de Penelton, Roger, 4
de Penelton, Siward, 4
de Penholton, Adam, 4
de Penholton, Robert, 4
de Penholton, Thomas, 4
de Russy, Edmund, 167
Deekens, Amelia Catherine, 292
Dekker, Joseph H., 267
Dennis, Robert, 11
Denson, Velma, 331
Dent, Cybil, 61
Deshazo, Martha, 140
Dew, Benjamin F., 141
Dew, Thomas, Capt., 247

Filler, John M., 254
Finley, George, 417
Finley, George R., 417
Finley, Raymond F., 417
Finley, Roxie A., 417
Finley, William, 417
Finn, Clara Emily, 167
Flanary, Phebe, 187
Flanary, Phoebe, 185
Flannery, Mary Jane, 319
Flannery, Sarah Jane, 101
Flaugher, Viola Melva, 348
Fleet, Mary, 247
Fleet, Mary Anne, 71, 72
Fleet, William, 71
Fletcher, Andrew, 243
Fletcher, Ida Gertrude, 107
Fletcher, Mary, 243
Fletcher, Thomas L., 243
Flippo, Littleberry Terrell, 219
Flippo, Littleton, 295
Flippo, Sallie Woolfolk, 295
Flippo, William S., 219
Fluornoy, Emily, 110, 111
Fluornoy, James, 111
Fluornoy, Samuel, 110
Foley, Frances, 368
Foley, Herbert, 429
Foley, Mary Edith, 429
Foley, Oscar, 429
Forrest, Capt., 328
Forrest, William Mentzel, 299
Forrester, Docia Ellen, 325
Forrester, Ed, 325
Forrester, Gertrude, 325
Forrester, James, 325
Forrester, Ora, 325
Forrester, Richard Miller, 325
Forster, Charles R., 263
Forster, Ruth L., 434
Forts, Elizabeth, 112
Fortune, Elizabeth La, 293
Foster, Lucy, 433
Foushee, Charles, 149
Foushee, Elizabeth W., 149
Foushee, William T., 148
Fowler, Orissavilla, 101
Fox, George, 3
Fox, James, 120
Fraley, Delle, 317
Fraley, Edgar, 317
Fraley, Ella, 317
Fraley, Ethel, 317
Fraley, James Buchanan, 317
Fraley, Lillian, 317
Fraley, Martin, 317

Franklin, Peachey, 73
Frazer, Martha Baker, 67
Frazier, Elizabeth, 312
Frazier, Joseph Coulton, 127
Frazier, Martha E., 312
Frazier, Stella, 416
Freeland, James, 42
Freeland, Mace, 43
Freeland, Spice, 26, 42, 43
Freeze, Martha, 326
Frolmes, Bertha, 211
Fudge, Nancy Margaret, 268
Fudge, William, 417
Furnish, Elizabeth, 349
Furnival, Christine, 299
Furquereau, Joseph M., 174
Furr, Mary, 408
Gadsden, Edward Miles, 173
Gaines, Anne, 32
Gaines, Benjamin, 32
Gaines, Catherine, 34
Gaines, Dannie, 272
Gaines, Edmund, 34, 84
Gaines, Edmund Pendleton, 9
Gaines, Frances, 32
Gaines, Francis, 34
Gaines, Henry, 32, 34
Gaines, Henry Leon, 272
Gaines, India O., 272
Gaines, Isabella, 32, 35
Gaines, James, 22, 32, 34
Gaines, Jefferson Jones, 272
Gaines, John Edmond, 272
Gaines, Joseph, 34
Gaines, Judith, 49
Gaines, Mary, 34
Gaines, Nancy Ann, 49
Gaines, Philip, 32
Gaines, Philip B., 272
Gaines, Richard, 32, 34, 49
Gaines, Richard Edward, 34
Gaines, Robert, 32
Gaines, Sarah, 35, 272
Gaines, Thomas, 11, 32, 34
Gaines, Virenda Alethea, 151
Gaines, William, 32, 34
Gaines, Willie J., 272
Gallegos, Eligio, 355
Garber, J. Lindley, 260
Garber, Pendleton, 260
Garber, S., 260
Garland, David Shepherd, 201
Garland, Frances Maria Anna, 58
Garland, Hudson Martin, 144, 145
Garland, James, 144, 145
Garland, John, 145

Garland, Priscilla, 76
Garland, S., 61
Garland, William, 58
Garnett, Catherine Stockton, 221
Garnett, Eldredge Brockman, 220
Garnett, Frances A., 118, 221
Garnett, Helen L., 220
Garnett, James B., 220
Garnett, James Muscoe, 141
Garnett, John K., 141
Garnett, John Muscoe, 141
Garnett, John P., 220
Garnett, Mary Susan, 141
Garnett, Reuben, 141
Garnett, Richard, 221
Garnett, Virgil A., 220
Garnett, W. W., 223
Garnett, William W., 220
Garrett, Benjamin Othello, 430
Garrett, Cord Webb, 430
Garrett, Dorothy Elizabeth, 430
Garrett, Emaline, 272
Garrett, Ernest Walton, 430
Garrett, Harvey Campbell, 430
Garrett, James Pendleton, 430
Garrett, Jennie B., 430
Garrett, Isaac, 230
Garrett, Lelia Sallee, 430
Garrett, Nannie Agee, 230
Garrett, Radford Agee, 430
Garrett, Robert Wilson, 230
Garthright, Mary Cordelia, 397
Garvin, Isabella, 287
Gatewood, Catherine, 139
Gatewood, Hannah, 170
Gatewood, Philip, 73
Gatewood, Reuben, 75
Gathright, Robert Lee, 253
Gatlin, Thomas Hardy, 250
Gaunt, Lewis Corbin, 153
Gay, Annie E., 245
Gay, Curtis P. Martin, 126
Gay, Elizabeth, 126
Gay, James, 126
Gay, John, 126
Gay, John Dunlap, 126
Gay, Mary, 126
Gay, William T., 126
Gaylor, Andrew Joseph, 102
Gaylord, Emma, 166
Gee, Martha Ann, 85
Gerrell, Bland, 123
Gerrell, Edmond W., 123
Gerrell, James Henry, 123, 138
Gerrell, John Bland, 139
Gerrell, Josephine, 139

Gerrell, Louisa A., 139
Gerrell, Lucy Ann, 123
Gerrell, Margaret F., 139
Gerrell, Margaret Herndon, 123, 229
Gerrell, Mary Elizabeth 123
Gerrell, Mary E., 138
Gerrell, Mildred Thomas, 123
Gerrell, Robert Henry, 139
Gerrell, Robert Yates, 123
Gerrell, Susan Alice, 139
Gerrell, William Jefferson, 123
Gibbs, Edward Allen, 86
Gibney, Robert A., Dr., 125
Gibney, Virgil Pendleton, 125
Gibson, Albert Gaines, 382
Gibson, Andrew Jackson, 382
Gibson, Blair Thompson, 382
Gibson, Frances Hite, 290
Gibson, George Gose, 382
Gibson, Nancy, 219
Gibson, Percy, 189
Gibson, Rachel, 47
Gibson, Rosa Belle, 382
Gibson, Samuel, 382
Gibson, William G., 382
Gibson, Wirt W., 382
Gilbert, Benjamin, 85
Gilbert, Gertrude, 272
Gilbert, Martha, 85
Gillaspie, Emma, 236
Gilliam, 310
Gilliam, Eliza V., 411
Gilliam, Louisa F. 'Peters,' 311
Gilliam, Mrs. Annie S., 310
Gillenwater, Melissa Helen, 312
Gillenwater, William, 312
Glenn, Doris, 276
Glenn, Martha, 102
Glenn, Mary, 102
Glenn, Nathan, 102
Glenn, Sarah, 124
Goad, Lou, 367
Godsey, Robert Drewry, 405
Goldborough, Carolyn, 92
Goldsborough, Edmund Lee, 290
Golden, Sarah, 208
Gooch, Dabney Philip, 145
Gooch, Elizabeth, 145
Gooch, Fleming, 145
Gooch, Julia, 145
Gooch, Mary, 145
Gooch, William B., 75
Goodlet, Margaret, 147
Goodloe, Eliza, 227
Goodloe, Elizabeth, 227
Goodloe, George Philip, 227

Hamilton, Martha J., 319
Hamilton, Thomas, 26
Hamilton, William Stevens, 319
Hammack, Jennie Mae, 359
Hammonds, Mary, 322
Hancock, Anne Elizabeth, 141
Hanes, Mace, 49
Harbutt, William, 11
Harden, Mrs. Florence, 150
Hardin, Lulu, 431
Hardin, Sarah, 263
Hardin, Thomas, 430, 431
Hardman, David P., 235, 236
Hardman, Eliza J., 236
Hardman, Elizabeth S., 235
Hardman, George E., 235
Hardman, George G., 236
Hardman, John R., 235
Hardman, Lucy C., 236
Hardman, Nancy Hood, 236
Hardman, Rezin Constant, 236
Hardman, Sarah A., 235
Hardwick, Elizabeth, 114
Hardwick, Nancy A., 60, 61, 112
Hardyman, 65
Harman, Eliza, 203, 204
Harman, William, 204
Harmon, Viola, 316
Harrell, Charles I., 275
Harrell, Omer, 324
Harris, Anne Lewis, 179
Harris, Catherine, 296
Harris, Catherine Mary, 98, 99
Harris, Charlotte Rebecca, 175
Harris, Elise E., 425
Harris, Frederick, 98, 175
Harris, George Washington, 256
Harris, Innis G., 425
Harris, Innis Durette, 425
Harris, John, 179
Harris, John F., 249
Harris, Lucy, 317
Harris, Marion M., 425
Harris, Samuel, 29, 30
Harrison, Andrew, 54
Harrison, Burr, Dr., 80
Harrison, Jane Cary, 107
Harrison, Jean, 54
Harrison, John Pendleton, 54
Harrison, Mary F., 172
Harrison, Mildred, 54
Harrison, Mollie, 314
Harrison, Patsy, 54
Harrison, Reuben, Maj., 122
Harrison, Robert, 54, 200
Harrison, Robert H., 172

Harrison, Thomas, 54
Harrison, William, 54, 72, 247
Harrison, William L., 172
Harrower, Alexander Gray, 249
Hart, Cassandra, 111
Hart, D., 111
Hart, Eli, 111
Hart, Jacob, 279
Hart, James T., 245
Hart, Mary, 279
Hart, Mary Anne, 264
Harvey, Charles, 149
Harvil, Alice, 338
Harwood, Christopher, 44
Harwood, Elizabeth, 44
Harwood, Maria Pendleton, 173
Harwood, William, 44
Harwood, William, Capt., 44, 173
Hastings, George Stuart, 292
Hatcher, Louis Berckmans, 287
Hatsell, Edward, 232
Haughton, Hattie, 307
Hawes, Clara, 355
Hawk, Everett, 344
Hawk, Ivy Caroline, 344
Hawkins, Alex, 122
Hawkins, Cordella, 122
Hawkins, Eliza, 122
Hawkins, Fannie G., 350
Hawkins, Fanny, 122
Hawkins, Huldah, 122
Hawkins, Isabella, 122
Hawkins, James H., 122
Hawkins, John T., 122
Hawkins, Lucy, 122
Hawkins, Martha, 122
Hawkins, Sally, 122
Haynes, Caleb, 410
Haynes, Margaret, 442
Hays, Malinda Jane, 60
Head, John O., 61
Headrick, Gibson Clark, 125
Headrick, Rachel, 125
Heard, Carrie, 211
Hearin, Charles William, 335
Hearin, Emmette Holcombe, 335
Hearin, Florence, 335
Hearin, Harry Smith, 335
Hearin, John, 335
Helton, George, 75, 403
Helton, Jim, 403
Helton, Oliver, 342
Helton, Sam, 402
Henderson, Emily, 212
Henderson, Joseph, 49
Hendrix, Elijah W., 189

Hendrix, Eliza, 189
Henley, Columbia B., 248
Henley, Laura, 215
Henley, Maria Elizabeth, 248
Henley, Mary Straughan, 248
Henley, Samuel Straughan, Dr., 248
Henley, T.M., 72
Henley, Thomas, 248
Henley, Thomas Baylor, 248
Henley, Wilma T., 248
Henry, Patrick, 168
Henties, Cora D., 414
Herdsman, Rev., 59
Herndon, Carrie, 319
Herndon, Edward, 63
Herndon, Joseph, 40
Herndon, Julian, 196
Herndon, Thomas, 122
Herndon, Vivian Inez, 319
Hersey, Sarah White, 160
Hewell, Virginia, 220, 221
Hewitt, Hester Rogers, 266
Hewitt, Imla, 266
Hicks, Alice, 40
Hicks, Curtis Kejlar, 274
Hicks, Elizabeth E., 120
Hicks, John R., 341
Hicks, Joseph, 120
Hicks, Louisa, 120
Hicks, Martin, 64
Hicks, Mary E., 120
Hicks, Roy, 426
Hicks, Ruth, 392
Hicks, Sally Ann, 120
Hicks, Thomas, 68, 69, 133
Hicks, William Sanford, 120
Hidden, Lois Elizabeth, 355
Higdon, Thomas, 247
Hightower, Edward Taylor, 198
Hightower, John, 198
Hightower, John Alexander, 198
Hildrup, Albert, 426
Hildrup, Edward, 425
Hildrup, Leroy, 426
Hildrup, Robert Warner, 425
Hill, Edward, 184
Hill, Elizabeth, 185
Hill, Hiram, 185
Hill, James, 185
Hill, Jemima, 185
Hill, John, 12, 185
Hill, Margaret, 185
Hill, Martin, 185
Hill, Mary "Polly," 184
Hill, Nancy, 126
Hill, Ona Belle, 417

Hill, Polly, 185
Hill, Robert, 185
Hill, Tennie, 401
Hill, William, Rev., 73
Hillhouse, Dobbin, 254
Hilton, Charles, 369
Hilton, Charles Talliaferro, 369
Hilton, George, 74
Hilton, Hattie, 323
Hilton, John, 323
Hilton, Mary Pendleton, 369
Hilton, Roand, 369
Hinson, Annalee (Andrews), 404
Hinson, Katherine, 439
Hinson, Thomas A., 439
Hirams, S., 121
Hite, Joseph S., 84
Hite, Mary A. M., 84
Hite, Stephen Lewis, 84
Hobbs, Cyrus B., 147
Hodges, Walter Lee, 269
Hoffman, Alice, 367
Hoffman, Helen, 383
Holderby, William, 42
Holladay, Helen B., 352
Holladay, Isabella Park, 351, 352
Holladay, Lillian M., 352
Holladay, Taverner, 351, 352
Holliday, Jane Kimbrough, 177, 399
Holliday, William, 117
Holloday, Lewis, 63
Holmes, Priscilla, 53
Holmes, Catherine, 127
Holsonbake, Mary Evelyn, 321
Holsonbake, Wade, 321
Holstun, James Drayton, 249
Honaker, Etta, 313
Honaker, Henry, 413
Honaker, Lyda Anna Eliza, 413
Hooker, R. W., Rev., 225
Hoomes, Benjamin, 42, 71
Hoomes, Judith Allen, 170
Hoomes, Martha, 71, 72
Hoomes, Richard, 170
Hope, Margaret, 439
Hope, Nancy, 438
Hope, W. Byron, 413
Hopkins, Samuel, 26
Horne, Polly, 317
Horsley, Isabella, 76
Horsley, Mary Cabell, 75, 76
Horsley, William, 75
Horton, Aby C., 181
Horton, Eliza, 181
Horton, Enoch, 181
Horton, James Harvey, 181

Lee, Sarah, 426
Lee, Susan P., 291
Leeper, Emily Ann, 390
Leeper, William Dudley, 390
Legg, James M., 189
Legg, John Craig, 189
Legg, Margaret D., 189
Legg, Monroe W., 189
Legg, William Huston, 189
Leigh, William, 12
Lemaster, Mahala Delphie, 403
Lemmons, Mary Jane, 234
Lewis, Annie, 26
Lewis, Catherine Ann, 146
Lewis, Delia Maria, 147
Lewis, Edward, 66
Lewis, Elizabeth C., 146
Lewis, Frances Ellen, 147
Lewis, Hulda, 157
Lewis, Huldah, 218
Lewis, Huldah E., 123
Lewis, James, 27
Lewis, James B., 147
Lewis, James S., 146
Lewis, Joel, 136
Lewis, John, 94
Lewis, John A., 146
Lewis, Lucinda, 123
Lewis, Lucy Ellen, 136
Lewis, Mahala A., 123
Lewis, Martha H., 147
Lewis, Mary Jane, 146
Lewis, Nancy, 171, 175
Lewis, Nancy "Anne," 94
Lewis, Philip Pendleton, 123
Lewis, Robert C., 147
Lewis, Trueman, 218
Lewis, William, 123, 218
Lewis, William Henry, 146
Licklider, Alice, 388
Lightfoot, Goodrich, 180
Lightfoot, John, 180
Lightfoot, Pendleton Goodrich, 180
Linder, Artie, 421
Lindsay, Charles, 236
Lindsay, Elizabeth Ann, 236, 237
Lindsay, Reuben L., 220
Lippard, George, 122
Lipscomb, Caroline, 96
Lipscomb, Fanny, 331
Lipscomb, Katherine, 140, 248
Lipscomb, Spotswood, 96
Little, Albert Johnson, Judge, 275
Little, Robert C., 174
Livingston, Herman T., 93
Livingston, John Callendar, 165

Livingston, Mrs., 56
Lloyd, Ada (Harvuot), 297
Lloyd, Mary Tayloe, 165
Locker, Sallie B., 428
Lohr, James Henry, 220
Long, Edward Pendleton, 150
Long, Ellis, B., 150
Long, Ellis Barcroft, 149
Long, Gertrude Summerville, 150
Long, Helen Mary, 150
Long, John, 149
Long, John Ricards, 150
Long, Joshua, 70
Long, Lillie, 427, 428
Long, Virginia Henrietta, 150
Longstreet, Gen., 173, 273
Loone, Allen, 88
Loone, Sarah, 88
Loone, Westley, 88
Loudder, Pauline, 325
Love, James Clyde, 391
Love, John William Pendleton, 391
Love, Virginia T., 391
Lovejoy, Gladys, 324
Lowe, Alice, 426
Lucas, Ambrose, 59
Lucas, Henry, 59
Lucas, Lucinda, 59
Lucas, Rachel, 100
Lucas, Sarah Ann, 59
Lucas, Zachariah, 58
Luke, William H. W., 98
Lumpkin, Laura A., 172
Lumpkin, Josephine, 247
Lumpkin, Richard, 247
Lundquist, Alida Maria, 285, 286
Lurton, Sarah, 208, 209
Lyles, Albert Rufus, Dr., 389
Lyles, Miriam Eunice, 389
Lyles, Moses, 389
Lyles, Pauline Lavinia, 389
Lynn, David, 326
Lynn, Mary Elizabeth, 326
Lynne, Lucy, 27
Lyster, Morton J., 329
Lyte, William Francis, 413
Machon, Anna J., 343
Macon, John, 42
Macon, Mary, 42
Madden, Nancy, 306
Maddison, John, 15
Maddison, Mary, 15
Madison, Frances, 32
Madison, Henry, 36
Madison, James, 32, 92
Madison, Sarah, 35, 37

Madsen, Ernest Christian, 299
Magruder, Catherine Anne, 262
Magruder, Elizabeth Bankhead, 167
Magruder, Gen., 285, 286
Magruder, Owen, 262
Mahan, Elizabeth, 304
Mahan, Frances A., 304
Mahan, Henry, 304
Mahan, Henry W., 305
Mahan, Josephine, 304
Mahan, Peter, 304
Mahan, Rosa, 305
Mahone, John, 39
Majors, Isabella, 223, 224
Maley, Johnson, 157
Mallory, Lucretia, 265
Maness, Francis Asberry, 182
Manion, James, 232
Manion, James A., 233
Manion, John A., 233
Manion, Mary C., 233
Manion, Nancy J., 233
Manion, Reuben O., 232, 233
Manion, Sallie Elizabeth, 233
Mann, Michael, 133
Mann, Phebe, 133
Mann, William, 247
Mansfield, Eller H., 233
Mansfield, Henry C., 233
Mansfield, James, 124
Mansfield, James R., 233
Mansfield, John A., 233
Mansfield, John W., 233
Mansfield, L.V., 233
Mansfield, Mary E., 233
Mansfield, Nannie, 233
Mansfield, Oliver A., 233
Mansfield, Robert T., 233
Mansfield, Thomas, 233
Manus, Jacob, 318
Manus, Mary J., 318
Manus, Reuben, 318
Marcy, Cornelia, 167
Marcy, William Learned, 167
Markert, Harry, 368
Markert, Robert Harry, 368
Marion, Lucy E., 324
Marshall, Edward W., 239
Marshall, James M., 90
Marshall, John, 90, 92
Marshall, Marjoria Washington, 433
Marshall, Sallie A., 361
Martin, 191
Martin, Agnes, 183
Martin, Brumby, 249
Martin, Denny, 190

Martin, Elizabeth, 433
Martin, Fanny, Mrs., 208
Martin, Marguerite, 337
Martin, Mary, 393, 394
Martin, William Peters, Rev., 37
Mason, George, 46
Mason, George Washington, 377, 378
Mason, Idelle Lucy, 378
Mason, James M., 163
Mason, Mary Etta, 378
Mason, Wallace A., 321
Massey, Benjamin, 70, 123, 124
Massey, James, 124
Massey, Nina E., 246
Massey, Silas, 124
Massey, Thomas, 124
Massoc, William, 139
Massoc, Frances, 139
Matney, Esther Octavia, 424
Matthews, Lucy, 195, 196
Mattox, Verina Davis, 384
Maupin, Charlie, 319
Maupin, Dora B., 319
Maupin, Thomas, 319
Mavis, 319
Maxwell, Amelia, 90
Maxwell, Anna, 137
Maxwell, John, 190
May, Phillip, 43
Mayo, Claud, Cdr., 285
Mays, David John, 5, 19
Maze, Ina Farris, 368
Maze, John T., 128, 234
McAdoo, Alisa, 193
McAdoo, William, 193
McBride, Maggie, 322, 412
McCallister, Susie, 191
McCarthy, Daniel Stephens, 177
McCartney, Richard Seton, 337
McClain, Artemecia, 134, 135
McClain, George, 134
McClay, Evaline, 349
McClellan, George B., 166
McConnell, Archibald F., 125
McConnell, Cyrus, 125
McConnell, Isaac Perry, 125
McConnell, Ovia McCracken, 125
McConnell, Melissa, 125
McConnell, Sally M., 125
McCord, Frances, 414
McCormick, Deborah Elizabeth, 349
McCormick, Orris, 349
McCurry, Lou Vesta, 403
McDaniel, Edward Jackson, 102
McDaniel, Elizabeth, 102
McDaniel, James Pendleton, 102

Pendleton, Beckham, 429
Pendleton, Bedford Horner, 406, 442, 443
Pendleton, Ben, 350, 394
Pendleton, Ben K., 318
Pendleton, Benjamin, 26, 30, 38, 39, 42, 43, 50,
55-57, 63, 72, 74, 88, 89, 103, 104, 115, 139,
142, 143, 190, 193, 194, 278, 393, 394
Pendleton, Benjamin D., 104
Pendleton, Benjamin F., 140, 350
Pendleton, Benjamin Fleet, 141, 252
Pendleton, Benjamin Franklin, 94, 187, 216, 317
Pendleton, Benjamin L., 378
Pendleton, Benjamin Strother, 89, 160, 279, 280
Pendleton, Bennett, 424
Pendleton, Bentley Gaines, 257
Pendleton, Berryman H., 132, 240
Pendleton, Bertha, 320, 359, 395, 410
Pendleton, Bertha Ernestine, 278
Pendleton, Bertie, 441
Pendleton, Bertie E., 345
Pendleton, Bessie, 364, 373, 404, 422
Pendleton, Bessie C., 381
Pendleton, Bessie D., 330
Pendleton, Bessie E., 406
Pendleton, Bessie Gould, 384
Pendleton, Bessie Jane, 342
Pendleton, Bessie K., 317
Pendleton, Bessie M., 436
Pendleton, Bessie May, 190
Pendleton, Bessie Noma, 321, 416
Pendleton, Bettie, 59
Pendleton, Beula, 217
Pendleton, Beverly Neal, 307, 405, 406
Pendleton, Beverly Walker, 286
Pendleton, Billie J., 411
Pendleton, Blanche, 436
Pendleton, Blanche Clara, 199
Pendleton, Bonnie, 325, 439, 442
Pendleton, Bonnie H., 443
Pendleton, Bonnie Laura, 190, 323
Pendleton, Boyakin, 336
Pendleton, Boyd, 394
Pendleton, Bracken, 244
Pendleton, Brady, 328
Pendleton, Brault C., 427
Pendleton, Brian, 5, 10
Pendleton, Brodie Herndon, 296
Pendleton, Brookes Stevenson, 337
Pendleton, Brooksie Elizabeth, 321
Pendleton, Brooksie May, 342
Pendleton, Buster Willie, 325
Pendleton, Byrd Page, 293
Pendleton, C. C., 288
Pendleton, Caldonia, 379
Pendleton, Calley Dona, 311
Pendleton, Callie, 358

Pendleton, Callie D., 190
Pendleton, Callie R., 313, 317
Pendleton, Campbellina, 176
Pendleton, Candis L., 365
Pendleton, Carita, 274
Pendleton, Carl Lester, 359, 429
Pendleton, Carl Macon, 375, 376
Pendleton, Carlos, 410
Pendleton, Caroline, 108, 224, 338
Pendleton, Caroline Augusta, 119, 223
Pendleton, Caroline Cabell, 199
Pendleton, Carrie, 114, 425
Pendleton, Carrie Crismond, 351
Pendleton, Carrie Mae, 418
Pendleton, Carrie Strother, 269, 391
Pendleton, Carson, 334
Pendleton, Cary Verdier, 280
Pendleton, Cassandra Bernice, 413
Pendleton, Catherine, 15, 21, 26, 46, 79, 188,
319, 335, 382, 441
Pendleton, Catherine "Caty," 42
Pendleton, Catherine Anne, 78, 140, 146, 248,
249, 251
Pendleton, Catherine Anne Bowie, 80
Pendleton, Catherine Bowie, 47, 81
Pendleton, Catherine E.T., 151, 262
Pendleton, Catherine Harrison, 263, 387
Pendleton, Catherine Huntington, 298
Pendleton, Catherine Kimbrough, 295
Pendleton, Catherine M., 349, 397
Pendleton, Catherine May, 405
Pendleton, Catherine Peebles, 274
Pendleton, Catherine "Kitty" Robertson, 55
Pendleton, Catherine Sarah, 393
Pendleton, Catherine Thornton, 89, 160
Pendleton, Catlett, 47
Pendleton, Cecil Richmond, Dr., 316
Pendleton, Cecily, 7
Pendleton, Cenara, 232, 361
Pendleton, Champney, 69, 133
Pendleton, Charles, 240, 305, 345, 403, 404,
407, 410, 48, 419
Pendleton, Charles A., 244, 258, 342, 369, 379
Pendleton, Charles Arthur, 341, 421
Pendleton, Charles B., 107
Pendleton, Charles Clayton, 409
Pendleton, Charles Clinton, 316
Pendleton, Charles D., 336
Pendleton, Charles David, 432
Pendleton, Charles Dix, 201
Pendleton, Charles Douglass, 313
Pendleton, Charles E., 344, 422, 439
Pendleton, Charles Edward, 219, 258
Pendleton, Charles Eldridge, 189
Pendleton, Charles Elihu, 309
Pendleton, Charles H., 357

Pendleton, Charles Henry, 164, 190, 282
Pendleton, Charles Kimbrough, 175, 295, 296
Pendleton, Charles Lewis, 94, 169
Pendleton, Charles Lilburn, 237
Pendleton, Charles M., 212
Pendleton, Charles Mason, 163
Pendleton, Charles Micajah, 277
Pendleton, Charles Pottie, 180
Pendleton, Charles Rittenhouse, 158, 274, 392
Pendleton, Charles S., 409
Pendleton, Charles Sumner, 309, 409
Pendleton, Charles V., 384
Pendleton, Charles W., 319
Pendleton, Charles Wilgus, 431
Pendleton, Charles William, 180, 302
Pendleton, Charlie, 364
Pendleton, Charlotte, 73, 93, 290
Pendleton, Charlotte Adelaide Smith, 105
Pendleton, Charlotte Austin, 105
Pendleton, Charlotte Elizabeth, 314, 414
Pendleton, Charlotte T. 149
Pendleton, Chesley, 63, 64
Pendleton, Chesley Buckner, 356, 427
Pendleton, Chesley Thacker, 64, 121, 227, 228, 355, 356
Pendleton, Christopher, 78, 112, 113, 307, 406, 407
Pendleton, Christopher C., 312, 412
Pendleton, Clara, 199
Pendleton, Clara Alexander, 199
Pendleton, Clara Etta, 310
Pendleton, Clara Frances, 382
Pendleton, Clara L., 432
Pendleton, Clara Mae, 348
Pendleton, Clarabella, 345
Pendleton, Clare Cassandra, 314
Pendleton, Clarence, 241, 358, 423, 427
Pendleton, Clarence Bascom, 409
Pendleton, Clarence Clark, 335
Pendleton, Clarence E., 374
Pendleton, Clarence Everett, 264
Pendleton, Clarence M., 266, 389
Pendleton, Clarence N., 311
Pendleton, Clarinda Huntington, 177, 296, 297
Pendleton, Clarissa, 129, 234
Pendleton, Clarissa S., 255
Pendleton, Clark Asbury, 322
Pendleton, Claud Ernest, 267, 390
Pendleton, Claude Barnhart, 346
Pendleton, Claude Howard, 313
Pendleton, Claude L., 214, 349
Pendleton, Claudia Clara, 281
Pendleton, Claudia L., 162
Pendleton, Cleveland, 344, 423
Pendleton, Clifford, 438
Pendleton, Clyde, 429

Pendleton, Clyde C., 422
Pendleton, Clyde D., 367
Pendleton, Clyde Elmer, 267
Pendleton, Clyde Fugate, 404
Pendleton, Cole, 407
Pendleton, Coleman, 49, 85, 272
Pendleton, Conley, 288
Pendleton, Conley F., 311
Pendleton, Conner Spillman, 265
Pendleton, Constance, 273, 303
Pendleton, Cora, 311
Pendleton, Cora Albina, 250, 372
Pendleton, Cora B., 310
Pendleton, Cora E., 311
Pendleton, Cora Evelyn, 342
Pendleton, Cora Harris, 328
Pendleton, Cordelia, 186, 210, 315, 347
Pendleton, Cordie Lee, 435
Pendleton, Cornelia, 207, 285, 339
Pendleton, Cornelia Ann, 366, 433
Pendleton, Cornelia Chisholm, 277
Pendleton, Creed, 100
Pendleton, Cunningham, 394
Pendleton, Curtis, 41, 64, 66-68, 117, 125, 126, 229
Pendleton, Curtis Ray, 408
Pendleton, Cynthia A., 132, 241
Pendleton, Cyrus Neville, 117-120, 226
Pendleton, Daisy, 362
Pendleton, Daisy Deane, 267
Pendleton, Daisy Mae, 416
Pendleton, Daniel C., 309
Pendleton, Daniel Farmer, 81, 153
Pendleton, Daniel Micajah, 205, 206, 258
Pendleton, Daniel N., 381, 437
Pendleton, Daniel Ward, 79
Pendleton, David, 114, 329
Pendleton, David Edward, 242, 367
Pendleton, David Elliott, 330
Pendleton, David Ellis, 150, 260
Pendleton, David Elmer, 240, 365
Pendleton, David Elva, 435
Pendleton, David F., 310
Pendleton, David H., 84, 156, 271
Pendleton, David Harris, Dr., 99, 180
Pendleton, David J., 129, 131, 231, 236, 237, 239
Pendleton, David M., 302
Pendleton, David Ramsey, 195, 331
Pendleton, David W., 327
Pendleton, David Wrightly R., 408
Pendleton, Dawson R., 374
Pendleton, Deamy, 381
Pendleton, Delia, 436
Pendleton, Della, 251, 376, 422
Pendleton, Dennis, 438

Pendleton, Derinda Elizabeth, 326, 416
Pendleton, Derinda M., 192
Pendleton, Dewey Ellwood, 328
Pendleton, Diadamia Hannah, 159, 278
Pendleton, Dillard, 104, 197
Pendleton, Dinah, 183
Pendleton, Docia Lee, 407
Pendleton, Docky H., 379, 436
Pendleton, Dolly Odessa, 325
Pendleton, Dolores "Do" Marene, 368
Pendleton, Donnelly, 408
Pendleton, Dora A., 255
Pendleton, Dora Blanche, 404
Pendleton, Dora E., 379, 423
Pendleton, Dora L., 328
Pendleton, Dorcas, 84
Pendleton, Doris, 437
Pendleton, Doris M., 397
Pendleton, Dorothy, 322, 334, 404, 434
Pendleton, Dorothy E., 437
Pendleton, Dorothy V., 415
Pendleton, Dorsey E., 367
Pendleton, Dorsie Edward, 422
Pendleton, Douglas, 198
Pendleton, Douglas Schley, 199
Pendleton, Dovey Jane, 326, 417
Pendleton, Drew Brasher, 394
Pendleton, Dudley Digges, 171, 289, 397, 398
Pendleton, Dudley Fleet, 252
Pendleton, Dulcena, 182, 240, 304
Pendleton, Dulcena J., 239
Pendleton, Dulcinda, 129
Pendleton, Dwight Lyman, 177, 298
Pendleton, E. C., 259
Pendleton, E. D., 239
Pendleton, Easter, 305
Pendleton, Eberle, 112, 214
Pendleton, Edella G., 397
Pendleton, Edgar, 358
Pendleton, Edith, 282, 411, 423
Pendleton, Edith Alice, 316, 415, 443
Pendleton, Edith D., 367
Pendleton, Edith M., 241
Pendleton, Edith May, 351, 425
Pendleton, Edith May St. George, 281
Pendleton, Edmond, 57, 117, 239
Pendleton, Edmond Harris, 194, 327, 328
Pendleton, Edmonia, 136, 137
Pendleton, Edmund, 5, 9, 10, 14, 18-26, 28-30,
35-39, 46, 52, 53, 55, 57, 66, 76, 78, 79, 82, 91-
93, 95, 96, 104, 106, 124-126, 131, 132, 141,
149, 150, 163, 174, 190, 194, 202, 203, 205, 207,
240, 273, 282, 292, 337
Pendleton, Edmund Allen, 94, 168, 171, 286,
287, 395, 396
Pendleton, Edmund B., 71, 135, 136, 218

Pendleton, Edmund Boyd, 91, 163
Pendleton, Edmund Cole, 301
Pendleton, Edmund Embree, 329, 420
Pendleton, Edmund Gaines, 84, 195, 330
Pendleton, Edmund H., 103
Pendleton, Edmund Henry, 52, 53, 77, 93, 167
Pendleton, Edmund J., 127, 284
Pendleton, Edmund Lewis, 168
Pendleton, Edmund Littleton, 295
Pendleton, Edmund Micajah, 224, 338
Pendleton, Edmund Monroe, 85, 158, 159, 277
Pendleton, Edmund P., 153
Pendleton, Edmund Piper, 155, 270
Pendleton, Edmund Porter, 399
Pendleton, Edmund Randolph, 284, 337
Pendleton, Edmund Strachan, 175, 295
Pendleton, Edmund Tebeau, 158
Pendleton, Edmund Waller, 119, 120, 224
Pendleton, Edna, 76, 145, 216, 319, 330, 411
Pendleton, Edna C., 411
Pendleton, Edna Earl, 267
Pendleton, Edna Frances, 389
Pendleton, Edna Margaret, 365
Pendleton, Edward, 46, 78, 214, 239, 343
Pendleton, Edward Crawley, 287
Pendleton, Edward D., 226
Pendleton, Edward Franklin, 432
Pendleton, Edward Gray, 163
Pendleton, Edward Henry, 79
Pendleton, Edward Leslie, 363, 431, 432
Pendleton, Edward M., 310
Pendleton, Edward Spears, 362, 431
Pendleton, Edward Walter, 264
Pendleton, Edwin, 116, 117, 147, 250, 374
Pendleton, Edwin Conway, 198, 333, 334, 420
Pendleton, Edwin Dudley, 307, 404
Pendleton, Edwin H., 78
Pendleton, Edwin Morgan, 337
Pendleton, Edwin Taylor, 199
Pendleton, Effa, 239
Pendleton, Effa L., 411
Pendleton, Effie, 342
Pendleton, Effie Lee, 244
Pendleton, Elbert M., 185, 312, 313
Pendleton, Eldon David, 365
Pendleton, Eldridge Honaker, 413
Pendleton, Eldridge Howard, 186, 190, 313
Pendleton, Eldridge McKinley, 316
Pendleton, Eleanor, 51, 89, 90, 123, 230, 320,
433
Pendleton, Eleanor Agnes, 283
Pendleton, Eleanor Chinn, 263, 388
Pendleton, Eleanor Ford, 297
Pendleton, Eleanor Love, 292
Pendleton, Elena M., 422
Pendleton, Eliott Hunt, 93, 166, 284

Pendleton, Essie Lee, 267
Pendleton, Esta, 404
Pendleton, Ester R., 435
Pendleton, Ethel, 328, 412, 419, 423
Pendleton, Ethel A., 410
Pendleton, Ethel Lenoir, 370
Pendleton, Ethel Mae, 377
Pendleton, Etta Louise, 413
Pendleton, Eugene, 190, 242, 250, 286
Pendleton, Eugene B., Dr., 177, 298, 299, 399
Pendleton, Eugene Banks, 212, 348, 349
Pendleton, Eugene Barbour, 299, 400
Pendleton, Eugene Beauharnais, 168, 285, 286
Pendleton, Eugene Reynolds, 372
Pendleton, Eugene Robinson, 370
Pendleton, Eugenia, 116, 219
Pendleton, Eula Fay, 415
Pendleton, Eustace B., 350
Pendleton, Eva, 328
Pendleton, Evalina, 356
Pendleton, Evan, 114
Pendleton, Everett, 3, 5
Pendleton, Everett S., 340
Pendleton, Ewell William, 418
Pendleton, Ewing E., 328
Pendleton, Exce Opal, 342
Pendleton, Ezekiel B., 411
Pendleton, Fannie, 207, 214
Pendleton, Fannie Caroline, 327
Pendleton, Fannie Elizabeth, 351, 425, 426
Pendleton, Fannie L., 317, 336
Pendleton, Fanny, 247
Pendleton, Fanny Cisire, 379
Pendleton, Fanny R., 127, 133
Pendleton, Fay, 330
Pendleton, Fay Elenor, 365
Pendleton, Faye, 421
Pendleton, Felix, 114
Pendleton, Fern, 330
Pendleton, Festus Ray, 368
Pendleton, Fidella, 345
Pendleton, Fletcher, 410
Pendleton, Flonnie, 429
Pendleton, Flora, 328, 401
Pendleton, Florence, 226, 366
Pendleton, Florence Belle, 242, 367
Pendleton, Florence C., 252
Pendleton, Florence V., 188
Pendleton, Flory, 409
Pendleton, Frances, 39, 41, 46, 53, 56, 61, 64, 69-71, 100, 108, 110, 114, 122, 137, 181, 209, 354, 364
Pendleton, Frances "Fanny," 69, 129, 130, 222, 352
Pendleton, Frances A., 240, 366
Pendleton, Frances Ann, 105, 197

Pendleton, Frances Anne, 119, 220, 221
Pendleton, Frances Catherine, 321
Pendleton, Frances Coleman, 51, 90
Pendleton, Frances Crutchfield, 388
Pendleton, Frances E., 152
Pendleton, Frances Eleanor, 431
Pendleton, Frances Ellen, 246
Pendleton, Frances Emiline, 210
Pendleton, Frances G., 199
Pendleton, Frances Garland, 58
Pendleton, Frances I. C., 169
Pendleton, Frances J., 223
Pendleton, Frances Jane, 154
Pendleton, Frances Lawrence, 174, 294
Pendleton, Frances Rucker, 198
Pendleton, Frances Samuella, 55, 99
Pendleton, Francis, 6, 7, 11, 323
Pendleton, Francis Key, 166, 275, 283
Pendleton, Francis L., 396
Pendleton, Francis M., 134, 243
Pendleton, Francis R., 388
Pendleton, Francis Rittenhouse, 159
Pendleton, Francis Walker, Dr., 95, 172, 174
Pendleton, Frank, 38, 39, 111, 204, 363, 421
Pendleton, Frank Burk, 439, 443, 444
Pendleton, Frank Leslie, 257, 384
Pendleton, Frank Sampson, 199
Pendleton, Franklin P., 237, 364
Pendleton, Fred, 418
Pendleton, Fred Champion, 242
Pendleton, Fred H., 318
Pendleton, Freda, 273
Pendleton, Frederick Harry, 99
Pendleton, Frederick William, 269
Pendleton, French Strother, 82
Pendleton, Fulton, 114
Pendleton, G. L., 377
Pendleton, G. Luther, 375
Pendleton, G. W., 213
Pendleton, Gabriel, 49
Pendleton, Gail, 403
Pendleton, Gail Albert, 390
Pendleton, Garland E., 323
Pendleton, Garnett, 222, 352
Pendleton, Garnett Peyton, 162, 280
Pendleton, Garett A., 425
Pendleton, Garrett, 423
Pendleton, General, 381
Pendleton, George, 2, 5-7, 14, 135, 248, 284, 371, 437
Pendleton, George A., 434
Pendleton, George Allen, 138, 167, 246, 258
Pendleton, George Alvin, 239, 240, 242, 365
Pendleton, George Baylor, 249, 371
Pendleton, George Beckham, 359
Pendleton, George C., 330, 331, 420

Pendleton, George Cassety, 195, 328, 329
Pendleton, George Clark, 314
Pendleton, George Cyrus, 226
Pendleton, George E., 425
Pendleton, George Ebley, 214
Pendleton, George Edmund, 248
Pendleton, George Edwin, 388
Pendleton, George H., 271, 304, 344, 403, 412, 422
Pendleton, George Hampton, 416
Pendleton, George Hiram, 381, 437
Pendleton, George Hunt, 93, 165, 166, 283
Pendleton, George M., 139
Pendleton, George Macon, 72, 140, 250, 251
Pendleton, George Paxton, 297
Pendleton, George Pinckney, 210, 342, 343
Pendleton, George Raney, 372, 434
Pendleton, George Robert, 251, 375
Pendleton, George T., 259, 379, 387
Pendleton, George Taylor, 152, 262, 263
Pendleton, George W., 108, 197, 207, 208, 346, 347
Pendleton, George Walter, 250, 373, 374
Pendleton, George Washington, 79, 81, 110, 151, 153, 154, 187, 210, 255, 379
Pendleton, George Wilson, 209
Pendleton, Georgie Alice, 339
Pendleton, Gertrude, 377, 437
Pendleton, Gertrude Adala, 275
Pendleton, Gertrude Owen, 387
Pendleton, Gertrude Powell, 337
Pendleton, Giles, 410
Pendleton, Ginever, 437
Pendleton, Girta, 363
Pendleton, Gladys, 324, 394, 418, 441
Pendleton, Gladys L., 317
Pendleton, Gladys R., 434
Pendleton, Golden, 423
Pendleton, Goldie, 436
Pendleton, Grace, 150
Pendleton, Grace L., 252
Pendleton, Grace LaBelle, 313
Pendleton, Grace Mae, 412
Pendleton, Gracie, 315
Pendleton, Grady Reasons, 376
Pendleton, Gradys, 315
Pendleton, Grover, 401
Pendleton, Grover C., 406
Pendleton, Grover Cleveland, 339, 358, 428
Pendleton, Guerdon Huntingdon, 95, 174
Pendleton, Gus, 363
Pendleton, Guy Briggs, 302
Pendleton, Guy Chetwood, 351
Pendleton, H. H., 213
Pendleton, Hailes Janney, 204
Pendleton, Hall P., 331

Pendleton, Hallie Woodford, 362
Pendleton, Hamilton J., 143, 144
Pendleton, Hammett Claggett, 293
Pendleton, Hampton Flanary, 308
Pendleton, Hampton Lloyd, 407, 415, 443
Pendleton, Hampton W., 319, 416
Pendleton, Hannah, 134, 156, 235, 242, 243
Pendleton, Hannah B., 170
Pendleton, Hannah F., 311
Pendleton, Hannah L., 411
Pendleton, Hap F., 407
Pendleton, Harold Worth, 312
Pendleton, Harriet, 58, 284
Pendleton, Harriet Ella, 250
Pendleton, Harriett, 84
Pendleton, Harris, 327, 418
Pendleton, Harrison Burton, 315, 415
Pendleton, Harry Curtis, 366
Pendleton, Harry Easton, 331
Pendleton, Harry Holladay, 352, 426
Pendleton, Harry Leigh, 296
Pendleton, Harry Monroe, 426
Pendleton, Harry W., 288
Pendleton, Harvey B., 126, 232, 361
Pendleton, Harvey Eldridge, 191, 324, 325
Pendleton, Harvey Hart, 279
Pendleton, Harvey Russell, 325
Pendleton, Hattie, 286, 407, 439
Pendleton, Hazel Vivian, 418
Pendleton, Helen, 428
Pendleton, Helen Anne Catlett, 82
Pendleton, Helen Boteler, 289, 398
Pendleton, Helen M., 420
Pendleton, Helen Maria, 79
Pendleton, Helen N., 149, 260
Pendleton, Helen Newsome, 277
Pendleton, Helen S., 361
Pendleton, Helena Bernice, 368
Pendleton, Hena, 364
Pendleton, Henley Chapman, 156
Pendleton, Henrietta, 170, 288, 334
Pendleton, Henrietta "Hattie Mae," 359, 429
Pendleton, Henrietta Grymes, 161
Pendleton, Henry, 1, 5-12, 14, 16-19, 21, 25, 28-30, 33-37, 41, 45-47, 51, 54, 55, 62, 63, 65-67, 77, 78, 83, 88, 92, 96, 97, 116, 117, 147, 168, 176, 178, 209, 214, 219, 222, 246, 314, 371
Pendleton, Henry A., 259, 302, 340
Pendleton, Henry Clay, 152-154, 247, 264, 368-370
Pendleton, Henry Ervin, 223
Pendleton, Henry H., 179, 258
Pendleton, Henry K., 317
Pendleton, Henry Leavell, 353
Pendleton, Henry Lee, 372
Pendleton, Henry T., 59, 60, 207

Pendleton, Herbert, 374
Pendleton, Herbert Beeson, 301
Pendleton, Herbert Ellsworth, 385
Pendleton, Herbert Elmer, 367
Pendleton, Herbert George, 201, 335
Pendleton, Herman, 438
Pendleton, Herman R., 422
Pendleton, Herschel, 338
Pendleton, Hettie E., 357
Pendleton, Hezekiah, 144
Pendleton, Hilah White, 303
Pendleton, Hiram, 228, 256, 358
Pendleton, Hiram Kilgore, 102, 186, 187, 191, 323
Pendleton, Hoke James, 412
Pendleton, Holmes, 341
Pendleton, Homer Alexander, 314, 413, 414
Pendleton, Homer B., 324
Pendleton, Homer Herman, 373
Pendleton, Horace, 324
Pendleton, Howard, 287
Pendleton, Howard Ferris, 431
Pendleton, Howard Jackson, 315
Pendleton, Hubert Monroe, 325
Pendleton, Hugh, 168, 174, 287
Pendleton, Hugh C., 352
Pendleton, Hugh Claiborne, 116, 117, 218, 219
Pendleton, Hugh Halsell, 413
Pendleton, Hugh Nelson, 95, 171, 174, 290, 398
Pendleton, Hugh Ward, 287
Pendleton, Hughella, 173
Pendleton, Huldah, 65, 123, 124
Pendleton, Hunter, 303
Pendleton, Hunter Ashby, 371, 372
Pendleton, Huntington King, 177, 297
Pendleton, Hurshel Hastin, 441
Pendleton, Huston C., 309
Pendleton, Hyacinth, 249
Pendleton, Hyatt Fleet, 376
Pendleton, Ida, 232, 243, 285, 340
Pendleton, Ida Bell, 346
Pendleton, Ida C., 427
Pendleton, Ida Davis, 302
Pendleton, Ida Ewing, 179, 301
Pendleton, Ida Frances, 348
Pendleton, Ida M., 253
Pendleton, Ida May, 267
Pendleton, Ida Pearl, 422
Pendleton, Ida R., 241
Pendleton, Ida Victoria, 310
Pendleton, Illa Corene, 325
Pendleton, Inez Maud, 267
Pendleton, Ira Joseph, 307
Pendleton, Ira Lynn, 404
Pendleton, Ira M., 185, 243, 312
Pendleton, Ira Nash, 100, 181, 182, 303, 307

Pendleton, Ira Newton, 304, 386, 400, 401
Pendleton, Ira Quillen, 309
Pendleton, Ira S., 409
Pendleton, Irene B., 434
Pendleton, Irene R., 346
Pendleton, Irma Louise, 321
Pendleton, Isaac, 38, 39, 45, 60, 61, 112, 113, 115
Pendleton, Isaac Arlo, 409
Pendleton, Isaac H. "Ike," 310
Pendleton, Isaac Newton, 102, 188
Pendleton, Isaac Purnell, 92
Pendleton, Isaac T., 61, 113, 114
Pendleton, Isaac Thomas, 235, 362
Pendleton, Isabel A., 326
Pendleton, Isabel R., 292
Pendleton, Isabel Virginia, 308
Pendleton, Isabella, 15, 16, 19, 21, 24, 32, 249
Pendleton, Isabella E., 284
Pendleton, Isabella Lawrence, 398
Pendleton, Isabella V., 184
Pendleton, Isaiah, 127, 233, 234
Pendleton, Isold, 4
Pendleton, Iva, 340
Pendleton, Ivan V., 374
Pendleton, Ivy, 100
Pendleton, Ivy Jane, 358
Pendleton, Ivy Taylor, 102, 187
Pendleton, J. L., 326
Pendleton, Jack, 421
Pendleton, Jack H., 335, 421
Pendleton, Jackson, 65, 70, 71, 136
Pendleton, Jacob, 200
Pendleton, Jacqueline, 252
Pendleton, James, 18, 19, 21, 28, 29, 31-33, 35-39, 42, 43, 46, 47, 49, 51, 52, 57, 60, 61, 67, 72, 73, 74, 81, 83, 84, 100, 108, 111, 114, 140, 148, 152, 188, 193, 200, 208, 247, 248, 335, 359, 381
Pendleton, James A., 56, 100, 101, 185, 326
Pendleton, James Albert, 161, 258
Pendleton, James Aubrey, 158
Pendleton, James B., 143, 253
Pendleton, James Blackstone Taylor, 283
Pendleton, James Bowie, 47, 82
Pendleton, James C., 88, 159
Pendleton, James Church, 394
Pendleton, James Coleman, 84, 156, 159, 277, 278
Pendleton, James Coral, 420
Pendleton, James Crew, 112, 215
Pendleton, James Dudley, 107, 203, 207, 337
Pendleton, James E., 316, 362, 415, 439
Pendleton, James E. Wilson, 382, 439
Pendleton, James Eldridge, 313, 413
Pendleton, James F., 184, 309
Pendleton, James Frederick Arthur, 323

Pendleton, James French, 82, 153, 155, 264, 269, 270

Pendleton, James G., 255, 379

Pendleton, James H., 155, 211, 214, 228, 339, 347, 356

Pendleton, James Henry, 78, 147, 210, 345

Pendleton, James I., 342

Pendleton, James Ira, 389, 441

Pendleton, James L., 218, 292

Pendleton, James Lake, 398

Pendleton, James Lawrence, 95, 173

Pendleton, James Lee, 214

Pendleton, James Lewis, 108, 208

Pendleton, James Lucas, 103, 192

Pendleton, James M., 53, 94, 127, 183, 304, 307, 386, 402, 406

Pendleton, James M. Jones, 94

Pendleton, James Madison, 118, 119, 221, 222, 295

Pendleton, James Malcolm, 354

Pendleton, James Marion, 190, 322, 323

Pendleton, James McFall, 278

Pendleton, James Monroe, 219, 225, 255, 310, 351, 378, 411, 412

Pendleton, James Montague, 226, 355

Pendleton, James P., 156

Pendleton, James Philip Bosman, 162, 287

Pendleton, James Presley, 307, 405

Pendleton, James R., 232, 361

Pendleton, James Ray, 438

Pendleton, James Rice, 362, 431

Pendleton, James Richard, 110, 210, 211, 342, 348

Pendleton, James Russell, 431

Pendleton, James S., 207, 411

Pendleton, James Samuel, 309, 410

Pendleton, James Sheffey, 268

Pendleton, James Shepherd, 58, 106, 201

Pendleton, James Strother, 264, 388, 389

Pendleton, James T., 143, 259, 350

Pendleton, James Taylor, 80

Pendleton, James Trigg, 182, 304, 401, 440, 441

Pendleton, James Vance, 144, 256

Pendleton, James W., 315

Pendleton, James Walter, 201

Pendleton, James William, 89, 160, 238, 248, 364

Pendleton, Jane, 69, 102, 188

Pendleton, Jane Agnes, 121, 226

Pendleton, Jane Ann, 298

Pendleton, Jane Byrd, 174, 292, 294

Pendleton, Jane Claybrooke, 176

Pendleton, Jane Frances, 166, 283

Pendleton, Jane Garland, 58, 105

Pendleton, Jane Kimbrough, 299

Pendleton, Jane L., 318

Pendleton, Jane Marie, 442

Pendleton, Jane R., 145

Pendleton, Jane Stafford, 300

Pendleton, Janet R., 355

Pendleton, Janul, 410

Pendleton, Jean Frances, 276

Pendleton, Jean Lowrie, 276

Pendleton, Jean Washington, 297

Pendleton, Jefferson, 358, 427

Pendleton, Jefferson D., 343

Pendleton, Jeffrie, 442

Pendleton, Jemima, 31, 32, 49, 100, 184, 185, 311

Pendleton, Jemima Elizabeth, 189, 320

Pendleton, Jemima J., 188

Pendleton, Jemima Jane, 187, 317

Pendleton, Jennie, 208, 340

Pendleton, Jerry, 379

Pendleton, Jesse, 88, 244, 368

Pendleton, Jesse Caswell, 372, 434

Pendleton, Jesse Clark, 324

Pendleton, Jesse Emry, 305

Pendleton, Jesse Frank, 344

Pendleton, Jesse Hayden, 310

Pendleton, Jesse J., 427

Pendleton, Jesse Johnson, 335

Pendleton, Jessie, 213, 250, 416

Pendleton, Jessie N., 377

Pendleton, Jessie Read, 199

Pendleton, Jessie Strother, 265

Pendleton, Jessie Wright, 322

Pendleton, Jewel, 436

Pendleton, Jimmy, 322

Pendleton, Joanna, 46, 78, 114, 148

Pendleton, Joe Lamar, 298

Pendleton, Johanna, 364

Pendleton, John, 1, 7-9, 14-16, 18, 19, 21-26, 28-30, 33, 35-39, 41, 43, 47, 51, 53, 54, 56, 57, 60, 63, 64, 66, 67, 70, 73, 74, 79, 80, 83, 94, 101-103, 115, 117-119, 121, 126, 127, 134, 143, 144, 149, 156, 168, 188, 190, 225, 230, 252, 255, 262, 265, 271, 287, 304, 323, 350, 361, 371, 381, 401, 402

Pendleton, John A., 228, 355, 356, 358

Pendleton, John Alfred, 403

Pendleton, John Ally, 309, 410

Pendleton, John Asbury, 189, 321

Pendleton, John Bard, 53

Pendleton, John Barrett, 175, 294, 299, 300

Pendleton, John Baylor, 141, 251, 252

Pendleton, John Bell, 186

Pendleton, John Benjamin, 197, 332

Pendleton, John Bickerton, 55, 97

Pendleton, John Bowie, 81, 154, 155

Pendleton, John Calhoun, 154

Pendleton, John Chester Backus, 282

Pendleton, Lucy E., 69, 117, 133
Pendleton, Lucy Gaylord, 166, 283
Pendleton, Lucy H., 350
Pendleton, Lucy J., 219, 380
Pendleton, Lucy Jane, 108, 134, 208, 243
Pendleton, Lucy K., 389
Pendleton, Lucy Katherine, 265, 389
Pendleton, Lucy May, 362
Pendleton, Lucy Nelson, 290
Pendleton, Lucy Virginia, 200
Pendleton, Lucy W., 174
Pendleton, Lucy Welford Randolph, 161
Pendleton, Luelle, 273, 274, 391
Pendleton, Lula, 239
Pendleton, Lula Caldonia, 380
Pendleton, Lula Elizabeth, 251, 377
Pendleton, Lula J., 426
Pendleton, Lulu, 214
Pendleton, Lulua, 358
Pendleton, Luther E., 341
Pendleton, Luther Douglas, 189, 322
Pendleton, Lydia, 307
Pendleton, Lyle Turner, 390
Pendleton, M. Elizabeth, 211
Pendleton, M. Jackson, 340
Pendleton, Mable, 329
Pendleton, Mace, 43, 74-76
Pendleton, Mace C., 144
Pendleton, Mace Coleman, 75, 143
Pendleton, Madaline, 214
Pendleton, Madeline Ruth, 281
Pendleton, Madge, 413
Pendleton, Madison Henry, 177
Pendleton, Madison Strachan, 296
Pendleton, Madison, Dr., 96, 175
Pendleton, Mae Louise, 432
Pendleton, Maggie, 352, 411
Pendleton, Maggie B., 326
Pendleton, Maggie K., 411
Pendleton, Maggie P., 403
Pendleton, Mahaly, 74
Pendleton, Mahetta, 217
Pendleton, Malinda, 60, 84, 103, 110, 184, 308
Pendleton, Malinda A., 102, 186
Pendleton, Malinda V., 311
Pendleton, Malvina Rice, 121, 227
Pendleton, Mamie B., 324
Pendleton, Mann Randolph Page, 174, 293
Pendleton, Mara Rebecca, 307
Pendleton, Marc Davis, 438
Pendleton, Marcellus E., 362
Pendleton, Marcus, 214
Pendleton, Marella Elizabeth, 366
Pendleton, Margaret, 40, 47, 80, 103, 174, 193, 259, 322, 360, 408, 442
Pendleton, Margaret Anna, 194

Pendleton, Margaret Elizabeth, 338, 390
Pendleton, Margaret Ellen, 78, 148
Pendleton, Margaret Ethel, 389, 440, 441
Pendleton, Margaret Jane, 153, 439
Pendleton, Margaret Josephine, 179
Pendleton, Margaret Malinda, 84
Pendleton, Margaret Vance, 384
Pendleton, Margarette, 349, 366
Pendleton, Margerie, 364
Pendleton, Marguerite, 384
Pendleton, Maria, 219
Pendleton, Maria Gertrude, 276
Pendleton, Maria Jackson, 117, 137
Pendleton, Maria Louisa, 141, 251, 375
Pendleton, Maria W., 51, 52, 92
Pendleton, Marianne, 78, 147
Pendleton, Marie Lucinda, 282
Pendleton, Marion A., 264
Pendleton, Marion Childs, 274, 276, 393
Pendleton, Martha, 32, 41, 49, 65, 66, 73, 114, 129, 234, 258, 322, 342, 351, 412, 429
Pendleton, Martha "Molly, " 307
Pendleton, Martha "Patsy, " 69, 130
Pendleton, Martha "Patsy" Curtis, 71
Pendleton, Martha A., 186, 218, 232, 380
Pendleton, Martha Adeline, 189, 320
Pendleton, Martha Anna Priscilla, 157, 272, 273
Pendleton, Martha Anne, 58, 136
Pendleton, Martha Carter, 174
Pendleton, Martha E., 97, 215
Pendleton, Martha Eliza, 92, 93, 165
Pendleton, Martha Elizabeth, 210, 310, 343
Pendleton, Martha J., 228, 255, 340
Pendleton, Martha Jane, 138, 182, 306, 339
Pendleton, Martha Jane "Mattie," 235
Pendleton, Martha L., 326
Pendleton, Martha M., 76
Pendleton, Martha Todd, 55
Pendleton, Martha V., 407
Pendleton, Martha Victoria, 308
Pendleton, Martin Eugene, 239
Pendleton, Martin J., 131, 238
Pendleton, Mary, 7, 12, 19, 25, 32-34, 38-42, 50, 54, 55, 61, 72, 81, 86, 114, 119, 129, 147, 174, 212, 214, 216, 234, 274, 285, 335, 342, 348, 364, 380, 423, 428, 442
Pendleton, Mary "Molly," 100, 185
Pendleton, Mary "Polly," 56, 63, 66, 101, 115
Pendleton, Mary A., 378, 442
Pendleton, Mary Alice, 269
Pendleton, Mary Allen, 125, 231
Pendleton, Mary Alsop, 351, 425
Pendleton, Mary Ann, 70, 71, 228, 356
Pendleton, Mary Anne, 72, 79, 94, 140, 148, 149
Pendleton, Mary Arizona, 345, 424
Pendleton, Mary Belle, 353, 426

Pendleton, Mary Burnley, 98, 179
Pendleton, Mary C., 140, 259, 349, 379, 435, 436
Pendleton, Mary Catherine, 139, 219, 249, 250, 255, 380
Pendleton, Mary Davis, 312
Pendleton, Mary "Mollie" Duncan, 307
Pendleton, Mary E., 121, 127, 188, 211, 227, 253, 285, 425, 432, 435
Pendleton, Mary Eleanor, 152, 163
Pendleton, Mary Eliza, 135, 136, 200
Pendleton, Mary Elizabeth, 76, 138, 145, 326, 413
Pendleton, Mary Elizabeth "Betty," 218
Pendleton, Mary Elizabeth "Mollie," 187
Pendleton, Mary Ella, 437, 443
Pendleton, Mary Ellen, 229, 360, 361
Pendleton, Mary Emma, 251, 375
Pendleton, Mary Estell, 408
Pendleton, Mary Frances, 226, 354, 389
Pendleton, Mary H., 386
Pendleton, Mary Hugh, 247
Pendleton, Mary J., 330
Pendleton, Mary Jane, 104, 105, 136, 156, 189, 192, 196, 198, 228, 271, 320, 357
Pendleton, Mary Katherine, 390
Pendleton, Mary Kent, 338
Pendleton, Mary L., 366
Pendleton, Mary Laura, 349
Pendleton, Mary Leche, 262
Pendleton, Mary Lloyd, 166
Pendleton, Mary Louisa, 157
Pendleton, Mary Louise, 159, 384
Pendleton, Mary Lucas, 103, 192
Pendleton, Mary M., 162, 235, 357
Pendleton, Mary Macon, 73
Pendleton, Mary Nelson, 173
Pendleton, Mary Overton, 97, 177, 178
Pendleton, Mary Pearl, 204, 337
Pendleton, Mary R., 433
Pendleton, Mary Randolph, 161
Pendleton, Mary Rickard, 279, 394
Pendleton, Mary Spencer, 204
Pendleton, Mary Sula, 372
Pendleton, Mary T., 193
Pendleton, Mary Unity, 295
Pendleton, Mary Valonia, 356, 427
Pendleton, Mary Virginia, 155, 268
Pendleton, Mary Washington, 296, 400
Pendleton, Mary Whitehead, 297
Pendleton, Mary Zella, 158
Pendleton, Matilda, 7
Pendleton, Matilda Chaffee, 150
Pendleton, Matilda Winston, 55, 97
Pendleton, Matthew, 7, 8
Pendleton, Matthew Clinton, 434

Pendleton, Matthew Rainey, 250, 374
Pendleton, Mattie, 240, 320
Pendleton, Mattie E., 371
Pendleton, Mattie Irene, 413
Pendleton, Mattie Lee, 362, 430, 431
Pendleton, Mattie Lou, 377
Pendleton, Maude Menefee, 266
Pendleton, Maudie, 424
Pendleton, Maxie Elizabeth, 315, 414
Pendleton, Maxie Marvin, 351
Pendleton, Maxine Jeanette, 414
Pendleton, May, 313, 437
Pendleton, May Anna, 35
Pendleton, May Pearl, 323
Pendleton, Melvin C., 102, 190, 192
Pendleton, Melvina E., 240
Pendleton, Mentie, 441
Pendleton, Mercedes Lamar, 367
Pendleton, Merrettie, 241
Pendleton, Micajah, 43, 58, 60, 75, 76, 104, 106, 107, 110-112, 144, 202, 205, 214
Pendleton, Michael, 134, 242
Pendleton, Mildred, 32, 43, 53, 95, 168, 171, 367, 437
Pendleton, Mildred Edmonia, 172, 290
Pendleton, Mildred F., 234
Pendleton, Mildred Kathryn, 413
Pendleton, Mildred Lee, 293
Pendleton, Mildred Louise, 174, 293
Pendleton, Mildred Ruth, 368
Pendleton, Mildred Thomas, 65
Pendleton, Milford Lyman, 368
Pendleton, Miller Vance, 383
Pendleton, Millie, 215
Pendleton, Mina, 43, 44
Pendleton, Mina B., 347
Pendleton, Minerva, 187
Pendleton, Minerva Jane, 84
Pendleton, Minerva Jemima, 102, 191
Pendleton, Minnie, 382
Pendleton, Minnie A., 341
Pendleton, Minnie Frances, 438
Pendleton, Minnie May, 373
Pendleton, Mollie, 364, 401, 402
Pendleton, Mollie E., 190
Pendleton, Monte W., 424
Pendleton, Morgan Mitchell, 256, 381
Pendleton, Morris, 428
Pendleton, Musa May, 266
Pendleton, Myrtle, 329, 408, 410, 438
Pendleton, Myrtle B., 310
Pendleton, Myrtle Hewitt, 267, 390
Pendleton, Myrtle Verina, 384
Pendleton, Mystie M., 357
Pendleton, N. Collman, 406
Pendleton, Nana Lee

Pendleton, Pete, 362
Pendleton, Peter Henry V., 382
Pendleton, Phereba Delane, 438
Pendleton, Philander Barclay, 224, 353
Pendleton, Philip, 1, 2, 5, 8, 9-19, 21, 25, 26, 28-34, 37, 41-45, 47-49, 51, 52, 56, 62, 64, 65, 68, 70-72, 77, 86, 88, 90, 92, 145, 149, 150, 165, 218, 230, 258, 386, 438
Pendleton, Philip Barbour, 96, 177, 300
Pendleton, Philip Baylor, 72, 139, 140, 248, 249, 251, 371, 433
Pendleton, Philip C., 282
Pendleton, Philip Campbell, 371
Pendleton, Philip Cargill, 300
Pendleton, Philip Childs, 271
Pendleton, Philip Clayton, 51, 91, 162-164, 281
Pendleton, Philip Coleman, 85, 157, 158, 274, 392, 393
Pendleton, Philip Davis, 302
Pendleton, Philip Edmund, 90
Pendleton, Philip Harper, 144, 256
Pendleton, Philip Henry, 175, 181, 303
Pendleton, Philip Nelson, 276
Pendleton, Philip Peter, 79, 150, 260
Pendleton, Philip Randolph, 161
Pendleton, Philip Thomas, 159, 276
Pendleton, Philip Yancey, 177, 297
Pendleton, Philola, 274
Pendleton, Phoebe, 253
Pendleton, Pleasant H., 61
Pendleton, Polk, 402
Pendleton, Polly, 58, 59, 65, 121, 143, 310, 311
Pendleton, Polly Ann, 308, 408
Pendleton, Pompey, 141
Pendleton, Presley, 69, 126, 131, 132, 237
Pendleton, Presley A., 131, 239
Pendleton, Preston, 68, 69, 131, 132, 134
Pendleton, Prince E., 259
Pendleton, Priscilla, 26, 42, 44, 139, 247
Pendleton, Prudence, 61
Pendleton, R., 288
Pendleton, R. D., 328
Pendleton, R. E., 259
Pendleton, Rachel, 15, 16, 21, 25
Pendleton, Rachel A., 192, 193
Pendleton, Rachel E., 326
Pendleton, Rachel Elizabeth, 327, 418, 419
Pendleton, Ralph C., 279
Pendleton, Randolph Tucker, 337
Pendleton, Raney, 347
Pendleton, Ray, 363
Pendleton, Ray W., 341
Pendleton, Raymond, 428
Pendleton, Raymond Thomas, 387
Pendleton, Rebecca, 49, 84, 85, 100, 152, 183, 263

Pendleton, Rebecca Jane, 187, 318
Pendleton, Reginald Noel, 288, 397
Pendleton, Reid, 303
Pendleton, Rennie Hurley, 216
Pendleton, Reuben, 39, 55-60, 100, 101, 189
Pendleton, Riba N., 412
Pendleton, Rice, 41, 64, 66-69, 117, 120, 128, 129, 133, 134, 228, 229, 235, 236
Pendleton, Richard, 7, 38, 39, 58-60, 108, 109, 111, 112, 215, 247, 312, 335, 366, 371, 394
Pendleton, Richard "Dick," 279, 394
Pendleton, Richard A., 259, 386
Pendleton, Richard B., 143
Pendleton, Richard Hundley, 370
Pendleton, Richard J., 155, 267
Pendleton, Richard McFall, 394
Pendleton, Richard S., 200, 344, 345
Pendleton, Robbinette, 250
Pendleton, Robert, 42, 49, 68, 70, 84, 100, 114, 136, 138, 149, 185, 188, 213, 231, 237, 304, 312, 363, 409
Pendleton, Robert A., 288
Pendleton, Robert Aldrich, 201
Pendleton, Robert Aldridge, 106, 200
Pendleton, Robert C., 313
Pendleton, Robert Carter, 95, 162, 172, 258
Pendleton, Robert Edmund, 162, 330
Pendleton, Robert H., 108, 113, 207, 435
Pendleton, Robert Hardwick, 61, 112, 113, 216
Pendleton, Robert Henry, 336, 378, 435
Pendleton, Robert James, 246, 247, 369
Pendleton, Robert K., 411
Pendleton, Robert Kennus, 184, 310
Pendleton, Robert L., 162, 239, 288, 364, 365, 397, 412
Pendleton, Robert Lavelle, 377
Pendleton, Robert Lewis, 136, 170, 245, 246, 288
Pendleton, Robert Melvin, 187, 317, 318
Pendleton, Robert Milton, 338
Pendleton, Robert N., 76, 145
Pendleton, Robert Nelson, 171, 290
Pendleton, Robert Patton, 310, 411
Pendleton, Robert Randolph, 280
Pendleton, Robert S., 246, 319
Pendleton, Robert Shepherd, 89, 162
Pendleton, Robert Stevenson, 337
Pendleton, Robert Taylor, 94, 170
Pendleton, Robert Trigg, 401
Pendleton, Robert Walker, 408
Pendleton, Robert Ward, 79, 150
Pendleton, Robert Yates, 65, 122, 123, 229, 230, 361, 362
Pendleton, Roberta, 344
Pendleton, Roberta Ellis, 200
Pendleton, Roberta Lewis, 169

Rose, William H., 106, 201, 202
Ross, David, 22
Ross, Henrietta, 322
Ross, James R., 256
Ross, John, 22
Ross, Reuben, 221
Roundtree, Polly (Mary), 128, 129
Rowntree, John, 128
Roy, Elizabeth, 19, 22
Roy, John, 20
Royall, John M., 292
Royall, Mary J., 292
Royall, Samuel, 292
Rucker, Ambrose, 38
Rucker, John, 57
Rucker, Margaret, 102
Rucker, Mary, 296, 297
Rucker, Sarah Elizabeth, 57
Ruffin, Martha, 31, 32
Russell, June Etta, 324, 325
Russell, Thurman, 360
Russell, William, 324
Rust, Sophia, 149
Ryan, Sarah, 70
Sale, Benjamin P., 252
Sale, Ella West, 252
Salmon, Katherine, 388
Sampson, Charles E., 132
Sanders, Louisa, 105
Sanders, Roy, 414
Sandusky, George William, 153
Sapp, Rachael, 62
Sargent, Rebecca, 305
Sattley, Archibald, 87
Sattley, Charles E., 87
Savage, William Vann, 405
Saxton, Joseph, 333
Saxton, Mary Riddle, 333
Sayles, Louis, 440
Sayles, Nicholas, 440
Sayles, Norma, 440
Sayles, Patsy, 440
Sayre, Andrew Noble, 329
Scaling, Marguerite, 303
Schenck, Ann Pendleton, 167
Schenck, Dorsey Noah, 167
Schenck, Ernest Wharton, 167
Schenck, George Elliot Pendleton, 167
Schenck, Grace Fitz, 167
Schenck, Ida Sutphin, 167
Schenck, John Bard, 167
Schenck, Nathaniel, 167
Schenck, Pendleton, 167
Schenck, Robert C., 82
Schenck, Spotswood Dandridge, 167
Schenck, Susan Bowler, 167

Schmir, Susan, 242
Scobee, Elizabeth Ann, 236
Scobee, Emma Amelia, 238
Scobee, James W., 238
Scobee, Mary C. "Kate," 238
Scobee, Rezin A., 236
Scobee, Rice Pendleton, 237
Scobee, Robert, 236, 237
Scobee, Robert S., 238
Scott, Catherine, 110
Scott, Duke, 307
Scott, Edward Waller, 107
Scott, Frances Ann, 107
Scott, Henrietta, 285
Scott, Hugh Roy, 107
Scott, James Pendleton, 107
Scott, Lucy Ann, 110
Scott, Mary Camden, 107
Scott, Mary Frances, 110
Scott, Robert Garland, 107
Scott, Thomas, 110
Scott, William, 107
Scott, William Preston, 107
Scott, William Waller, 107
Scully, Alice Pendleton, 398
Scully, Cornelius Decatur, 398
Scully, Elizabeth Negley, 398
Scully, John Pendleton, 398
Seamore, William, 12
Seaton, Elizabeth, 211
Seay, John, 58
Seigler, Alice, 320
Seigler, Crawford C., 320
Seigler, Homer N., 320
Seigler, Mamie E., 320
Seigler, Minola, 320
Seigler, Myrtle R., 320
Seigler, Nannie B., 320
Seigler, Robert, 320
Seigler, Robert Franklin, 320
Seigler, Rosa, 320
Sergent, Mollie, 315
Settle, Sarah Ann, 87
Shacklett, Mary, 387
Shanks, Sarah Belle, 211
Shanks, David, 211
Shanks, Emma, 211
Shanks, Francis M., 211
Shanks, Mack Richard, 211
Shanks, William Edward, 211
Sharp, Frances Narcissa, 108, 208
Sheffey, Elizabeth Madison, 267
Sheffield, Bertha Mae, 323
Shelby, Isaac, Gov., 124
Shelton, Abraham, 48
Shelton, Anne, 329, 330

Spencer, Sarah, 48
Spencer, William, 443
Spencer, Winnie Mae, 369
Spindle, Elizabeth, 351
Sprague, 78
Spratling, Mary, 188
St. Clair, Glenn Moore, 269
Stacy, Mary A., 143
Stafford, Alma Florence, 300
Stafford, Charles, 300
Stallings, McClendon M., 322
Standley, George, 183, 184
Standley, Granville H., 184
Standley, John, 184
Standley, Mary J., 184
Standley, Matilda, 184
Standley, Richard, 183
Standley, Sarah, 184
Stanley, Carrie C., 338
Stanton, Bluford, 85
Stanton, Ganid Power, 338
Staples, Joseph, 58
Starke, Thomas, 12
Starnes, Virgie B., 301
Steele, 340
Steele, Frances, 282
Steele, Georgia E., 340
Steele, John J., 340
Steele, Mamie M., 340
Steinle, Howard, 413
Stephens, Benjamin, 40
Stephens, Christopher C., 360
Stephens, Cora A., 360
Stephens, Elijah, 228
Stephens, Maudaunt T., 360
Stephens, Nancy Jane, 228
Stevens, Harriet, 88
Stevens, Tom, 238
Stevenson, Mary Brookes, 337
Stevenson, R. L., 64, 70
Steward, Nancy, 78
Stewart, Agnes, 416
Stewart, Edwin C., 426, 427
Stewart, Ellen, 312
Stewart, Henry, 312
Stewart, John P., 427
Stewart, Katherine, 427
Stewart, Mary Louise, 427
Stewart, Susie Pearl, 325
Stiles, Abraham, 119
Stiles, Margaret, 376, 377
Stites, Edith, 388
Stites, Katherine, 388
Stites, Madeline A., 388
Stites, Stephen Louis, 387
Stith, Herbert Davis, 261

Stockton, Theodosia, 221
Stockton, Helen, 289
Stokes, LeRoy, 346
Stokes, Mary C., 344
Stokes, W. P., 344
Stone, Benjamin Allen, 196
Stone, Dillard, 196
Stone, Esther, 306
Stone, Helen R., 305
Stone, Ira Trigg, 305
Stone, James B., 305
Stone, John, 305
Stone, John Edward, 196
Stone, Lydia V., 306
Stone, Margaret Ann, 196
Stone, Martha, 364
Stone, Martin G., 305
Stone, Nancy M., 305
Stone, Robert Brown, 196
Stone, Samuel Stephen, 305
Stone, Verda D., 415
Stone, William, 415
Stonebraker, Urilla, 86
Stowell, 58
Straker, Phereba Christine, 437, 438
Stratton, Sarah Emaline, 341
Stratton, William G., 90
Strecker, G. Louis, 138
Strong, Harriet, 309
Strong, Martha, 307
Strong, Martha Elizabeth, 312
Strong, Polly, 307
Strong, Thomas, 309
Strong, William Hiram, 308
Strother, Benjamin, 88
Strother, David Hunter, 9
Strother, Elaina, 270
Strother, Elizabeth, 88, 89, 270
Strother, James, 270
Strother, John, 82
Strother, Joseph, 78
Strother, Nancy, 82, 270
Strother, Pendleton, 270
Strother, Philip Williams, 270
Strother, Sadie, 270
Strother, Sarah, 78
Stuart, James W., 382
Stubblefield, George, 65
Stubblefield, Harry, 65
Sturgill, Sarah, 311
Sullivan, 194
Sullivan, Henry, 195
Sullivan, Priscilla, 214
Summer, J. W., 191
Summers, Ava Irene, 302
Summers, Noah, 84

Sumpter, Josephine, 406, 407
Sumpter, Lafayette, 406
Sumpter, Mary Jane, 406
Surratt, John, 286
Sutton, Anne Lewis, 171
Sutton, Betty Burwell, 171
Sutton, Edmund Pendleton, 170
Sutton, Hugh Carter, 170
Sutton, Jane, 325
Sutton, John Carter, 170
Sutton, Lucy Carter, 171
Sutton, Norbornne E., 170
Sutton, Patrick H., 171
Sutton, Robert W., 170
Sutton, Sarah Jane, 171
Sutton, William Carter, 170
Swan, Almira Dawson, 220
Swan, Annie Wayland, 220
Swan, Charles E., 220
Swan, Charles William, 220
Swan, Cordelia C., 220
Swan, Emily Pendleton, 220
Swan, James Alexander, 219, 220
Swan, Lucy Jane, 220
Swan, Mary Ann, 218, 219
Swan, Robert, 218, 220
Swan, Robert Henry, 220
Swan, William Duval, 220
Swanson, Levi, 56
Swearingen, Nancy U., 254
Swift, Bertha Eugenia, 277, 278
Swift, Richard, 277
Swilley, A. A. C., 376
Swilley, C. D., 376
Swilley, Edward S., 376
Swilley, George William, 376
Swilley, Lawson, 376, 377
Swilley, M. F., 376
Swilley, Martha Ann, 377
Swilley, Maude Estelle, 376
Swilley, Walter Lee, 376
Swilley, William M., 376
Swilley, Z. E., 376
Sydnor, Robert, 36, 37
Synan, Mary L., 265
Tadlock, Otto James, 415
Taft, William H., 296
Taliaferro, A. P., 270
Taliaferro, Emily F., 270
Taliaferro, Francis, Capt., 65
Taliaferro, Ida L., 397
Taliaferro, Mamie, 270
Taliaferro, Mary A., 270
Taliaferro, Mary Elizabeth, 145
Taliaferro, Sallie P., 271
Taliaferro, Van, 270, 271

Talley, Mary Caroline, 436
Talmadge, Ann P., Mrs., 277
Talmadge, Elizabeth, 277
Tandy, Charles E., 116
Tandy, Henry, 12, 115, 116
Tandy, Jesup M., 116
Tandy, John Davis, 116
Tandy, Mills, 116
Tandy, Nathaniel Mills, 116
Tandy, Samuel R., 116
Tandy, William, 119, 221
Tarpley, Margaret, 147
Tarpley, William, 147
Tarr, Edward E., 383
Tayloe, William, 31
Taylor, 188
Taylor, Agnes Kirkland, 282
Taylor, Ann, 26
Taylor, Ann Pendleton, 47
Taylor, Anne, 18
Taylor, Benjamin F., 228
Taylor, Benjamin R., 233
Taylor, Catherine, 26
Taylor, Edmund, 26, 35, 36
Taylor, Elizabeth, 27, 47, 79, 80, 239, 321
Taylor, Elizabeth January, 151, 152
Taylor, Emma H., 162
Taylor, Ethel, 416
Taylor, Francis, 18
Taylor, George, 288
Taylor, Harrison Pirtle, 348
Taylor, Ira, 306
Taylor, Isabella, 26
Taylor, James, 11, 18, 21, 26, 27, 31, 47, 79, 80,
99, 182, 307
Taylor, James Calvin, 327
Taylor, James N., 306
Taylor, John, 21-23, 26, 27, 31
Taylor, John B., 86
Taylor, John Gibson, 47, 80
Taylor, John P., 348
Taylor, Joseph, 27
Taylor, Mary, 11, 18, 19, 21, 26, 37, 47
Taylor, Mary J., 113
Taylor, Mary Lyell, 31
Taylor, Mildred, 24
Taylor, Nathaniel, 47, 80
Taylor, Philip, 27
Taylor, Rad, 189
Taylor, Robert, 53
Taylor, Robert Dudley, 298
Taylor, Robert R., 227
Taylor, Rosamond, 182
Taylor, Samuel, 306
Taylor, Sally, 306
Taylor, Sara 'Sally,' 189, 190

www.ingramcontent.com/pod-product-compliance
Lightning Source LLC
Chambersburg PA
CBHW080222270326
41926CB00020B/4122